Eighth Edition

Quantitative Approaches in Business Studies

Clare Morris

MA (Oxon), MSc, PhD (Bristol), C Stat
Professor Emeritus, University of Gloucestershire

Financial Times
Prentice Hall
is an imprint of

PEARSON

Harlow, England • London • New York • Boston • San Francisco • Toronto • Sydney • Singapore • Hong Kong
Tokyo • Seoul • Taipei • New Delhi • Cape Town • Madrid • Mexico City • Amsterdam • Munich • Paris • Milan

Pearson Education Limited

Edinburgh Gate
Harlow
Essex CM20 2JE
England

and Associated Companies throughout the world

Visit us on the World Wide Web at:
www.pearsoned.co.uk

———————————————

First published 1983 Macdonald & Evans Limited
Second edition 1989 Pitman Publishing, a division of Longman Group UK Limited
Third edition 1993 Pitman Publishing, a division of Longman Group UK Limited
Fourth edition 1996 Pitman Publishing, a division of Longman Group Limited
Fifth edition 2000 Pearson Education Limited
Sixth edition 2003 Pearson Education Limited
Seventh edition 2008
Eighth edition 2012

ISBN: 978-0-273-73863-3

British Library Cataloguing-in-Publication Data
A catalogue record for this book is available from the British Library

Library of Congress Cataloging-in-Publication Data
A catalog record for this book is available from the Library of Congress

10 9 8 7 6 5 4 3 2
15 14

Typeset in 10.5/13.5pt Minion by 35
Printed in Malaysia (CTP-VVP)

Brief contents

Contents

Supporting resources

Visit **www.pearsoned.co.uk/morris** to find valuable online resources

MyMathLab Global

- Online homework and assessment system
- Unlimited question practice due to algorithmically generated questions
- Personalised feedback
- Access to the Pearson eText
- Excel supplements and datasets
- Worksheets
- Multiple choice questions
- Weblinks

For instructors

- Complete, downloadable instructor's manual including teaching hints, solutions and suggestions for work
- A full suite of PowerPoint slides that can be downloaded and used as OHTs

For more information please contact your local Pearson Education sales representative or visit **www.pearsoned.co.uk/morris**

Guided tour

Chapter 1

TOOLS OF THE TRADE:
BASIC NUMERACY SKILLS

Chapter prerequisites Before starting work on this chapter, try the short test of basic mathematical skills below; you will find the answers in Appendix 9 and, according to which questions you find difficult, you will be directed to the appropriate section of this chapter. This will save you time and prevent your having to read through a lot of things that you can already cope with. If, however, you get more than half of the test questions wrong I would advise you to read the entire chapter.

Learning outcomes By the end of your work on this chapter you should be able to:

1 carry out the four operations of basic arithmetic (addition, subtraction, multiplication and division) with positive and negative integers, fractions and decimals;

2 round off the results of your calculations to a given number of decimal places or significant figures;

3 perform calculations involving percentages;

4 handle expressions involving powers and roots of a variable;

5 remove brackets from algebraic expressions;

6 construct a linear equation or inequality from a verbal problem;

7 solve linear equations;

8 solve a pair of simultaneous equations;

9 plot the graphs of linear equations or inequalities;

10 make efficient use of your calculator.

7

Chapter prerequisites – placed at the beginning of specific chapters, the prerequisites show the essential knowledge required to complete the chapter.

Learning outcomes – numbered points at the start of each chapter show what you can expect to learn from that chapter, and highlight the core coverage.

Quantitative methods in practice – real-world examples that appear at the beginning of every chapter, high-lighting key quantitative issues, and discussing them in both practical and theoretical terms.

CHAPTER 9 • CHECKING A THEORY: HYPOTHESIS TESTING

Quantitative methods in practice

Boys educated at single-sex schools 'more likely to divorce by early 40s'

'When we examined the risk of divorce or separation by age 42 for those who had ever been married, there was a statistically significant increased risk of divorce or separation for men from single-sex schools,' IoE emeritus professor Diana Leonard said.

www.telegraph.co.uk, 2 December 2009

Man-made climate change blamed for 'significant' rise in ocean temperature

Peter Challenor, of the National Oceanography Centre in Southampton, said the overall picture is clear – the oceans are warming up. 'I'm convinced of that. Everything is consistent with it. The slope [of the graph of ocean temperature against time] is statistically significant, whereas the levelling off in recent years isn't statistically significant,' he said. 'This study has removed many of the nagging doubts about the details. It shows the warming is real.'

www.independent.co.uk, 20 May 2010

The phrase 'statistically significant', as used in the two quotes above, is becoming a familiar one in news reports. We hear that there is (or is not, depending on who is speaking) a 'statistically significant' link between the measles/mumps/rubella (MMR) vaccination of children and the occurrence of various serious disabilities; some scientists warn against 'statistically significant' relationships between mobile phone use and the development of various cancers; and so on.

In business and management, too, the expression raises its head. To mention just three examples: service providers want to know whether increases or decreases in the rate of complaints they receive are 'statistically significant' or just 'blips'; manufacturers need to ask whether quality improvement campaigns have produced a 'significant' reduction in the proportion of poor-quality products; and hospital managers would like to be able to claim 'statistically significant reductions' in patients' waiting times for surgery.

What does the phrase convey to you? One of the self-inflicted problems which statisticians have to grapple with is the fact that we use ordinary, everyday words to convey statistical ideas – but not with their ordinary, everyday meanings. So most people, hearing the phrase 'statistically significant', would probably think that it means 'really big' or 'important' or 'definite'. The true meaning is a good deal more complex, as you might guess from the controversial nature of the examples I have mentioned. It is related to the business of weighing evidence from a sample and deciding whether or not it supports a theory or *hypothesis*. In this chapter we use the concepts of sampling set up in Chapter 8 to explore this process of *hypothesis testing*.

The training manager's problem

Elizabeth Field is the training manager of a light engineering firm which employs a considerable number of skilled machine operators. The firm is constantly making efforts to improve the quality of its product, and so recently Elizabeth has introduced a new 'refresher' training course for workers who have been on the same machines for a long

224

Key rules – examples of key methods or terms are highlighted clearly throughout the text.

Quick check questions – at frequent intervals throughout each chapter, there are accessible questions that act as knowledge progress checks as you work through the content.

Exercises – there are a range of exercises at the end of every chapter, requiring the reader to combine the skills and knowledge learnt in the chapter to reach the answers.

CHAPTER 6 • A FIRM FOUNDATION: ELEMENTARY PROBABILITY

probabilities in this case by adding them. In fact, it would appear that this is a general rule, for if we return to the *a priori* definition of probability, then:

Probability of A or B happening
$$= \frac{\text{number of ways A or B can happen}}{\text{total number of possibilities}}$$
$$= \frac{\text{number of ways A can happen} + \text{number of ways B can happen}}{\text{total number of possibilities}}$$
$$= \frac{\text{number of ways A can happen}}{\text{total number of possibilities}} + \frac{\text{number of ways B can happen}}{\text{total number of possibilities}}$$
= probability of A happening + probability of B happening.

However, we must be a little careful when applying this result. The step we have taken in saying that the number of ways A or B can happen is the sum of the ways A can happen and the ways B can happen is only true if A and B cannot both happen at once – if, in statistical jargon, they are *mutually exclusive*. If A and B *can* occur simultaneously, then we will, in adding up the two sets of cases like this, be counting twice over those occasions on which both A and B happen.

This will be clear if we consider another example. If we throw an ordinary dice and ask what the probability is that an even number or one divisible by three will show, the addition rule in its simple form would suggest that the answer should be $p(\text{even}) + p(\text{divisible by 3}) = 3/6 + 2/6 = 5/6$. In fact, of course, the answer should be 4/6: one of the even numbers, 6, is also divisible by 3, and so the events 'even' and 'divisible by 3' are not mutually exclusive. The simple rule fails because it causes us to count 6 twice over.

There *are* ways of dealing with 'or' problems when the events are *not* mutually exclusive, as we will see later. For the time being, we state the rule in its simple form:

> When A and B are mutually exclusive events
> $p(\text{A or B}) = p(\text{A}) + p(\text{B})$.

The 'and' rule

Now consider the other type of combination, where we wish to find the probability of A *and* B happening at once. The problem discussed on p. 148 of throwing the two coloured dice so as to obtain a combination of one yellow and one green face can be broken down into the probability of getting a yellow on the first dice *and* a green on the second, *or* vice versa. The first of these, a yellow on the first and a green on the second, we saw could occur in four ways, giving a probability of 4/36. Now the chance of a yellow on the first is 2/6, as is the chance of a green on the second, so it looks as if what we have done here is to *multiply* the two separate probabilities to get the combined one:

> Probability of A and B happening = probability of A × probability of B.

But once again, there is a cautionary note to be sounded in the application of this result. In the example we have just looked at, the colour that showed on the second dice was clearly independent of what showed on the first; the fact that the first produced a yellow face did not make it any more, or any less, likely that the second would show a green one.

150

CHAPTER 14 • PLANNING AN INVENTORY POLICY: STOCK CONTROL AND SIMULATION

much the same way as we have found the stock-holding cost. The average amount by which stocks run out is half of the maximum stock-out, which means $\frac{1}{2} \times 50$ or 25 frames; each costs 5p per month, but the out-of-stock situation actually arises for only $\frac{1}{4}$ of the cycle, so that the stock-out cost altogether will be $25 \times 5 \times \frac{1}{4}$ or about $15\frac{1}{2}$ pence.

Policy 2 therefore has a total cost of $15.5 + 76.5 + 100 = 192$ pence per month, as opposed to the 202 pence per month for Policy 1; so in this case it would be slightly cheaper to run out of stock by 50 frames, rather than reduce the size of orders. In another case, where the balance between the various components of the total cost was different, we might come to a different conclusion. There is no easy way of deciding in advance which policy would be best, other than to work out the total cost of each.

Quick check questions

1 Why does the graph of the stock cycle in Figure 14.2 involve vertical components where q increases suddenly, while that in Figure 14.5 has a more gradual upward slope?

2 Look back at question 3 of the 'Quick check questions' on p. 359. What will be the total annual cost of the policy of ordering 400 items at a time?

3 Now using the data provided in the earlier questions, find the total cost if 500 items rather than 400 were ordered at a time. What do you notice?

Answers:
1 In a situation where replacement stock is being delivered in a single order, the stock will increase suddenly – hence the vertical segments in Figure 14.2. Where items are being manufactured and used at the same time, the build-up of stock will be more gradual, giving a graph like that in Figure 14.5.
2 When 400 items are ordered, the ordering cost per year is $£12 \times 1800/400 = £48$ per year. The stock-holding cost is $0.5 \times 400 \times 0.24 = £48$ per year also (why are the two costs equal?). So total cost of this policy is £96 per year.
3 If 500 items are ordered at a time, then ordering cost = $£12 \times 1600/500 = £38.40$, while stock-holding cost = $0.5 \times 500 \times 0.24 = £60$ per year, giving a total cost of £98.40. So even though the order size has been increased by 100 items or 25 per cent, the total cost has only increased by £2.40, indicating the stability of the solution, or its lack of sensitivity to changes in the order size. This point is discussed further in the next section.

The effect of errors in estimates

You may have noticed that a good deal of 'supposing' has gone on in the preceding sections. We 'supposed' that the stock-holding costs had been worked out to be $\frac{1}{2}$p per frame per month, we 'supposed' that the charge for placing an order was £3, and so on. Now, in practice, some of these suppositions may well turn out to be wide of the mark. Certainly if we are planning a stock policy for the whole of next year, it is quite likely that the order cost *will not* stay put at £3, but will increase during the year. Similarly, the demand, which we need to know in order to solve the problem, will certainly vary and the same could well apply to all the other quantities required in the solution of the problem.

So a point that might justifiably worry John Williams when we present him with our recommendations as to his 'best' stock policy is: 'What happens if some of these figures

364

EXERCISES

EXERCISES

Further examples on the work of this chapter can be found on the Companion Website.

1 Tabulate the data contained in the following extract from a company report:

> This year saw an increase of 20 per cent over last year's total of 11 000 customers. We classify our customers, one-quarter of whom are overseas, as 'regular', 'occasional' or 'dormant', according to the number of orders they have placed in the past year. Overall, 'regular' customers formed 60 per cent of the total, and only 10 per cent were classed as 'dormant', though among overseas customers the proportions in the three categories were 3:2:1.

2 Produce a diagram illustrating the data of Exercise 1 suitable for inclusion in the report.

3 A sample of 1000 receipted bills was taken from a firm's files, and checked for errors. Of the bills 105 contained errors which were classified as follows:

In firm's favour by		In customer's favour by	
under 5p	32	under 5p	29
5p but under 10p	11	5p but under 10p	18
10p but under 15p	4	10p but under 15p	7
15p but under 20p	1	15p but under 20p	0
20p or more	1	20p or more	2

Construct a diagram to represent the data.

4 The council of a seaside resort has carried out a small-scale survey to find out how far day visitors travel to the resort. The raw results are as follows (figures in miles):

> 12, 23, 14, 27, 14, 8, 19, 27, 25, 11, 17, 32, 22, 25, 42, 13, 9, 36, 16, 5, 13, 22, 28, 6, 29, 37, 24, 24, 7, 28, 34, 56, 21, 39, 12, 18, 25, 45, 33, 31.

Tabulate these figures in a manner that could be used at a council meeting.

5 Get hold of a list of postal charges for first-class letters and from it draw a suitable graph showing charge against weight, which could be used in a firm's post room.

6 Look at *Social Trends, Economic Trends, Regional Statistics* or other government statistical publications, noticing what kinds of diagrams are used to present particular types of data. Be critical! (You can find these publications via www.statistics.gov.uk.)

7 Collect examples of bad or misleading diagrams from the press (pseudo-scientific advertisements are a rich source), and look out, too, for articles in which numerical information is presented in narrative style.

8 For the data in the file STUD.XLS/STUD.DAT draw up (a) a frequency distribution of ages for male and female students; (b) a table showing subject of first degree and gender. For each of these tables, construct a diagram suitable for use in a presentation to potential students of the course in question.

9 For the data in the file MACH.XLS/MACH.DAT, produce a cumulative frequency table of weights of packets for the three machines, and display the results on a single ogive.

10 For the data in the file QUAL.XLS/QUAL.DAT, plot a scattergraph of floorspace against takings. What can you conclude from the graph?

→

91

Step 1 Take a sample test

Sample tests enable you to test yourself to see how much you already know about a particular topic and identify the areas in which you need more practice. Click on the **Study Plan** button in the menu and take a sample test for the chapter you are studying.

Step 2 Review your study plan

The results of the sample tests you have taken will be incorporated into your study plan, showing you what sections you have mastered and what sections you need to study further, helping you make the most efficient use of your self-study time.

Step 3 Have a go at an exercise

From the study plan click on the section of the book you are studying and have a go at the series of inter-active **Exercises**. When required use the maths panel on the left hand side to select the maths functions you need. Click on **more** to see the full range of functions available. Additional study tools such as **Help me solve this** and **View an example** break the question down step-by-step for you, helping you to complete the exercises successfully. You can try the same exercises over and over again, and each time the values will change, giving you unlimited practice.

Step 4 Use the E-book to help you

If you are struggling with a question, you can click on the **textbook** button to read the relevant part of your textbook again.

Preface

It is now more than 25 years since the first edition of this book appeared. In the intervening period the range of computer-based tools available to students and teachers has increased enormously, with Web-based material in particular providing an invaluable resource which has been heavily exploited in this new edition. However, the essential needs of students studying quantitative methods as part of a business course have changed very little. Thus the premise of the book remains a recognition that such students have neither the inclination nor, in many cases, the underpinning mathematical experience to follow a rigorous course in applied statistics and operational research. They do, however, have other skills – in problem-solving, communication and business operations – which must be exploited by anyone attempting to interest them in a quantitative approach to business problems.

Accordingly, the book has a high proportion of words, and a correspondingly low proportion of numbers, mathematical symbols and technical terminology. Few proofs of results are given; instead, the effectiveness of the methods is demonstrated by the fact that they give sensible and useful solutions to practical problems. By adopting a problem-driven approach, I hope to convince readers that quantitative methods, while not always easy to get to grips with, really do have something irreplaceable to offer as a tool for managers.

The range of topics covered is probably larger than would be covered in most HNDs, level 1 undergraduate or MBA quantitative methods courses, particularly in Part 4 of the book. The topics included in any individual course will naturally reflect the interests of the teacher and the specialist needs of the students involved. I have therefore tried to make the chapters of Part 4 as independent as possible of each other. Where there is a dependence on preceding material, the fact is indicated in the list of prerequisites at the start of the chapter. Further details of possible topic sequences will be found in the section 'How this book is organised' on p. xix. These chapters are perforce introductory in character and do not claim to cover the needs of courses where operational research techniques form a substantial part of the content; however, they should be adequate as a demonstration of the quantitative modelling approach, its power and versatility.

In producing this eighth edition, the opportunity has been taken to make a number of modifications. The chapter on Excel and other software has been removed and replaced by a short note in Appendix 1, since it is now likely either that students will already have spreadsheet skills, or that they will be taught to use a spreadsheet as a separate part of their course. I have decided not to include material on other software, such as Minitab and SPSS, partly in the interests of keeping the size of the book within bounds, and partly because evidence suggests that, while statisticians (including myself) have reservations about the statistical routines in Excel, it is certainly the most widely used numerical tool on business courses.

In most chapters, the 'real-world' examples at the start are new ones. In addition to the exercises, there is now a more substantial 'case study' at the end of each chapter, generally requiring an answer in the form of a management report or some other type of realistic business-based output.

A number of other changes and updatings have been made throughout the text, and some errors and obscurities in the previous edition have been corrected, often as a result of comments from users. I am grateful to all those who have taken the trouble to draw these matters to my attention, and hope that they will continue to do so in respect of the new edition. I am also grateful to the adopters and other colleagues who reviewed the seventh edition and made helpful suggestions for changes and additions to the present edition, most of which have been incorporated. I have not attempted totally to remove mentions of non-metric units such as gallons and miles, but hope I have brought the units throughout in line with the rather mixed usage that currently prevails in the UK.

The Companion Website for the book has also been extensively revised and expanded, and includes, in response to requests from both lecturers and students, more examples with full solutions. Many links to websites of related interest are provided, and it is hoped that following some of these will lead students not only to a better understanding but to greater enjoyment of the subject. All of this material can now be found within the new MyMathLab Global course for this book. MyMathLab Global is an online tutorial and self-study system which enables students to create a personalised study plan, test their understanding of the course material and use practice examples to improve their technical skills.

It should be noted that, while all the websites referenced in the book were live at the time of writing, of course there can be no guarantee that any of these will remain available during the period that the book remains in print.

Clare Morris
Bristol
July 2011

Acknowledgements

We are grateful to the following for permission to reproduce copyright material:

Tables

Table on page 201 from *General Election 2010 – An Overview*, Ipsos MORI; Table on page 323 from HESA 2011, www.HESA.ac.uk; Table on page 329 adapted from Vehicle Ownership and Income Growth, Worldwide: 1960–2030, *The Energy Journal*, 28 (4), pp. 163–190 (Dargay, J., Gately, D. and Sommer, M. 2007), Table 1, reprinted with permission from The Energy Journal.

Text

Appendix 3 from *Statistical Tables for Science, Engineering, Management and Business Studies*, 3rd ed., Macmillan, London and Basingstoke (Murdoch, J. and Barnes, J.A. 1986) Table 1, reproduced with permission of Palgrave Macmillan; Appendix 4 from *Statistical Tables for Science, Engineering, Management and Business Studies*, 3rd ed., Macmillan, London and Basingstoke (Murdoch, J. and Barnes, J.A. 1986) Table 2, reproduced with permission of Palgrave Macmillan; Appendix 5 from *Statistical Tables for Science, Engineering, Management and Business Studies*, 3rd ed., Macmillan, London and Basingstoke (Murdoch, J. and Barnes, J.A. 1986) Table 3, reproduced with permission of Palgrave Macmillan; Appendix 6 adapted from *Statistical Tables for Biological, Agricultural and Medical Research*, Longman Group Ltd. (Fisher, R.A. and Yates, F.) Table IV, reprinted by permission of Pearson Education Ltd.; Appendix 7 from *Statistical Tables for Biological, Agricultural and Medical Research*, Longman Group Ltd. (Fisher, R.A. and Yates, F.) Table VII, reprinted by permission of Pearson Education Ltd.; Appendix 8 from *Statistical Tables for Biological, Agricultural and Medical Research*, Longman Group Ltd. (Fisher, R.A. and Yates, F.) Table III, reprinted by permission of Pearson Education Ltd.; Box on page 38 from Aer Lingus flies high over rival Ryanair, say passengers, *Irish Independent* (Sheehan, A.), 23 June 2010; Box on page 219 from *Ipsos MORI July Political Monitor for Reuters*, Ipsos MORI; Box on page 258 from http://media.ford.com/article_display.cfm?article_id=16001; Box on page 375 from The website of the millennium maths project, http://plus.maths.org/issue10/interview/index.html, this article first appeared in Plus magazine (http://plus.maths.org), a free online magazine about mathematics aimed at the general public; Newspaper Headline on page 406 from Don't cut interest rates, building societies tell Bank of England, *The Telegraph*, 3 February 2009, www.telegraph.co.uk, copyright © Telegraph Media Group Limited 2009; Newspaper Headline on page 406 from Zimbabwe's inflation rate surges to 231,000,000%, *The Guardian* (McGreal, C.), 9 October 2008, www.guardian.co.uk, copyright Guardian News & Media Ltd. 2008; Box on page 428 from Simulation and optimisation join forces to schedule London's water, Robert Simons, MP in Action, January 1996, www.eudoxus.com/mpac9601.html; Box on page 449 from Olympic Park master plan submitted, *Sports Management*, 8 February 2007, © Cybertrek Ltd. Tel: +44 (0) 1462 431385.

In some instances we have been unable to trace the owners of copyright material, and we would appreciate any information that would enable us to do so.

Note to the reader

Although I hope that you are going to find this book fairly readable, it would be silly to pretend that you can read it – or any other textbook on a numerical subject – in quite the same way as you would read, say, a detective story, or even a textbook in a more 'wordy' subject such as law or sociology. Since I naturally want you to benefit as much as possible from reading this book, and since it may be some time since you last studied a numerical subject, you may find the following points helpful.

At the start of each chapter you will find a list of the prerequisites for reading that chapter – the things which you need to understand in order to follow the material contained in the chapter. If you are doubtful about any of these, go back to the section in which the topic was covered (you will find a reference given) and check your understanding of that topic. *Don't* just carry on into the chapter hoping for the best – that's the way to get confused and demoralised! To a large extent mathematics and statistics are cumulative subjects, in which one topic builds on another, so it is important to get each stage clear before going on to the next.

You will also find at the start of the chapters a list of the things that you should be able to do by the end of the chapter; when you have read the chapter, and gone through some of the exercises at the end – particularly the more straightforward problems – then waited a few days for the material to fall into place, you can use this list to check that you have grasped the main points of the chapter. You may also find that these lists are useful when you come to revise for examinations, in reminding you of the major areas within each topic.

At key points within each chapter, you will find short sets of 'Quick check questions', with answers immediately below. These questions, which often explore your understanding of concepts rather than requiring you to carry out calculations, will help you to ensure that you are comfortable with one set of important ideas before proceeding to the next. You are strongly advised not to skip these questions, but to look back over the preceding material, or to seek help from your tutor, if you have difficulties with any of them.

Always have a pencil and paper to hand when you are reading the book, so that you can follow the workings of problems for yourself, or perhaps work out in more detail steps of a calculation which I have abbreviated. And do not worry too much if you feel you need two or three readings of some of the sections, plus some work on practical examples, before they make complete sense – this is quite usual when getting to grips with numerical ideas.

Finally, and most importantly, remember that all the skills that you bring to bear in other areas of your work – your ability to communicate effectively, your knowledge of business, your problem-solving skills, and above all your plain common sense – can be used in the numerical context too. Is this a sensible result? Is it about the size of answer which I would have expected to get? Is it realistic in terms of the original problem we set out to solve? These are the kinds of questions you should constantly be asking yourself as you work through the book, so that by the end numbers, and the ability to handle them effectively, will be just another of your everyday skills.

How this book is organised

Although most of the topics in this book appear in many courses on quantitative methods for business and management, you may find that your course does not include all of them. Or perhaps you are reading the book for interest only, and would like to be able to skip some material without getting lost.

For your guidance, here is an indication of how the book fits together, and of possible routes through it. You will find more detailed information about the prerequisites for understanding each chapter at the start of the chapter. The order in which topics are covered is to some extent a matter of taste; I have tried to provide a logical structure by subdividing the book into four parts, but there are many other possible and equally logical orders which you could follow.

The introduction is a preliminary chapter which explains the role of quantitative methods in business. You are strongly recommended to read this first!

Chapter 1 is necessary only if you are not very confident of your basic mathematical skills; try the test at the start to find out if you have the level of ability needed for later work.

Chapters 2–4 should be read sequentially, and cover the essentials of what is called descriptive statistics.

Chapter 5 on index numbers could be omitted without affecting later work.

Chapters 6–9 are also sequential; they cover probability and the problems of drawing conclusions from sample data, and could be left out if you are only interested in the descriptive aspects of the subject. Chapter 10 covers specific applications of statistics in quality improvement, and could be omitted if you are not interested in this area.

Chapters 11–13 are chiefly devoted to regression, an important method, widely used in a business context. The greater part of these chapters can be read without reference to Chapters 6–10, though a small part of the content requires an understanding of the concept of statistical significance.

Chapter 14 shows how we can use quantitative methods to model business problems, using the mathematical approach to inventory control to illustrate the ideas. It also introduces the technique of simulation, which requires you to recall some of the material on distributions from Chapter 6.

Chapter 15 covers forecasting, another very important area for business applications. This chapter does not depend on previous work, and could be read much earlier in the sequence if you wish.

Chapters 16–18 are each devoted to a separate topic in operational research, and each is pretty well freestanding.

Finally, Chapter 19 provides some advice on applying all the methods of preceding chapters to practical problems encountered in project work and elsewhere. Though this chapter does require you to recall some material from earlier work, it could be read independently without too much difficulty.

The book makes references throughout to the Microsoft Excel spreadsheet as a tool for calculations. The reader may have to customise Excel 2007 and incorporate the Analysis Tools and Solver add-ins to follow the methods given in the text. Appendix 1 contains a note about this and other software for quantitative methods.

Introduction

Why quantitative methods?

It would be an odd feature if a text on, say, accounting were to begin with a chapter called 'Why Accounting?'. Everyone studying business and management knows that any decent manager needs to have a good understanding of accounting principles and ideas, to be able to read a balance sheet, to know about different ways of assessing the financial health of an organisation, and so on. Most students of business, even before they start their course, have a fair idea as to the role that accounting plays within a company.

But the same can't be said for quantitative methods. The word 'statistics', when it arises in everyday life at all, is usually in the context of 'government statistics' – the unemployment statistics, economic statistics about inflation and interest rates, and so on. Occasionally a phrase such as 'statistically significant' may stray into a news bulletin – as in 'the new drug is said to produce a statistically significant improvement in the recovery rate of patients' – but very few people have a real understanding of such phrases (though by the time you have completed Chapter 9 you should be one of them).

So it is hard for a student starting out on a business course to have any idea what to expect from a quantitative methods course. In this chapter I will try to give you an idea of the important contribution which statistical and mathematical methods – the bunch of techniques generally covered under the title 'quantitative methods' – can make to the effective running of an organisation, to good decision-making and to efficient operations.

Data and information

You are going to encounter the word 'data' quite a lot in the next few chapters. It is the term used to describe the raw material of quantitative methods, which gets presented, manipulated and analysed using the various techniques we will study. Examples of so-called 'raw' data – that is, before it has been processed in any way – would be the results of a market research questionnaire, the wages of a group of employees, the values of a portfolio of shares, or the point-of-sale (POS) information collected by a large supermarket such as Tesco about its customers' purchases.

Data in this form conveys very little to most people, particularly when there is a huge amount of it (as there would be in the case of Tesco's POS records). It needs to be organised and processed before it becomes useful – in other words, it must be turned into *information*. One way of looking at quantitative methods is as a collection of techniques for organising, presenting, summarising, communicating and drawing conclusions from data, so that it becomes informative.

This processing may have a number of objectives:

- We may simply want to communicate some important facts about the data items, or to use them to back up an argument or explanation. For example, company annual reports and accounts often include statistical diagrams such as pie charts, showing how the year's profit was split up into dividends, tax and retained profits. The trend of profits over time may be presented as a line graph, and so forth. This aspect of the analysis of data is covered by Chapters 2–5.

- We may want to make deductions from the data about a wider situation. For example, perhaps we have done a small-scale survey of 500 people and found that 35 per cent of electricity users in a town would consider switching to another supplier. What does that enable us to conclude about the proportion of the whole population in the town who would consider switching suppliers? Clearly there is an element of uncertainty here, since we feel instinctively that a small survey is not guaranteed to give exactly the same proportion as we would get if we asked the whole population.

  Chapters 6–11 cover this sort of situation. The endpoint in a business context is often the making of a decision – shall we go ahead with a big drive to get electricity consumers to change supplier? – and having reliable numerical information is a crucial part of that decision-making process.

- We may want to build a model of the main features of a management problem – not in the sense of a physical model, but in the form of an equation, a graph, a computer program, etc. Such models underlie the ways that motor-car manufacturers choose to lay out their plants, the routeing of large fleets of delivery vehicles, the scheduling of airline flights, the forecasting of demand for fast-moving consumer goods. It is essential, if a model is to be useful rather than misleading (or possibly downright dangerous), that good-quality, reliable data is used in its construction.

  Chapters 12–18 cover various approaches to quantitative modelling, emphasising the use to which the results of the modelling process may be put, and the limitations that, inevitably, are present in all such methods.

Whichever kind of analysis we are carrying out, then, quantitative methods have an important role to play in underpinning the running of an organisation.

Leave it to the experts?

Your reaction to this might be 'Yes, I can believe all that, but I have no ambition to become a member of an operational research department, or to join the Government Statistical Service. So do I really need to know how to do these things myself?'

The answer is yes – and no. Certainly it is unlikely that, as a general manager or a functional specialist in an area such as marketing or human resource management, you would find yourself carrying out complex statistical analyses or building elaborate models. But you do need to know what can be done – what sort of methods are available, their capabilities and limitations – so that in simple cases you can do the analysis yourself (with the aid of a suitable computer package), and in more complex cases you can have an intelligent discussion with an expert.

There is an analogy to be drawn here with computing. No manager needs to know a great deal of technical detail about networking, communications or the way a PC handles information internally. But all managers need to be able to make use of computer-based tools such as spreadsheets and databases, and to have some idea what is and is not a reasonable demand to make of their company's systems. Otherwise they are at the mercy of the experts, who can 'blind them with science', and may not fully appreciate the needs and best interests of the business. Likewise with quantitative methods: a good appreciation of the power of the methods is needed so that best use can be made of expert resources, whether in the human form of business statisticians and operational researchers, or in the form of powerful computer packages.

Is it maths?

There is one more point that may help you understand 'where we are coming from' in the remainder of this book. Many newcomers to statistics and quantitative methods perceive these topics as a branch of mathematics, and so bring their preconceptions about that subject to their studies. After all, quantitative methods involve numbers, use formulae, require some manipulation of figures, etc.; isn't that maths?

It's certainly true that these methods are based on mathematical ideas, and make use of them in solving business problems. You therefore need to be comfortable with some fairly basic mathematical ideas and processes, and Chapter 1 is aimed at making sure that you have the necessary level of proficiency.

But there are some important differences. For example, in the kind of mathematics you may have studied previously, the answer to a calculation was probably its most important aspect, and you may have worried about getting it right to two or more decimal places.

With quantitative methods, of course answers *are* still important, but they are not the end of the story. They need to be interpreted in practical terms before they become useful aids to the solution of business problems. Likewise, the precise value of an answer to umpteen decimal places may not matter very much – it may only be the value to the nearest hundred or even thousand which, in the context, is of interest to us.

This also helps explain another feature that sometimes worries students – the fact that different versions of formulae and methods are used in different textbooks or by different experts. Very often the differences are just in the way things are expressed, and the results at the end are actually the same; but sometimes there will be small differences in the final results. In some cases, we may actually have several different measures for the same concept – for instance, in Chapter 4 we will see that there at least three ways of defining the 'typical' value in a set of numbers.

This can be upsetting to a student who wants to know 'which is right and which is wrong'. You need to get used to the idea that very often it's a matter of opinion which measure is the best one to use in a given situation, and there may be a good case for several options, so there *is* no 'right and wrong'. Grasping this idea from the start can save you much anxiety later on.

What's in it for me?

It has to be admitted that, at present, many managers, particularly in UK industry and commerce, would happily admit that they know nothing about quantitative methods, and have never felt the need to learn any. However, there is also plenty of evidence to suggest that in the most successful economies, managers have good levels of awareness of these methods and how they can contribute to the successful running of a business. So if you reach a reasonable level of proficiency, and are able to make use of the tools we are going to be discussing in a practical way, you will certainly have a competitive edge in your career.

Part 1

NUMBERS –
HOW WE HANDLE THEM

This part covers the essential tools which you will need to use in order to get the most out of your reading of the rest of the book. Chapter 1 summarises the mathematical methods required, with material to help you revise and improve your understanding of these methods if necessary, and exercises to help you discover if you have done so satisfactorily.

Chapter 1

TOOLS OF THE TRADE:
BASIC NUMERACY SKILLS

Chapter prerequisites

Before starting work on this chapter, try the short test of basic mathematical skills below; you will find the answers in Appendix 9 and, according to which questions you find difficult, you will be directed to the appropriate section of this chapter. This will save you time and prevent your having to read through a lot of things that you can already cope with. If, however, you get more than half of the test questions wrong I would advise you to read the entire chapter.

Learning outcomes

By the end of your work on this chapter you should be able to:

1 carry out the four operations of basic arithmetic (addition, subtraction, multiplication and division) with positive and negative integers, fractions and decimals;

2 round off the results of your calculations to a given number of decimal places or significant figures;

3 perform calculations involving percentages;

4 handle expressions involving powers and roots of a variable;

5 remove brackets from algebraic expressions;

6 construct a linear equation or inequality from a verbal problem;

7 solve linear equations;

8 solve a pair of simultaneous equations;

9 plot the graphs of linear equations or inequalities;

10 make efficient use of your calculator.

TEST

1 $-3 + 4 =$ 2 $-5 \div 2 =$ 3 $\dfrac{3}{8} + \dfrac{4}{5} =$ 4 $\dfrac{7}{8} \times \dfrac{3}{5} =$

5 $2 \div \dfrac{1}{2} =$ 6 $0.05 \times 2.5 =$ 7 $8 \div 0.2 =$

8 Convert $\dfrac{5}{12}$ to a decimal.

9 Express 0.28 as a fraction.

10 What is 67.469 to three significant figures?

11 16% of 8 =   12 18 as a percentage of 64 =

13 The price of an item including the dealer's 20 per cent mark-up is £36. What did it cost before the mark-up?

14 $x^2 \times x^4 =$ 15 $\sqrt{x^{16}} =$

16 $2(3a + b) - (a - 2b) =$

17 If it costs £6 to drive k miles then what is the cost of driving 4 miles?

18 Items priced at m pence per dozen are repacked in boxes of 100. What will the cost of such a box be, in pounds?

19 There are f female workers and m male workers in a factory. Write down an algebraic expression to show that the total workforce must be less than 150.

20 $3x - 5 = 10$; $x =$ 21 $\dfrac{4}{y} = \dfrac{7}{8}$; $y =$

22 $\begin{cases} 3p + 2q = 9 \\ 4p - 6q = 25 \end{cases}$ Find p and q.

23 Where does the graph of $s = 3t + 5$ cross the t-axis?

24 Which of these graphs, (a), (b) or (c), could be the graph of $y = x^2 + 3x - 4$?

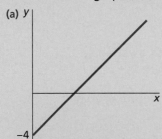
(a)

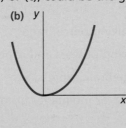
(b)

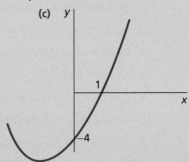
(c)

25 On which side of the line in the following diagram will inequality $x > 2y$ be satisfied?

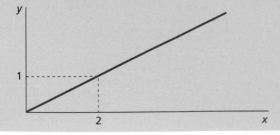

Almost everybody's problem

If you are reading this book then you are almost certainly not a mathematician. You have probably chosen to do a course in business studies, management or accounting, only to discover that among the obviously relevant and useful subjects, such as economics and law, you are expected to study mathematics (possibly disguised under the title of statistics, but that doesn't fool you).

To this news, if you are like 99 per cent of students in my experience, your reaction was close to horror. It is quite probably several years since you last studied mathematics, and your recollections of those days may not be very pleasant. But in fact your apprehension is groundless. What you will be studying in this book is not mathematics for its own sake, however appealing that may be to some of us, but *useful* mathematics – the sort of mathematics that can lead quickly and effectively to the solution of practical, business-oriented problems.

However, it would be misleading to pretend that you are not going to need to dredge up a little of what you learned at school, and this first chapter is designed to help you do just that. There is probably hardly anything that will be completely new to you; there will be some things that you once knew but have forgotten, others that you have heard about before but that may not have made much sense the first time around. You will find plenty of exercises to practise on, since practice is essential in achieving facility in the basic techniques we will be calling on later in the book.

And, in case you suspect that some topics are included just because they are good for you and cannot conceivably have any relevance to business, you will find a reference at the beginning of each section to the points at which the material of that section will be needed in later chapters.

Numbers and how we combine them

This is fundamental to all later work.

It is often helpful to think of all numbers as strung out in a straight line as follows:

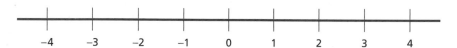

In the middle we have zero, to the right are the *positive* whole numbers +1, +2 . . . (we do not usually bother to write the + sign) and to the left are the *negative* whole numbers −1, −2 . . . The '. . .' here indicates that the numbers can be continued without limit in either direction.

An integer is a 'whole number'.

In between the integers, positive and negative, we can think of the entire line as being filled up with the remaining non-integer numbers – fractions and/or decimals which we will be returning to later.

For most people, adding positive integers is no problem; the difficulties start to appear with the minus signs. This is where the idea of the number line can be quite helpful. Consider the expression $42 - 36 + 27$. Should we say '36 + 27' first, and then take the answer away from 42, or should we take '42 − 36' and then add on the 27?

In fact, with + and − signs we are safe in performing the operations from left to right, unless there are brackets telling us otherwise (of which more later). Looking at it another way, saying 'subtract 36' is exactly the same as saying 'add the negative number −36', so the whole expression can be thought of as '42 plus −36 plus 27'. In other words, subtraction means adding negative numbers. So on the number line, adding corresponds to moving to the right, subtraction to moving to the left.

Taking a simpler case, $4 - 9 + 2$ can be interpreted as: start at 4 on the line, move 9 steps to the left (which brings us to −5) and then 2 to the right, ending up at −3. Of course, after a while you will not need to use the line explicitly, but this is the basis of 'rules' you may have learned, such as 'in subtraction put the sign of the larger to the difference'.

Another example:

$$-6 - 7 + 4 = -13 + 4 = -9.$$

When it comes to multiplication and division, there are a few different ways of writing things which you should be aware of: 2×6 is often written as 2*6, especially when using a spreadsheet, and $4 \div 2$, 4/2 and $\frac{4}{2}$ all mean the same thing.

As far as multiplying or dividing negative numbers goes, this is one of the few cases where I would advise you to remember some rules (they can be proved, but in a rather long-winded way):

> Two *like* signs (two pluses or two minuses) multiplied together or divided give a positive answer.
>
> Two *unlike* signs (one plus and one minus) multiplied together or divided give a negative answer.

For example,

$$(-2) \times (-4) = 8 \qquad 12 \div (-6) = -2 \qquad -8/-2 = 4.$$

In division, if the result is not a whole number – that is, if the number being divided is not an integer multiple of the *divisor* (the dividing number) – then the remainder can be expressed as either a fraction or a decimal. To express it as a fraction, simply put the remainder over the divisor. For example, 20/7 = 2 with remainder 6, or $2\frac{6}{7}$. We will find out how to turn this into a decimal later.

One final point on the four basic rules of arithmetic: there is a standard convention about the priority which operates if you have + and − signs mixed up with × and ÷. The rule is that the multiplications and divisions are done first, unless there are brackets indicating otherwise. For instance, $2 \times 6 + 5 = 12 + 5 = 17$, *not* $2 \times 11 = 22$. If we wanted this, we would have to put $2 \times (6 + 5)$, to show that the addition is to be done first. There is, however, no difference in meaning between $\frac{-1}{2}$, $\frac{1}{-2}$ and $-\frac{1}{2}$; we usually prefer to attach the minus sign to the front of the expression, as in the last of the three expressions, but it really does not matter. It is important to remember these rules about the order of operations, since they are implicit in the way many computer packages work.

Exercise 1

1 $-5-4-7$	2 $6+4-10$	3 $2+2-2$	4 $-11+18+25$
5 $16-9+7$	6 $-8+3+2$	7 $6\times(-2)$	8 $18\div(-3)$
9 $(-4)\times(-6)$	10 $27/-3$	11 $\dfrac{-16}{-8}$	12 $3\times7+4$

Operations with fractions

You will need to be able to handle addition, subtraction and multiplication of fractions when we come to discuss probability in Chapter 7. Although it *is* possible using an electronic calculator to turn all your fractions into decimals and use the calculator to work out the arithmetic, doing so would waste a great deal of time, and in many cases the results are easier to interpret when expressed in fraction rather than decimal form.

There are actually three ways of writing fractions – as decimals, percentages or 'ordinary' fractions such as $\frac{1}{2}$ or $\frac{3}{4}$ – but we will concentrate in this section on the last of the three ways, leaving the first two to later sections. For addition and subtraction, the magic words are 'common denominator'. Actually there is nothing magic about it: the point is that trying to add sixths and sevenths is like trying to add apples and bananas – they are quite different things; we must express them in the same terms before we can do anything with them:

> To add or subtract fractions, express them in terms of a common denominator.

For example, to add $\frac{5}{6}$ and $\frac{2}{7}$ we must write them both with the same bottom line or *denominator* – in this case both can be written in terms of forty-seconds as

$$\frac{35}{42}+\frac{12}{42}=\frac{47}{42}$$

(or $1\frac{5}{42}$, but we do not generally use such 'mixed' fractions).

It is easy to see why we chose 42 here – it is 6×7. Sometimes a smaller number will do, but if you find it difficult to spot this, multiplying the denominators of the fractions always works.

Another example:

$$\frac{4}{5}-\frac{1}{4}=\frac{16}{20}-\frac{5}{20}=\frac{16-5}{20}=\frac{11}{20}.$$

Cancellation of fractions sometimes causes confusion but to *cancel* a fraction simply means to divide the top and bottom by the same figure; for example, $4/8 = 1/2$, $12/16 = 3/4$. It is generally preferable to express a fraction in its lowest terms, that is, to cancel it as far as possible. Notice that, as what we are really doing here is saying $12/16 = (3 \times 4)/(4 \times 4) = 3/4$, we are dividing the whole of the top and bottom of the fraction by 4. It follows that it is *not* permissible to say $(4 + 1)/2 = (2 + 1)/1 = 3$, because we have not divided the *whole* of the top by 2, but only part of it. If you are tempted to perform a cancellation like this where plus and minus signs are involved, either leave well alone, or put in some simple numbers to see whether the operation is really valid. In the example above, $(4+1)/2 = 2\frac{1}{2}$, whereas the 'cancelled' expression $= 3$, so clearly this does not work.

Multiplication is the easiest of all fraction operations:

> To multiply fractions, multiply the tops or numerators and the denominators of the fractions separately.

Examples:

$$\frac{1}{5} \times \frac{5}{7} = \frac{1 \times 5}{5 \times 7} = \frac{5}{35}, \quad \frac{2}{3} \times \frac{8}{9} = \frac{16}{27}, \text{ etc.}$$

Of course, in the first case here we could cancel by 5, to reduce the fraction to $\frac{1}{7}$.

For division, the rule is:

> Turn the divisor upside down and multiply by this number.

Example:

$$\frac{5/6}{2/3} = \frac{5}{6} \div \frac{2}{3} = \frac{5}{6} \times \frac{3}{2} = \frac{15}{12} = \frac{5}{4},$$

cancelling by 3. We could have cancelled at an earlier stage but if you are doubtful about cancellation it is safer to leave it until the end, when you have only one fraction to deal with.

Another example:

$$\frac{3}{16} \div \frac{7}{8} = \frac{3}{16} \times \frac{8}{7} = \frac{24}{112} = \frac{3}{14},$$

cancelling by 8.

A phrase you may have heard in the past is '*of* means *multiply*'. This simply means that to get a certain fraction of a number, you multiply the number by that fraction. For example, two-thirds of $12 = \frac{2}{3} \times 12 = \frac{2}{3} \times \frac{12}{1} = \frac{24}{3} = 8$. Notice too that a whole number can always be written as a fraction with 1 as the denominator, as we have done with the 12 here.

Finally, if you have to deal with negative fractions, exactly the same rules apply as for operating with negative integers.

Now try the following exercise.

Exercise 2

1 $\frac{1}{6} \times \frac{7}{8}$ 2 $\frac{1}{4} - \frac{1}{3}$

3 $\frac{1}{11} + \frac{1}{22}$ 4 $-\frac{1}{2} + \frac{3}{4} - \frac{1}{8}$

5 $\frac{2}{7} \times 9$ 6 $\frac{2}{5} \div \frac{4}{7}$

7 $10 \div \frac{1}{2}$ 8 $\frac{3}{4} \times \frac{1}{4} \div \frac{4}{5}$

9 $\left(\frac{3}{8} - \frac{3}{4}\right) \div \frac{4}{3}$ 10 $\left(\frac{1}{9} + \frac{5}{6}\right) \times \frac{3}{17}$

Decimals: a special kind of fraction

Now that everyone uses calculators, nearly all the calculations you perform will be done in terms of decimals, but you cannot abdicate all responsibility for the accuracy of your calculations to the calculator because it is easy to press a wrong key in the course of entering the figures. So a familiarity with the rules for handling decimal points – in order that you can check that the answer is roughly what it should be – is, if anything, even more necessary now.

Sometimes one hears the expression 'decimal fractions' used, and the phrase gives the clue to what decimals really are – a system of fractions based on multiples of ten. When we write 0.75, for example, this is a shorthand for 'seven tenths and five hundredths' – the seven, one place to the right of the decimal point, represents tenths; the five, two places to the right, represents hundredths, and so on. But it would be tedious to have to convert back to fractions every time we wanted to operate with decimals, so there are a few simple rules to enable us to use them directly.

Addition and subtraction work much as for integers, as long as you remember to keep the decimal points lined up – that is, add tenths to tenths, hundredths to hundredths, etc. For instance, to add 2.15 and 3.4 we think of the 3.4 as 3.40, then add the 5 to the 0, the 1 to the 4 and the 2 to the 3, to get 5.55.

In multiplication, the number of decimal places in the answer is the total of the number of places in the figures being multiplied. For example,

$$3.2 \times 0.5 \times 0.2 = 1.60 \times 0.2 = 0.320$$

(notice that the final zero must be included in the count of places).

Multiplication by 10, 100, etc., is particularly easy because the decimal system is based on tens. To multiply by 10, 100, etc., move the decimal point one, two, etc., places to the right.

You may say, 'But suppose there isn't a point?' However, you can always think of a whole number such as 54 as being 54.0, so the point is there implicitly. Thus $54 \times 100 = 5400$, $3.9 \times 10 = 39$, and so on.

Division is a bit more complicated. What we do is to get rid of decimals in the denominator altogether by shifting the point the same number of places to the right in numerator and denominator – in other words, multiplying top and bottom by 10, 100 or whatever. We can do this because multiplying the top and bottom of a fraction simultaneously by the same figure makes no difference to its value. Once we have got rid of the decimals in the denominator in this way, we are back to division by an integer, and all we have to do is keep the point in the answer in the correct place:

$3.2/0.2 = 32/2$ (multiplying top and bottom by 10) $= 16$
$3.2/0.02 = 320/2$ (multiplying by 100) $= 160$
$0.32/0.2 = 3.2/2 = 1.6$, and so on.

To divide by 10, 100, etc., we move the point (or implied point) one, two, etc., places to the left, for example $4.3/100 = 0.043$.

Frequently we have to turn fractions into decimals, or vice versa. To turn a fraction into a decimal, divide the denominator into the numerator according to the usual process of division, as in $4/5 = 0.8$, $5/16 = 0.3125$, etc. Sometimes the process does not stop, but repeats itself after a certain number of decimal places. For example, $1/3 = 0.333...$, $6/7 = 0.857\ 142\ 857\ 142\ 8...$ This is called a *recurring* decimal. There are numbers – π is one you may have come across – that are decimals that neither repeat nor stop; they just carry on for ever with no discernible pattern!

You should remember the decimal equivalents of a few commonly used fractions: $0.5 = \frac{1}{2}$, $0.25 = \frac{1}{4}$, and so on.

The process the other way round – to write a given decimal as a fraction – is easy. If we want to turn 0.18 into a fraction, we have only to recall that this means 'one tenth and eight hundredths', that is, eighteen hundredths or 18/100. If you wish you can cancel this to 9/50.

Significant figures and rounding

Throughout all your calculations you will need to be able to round off answers to a certain number of decimal places or significant figures. Although your calculator probably spits out up to eight decimal places, it may not be sensible to quote them all – if, for instance, you are working in pounds and pence, there is no point in quoting an answer of £45.873 438. Indeed, the last few digits may not even be worth believing. There is no 'right' number of figures to quote in a given situation; you have to develop a feeling based on such things as the figures which went into the calculation, what you want to use the answer for, and so on. We will mention this at appropriate points in later chapters, but at the moment we will simply discuss the mechanics of rounding.

If we want to round a number to a given number of decimal places, the rule most commonly applied is that 5 and upwards are rounded up, everything below 5, down. So 3.675 to two decimal places is 3.68, 0.0689 to three places is 0.069, and so forth. This system does lead to slight bias in that rather more figures are rounded up than down (those ending in 5, 6, 7, 8 and 9 go up as against only 1, 2, 3 and 4 going down), but this is only important in situations where there are a lot of figures ending in 5s to be rounded. So although alternative methods have been devised to get round this problem we will stick to the common rule.

Another way to specify the accuracy required of a number is to require a certain number of *significant figures*. A figure is significant if it carries information; in this sense the zeros on the end of 15 000 or immediately after the decimal point in 0.0035 are not significant, but the zero in 7053 is. Thus 34 722 to three significant figures is 34 700; 0.002 56 to two significant figures is 0.0026; 7045 to three significant figures is 7050, and so on.

Exercise 3

1 Express 4/9 as a decimal to three places.

2 0.63/0.009   3 0.045 × 320   4 7.2/0.06

5 What is 16 527 to two significant figures?

6 Express 0.85 as a fraction.

7 3.5 × 1.2   8 0.005/0.05   9 400 × 0.0025

10 What is a quarter of 0.08?

Percentages

A percentage is really only a fraction in which the denominator is always 100, so that we do not bother to write it – or rather, the writing of '/100' has degenerated into the % sign. The term 'per cent' on its own means nothing, unless we specify per cent of *what*. For example, the statement 'prices are 10 per cent lower during the sale' is meaningless unless we say 'lower than list price' or 'lower than last week's price' or whatever.

The idea of expressing fractions as percentages is that for most people it is a good deal easier to visualise an amount such as 70 per cent, that is 70/100, than something such as 13/17. So it has become conventional to use 100 as a sort of standard denominator.

We actually use percentages in two different ways. First:

> To find a given percentage of a quantity, multiply the quantity by the percentage figure over 100.

For example,

$$16\% \text{ of } 40 = \frac{16}{100} \times 40 = \frac{640}{100} = 6.4.$$

All that we are doing here is recalling that 16 per cent means 16/100, and finding sixteen hundredths of 40.

Second:

> To express one quantity as a percentage of another, put the first over the second and multiply by 100.

For example,

$$£6 \text{ as a percentage of } £8: \frac{6}{8} \times 100 = \frac{600}{8} = 75\%.$$

Again, you should remember a few common percentages as fractions and vice versa, such as $50\% = \frac{1}{2}$, $25\% = \frac{1}{4}$, and so on.

To convert decimals into percentages, or the other way round, is a matter of moving the point. For instance, 0.08 as a percentage is 8 per cent (multiply by 100, i.e. move the point two places right) and 68 per cent as a decimal is 0.68 (move point two places left).

In dealing with practical problems involving percentages, be very careful to ask, 'Percentage of what?' As an illustration, suppose that we are told that a bill which includes $17\frac{1}{2}$ per cent VAT comes to £16. What was it before the VAT was added? The $17\frac{1}{2}$ per cent here is *not* $17\frac{1}{2}$ per cent of £16; it is $17\frac{1}{2}$ per cent of what the bill was *before* the VAT was added – the thing we are trying to find. If we call this amount x, what we can say is that $x + 17\frac{1}{2}$ per cent of x comes to £16, or in symbolic terms:

$$x + \frac{17.5x}{100} = £16.$$

So $\dfrac{117.5x}{100} = £16$

whence $\quad x = £16 \times \dfrac{100}{117.5} = £13.62.$

Exercise 4

1 What is 8 per cent of 40?

2 Express 17 per cent as a decimal.

3 Express 45 as a percentage of 108.

4 A price of £12.50 is increased by 20 per cent. What is the new price?

5 An item now priced at £12 carries a label 'Original price reduced by 25 per cent'. What was the original price?

6 The number of customers of an online store has increased by 12 per cent since last year. If there were 850 customers last year, how many are there now?

7 In a class of 56 students, 51 pass the final assessment. What is the percentage pass rate, to the nearest whole per cent?

8 What is 20 per cent of 80 per cent?

9 The amount of non-recyclable waste produced by a small factory has decreased by 30 per cent compared with last year. This year 16 tonnes were produced. What was last year's amount, to one decimal place?

10 An investment attracts 5 per cent interest per year. If you invest £200 at the start of year 1, and interest is added on the last day of the year, how much will you have in your account at the start of year 3?

Letters for numbers

As far as most people are concerned, I suppose of all the branches of mathematics they have studied at school, algebra seems the most rarefied and abstract. Certainly the higher reaches of algebra *can* be very abstract, but the kind of algebra we need to use is about as practical as it could be. The main purpose of using letters to represent numbers or quantities – which is what our kind of algebra is about – is that it enables us to express practical truths about the real world neatly, succinctly and in more general terms than we could if we insisted on sticking to definite numbers all the time.

To take a specific example: if you want to explain to someone how to find the area of a rectangle 4 cm by 3 cm, you can tell them to multiply 4 by 3. But if you call the length of the rectangle l and its width w, then you can say that the area is $l \times w$ – this will be true for *any* values of l and w. Again, consider the rule we have just encountered for expressing one quantity as a percentage of another: 'Put the first quantity on top of the second and multiply by 100'. What a mouthful! But if the first number is denoted by x and the second by y, then the rule boils down to $\frac{x}{y} \times 100$ – and once again, it holds good for whatever values of x and y we want to use.

This is the great strength in using letters to represent numbers – we are then able to write down rules, expressions and so on that are completely general, so that to find the answer in a particular case, all we need to do is substitute our particular values of x and y or whatever into the appropriate algebraic expression.

You will be coming across this application of algebra – the use of formulae to express rules – over and over in later chapters. But there are also some specific techniques that will be needed; we will begin with powers and roots, which will be referred to particularly in Chapter 16 on compound interest.

Powers and roots

We write x^2 as a shorthand for $x \times x$, x^3 to mean $x \times x \times x$, and in general x^n to mean x multiplied by itself n times. If we wish to multiply two such numbers together, say $x^m \times x^n$, where n and m are whole numbers, we will have

$$\underbrace{(x \times x \times x \times \ldots \times x)}_{m \text{ times}} \times \underbrace{(x \times x \times x \times \ldots \times x)}_{n \text{ times}};$$

that is, x multiplied by itself $m + n$ times altogether, which can be written as x^{m+n}. So we have the first rule for operating with indices (indices is the plural of index, which means the n in x^n):

> In multiplication, *add* the indices.

We can develop the rule for division in the same way. If we have x^3/x^2, we can cancel to get x^1 (this is, of course, the same as x, since we do not usually bother writing the 1). Similarly, if we have x^m/x^n, with $m > n$, cancelling gives x^{m-n}, suggesting the division rule:

> In division, *subtract* the indices.

This in turn gives a meaning to a negative power of x. Consider x^2/x^3; by cancellation this becomes $1/x$, but by the division rule we have just derived it must also be equal to $x^{2-3} = x^{-1}$. So to be consistent we have to interpret x^{-1} as meaning $1/x$, and more generally x^{-n} as meaning $1/x^n$. We can also use the division rule to give x^0 a definition. Of course, x^2/x^2 is just 1, but it is also, by the division rule, $x^{2-2} = x^0$. Thus x^0 has to be equal to 1; and, there being nothing special about x, we can say:

> Anything to the power 0 is 1.

Finally, what about fractional powers, such as $x^{\frac{1}{2}}$? By the multiplication rule, $x^{\frac{1}{2}} \times x^{\frac{1}{2}} = x^{\frac{1}{2}+\frac{1}{2}} = x^1$; in other words, $x^{\frac{1}{2}}$ is the thing which, when multiplied by itself, gives x. This is what we call the *square root* of x; so $x^{\frac{1}{2}}$ means $\sqrt{x}$. Similarly. $x^{\frac{1}{3}}$ means $\sqrt[3]{x}$, the cube root of x, and in general

> $x^{1/n} = \sqrt[n]{x}$, the nth root of x.

(that is, the number that, multiplied by itself n times, gives x).

To see how all these rules work in combination, we will simplify the following:

$$\frac{y^4 \times y^2}{\sqrt{y^3}} = \frac{y^{4+2}}{y^{3/2}} = \frac{y^6}{y^{3/2}} = y^{6-3/2} = y^{9/2}.$$

If you find these complicated powers a bit difficult to get hold of, try putting in numbers rather than letters. For example,

$$4^{\frac{1}{2}} = \sqrt{4} = 2, \qquad 2^{-2} = \tfrac{1}{4} \text{ or } 0.25,$$

and so on. (Strictly $\sqrt{4} = \pm 2$, since $(-2)^2 = 4$.)

Exercise 5

Simplify:

1 $y^4 \div y^2$ 2 $\sqrt[3]{\sqrt{x}}$ 3 x^3/x 4 $p^2 \times pq \times q^2$ 5 $1/n^3$

6 $a \times \dfrac{b}{a^2}$ 7 $y^2 \times y^2$ 8 $3x^2/9x$ 9 $\dfrac{x^2 \times x^4}{\sqrt{x}}$ 10 $\sqrt{(16x^4)}$

Note: when we write two symbols next to each other with no sign between, as in question 4 above, they are interpreted as being multiplied.

The use of brackets

In several of the formulae we shall be encountering in later chapters you will find brackets used to clarify the order in which operations are to be carried out. The basic rule for dealing with these is that operations in brackets are done first.

Suppose we want to find the value of $4(6y + 3)$ when y is 9. We must work out the $6y + 3$ first, which comes to $6 \times 9 + 3 = 54 + 3 = 57$ (remember that $\times$ comes before +) and then multiply this by 4 to get 228. So the 4 multiplies *everything* inside the bracket, and this applies also when we have a letter rather than a number outside. For example,

$$2p(3p - 8) = 2p \times 3p - 2p \times 8 = 6p^2 - 16p.$$

Be careful if there is a minus sign outside the brackets: remember the rules for multiplying by a negative number, for example

$$-2x(x - 1) = -2x^2 + 2x.$$

Even if there is no number or other expression in front of a bracket, just a minus sign, the same applies:

$$8x - (x - 1)$$

means

$$8x - 1(x - 1) = 8x - x + 1 = 7x + 1.$$

It is important to realise that if we write $6x^2$ what we mean is 'square x first and then multiply by 6', whereas $(6x)^2$ means 'multiply x by 6 and then square the result'. In later statistical work we will encounter a case where this distinction is very important. Also note that xy and yx mean the same thing.

Where there are two bracketed expressions to be multiplied together, a useful mnemonic to help you ensure that you have included all the terms is FOIL, standing for First, Outer, Inner and Last:

$$(x - 2)(x + 3) = x^2 + 3x - 2x - 6 = x^2 + x - 6.$$
$$\quad\quad\;\; \text{First} \;\; \text{Outer} \;\; \text{Inner} \;\; \text{Last}$$

With more than two bracketed expressions, it is easiest to multiply out two at a time:

$$(x + 2)(2x - 1)(x + 3) = (2x^2 + 3x - 2)(x + 3)$$
$$= 2x^3 + 9x^2 + 7x - 6.$$

Finally, if you encounter brackets within brackets, remove the inner ones first:

$$4[x + 3(x - 2)] = 4(x + 3x - 6)$$
$$= 4(4x - 6)$$
$$= 16x - 24.$$

Exercise 6

Simplify 1–3:

1 $3x(2x - 6)$ 2 $(a - 1)(a + 2)$ 3 $x(3y + z)$

4 Find $8x^2$ and $(8x)^2$ when $x = 2$.

5 Evaluate $3pq(q - p)$ when $p = 5$ and $q = \frac{1}{2}$.

6 $(x + y)(x - y)(2x - 1)$

7 $2(a + b) - 3(a - b)$

8 The proprietor of a sandwich bar represents the cost of bread for each sandwich by B pence, and the cost of the filling by F pence. So the cost of making 12 sandwiches can be represented by $12(B + F)$. Explain why the brackets are needed in this expression.

9 What is wrong with this piece of algebra?

$$2(x + y) - x(x + y) = 2x + y - x^2 + xy$$

10 Simplify $x[2x - 3(y - 2)]$.

Solving equations

Throughout the rest of this book, particularly in Chapter 12 where we discuss regression, and to a lesser extent Chapters 8 and 9, you will come across equations that have to be solved, or algebraic expressions that have to be manipulated – two very similar processes in practice.

We speak of *solving* an equation when we express an unknown quantity in terms either of other quantities or of numbers. We can only solve a single equation for *one* unknown quantity; if there is more than one, then more than one equation will be required. In this section, we will concentrate on a single equation involving a single unknown, and in fact we will deal only with *linear* equations – those that do not involve any powers of x higher than the first. You may have grappled with quadratic equations – those including x^2 terms – at school, but as we do not need those anywhere in later chapters we will not discuss them.

Our aim in solving an equation, then, is to isolate x – or whatever the unknown quantity may be called – on one side of the equals sign (usually the left, but there is no reason why it must be); we can work towards this end by all the legitimate processes of algebra – adding and subtracting things, multiplying or dividing by things – as long as we do the same to both sides of the equation at every stage. This is the only real rule in solving equations; other rules you may have learnt, such as 'change side, change sign' or 'cross multiplication', are really only special cases of this general rule.

Suppose we have the equation $3x + 2 = 9$. We want to isolate x on the left-hand side. As a first step towards this, let us get rid of the +2 by taking 2 away from each side:

$$3x + 2 - 2 = 9 - 2,$$

that is $3x = 7$, since $+2 - 2 = 0$.

Now get rid of the 3 from the left-hand side by dividing by 3:

$$\frac{3x}{3} = \frac{7}{3},$$

that is $x = \frac{7}{3}$ or $2\frac{1}{3}$.

Let us work through another example:

$$\frac{4}{y} = \frac{7}{2}.$$

The y here is on the bottom of a fraction, which we certainly do not want. Get rid of it from the bottom by multiplying through by y:

$$\frac{4}{y} \times y = \frac{7}{2} \times y, \text{ or } 4 = \frac{7y}{2}.$$

(If you find it hard to remember that $\frac{7}{2} \times y$ is the same thing as $\frac{7y}{2}$, note that y can always be thought of as $\frac{y}{1}$.) Now multiply each side of the equation by 2, obtaining $8 = 7y$. Finally, divide both sides by 7 to get $y = 8/7$.

The same sorts of processes apply if we are trying to transform a formula rather than solve an equation. For example, given the equation $A = l \times b$ for the area of a rectangle, we can get b in terms of the other two variables by dividing both sides by l, to give $b = A/l$.

Let us take a more complicated case: the formula $1/u + 1/v = 1/f$ relates the distances of object and image in a lens of a certain focal length. Suppose we want to find v in terms of u and f. First, subtract $1/u$ from each side:

$$1/v = 1/f - 1/u = \frac{u - f}{uf},$$

putting the right-hand side over a common denominator. Now invert both sides to get

$$v = \frac{uf}{u - f}.$$

We have contracted some of the steps here, as you will be able to do when you are familiar with the processes; but if in any doubt, ask yourself, 'What am I doing to *this* side of the equation? Have I done it to the *other* side too?'

A final example before you try to solve some equations yourself: if $y + z^2 = x$, find z in terms of y and x:

$$z^2 = x - y, \text{ and so } z = \pm\sqrt{x - y}.$$

Exercise 7

Solve the following equations. (Some of them look as if they might be quadratics – but they aren't!)

1 $x + 2 = -3$ 2 $2 + x = 3 - x$ 3 $6x^2 = 54$

4 $2x + 3 = 5$ 5 If $v = u + ft$, find f.   6 $x^2 - 2 = x^2 + 4x + 8$

7 If $P = R - (F + nV)$, find V.   8 If $(a + b)^2 = 16c$, find a.   9 If $\sqrt[3]{x^2 y} = 3z$, find y.

10 $x + 4 = 12 - 3x$

Equations from problems

When you are concerned not so much with handling algebraic expressions for their own sake as with using them in the course of solving practical problems, the major difficulty may well be, not solving the equation, but extracting it from the 'wordy' problem in the first place. The line of approach can best be demonstrated by an example, since this is not an area where cut-and-dried 'rules' can be laid down.

Suppose we are told that a return bus ticket for a certain trip costs half as much again as a single one, and that when a passenger books three return and two single tickets she pays £3.25. How much does each type of ticket cost?

The first step is always to give the unknown quantity a name. Here we appear to have two unknown quantities – the price of a single ticket and that of a return – but they are related in such a way that if we call the price of a single ticket £x, then a return costs $1.5 \times £x$. Thus the statement of the problem can be reduced to

$$3 \times 1.5 \times x + 2 \times x = 3.25$$

whence

$$4.5x + 2x = 6.5x = 3.25$$

so that $x = 0.50$. A single ticket costs 50p, therefore, and a return 75p.

This was, of course, a very easy example. In more complicated cases, it can help to get to the general expression via particular figures. For example, if we are told that a firm orders items in boxes of x at a time, and are asked how many boxes will be needed to supply 500 items, we can get an idea of how to proceed by saying: 'Suppose they came in boxes of 50 at a time; how many would then be needed to supply 500 items?' The answer is clearly 10. What have we done to get this? Obviously, divided the 50 into the 500. So more generally, if the boxes contain x items, we will divide x into 500 to find that $500/x$ boxes are needed.

Some unfamiliar symbols

Many of the problems we will be concerned with, especially in Chapter 17, are expressible not as equations but as inequalities: the number of workers needed to operate a production line is at least eight, we cannot spend more than £500 on this new machine, and so on.

Just as we use = to represent the fact that two quantities are equal, so we have symbols to represent these inequalities:

$$a \leqslant b \text{ means } `a \text{ is less than or equal to } b`.$$

So we might say $x \leqslant 100$ to express the fact that a sum of money, x pence, is never greater than £1. Or, if y denotes the number of students out of a class of 20 who pass an exam, we could say $y \leqslant 20$, because obviously 20 is the maximum number who can pass.

In a similar way,

$$p \geqslant q \text{ means } `p \text{ is greater than or equal to } q`.$$

If I am manufacturing p items in a week and already have advance orders for 16, I might say $p \geqslant 16$ to express the fact that I must make at least 16 items.

If you find it confusing to recall which symbol is which, notice that the bigger end of the symbol points to the bigger quantity.

There are also two other symbols, related to these but not quite so widely used, < and >. These mean 'less than (or greater than) but not equal to'. So if you have got only enough raw material to make 20 items, you could write 'number of items < 21'.

Exercise 8

1 The cost of a journey is reckoned to be 50p plus 5p per mile. Write down an expression for the cost of travelling m miles.

2 I am buying handkerchiefs and socks for my family's Christmas presents – a box of handkerchiefs costs £1.50 and a pair of socks £1.25. I don't want to spend more than £12 altogether. If I buy h boxes of handkerchiefs and s pairs of socks, write down an expression representing my financial limitation.

3 A spoon costs twice as much as a fork, and six forks and ten spoons cost £20.80. How much does a spoon cost?

4 Balloons can be bought in packets of 12 for 25p, or separately for 3p each. Write down an expression for the cost of buying y balloons ($12 < y < 23$).

Simultaneous equations

You will need to be able to solve simultaneous equations – a pair of linear equations with two unknowns – to cope with material in Chapter 17. The equations are called simultaneous because we have to consider them both at once if we are to be able to solve them.

There are two methods that may be used to solve a pair of simultaneous linear equations with two unknowns, often called x and y. If you have studied this topic before, then continue to use the method with which you are familiar; if you are coming to the subject with no prior knowledge, I recommend you read the explanation of both methods and then choose the one which you find easiest.

Both methods are best illustrated using an example:

$$2x + y = 4, \tag{1}$$

$$3x - 2y = 7. \tag{2}$$

Both methods involve moving from two equations with two unknowns to one equation with one unknown, which we already know how to solve. However, the process by which this is achieved varies between the two approaches.

Method A

In this method we use one equation to express one of the variables in terms of the other, and then substitute this into the other equation. We will choose to use equation (1) above to express y in terms of x, as this is the easiest option. (Can you see why? It's because we only have a single y in equation (1).)

Manipulation of equation (1) gives

$$y = 4 - 2x. \tag{3}$$

Now we replace the y in equation (2) by $4 - 2x$, to get

$$3x - 2(4 - 2x) = 7.$$

Removing the brackets gives

$$3x - 8 + 4x = 7,$$

so

$$7x - 8 = 7,$$

and hence

$$7x = 7 + 8 = 15,$$

so that $x = 15/7$. Now we use equation (3) to tell us the value of y:

$$y = 4 - 2 \times (15/7) = 4 - 30/7 = 28/7 - 30/7 = -2/7.$$

So the solution is $x = 15/7$, $y = -2/7$. It is always a good idea to check your answer by putting the x and y values you have found back into the original equations. Here we have, from (1),

$$2x + y = 30/7 - 2/7 = 28/7 = 4,$$

and from (2)

$$3x - 2y = 45/7 - (-4/7) = 45/7 + 4/7 = 49/7 = 7,$$

so that both equations are satisfied by the solution.

This method will always work except in two special situations:

(i) where the original equations are *inconsistent* – that is, they just cannot both be true at once (e.g. $x + y = 9$ and $x + y = 7$);

(ii) where the original equations are really the *same* equation – for example, $2x - y = 4$ and $x = 2 + \frac{1}{2}y$.

You might like to try solving these equations, to see where the method breaks down.

Method B

In the second method, we aim to get the same number either of xs or of ys in the two equations, so that we can get rid of one variable by either adding or subtracting the equations, to give a single equation in one variable which we already know how to solve. To achieve this end, we may operate on either or both of the equations according to the rules of algebra, as long as we remember the cardinal rule that we must perform an operation *throughout* an equation – that is, to both sides.

Here, if we multiply the top equation by 2 and leave the bottom one alone, we get

$$4x + 2y = 8$$
$$3x - 2y = 7$$

which, added, give

$$7x = 15, \text{ since } +2y - 2y = 0.$$

Thus $x = 15/7$, and we can now substitute this value in either of the *original* two equations to find y. Choosing the original first equation, because it is slightly simpler:

$$2 \times 15/7 + y = 4$$
$$\text{i.e. } 30/7 + y = 4$$
$$\text{i.e. } \quad y = 4 - 30/7$$
$$= -2/7.$$

This agrees with the result obtained by method A.

Exercise 9

Solve, where possible, the following pairs of equations:

1 $2x + y = 3$; $x - y = 6$.

2 $7x + 2y = 11$; $4x + 3y = 10$.

3 $x - y = 4$; $2x = 2y + 8$.

4 $2x + y = 1$; $2x - 3y = 9$.

5 $x + y = 3$; $x - 2y = 3$.

6 Find two numbers, one of which is twice the other, and whose sum is 18.

7 $a + 2b = 14$; $2a - b = 13$.

8 $2x + y = 7$; $4x + 2y = 3$.

9 Peter is three years older than Ahmed, and their combined ages add up to 31. How old is Peter?

10 $x/y = 5$; $2x + y = 33$.

Straight line graphs

In Chapters 12, 14 and 17, there will be quite a lot of graphical work, so it is important that you should be able to plot or sketch simple graphs without too much trouble.

The idea behind almost all graphs is to show pictorially the relationship between two quantities, often called x and y, though it is a good idea not to get too attached to this notation. Graphs that result in straight lines are going to be particularly important to us, since a straight line is the only form one can be quite definite about; plotting it accurately is simply a matter of using a ruler, whereas plotting any kind of curve involves some degree of skill and judgement. Moreover, to plot a straight line graph we need know only two points on the line (three if we want an extra point for checking purposes), whereas to obtain a reasonably accurate curve, a whole set of points is needed.

It is therefore useful, and saves wasting time, if you are able to recognise when an equation will result in a straight line graph. Consider the case of a manufacturer who, in producing some commodity, has fixed costs of £300 plus a variable cost of £2 per item. We will call the number of items being made n, and will construct a graph to show the relationship between the number of items made and the total cost of making them.

If no items at all are made, there will still be the fixed costs of £300 to pay, so when $n = 0$, cost = £300. The total cost will then increase by £2 for every extra item that is made; so 10 items will cost £320, 20 items will cost £340, and so on. It is clear that the graph representing the relationship will climb at a steady rate – that is, it will be a straight line. The graph is shown in Figure 1.1 and illustrates a number of general points about graph-plotting.

First, we have chosen to put the number of items being made on the horizontal axis, and the costs on the vertical axis. This is in accordance with the convention that the *independent* quantity goes horizontally and the *dependent* one vertically; in this case cost depends on the numbers of items being made. Of course it is not always totally clear which is the dependent quantity, so in some cases there may be scope for alternative ways of plotting. However, it is fairly safe to say that amounts of money – costs, profits, revenues and so on – are nearly always plotted on the vertical axis.

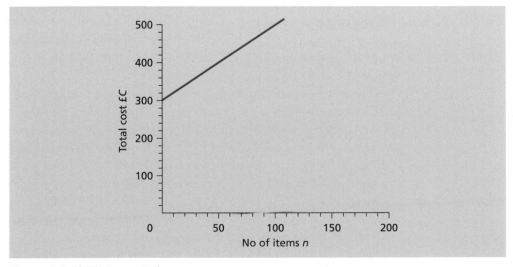

Figure 1.1 Plotting a graph

The second thing to notice is the choice of scales. The question of the *range* of *n* values we choose to plot is one to which we will return later, but for now you should notice that the *n*-scale goes up in steps of 10, and the cost-scale in steps of £20. When you are using graph paper that is divided into multiples of ten squares, it is asking for trouble to choose a scale that goes in multiples of seven, or three, or some other amount not easily related to ten; you are very likely to go wrong in trying to estimate intermediate values by eye. It is much safer, therefore, to use steps of 5, 10 and so on which are easily related to the subdivisions on your graph paper.

I hope it is hardly necessary to point out that the scales on both axes increase by *equal* steps; it would be quite wrong, and could result in some very funny-shaped graphs, if we started off with one large division on the scale representing ten items, and then suddenly changed half-way along the axis to one division representing twenty.

If we now look at the graph line itself, we see that it commences when no items are being made at a cost of £300, as already calculated, and then climbs by £20 for every ten items made. We can relate these facts to the equation representing the line, as follows. The total cost, £*C* say, is given by the fixed cost of £300 plus £2 per item made – that will be £2*n* for *n* items. Thus $C = 300 + 2n$ is the equation of the cost line. Now, comparing this with the graph, you can see that the 300 – the 'fixed' part that does not change with *n* – is represented by the point where the graph crosses the vertical axis. This point is known as the *intercept*:

The intercept is the value of *C* where $n = 0$.

As for the £2 per item, that gives us the *slope* of the line:

The slope of the line is the amount by which *C* increases for each increase of one unit in *n*.

We could find this slope by taking any convenient increase in *n*, and dividing it into the corresponding increase in *C*.

In fact, any straight line equation will have the form $y = a + bx$, where *a* and *b* are some numbers, and *x* and *y* are the variable quantities. Comparing this general equation with the cost equation just discussed, which had values of 300 for *a* and 2 for *b*, you can see that *a* is going to tell us where the graph crosses the vertical axis (assuming that the horizontal scale starts from zero) and *b* tells us the slope. By giving *a* and *b* different values, we can obtain all possible straight lines.

For example, equations in which *a* is zero will pass through the origin of the graph; particular cases would be $y = 2x$ and $C = \frac{1}{2}n$. If we wish to have a line which slopes *down-hill* from left to right, then we must give the slope a negative value, expressing the fact that as *x* increases, *y* gets smaller. So, for instance, the graph of $y = 20 - 2x$ is as shown in Figure 1.2.

It is easy to see why equations involving powers of *x* higher than 1 cannot result in straight lines. If we had $y = x^2$, then as *x* increases from 1 to 2, *y* will increase from 1 to 4 – an increase of 3. But as *x* goes from 2 to 3, the corresponding *y*-increase is from 4 to 9, a change of five units. In fact the bigger *x* gets, the faster *y* increases, so we no longer have the steady rate of increase that would produce a straight line.

Having said this, however, I should warn you that sometimes straight line equations may arise in a form which does not immediately look like $y = a + bx$. For example,

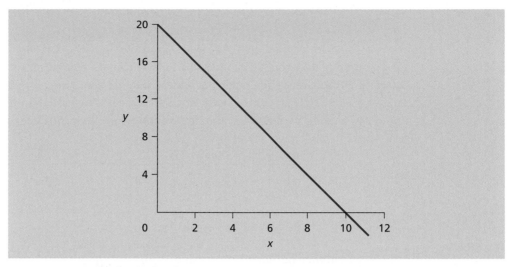

Figure 1.2 Graph of $y = 20 - 2x$

$x/y = 6$ looks as if it involves a y on the bottom of a fraction – a y^{-1}, in fact – but a bit of algebraic juggling turns the equation into $x = 6y$, or $y = \frac{1}{6}x$, the equation of a line through the origin with a slope of $\frac{1}{6}$. So you must be prepared for such possibilities.

Having recognised an equation as giving a straight line, how should you go about plotting it? It is safest to find three points on the line, two for plotting and one for checking. Take $y = 20 - 2x$, and suppose we want to plot it for values of x from 0 to 10. We could use $x = 0$, 1 and 2 as our three points, but it is much safer to use values as far apart as possible, since this will minimise the effect of any errors in plotting, as is shown by Figure 1.3. So we choose $x = 0$, which gives $y = 20$; $x = 5$, giving $y = 10$; and $x = 10$, for which $y = 0$. We plot points at 0 on the horizontal scale and 20 on the vertical; and at 10 on the horizontal and 0 on the vertical; join them together and then verify that the third point, $x = 5$ and $y = 10$, does indeed lie on the line we have plotted.

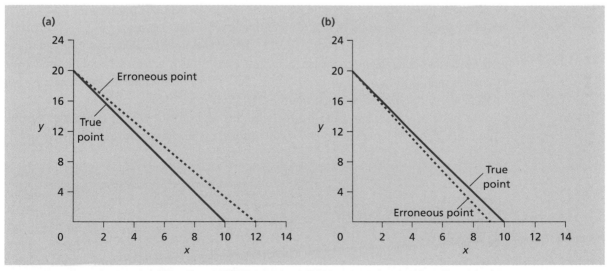

Figure 1.3 The need to use points as far apart as possible when plotting straight line graphs: (a) small error in plotting gives large errors as x increases; (b) small error in plotting gives only small errors throughout

Other types of graph

If for some reason you have to plot a graph which you recognise will *not* give a straight line, the process is not dissimilar, but you need to use a lot more points in order to be able to draw a smooth curve through them. In this case it is easier to set out the calculation of points as a table. To plot $y = x^2 + 3x$, for example, I would recommend a layout as follows:

	x	0	1	2	3	4	. . .
	x^2	0	1	4	9	16	. . .
+	$3x$	0	3	6	9	12	. . .
	y	0	4	10	18	28	. . .

Points would then be plotted at $x = 0$ and $y = 0$, $x = 1$ and $y = 4$, etc., and as smooth a curve as possible drawn through them. If you find it very difficult to get your curve to go through one particular point, go back to check your calculation – the point might be in the wrong place!

Graphing inequalities

Before we end this section, we will take a brief look at how inequalities, introduced on p. 22, can be shown graphically. Taking a very easy case first, consider $y \geqslant 6$.

We want to identify the region of the graph in which the value of y is equal to, or bigger than, 6, regardless of what is happening to x. It is not hard to see that that will be true everywhere on and above the horizontal line through $y = 6$. We generally choose to indicate this on the graph by shading the side of the line where the inequality is *not* satisfied, as shown in Figure 1.4.

A more complicated case would be $3x + 5y \leqslant 15$. We begin by plotting the line $3x + 5y = 15$; the easiest way to do that is to note that x is 5 when y is zero, and y is 3 when x is zero. Then we must decide on which side of this line the inequality is satisfied. Take some simple point below the line, such as the origin. Here $3x + 5y$ is zero, which is certainly less than or equal to 15, so the side of the line including the origin satisfies the inequality but points above the line do not (see Figure 1.5).

We have been concentrating throughout this section on what is called the *positive quadrant* – the region of graphs in which both x and y are positive. In many of the

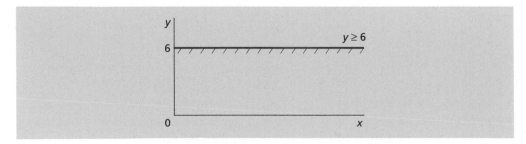

Figure 1.4 Graphing a simple inequality

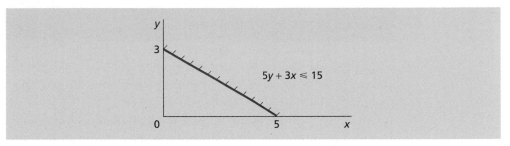

Figure 1.5 Graphing a more complicated inequality

practical applications we are concerned with, that will be the region of interest, because real variables such as costs, quantity produced, numbers of employees and so on cannot be negative. Nevertheless, you should not forget that there *are* cases where we might need to extend our graphs to cover negative regions; an example would be the profit graph of a firm making a loss – that is to say, a negative profit.

Sketching graphs

Don't imagine that you necessarily have to plot a graph using graph paper in order to get an idea of the relationship between two quantities. Very often it's sufficient to identify a few key facts – such as whether the graph passes through the origin and whether its slope is positive or negative – and then roughly sketch the overall shape of the graph. You need only worry about plotting points accurately if you need to be able to read off precise values from the graph, or if you are using it to find the exact solution of a problem.

We've spent quite a long time discussing graphs, because they are fundamental to many topics later in the book. Try the following exercise to make sure you have understood the sections.

Exercise 10

1   Which of the following equations would give straight line graphs:
    (a) $y = 2x - 17$; (b) $xy = 4$; (c) $p = 6q + 44$; (d) $2/x = 5/y$?

2   Find the slope of the graphs in question 1 which give straight lines.

3   Plot the graph of $R = 200n - 8n^2$ for values of n between 0 and 30.

4   Show on a single graph the regions satisfying $x > 4$ and $3x + 2y > 12$.

5   Sketch the graph of $y = 2x + 1$.

6   Where does the graph of $6x - 7y = 21$ cross the x-axis?

7   Does the graph of $y = x(x - 3)$ pass through the origin?

8   The equation $n = 20(200 - p)$ relates the price of an item in pence, p, to the number of items sold per week, n. Where does this graph cross the n-axis? What does this represent in practical terms?

9   Describe the region defined by the inequality $2x + 5y < 20$.

10 Draw up the table needed to plot the graph of $C = 4n(n - 10)$ for values of n from 0 to 20.

Making use of graphs

In the previous sections we discussed plotting graphs and inequalities without reference to what practical situation they might represent. We will now take a brief look at the applications to which they may be put.

One of the most important of these is in the solution of equations. For instance, if we have the graph of $y = 2x + 3$ (a straight line) then the point where this crosses the x-axis – that is, where $y = 0$ – gives the solution of the equation $0 = 2x + 3$, or, as we would more usually express it, $2x + 3 = 0$. This is a very simple equation which could easily be solved without the use of a graph, but the same method works for the more complex equations, such as quadratics, which give rise to curves.

To find the solution of the quadratic $x^2 + 2x - 15 = 0$, as an example, we would plot the graph $y = x^2 + 2x - 15$ as explained on p. 28, and then look for the points at which the curve crosses the x-axis (where $y = 0$). These turn out to be $x = 3$ and $x = -5$, which are exactly the values satisfying the quadratic, as you can check for yourself.

Perhaps even more important is the use of graphs to solve two equations simultaneously. The points at which two equations are simultaneously satisfied are the points at which their graphs cross, as you can verify by plotting the graphs of one of the pairs of simultaneous equations you solved in Exercise 9. This gives us a method for solving two simultaneous equations even when one of them is not linear and the methods of the section on simultaneous equations (p. 23) will not work.

A business application

All these points are best illustrated by taking a look at one of the major applications of graphical methods in business – the *break-even graph*. The idea behind this is simple: a firm is said to break even when costs are just balanced by revenues. The break-even point is, in fact, the point at which the firm begins to make a profit.

Suppose that we return to the item whose production costs were discussed on pp. 25–6, giving rise to the straight line cost equation $C = 300 + 2n$ where n was the number produced. We will now imagine that the demand for the product is related to the price being charged for it by the equation $n = 600 - 50p$, where n is the number sold at a price p pounds. This means that if a price of £2 is charged, 500 items will be sold; at £3 each, the number sold will be 450, and so on.

We can manipulate this expression to give price in terms of number sold, using the processes discussed on p. 20, to get $p = (600 - n)/50$, or $p = 12 - 0.02n$. This is the price at which n items could be sold, so the revenue generated by the sale of these n items will be price × quantity. The revenue equation is thus $R = n(12 - 0.02n)$, or $R = 12n - 0.02n^2$. Notice here how we use meaningful notation – R for revenue, n for number – rather than x and y.

To find the output at which the firm will break even, then, all we need do is plot, on the same pair of axes, the revenue and cost graphs. A point that often causes problems in cases of this kind, though, is what sort of range of values of n we should be looking at. Should we draw up tables of values for C and R with $n = 1, 2, 3 \ldots$, or with $n = 1000$,

2000, 3000 . . . ? Well, it is pretty clear that since we are talking about a commodity where the fixed costs of production are £300, while prices, as we have just seen, are of the order of a few pounds, we are going to have to sell a fair number before we even cover the fixed costs, let alone start making a profit.

So we try a couple of values of n of the order of several hundreds, to get a better idea of what sort of range we should be considering. If $n = 500$ then the costs are $300 + 2 \times 500 = £1300$, while the revenue generated is $12 \times 500 - 0.02 \times 500 \times 500 = £1000$, so a loss is being made. If $n = 300$, then in a similar way the costs are £900 and the revenue £1800 (you should check these calculations), so a profit of £900 is made. Thus the change from profit to loss comes somewhere between $n = 300$ and $n = 500$.

Knowing this, we choose to set up a table as follows:

n	50	100	150	200	250	300	350	400	450	500
$C(£)$	400	500	600	700	800	900	1000	1100	1200	1300
$12n$	600	1200	1800	2400	3000	3600	4200	4800	5400	6000
$0.02n^2$	50	200	450	800	1250	1800	2450	3200	4050	5000
$R(£)$	550	1000	1350	1600	1750	1800	1750	1600	1350	1000

It is clear from the table that the firm begins to make a profit at some output below 50 items; there is already a profit at $n = 50$, but we know there must be a loss at $n = 0$, where there is no revenue to offset costs of £300. A profit ceases to be made between 450 and 500 items. To determine the values more exactly, the two curves, one for revenue and one for costs, are plotted as shown in Figure 1.6, from which the approximate break-even

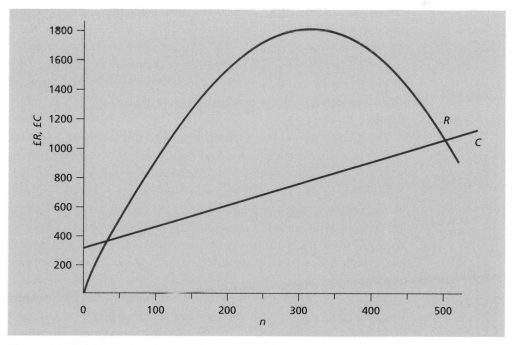

Figure 1.6 Break-even graph

points can be read off as $n = 32$ and $n = 468$. Strictly speaking, only the first of these is called a break-even, though of course it is as important to know where you stop making a profit as where you start to make one!

Exercise 11

1 A firm has fixed costs of £500 and a variable cost of 50p per item. It sells its product at a price of 80p per item, regardless of the number sold. Draw a graph to find at what output the firm breaks even.

2 Draw a suitable graph to determine the solution of the equation $x^2 - 6x + 5 = 0$.

3 A firm has the choice of two machines: machine A will give a fixed cost of £20 plus £1 for every 100 items produced; machine B has no fixed costs, but will incur variable costs at a rate of £1 multiplied by the square of the number of hundreds of items produced. At what output does machine A become cheaper than machine B?

A word about calculators

Although it is important that you should be happy with the mathematical skills described in this chapter, it would be silly to ignore the fact that the great majority of calculations are now carried out using either a calculator or a computer package such as a spreadsheet. Reference will be made throughout the book to the use of Microsoft Excel for carrying out statistical calculations and for plottings charts and graphs. However, for your quantitative work you will also need to have a calculator and know how to use it effectively. This section therefore offers a little advice on getting the most out of your calculator.

I will not constantly mention the fact that you should be using a calculator for your computations – that goes without saying. What I will do is point out particular processes that can be speeded up by making efficient use of such things as the constant key or the memory on your calculator. It would be impossible to tell you what key sequences to use, since there are so many different models of calculator on the market, and each has its own quirks of operation. It is up to you to read the booklet that came with your calculator when you bought it, and make sure you exploit to the full all those buttons you have paid for.

If you are about to buy a calculator before embarking on your course, the minimum you need is a machine with the four basic functions ($+, -, \times, \div$) plus a memory (preferably one with both M+ and M− facilities) and a square root. Many of you will already have scientific calculators, which can compute means, standard deviations and so on automatically – that is, without requiring the user to understand the details of the calculation. You should certainly know how to use these facilities, and they come in very handy for checking answers, but many examinations, particularly those set by external bodies such as the accountancy institutes, will not permit you to quote the results from such a calculator in isolation. They preface exam papers by a statement such as 'All workings must be shown to obtain full credit'. Be careful, therefore, not to become too dependent on your calculator if you are doing a course of this kind.

Below is a set of exercises to make sure you are comfortable with your calculator and get the best out of it. If you get stuck on any of them, go back to the instruction manual!

Exercise 12

You should be able to perform all these calculations on a four-function, single-memory calculator with per cent key and square root, *without* having to write down any intermediate steps.

1 17×82

2 $83 + 66 + 947$

3 $54 - 76 + 12$

4 $95 \div 8.3$

5 $0.002 \times 10\ 304$

6 $12 \times 8 + 13 \times 11$

7 $11/7 + 5/3 + 9/13$

8 $16 \times 16 + 17 \times 17 + 18 \times 18$

9 $14 \div \sqrt{2}$

10 $\sqrt{8} \times 4$

11 Find the total cost of three loaves at 58p each, 2 kg of cheese at £4.20 per kg, and six lettuces at 65p each.

12 There are 2.54 cm in 1 inch. Convert the following set of lengths to inches: 8 cm, 27 cm, 33 cm, 49 cm, 72 cm.

13 An examination is marked out of 80. What is the percentage mark of a student who gets 66 out of 80?

14 In the same exam, five students gain 23, 37, 44, 59, 73 out of 80. Convert all these marks to percentages (nearest whole per cent).

15 What is 33 per cent of £900?

16 Find the cost inclusive of $17\frac{1}{2}$ per cent VAT of an item that without VAT costs £17.

17 $\sqrt{\dfrac{8 \times 13 + 517}{86}}$

18 $\dfrac{11 + 17.3}{2.8 \times 4.3 + 3.6 \times 9}$

19 $1.1 + 1.1^2 + 1.1^3 + 1.1^4$

For calculators with an M− key:

20 $2.3 \times 6 - 1.9 \times 4$

21 $\sqrt{\dfrac{263}{7} - 4.9^2}$

22 $\dfrac{16}{8 \times 18.2 - 4 \times 13.7}$

23 $2 \times 3 + 4 \times 5 - 6 \times 7$

24 A shopkeeper pays his wholesaler for a dozen items at £1.72 each, 40 at £8.84 each, and 200 at 63p each, and receives a refund for 60 items costing 52p each which he returns. How much does he pay when 8 per cent cash discount has been deducted?

Case Study

Partywhizz!

You are planning a reception for some of your company's important clients, and have asked the catering company Partywhizz to provide you with a quote for the event. Partywhizz offers you a choice of two tariffs: tariff A costs £80 for up to eight guests, then £7.50 per head thereafter, while tariff B costs £9 per head with no minimum number of guests.

Draw up a table to show the cost of the event for up to 25 guests, preferably using Excel. Display the data on a graph, and write a short report for your manager summarising your recommendations as to which tariff you should choose.

Further reading

If you have worked carefully through the material of this chapter, plus the exercises, and not had too much difficulty, you should be well equipped to tackle the rest of the book. However, if you feel your difficulties need a more thorough revision of basic maths, you may find the following book helpful:

Morris, C. (with Thanassoulis, E.) (2007), *Essential Maths*, Palgrave.

Part 2

NUMBERS –
A MEANS OF COMMUNICATION

In this part we will discuss why we need to be able to communicate numerically as well as verbally. We will examine some of the ways in which we can best gather numerical information and convey it to other people, and see how we can make the most of numerical information that other people are trying to convey to us.

Chapter 2

OBTAINING THE FIGURES:
DATA AND DATA COLLECTION

Learning outcomes

There are no prerequisites for understanding this chapter. By the end of your work on this chapter you should be able to:

1 recognise qualitative and quantitative, discrete and continuous scales of measurement, and decide which type would be suitable in a given case;

2 explain the difference between primary and secondary data, and decide in practical cases which type could most appropriately be used;

3 define the major methods of selecting a sample from a population, and comment on their advantages and disadvantages;

4 design a simple questionnaire, and make constructive criticisms of those designed by other people;

5 name some of the more important sources of published statistical data;

6 make use of the Internet to access and search for data;

7 show awareness of the potential, and the problems, offered by electronic data collection.

Quantitative methods in practice

Aer Lingus flies high over rival Ryanair, say passengers

Aideen Sheehan Consumer Correspondent, *Irish Independent*, **Wednesday 23 June 2010**

It was a tale of two airlines as Aer Lingus came near the top of the class and Ryanair near the bottom in a passenger survey.

The findings were based on a poll of over 5,700 passengers who rated the last airline they had used based on their cabin staff, cleanliness, seating arrangements, legroom, baggage allowances, handling of delays and value for money.

The survey by 'Which? Holiday' magazine rated Aer Lingus second, whereas Ryanair came second-last among short-haul carriers.

Aer Lingus got an overall satisfaction rating of 71pc, just behind winners Swiss at 72pc, and well ahead of big name rivals such as KLM, Lufthansa, BMI and British Airways. Air Malta was the third-favourite with passengers.

However, Ryanair's satisfaction rating came in at just 42pc, ahead of worst-rated Thomas Cook Airlines at 37pc, and below 16 other short-haul airlines.

. . .

Impressions

'Our rigorous research shows that while the cost of flights is important to customers, it's things like friendly cabin staff and reasonable luggage allowances that leave a lasting impression, said "Which? Holiday" head of research Rochelle Turner.'

But Ryanair dismissed the results of the survey.

Spokesman Stephen McNamara said: 'The "Which?" survey reflects the opinions of 5,700 people who like to complain, whereas Ryanair is the choice of 73 million people who like good value, cheap fares, the least lost baggage and best punctuality of Europe's leading airline,' he said.

'The reality is, if people weren't flying with us because of something we would change it.'

Aer Lingus, meanwhile, welcomed the results. 'This is testament to Aer Lingus's winning combination of great-value fares and excellent customer service,' said spokesman Declan Kearney.

The article quoted above is not unusual. Every day, dozens of news items appear which discuss the results of surveys, or claim that 'a representative sample' of the public thinks this or that. Businesses, too, rely on gathering data in this way – about their customers' opinions, the potential market for new products, and so on. And governments need to collect information, relating not just to people, but to economic conditions, prices and other aspects of life in a country or region.

But unless the information gathered is accurate and complete, it can be worthless, not to say downright misleading; inaccurate data used as a basis for making decisions can have a disastrous effect on the running of a company or a country.

The article above mentions some of the issues that impact on the accuracy of survey results – for example, we're told that 'over 5,700' passengers were questioned, which sounds like a very large number, but is clearly only a tiny fraction of the total number of people who had taken flights during the relevant period. We're also told that the survey was carried out by 'Which? Holiday' magazine, so did it just survey its readers, who arguably are unlikely to be a representative sample of the flying population at large? What we aren't told is how the survey was carried out – was it done by face-to-face interviews, via a postal survey, or by some other method? All of these factors can have a significant impact on the reliability of the survey findings. Indeed, the Ryanair spokesman quoted in the article highlights some of these questions when he says 'The "Which?" survey reflects the opinions of 5,700 people who like to complain, whereas Ryanair is the choice of 73 million people'. In other words, he's speculating that the survey is based on a small and unrepresentative sample.

In this chapter we explore some of these issues: how can we collect sufficient quantities of reliable data for a particular purpose, and what strategies for data collection are open to us? How can we look with a critical eye at data which has been collected by other people, and assess how reliable and up to date it is? We will also take a look at the use of computer resources in gathering data. We will see how the Internet can be used to search for sources of data in the public domain, and we will examine the opportunities that are opening up as a consequence of the possibility of gathering enormous amounts of data electronically – and some of the special problems this possibility can create.

But before we can discuss methods for collecting data, we need to be a little more precise about what 'data' actually means, and the different types of data we will encounter in practical situations. The next section addresses these issues.

A multiplicity of measurements

At first sight it would appear that many of the facts about a business are simply not measurable in the ordinary sense in which we use that term. How, for example, could we 'measure' in any straightforward numerical way the efficiency with which a worker performs his or her job, or the reaction of a consumer to a new variety of chocolate biscuit? And yet numerical measurements are what, ideally, we are after; mere verbal information can never convey the same accuracy. To take a rather trivial example: if you were looking at the profitability of various companies with a view to purchasing shares in one of them, I doubt whether you would be very satisfied to be told, 'Oh, we made a nice little profit last year', or 'Well, last year's performance *was* a bit disappointing'! Only the actual *figures* for profit, dividends declared and so on can convey the facts you want in an unequivocal way. And the same applies, in a less obvious fashion, to almost any kind of information you can think of.

Of course, there *are* variations in the *way* in which different kinds of information can be quantified – that is to say, rendered into numerical terms. In fact, we might define a sort of hierarchy of measurements, in ascending order of precision.

Descriptive classes

First of all we have information that is purely qualitative or descriptive, so that about the best we can do is to classify it into groups or classes according to the characteristics we are interested in, and then count the number of items in each class. For instance, a biscuit manufacturer might classify the various lines produced into 'plain', 'chocolate-covered' and 'cream-filled', and then count how many lines fall into each category. Naturally, it is important to make sure that, as far as possible, the categories are unambiguous and do not overlap, otherwise questions arise as to which category an individual item belongs to – for example, into which group should our biscuit manufacturer place lines that are both chocolate-covered and cream-filled? Such problems apart, however, even such an apparently crude system of 'measurement' can convey a good deal of useful information such as which category has the most members, whether items are evenly spread over all the categories, and so on. Information of this kind is often called 'categoric' or 'nominal'.

Ordered classes

Our second 'level of measurement' arises in situations where, as before, items can be grouped into classes according to some characteristic, but this time there is an *order* among the classes. One obvious example is the way in which most British degree courses classify their results – first, upper and lower second, third, pass and fail. The ordering here is clear, but no one would claim that all students within each class are in any sense identical in their performance. The same sort of system would apply to the social class groupings employed by sociologists, whereby people are classified as A, B1, B2 and so on; again there is a clear order *among* the classes, but no necessary equivalence of individuals *within* classes.

Rankings

One step more precise again is what we might call a *ranking* of items; you may be familiar with this from the idea of 'places' – first, second, third and so on – in class or subject, employed at school. This differs from the previous case in that each individual item is given a definite position in the ranking, which may or may not be the same as that for any other item. In the case of 'places' at school, of course, the rankings are usually derived from the actual marks obtained by pupils, but the system is particularly useful in situations where proper numerical measurements such as marks are difficult or impossible to obtain.

Consider, for example, the position of a supervisor required, when promotion is under consideration, to report on the efficiency of the workers in his or her charge. A whole conglomeration of separate measurements might be needed for this purpose – how fast the workers perform their tasks, how good the finished quality is of the goods they produce, how often they have been absent during the past month, and so on. But simply ask the supervisor to *rank* the workers according to their efficiency, and he or she probably will not have too much trouble deciding who is the best, who comes second, and so on, down to the absolutely useless! So the multitude of measurements needed can be reduced to the set of rankings 1, 2, 3 . . . For this reason, rankings are immensely useful, particularly in situations that would have too many dimensions to measure individually; another example might be provided by the market researcher who wants to assess the consumer reaction to a new range of products: 'Which of these do you like most? Least? . . .' Because ranking involves putting things in order, such data is often called *ordinal*.

Moreover, the set of 'measurements' with which we end up when we have ranked items is of a particularly simple kind – it is just the set of whole numbers 1, 2, 3 . . . So, even in cases where it is perfectly possible to get a genuine numerical measurement, we often resort to rankings in order to simplify further calculations. After all, it is a good deal easier to say 'Northern Sales Region was third in terms of turnover last year' than 'The turnover last year in Northern Sales Region was £247 346.10'! Inevitably, we have lost detail in making the transition from one statement to the other – in this case, the detail being precisely what the turnover was – but in many cases that is a penalty we are prepared to pay in the interests of simplicity and clarity.

Measurements

Finally, at the top of our hierarchy of scales of measurement, we come to what is probably understood by 'measurement' in the colloquial sense – quantities that can be assigned a definite, unique position on a numerical scale. The examples which could be given are endless – weights of bags of sugar, densities of samples of metal, ages of customers in a store – you can continue the list for yourself. Quantities such as these, which can be measured numerically and which have different values for different people or items, are often referred to as *variables*, because their value varies from one item to another. (You will find that some books on statistics distinguish two kinds of measured data, called 'interval scale' and 'ratio scale'. However, we will not go into the details of these scales.)

Within this final category, there is one more important subdivision of which you need to be aware. When official statistics are being held up to ridicule, one figure commonly cited to demonstrate the silliness of the whole business is that 'the average British family has 2.3 children' or whatever. Whoever saw 0.3 of a child? What peculiar ideas these statisticians have! Now although of course this is a caricature (for reasons which I hope you can see!) there is a valid point being made – namely, that numbers of children in families are always *integers* – that is, whole numbers. In exactly the same way, numbers of rooms in houses, number of employees or production of motor cars in a factory will always take only integer values.

Variables of this kind are called *discrete* (note the spelling) variables; they can take on only certain definite and separate values. These values are nearly always integers, but not invariably so; one often-cited example of a discrete variable that takes non-integer values is British shoe sizes.

The other type of variable, which can take on absolutely any value (perhaps restricted to a certain limited range) as long as we can measure it accurately enough, is called a *continuous* variable. Things such as height and weight would come into this category; we do not expect to find people with heights much above 7 feet or below 3 feet, but within this range, given a sufficiently accurate tape-measure, we could encounter any height – there is no rule, as yet, which says that people *must* have heights in tidy multiples of 1 inch!

Like many definitions within statistics, the ideas of 'discrete' and 'continuous' variables are not watertight – to some extent they depend on how we decide to measure things – and there is a kind of grey area where we might treat a variable as either. Wages, for instance, are strictly discrete, since one's pay must be a whole number of pence; however, for practical purposes we might regard wages as measured on a continuous scale since the discrete steps are so very tiny compared with the actual amounts being considered.

By now you may well be thinking that this discussion of different types of measurement is all very well, but somewhat philosophical. However, it *is* also very practical, for two reasons. First, you may well be in a position at some time in your career of having to devise a way of measuring some hitherto unquantified variable – such as the nuttiness of different recipes of chocolate bar – in which case a knowledge of different possibilities will be very useful. Second, when we discuss in Chapters 3 and 4 methods for presenting and summarising information, we will find that the means at our disposal depend very much on the type of information concerned, whether it is quantitative or qualitative, discrete or continuous, and so on.

Quick check questions

Which of the following statements are true?

1 A discrete variable is one which can take only a whole-number value.

2 A continuous variable can't take negative values.

3 Measured variables can be converted into rankings.

Answers:
1 is false – the key feature of a discrete variable is that there are gaps between the possible values of the variable, but those values need not be integers.
2 is also false – think of temperature measured in degrees centigrade, where temperatures below freezing are negative.
3 is true – the marks of a group of students can be converted to indicate who was ranked first, second and so on in the class.

Whence information?

Now that we have some idea of the kinds of information we are going to be discussing, we can address ourselves to the problem of getting hold of it. In some respects this is rather a chicken-and-egg question – how you collect the information depends on what you want to do with it. For this reason, you will find that many elementary statistics textbooks defer a discussion of how information is obtained until after they have talked about the techniques available for analysing it. Although there are good arguments in favour of this approach, it *is* a little like cooking the dinner before you have bought the ingredients; so, at the expense of a bit of cross-referencing later on, we will adopt the alternative course.

Two definitions before we continue will enable us to use more compact terminology than we have done so far. We have been talking about 'measurements', or even more vaguely 'information', but from now on we will refer simply to 'data' – the set of facts, figures or whatever, with which we are concerned in a particular problem. It will also be useful to talk about the 'population' – the statistician's term, not just for a collection of people, but for *any* collection of items about which we have, or wish to obtain, data. Thus we could refer to the population of sheep in the county of Powys, the population of bags of sugar filled by a machine, and so on.

Getting hold of data is rather like doing your maths homework at school: there are basically three ways to go about obtaining the answers. You can find the items yourself, 'borrow' them from someone else, or hope to find them in a textbook. Data found for yourself is called *primary* data; anything else, whether obtained from published sources or directly, perhaps from a colleague in your organisation, is *secondary*. There are arguments for and against both types, knowledge of which will enable you to make an informed choice in a practical situation.

It is certainly true that the only data items you can be sure of having tailor-made to your requirements are those that you collect yourself. They are also likely to be much more up to date than anything from a published source; the most rapidly published of the government's statistical periodicals, for example, tends to be about six weeks out of date.

On the other hand, large organisations, particularly the government, are able to obtain access to information that you, as a private individual or a representative of your firm, are unlikely to discover. The government actually imposes a statutory requirement on organisations to provide certain details about wages, hours worked and so on, thus ensuring a completeness of coverage which you could not possibly obtain; it also has at its disposal large resources of money and staff entirely devoted to the collection and processing of statistical data. Thus a figure such as the Retail Price Index, for example, possesses a generality, in terms of the number of prices that go into its calculation, coverage of prices over the whole country, and consideration of price variations between different types of retail outlet, which no individual could hope to emulate.

Other large organisations, too, can obtain data not available to the casual enquirer. A trade organisation such as the Federation of Motor Manufacturers and Traders may ask all its members to supply returns concerning their turnover, profits and other matters. They will be willing to provide this information, secure in the knowledge that it will be used for the benefit of their entire industry – and that if it *is* published, it will appear in the anonymity of a large collection of data referring to many member firms. The reaction if one individual firm were to ask its nearest rival to provide such details can be imagined!

Then there are questions of time and cost to be considered. Data collection can be an expensive business – why go to the trouble of 'doing-it-yourself' when a trip to the nearest library subscribing to the government's *Monthly Digest of Statistics*, a few minutes on the Internet or a telephone call to Darren in the accounts department could produce the same results? Ultimately, like many such questions we will encounter later in the book, the 'primary or secondary' problem resolves itself into a matter of compromise: are we prepared to settle for secondary data that may not be *exactly* what we were looking for, but that is available here, now, and quite cheaply; or is the accuracy of the data such an important feature that we are prepared to pay for it in terms of time, money and effort?

Collect-it-yourself

Whom shall we ask?

Assuming that we have decided to try to obtain our data first hand, the immediate problem we face is to define the population we are interested in. This sounds pretty obvious, but it is vital that we are very precise about this definition, particularly if we are going to rely on outside help, such as part-time market research interviewers, to do some of the data collection. It is no use telling your interviewers to question 'housewives'; does this mean people who are solely occupied in work within the home or do you want to include those who have outside jobs? And does *housewives* include single mothers who are at home taking care of children? What about fathers who are doing the same? If you intended the term to be interpreted in one way, and your interviewers interpret it differently, your results may be invalid and even downright misleading.

Even when we have managed to specify the population in a sufficiently detailed way, we almost certainly will not be able to collect information from absolutely every member of that population. Even the government in the ten-year census, the completion of which is a statutory requirement, cannot obtain totally complete data; there will always be those who for reasons of their own do not wish to give the government details of their present address! More important, in most practical cases, are considerations of time and money. Manufacturers carrying out nationwide market research surveys would have colossal bills were they to attempt total coverage of their target population, and the mass of results would probably take months to analyse. When the question at issue is, say, the reaction of schoolchildren to a new curry-flavoured potato crisp, it clearly just is not worthwhile going to such lengths to carry out a census (the term, incidentally, applies not only to the ten-yearly census but to any data-collection operation that covers an entire population).

So, in most cases, we have to be content with taking a *sample* from the population, and hoping that the results we get from our sample will not be too far from those which would apply to the rest of the population. Actually, it is not only a question of hoping – if we select our sample in the right way we can be quite precise about how reliable the results we get will be. But what is the right way? And what are our criteria for 'rightness' in this context?

What sort of sample?

A simple random sample

Most people would, I think, agree that a well-selected sample should represent the population from which it is taken fairly – that is, it should not be *biased* towards any particular part of the population. We might go further and demand that to be completely fair, every member of the population should have *exactly* the same chance of being included in our sample. If we make this demand, we are asking for a *simple random sample*, and it is not hard to see how we might achieve such a sample, certainly from a fairly small population. We could put all the names or identifying numbers of the members of the population on to identical pieces of paper, put them in a hat, shake it well, and pull out as many as we need for our sample.

If we have a large population, however, we would need a very big hat to carry out this process; but actually with the aid of a table of *random numbers* such as those in Appendix 2 we can *simulate* the pulling-out-of-the-hat procedure quite simply even for large populations – especially if we also happen to have a computer handy. All we need to do is assign a number to every member of our chosen population (and this is often already done – workers have works numbers or National Insurance numbers, bank accounts have account numbers, and so on). Then we read off numbers from the table – in three-digit sets if the numbers assigned to our population have three digits – and our sample consists of the members of the population with the corresponding numbers. You'll be encountering the term 'simulate' again, and learning more about random numbers, in Chapter 14. For now, we can see how the process works by looking at a simple example.

Suppose we want to choose three out of eight workers in a production team to receive special experimental training, and in order for the experiment to work the choice has to be random. Then, if we are too idle to write the eight names on bits of paper and put them in a hat, we give each of them a number: 1 Adams, 2 Brown, 3 Carter, 4 Davies, 5 Evans, 6 Finch, 7 Goss, 8 Hall. Then we look at row 16 say, of the Appendix 2 table, and find that the first three numbers within the range 1–8 are 5, 6 and 1 (we ignore the 9s because they are outside the range of interest). So our sample will consist of Messrs Evans, Finch and Adams.

A computer can generate the random numbers for us, and even, if the details of the population are stored within it, print out for us a list of the members of the sample. This is exactly what Ernie does when choosing premium bond winners – in fact it is really just a glorified electronic hat. Some scientific calculators, too, include a random number key, and there are facilities for generating random numbers in Excel.

A stratified sample

This all seems very satisfactory, and certainly fits in with our intuitive ideas of what constitutes a 'fair' sample. But there are at least two valid criticisms to be levelled at the method. First, it requires that we have a 'list' of all the members of our population – the technical name for such a list is a *sampling frame*. In many cases this is not too serious a problem; market research enquirers often use the electoral roll, and organisations such as the AA and the Consumers' Association generate income by selling lists of their members to commercial firms. Bias may creep into your sample, though, if you use as your sampling frame something such as the telephone directory; ownership of a land-line telephone is quite strongly linked to social class/income bracket. However, the defect *can* usually be got around, and in any case also applies to many other methods of sampling.

More serious is the problem that you may actually get a perfectly respectable simple random sample which is nevertheless very *un*representative of its *parent* population. For instance, if you took a simple random sample of 20 workers from a firm with a workforce of 200 part-time and 800 full-time staff, all the names which came out of your hat *might* be those of part-time workers – in which case, if your enquiry was concerned with the adequacy of canteen facilities in the firm, you might get very odd results because all the part-timers go home before lunch. To overcome this drawback, an alternative type of sample called a *stratified sample* has been devised.

The origin of the word is the Latin *stratum* meaning a layer, and the sample is designed to give fair representation to the various 'layers' or subgroups within a population. In the example above, for instance, we could insist that our sample of 20 workers must contain 4 part-timers and 16 full-timers, so as to reflect accurately the proportions of the two groups in the whole workforce. Within each group, the 4 and the 16 would be chosen randomly as already described. This way, the sort of anomaly described above just cannot arise.

A multi-stage sample

With any kind of random selection, simple or stratified, further difficulties may become apparent when we look at the names that emerge from our 'hat'. If the first is P Smith of Dover, the second H Macdonald of Inverness and the third J Williams of Aberystwyth, it is clearly going to be a slow and expensive business for someone to rush about the country interviewing them. Ruling out for the moment the possibility of a postal questionnaire, which we will consider later in the chapter, we could surmount this difficulty by adopting *multi-stage sampling* instead. With this method, the country is first of all divided up into a small number of large areas – the Independent Television Regions are popular ones for use in market research surveys – and two or three of these are chosen at random in the usual way. Then within the selected areas, we subdivide into, perhaps, parliamentary constituencies or local authority regions, and choose a few of *these* at random. So the process continues, working through to streets and finally to individuals, the advantage of the method being that those selected at the last stage will be concentrated geographically into a few areas, thus cutting down greatly on the amount of travelling required of interviewers.

A quota sample

Where a great deal of accuracy is not required in the final results, the demand for random sampling is often abandoned altogether in favour of an easier-to-implement alternative known as *quota sampling*. If you have ever been stopped in the street by a person – usually female – with a clipboard, and asked to give your views on a new sort of chocolate or last night's TV programmes, you were probably part of a *quota* that the interviewer had been told to fill: 20 white-collar males aged 30–65, 15 unemployed housewives aged 18–30, and so on. The advantage of this method to the interviewer is that, while the correct proportions of different subgroups in the population are preserved, she can choose *anyone* who satisfies the criteria of a particular subgroup as her victim. Perhaps this is the place for a note on the confusion caused by the colloquial understanding of 'random' as 'haphazard'; one hears statements like 'We interviewed a sample of ten people randomly in the street as they came along'. Now this may be haphazard, but it certainly is not random in the statistical sense of everyone having the same chance of selection; people who just happened not to be passing when the survey was being carried out had no chance at all of selection. In the same way, a quota sample is non-random because, if you are an Irish bus conductor who happens to pass the interviewer when she has already filled her quota of Irish bus conductors, then your chance of selection is nil.

The method is also subject to interviewer abuse, in that an interviewer who is tired of standing in the rain trying to fill her quota of former train drivers aged over 90 may well get fed up, fill in the details of the next person to pass in the relevant box and go home! However, reputable research agencies carry out checks designed to eliminate 'fiddling' of this kind by interviewers, though there *is* an authenticated case of a single interviewer filling in all 500 forms in his quota himself – all with different, imaginary details, of course!

A systematic sample

Yet another kind of sample, perhaps the simplest of all, is the *systematic sample*, whereby, if we want a sample which is 10 per cent of the population, we go through our sampling frame selecting, say, every tenth person beginning with person number 7. Again, this is not strictly random since persons 11, 12 . . . 16, and all the other 'in-between' ones, have no chance of selection; but it is almost as satisfactory in many cases. The only situation where such a sample *might* introduce bias is where your pattern of sampling picks up some underlying pattern in the population; for example, if you choose to examine every 20th screw produced by a machine in order to check the quality of production, and the machine has developed a vibration causing it to hiccup every 20 screws, then you could well gain the impression, should you happen to coincide with the hiccups, that the entire production is faulty, whereas in fact the other 19 (95 per cent of the output) are perfectly satisfactory. However, in most situations this is not likely to arise; there is no reason to suppose, for instance, that if you choose to question every tenth worker emerging from a factory gate about their political views, they will carefully line up inside so that every tenth person has views either of the darkest blue or the brightest red, simply in order to invalidate your sample!

Deductions from samples

Whichever sampling method you choose to use, one thing is certain: data obtained from a sample will not give you totally accurate information about a population in the way that a complete census would. This is simply common sense: just because a sample pack of mixed nuts contains 20 per cent almonds, no one would expect the entire population to contain exactly the same proportion.

However, for certain kinds of sample – namely, those whose selection includes a random element – what we can do is make definite quantitative statements about how much the sample could be in error, relative to the entire population. We will see how to do this in Chapter 8. At present it is sufficient to note that for this reason, such samples (they include simple random, stratified and multi-stage samples) are to be preferred to those (such as quota samples) in whose selection no random element is allowed to operate.

Quick check questions

1 To get a systematic sample of 5 per cent of the items from a production line, what instructions would you give the person doing the sampling?

2 How does a stratified sample differ from a quota sample?

3 A survey on customer satisfaction at a bank is carried out by asking everyone who visits the bank on a particular day to complete a questionnaire. Is this a random sample of customers?

Answers:
1 The instructions should be 'take every 20th item'.
2 In a stratified sample, the selection of individuals within each subgroup (stratum) is random, whereas with a quota sample this is not the case.
3 No – customers who don't visit the bank on the day of the survey have no chance to be included.

How shall we gather the data?

Observation

There is a saying, 'If you want a job doing, do it yourself'. We might modify that to 'If you want data items collecting, collect them yourself'. The only way in which we can be sure that we are getting the facts we want, all the facts we want and nothing but the facts we want is to gather them by personal observation. This, of course, is what 'pure' scientists are doing all the time; there is no point in asking a mouse to rate its chances of finding a piece of cheese in the middle of a maze on a scale from 1 to 10 – you just have to let it try, and watch what happens.

In the same way, the only way we can determine with certainty how many slices of bread a family consume per day is to watch them doing it; if we rely on asking for the information, they may well make a guess because they do not really know, or deliberately misinform us because they feel they eat too much and do not like to admit it, or say 'Well, it depends whether Aunty Mary comes round for supper', and so on. Of course, it is unlikely that we could station an observer in every household in our sample, so in areas such as market research direct observation is not used much.

However, there are certain types of investigation where businesses can make use of this kind of direct data gathering, particularly by electronic means. For example, call centres routinely monitor the length of calls from customers; police authorities gather data about the length of time taken to respond to emergency calls; and supermarkets can store information about the purchases made by each customer. We will come across another case in Chapter 5, when we discuss the Retail Price Index: the government employs people across the country to go into shops on a particular day each month and gather details of the prices of various items of food, clothing and so on, in order to provide information for the calculation of the index. So the use of direct observation as a way of gathering data should not be overlooked.

Questionnaires

This is probably the most familiar data-gathering situation, at least to members of the general public. As mentioned earlier, few people can have avoided the experience of being accosted by a person with a clipboard who wants 'a few minutes of your time' to complete a questionnaire about some product or service. This is how the 'Which? Holiday' survey described in the *Irish Independent* article at the start of the chapter will have been conducted.

But in addition to the considerations about the nature of our sample covered earlier in the chapter, the quality of information from a questionnaire depends crucially on the way in which the questions are designed and put together. There has been a great deal of research in this area: even issues such as the effect of printing the questionnaire on different colours of paper, and the size of printing used, have been investigated.

We will confine ourselves to a few more basic guidelines to be borne in mind when designing a questionnaire. Some of these may appear to be a matter of common sense, as indeed they are; but you only have to look at a few examples of the kinds of questionnaire which are in general use to see that putting that common sense into practice is not so easy!

- **Keep it short**: this applies to both the individual questions and the overall questionnaire, and is particularly important in relation to the place where the questionnaire is to be answered – a questionnaire to be sent by post and answered in the respondent's home can be longer than one that will be completed on a windy tube-station platform. You need, of course, to make sure you cover all the essential points – but don't get carried away and ask unnecessary questions.
- **Use a logical sequence**: respondents like to be able to see what you're getting at.
- **Progress from simple to more complex questions**: start with things that are easy and quick to answer, and leave anything more complicated or sensitive for later.
- **Provide codified responses as far as possible**: opinions are often expressed on a scale called a *semantic differential* – from 1 (= strongly agree) to 5 (= strongly disagree), for example. You may also come across the term 'Likert scale' for this kind of scale with a number of ordered points from which a respondent may choose. There are lots of arguments about how many points to use (5, 7 and 10 are all popular), whether to have

an odd number of points (so that a 'neutral' response is possible) or an even number (which forces respondents to express a view one way or the other). It is also important to realise that the numbers in such a scale are not, to use our earlier terminology, real 'measurements' – in the respondent's interpretation, the difference between, say, a 1 and a 2 may not be the same as that between a 4 and a 5.

- **Don't force respondents into a straitjacket**: if you are not sure whether the choice of response you have provided covers all the possibilities, include a category such as 'other – please specify'. For example, a question 'Please indicate highest level of educational achievement' might provide possible responses 'GCSE/A-level/first degree/higher degree/ professional qualification/other (please specify)' to allow for variations such as people with overseas qualifications.

- **Avoid leading questions**: if you ask 'Do you agree that the workers are being oppressed by global capitalist managements?', it's pretty clear where you are coming from, and this can influence the responses you receive.

- **Avoid ambiguity/'portmanteau' questions**: a question that asks 'Do you find the lecturer's voice clear and her handwriting legible?' and receives the answer 'no' gives no indication whether it's the voice that is the problem, or the handwriting, or both.

- **Use a pilot survey to test and modify your questions**: the only way to find out whether your questions make sense and will be understood by your target sample is to try them out on a small group. Make sure, though, that it's taken from an appropriate population – if you are designing a survey on the experience of over-60s on the Internet, it's no good piloting it on a group of under-25s in your company's computer department.

- **Think about how you will analyse the results of the survey**: thinking ahead can save a lot of hassle later. For example, questions that allow respondents to select a variable number of options in a list are not so easily coded for computer input as those that ask for a fixed number of options to be selected ('the most important' or 'your three favourites', for example).

Administering the questionnaire

When it comes to actually obtaining the responses to our well-designed questions, we have a choice of four basic approaches:

1 We can use a *postal survey* – that is, send the questionnaires by post to our selected sample, and let people return their answers also by post. Naturally, unless a stamped addressed envelope is provided, the response will not be very good. Even when this is the case, response rates of around 15 per cent are considered to be good in many surveys. And not only does this mean you must send out 10 000 questionnaires if you want to get 1500 replies; the results may actually be biased by the non-responses. For example, in a customer satisfaction survey, people who are dissatisfied with a product are more likely to respond than those who are quite happy, human nature being what it is! Thus a manufacturer can get an exaggerated idea of the extent of dissatisfaction.

The response rate can sometimes be boosted by devices such as entering all respondents into a free prize draw – though this requires them to give their names and addresses, and so may have a different kind of distorting effect. Non-responses can be followed up to see if they have special characteristics, so that this can be allowed for in subsequent analysis – but the follow-up process can be expensive and time-consuming.

A final problem with postal surveys is that often it is hard to make sure the intended recipient completes the survey. This is particularly true with business surveys – the kind of thing you might find yourself doing as part of a project. People doing the same job in different organisations may have different job titles; if you want to be sure that it is the person responsible for health and safety who completes your survey, you may need someone in the human resources section in one company, a production engineer in a second, and a specialist safety officer in a third. So to whom should you address your questionnaire?

2 To try to overcome some of these problems, *telephone questionnaires* are often used, particularly in what is called 'business-to-business' research. Telephoning and speaking to someone in the company means you can ensure you get through to the right person. The telephone directory also provides a convenient sampling frame in this case.

On the other hand, using the phone isn't always suitable for long or complex questionnaires, with a lot of open-ended questions. And it is very easy for an exasperated respondent to put the phone down! Moreover, if your target population is the general public, the fact that many households still do not have telephones, and that possession of a telephone is linked to income, may mean that you cannot reach a suitable sample by this means.

3 Recently the use of *Internet-based questionnaires* has become more widespread. Clearly you can only use this method when your target populations all have e-mail, and you can access their addresses (or where you are not too worried about the statistical 'respectability' of your sample). There are ways of anonymising responses so that the sender of a reply cannot immediately be identified with his or her e-mail address, and of course having responses already in electronic format can have enormous advantages when it comes to processing the results. While the method presents all the challenges of questionnaire design plus a number of additional problems, it is likely that the use of the Internet as a resource for surveys will continue to grow.

4 *Face-to-face interviews* are still a very popular means of administering a questionnaire. The method has many advantages: interviewers can use prompts, such as pictures of the products being researched, which they can show to respondents. They can try to ensure that answers are accurate – for example, by asking not just 'Do you eat Weety Smashers for breakfast?' but 'Can you show me your packet of Weety Smashers?'. They can also be trained to complete the questionnaire form correctly, thus reducing problems of data input and the risk of errors – in fact, many interviewers now use laptop computers to enter the responses directly into a database for analysis.

On the other hand, interviewer bias is not unknown: even the tone of voice adopted in asking a question may have an effect on the response elicited. Much research has been done on issues such as the effect of interviewer gender and its interaction with respondent gender. (For example, does a male respondent give different responses to a female interviewer from those he would give to a male interviewer?) So we cannot simply assume that, because we use trained interviewers, responses will be completely unbiased.

It is probably becoming clear that the design and administration of surveys is a topic on which entire books could be – and have been – written. Some references for further reading on the topic are given at the end of the chapter. However, it is an area where a bit of practical experience is probably worth many hours of theoretical study; so in the exercises you will find some suggestions for small-scale surveys that you yourself could design and analyse, either individually or in a group. Take advantage of the opportunity to indulge your curiosity on an entirely legitimate pretext!

<h1>Where to find second-hand statistics</h1>

If, on reflection, you have decided that the data you need should already have been collected by someone, how do you decide where to begin looking? You have the choice of an enormous range of data sources, both print and electronic, which can be quite daunting to the novice researcher. It would be both tedious and impractical to attempt to give lists of publications and websites in any detail; instead, I will mention just a few of the major sources of each type, and then give you some ideas as to how you might go about finding others.

Print resources

A visit to your university library, or to a well-stocked public reference library, will show that there is an enormous amount of statistical information gathered and published by national and local government, trade federations and international agencies such as the United Nations. Broadly speaking, these can be grouped into general publications, bringing together a range of topics, and specialist publications, which focus on a particular area such as the national income or employment.

Most official government statistics in the UK are collected and published via the Government Statistical Service. This publishes the *Monthly Digest of Statistics*, which as its name suggests is a compilation of statistics on all sorts of topics, ranging from wages to weather, from road accidents to retail prices, appearing once a month. This is always a good place to begin looking for statistical information on fairly broad issues, as are the various *Abstracts* made from the *Monthly Digest* at the end of the year or less frequently. These include the *Annual Abstract*, a general collection, and the more specialised *Economic Trends* and *Social Trends*, which often contain articles and more appealing graphical or diagrammatic presentations of information as well as tables of data relating to their specialised areas.

If these major publications fail to produce the data you need, probably the best course of action is to consult the *Guide to Official Statistics* also produced by the Government Statistical Service. This has an exhaustive index in which, taking a topic at random, the entry under 'margarine' contains references to *Business Monitors* PQ229.1 and 2, the *Monthly Digest*, *Annual Abstract*, *Scottish Abstract*, *Statistical Information Notice* and the *Census of Production* reports.

If the information you require is of an international character, the *Statistical Yearbook* produced by the United Nations may be of help; while for detailed information about particular industries, publications of the trade federation or association concerned might be useful – though these are often available to the general public only at great expense.

Electronic resources

If you are searching for information produced by an agency of the UK national government, probably the best place to begin is the site **http://www.statistics.gov.uk/** which is the homepage of the National Statistics website. From here you can locate downloadable statistics on a wide range of topics, search for data, find out what print sources of data are available on a particular topic, and much more. The site is organised around 13 themes:

agriculture, fishing and forestry; health and care; education and training; commerce, energy and industry; economy; natural and built environment; transport, travel and tourism; labour market; compendia and reference; crime and justice; population and migration; social and welfare; and 'other' – so you can see how comprehensive it is. It is also very user-friendly and easy to navigate.

If you want international rather than British statistical data, then a good starting point is the United Nations Statistics Division's homepage at **http://www.un.org/depts/unsd/**. This provides links to some free access datasets, information about others that are available on subscription or in hard copy, and a very useful set of links to the sites of various national statistical services and of international organisations dealing with statistical data.

Should you need to find information about a specific company or organisation, then the relevant homepage is usually a good place to start; the sites of quality newspapers such as the *Financial Times*, the *Guardian* and the *Independent* also often contain statistical information, particularly about companies and about issues of public concern such as education and health services.

Links to many of these sites and others will be found on the Companion Website, together with some suggestions for accessing particular sets of data, just to get you started. As you will know if you have made any use at all of the Internet, the wealth of available information is almost unlimited, and the main problem when researching data on a particular topic is to stay focused, and not to get side-tracked into fascinating but irrelevant byways!

Whatever the source in which you eventually track down the published data you are seeking, there are some general points to be borne in mind when consulting it. Do make sure that you read any explanatory notes which accompany the publication – with the *Monthly Digest*, for example, there is a once-yearly booklet explaining terminology used in that year's *Digests*. *Do* read all footnotes to tables – they will draw your attention to factors that may have distorted the figures in the tables, such as industrial action by civil servants which may have resulted in some data being unavailable, changes in definitions of the quantities in the table which may produce sudden discontinuities in the data, and so on.

Be sure, too, to note carefully what units of measurement are being used. Many official statistics deal in very large numbers, and in the interests of simplicity are often measured in thousands, hundreds of thousands or millions. For example, in tables dealing with the population of countries, figures are generally given in millions, so the population of the UK would be given as 61 rather than 61 000 000. Failure to be clear about units can lead to some serious confusion, especially if, for instance, percentage figures are incorrectly read as absolutes, or vice versa.

Points for further thought

We have concentrated, in this chapter, mainly on sampling from human populations, but of course it is often necessary to take samples from other populations too, and sometimes this can be quite difficult. Consider, for example, a brewery which requires that, as a final quality check, no lorry-load of crates of bottled beer should leave the loading bay unless four crates have been randomly chosen and the bottles in those crates checked to ensure that they are correctly capped. There will be a great temptation to select crates that are on the top of the lorry-load, and thus easily accessible, rather than those that are right at the bottom or in the middle – yet the ones on the bottom may actually have a much greater chance of being damaged. The sample that results from choosing only crates from the top layer may thus give a biased impression of the magnitude of the problem. We will be returning to consider sampling of this kind in Chapter 10 where we discuss statistical process control.

There are also many difficulties associated with allowing individuals in a sample to self-select. This is what the Ryanair spokesman quoted in the article at the start of the chapter is getting at when he says the survey 'reflects the opinions of 5700 people who like to complain'. Notorious examples of this kind of difficulty occur with the kind of phone-in 'survey' of readers' or viewers' opinions of which the media have become rather fond in recent years. If a newspaper asks its readers to telephone and indicate whether they agree or disagree with the proposition that the British monarchy should be abolished, it is likely that only those with strong views – whether pro- or anti-monarchy – will bother to respond, not to mention the fact that the readership as a whole will be inclined to have political views that accord with those of the newspaper. The results of such a survey are therefore almost certain to be biased – yet they are frequently discussed as though they represent the views of the population as a whole.

These illustrations make it clear that one of the major objectives in selecting a sampling method must be the elimination of bias in the results. Whenever you are designing a sample for your own use, or examining the results of someone else's survey-based research, you should be very alert to possible sources of bias, and adjust your attitude to the results accordingly.

A word of warning

You should now have a fair idea of the various ways in which we may go about obtaining numerical information, but there is one principle that should be borne in mind when doing so, by whatever means. Simplicity should be the keynote; collect no more data than you actually need for the enquiry on hand. There is a great temptation, particularly when designing an investigation yourself, to collect data that *might* come in useful, or even to ask questions from force of habit. For instance, many questionnaires include a question as to the gender of the respondent. But unless this is really relevant to the topic of the enquiry – unless you suspect that males and females may differ in their responses in some manner pertinent to the enquiry – the question is pointless. Not only is it a waste of time to collect redundant data; when we concern ourselves in the next few chapters with the presentation and summarisation of data, we will find that presenting even relatively small amounts of data is quite time-consuming. Certainly we do not want to have to spend time and effort dealing with information that is never going to be used.

This is particularly important when you are gathering data via the Internet. You need to be very organised about keeping track of any data you download – what the variables are, the source of the data in case you need to refer back, and so on. Files of data should also be carefully managed, with meaningful names that give an indication of the file contents, and version control is essential – you don't want to discover that you have mistakenly deleted the latest version of a file and retained an out-of-date one. Much wasted time can be avoided by practising this kind of 'good housekeeping'.

EXERCISES

*Further examples on the work of this chapter can be found on the **Companion Website**.*

1 What kind of sample do you think might best be used in each of the following enquiries?

   (a) You want to select a 10 per cent sample of all people collecting their social security payments on a certain day, to take part in an investigation of the effects of unemployment.

   (b) You want to select a sample of 200 employees, covering all grades, both manual and non-manual, from the workforce of a large factory employing 1500 people. The object of your survey is to determine respondents' reactions to a proposal to resite the factory in new premises some miles from its old site.

   (c) You want to determine by examining a sample of customers at a large supermarket what proportion of them are male.

   (d) You want to take a sample of receipted accounts from records stored on your firm's computer, with a view to analysing the occurrence of errors.

2 Which of the following do you think are discrete and which continuous variables?

   (a) The weights of bags of fruitdrops (nominally 100 g and 200 g bags) filled by an automatic machine.

   (b) The numbers of sweets in these bags.

   (c) The stock levels of a retail shoe dealer.

   (d) The stocks of grain held by a wholesale animal feed merchant.

3 Criticise and, if necessary, suggest improved versions of the following questions taken from a (hypothetical) survey carried out by the town council of a popular holiday resort among its residents.

   (a) 'Don't you mind all the litter and mess that summer visitors create?'

   (b) 'How would you describe your social class?'

   (c) 'Does the council provide adequate facilities for visitors, and if not what further facilities do you think are needed?'

   (d) 'Do you think you would use a town swimming-pool if one were built?'

4 Reread the extract from the *Irish Independent* given at the start of this chapter. Then try to draft a few of the questions which might have been included in the passenger survey. What kind of difficulties might you expect to encounter in carrying out such a survey? How might the sample of respondents have been selected?

5 Visit the website www.yougov.com. This is an interesting site (the title 'yougov' is short for 'you govern') which invites members of the general public to express their views on various topical British issues, such as the reform of the House of Lords. Some of the enquiries are simple 'agree/disagree' votes, but some are multi-question surveys. You can get useful experience both by looking critically at the way the questions are posed and by answering them yourself. In some cases you can even get paid for taking part!

6 Suggest ways in which the following might be measured.

   (a) The efficacy of a new training programme for recruits to a company.

   (b) The market potential of a new kind of biscuit.

   (c) The 'favourability' of workers towards a new kind of protective clothing for use in a factory.

   (d) The overall level of academic achievement of applicants for an advertised post.

7 Use government and other statistical publications to try to find the answers to the following and suggest how the information you have found might be of use to a business.

(a) How many cars were exported to the UK from Japan last year? How many cars were imported from Japan to the UK? Is there a difference between the two figures, and, if so, what might be the reason for this?

(b) What region of the UK has the highest percentage of homes with central heating?

(c) What was the average consumption per head in the UK last year of (i) potatoes, (ii) bread, (iii) cakes and biscuits?

(d) How many butchers' shops were there in England last year, and what was their turnover?

(e) How many first-class letters were posted in the UK inland mail system last year?

8 Select one of the following survey scenarios, and carry out the following process:

(a) Discuss the design of a sample to be used for the survey, paying attention to the sampling frame you would use (if any) and the problems you might expect to encounter.

(b) Draft the questionnaire you would use for the survey (aim for 6–10 questions), in a format which could be used if analysis were to be carried out using a computer.

(c) Carry out a pilot survey on 25–40 people using your questionnaire. (If you are going to carry out this exercise on private premises – for example, in your college canteen, in a local shopping centre, etc. – make sure that you have permission to do so from the relevant authority before you start.)

(d) Show, using the results of your pilot survey as illustrations, how you would present the findings of the survey.

(e) Discuss any problems which have come to light in carrying out the pilot survey, and indicate any changes you would wish to make if you were to undertake the study on a larger scale.

Scenarios for question 8

(i) You are considering launching a small-scale catering business, dealing with functions such as wedding receptions and private parties. As part of your market research, you want to find out whether, when attending a function of this kind, the general public prefer a finger buffet, fork buffet or sit-down meal; how much they would be prepared to pay for this type of catering; what venue they prefer; their views on hotel *vs* private catering; and any other relevant points.

(ii) You are about to start up a new sports club in your institution or company, and wish to find out how colleagues spend their leisure time – what kinds of sporting and fitness activities they engage in; what sort of expenditure this involves; what portion of time these activities occupy, etc.

(iii) You are employed in a marketing function for a small company retailing environmentally friendly cleaning products by mail order. You wish to carry out a survey to ascertain the views of consumers in this area: whether they are prepared to pay a premium for such products; whether they would consider mail-order purchase; how frequently they make such purchases, etc.

(iv) You would like to initiate a car-sharing scheme in your organisation and wish to find out how much interest there would be in such a scheme; how it might best be run, etc.

9 What sources of data might you use to find the following:

(a) The number of customers of a large supermarket who purchased a large white organic loaf during the last week?

(b) The proportion of trains run by a particular train operator which arrived on time at their destination during the last month?

(c) The proportion of lightbulbs sold by a supermarket chain which fail to operate when fitted?

10 The *London Evening Standard* newspaper regularly carries out polls via its website (see the link at the Companion Website). At the time of writing (October 2010), one of the polls featured asks the question 'Has the Government [of the UK] cut our military capacity too far?' Discuss the extent to which the results of such a 'survey' can be useful, and the limitations which should be borne in mind when examining those results.

Case Study

The FitCavern Health Club

The FitCavern chain of health clubs is considering opening a new branch in your local area, and has engaged you as a marketing consultant to do some initial research on its behalf.

The objective of the research is to determine the local demand for such a facility. You have been provided with the following information. The population of the catchment area is approximately 50 000. This is made up as follows:

Age group	Male	Female
Under 18	5290	5670
18–30	3910	4320
31–50	5980	6480
51–70	4600	5670
71 and older	3220	4860

Your budget for the data-collection stage of the project is £2000, and you estimate that face-to-face interviewing will cost roughly £1.25 per interview, whereas a postal survey will cost £1 per survey sent out.

Write a short report for FitCavern, covering the following points:

(a) The size and composition of the sample you would use, and the method you would choose for gathering the data (you should include an explanation of the reasons for your recommendations).
(b) A draft questionnaire of 8–10 questions.
(c) An indication (without any calculations) of how you would propose to summarise and analyse the survey responses.
(d) Any limitations to your approach which need to be borne in mind.

Your report should be addressed to the Business Development Manager of FitCavern.

Further reading

Barnett, V. (2002), *Sample Survey Principles and Methods*, 3rd edn, Arnold.

A thorough but approachable introduction to the theory and practice of sampling.

Deming, W.E. (1960), *Sample Design in Business Research*, Wiley.

Not an easy read, but a classic treatment of the subject by one of the most influential business statisticians of the twentieth century.

Fink, A.G. (2004), *The Survey Kit*, 2nd edn, Sage.

A set of ten short books each covering a specific aspect of survey design and analysis. Titles include *How to ask survey questions* and *How to design survey studies*. The books go into considerable technical depth, but form an invaluable resource for anyone getting seriously involved in this topic.

Chapter 3

PRESENTING THE FIGURES:
TABLES AND DIAGRAMS

Chapter prerequisites

Before starting work on this chapter, make sure you are happy with the following topics:

1 calculation of percentages (see Chapter 1, pp. 15–16);

2 plotting points on graphs (see Chapter 1, pp. 25–9).

Learning outcomes

By the end of your work on this chapter you should be able to:

1 examine a set of numerical data and extract from it the major features, without resorting to long calculations;

2 carry out rough 'check' calculations to verify the accuracy of operations performed by a calculator or computer;

3 construct one-, two- and three-way tabulations of data, and include derived statistics as appropriate;

4 make an informed choice of method of diagrammatic presentation for a given set of data, and draw the chosen diagram (pictogram, bar chart, pie chart, statistical map);

5 plot simple numerical graphs;

6 construct grouped or ungrouped frequency tables from raw numerical data and display the data by means of a histogram or ogive;

7 critically interpret other people's tabular and diagrammatic presentations of data;

8 use the resources of a suitable software package to produce graphical displays.

Quantitative methods in practice

Morrisons uses graphs for better communication

In the previous chapter we talked about the different types of data and how they can be gathered. But of course, all the data in the world is no good to an organisation or individual unless they can decipher what the data is telling them, and get the message across to others. So in this chapter we will be considering ways of presenting data effectively.

The website of any large public company can provide both good and bad examples of data presentation. Consider the three examples below, all of which are taken from the corporate website of the Morrisons supermarket chain.

The first is a line graph which shows the price of Morrisons' shares over a six-month period.

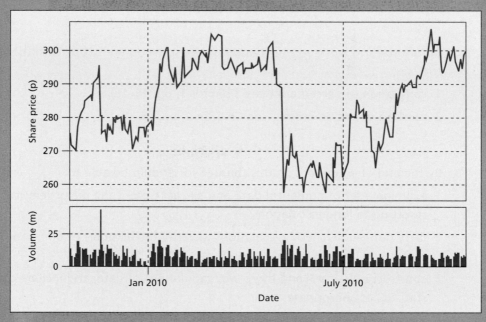

The second involves two different types of chart, a variant of a bar chart and a doughnut chart, to illustrate how the carbon emissions generated by Morrisons' activity have been reduced over a five-year period, and how the emissions break down between different sources.

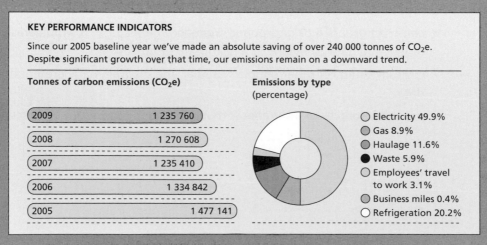

KEY PERFORMANCE INDICATORS

Since our 2005 baseline year we've made an absolute saving of over 240 000 tonnes of CO_2e. Despite significant growth over that time, our emissions remain on a downward trend.

Tonnes of carbon emissions (CO_2e)

2009	1 235 760
2008	1 270 608
2007	1 235 410
2006	1 334 842
2005	1 477 141

Emissions by type (percentage)

- Electricity 49.9%
- Gas 8.9%
- Haulage 11.6%
- Waste 5.9%
- Employees' travel to work 3.1%
- Business miles 0.4%
- Refrigeration 20.2%

The final example makes use of a map to show how Morrisons' market share differs between different regions of the UK.

Scotland
16.1%
(15.1*)

Lancashire
and North East
16.6%
(16.4*)

Yorkshire
22.0%
(21.4*)

East England
11.7%
(11.3*)

Wales and West
12.4%
(12.2*)

Central
12.5%
(12.2*)

London
6.7%
(6.5*)

South West
15.3%
(14.1*)

South and
South East
6.1%
(6.1*)

There are things about these graphs that could be criticised, and we'll be returning to that at the end of the chapter. But for the present, just note how quickly the charts convey quite complex information. Imagine, for example, that the share price data was presented as a list of daily closing prices – would you be so aware of the big drop in the price that took place around the beginning of June 2010?

If large organisations such as Morrisons can make effective use of charts and tables to get their point across, then so can you. This chapter will show you how.

The management trainee's problem

Charles Andrews has been working for about six months as a placement student with WeatherGood Ltd, a medium-sized firm which manufactures weatherproof outerwear for the specialist outdoor activities market. Recently, the firm has been trying to increase its sales by diversifying from the sports shops and camping centres, which have hitherto formed its major outlets, into department stores and other more general clothing retail stores. The first major task that Charles has been given is to write a detailed report on the success of this diversification.

He *thought* he had done a pretty good job on the report; he spent a lot of time getting hold of really detailed facts and figures, often collecting the information himself rather than asking other people within the firm, just to be on the safe side. But now he has all the data, he is finding it a rather daunting task to get to grips with what it is actually telling him – like most people, he does not find it easy to take in a large quantity of information expressed in numerical form.

This chapter presents some of the methods and ideas which Charles might find useful in reducing his mountain of data to a concise and informative report.

'Eyeballing' data

This is the expression which is often used to describe the process of looking at data and drawing intelligent conclusions without carrying out any calculations at all. This is a skill which needs to be developed with practice; however, the following example illustrates the kind of thinking which is involved.

Suppose that one of the sets of data which Charles has collected gives monthly sales of pairs of thick walking socks (in numbers of units) over the past 12 months, broken down into the company's three sales regions. The data is as follows:

Month	North	Midlands	South
Jan	120	83	160
Feb	90	61	113
Mar	60	30	92
Apr	70	45	75
May	70	48	73
June	90	59	94
July	110	77	124
Aug	140	106	168
Sept	90		125
Oct	40	27	101
Nov	30	19	73
Dec	170	114	2004
	1080		1402

The most obvious feature here is probably the missing value for September in the Midlands region. Of course, this does not mean that no socks were sold in that month – that would be shown by a zero. It is more likely to mean that for some reason the September figure wasn't available. Missing values do occur quite often, particularly in sets of data which are derived from questionnaires, where someone may not wish to answer a certain question. Deciding what to do about them can be quite a challenge; here there are various expedients which Charles could adopt, such as chasing up the missing figure, or trying to fill the gap in the table by inserting a figure which is in line with the general pattern of the sales.

A second point which you may have spotted is that there is something odd about the December figure for the South – it is much bigger than any of the other figures. Moreover, without actually working out the total for the year, you can see that it isn't consistent with the given figure for December – it's much too small if the December figure is correct. What has actually happened, as you can confirm, is that the December figure should really be 204, but an extra zero has been inserted, probably due to a keyboarding error. Other common kinds of errors when inputting data include transposition errors, where two digits are interchanged, so that for example 256 appears as 265.

Finally, what about the overall pattern which the figures reveal? If you are familiar with the context for a set of data, then you should be able to see why it follows a particular pattern. Here, it's clear that sales are generally highest in the South, followed by the North and then the Midlands. The month-to-month pattern is, however, very similar for all regions, with higher sales in the winter, when the socks will be purchased for skiing or as Christmas presents, and during the summer holiday period.

There is nothing particularly surprising here, but it is always a good idea to examine your data in this way before launching into calculations, plotting charts, and so on. Spotting errors in the data at this stage can save a lot of trouble later, while noting any patterns which are present can give you an indication as to what to expect from further analysis.

The narrative approach

Having had an initial look at the data, the next step is to try to present it in an informative and easily accessible format. One possibility is to use the so-called *narrative method* of presentation, that is, embedding the figures in sentences of English prose. For example, in the case of the WeatherGood data, Charles might have written:

> While sales of female-sized anoraks in the north-western sales division hardly increased at all over last year's total of 3500 items, the situation was much brighter in the Scottish division with 4300 items sold compared with last year's disappointing figure of 2700.

This approach can be very effective in certain situations; you need look no further than the financial pages of your daily newspaper to find articles in which the annual report and accounts of some major public company are summarised, including the salient figures, in a couple of well-designed paragraphs.

But the point about such articles is that they are generally concerned to present only a few key figures, not a mass of numerical information. The effectiveness of such a method of presentation diminishes sharply as the amount of data increases, and if the recipient of the information wants not only to get a general 'feel' for the figures, but actually to use them – perhaps to try to relate the behaviour of one set of figures to that of another, or to look for patterns in the values of a quantity – he or she will probably have to do quite a lot of sorting out to assemble the data required, which may be widely scattered throughout the article, interspersed with other figures which are totally irrelevant as far as one particular user is concerned.

This is not to condemn the narrative approach altogether, nor to suggest that all reports on numerical data should consist entirely of columns of figures unmixed with any word of English. That would be even harder to swallow than the opposite extreme! It is *always* a good idea to include a few sentences of verbal explanation of any method of data presentation you choose to use – be it a graph, table or whatever – in order to point out, for the benefit of your readers, what you consider to be the important features of the data; that way, even if they never bother to look at the data at all, you can at least feel assured that the major points have been got across. But you will increase the likelihood that they *will* look at the figures properly if, rather than leaving them to a do-it-yourself job, you present your data in the form of a well-arranged *table*.

The dos and don'ts of effective tabulation

The major principle to bear in mind when designing a table – or, for that matter, any of the other forms of data presentation that we will be looking at later – is that your objective is *simplification* of the task of grasping the information contained therein. If it takes readers 20 minutes to work out just what the figures in column 6(b) are supposed to mean, then your presentation, however ingenious, has failed, and you might as well have given them the raw data and told them to get on with it! Of course, the person who has designed a table is not always the best one to judge whether it is clear or not – naturally it will be clear to *them*! So it is a good idea, if you have really complicated information to get across, to find a guinea pig who will look at your proposed table and tell you if it is clear.

Nevertheless, there are several general points which can be made about good table construction; we will illustrate them by using some of the data from the WeatherGood Ltd report mentioned above. For the present, we will concentrate primarily on tabulation of qualitative data, leaving a discussion of quantitative data until later (in the section 'Tabulating quantitative data', p. 73).

The relevant section of the report originally read as follows:

> Although in 2007 much the larger part of our profits was generated by the heavy-duty 'HailGood' range, which contributed £700 000 to a total profit before tax of £900 000, the policy of diversifying our retail outlets has altered this situation. In 2008 profits from 'HailGood' sales had increased to £820 000, but those from our lighter 'RainGood' range had gone up from £200 000 to £460 000 over the same period. By 2009 this trend was even more pronounced, with 'RainGood' sales accounting for £680 000 out of a total profit of £1 610 000.

Relatively simple though the information in this paragraph is, it does illustrate some of the defects of a narrative presentation. In particular, the figures are not given for each year in the same order, and in fact for two of the years you would need to calculate the sales of one type of product by subtracting the figure given for the other from the total, since only one is given explicitly.

We might start by drawing up the simplest possible type of table to show just the *total* profit for each year. This will be a one-way table, since we have profits classified according to just one criterion – the year in which they occurred. Our first attempt might look something like this:

2007	900 000
2008	1 280 000
2009	1 610 000

All the facts we wish to convey are there, but as a table this has several defects. It would be good to know what the figures in the two columns represent – it is pretty clear that the first lot are dates, but you would have to refer to the text to find out that the second column shows profits – and searching about for that information will not put your readers in a good mood! So why not include a self-explanatory *heading* to each column? And while we are at it, a *title* for the whole table would not be a bad idea. That would give us the following:

Total profits of 'WeatherGood' for the last three years

Year	*Profit*
2007	900 000
2008	1 280 000
2009	1 610 000

This is certainly an improvement; the italic typeface of the headings helps to clarify the fact that they are not part of the data, and the title tells us exactly what is in the table. However, one defect of the first attempt has not yet been corrected. If you look at the profit figures, your eye almost certainly scans down the first digit or two of each entry in the column, and receives the impression that profits have declined drastically! True, this impression should not last very long, because a second glance would show that there is an extra 0 on the end of the second and third year's figures. Nevertheless, it is another minor irritation which can easily be eliminated by making sure that the *right*-hand ends of all figures are lined up. It would, of course, be even more annoying if you wanted to add the figures up, because digits to be added would not be under each other, and you might easily make a mistake. (If you are constructing your table using a spreadsheet such as Excel, this aligning will be done automatically.)

The table is also rather cluttered up with zeros. Since *all* the profits are expressed as a round number of tens of thousands of pounds, why not knock off the zeros and indicate in the column heading that the units are tens of thousands of pounds? At least, we are *assuming* the profits are in pounds, and not dollars or yen – the table as it stands does not actually indicate this. So let us include *that* in the column heading, too. The result of all these changes will be:

Total profits of 'WeatherGood' for the last three years

Year	*Profit (£0000s)*
2007	90
2008	128
2009	161

This is much better, but there are still one or two things we could do to improve it, particularly if it were to be given to someone with no further explanation as a summary of 'WeatherGood's' performance. The sceptical recipient might well respond 'Who says so?' In other words, where did the data come from? Even a more kindly disposed recipient might need to know the *source* of the data, so that if necessary he or she could go back to that source to get further details which he or she might need, but which are not given in the table as it stands. For this reason, every table should include a statement of the source from which it derives its figures, even if it's only of the form 'Company records' or 'Personal observation'.

The final change is to add the words 'Before tax' to the title, to make it absolutely unambiguous. So the ultimate version of the table is reached:

Total before-tax profits of 'WeatherGood' for the last three years

Year	Profit (£0000s)
2007	90
2008	128
2009	161

(*Source*: Company annual reports.)

More complicated tables

We made rather a meal out of drawing up the very simple table in the previous section, but all the points made apply, if anything with greater force, in constructing more complex tabulations. For instance, if we wished to include the breakdown into the two ranges 'HailGood' and 'RainGood' in the table, then we would require a two-way construction, because we have two classifications of the data – by years, and also by range. We *could*, it is true, show just the 'HailGood' profits and the total, but this would be undesirable for two reasons – first the obvious one, that anyone who wants to know about the profits on 'RainGood' will have to do a subtraction sum, which is annoying and might lead to errors; and second, because as far as possible it is preferable to have *non-overlapping* categories. For example, a table of births that shows four columns, headed 'Male', 'Female', 'Born outside marriage' and 'Total', is confusing because, of course, the 'Total' column *is* not the total of the other three – the babies who are counted as 'Born outside marriage' also appear in either the 'Male' or 'Female' column.

The best way, then, of giving the information as to the two ranges is to have the years, as before, as one set of 'headings' and the two types of product as the other. Which we put horizontally, and which vertically, are to a large extent a matter of choice, though it usually looks better to have more rows than columns in a table. There is also the point that we find it more convenient to scan a column of figures than a row mainly because we can then take in just the important first few digits (which will all be lined up under each other) more easily – so any figures which are likely to need comparing should ideally go in columns. The need to have figures which are to be totalled also underneath rather than beside each other is less great now that the addition will probably be done with a calculator, but could still be borne in mind.

All this having been said, we have one possible tabulation (Table 3.1) for the more detailed profits data:

Table 3.1 Before-tax profit breakdown of 'WeatherGood' for the past three years

Year	HailGood	RainGood
2007	70	20
2008	82	46
2009	93	68

All figures in £0000s.

(*Source*: Company annual reports.)

You'll notice that we have adopted the alternative policy here of indicating the units of the data in a footnote to the table, rather than having to repeat the statement in each column heading. Now that things are getting more complicated, use has also been made of ruled lines to distinguish between row and column headings and actual data. The table is quite useful as it stands, but although we can see at a glance that both ranges are generating increasing amounts of profit, and maybe even that the balance between the two ranges is altering in favour of 'RainGood' as time goes on, a few so-called *derived* statistics – that is, figures calculated from the original data to assist the reader – would make things much clearer.

First, we could put in a 'Total' column – clearly distinguished, of course, from the other two – but even that is not a great deal of help on its own. So the 'RainGood' profits went up from 20 out of 90 to 68 out of 161 over the three years – what does that tell us?

To most people, those fractions do not convey very much, because both their numerators and denominators are different. If they were expressed as percentages, however, it would be a different matter; we could then see how the shares of the profits accounted for by the two ranges of product have altered over the three-year period, without being distracted by the fact that the overall profits have also increased.

So we will add to our table the percentage figures, putting them in brackets to separate them from the actual profits. The table (Table 3.2) now looks like this:

Table 3.2 Before-tax profit breakdown of 'WeatherGood' for the past three years

Year	HailGood	RainGood	Total
2007	70 (78)	20 (22)	90
2008	82 (64)	46 (36)	128
2009	93 (58)	68 (42)	161

All figures in £0000s. Bracketed figures are per cent of year's total.

(*Source*: Company annual reports.)

We could, of course, have indicated the percentage figures by a subsidiary heading rather than by a footnote; naturally, too, the percentages for each year total to 100 per cent, which could provide a useful check particularly in a situation where there might be more categories.

When we want to go one stage further again and tabulate data that is classified in three ways, we encounter the problem of drawing up our tables on a two-dimensional sheet of paper – there is no way in which we can use a separate direction for each classification. This means that inevitably we will have to repeat one of our sets of headings. This will become clear if we continue using the data above, but now imagine that we also have the figures broken down into profits on male and female garments. Then we might produce the tabulation shown below (Table 3.3):

Table 3.3 Before-tax profit breakdown of 'WeatherGood' for the past three years

Year	HailGood		RainGood		Total		Overall total
	M	F	M	F	M	F	
2007	40	30	14	5	55	35	90
2008	45	37	34	12	79	49	128
2009	53	40	46	22	99	62	161

All figures in £0000s.

(*Source*: Company annual reports.)

You can see that we have had to repeat the male/female column headings. Of course, this is not the only way of setting out the table – there are actually six different possible arrangements of the data, and which you choose depends very much on what you want to get out of the table. As arranged here, the table makes comparisons between the male and female figures for each product range easy, but we no longer have the overall total profits for each product range separately. If that were the major point of interest, then we might select one of the other ways of drawing up the table. We have also omitted the percentage figures, in the interests of clarity. We *could* have included them – and, for that matter, more subsidiary totals – but only at the expense of further complicating the table. In general, if you do want to fit in a lot of information of this kind, and certainly if you want to include more than three classifications of the data, it is better to draw up two or three smaller tables rather than try to cram everything on to one.

The construction of good tables is made much easier these days by the availability of computer packages, which can be used to try out several formats of a table very quickly. You should get into the habit of using the computer packages to which you have access in this way; too often students do not want to use a package unless they know exactly what they are going to do with it, whereas the great strength of computing power is in its ability to perform 'try-it-and-see' exercises without taking up time and effort.

Moreover, in a business context you might well wish to keep the format of a table fixed over a period of time, while constantly updating the figures within it. Again, this is precisely what a spreadsheet enables you to do; the skeleton of the table can be stored and the figures in it revised as the need arises. You will find more details about using Excel for tabulation in the section 'Tables and diagrams with Excel' on p. 86, and in the MyMathLab Excel guide.

If you want to look at further examples of excellent tabulation techniques (as well as some examples of highly ingenious but totally impenetrable data presentations!) you cannot do better than to dip into the publications of the Government Statistical Service, particularly the summary publications such as *Social Trends* and *Economic Trends*. You will also notice that in these volumes, considerable use is made of charts, diagrams and so on to present the data of the tables in even more easily assimilated form.

Easily digested diagrams

Having gone to the trouble of presenting your data in the form of a well-designed table, you may feel that you have done your duty by your readers, and that if they *still* will not take note of the figures, then that is just their own silly fault. But to many people even the best-organised table still consists of a mass of figures, which as far as they are concerned is an incentive to turn the page as quickly as possible. A picture of some sort, however, is a different matter, especially if it makes use of colour or striking images to attract the eye. It is this fact that advertisers are exploiting all the time, and it is this fact that you, too, must learn to exploit in devising effective presentations for your numerical data. We will discuss the principles behind the various types of chart first, and then see how they can be constructed using software such as Excel.

The pictogram

You will almost certainly be familiar with at least the first two types of statistical diagram we are going to look at. The first, called the *pictogram*, is widely used in the press since it combines eye-catching quality with being easy to understand. You will find in Figure 3.1 a pictogram representing the data about total 'WeatherGood' sales shown in Table 3.1. As you can see, the idea is simply that we represent every £100 000 of profit by one little

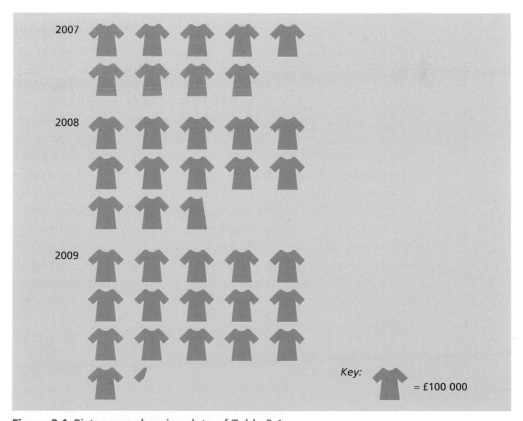

Figure 3.1 Pictogram showing data of Table 3.1

drawing of an anorak – chosen because the image represents the firm's products. Then the growth in profits over the three years is shown quite graphically, and we can even get some idea of the actual size of the profits in each year.

It will not, however, be a very accurate idea – just what does an anorak with one sleeve removed, as shown for 2008, represent? Clearly it will be something over £50 000, but to find out the exact figure we would have to return to the original source of the data, which should therefore always be stated. This inability to convey accurate figures limits the usefulness of pictograms to cases where you want to convey a general impression of a set of figures – preferably with not too many categories of classification – without worrying too much about the details.

There is another possible drawback to the use of pictograms that you should be aware of, although I hope you will not try to exploit it! That is, that, like many forms of data presentation, they *can* be used to give a misleading impression of a set of data. For instance, suppose that 'WeatherGood' has increased its sales of ladies' overtrousers from 3000 to 6000 pairs during the period 2007–9. It *might* try to show this growth by drawing two pairs of trousers, the second twice as long as the first. But if that is the case, then they should also be twice as wide, so that the actual *area* of the drawing, which is what strikes the eye, will be four times as great. Indeed, if the drawing is skilful and gives a three-dimensional impression, we might even make our assessment of the growth in sales from the *volume*, which will be eight times as great! In this way, the increase is made to appear much more impressive than it actually is. The honest way, of course, would be to represent the 2009 sales by *two* pairs of trousers, each the same size as that used for the 2007 figure; and in general, you should always decide on a standard 'unit' for a pictogram, and not alter its size.

The pie chart

The second type of diagram, the *pie chart*, is also much used in newspapers, government publications and so on. The word 'pie' in a mathematical context probably conjures up vague recollections of the formula for the area of a circle, but in fact here it refers to the ordinary concept of a pie as a round thing with apples or mincemeat in it! The idea is that we use the whole 'pie' or circle to represent some set of data, and break it down into various 'slices' to illustrate how the data breaks down into different categories. For example, if we want to show how the 2009 profits of 'WeatherGood' were made up (Table 3.3) we will need to divide our 'pie' into four 'slices', one for HailGood (male), one for HailGood (female), and one each for RainGood male and female. If we want to find what angle the 'slice' representing HailGood (male) should contain, we have to note that the entire circle, containing 360°, is to represent the total profits for the year, £1 610 000. So, since HailGood (male) contributed £530 000 of this, its 'slice' should contain an angle which is 530 000/1 610 000 of the 360. Thus we have

$$\text{angle for HailGood (male)} = \frac{53}{161} \times 360 = 119°$$

and similarly

$$\text{angle for HailGood (female)} = \frac{40}{161} \times 360 = 89°$$

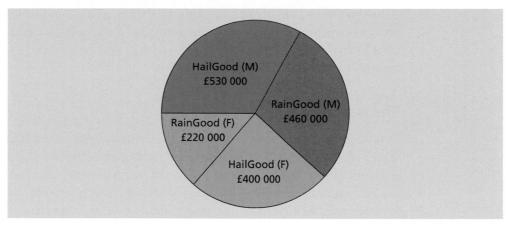

Figure 3.2 Pie chart of data in Table 3.3

$$\text{angle for RainGood (male)} \quad = \frac{46}{161} \times 360 = 103°$$

$$\text{angle for RainGood (female)} = \frac{22}{161} \times 360 = 49°.$$

Today, of course, a computer package would probably be used to draw the chart, making the hand-calculations unnecessary. The chart for the 'WeatherGood' data is shown in Figure 3.2 using the convention (fairly common but by no means universal) of drawing the 'slices' in decreasing order of size, starting from a horizontal line on the left of the 'pie'. The chart certainly brings out the differences in size between the contributions of the different categories, but the criticism we applied to the pictogram is even more relevant here: for conveying accurate information, the pie chart is useless. In fact, whereas with the aid of the key the pictogram did at least give us a vague idea of the size of the figures involved, the pie chart can do no such thing unless we actually write the numbers in each sector, as has been done here. Alternatively, the percentages are often shown.

One difficulty with pie charts is that the human eye is not very good at judging small differences in angles, particularly if there are many small angles of almost the same size. It is therefore not a good idea to use this as a way of displaying the data if there are more than about six categories involved.

But perhaps the most limiting factor about this method of data representation is that it really is not suited to a comparison of the breakdown of several different sets of data – for instance, the profit breakdowns in Table 3.3 over a number of years. The reason for this is easily seen if you recall that the total area of the 'pie' in each case would represent the total profits for the year; so the circle we drew for, say, 2007 would represent a total profit of £900 000. But in that case the circle for 2008 would have to have an area representing a profit of £1 280 000; so the ratio of the *areas* of the two circles would be 90:128. However, we draw circles not to a given area, but with a given *radius*, and you may remember that the connection between area and radius is that area = π × radius squared. You can perhaps begin to see that determining the radii we should use in order that the areas of our two circles should be in the ratio 90:128 is going to involve some messy calculations!

Roughly then, we can say that a pie chart will give a reasonable impression of the breakdown of one set of data into not more than about half a dozen categories, but if we want to compare the way in which several sets of data break down, we need to adopt an alternative method.

The bar chart

This alternative method is provided by the various forms of *bar chart*. The simplest of these is shown in Figure 3.3, which represents the data of Table 3.1. The diagram is almost self-explanatory, but a couple of points are worth mentioning. The width of the bars has no significance at all – it is simply chosen for convenience, as is the size of the gaps between the bars. It is a good idea always to leave *some* gap, and not put the bars directly next to each other, as this aids the clarity of the diagram. The other thing to note is that the vertical scale *must* start at zero; however tempting it may be to save paper by beginning at, say, £800 000, to do so would be quite misleading, as it would distort the relationship between the heights of the different bars. You can easily see this by placing a sheet of paper across Figure 3.3 at 80 on the vertical axis, and seeing how the apparent relationship from year to year is altered.

The strength of the bar chart, however, lies not so much in this simple type as in the facility with which the bars may be subdivided to illustrate more complex classifications of the data. For example, in Figure 3.4 we have a *compound* bar chart showing the data of Table 3.2. In this format we retain the information about *total* profit each year in an easily read form, since the height of each bar overall represents that total. If, however, we were less concerned to retain this information, but more anxious that the individual 'HailGood' and 'RainGood' totals should be easily accessible, we might prefer the *multiple*

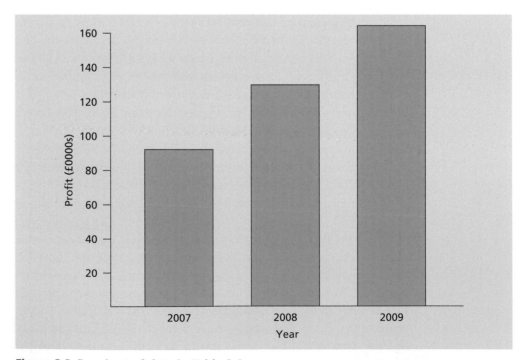

Figure 3.3 Bar chart of data in Table 3.1

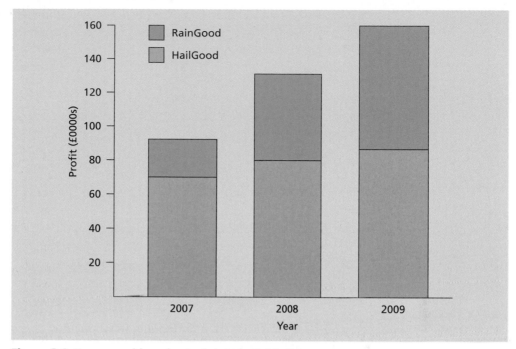

Figure 3.4 Compound bar chart of data in Table 3.2

bar chart format shown in Figure 3.5. Note there also the use of gaps to distinguish one year's data from the next, while the bars *within* each year are placed next to each other. Yet a third option is provided by the *percentage* bar chart (Figure 3.6) where, of course, each year's bar has the same height, representing as it does a total of 100 per cent, but the changing balance between the two product ranges is clearly brought out.

You will realise by now that the bar chart is by far the most versatile, as well as the most accurate, form of statistical diagram that we have looked at so far. Precisely because of this versatility, there is rarely one 'right' way of presenting data such as this, and you should

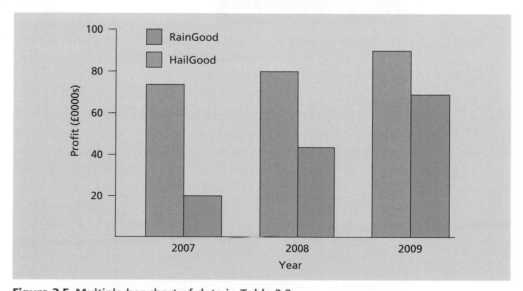

Figure 3.5 Multiple bar chart of data in Table 3.2

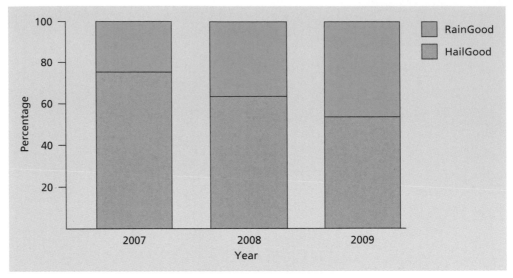

Figure 3.6 Percentage bar chart of data in Table 3.2

find plenty of scope for imagination in deciding which method best suits the use which you wish to make of the diagram.

Again, use of a computer package greatly facilitates experimenting with different types of diagram (see the section 'Tables and diagrams with Excel', p. 86).

There are, of course, many other types of diagram by which we can convey numerical information; if you look in the publication *Regional Statistics* issued from time to time by the Government Statistical Service, for instance, you will find plenty of examples of *statistical maps*, and *Which?*, the Consumers' Association magazine, is a rich source of less orthodox ways of getting facts across by means of diagrams. But although you can enjoy yourself inventing your own original methods, do not lose sight of the essential objective of the exercise – to make the data more easily and attractively accessible to the reader.

Quick check questions

1 You are drawing a pie chart to represent the fact that your company's total workforce breaks down into 600 full-time and 250 part-time staff, together with 150 on short-term consultancy contracts. What would be the angle of the pie-chart sector representing part-time staff?

2 What scale should be used on the horizontal axis of a bar chart?

3 Why is it incorrect to show the vertical scale of a bar chart starting from a value other than zero?

Answers:
1 The angle would be 90°, or $\frac{1}{4}$ of the total 360°, since 250 is $\frac{1}{4}$ of the total workforce of 1000.
2 The scale chosen for the horizontal axis of a bar chart is entirely a matter of convenience – it does not have any statistical meaning. All bars should of course be the same width, and be separated by gaps.
3 If you start the vertical scale of your bar chart from a point other than zero, you will distort the relationship between the heights of the bars, thus giving a misleading impression of the data.

Tabulating quantitative data

Ungrouped frequency tables

Thus far, almost everything we have said on the subject of data presentation has applied to qualitative data – we have drawn up tables for the descriptive categories 'HailGood' and 'RainGood', 'Male' and 'Female', and so on, and then constructed diagrams from these tables. The position is rather different, however, if we are dealing with actual measurements, and we need to devise new types of table to deal with the difference.

Take the following statement from the 'WeatherGood' report as an example:

I contacted a sample of 25 department stores who stock our products, and asked them to tell me how many ladies' anoraks they had sold during the winter quarter. The results are given below:

4	7	10	11	14	18	19	20	20	22	23	25	25
27	28	30	33	34	37	37	38	45	48	50	52	

Now, as it stands, this information is not particularly easy to assimilate. You can see that the largest number sold was 52, and the smallest 4, but apart from that it would be hard to draw any conclusions as to the pattern of sales. The data has been arranged in ascending order of size, but that is not really enough; we will have to make much more drastic simplifications if we are to make the figures really easy to grasp.

This is, in the terminology of the section on measurements in Chapter 2, a set of *discrete* data; since the shops presumably do not deal in fractions of an anorak, the sales figure has to be a whole number. So we could write down a list of all the sales figures which *might* arise, and then count how many times each of them *did* arise. There is not much point in starting below 4, as we have already observed that 4 is the lowest value in the data; equally we can stop at 52. That still leaves us with a lot of possibilities, though, many of which never occur at all:

No. sold	No. of stores	No. sold	No. of stores	No. sold	No. of stores
4	1	20	2	36	0
5	0	21	0	37	2
6	0	22	1	38	1
7	1	23	1	39	0
8	0	24	0	40	0
9	0	25	2	41	0
10	1	26	0	42	0
11	1	27	1	43	0
12	0	28	1	44	0
13	0	29	0	45	1
14	1	30	1	46	0
15	0	31	0	47	0
16	0	32	0	48	1
17	0	33	1	49	0
18	1	34	1	50	1
19	1	35	0	51	0
				52	1

This arrangement is known as an *ungrouped frequency table*, the *frequencies* being the number of times each value in the table occurs. For example, 25 has a frequency of 2. We often denote the frequencies by the letter *f*, and the values themselves – in this case, the numbers of items sold – by *x*. An arrangement like this can be quite useful if we have to deal with a fairly small number of discrete possibilities confined to a limited range; but in the present case the values cover far too large a range for this kind of table to effect much simplification, and we resort to the further step of *grouping* the values.

Grouped frequency tables

By 'grouping' the data we mean constructing a set of non-overlapping groups or classes, which between them cover the whole range of the data we are interested in. We can then count how many of the data values fall within each class.

In order to decide where each class shall begin and end, we recall that we must cover the range of the data – from 4 to 52 – but there is no reason why we need actually start at 4, or finish dead on 52. Life is considerably simplified, especially later on when we come to calculate means and so on, if we choose round numbers as our class boundaries as far as possible. We do not want, either, to have too many classes, otherwise the final table will not be much simpler than the original data. On the other hand, if we have too *few* classes, we will have thrown away too much information about the data – for make no mistake, we *are* throwing away information, however we group the figures. If the classes are sensibly chosen, however, we will effect considerable simplification while retaining the essential features of the data.

Suppose, then, that we choose to make our classes 0 to 9, 10 to 19, and so on. This will give us six classes to cover the data, which is perhaps a little on the low side, but is probably preferable to the eleven we should need if we used 0 to 4, 5 to 9, and so on. There will be just two values in the first class – 4 and 7 – as we can see by reference to the original data. Similarly, counting up the numbers of items in the other classes, we arrive at the *grouped frequency table* (Table 3.4):

Table 3.4

Class	Frequency
0–9	2
10–19	5
20–29	8
30–39	6
40–49	2
50–59	2

You can see how this arrangement of the data immediately makes it clear, for example, that the commonest number of anoraks sold was between 20 and 29, and that values in the two highest classes did not occur very often. If this table were given, however, to someone who did not have access to the original data – which would probably be the case in practice – they would have no way of knowing whether the '2' in the frequency column for the first class indicates that there is one store that sold no anoraks at all, or whether both those two in fact sold nine anoraks. This is what was meant by the loss of information which is the price we pay for simplification.

There are several things that we have taken for granted in drawing up this table but that are not really essential. The first is that all the classes are the same size. We will discover later that this does have many advantages, but there is no reason why, for instance, we should not choose to have classes 20–24, 25–29, 30–34 and 35–39 in the middle of the table where a lot of the values occur, but larger classes 0–9, 10–19 and 50–59 at the ends where the values are more scattered. The second point is that here we *knew* where to start and end the table, because we had the figures in front of us and could see that they ranged from 4 to 52. If, however, we had been sending someone out to collect the data, and wished to give them the table so that as they went along they could enter the data values they found into the appropriate class, then we would have very little idea where to stop the table. It is pretty clear that we must begin, at worst, at zero, since no store can sell fewer than that number of anoraks; but the easiest way to cope at the upper limit is to make use of an open class, such as '50 and upwards', to ensure that, whatever the highest value encountered may be, it will find a place in our table.

One final matter before we leave this set of figures: we can easily check that we have included all the data when constructing the table, by making sure that the 'frequency' column adds up to 25, the total number in our sample. The information given in the frequency table is often referred to as a *frequency distribution*, since it shows how the frequencies are distributed among the various classes.

Another example

Table 3.4 was easy to construct because we knew, since the data were discrete, exactly what values we might expect to occur. If, however, we have continuous data, the situation is rather different. Consider, as an illustration, this set of data, again taken from the 'WeatherGood' report, representing the average number of miles travelled by representatives for each effective call they make:

10.1	43.6	12.9	37.4	33.2	27.4	39.7	36.3
34.0	47.0	25.5	51.7	37.6	28.5	47.9	36.8
37.9	28.0	33.8	38.5	39.6	33.7	32.0	22.6
25.9	17.3	55.0	44.7	32.5	11.2	37.0	36.4
31.1	24.0	46.8	43.3	58.0	44.1	35.0	40.0

It is clear that these values have been quoted to the first decimal place only, but of course they are actually values of a continuous variable. So the kind of class boundaries that we used in our first frequency table will not cover this case; there, we were able to specify a class as, for example, '10–19' because, knowing that the data represented numbers of anoraks sold, we could be sure that we would never encounter a value of 19.5 which might, as it were, fall down the hole between these two classes. But in the present case, if we had classes '30–39' and '40–49' then the value 39.7 occurring in the table above would not be covered by either.

Nor can we take the apparently obvious step of making the classes '30–40' and '40–50', because that would give us an ambiguity as to where the value 40.0 should be placed. So we resort to the rather long-winded but safe expedient of making our classes '10 but under 20', '20 but under 30', and so on; that way, every value up to 20, including 19.9999 should we happen to be working to that level of accuracy, would be placed in the first class, but 20 would definitely belong in the second. (Of course, there is nothing to stop you always using this system, even when the data is discrete – though that can lead to problems later in working out averages, as we will see.)

Having got round this problem, there is another minor difficulty associated with tabulating the data. In the previous example, the figures were already arranged in increasing order of size, so that it was easy to count how many values there were in each class. Here, we have a haphazard arrangement of the data, but there is no need to rearrange it in order before drawing up the frequency table if we make use of a *tally*.

This means that, rather than dotting about the raw data trying to count, say, all the values in the '20 but under 30' class, we proceed through the table in an orderly manner, either going down columns or along rows, and for each value encountered we place a tally or mark opposite the appropriate class. When the table has been completely covered in this way, we simply have to count the number of marks opposite each class to arrive at the frequency – the process of counting up being considerably easier if we place every fifth tally across the preceding four, so that a count in multiples of five can be made quickly. The whole process is illustrated in Table 3.5.

Table 3.5

No. of miles per effective call	Tally	No. of representatives
10 but less than 20	IIII	4
20 but less than 30	IIII II	7
30 but less than 40	IIII IIII IIII III	18
40 but less than 50	IIII III	8
50 but less than 60	III	3

Again, the accuracy of our tabulation can be checked to a certain extent by making sure the frequencies total to 40, since that was the number of items in our raw data.

Tables of this kind are useful in showing such features of the data as the range, whereabouts the majority of values occur, and so on. But often we want answers to a somewhat different type of question: not 'How many representatives did between 30 and 40 miles per call?' but 'If we define an efficient representative as one who has to travel under 40 miles per effective call, how many of this sample count as efficient?' In other words, what we want is the number of items *less than* a certain value, and the question is most conveniently answered by converting the table above into a *cumulative* frequency table.

We will begin this table with a class 'under 10', which will, of course, contain none of the representatives, since they all did at least 10 miles per call. In the next class, 'under 20', we have just the four salespeople who did 10 but under 20 miles per call. In the next class, however, which is 'under 30', we have both the 4 in the '10 but less than 20' group, *and* the 7 in the '20 but less than 30' group – that is, 11 representatives altogether. You can now see why we call this a cumulative frequency table – as we proceed through the table, we accumulate more and more of the frequencies until we end up with all 40 salespeople in the 'under 60' class. The complete cumulative table is shown in Table 3.6.

Table 3.6

No. of miles per effective call	No. of representatives
Less than 10	0
Less than 20	4
Less than 30	11
Less than 40	29
Less than 50	37
Less than 60	40

We could have constructed the table from the opposite end, as it were, by asking how many representatives did 50 or more miles, 40 or more, and so on; but as this arrangement would effectively convey the same information as the 'less than' table above, it is not usually used, and if a 'cumulative frequency table' is referred to, you are safe in assuming that a 'less than' table is meant.

A word of caution needs to be said on the subject of constructing cumulative tables for *discrete* data. If we revert to our data concerning numbers of anoraks sold, where the classes used were 0–9, 10–19, etc., then the first class in a cumulative table produced from these figures would be, not 'less than 9', but 'less than 10', because the value 9, should it occur, is actually included in the first group. For this reason, try not to succumb to the temptation to turn the ordinary frequency table into a cumulative one by merely tacking on the cumulative frequencies down the side; it really is worthwhile, particularly to avoid confusion in this sort of discrete situation, going to the effort of writing out a *separate* cumulative table.

Diagrams from frequency tables

The kinds of diagrams we discussed in the section 'Easily digested diagrams' (see p. 67) – bar charts, pie charts and so on – are very well suited to the presentation of qualitative data, but we need to develop rather different methods to cope with quantitative data such as we have tabulated in the preceding section. We will look specifically at two such methods – the *histogram*, by means of which an ordinary grouped frequency table may be represented, and the *ogive*, constructed from the cumulative frequency table.

The histogram

Probably the easiest way to introduce the histogram is to discuss the one in Figure 3.7, which displays the data on representatives' mileages per call discussed above. At first sight this may appear to you to differ very little from a bar chart, but a closer examination should reveal some important differences. Most significant is the fact that the width of each 'block' in the histogram is no longer simply a matter of convenience; there is a genuine numerical scale on the horizontal axis, and the width of each block relates to this. If one of our classes happened to be twice the width of the others, then the block representing that class would also be twice as wide. For the same reason, there are no gaps

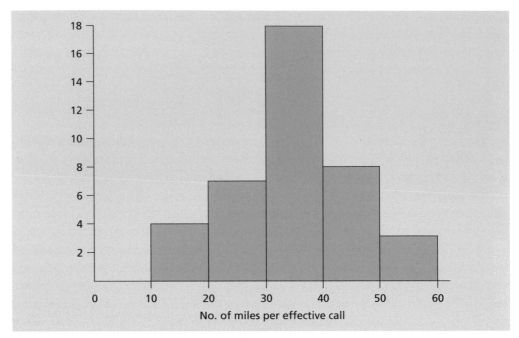

Figure 3.7 Histogram to show data of Table 3.5

between the blocks; the first represents all values from 10 up to 19.999 99 . . . , which takes us right up to 20, the beginning of the next block.

If you inspect the vertical axis of the histogram, you may well suspect that the printer – or the author! – has forgotten to include the label for this axis. The numerical scale is there, but why no explanation as to what it is measuring? In fact the omission is deliberate because the vertical scale itself is not measuring anything. If you give a histogram a cursory glance, what surely makes the impression on your eye is not so much the *height* of each block as the overall *area* occupied by the histogram, and the shape of that area. This does not make much difference if all the classes are the same width, in which case the height of each block and its area are proportional; but it becomes absolutely crucial if we have one or more non-standard classes.

To see why this should be, imagine that the first two classes of the data in Table 3.5 are combined, giving a class '10 but less than 30' with a frequency of 11. If we were to represent this combined class in the histogram by a block extending from 10 to 30, and having a height of 11, as shown in Figure 3.8(a), we would give a very misleading impression that a large proportion of the representatives did under 30 miles per sale; this impression is conveyed by the large area occupied by the 10–30 block. What we want to do is combine the blocks in such a way that the overall area of the new 'combined' block is exactly equal to the areas of the original two blocks added together, so that the impression of area given by the diagram does not alter.

This can be done by adjusting the height of the new combined block in such a way that its area represents a frequency of 11 on the same scale as all the other blocks. Since this class is now twice as wide as all the other classes – we might say it has a width of two standard classes – we need only plot a block 5.5 units in height to produce an area of 11 units. This is shown in Figure 3.8(b) where you can also see how the area of the new combined block is just the same as that of the two original blocks, the added and removed pieces (shaded in the figure) being equal.

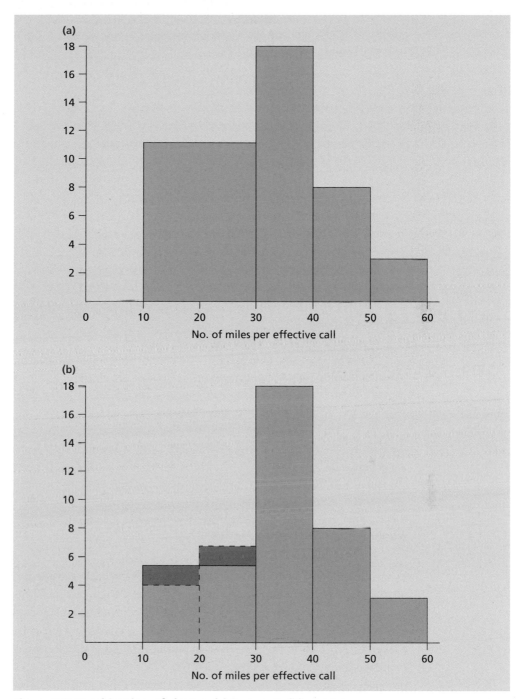

Figure 3.8 Combination of classes: (a) incorrect; (b) correct

In general, if we have a class that is twice the width of the other, 'standard' classes in the distribution, we must plot that block of the histogram with a height equal to half the frequency; if we have a class three times as wide as the standard, the height of its block will only be one-third of the frequency, and so on. It would clearly be quite wrong, then, to label the vertical axis of the histogram 'frequency' or 'number of representatives' – that would suggest that there were 5.5 representatives who did 10 but under 30 miles per call!

Table 3.7 Distribution of numbers of calls made by representatives in one day

No. of calls	No. of representatives making this no. of calls
3	1
4	3
5	7
6	11
7	10
8	4

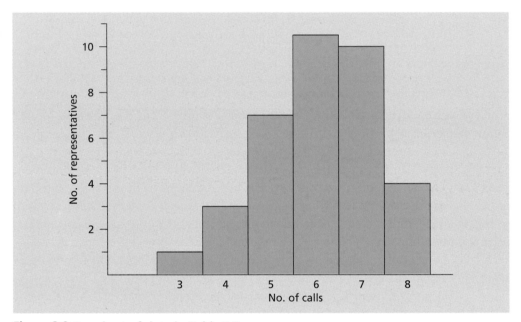

Figure 3.9 Bar chart of data in Table 3.7

You will sometimes find the label 'relative frequency' used, but there is really no need for any label; if you feel you *must* show the scale, then an *area* scale is the right way to do it.

This histogram represented data that were definitely continuous, but there is something of a 'grey area' between histograms and bar charts when it comes to discrete data. For an ungrouped frequency table such as that in Table 3.7, we really are back with bar charts, as shown in Figure 3.9.

With a grouped discrete table, however, such as that in Table 3.4, you will find several versions of the labelling of the horizontal axis, as shown in Figure 3.10, in use. Certainly the diagram should be treated like a histogram in terms of the adjustment needed if there are some non-standard classes.

One final headache about drawing histograms is the problem of open classes: how do you show a class '60 and over' on a histogram? The simple answer is that you do not; if you really want to draw a histogram for a distribution which has such a class, you will have to begin by assuming some upper limit to the open class – usually on common-sense grounds. For example, a class '90 and over' in an age distribution might well be closed at 100 on the grounds that hardly anyone lives longer than that. Sometimes, if such a 'closing

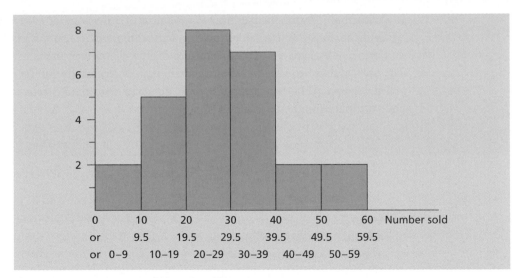

Figure 3.10 Histogram of data in Table 3.4

assumption' has had to be made, the corresponding block of the histogram will be enclosed by a dashed line, intended to show that the point of closure is only conjectural.

By now you are probably beginning to think that histograms are more trouble than they are worth – a point of view with which I would, on the whole, concur. They provide a useful picture of the general shape of a distribution, but cannot be used to give any further information about its characteristics – a defect which renders them very much inferior to graphs of cumulative frequency tables, to which we now turn.

The ogive

Such a graph for the data of Table 3.6 is shown in Figure 3.11. It is termed an *ogive* (pronounced variously with hard or soft 'g'), from its characteristic shape, which is similar

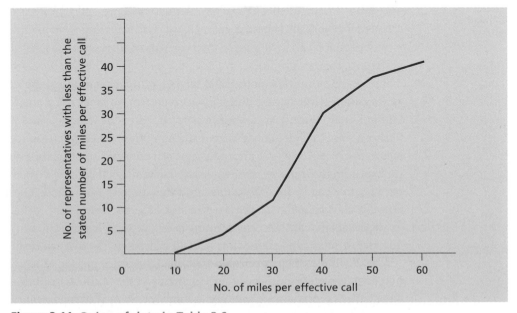

Figure 3.11 Ogive of data in Table 3.6

to that of half of an ogival arch in architectural terminology. It always has this upward-climbing shape, of course, since the cumulative frequencies grow steadily larger.

The ogive is easy to plot, as it is just an ordinary graph of the cumulative frequencies. The only possible confusion will arise if you have neglected the advice given in the section 'Tabulating quantitative data', p. 73, and added the cumulative frequencies to the side of your ordinary frequency table like this:

	f	Cum. f
10 but less than 20	4	4
20 but less than 30	7	11

and so on. In that case you may well wonder whether to plot the cumulative frequency 11 opposite to 20, or 30, or somewhere in the middle. If, however, you had taken the trouble to write out a new table:

Less than 20	4
Less than 30	11

etc., it would be quite clear to you that the frequency 11 is to be plotted above 30 on the horizontal axis. Incidentally, the convention of putting the class boundaries on the horizontal axis and the cumulative frequencies on the vertical axis is absolutely standard – an ogive plotted the other way round looks very funny to a statistician.

There are two things about the ogive of Figure 3.11 that may strike you as strange, particularly if you have come across such graphs before. One is that the points of the graph are connected by straight lines rather than a smooth curve. This is not merely because the author is incapable of drawing a 'smooth curve' which does not look like a string of telegraph wires; there is a logical reason for it. When we connect up the points of the graph in *any* way we are making some kind of assumption about how the points within each class are distributed. But at least, with a straight line, we *know* what we are assuming – namely, that the values in each class are spread uniformly throughout the class. With a so-called smooth curve, there is no knowing *what* assumptions are involved – and probably no two people's curves will be the same anyway; hence the author's preference for straight lines.

The second thing is that the label on the vertical axis of the graph no doubt strikes you as very long-winded; and indeed, you *could* simply label it 'cumulative frequency'. But, labelled as in Figure 3.11, we have a clear statement of exactly *what* the graph is designed to show – and, incidentally, a demonstration of why the ogive is so much superior to the histogram in terms of the information it can convey. Suppose, for example, that we wish to determine how many salespeople are efficient, if efficient is defined as doing 45 miles per effective call or less. We cannot find this directly from Table 3.6, since 45 is midway between class boundaries; but if we go along the horizontal axis to 45, and then up to the graph and across to the corresponding point on the vertical axis, we can read off that the number of salespeople doing less than 45 miles per effective call is about 33.

We will find in the next chapter that the ogive, once plotted, can give us measurements that form a useful summary of the behaviour of the entire distribution, by very much the same simple procedure we have just carried out. So by plotting it you are not merely giving a useful display of the data, but preparing for further operations on that data in the future.

Although histograms and ogives are still the types of statistical diagram most widely used and included in examination syllabuses, there are several more recent arrivals on the scene, generally included under the title of Exploratory Data Analysis (EDA). You will find a discussion of these approaches in some of the references listed in the Further reading section, and one of them, the oddly named 'box-and-whisker' diagram, is illustrated in Chapter 4.

Some simple graphs

We have already discussed a few graphs in Chapter 1, in the sections on straight line and other types of graph, and we will be encountering many more in later chapters. But the graphs examined in Chapter 1 were those of algebraic expressions, particularly straight lines, whereas the object of the present section is to look at some numerical graphs which can be used as an effective way of presenting data. In particular, we will get away from the idea of a graph as a smooth or continuous curve, and discover that in many cases, it would be quite wrong, even impossible, to try to draw such a curve through a set of points.

A 'spiky' graph

Take the following set of figures, again abstracted from the 'WeatherGood' report mentioned at the beginning of the chapter, which give the total revenue generated by the sales of 'HailGood' outerwear for the years 2007–9, summarised quarterly. The figures are in £0000s:

Year	Quarter	Sales revenue
2007	1	256
	2	220
	3	130
	4	283
2008	1	260
	2	225
	3	137
	4	288
2009	1	264
	2	227
	3	141
	4	290

It is clear simply from a glance at the figures that there is a pattern in the sales for each year, which vary in a fairly regular manner from quarter to quarter. However, the pattern is made much clearer by plotting the data on a graph, with time on the horizontal axis and revenue on the vertical axis, as in Figure 3.12. But it is certainly not possible to join the points of this graph by smooth curves; nor should we try to do so. The lines connecting the points here have no function except to emphasise the shape of the pattern

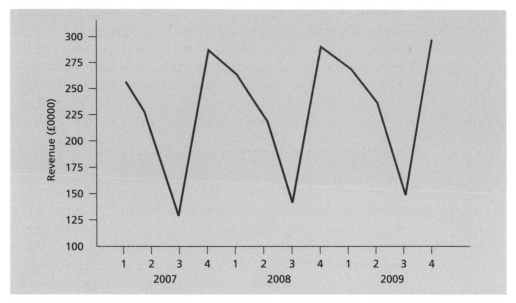

Figure 3.12 Graph of 'WeatherGood' quarterly revenue

produced by the figures; there can be no question, for example, of reading off an inter-mediate figure of 181 as the sales half-way between the second and third quarters of 2008, as one might do with the sorts of graph we looked at in Chapter 1. Nevertheless, such graphs are very useful if we wish to identify the kind of patterns inherent in data of this kind; we will be encountering them again in Chapter 13.

A 'stepped' graph

In other cases, the appropriate way of connecting the points of the graph is not by jagged straight lines, as in Figure 3.12, but by a 'stepped' form of line. If, for instance, 'WeatherGood' want to show graphically the interest rates which it has been charged by its bank on loans over the past few years, it could do so as shown in Figure 3.13. The graph

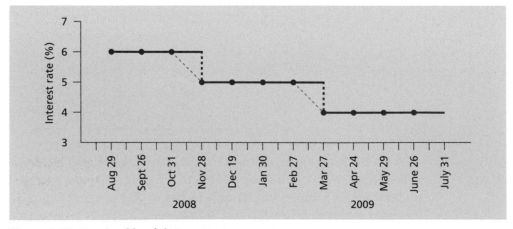

Figure 3.13 Graph of bank interest rate

takes this 'stepped' shape because the interest rate will remain constant for a certain length of time, then change suddenly and immediately to a new value. The vertical parts of the graph again have no significance – they are there merely to connect the horizontal sections. It would be very misleading here if we tried to connect the points in some other way, perhaps as shown by the diagonal lines in Figure 3.13. These would suggest that an interest rate of 5.5 per cent was being charged on 15 November, whereas of course such a rate never applied – the rate actually decreased at one jump from 6 per cent to 5 per cent.

A scattergraph

There is a third type of graph, more extreme than either of the two we have looked at so far, where we make no attempt to connect the points in any way whatsoever. Such a graph is shown in Figure 3.14, and you can see at a glance why it goes by the name of *scatter-graph*. The object of the graph is to demonstrate what sort of relationship, if any, exists between two quantities – in this case, the amount 'WeatherGood' spends on advertising 'HailGood' outerwear and the sales revenue generated by that product group. The firm presumably hopes that larger advertising expenditures will result in larger sales, and the scattergraph showing both quantities over a period of five years suggests that something of the kind is indeed true; the larger values of sales revenue occur at larger values of advertising expenditure, and the smaller sales revenues at smaller advertising expenditures. The points also seem to cluster around a curve of the approximate shape indicated by the line, which might suggest a further line of investigation if we wanted to determine the relationship between the two quantities more exactly. We will be pursuing this topic in Chapter 11; at present we mention the scattergraph simply as yet another example of a graph far removed from the smooth graphs which are probably most familiar to you from schoolwork.

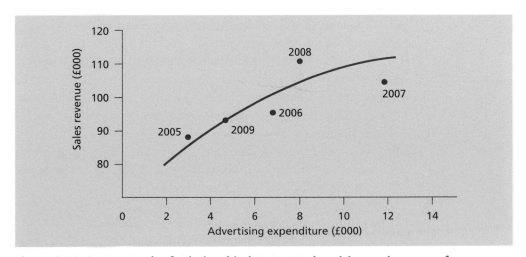

Figure 3.14 Scattergraph of relationship between advertising and revenue for 'HailGood' outerwear

Quick check questions

1 A grouped frequency table has six classes with frequencies 2, 8, 17, 21, 16, 9. Find the corresponding cumulative frequencies you would need to calculate in order to plot a 'less than' ogive.

2 You want to draw a diagram to show how the volume of waste paper produced by your organisation has declined over the past ten years. The best format would be (a) a bar chart; (b) a pie chart; (c) a line graph?

3 Describe in your own words the difference between a histogram and a bar chart.

Answers:
1 The cumulative frequencies are 2, 10, 27, 48, 64, 73.
2 A line graph would be best here, as it would emphasise the downward movement of the figures. A bar chart would be next best, but a pie chart is definitely not suitable in this situation.
3 A histogram has a properly scaled horizontal axis, with the widths of bars corresponding to the widths of the classes in the underlying frequency table. A bar chart generally shows qualitative data, and the widths of the bars are simply a matter of convenience.

Tables and diagrams with Excel

If you already have your data stored as an Excel worksheet, you can make use of the facilities offered by the spreadsheet for tabulation and graphing, though these are not always ideal, as we will see.

Frequency tables

There are two ways of constructing frequency tables using Excel, both of which require you to begin by setting up a column containing the class limits. For example, if we want to tabulate the numbers of full- and part-time employees from the data in EMP.XLS, we put the numbers 0 and 1 into two adjacent cells of a spare column in the worksheet – say E1 and E2. We then select cells F1 and F2, and enter into these the array formula =FREQUENCY(A2:A61, E1:E2) (remembering to use CTRL–SHIFT–ENTER simultaneously to enter an array formula). Excel counts the number of occurrences of 0 and 1, and displays the frequencies in cells F1 and F2 respectively. Thus we see that there are in fact 42 full-time and 18 part-time employees in the data set.

If we are constructing a grouped frequency table, the Excel convention is that all values up to, and including, the specified class limit are included in the frequency count. So, if we were tabulating the age data our first step might be to use Excel =MAX and =MIN functions to examine the range of ages involved; this reveals that the highest age is 57, and the lowest is 17. If we then enter 20, 30, 40, 50, 60 into (say) cells H1 to H5, to represent our chosen class limits, and place the function =FREQUENCY(C2:C61, H1:H5) in an array I1 to I5 as described above, the frequency placed in cell I1 will be the count of all employees aged 20 and under – that is, 2. Similarly in I2 we have the number of employees aged 21–30, and so on. Once the frequency table has been constructed as described, it is a good idea to change the formulae in the frequency column to values, using EDIT/PASTE SPECIAL. This will prevent the values changing should you wish to move the table around. The class limits can then be overwritten with something more meaningful, such as our '21 and up to 30' format, and the columns given suitable titles.

The alternative way to draw up a frequency table is to use the DATA ANALYSIS command in the DATA menu. This gives access to a wide range of statistical tools; the relevant one is HISTOGRAM, which, contrary to what you might think, does not merely plot histograms but also draws up frequency and cumulative frequency tables. Again, we need to have the class limits already set up in a column. The HISTOGRAM dialogue box requires you to enter the range of cells containing the data, the *bin range*, which is the range of cells containing the class limits, and a destination range for the output – the default is that it will be placed in a new ply of the worksheet. If you specify a range in the current ply make sure it is not going to overwrite anything important! You can check boxes to obtain cumulative as well as raw frequencies (though these will always be in per cent format), and if you want an actual histogram to be plotted, you'll have to check the 'chart output' box.

Table 3.8 shows the written output produced by Excel using this command, with the EMP ages as the input range, and Figure 3.15 is the corresponding diagram. As you can see, it is really more of a bar chart than a histogram – there are gaps between the bars, and no adjustment has been made to take account of the unequal classes. Moreover, the labels

Table 3.8

Bin	Frequency	Cumulative %
20	2	3.33%
30	8	16.67%
40	30	66.67%
60	20	100.00%
More	0	100.00%

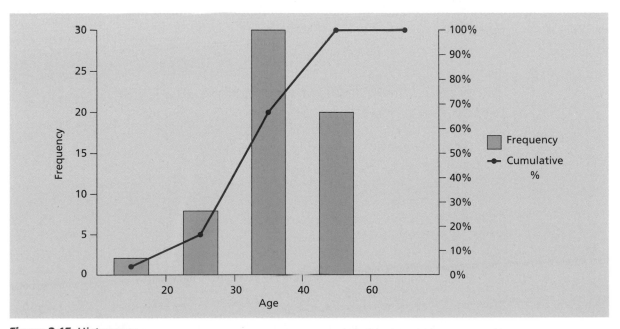

Figure 3.15 Histogram

on the axis (20, 30, etc.) are placed at the mid-points of the bars when they should be at the upper limits. Some of these problems can be overcome by clever tricks if you know your way around Excel but, on the whole, this way of producing a histogram is perhaps best avoided.

Diagrams

Spreadsheets probably have the edge over other statistical packages where diagrams are concerned, providing numerous variations on bar charts, pie charts and other types of special chart as well as straightforward *xy* graphs. A quick way to obtain charts is to use the various chart options in the CHART group on the INSERT tab. (Note that the bar charts produced in this way sometimes have a vertical axis which doesn't start from zero – to get a proper bar chart you may need to rescale this axis.) There are facilities for improving the layout of graphs by adding titles, legends, labels on axes, and so on. Figures 3.16 and 3.17 show respectively a pie chart of the employee status figures from EMP.XLS, and an ogive of the age data from the same data set (plotted using an *xy* graph).

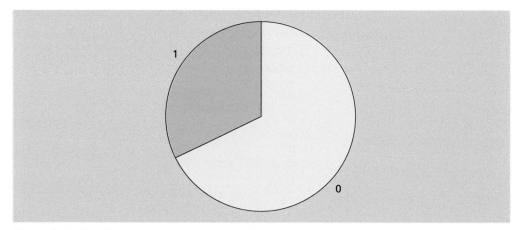

Figure 3.16 Pie chart of employee status data

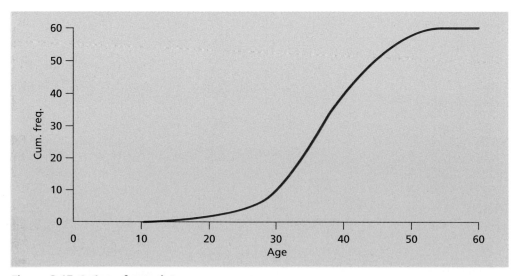

Figure 3.17 Ogive of age data

There are many tools in Excel for giving your graphs a professional finish, by plotting in colour, adding labels, and so on. Perhaps the main advantage of using a computer package to construct your tables and diagrams is that you can try lots of different formats very quickly on the screen, and select for printing the one that best meets your needs. However, it is important not to be persuaded to use a particular format simply because it is provided by your software. For example, Excel offers three-dimensional pie charts and bar charts, but these rarely improve the clarity of the information communicated by the diagram; use them only if you are more interested in impact than in conveying quantitative information.

How *not* to do it

Before we leave the topic of visual presentation of data altogether, one final note of caution: we have been discussing the *honest* presentation of figures by means of diagrams, and I hope that is what you are interested in doing, but it *is* possible to make use of these methods in a deliberate attempt to *mis*represent a situation. Beware, for instance, of the graph with no label on the vertical axis, perhaps even no scale at all, as in Figure 3.18(a); treat with caution the graph in which the vertical axis is broken without any indication to the reader, as in Figure 3.18(b) (sometimes one is forced to do this, but the

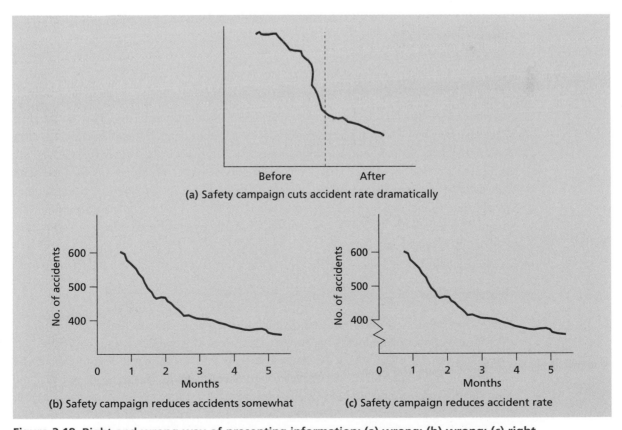

Figure 3.18 Right and wrong way of presenting information: (a) wrong; (b) wrong; (c) right

reader's attention should be drawn to the fact by showing a deliberate break in the scale, as Figure 3.18(c) illustrates). Not everyone will be as honest as you! For more illustrations of both good and bad data presentation, see Further reading on p. 93.

Back to the Morrisons charts

Let's round off this chapter by having another look at the charts from the Morrisons website which were introduced in the first section of the chapter (pp. 58–9).

Share prices

The first graph shows the behaviour of the share price over time. The units – pence – are shown on the vertical axis. The vertical scale does not start from zero; what would the graph look like if it did? Suppressing the zero means that the vertical scale is somewhat exaggerated, but in a graph primarily designed to show movements in share price that is probably appropriate. Certainly the so-called volatility of the share price – the random small-scale ups and downs – is made very clear, as is the big fall in price around June 2010. (You might like to try to find out what happened at that point to cause this – an announcement of reduced profits? Some kind of acquisition activity?) It might be easier to focus on the long-term behaviour if some of the small-scale rises and falls were 'ironed out', or 'smoothed', to use the statistical term. We will be looking at ways of doing this in Chapter 15.

Carbon emissions

The bar chart showing tonnes of carbon emissions is slightly odd, since the ends of the bars have been rounded off – this would make it difficult to read off values against a scale, but actually no proper scale is provided in this case, though the values represented are indicated on the bars. The 'doughnut' shape adopted for the 'Emissions by type' data has little to recommend it over a normal pie chart – it is in fact slightly more difficult to estimate the relative size of the sectors when the centre of the circle is not shown. The diagram does make clear, however, that electricity is responsible for the largest percentage of emissions by far.

Market share

The map layout used to display this data is quite striking, though there is something a bit strange about the regions – we have 'Lancashire and North East' and 'Yorkshire', but what has become of Cumbria? It would also be helpful to show the boundaries of the regions on the map. And it's necessary to read accompanying text to work out that the bracketed figures shown below the main ones are those for the previous reporting period. Nevertheless, the chart does make it very clear where Morrisons' areas of strength and weakness lie.

EXERCISES

*Further examples on the work of this chapter can be found on the **Companion Website**.*

1 Tabulate the data contained in the following extract from a company report:

   This year saw an increase of 20 per cent over last year's total of 11 000 customers. We classify our customers, one-quarter of whom are overseas, as 'regular', 'occasional' or 'dormant', according to the number of orders they have placed in the past year. Overall, 'regular' customers formed 60 per cent of the total, and only 10 per cent were classed as 'dormant', though among overseas customers the proportions in the three categories were 3:2:1.

2 Produce a diagram illustrating the data of Exercise 1 suitable for inclusion in the report.

3 A sample of 1000 receipted bills was taken from a firm's files, and checked for errors. Of the bills 105 contained errors which were classified as follows:

In firm's favour by		In customer's favour by	
under 5p	32	under 5p	29
5p but under 10p	11	5p but under 10p	18
10p but under 15p	4	10p but under 15p	7
15p but under 20p	1	15p but under 20p	0
20p or more	1	20p or more	2

   Construct a diagram to represent the data.

4 The council of a seaside resort has carried out a small-scale survey to find out how far day visitors travel to the resort. The raw results are as follows (figures in miles):

   12, 23, 14, 27, 14, 8, 19, 27, 25, 11, 17, 32, 22, 25, 42, 13, 9, 36, 16, 5, 13, 22, 28, 6, 29, 37, 24, 24, 7, 28, 34, 56, 21, 39, 12, 18, 25, 45, 33, 31.

   Tabulate these figures in a manner that could be used at a council meeting.

5 Get hold of a list of postal charges for first-class letters and from it draw a suitable graph showing charge against weight, which could be used in a firm's post room.

6 Look at *Social Trends*, *Economic Trends*, *Regional Statistics* or other government statistical publications, noticing what kinds of diagrams are used to present particular types of data. Be critical! (You can find these publications via www.statistics.gov.uk.)

7 Collect examples of bad or misleading diagrams from the press (pseudo-scientific advertisements are a rich source), and look out, too, for articles in which numerical information is presented in narrative style.

8 For the data in the file STUD.XLS/STUD.DAT draw up (a) a frequency distribution of ages for male and female students; (b) a table showing subject of first degree and gender. For each of these tables, construct a diagram suitable for use in a presentation to potential students of the course in question.

9 For the data in the file MACH.XLS/MACH.DAT, produce a cumulative frequency table of weights of packets for the three machines, and display the results on a single ogive.

10 For the data in the file QUAL.XLS/QUAL.DAT, plot a scattergraph of floorspace against takings. What can you conclude from the graph?

$\rightarrow$

11 At the beginning of 2009 Ms A purchased a number of shares in various companies, as follows:

Company name	Number of shares	Purchase price per share (p)
Equimix plc	500	113
Farringdon Holdings	800	83
Greenbridge	400	75

During the year she disposed of her entire holding of Equimix, selling at 130p per share, and also sold half her Greenbridge shares at 80p per share. She purchased a further 200 shares in Farringdon Holdings at 80p, and also bought 400 shares in Heavicast Ltd at 72p per share.

Expand the above table to show the changes in Ms A's investment portfolio over the year, and construct a suitable diagram to illustrate the information.

12 In a survey of customers' opinions of a certain supermarket chain, respondents were asked their opinion of ease of access of the chain's stores. The results showed that, of 347 car owners included in the survey, 230 rated the access 'excellent', 72 rated it 'fair' and the remainder 'poor'. For non-car owners, the numbers were 29, 51 and 63 respectively. Tabulate this information adding suitable derived statistics, and construct a diagram or diagrams to show the results.

13 Look at the websites of the other major supermarkets (Sainsbury's, Asda, etc.) and compare their use of charts and graphics with the examples from Morrisons in this chapter. (*See the* **Companion Website** *for useful links.*)

Case Study

Subrose supermarkets

A branch of the Subrose supermarket chain in your local town has recently carried out a survey as part of its policy of encouraging 'green' behaviour in its customers. The survey was as follows:

1 How far have you travelled today to get to Subrose?
    1.1 Under a mile
    1.2 1–2 miles
    1.3 More than 2 but less than 5 miles
    1.4 5 miles or over
2 What mode of transport did you use to reach the store?
    2.1 Walked
    2.2 Cycled
    2.3 Car
    2.4 Public transport (bus, tube, etc.)
    2.5 Taxi
3 What mode of transport will you use to get home with your shopping?
    2.1 Walk
    2.2 Cycle
    2.3 Car
    2.4 Public transport (bus, tube, etc.)
    2.5 Taxi

4 If a free bus service were provided covering locations within 5 miles of the store, how likely do you think you would be to use it?
   4.1 Would definitely use it all the time
   4.2 Might sometimes use it
   4.3 Probably wouldn't use it
   4.4 Definitely wouldn't use it
5 Please indicate your age:
   5.1 Under 18
   5.2 18–30
   5.3 31–50
   5.4 51–70
   5.5 Over 70

You have been asked, as a management trainee at Subrose, to give a short presentation of the results of the survey, which you will find on the website in an Excel spreadsheet called SUBROSE.XLS. The presentation is for the store manager and deputy manager, the regional sales manager, and the sales director.

Prepare 4–6 PowerPoint slides for the presentation, covering the key points from the survey. You should make use of appropriate charts and tables.

Further reading

Huff, D. and Geis, I. (1993), *How to Lie with Statistics*, Norton.

Although this is quite an old book, the content has not dated; written in a straightforward style which is easy to read, and assuming no statistical knowledge, it is a great guide to the ways in which statistics are, whether deliberately or accidentally, misused by advertisers, politicians and others.

Tufte, E.R. (1990), *Envisioning Information*, Graphics Press.

Tufte, E.R. (2001), *The Visual Display of Quantitative Information*, 2nd edn, Graphics Press.

These latter two titles, which make their content clear, are beautiful books – perhaps the only examples of coffee table statistics books!

Chapter 4

SUMMARISING THE FIGURES:
MEASURES OF LOCATION AND SPREAD

Chapter prerequisites Before starting work on this chapter, make sure you are happy with the following topics:

1 construction of frequency tables (see Chapter 3, pp. 73–7);

2 construction and interpretation of histograms and ogives (see Chapter 3, pp. 77–83).

Learning outcomes By the end of your work on this chapter you should be able to:

1 define and calculate the mean, median, mode, standard deviation, quartiles and range, for a given set of data;

2 select the most appropriate measures for use with a particular set of data, and explain your choice.

Quantitative methods in practice

What's typical?

Let's make CEOs justify their wages

The facts about income inequality in the UK are nothing less than mind-boggling. The average income of a FTSE 100 chief executive, according to the most recent Guardian survey of executive pay, is over £3m per year, including bonuses and pension contributions. This is more than 100 times median house-hold income. It is not uncommon for CEOs to earn 200, or 300 times as much as the median pay of their employees or, in the case of Terry Leahy's final year at Tesco, for a CEO to be paid 500 times the average take-home pay of his colleagues.

Martin O'Neill, guardian.co.uk, Tuesday 19 October 2010
http://www.guardian.co.uk/commentisfree/2010/oct/19/make-ceos-justify-wages

Here's a challenge to the myths of the mega-earners

The Association of British Insurers this week challenged the weak code of practice of executive pay con-sultants, the great bellows that inflate top pay. It is conflict of interest to sell all kinds of services to the very company executives whose pay they are advising on. The fastest way to pump up pay is to suggest to every company that their remuneration should be in the top quartile.

Polly Toynbee, guardian.co.uk, Monday 24 August 2009
http://www.guardian.co.uk/commentisfree/2009/aug/24/mega-earners-pay-commission

These two quotes illustrate how difficult it is to discuss incomes unless we can arrive at a sensible definition of what is 'typical'. There is a reference to the 'average take-home pay' in the first quote, and most of us probably think we understand what that means – but what about the 'median' in the same quote? And what is the 'top quartile' within which all companies think their pay should fall?

The problem of determining a few simple numbers which will somehow typify the behaviour of a large and complicated set of data is not, of course, peculiar to discussions about wages. Whenever we want to communicate the important facts about a customer survey, a production process or a portfolio of share prices in an effective way, we are faced with exactly the same situation. This chapter examines a set of measures that can be used to communicate in this way, and the methods for calculating them.

The trade union leader's problem

We will stay with the theme of wages for the moment, but consider a simpler example. The Grimchester plant of the Westward Packaging Company has for many years enjoyed good management–employee relations, but now this happy state of affairs is threatened by increasing industrial unrest. The root of the problem is that workers feel that they are underpaid, compared with their colleagues at Westward's nearby Greentown plant, and claim that this difference is due to differing ways of interpreting piecework pay agreements.

Westward's management is quite prepared to listen to the workers' grievances, but first it wishes to see some evidence on paper that the wages of the two groups really *are* different. So, full-time union official Arthur Hughes has been called in to try to put together some figures.

He realises immediately that, as each plant employs several thousand workers, it is not going to be practical to collect details about how much each one of them earns – especially as some of them are unwilling to give him the information. He therefore decides to use a sample of 150 workers from each factory. After consultation with a friendly statistician, he comes up with a *stratified sample* (see Chapter 2) designed so as to cover all groups in the workforce; management examines this design and agrees to accept the samples as representative.

Arthur therefore goes ahead and collects from all the people in his two samples the amount of take-home pay they received last week. This gives him two sets, each of 150 figures, all different because of differing amounts of tax, allowances and so on, and varying in size from £302 a week to £387 a week. He knows enough about data presentation to arrange the two sets into two frequency distributions which are shown below.

Weekly take-home pay (£)	No. of Grimchester workers	No. of Greentown workers
300 but under 310	3	4
310 but under 320	7	12
320 but under 330	33	17
330 but under 340	26	23
340 but under 350	24	38
350 but under 360	20	26
360 but under 370	18	16
370 but under 380	15	12
380 but under 400	4	2

However, he realises that this will not convey a great deal to Westward's management – in fact, in some ways it makes it appear that the Greentown workers are worse off, since there are more of them in the bottom class and fewer at the top! What he really needs is a few simple numbers that will *summarise*, in an easily understood fashion, the behaviour of the two samples.

What needs to be measured

To help us decide what kind of measurements would be useful to Arthur, it is a good idea to look at the histograms of the two samples. These are drawn in Figure 4.1; in interpreting them remember that because the last group has a range of £20, whereas all the others have ranges of only £10, the height of the last blocks in the histograms must be adjusted accordingly.

The most noticeable feature of the two histograms is perhaps the fact that the peak of the 'Grimchester' histogram is further over to the left than the peak of the 'Greentown' one, although both are contained within the same interval. Associated with this is the fact that the 'Greentown' one is much more symmetrical. And these facts really pinpoint the three properties of the distributions which need to be measured: the *location*, or roughly

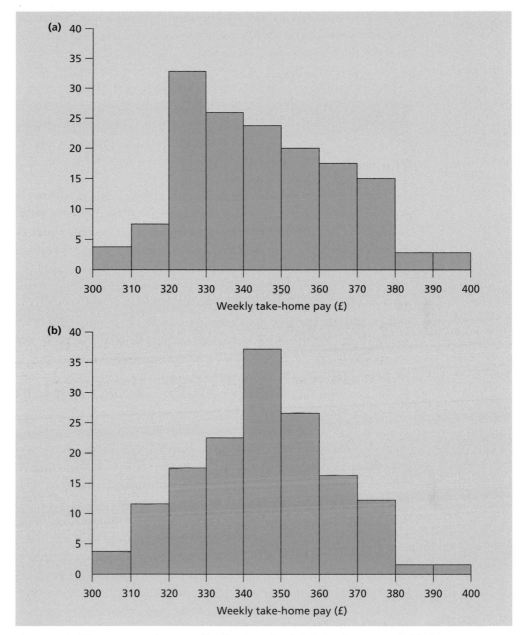

Figure 4.1 Histograms of wage distributions for (a) Grimchester and (b) Greentown workers

where on the pay-scale the values in the sample tend to be situated; the *dispersion*, or how scattered the values in the sample tend to be; and – rather less importantly – the *skewness*, or degree of asymmetry of the sample values.

We will find, however, that it is not sufficient to devise just one way of measuring each of these characteristics of a frequency distribution. Because different distributions behave in different ways, and because different types of measurement are suited to those differ-ent types of behaviour, quite a variety of ways of measuring the three characteristics have been developed. We are going to look at three ways of measuring location and three ways of measuring dispersion – measurements of the two features tend to go together in pairs.

We will not actually calculate any measures of skewness, since these are much less standardised than the other two types, but will merely look at skewness in a descriptive sort of way.

Measuring location

The mode

We have already, in fact, looked at one measure of location without being explicit about it, when we said in the previous section that 'the "Grimchester" histogram has its peak further over to the left'. We were suggesting here the idea that the 'peak' or most common value in a distribution gives us a clue to the 'typical' value for the distribution as a whole. The technical name for this most common value is the *mode*, and it is very easy to see, either by looking at the histogram or by inspecting the frequency table to find the highest frequency, whereabouts it occurs.

Actually, what we find in the case of a grouped frequency table like the ones here is not a *single* figure for the mode, but rather a modal class; in the case of the Grimchester data, the modal class is £320–£330, while for Greentown it is £340–£350. These certainly seem to support the Grimchester workers' idea that they are worse off – but let us look at some of the criticisms that could be levelled at this way of measuring the 'typical' wage.

First of all, it is rather imprecise – we have a range of £10 in each case. There *are* ways of deciding whereabouts in the modal class the actual mode must lie, but for the sort of data you are likely to encounter these methods give purely theoretical figures which may not in practice have much to do with the 'most common' value. This is clearly undesirable; so, too, is the fact that there may well be more than one mode in a distribution. Consider, for instance, the distribution you would get if you classified into 2-inch-wide groups the heights of all the members of your course. There would almost certainly be two 'peak' values if your course contains a mixture of males and females – one peak at around the average height for women, and another at the average height for men. There might even be exactly equal numbers in each of these 'peak' classes. So we should have two modes, which would lead to a good deal of ambiguity in talking about *the* mode. And there are situations where *more* than two modes exist – even where *all* values are modal!

Perhaps, though, the most serious drawback of the mode as a way of measuring the 'typical' value in a distribution is the fact that it completely ignores the data in the rest of the distribution. With the wages data, for example, it takes no account of the very considerable numbers of both groups who earn amounts quite a long way above or below the modal group. Indeed if the data had been grouped in a different way – perhaps in classes running '£295 but under £305', and so on – we might have come to a completely different conclusion about where the mode is, which is altogether an unsatisfactory state of affairs.

All these reasons combine to make the mode the least useful of the three measures of location we are going to examine. We certainly could not recommend it to Arthur Hughes as anything but a preliminary way of looking at his data, simplicity being about its one redeeming feature.

The mean

How to calculate the mean

The most familiar measure of the 'typical' wage in the two groups is, of course, the ordinary 'average' which is obtained by adding together the wages of all the people in the sample and dividing by the number of people involved. Another way of interpreting this procedure is to say that the average wage is the amount each worker would be getting if all their earnings were pooled and then shared out equally among them. The statisticians' term for this way of calculating the typical value in a distribution is the *mean* – strictly the *arithmetic* mean, to distinguish it from other kinds of mean which are sometimes used. As we are not going to encounter those other kinds, we will refer simply to the mean, an abbreviation which is generally understood to signify the arithmetic mean.

Although most people probably feel that they know what an average wage is, and could find one quite easily with the aid of a calculator, in practice for large amounts of data it may not be quite such a simple matter as it appears at first. Look again at the wage data for Grimchester, reproduced below.

Weekly take-home pay (£)	No. of workers
300 but under 310	3
310 but under 320	7
320 but under 330	33
330 but under 340	26
340 but under 350	24
350 but under 360	20
360 but under 370	18
370 but under 380	15
380 but under 400	4

We certainly cannot 'add up all the wages' as the simple description of calculating an average would suggest because we do not actually know what all the individual wages are! Of course, at some stage in the construction of the table Arthur Hughes must have had that information, but for the sake of simplifying the presentation of the information he has given up that level of detail, and – let's suppose – thrown the original figures away. So he has to begin by *choosing* a single wage to represent all the workers in each class; it may not be what each one is actually earning but the errors involved should not be too great. The most sensible representative value to choose is the *middle* wage in each group; so it is assumed that all the workers in the '£300 but under £310' class earn £305 per week, and so on. In fact, the assumption need not be quite so sweeping; all we really need, in order for this £305 figure correctly to represent all the workers in the '£300 but under £310' class, is that their average should be £305 (can you see why this is?).

So we now have a single value to represent each wage-group, and this class *mid-point* is often denoted by the letter *x*. A foolproof way of finding the *x*s, in cases where the class boundaries are not so easy to deal with as here, is to add up the upper and lower class boundaries and divide the result by 2. Thus a class '26 but under 34' in a distribution of ages would have mid-point (26 + 34)/2 = 30, a class '20–29' in a discrete mark-distribution would have mid-point (20 + 29)/2 = 24.5, and so on.

We also have a letter which is commonly used to denote the number of workers in each wage-group – the letter f, standing for 'frequency'. You will recall that this was the term applied in Chapter 3 to the number of items occurring in each group.

But having names for the various quantities involved does not help us to do the calculation. For that we need to return to our definition of the mean: 'add up all the wages and divide by the number of workers in the sample'. Does this mean add up all the x-values? That would certainly be the case if there were just *one* worker earning £305, one earning £315, and so on, but in reality there are *three* with £305, *seven* with £315, etc. So the total wages of all the workers in the sample *could* be found by taking £(305 + 305 + 305 + 315 + 315 + 315 + 315 + 315 + 315 + 315 + 325 + . . .) – in all, 150 figures to be added together, since there are a total of 150 workers in the sample.

However, doing the calculation of the total this way is a bit inefficient – especially when someone has gone to the trouble of arranging the data into a frequency table. The clue to a better method lies in realising that 305 + 305 + 305 is the same thing as 3×305 – in other words, successive addition is equivalent to multiplication. (It may be of interest to note in passing that this is how old-fashioned electro-mechanical calculators actually did multiplications. If one asked such a machine to multiply 37 by 42, one could watch it adding 37 to itself 42 times – which is why it took so long!)

Thus, to find the total wages of all workers in the sample, what we need to do is to take each wage, x, f times over: 3×305, 7×315, etc. The neatest way of doing this is to set out the calculation in three columns as shown below (this is very easily done with a spreadsheet).

Weekly take-home pay (£)	Class mid-point, x	No. of workers in class, f	fx
300 but under 310	305	3	915
310 but under 320	315	7	2 205
320 but under 330	325	33	10 725
330 but under 340	335	26	8 710
340 but under 350	345	24	8 280
350 but under 360	355	20	7 100
360 but under 370	365	18	6 570
370 but under 380	375	15	5 625
380 but under 400	390	4	1 560
		150	51 690

So the total income of all the 150 workers in the group is £51 690 – the total we get by adding up the 'fx' column. (Remember that fx means f multiplied by x, only we do not usually bother to write the multiplication sign.) Now, we want to share out this £51 690 equally among the 150 workers, so the mean wage per worker would be

$$\frac{51\ 690}{150} = £344.60.$$

(It is worth reminding ourselves that this figure is an approximation to the true mean, since we have used the class mid-points rather than individual wages in calculating it.)

Expressing the mean symbolically

This calculation is easy to carry out, but takes quite a long time to explain in words, as you can see! Fortunately, with the help of a symbol which may be new to you but which will prove very useful throughout our statistical work, we can summarise the process of finding the mean by one simple formula. The symbol is Σ – a capital sigma, the Greek form of s – standing for *summation*. It does not mean anything on its own, but can be read as 'add up all the', so that if, for example, we write Σx, this is to be understood as meaning 'add up all the xs'.

What we have to do in finding the mean is to add up all the 'f multiplied by x' terms, and then divide that total by the total number of items in our sample. With the aid of our Σ sign we can write 'add up all the fxs' as Σfx; and the total number of items in our sample is just Σf, the sum of the numbers of items in each class. We therefore arrive at the *formula for the mean*:

$$\text{Mean } \bar{x} = \frac{\Sigma fx}{\Sigma f}.$$

We have used the letter $\bar{x}$ (pronounced 'x-bar') here to stand for the mean; it is standard practice to denote the mean of a sample of values x as $\bar{x}$. Similarly, if the values were denoted by y then the mean would be $\bar{y}$, and so on. When we are talking about the mean of an entire population, rather than just a sample, we use the Greek letter μ (pronounced 'mew') – this is the Greek version of m, standing for mean. The convention of using ordinary Roman letters for sample values and Greek ones for population values is used for many measures other than the mean, as we will see later.

Of course, in the case where we do not have a frequency table but just a set of xs, we may regard the 'frequency' with which each x occurs as being 1, so that the formula then reduces to

$$\bar{x} = \frac{\Sigma x}{\text{no. of items}}$$

– the old familiar average.

One point worth noticing here is that the mean has the same units as the original data – the mean of a distribution of wages in £ will also be a wage in £. This is not just a detail, but can actually help you to notice if you have made a silly mistake in the calculation. For example, suppose in finding the mean wage of the Grimchester workers we had got our decimal point in the wrong place and arrived at an answer of 3446.00. A 'mean' of 3446 does not look too bad – but an average weekly wage of £3446 for a group of workers, none of whom gets more than £400, looks very unlikely indeed!

Before going any further, you might like to test your understanding of the story so far by calculating the mean for the Greentown workers. You can do this by repeating the calculation we have done above, making best use of the 'memory' facility on your calculator to total the fx terms as you work them out. Alternatively, if you have a statistical calculator you may be able to compute the mean directly – read your instruction booklet to find out how to enter the data. And if you are going to use Excel or another computer package, read the last section of the chapter to find out more about how to obtain the mean in that way.

Whichever way you do the calculation, if you get it right, you should reach an answer of £344.60 – exactly the same figure as for the Grimchester sample! So for Arthur Hughes's purposes the mean certainly is not a very satisfactory measure of the typical wage, since it seems to suggest that there is no difference between the two groups. From our more dispassionate standpoint, however, let us try to find out *why* two such apparently different distributions should have the same mean.

What does it tell us?

The root of the matter really lies in the fact that the mean is very much affected by the extreme values in a distribution. To see this, one need only consider the set of figures 2, 4, 6, 8, 80, which has mean 20. The mean here is clearly *not* a good representative value, either for the 'majority' values, which are all below 10, or for the 'rogue' value 80. It has been 'pulled over' towards the one very high value in the distribution, which makes it a rather unreliable measure in such a case.

Something similar is going on with the Grimchester data. Although a lot of the workers earn less than £340 per week, there is a substantial number with much higher wages, which is why the mean turns out to be identical to that for the Greentown data, although the peak or modal group for the latter data is £20 higher. So it looks as if the mean might not be quite suitable as a measure of the 'typical' value in the case of a very *un*symmetrical distribution, but is certainly a good guide with fairly symmetrical data like the Greentown wages.

There are one or two other factors which also need to be taken into account when deciding whether to use the mean as one's measure of location. If we had had an open class (such as 'over £380') at either or both ends of our data, we would have had difficulty in assigning a mid-point to that class, and in fact we would have had to make some *assumption* as to where the class ended (perhaps at £420) before we could get any further with the calculation of the mean. But, of course, such an assumption might be quite wrong, introducing an element of unreliability into our mean value (though if there are not very many values in the open class, the error will not be serious).

On the 'pro' side, one strong point in favour of the mean is that it does take into account every item of data, which was certainly not the case with the mode. It is also easy to calculate automatically – we have seen how to do it with a calculator, and later we will see how simply it can be found using a computer package. Moreover, it lends itself well to further calculations – for example, if we know the means of two separate samples (and their sizes), we can combine them to get an overall mean for the two samples together, as the following example demonstrates.

Suppose a firm has taken samples from its receipted bills in order to find out how many contain errors, and has discovered that there are 80 that contain errors favourable to the customer (i.e. the bill is *lower* than it should be). The average size of these errors is 4p. Among the 120 errors that are in favour of the firm (the bills are too *high*), the mean size of error is 3p per bill. The problem is to find out if, taken overall, the errors produce a surplus or a deficit for the firm. Now, it would be quite wrong to say, '4p on average for the customer and only 3p on average for us – that means an average of 1p for the customer altogether'; what we *must* take into account is the relative *size* of the two groups of erroneous bills. Eighty bills each with an average error of 4p give a total of £3.20 in favour of the customers, while 120 bills each with an average error of 3p give a total of £3.60 in favour of the firm, so in fact over the whole 200 bills the average error is (£3.60 − £3.20)/200 = 0.2p per bill in favour of the firm.

But perhaps the most important reason why the mean has become the standard measure of location lies in the fact that, given the mean of a sample, it is relatively easy to make sensible deductions about the mean of the entire population from which the sample was taken. We will look in detail at how this works in Chapter 8.

On the whole then, the mean has more 'pro' than 'con' properties, and certainly is the measure of location you will encounter most commonly. But for use in the cases we have pointed out where it *does* have drawbacks, we need a third type of measure.

Quick check questions

1 Explain in your own words what $\sum fx$ means.

2 If for a particular frequency distribution $\sum fx = 2500$, and this is based on a sample of 50 values, what is the mean of the distribution?

3 Without doing any calculations, say which of the two sets of data

6, 14, 19, 21, 25
12, 14, 19, 21, 25

will have the smaller mean.

Answers:
1 $\sum fx$ means 'multiply each value x by its corresponding frequency f and then add them all together.
2 The mean is 2500/50 = 50.
3 The first set will have a smaller mean, since the more extreme value 6 (as against 12 in the second set) will reduce the value of the mean.

The median

If you were to give a pack of cards to someone and ask them to choose one at random, my guess is that 99 people out of 100 would *not* choose the bottom or the top one, but would take one from somewhere in the middle of the pack; they would feel that the top or bottom card might somehow be more special than one in the middle. In the same way, if you were a sociologist conducting a piece of research, and wanted to interview a 'typical' child out of a family of three, I expect you would prefer to use the middle child as being in some way more representative, less extreme than either of the other two.

This intuitive feeling we have that a middle value should be in some sense a representative value has been made use of by statisticians in devising the third measure of location we are going to examine – the *median*. We define the median as follows:

The median of a set of data is the middle value when the data
has been arranged in order of size (either increasing or decreasing).

For example, if seven metal bars produced by a machine have lengths as follows:

6.2, 4.9, 8.7, 3.4, 6.6, 5.2, 5.2 cm

then in order to find the median length we would first of all rearrange the lengths in, say, ascending order:

3.4, 4.9, 5.2, 5.2, 6.2, 6.6, 8.7.

Then the median would be the length of the middle, that is the fourth, bar, which is 5.2 cm.

If we had eight bars rather than seven, the situation would be slightly different. Suppose that an extra bar is added to the seven above, giving

3.4, 4.9, 5.2, 5.2, 5.7, 6.2, 6.6, 8.7

as the eight lengths. The mid-point of the data now occurs *between* the fourth and fifth lengths – between 5.2 and 5.7 cm in other words. We take as the actual median the length that is half-way in between these two – in this case it will be $(5.2 + 5.7)/2 = 5.45$ cm.

It was easy enough with such small sets of data to see whereabouts the median was going to be, but if we have a very large amount of data it may not be quite so simple, so it is useful to have a standard way of finding the position of the median. We have seen that with seven numbers the median is the fourth; with eight it is the $4\frac{1}{2}$th. In general:

> In a set of n numbers, the median will be the $(n + 1)/2$th number.

You can check that this does indeed give 4 when $n = 7$ and $4\frac{1}{2}$ when $n = 8$. Actually if we have a very large amount of data, so that n is big, then adding 1 to n is not going to make a lot of difference; if $n = 500$, for example, then the median should strictly be the $(500 + 1)/2$th $= 250\frac{1}{2}$th item – half-way between the 250th and the 251st – but we will not be much in error if we take it as the $500/2$th $= 250$th item instead. In the remainder of the chapter we will not worry about adding the 1 to n as long as n is over 50.

With this in mind, we can now look at the wages data on p. 96 again with a view to finding the median wage for each group. As there are 150 workers in each sample, the median in both cases will be the wage earned by the 75th worker. So all we need do is to arrange the individual wages in increasing order and pick out the 75th – but we do not *know* the individual wages! As we already found when calculating the mean, the loss of that individual information was the price we paid for the simplification produced by grouping the data.

It is quite easy to find out which *group* the median wage falls into; if we convert the data to a *cumulative* frequency table (see the section on tabulating quantitative data in Chapter 3) we can see immediately where the 75th wage will lie:

Weekly take-home pay (£)	No. of Grimchester workers	No. of Greentown workers
Less than 300	0	0
Less than 310	3	4
Less than 320	10	16
Less than 330	43	33
Less than 340	69	56
Less than 350	93	94
Less than 360	113	120
Less than 370	131	136
Less than 380	146	148
Less than 400	150	150

As only 69 Grimchester workers are getting less than £340/week, but 93 of them are getting less than £350/week, the 75th wage must be somewhere in the £340–£350 bracket.

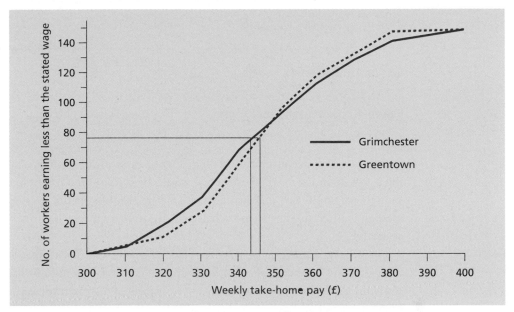

Figure 4.2 Ogives for wages of Grimchester and Greentown workers

We would, however, like to be more precise about this. Fortunately there is a very simple way to find out a more specific value for the median. The cumulative frequency table should remind you of the *ogive* – the graph we discussed in Chapter 3 (pp. 81–3), which showed how many items were below a given value. The ogive plotted from the wage data above is drawn in Figure 4.2 and it is a simple matter to read off from the graph the wage earned by the 75th worker in each group. The *median wage* is £342.50 for the Grimchester workers and £345 for the Greentown workers.

So there is a difference between the two groups if we use the median as our measure of location, even though the two mean wages were the same. Again, we can see why this occurs by taking some rather simpler figures as an illustration. If we return to the set of figures 2, 4, 6, 8, 80 which we used on p. 102 to show how the mean – 20 – is not really a very good 'typical' measure for such lopsided data, we can see immediately that the median here is the third figure, 6. This is certainly more representative of the four low figures in the set than is the mean, demonstrating how the median, by ignoring the extreme values – in fact, ignoring *everything* but the middle value – manages not to be 'pulled' towards the odd atypical high or low item.

Hence in the wages case, the median is less affected than the mean by the minority of Grimchester workers who earn really high wages, and might be regarded as a fairer representation of the bulk of lower-paid workers. With the Greentown data, we have a much more symmetrical distribution, so there is far less difference between median and mean. This gives us the key to one way in which you can decide, for a particular set of data, which measure to choose: if the data is very unsymmetrical, the median may well be a better choice; if the data is pretty symmetrical there will be little to choose between the two and the mean would probably be chosen for the reasons discussed above.

Two other factors which might cause us to opt for a median in preference to a mean are that its calculation does not require us to make any assumptions about closing open classes at the top or bottom of the distribution, and that it can be used even in situations where we cannot get a proper measurement of the data, but can only rank it in order (see

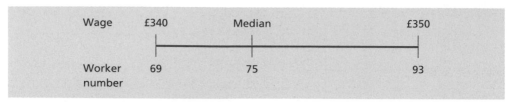

Figure 4.3 Calculating the median

Chapter 2). For instance, if we arranged workers in order of their efficiency in performing a job, then the median efficiency would be represented by the middle worker, even
though we could not perform any actual calculations on the data. For this reason the
median is often used in areas such as sociology where it may be difficult to quantify data
accurately.

One final point before we leave the topic of measures of location. For those of you who
like calculations, and dislike plotting graphs, it *is* possible to find the median of a grouped
distribution without drawing an ogive, by means of a straightforward proportion calculation as shown in Figure 4.3. We decided that the median for the Grimchester data must
fall in the group £340–£350. Now there are 69 workers earning less than £340, so person
number 75, who gets the median wage, is the sixth person in a group which contains
24 people altogether; that is, he or she is a quarter of the way through the group. But
the group covers a range of £10, so the median is a quarter of £10 *above* £340, at £342.50,
as we already found from the ogive. Reference to Figure 4.3 may help to clarify this
argument and you are advised, if you wish to perform this calculation, always to draw
a similar diagram.

Quick check questions

1 Which value will be the median in a set of eleven numbers?

2 Without doing any calculations, can you say whether the mean of the set of
   figures 2, 10, 11, 12, 13 will be less than or greater than the median?

3 Does it make any difference to the value of the median whether the data is
   arranged in ascending or descending order?

Answers:
1 The median will be the sixth value when the numbers are arranged in order.
2 The mean will be less, since the extreme value of 2 at the low end of the data will affect
   the mean, but not the median.
3 No, the median is the middle figure whichever way the data is arranged.

A worked example

Before we go any further, here is an example to consolidate what we have learned so far
in this chapter.

A college admissions section wishes to examine the profile of applicants for a certain
degree programme, and among other data has collected the following distribution of ages
for last year's applicants:

Age	No. of applicants
17	3
18	74
19	47
20	18
21	11
22	8
23–25	10
Over 25	6

What would the mean and the median of this set of data be, and which might be more useful in this case?

The way the data has been grouped is a bit strange, but let us assume we are stuck with it and cannot go back to find the exact ages of all the people over 22. Then before we can make any progress on computing the mean, we need to make an assumption about the upper limit – in other words, how old is the oldest applicant likely to be?

In practice, we could get some further information to help us with this assumption. If, for example, the programme is a strictly vocational one then it is unlikely that older people are going to be interested, whereas if it is in one of the humanities – history, say, or a language – there might even be some people of pensionable age applying. But in the absence of this information, let us say fairly arbitrarily that we think none of the applicants is likely to be over 40. In any case, the results will not be very sensitive to the assumption, since only a small proportion of the data lies at this end of the distribution.

With this assumption, we can rewrite the frequency table replacing the last two classes by their mid-points. When it comes to doing this, age is a slightly odd variable: it is a continuous quantity that is nearly always reported in discrete form. Moreover, if someone says they are 25, they could actually be any age up to 25 years and 364 days, so the mid-point of the class 23–25 is 24.5, not 24 as might at first appear. The age will be x in this case, and the number of applicants will be f, so we can compute fx:

x	f	fx
17	3	51
18	74	1332
19	47	893
20	18	360
21	11	231
22	8	176
24.5	10	245
32.5	6	195
	$\Sigma f = 177$	$\Sigma fx = 3483$

Then the mean will be 3483/177 = 19.68. So this is the average age of all applicants – and it should be pretty close to what we would get if we had access to all the individual ages.

When it comes to the median, we need to convert the table to the cumulative frequency format:

Age	Cum. no. of applicants
Under 17	0
Under 18	3
Under 19	77
Under 20	124
Under 21	142
Under 22	153
Under 23	161
Under 26	171
Under 40	177

The median will be the age of the $(177 + 1)/2 = 89$th person (or the 88.5th if we do not worry about the +1). This person is not included in the 'under 19' group, but *is* included in 'under 20'. So they must be aged 19. Thus 19 is the median age. We can actually go further and, using the proportion calculation, find that it is 19.26 years.

The mean is higher than the median here, which should not be too surprising – the age distribution is very skew, with a long 'tail' of applicants on the upper end. Since this is the case, it might be preferable to quote the median rather than the mean as a 'typical' age – though there is not much to choose between them.

Measuring spread

The range

The second feature of frequency distributions which we decided it would be useful to be able to measure was the degree to which the values in the distribution were spread out or squashed together – the degree of *spread* among those values. If you were asked the question, with reference to our two sets of wage data, 'How spread out are the wages in the two groups?', you might well reply 'Both samples contain wages ranging from £300 to £400 a week'.

This, the simplest measure of spread, is called, not surprisingly, the *range*, and might be defined as follows:

> The range is the difference between the highest and lowest values in a distribution.

So here we would say the data ranges from £300 to £400, or that there is a range of £100 in each of the samples. But immediately we see one of the chief drawbacks to the range: it gives us the same answer for both groups, even though we can see by looking at the ogives in Figure 4.2 that actually the Greentown wages are a good deal more compact than those for Grimchester.

The cause of this, and the consequent unreliability of the range, is that it ignores all but the two extreme items in the distribution, so what goes on in the middle makes no difference at all to it. Moreover, just one 'rogue' value in a set of data – maybe due to an error in measurement – can produce a quite misleading value of the range. Our old example of the figures 2, 4, 6, 8, 80 has a range of $80 - 2 = 78$, even though the first four numbers only have a range of $8 - 2 = 6$ among themselves.

So, like its companion measure the mode, the range is really only useful when we want a quick idea of the variability in a set of data without having to go to the trouble of doing any calculations. For more precise information, other forms of measure of spread are needed.

The standard deviation

One of the defects of the range is that it is a sort of absolute measure – it tells us about the variation between the highest and lowest items in a distribution, but gives us no idea how those items relate to the mean. And yet this is just what we would like to know if we want to assess the usefulness of the mean as a 'typical' value for the distribution – if all the items in the distribution are pretty near to the mean then clearly it represents them well; if some of them are quite a long way from the mean, then it is not such a good representative for those items.

The measure that has been devised precisely to do this job of telling us how near, on the whole, the values in the data are to the mean is called the *standard deviation*, and because it is a measure that may seem a bit complicated at first sight, we will see how it is devised first of all for a very easy set of numbers – the figures 1, 2, 3, 5, 9.

An easy example

We obviously need to find the mean of these numbers first before we can start looking at how the numbers relate to this mean. The numbers add up to 20, so their mean is 4. If we refer to the numbers in the distribution, as we did earlier in the chapter, as x, then the simplest way to find out how far the x is from the mean is to look at $x - \bar{x}$ for each x. This will actually tell us, not just how far x is from $\bar{x}$, but also which side of $\bar{x}$ it is; numbers *below* $\bar{x}$ will give a negative $x - \bar{x}$, those above, a positive one. So we get $x - \bar{x}$ values of $1 - 4$, $2 - 4$, $3 - 4$, $5 - 4$ and $9 - 4$, or $-3, -2, -1, 1$ and 5. These are shown in the second column of Table 4.1.

What we really want is not just these individual values, but something that will tell us how far, *on the average*, an x is from the mean. So if we add up all the $x - \bar{x}$ terms – the usual name for these is *deviations* because they tell us how much the xs *deviate* from the mean – and then divide by 5, we should get the kind of measure we are after. But when we total the deviations, we find $-6 + 6 = 0$! And this is not just a freak of the set of numbers used; if you repeat the process with *any* set of numbers you will find the same thing happening – roughly because the mean is 'in the middle' of the data. So as a sensible measure of spread, this is rather a non-starter.

The problem was, of course, caused by the minus signs, which cancelled out the positive deviations to give a zero total. We *could* try just ignoring them, and operating with what is called the *absolute value* of $x - \bar{x}$ – that is to say, the value ignoring any minus sign, often written as $|x - \bar{x}|$. However, arithmetic with these absolute values is awkward, and so, although there *is* a measure based on them (called the *mean absolute deviation*), we generally prefer to use an alternative way of eliminating the minuses. What we do is to *square* each of the deviations. That will certainly get rid of the troublesome minus signs (the square of a negative number is always positive) and, at the same time, we will not lose any important information about the deviations. If an x is a long way from $\bar{x}$, then $x - \bar{x}$ will be big, and so will $(x - \bar{x})^2$; if x is near to $\bar{x}$, then $x - \bar{x}$ and $(x - \bar{x})^2$ will both be small.

This process gives 9, 4, 1, 1 and 25 as the squared deviations, totalling 40 altogether. The figures are shown in the third column of Table 4.1.

Table 4.1

x	$x - \bar{x}$	$(x - \bar{x})^2$
1	−3	9
2	−2	4
3	−1	1
5	1	1
9	5	25
		40

The average squared deviation per point is thus 40/5 = 8, and we *could* use this as our measure of spread. In fact, it *is* sometimes used, and so has been given a special name – the *variance*. But it has one snag: because we squared all the deviations, the units in which the variance is expressed are the square of the original units. For example, if we started out with a set of lengths in centimetres, the variance will be in square centimetres; if our original data were percentage marks in an exam, the variance would be in squared percentages (!) and so on. This is clearly not desirable – we would like our measure of spread to have the *same* units as our original data, so the last step in constructing it is to take a square root, in our case $\sqrt{8}$ or 2.828. And this, finally, is the standard deviation.

Expressing it symbolically

We can build up a formula for calculating the standard deviation for other sets of data if we recap the process we have followed in terms of x and $\bar{x}$. What we did was to take the sum of the $(x - \bar{x})^2$ terms, average them out among the items of our distribution, and then take the square root of the result. So using the Σ sign we introduced in the section 'Measuring location', p. 98, we can define the standard deviation thus:

$$s = \sqrt{\frac{\Sigma(x - \bar{x})^2}{\text{no. of items}}}.$$

Doing the calculation like this was quite easy for our set of data 1, 2, 3, 5, 9, because the mean was a simple whole number. You can imagine, however, that if we had a set of data whose mean was a complicated decimal, subtracting it from each data value separately, then squaring the differences, and so on, would be rather a messy business. Fortunately, with a little algebraic manipulation we can put the formula into a more convenient form. We will not give the details, though if you are mathematically minded you might like to verify the result for yourself by multiplying out the term $(x - \bar{x})^2$ in the formula above. After doing so, and rearranging terms, we find

$$s = \sqrt{\frac{\Sigma x^2}{\text{no. of items}} - \bar{x}^2}.$$

In other words, rather than having to subtract the mean from each x-value individually and then square the resulting differences, we square the xs alone and then just subtract $\bar{x}^2$ once at the end. For our data 1, 2, 3, 5, 9 this gives us

$$s = \sqrt{\frac{1 + 4 + 9 + 25 + 81}{5} - 4^2}$$

$$= \sqrt{\frac{120}{5} - 16} = \sqrt{24 - 16}$$

$$= \sqrt{8},$$

exactly the same answer as we obtained in the previous section.

As you can see, we have used s to denote the standard deviation of the sample; in line with what we said earlier in connection with the mean, the Greek version of s, which is σ (pronounced sigma), would be used if we were talking about the standard deviation of an entire population. (This is a small sigma – do not confuse it with the big sigma Σ used to mean 'add up'.)

You can of course compute the standard deviation using the statistical functions on your calculator, or a computer package. If you do this, you may come across some puzzling discrepancies between the hand-calculated version using the formula above and the value obtained from the calculator or computer. Indeed, you may discover that you have a choice of two standard deviation buttons on your calculator, probably labelled 'SD$_n$' and 'SD$_{n-1}$' or something similar. The reason for this is that the formula we used above, where the sum of the squared deviations is divided by n, is fine if we have data about an entire population; but if we only have a sample, then the value we get from this formula is likely to be a slight underestimate of the population standard deviation – we say the sample value gives us a biased estimate of the population value.

Common sense suggests why this might be: if we take a sample – particularly a small one – from a population, we may end up with values that are closely bunched together, and therefore do not fully reflect the variability in the population as a whole. To correct for this, the sum of squared deviations should be divided, not by n but by $n - 1$ (this can be proved mathematically – it is not just a 'fiddle factor'!). Actually if n is bigger than about 30 there is very little difference in the two figures, so it is not worth getting too excited about which version you use. But the idea of estimating population values from sample data is an important one, which we will be encountering again in Chapter 8.

There is one further modification we must make to the formula before we can try to calculate the standard deviation for the wage distributions with which we began the chapter. In the case of those distributions, we had not *one* item in each class, but f items, where f was the frequency of that class. Consequently, when we come to calculate the standard deviation the x^2 term for each class will contribute to the total not just once, but f times – a total contribution of fx^2, precisely the same argument as when we found in calculating the mean that each class would contribute fx to the overall total wages. We also saw at that point that the number of items all together is equal to Σf; thus we can write the formula for standard deviation for a frequency distribution as

$$s = \sqrt{\frac{\Sigma fx^2}{\Sigma f} - \bar{x}^2}.$$

This is the version of the formula that we will use in all subsequent work, and that you are recommended to commit to memory, though you will find slight variations on it also used by other authors.

Returning to the problem

We are now in a position to calculate the standard deviation for the wages of the Grimchester factory workers. For the sake of completeness, since one is in practice nearly always calculating a mean and standard deviation simultaneously, the calculation of the mean is shown again.

The fx^2 column here was calculated not by squaring x and then multiplying by f, but by noticing that $fx^2 = fx \times x$, so we can find each fx^2 term by multiplying the fx figure once more by x. Again, you can make use of the memory facility on your calculator to add up the fx^2 column as you go along, or set up columns in a spreadsheet to compute the figures.

Weekly take-home pay (£)	Class mid-point, x	No. of workers in class, f	fx	fx²
300 but under 310	305	3	915	279 075
310 but under 320	315	7	2 205	694 575
320 but under 330	325	33	10 725	3 485 625
330 but under 340	335	26	8 710	2 917 850
340 but under 350	345	24	8 280	2 856 600
350 but under 360	355	20	7 100	2 520 500
360 but under 370	365	18	6 570	2 398 050
370 but under 380	375	15	5 625	2 109 375
380 but under 400	390	4	1 560	608 400
Total		150	51 690	17 870 050

As already calculated, we have the mean $\bar{x} = 51\,690/150 = £344.60$. Then the standard deviation is given by

$$s = \sqrt{\frac{17\,870\,050}{150} - 344.60^2}$$

$$= \sqrt{119\,133.667 - 118\,749.16}$$

$$= \sqrt{384.507}$$

$$= £19.61.$$

(Notice how we have retained three decimal places in the calculation before rounding to the nearest penny at the end.)

At this point, your reaction may well be 'So what?' One of the difficulties experienced by most people on encountering the standard deviation for the first time is that the calculation is rather complex, and when finally one arrives at the answer it is not straightforward to interpret. Bear in mind first of all that it is a measure of *spread around the mean*: the bigger the standard deviation, the more spread out the distribution. To develop more of a feeling for what it means, however, it will help if we look at it in the context of a comparison between two distributions.

To that end, and in order to practise carrying out the arithmetical procedures, you should now verify that the standard deviation of the Greentown wage distribution is £18.28 – that is, over £1 less than for the Grimchester workers (remember that if you do the calculation with a calculator or computer package, you may get a slightly different answer, for the reasons explained earlier). This fact demonstrates that though both groups have the same average wage, the Grimchester group is less consistent than the Greentown group, there being more members of the former who have wages quite a long way from the mean. This will be confirmed by looking again at Figure 4.1, which brings out the more compact form, dropping off quite sharply into the two 'tails', of the Greentown distribution.

The Greentown figures also exhibit another fact about the standard deviation which is useful in learning to interpret it. If we take a range of three standard deviations both above and below the mean, we arrive at an upper limit of approximately £344.60 + 3 × £18.28 = £399.44, and a lower limit of about £344.60 − 3 × £18.28 = £289.76. Between these two limits, the entire Greentown data is included; and you will find in fact that for any reasonably symmetrical set of data, a range of three standard deviations either side of the mean should include all but a few data items. We will come to understand more clearly why this should be when we examine the normal distribution in Chapter 7. Meanwhile, the fact will give you a very rough check on the correctness of your calculations, at least to the extent of showing up errors such as misplaced decimal points.

By now you may well have lost track of the fact that we originally set out to assist Arthur Hughes with his problem of comparing the wages of the two groups of workers. Let us therefore recap at this point, making use of the various measures we have developed so far. We have seen that, while both sets of workers have wages ranging from £300 to £400, and both earn the same average or mean wage, the differences in the way the wages are scattered within those ranges are reflected by the greater standard deviation of the Grimchester workers, while the fact that their distribution 'peaks' farther to the left (i.e. at a lower value) is shown by their lower median and modal wages.

We have seen how the standard deviation can show how spread out the data is around the mean, but what it will *not* tell us is whether the top end of the distribution tends to be more 'stretched out' than the bottom, or vice versa. To give that information, we need to introduce our third measure of spread.

Quick check questions

1 Your friend has calculated that $fx = 13$, and states that $fx^2 = 169$. Explain to him why this is not correct.

2 Find the standard deviation of the five numbers 6, 8, 12, 14, 20, using the same method as we used for the data 1, 2, 3, 5, 9 at the start of this section.

3 You have a set of data which represents weights in kg. What would be the units associated with the standard deviation?

Answers:
1 By squaring 13, your friend has squared both the *f* and the *x*, whereas fx^2 involves squaring only the *x* term, not the *f*.
2 The mean is 60/5 = 12, and the standard deviation is 4.90.
3 The units for the s.d. will also be kg – the standard deviation always has the same units as the original data.

The quartiles

One of the criticisms we levelled at the range as a measure of spread was the fact that by using the extreme upper and lower limits of the data it might well fail to give us an adequate indication as to how the main part of the data was spread out. One way to avoid this is to look at the range, not among all 100 per cent of the data, but among, for instance, the central 50 per cent. We therefore ignore the extreme upper and lower 25 per cent of the data, on the grounds that these values might in some way be atypical, and we examine the amount of scatter between the values 25 per cent of the way and 75 per cent of the way through the distribution.

These two values are called respectively the first and third *quartiles*: the first, or lower, quartile Q_1 is the value one-quarter of the way through the ordered set of data; the third, or upper, quartile Q_3 is the value three-quarters of the way through the ordered set of data. The second quartile is, of course, the mid-point of the data, which we have already encountered in the guise of the median. This suggests that, as we were easily able to find the median by looking at the ogive of the data, we should be able to do the same for the quartiles. For the Grimchester workers, of whom there are 150, the lower quartile will be the wage earned by the $150/4 = 37.5$th worker, and the upper quartile the wage of the $3 \times 150/4 = 112.5$th worker. Reference to Figure 4.2 then shows that the lower quartile is £328.30 approximately, while Q_3 is £359.75. You can confirm that for the Greentown wages the figures are $Q_1 = £331.95$ and $Q_3 = £357.15$, as accurately as can be read from the graph. Of course, we could always use a proportion calculation, like the one illustrated on p. 106, rather than resorting to the ogive to find the quartiles.

Whatever means we have used to calculate them, the quartiles can convey a good deal of information to anyone who knows how to interpret them. First and most simply, they tell us that the central 50 per cent of Grimchester workers have wages ranging from £328.30 to £359.75, an *interquartile range* of £31.45, while for the Greentown workers this is £331.95 to £357.15 or £25.20. There is thus less variability in the wages of the central 50 per cent of Greentown workers, confirming the picture we obtained by comparison of the standard deviations. (You may also encounter the semi-interquartile range, which as its name suggests is half the interquartile range, in this case £15.73. Its interpretation is similar.)

Skewness

But the quartiles can tell us more. Looked at in conjunction with the median they can convey information about how unsymmetrical or *skew* the data is, and in what direction. For instance, if you look at the relationship between Q_1, the median and Q_3 for the Grimchester data, you will notice that Q_1 is closer to the median than Q_3, whereas for the Greentown data the quartiles are much closer to being equidistant on either side of the median. For a perfectly symmetric distribution they would, in fact, be exactly equidistant; the more skew the distribution is, the more the median will tend to be closer to one of the quartiles and further from the other. The more distant quartile is on the side of the longer 'tail' of the distribution, as you can see by relating the quartiles for the Grimchester data to the histogram of the data shown in Figure 4.1. The high value of Q_3 in this case is due to the effect of the quite large number of Grimchester workers receiving wages in the higher groups, who tend to 'pull' the upper quartile over to the right. This is called *positive skewness*. Conversely, of course, a distribution which had a long *left*-hand 'tail' would exhibit a Q_1 that was noticeably further from the median than Q_3, and would be said to have *negative skewness*.

Thus, to the informed person, the simple statement 'The Grimchester workers have a median wage of £342.50, lower quartile £328.30 and upper quartile £359.75' conveys information as to the general position, degree of variability and overall shape of the wage distribution. For this reason, it is particularly useful to use the median and quartiles as one's measures of location and dispersion in cases where the data is markedly unsymmetric. Where there is a reasonable degree of symmetry, however, the advantages mentioned earlier for the mean, most of which also apply to the standard deviation, make these the usual choice.

Box-and-whisker diagrams

An interesting way of presenting all the information contained in the median, quartiles and range of a set of data is provided by the *box-and-whisker diagram* or *boxplot*. A diagram of this kind based on the Grimchester/Greentown data is shown in Figure 4.4; it consists of a 'box' extending from the first to the third quartiles, with 'whiskers' stretching to the full extent of the range in each direction. Within the 'box', the position of the median is shown by a vertical line (or sometimes an asterisk). Thus a small box with long whiskers indicates a distribution with its central values very bunched, but long tails; a median much nearer to one end of the box than the other, a degree of skewness, and so on. In the particular case shown, the observations we have already made about the greater skewness of the Grimchester figures and the more compact centre of the Greentown ones are summed up in a neat and easy-to-understand way.

Such diagrams are widely available in statistical packages, though not as yet within Excel.

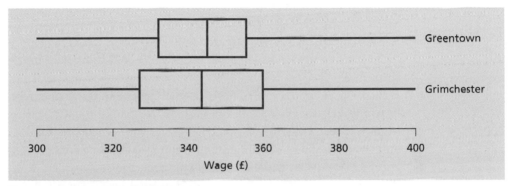

Figure 4.4 Box-and-whisker plot

Quick check questions

1 The lower quartile of a distribution of weights is 2.4 kg, and the upper quartile is 6.2 kg. Write a sentence to explain what this tells you about the distribution.

2 The median of the distribution mentioned in question 1 is 3.6 kg. What can you conclude about the shape of the distribution?

3 Mention one reason why the mean and standard deviation are used more often than the median and quartiles when summarising data.

Answers:
1 Fifty per cent of the data values lie between 2.4 kg and 6.2 kg; or alternatively 25 per cent of values lie below 2.4 kg and 25 per cent above 6.2 kg.
2 The median is closer to the lower than to the upper quartile. The distribution thus has a long 'tail' on the upper end.
3 The mean and standard deviation have become the usual way of summarising data because, as mentioned earlier in the chapter, given the mean and standard deviation of a sample we can make sensible deductions about the mean and standard deviation of the population from which the sample was taken.

Summary measures with Excel

There are a number of standard Excel functions which provide values of various summary measures:

- =AVERAGE (range) will return the mean of the data in the specified range (e.g., with the EMP data =AVERAGE (C2:C61) will give the average age of the sample of employees).
- =STDEV(range) will return the standard deviation of the data in the range, using the formula for sample standard deviation – that is, with the $n - 1$ divisor. If you want the *population* standard deviation (i.e. the version with the n divisor), use the command =STDEVP(range).

Other useful functions, which are pretty self-explanatory, are =MAX, =MIN, =MEDIAN, =MODE. The =QUARTILE function has a slightly more complicated format: =QUARTILE (range, n), where the integer n indicates which quartile is required. Both $n = 1$ and $n = 3$ return the usual first and third quartiles, while $n = 2$ gives the median and, rather less obviously, $n = 0$ and $n = 4$ give the minimum and maximum respectively.

A useful list of all Excel statistical functions is available in HELP by choosing STATISTICAL FUNCTIONS from the Index.

Alternatively, you can use the DESCRIPTIVE STATISTICS item under DATA ANALYSIS on the DATA tab to obtain a whole collection of summary statistics at once. You will be asked to specify a range for the output – as usual, make sure that you specify a clear space in the worksheet, or play safe and send the results to a new ply. If you check the SUMMARY STATISTICS box in the DESCRIPTIVE STATISTICS window, Excel will return a whole list of measures, including the mean, standard deviation, median, mode, maximum and minimum values, as well as some which we have not discussed (such as skewness and kurtosis), and some which we will mention in later chapters (such as standard error and confidence level). For a full discussion of all these features, visit the Excel workbook via the Companion Website.

If you prefer to compute means and standard deviations from a frequency table as we have done in this chapter, the spreadsheet format makes this very easy: by exploiting the way in which formulae can be copied around the worksheet using the relative addressing property, a table with columns f, x, fx and fx^2 can quickly be set up. You will find an example of this kind of table in the file MSD.XLS on the website; the information used there is the Grimchester/Greentown wage data discussed in this chapter, but you can overwrite it with other values of f and x. You should explore the contents of the various cells to make sure you understand what is going on.

Which should we choose?

You may feel by now that poor Arthur Hughes is no better off than he was at the beginning of the chapter, having passed from a situation where he has no means of summarising his data to one where he has perhaps too many methods to choose from. And we have only looked at the three most popular measures of location and dispersion – there are several more of each which we have not even touched on! Although one cannot lay down hard and fast rules for the use of these various measures, there is usually one that seems more appropriate than the rest in a given situation. We have already indicated that the mode and range are really only suited to giving us a quick idea of position and variability; the median and quartiles are the ones to choose if you have a noticeably skew distribution; while in most other situations the mean and standard deviation, by long historical usage as well as for the other reasons noted above, are the ones to use.

In the case of the wage data with which we have been mainly concerned in this chapter, my personal choice would be the median and quartiles – and it should certainly be Arthur Hughes's choice if he wants to support the idea that the Grimchester workers are worse off, since their median wage really is £2.50 less than that of their colleagues in Greentown. On the other hand, if management personnel know anything about statistics they will realise that the high upper quartile for the Grimchester workers means that some of them are really getting rather highly paid, so maybe their complaint is not justified after all!

Another example

To round off our discussion of descriptive statistics, let us return to the data concerning ages of college applicants for which we earlier calculated the mean, and complete the calculation of the standard deviation. We had already computed x, f and fx, so to get fx^2 we simply need to multiply the fx by the x column:

x	f	fx	fx^2
17	3	51	867
18	74	1332	23 976
19	47	893	16 967
20	18	360	7 200
21	11	231	4 851
22	8	176	3 872
24.5	10	245	6 002.5
32.5	6	195	6 337.5
			$\Sigma fx^2 = 70\ 073$

Since the mean of the data was found to be 19.68, we calculate the standard deviation as $\sqrt{(70\ 073/177 - 19.68^2)} = 2.93$. This fairly small value indicates that the ages of the majority of applicants are pretty close together; the very skew nature of the data, however, means that the 'plus or minus 3 standard deviations' check for the rough range of the data will not work in this case – in fact, this is a situation where it might be preferable to use the median and quartiles. The quartiles are 18 and 20, as you should verify, showing just how tightly bunched the data is apart from a few extreme values at the top end.

If you are daunted by the amount of arithmetic involved in finding means and standard deviations, take heart – you may never need to calculate them from scratch in this way. Generally, we would be using a spreadsheet, statistical package or at least a statistical calculator to do the hard work. However, if you are going to get some kind of feeling for what the measures actually represent, you need to have some idea of the underlying computations involved, so that the process is not a total 'black box'.

So what *is* typical?

At the start of this chapter we looked at a couple of quotes from online newspaper articles which cited what you will now recognise as various measures of location and dispersion. After the discussion in this chapter, we should be able to interpret more precisely what the quoted figures are telling us.

First we are informed that 'the average income of a FTSE 100 chief executive . . . is more than 100 times median household income'. We have to assume here that the phrase 'the average income' refers to the mean, so we are not quite comparing like with like – the average, particularly for very high earners, is likely to be skewed by the inclusion of some extremely high figures, and that average is being related to the median household income. When discussing incomes, it's often preferable to use the median rather than the mean, since, as we've seen in this chapter, wage distributions are likely to be positively skewed.

Then we learn that executive pay consultants are encouraging executives to believe that their pay should be 'in the top quartile'. We know that this refers to the pay of the highest-earning 25% of executives. There is a bit of a contradiction here – after all, *some-one* always has to be in the bottom quartile, otherwise it wouldn't *be* a quartile. The point is reminiscent of the old joke about a political speech: 'My party will ensure that all children achieve above-average reading levels'.

EXERCISES

*Further examples on the work of this chapter can be found on the **Companion Website**.*

1 The following sets of data represent the distribution of house prices in two counties. By calculating all three measures of location and dispersion for the two distributions, compare the position in the two counties. What can you say about the skewness of the data?

Price range (£000s)	No. of houses in Barsetshire sample	No. of houses in Cokeshire sample
260 but under 280	2	4
280 but under 300	5	11
300 but under 320	12	19
320 but under 360	20	15
360 but under 440	14	6
440 but under 560	6	4
560 and upwards	1	1

2 Calculate the mean and standard deviation for the two distributions 2, 5, 7, 8, 10 and 22, 25, 27, 28, 30, using the standard deviation key of your calculator or a suitable computer package if possible.

What do you notice about the means and the standard deviations of the two sets of data? Can you suggest a generalisation of this result? Confirm your guess by examining other sets of data of your own devising.

3 Do the same as in Exercise 2 for the two sets of data 2, 5, 7, 8, 10 and 6, 15, 21, 24, 30.

4 Look out for mentions in the press, TV and radio of the word 'average' (e.g. in accounts of wage negotiations) and discuss what particular form of 'average' or typical value might actually be being used in each case.

5 Can you think of any practical situations in which a modal value might actually be the best one to use?

6 Use the Excel spreadsheet MSD.XLS which is stored on the student part of the Companion Website to verify the calculations of the Greentown and Grimchester summary statistics as carried out in this chapter.

7 On the student part of the Companion Website you will find the data file MACH.XLS which gives the weights of packets of tea produced by three automated production lines. You have been asked to write a report on the performance of the three lines. Use Excel statistical functions to calculate suitable summary measures, and draft your report explaining what they indicate.

8 The measurement of performance in all areas of public life, from the effectiveness of schools to the funding of doctors' practices, is a major area of interest at present. One measure that has had a good deal of publicity Is the length of time hospital patients have to wait for routine surgery, once they have been put on a waiting list.

Here is some output from the Excel DESCRIPTIVE STATISTICS command, comparing the waiting time distributions for samples of patients awaiting the same minor operation at hospitals A and B. The variable WaitA gives the waiting time in weeks to the nearest whole week for A, and WaitB does the same for B.

WaitA		*WaitB*	
Mean	12.92	Mean	9.45
Standard error*	0.26	Standard error*	0.23
Median	13.00	Median	9.00
Mode	12.00	Mode	9.00
Standard deviation	3.05	Standard deviation	2.58
Sample variance	9.31	Sample variance	6.63
Kurtosis*	1.80	Kurtosis*	1.91
Skewness*	0.98	Skewness*	0.87
Range	17.00	Range	15.00
Minimum	7.00	Minimum	4.00
Maximum	24.00	Maximum	19.00
Sum	1835	Sum	1191.00
Count	142	Count	126.00

* This can be ignored.

(Note that this output has been formatted so that figures are given to two decimal places only – this makes it much easier to see what is going on.)

Write a brief report on these results, interpreting them in practical terms, indicating any reservations you have about your conclusions and any additional information which you believe would be useful in examining the figures.

9 You are working on placement for a company which manufactures toys, and you have been asked to help with a procurement exercise – the company is trying to decide between two suppliers of batteries. You've examined a sample of 100 batteries from each of the potential suppliers, and your analysis gives the following results:

Supplier A – mean lifetime of batteries is 162 hours of continuous operation, median = 166 hours, and standard deviation = 8 hours.

Supplier B – mean lifetime of batteries is 165 hours of continuous operation, median = 164, and standard deviation = 6.5 hours.

Draft a short report explaining to the management of your company what this information is telling you about the performance of the two samples, and how it can help in making a choice of supplier.

10 You know that the mean amount spent by a group of eight supermarket customers in a single visit to a store is £58.50, but you have lost the data relating to one particular customer. The expenditure of the other seven was as follows:

£42.20, £83.79, £10.40, £62.11, £71.77, £102.13, £59.74.

What was the expenditure of the missing customer?

Case Study

Carthorse Transport Ltd

You are an assistant to the logistics manager of Carthorse Transport, a small company which delivers fruit and vegetables to local stores. There have recently been some complaints from customers that deliveries are arriving late in the morning, so you have been experimenting with different routes from the depot to the town centre. Data relating to the times in minutes taken by vans on three possible routes has been gathered into boxplots, which are shown below.

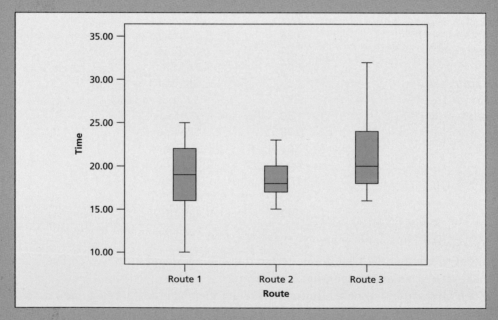

Write a short (two-page) report for the logistics manager, discussing the pros and cons of each route and making a recommendation. You should note that all the data was gathered during the same time period, 7–9 a.m.

(*Reminder*: in a boxplot, the two ends of the central 'box' are the lower and upper quartiles, the line within the box represents the median, and the 'whiskers' extend to the full range of the data.)

Further reading

If you want to do some further reading in this area and, indeed, that of the following five chapters, you will find that it is covered in any of the enormous number of business statistics texts. For a treatment which is rather more mathematically sophisticated than the one given here, try one of the following:

Clarke, G.M. and Cooke, D. (2004), *A Basic Course in Statistics*, 5th edn, Hodder Headline.

Anderson, D.R. *et al.* (2010), *Statistics for Business and Economics*, 2nd edn, CENGAGE Learning.

Chapter 5

MEASURING CHANGES:
INDEX NUMBERS

Chapter prerequisites   Before starting work on this chapter make sure you are happy with:

1 the ideas of percentages (see Chapter 1, pp. 15–16);

2 the use of the Σ sign (see Chapter 4, p. 101).

Learning outcomes   By the end of your work on this chapter you should be able to:

1 calculate a price index according to the Laspeyres (base-weighted) or Paasche (current-weighted) methods;

2 explain the difference between these two methods of calculation and the meaning of the indices obtained;

3 outline the purpose and use of the General Index of Retail Prices with the data upon which it is based;

4 make use of a price index to 'deflate' a series of figures (profits, revenues, etc.).

Quantitative methods in practice

Indexes everywhere

The term 'index', in the sense in which we're going to examine it in this chapter, is widely used in the media. Here are just two examples, which I gleaned in a quick Internet search:

> #### US markets slump on double-dip fears
>
> Wall Street plunged on Friday after disappointing economic data and worse-than-expected corporate earnings prompted fears of a double-dip recession.
>
> The Dow Jones Industrial Average fell 270 points to 10,088 – a 2.5pc fall – and the S&P 500 lost 2.9pc. All 30 components of the Dow closed lower. The tech-heavy Nasdaq index fell more than 3pc.

The Telegraph, 16 July 2010
http://www.telegraph.co.uk/finance/markets/7895992/US-markets-slump-on-double-dip-fears.html

> #### Review calls for index-linked pensions to be scrapped
>
> The link between retirement income and inflation was under threat tonight following controversial reforms proposed in a pensions review.
>
> The Pickering Review of pensions called for companies to have more control over their schemes, including allowing them to abolish index-linked pensions and benefits for surviving partners.

Mail Online, 27 October 2010
http://www.dailymail.co.uk/news/article-127364/Review-calls-index-linked-pensions-scrapped.html

In the first passage here, the Dow Jones Industrial Average, the S&P 500 and the Nasdaq are all indexes – or indices, to use the correct plural – which measure the behaviour of share prices on the New York Stock Exchange. They are based on different collections of companies – the Nasdaq only includes high-tech industries, the Dow Jones covers more traditional companies, and the S&P 500 is based on the prices of shares in 500 large publicly quoted companies.

In the second quote, we find a reference to 'index-linked pensions' – that is, pensions whose value is guaranteed to keep pace with the cost of living by linking them to an index – usually the Retail Prices Index – which measures price inflation.

But what exactly *is* an index? In essence, it's an extension of the idea of an average which we met in the last chapter (that's why the Dow Jones index is also called the Dow Jones Industrial Average). Thus we want to know what, on average, is happening to a set of share prices, or to the cost of a collection of consumer goods. The additional feature here is that there is a time factor involved – it's the average change in prices over a period of time which is of interest.

In this chapter, we will explore the idea of indices, looking at both the way they are constructed and the uses to which they are put.

The investor's problem

Susan White has been left a small legacy by her great-aunt. It is not enough to do anything very exciting with, and she does not need it for day-to-day living expenses or immediate purchases, so she has decided to invest it. But she feels she would like to have some fun out of her investment, so rather than placing the money somewhere 'safe' like a building society, she would prefer to buy a small number of shares in a reputable company.

However, she is finding it hard to decide which company to select. The amount concerned is too small to interest an investment consultant, so she has been to her personal financial adviser for advice, and he has provided her with half a dozen company annual reports to study, so that she can form an idea of the financial health – or otherwise – of the firm she finally chooses.

Naturally these reports, while they must satisfy certain statutory requirements, are designed to present the company's performance in as favourable a light as possible. In particular, Susan has noticed that, although the chairman's report will usually mention the effects of economic changes, the effect of inflation upon prices and profits is rarely mentioned. She is understandably concerned that the return on her investment should, if at all possible, at least keep pace with inflation. She is also curious to know when, for instance, one of the companies she is considering states that 'before-tax profits over the five years 2005–9 were £12, £13.5, £15.1, £17 and £19 millions respectively', how much of this increase can be ascribed simply to the firm's prices increasing in line with everyone else's, rather than to a genuine expansion in business.

In order to satisfy her curiosity, what Susan requires is a 'measure of inflation' – some kind of overall, average figure which will tell her how rapidly prices are changing. The most easily available and widely accepted measure of this kind is the Retail Prices Index (more properly known as the General Index of Retail Prices), but before we can discuss this particular index we need to examine the general concept of *index numbers*.

What is an index number?

Many of the complications in constructing a measure of price increases for our economy arise from the fact that people are free to spend their money on a tremendous variety of goods and services, and probably no two households dispose of their income in precisely the same way. Suppose, however, we simplify the discussion by imagining a community living on a remote island, who subsist entirely on a diet of potatoes. Then the sole factor determining the purchasing power of a family's wage will be the price per kilo of this staple commodity.

Let's say that the price of a kilo of potatoes was 80 pence in 2009, and went up to 85 pence in 2010. It is no good simply stating that 'the price went up by 5 pence'; an increase of 5 pence which raised the price from 5 to 10 pence per kilo would clearly have a more serious effect on people's standard of living than the present one which raises it from 80 to 85 pence per kilo, since the former price increase would halve the amount of potatoes they could purchase for a given wage, whereas the latter would reduce it by only about 6 per cent. So what is needed is a measure of how the price per kilo has increased *relative* to the price at some time in the past.

This is the basic idea behind all index numbers: they measure *changes* – in prices, quantities consumed, or whatever – *relative* to the situation at some period in the past. The period to which the changes are related is referred to as the *base period* (base year, base month, etc.).

We can construct a very simple kind of index, called a *price relative*, for the increase in the price of potatoes from 2009 to 2010, by defining

$$\text{Price relative for 2010 based on 2009} = \frac{2010 \text{ price/kilo}}{2009 \text{ price/kilo}} \times 100$$

$$= \frac{85}{80} \times 100$$

$$= 106 \ (\%) \ (\text{to the nearest whole } \%).$$

There are several things to notice about this very basic kind of price index for a single item, because they apply also to the more complex types of index we are going to look at later. First, the index is expressed as a percentage – hence the '× 100' in the calculation – but, because this applies almost universally, we do not usually bother to write in the % sign (which is why it is shown in brackets). There *are* one or two of the more obscure indices which use a 'per thousand' rather than 'per cent' form of expression, but you are not likely to come across them.

Second, and following on from this, we can deduce that the index for the base year will always be 100, since it will be calculated by

$$\frac{2009 \text{ price}}{2009 \text{ price}} \times 100 = 100.$$

An index greater than 100 therefore shows that the price has increased since the base year, while one below 100 indicates a decrease in price. All that the 2010 index of 106 is telling us is that potato prices have increased by about 6 per cent from 2009 to 2010.

We must beware, however, in interpreting changes in the index from one year to the next. If, for instance, the price of potatoes were to increase to 90 pence per kilo during 2011, then the index for 2011, still based on 2009, would be

$$\frac{90}{80} \times 100 = 113.$$

We could thus say, quite fairly, that potato prices have increased by 13 per cent from 2009 to 2011. What we could *not* do, however, would be to say 'The index has increased from 106 to 113 between 2010 and 2011, an increase of 7 per cent'. Each index is a percentage *of the base year* price, so the increase is 7 per cent of *that* price; the distinction is sometimes made by saying 'The index has increased by 7 percentage points'. If we wished to speak of the percentage increase between 2010 and 2011 we would have to express 7 as a percentage of the 2010 figure of 106, which would give about 6.6 per cent.

Diversifying the diet

The situation considered in the previous section was particularly simple because we did not have to worry about *how* the residents of our imaginary island might choose to spend their money – the only thing to spend it on was potatoes! But now suppose that they have diversified their diet somewhat to include not only potatoes but also milk and fish. The prices of these items over the past two years have been as follows:

	2009	2010
Fish (per kilo)	£6.50	£6.80
Potatoes (per kilo)	80p	85p
Milk (per half-litre)	60p	62p

There are two obvious ways of going about the construction of a price index taking all three commodities into account. First, we might try adding up the three prices and then constructing one overall price relative:

$$\frac{\text{Total cost of three items in 2010}}{\text{Total cost of three items in 2009}} = \frac{749}{712} \text{ (prices in pence)}$$

so the suggested index will be 105. Or we could try working out the three price relatives separately and then averaging them:

$$\frac{680}{650} \text{ (price relative for fish)} \times 100$$

$$+\frac{85}{80} \text{ (price relative for potatoes)} \times 100$$

$$+\frac{62}{60} \text{ (price relative for milk)} \times 100$$

$$= 314, \text{ giving an average of 105.}$$

Unfortunately, neither of these obvious methods is at all satisfactory, since both have the serious defect of completely ignoring the *amounts* of each item which people consume. The effect on a typical family's budget of an increase in the price of potatoes will be much more serious than the effect of a corresponding increase in the price of fish if they eat potatoes every day but fish only as an occasional special treat. Imagine, for example, that their annual consumption of fish is 10 kilos. Then the price increase on fish between 2009 and 2010 will add $10 \times 30p = £3$ to their annual food bill. But if they eat 5 kilos of potatoes per week, then their annual consumption will be 260 kilos, so the additional cost produced by the potato price increasing from 80 pence to 85 pence per kilo will be 260×5 pence $= £13$ – considerably greater than the effect of the fish price increase.

In other words, a small increase in the price of a heavily used commodity may have an effect just as serious, if not more so, upon the typical family's budget as a large increase in the price of a less popular commodity. Any sensible price index, purporting to demonstrate the effect of increasing prices upon people's budgets, must take this into consideration; yet both the 'indices' devised above give an equal weight to each of the three items. What is needed is a method of constructing a *weighted* index which will take account of the differing importance of items in the overall budget.

Weighting the index

By far the simplest way to deduce the importance of a certain item in a family's budget is to note how much they spend on that item – in other words, the *value* of their purchases of the item. This in turn will depend on the *quantity* of the item which they purchase. So an index which would correctly reflect the relative importance of the various items which people use could be defined as a price relative for their whole 'shopping basket' over a certain period (year, month or whatever):

$$\text{Price index} = \frac{\text{total cost of 'shopping basket' at present prices}}{\text{total cost of 'shopping basket' at base year prices}}.$$

And the total cost of the 'basket', of course, will just be the quantity of each item bought multiplied by the price of that item, added together for all the items in the 'basket'.

But here we come up against a snag: when we say, 'the quantity of each item bought', which quantity are we referring to – the amount that people bought in the base year, or the amount that they are buying *now*? If the prices have changed, then doubtless the quantities purchased have, too; the dearer rump steak becomes relative to sausages, the more likely people are to transfer some of their spending from rump steak to sausages, thus altering the quantities of each which would be bought. How are we going to take account of this factor in devising an index?

Base-weighting

There are actually two common systems in use, both of which involve the assumption that the quantities being purchased do not alter along with altering prices. The first system, sometimes known as the *Laspeyres* price index, after its inventor, assumes that people are still buying *now* the quantities which they bought in the base year. For this reason, the name I prefer for this method is the *base-weighted price index*. A verbal definition would be

$$\text{Base-weighted price index} = \frac{\text{total cost of base year quantities at current prices}}{\text{total cost of base year quantities at base year prices}}$$

expressed, as usual, as a percentage. If you are a formula-lover, you can easily devise one in this case, using the notations p_0, p_n to stand for the old and new prices, and q_0 to stand for the old or base year quantities. The amount spent on one item during the period would be quantity × price for that item; so, using the Σ symbol which was introduced in the last chapter, and which in this case we interpret as 'add up for all the items in the basket', we could say that the total cost of the base year quantities at current prices is $\Sigma q_0 p_n$ and that of the base year quantities at the base year prices is $\Sigma q_0 p_0$. Thus, including the conversion to percentages, we have

$$\text{Base-weighted price index} = \frac{\sum q_0 p_n}{\sum q_0 p_0} \times 100.$$

However, a much better way to remember how to calculate the index is to think of it simply as a price relative for the whole shopping basket, the quantities bought being those for the base year.

Current-weighting

You probably will not be too surprised to learn that the alternative method of calculation, known as a *Paasche* or, more meaningfully, a *current-weighted price index*, makes the alternative assumption that people were buying in the base year the same quantities as they are buying now. The verbal definition of this index is

$$\text{Current-weighted price index} = \frac{\begin{array}{c}\text{total cost of current}\\\text{quantities at current prices}\end{array}}{\begin{array}{c}\text{total cost of current}\\\text{quantities at base year prices}\end{array}},$$

once again expressed as a percentage. Using the notation previously introduced, together with the additional symbol q_n to represent the current (new) quantities, we can write this as

$$\text{Current-weighted price index} = \frac{\sum q_n p_n}{\sum q_n p_0} \times 100.$$

Calculating the indices

Before we discuss the pros and cons of these two methods of calculating an index, let us see how the calculations are actually done for the situation we have previously been discussing. The prices for the three commodities being consumed by our islanders are repeated below, together with the amounts of each which they consumed in the two years in question:

	2009		2010	
	Price	*Quantity*	*Price*	*Quantity*
Fish	650	10	680	12
Potatoes	80	260	85	250
Milk	60	200	62	190

The 2009 prices and quantities will be our p_0s and q_0s, and those for 2010 will be the p_ns and q_ns. If you examine the formulae for the two types of index you will see that we need to calculate four combinations of ps and qs: $p_0 q_0$, $p_0 q_n$, $p_n q_0$ and $p_n q_n$. The best way to lay out the calculation is in columns as follows:

p_0	q_0	p_n	q_n	$p_0 q_0$	$p_0 q_n$	$p_n q_0$	$p_n q_n$
650	10	680	12	6 500	7 800	6 800	8 160
80	260	85	250	20 800	20 000	22 100	21 250
60	200	62	190	12 000	11 400	12 400	11 780
				39 300	39 200	41 300	41 190

If you are used to using a spreadsheet, it is very easy to carry out this calculation – simply enter the appropriate formula into the top cells of the product columns, and then copy it down the entire column. You will find an Excel worksheet for doing this calculation at INDEX.XLS on the website.

So the base-weighted price index will be

$$\frac{\sum p_n q_0}{\sum p_0 q_0} = \frac{41\,300}{39\,300} = 1.050$$

which when expressed as a percentage is 105. The current-weighted index is

$$\frac{\sum p_n q_n}{\sum p_0 q_n} = \frac{41\,190}{39\,200} = 1.050$$

which in percentage terms is 105. So in this case the two systems give virtually the same result; we would have to go to more than two decimal places before we could distinguish any difference between them.

Why is this the case? After all, both prices and quantities have changed quite a bit over the two years. But the *proportion* of total expenditure taken up by each item remains very similar. Had these proportions changed drastically, we would have got values for the two indices that were more noticeably different, as you might like to confirm by experimenting with changes to the quantities in the example.

Deciding which to use

How, then, should we decide which system to use in a given situation? The chief drawback of the base-weighted system is that it uses weights that are out of date, since they refer to spending patterns in the base year. However, we have also seen that if the changes in quantities purchased are not too drastic, the use of old quantities does not result in serious inaccuracy; so this drawback need not be taken too seriously as long as we are not *too* far from the base year, or in a very rapidly fluctuating situation. And the base-weighting system has some very powerful compensating advantages.

The first of these is the fact that we do not require a knowledge of the quantities used in the current period in order to calculate a base-weighted index, which means that it can be calculated as soon as the current prices are known; a current-weighted index, on the other hand, could not be calculated until the end of the period, when information about current quantities becomes available. Second, and perhaps even more important, the *denominator* of the base-weighted index – the $\sum p_0 q_0$ term – remains the same from year to year, since it does not involve any current figures. So it can be calculated once and for all, then simply stored in the computer or wherever, to be used each time a new index is calculated. This may seem a trivial saving in effort when only three items are involved, but if you realise that the real-life Retail Prices Index involves hundreds of items, the saving in calculation time becomes quite significant.

Moreover, because the denominator of every price index based on the same year will be exactly the same, a series of index numbers calculated in this way can be compared directly with each other. The current-weighted index, in contrast to this, has a denominator that contains the term $\sum p_0 q_n$, and that therefore changes from one year to another, so that a series of index numbers of this kind can only be compared with the base year figure, and not directly with each other. Also, as already indicated, we must wait until the end of the period when the current quantities are known before computing a current-weighted index; so the disadvantages of the current-weighted index generally outweigh the advantages, except in situations where the quantities are changing substantially from one period to the next.

Several other more complex types of index number have been devised in an attempt to combine the advantages of base-weighting with those of current-weighting, or to provide various other, rather theoretical, advantages, but the two we have examined remain by far the most widely used and useful.

Quick check questions

1 Why is it necessary to use weightings in calculating a price index?

2 An item cost 47p in December 2009 and 51p in December 2010. What is the price relative for 2010 based on 2009?

3 Examine the effect on the current-weighted price index calculated above if the quantity of potatoes consumed in 2010 went down to 150 kg.

Answers:
1 Weightings are needed to reflect the relative importance of different items within the overall expenditure. A change in the price of a heavily used item will have more impact on overall expenditure than a change in the price of one which is only used in small quantities.
2 Price relative = 51/47 = 108.5.
3 The new current-weighted index is 104.8.

The Retail Prices Index

The government's General Index of Retail Prices, which has been in existence – though with substantial modifications – since 1914, measures the changes in the prices of a 'basket' of some 350 or so goods and services bought by the 'average family' from one month to the next. In this context the buying patterns of the 'average family' are deduced by means of the Family Expenditure Survey, an ongoing enquiry in which about 7000 families throughout the country keep a continuous record of all their spending. The sample is carefully structured so as to cover all sections of the population with the exception of one- and two-person pensioner households, and those in the top 3 or 4 per cent when classified by weekly income. These two categories of households are excluded because it is considered that their spending patterns differ substantially from those of the majority of households.

The actual method of calculation of the Retail Prices Index (or RPI as it is often called) is closely related to the base-weighted system which we examined in the sections 'Weighting the index' (p. 127) and 'Calculating the indices' (p. 128). The weightings for the various items included are obtained from the information provided by the Family Expenditure Survey, while the information as to the prices each month is gathered by numerous investigators throughout the country, who cover a wide range of types of retail outlet from hypermarkets to small travelling grocery suppliers. Some items, of course, do not vary over the country, and can be collected centrally; these include such things as postage and telephone charges. The overall weights total 1000, and up-to-date values of the weightings for individual categories are published in the *Monthly Digest of Statistics*.

When all the information has been gathered the index can be calculated, but, as you can imagine, this is quite a substantial task. By the time all the collating and computation have been done, the index is about four-and-a-half weeks out of date when it is announced. Naturally, deciding what items should go into the index, what base year should be used, when it should be changed and so on is an important part of producing the index, and so a standing advisory panel, consisting of members from a wide range of interested bodies, has been set up to guide the government in this respect.

As well as the overall index, separate indices are published, which together constitute the general index. The 'pensioner households' also have their own index, published separately from the main one.

It would not be fair to leave the topic of the RPI, however, without a mention of some of the criticisms levelled at it. The monthly announcement of the latest change in the RPI attained an almost mystical significance during periods of high inflation and so, not surprisingly, efforts to 'debunk' it have been made. It is certainly true, as many critics point out, that it is *not* a 'cost of living' index, since some items which have a very significant effect on people's standard of living are excluded from its calculation. Moreover, it makes no attempt to include any reflection of the *quality* of the goods or services purchased – admittedly a very difficult thing to quantify. The most sweeping criticisms – and the most difficult to respond to – are made by those who claim that the index is totally oriented to the standards of the 'consumer society', that it describes the requirements of a mythical 'typical family', and that it makes no attempt to reflect more imponderable, but possibly more important, factors than how many kilos of potatoes people can buy with their wages, such as how much pollution they have to put up with, or what educational and employment opportunities are open to them. There is also scope for argument about the *interpretation* of the index – you have probably heard or read discussions about the 'headline' and 'underlying' inflation rates.

In recognition of some of these deficiencies in the RPI, several alternatives have been proposed. You may see references to the Tax and Prices Index (TPI), which includes the impact of tax changes, or the Consumer Prices Index (CPI), which is an internationally agreed measure. The differences between these measures are largely in terms of which items are and are not included, though the method of calculation remains similar to that we have discussed above. Of course, the fact that using different measures leads to different values for the current level of inflation allows plenty of scope for economists to argue with each other! For a short and accessible discussion of the different measures, try visiting **http://www.guardian.co.uk/business/2007/may/16/businessglossary.**

What is the use of the RPI?

You are probably far better informed as to the applications to which the RPI, and index numbers in general, can be put, than your counterparts would have been not many years ago. The idea of 'index-linked' payments, designed to keep pace with inflation as measured by the RPI, is now a very familiar one – this is what is mentioned in the quote about pensions at the start of the chapter. The principle here is quite simple: if the general level of prices as indicated by the RPI rises by, say, 6 per cent over a period of three years then you are guaranteed a minimum return of 6 per cent on your savings, so that at least you will be no worse off, in terms of what you can buy with your money, than you were at the time you invested it. The RPI is also often referred to in wage negotiations, the government wishing at present to discourage wage increases greater than the inflation rate as measured by the RPI.

In an inflationary situation we should really make use of the RPI, or another appropriate index, whenever we wish to compare amounts of money – profits, incomes and so on – being paid at different points in time. This can be done very simply, as the following example will illustrate.

Suppose a worker was earning £1500 per month after deductions in 2008 and this rose to £1875 per month in 2009 – an apparent increase of 25 per cent. How much better off is she in real terms when the effect of inflation is taken into account?

Published values for the RPI give 212.9 as the value for December 2008, and 218.0 for December 2009, both figures being based on January 1987. In other words, goods and services which would have cost £212.90 in December 2008 would cost £218.00 in December 2009. So what could be bought for £1 at the end of 2008 would have cost only £212.9/218.0 = 97.7p at the end of 2009; that is, the 2009 £1 is worth only 97.7p or 97.7 per cent of what £1 was worth in 2008. The £1875 per month wage in 2009 is therefore worth only about £1875 × 97.7% = £1831.88 in 2008 terms, and so the real percentage increase in the worker's wage, looked at in terms of what she can buy with her money, is only (1831.88 − 1500)/1500 or about 22.13 per cent.

What we did in this example is called *deflating* the value of the wage – expressing it in terms of the value of money at some point in the past. To deflate a series, we multiply by ratios of values of the RPI which are less than 1 – the 'older' RPI value is in the numerator of the multiplier, as you can see by examining the calculations above.

The converse of this process is *inflation*, where we are increasing the value of an amount of money in line with increasing prices. For example, suppose a self-employed painter and decorator wishes to keep his hourly rates in line with the cost of living, as measured by the RPI. In 2007 he charged £18 per hour; how much should he charge in 2008 in order to keep pace with inflation?

The annual average RPI in 2007 was 206.6, and in 2008 it was 214.8. So it has increased in the ratio 214.8/206.6, and thus, to keep pace, the painter's charges must increase to £18 × 214.8/206.6 = £18.71 per hour. Here we are multiplying by a ratio which is greater than 1, with the more recent RPI in the numerator of the fraction.

Quick check questions

1 Use the values of the RPI given above to find by what percentage the cost of living increased between December 2008 and December 2009.

2 In the unlikely event that the cost of living became lower than it was in the base year, what would happen to the RPI?

3 You will sometimes hear the statement 'The rate of inflation is falling'. Does this mean that the RPI is getting smaller?

Answers:
1 RPI for December 2009/RPI for December 2008 = 218/212.9 = 1.024 = 102.4 per cent, so the increase is 2.4 per cent.
2 If the cost of living in a particular year is less than it was in the base year, then the index will be less than 100.
3 'The rate of inflation is falling' does not mean that the RPI is getting smaller – it just means that the year-on-year (or month-to-month) percentage increases in the RPI are getting smaller.

Advising the investor

We are now in a position to return to the problem mentioned in 'The investor's problem' on p. 123, and to advise the potential share-purchaser of the *real* behaviour of her chosen company's profits, when the effect of inflation is removed. You will recall that the quoted profits for the five years 2005–9 were, in millions of pounds, 12, 13.5, 15.1, 17 and 19. What has happened to the RPI, our 'measure of inflation', in the meantime? The published values for the annual average retail price indices for the five years in question are 192.0, 198.1, 206.6, 214.8 and 213.7 respectively, all based upon January 1987. So we can 'deflate' the quoted profit figures to their value in terms of the 2001 pound as follows.

The 2005 figure, of course, is unaltered. The 2006 figure must be multiplied by a factor of 192.0/198.1:

$$13.5 \times \frac{192.0}{198.1} = 13.084.$$

For 2007 we have

$$15.1 \times \frac{192.0}{206.6} = 14.033.$$

You should verify for yourself that the remaining calculations give 15.196 for 2008 and 17.070 for 2009, so the increase in the 'deflated' profits is not quite so impressive as the original figures would lead us to believe. If you care to calculate the percentage changes in the profit quoted and also those in the RPI from year to year over the period 2005–8, the reason for this will be brought home to you: the quoted profits are increasing at 11–12 per cent per year but simultaneously the RPI is increasing by around 3 per cent per year. Thus a part of the increase in profits is accountable for simply by price increases in line with inflation. Figure 5.1 emphasises this.

However, something surprising happens in 2009 – the RPI actually *decreases*, something which had certainly not happened since the index was re-based in 1987. This of course

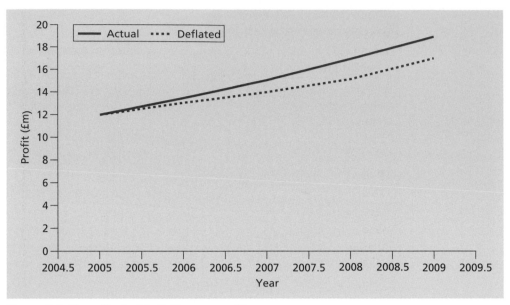

Figure 5.1 The effect of inflation on profits

shows the impact of the banking crisis and the global recession – prices had actually *fallen* on average. However, the index is now back on an upward trajectory.

Some technical considerations

There are one or two rather technical points we should consider before leaving the subject of index numbers. We have discussed the arguments for and against the two systems of weighting, but there are other decisions to be made in arriving at an index, notably as to what items should be included and what base year should be chosen. With the RPI, for example, it is clearly impossible to include every single item which people buy, while, with regard to the base year, if you look at the published values of the RPI you will find that within the last half-century it has been based successively on 1956, 1962, 1974 and currently 1987.

The choice of items to be included is crucial, since different selections could give quite different results. Clearly the items must be in fairly general use – one would not include in a food price index caviar or strawberries in January. From time to time the items will need to be altered so that the index keeps pace with changing consumer tastes; as items such as flat-screen television sets or calculators become more widely purchased, the index is modified to take account of such changes. Beyond this, it can only be said that some items are known to be good 'indicators' of inflation, responding more quickly to pressures for price rises. Ideally one should have a balance between this type of item and those that are more stable and less susceptible to sudden price increases.

The choice of a base period, and in particular the decision as to when the base period should be changed, is often problematical. The conventional wisdom states that a base year should be 'typical', a period of neither economic boom nor recession, and not exceptional in any other way; thus, for example, a year during which there has been a great deal of industrial unrest, reducing production levels or cutting down on public services, would not be a good candidate for a base period. It is obviously undesirable to let the index run for too long with the same base period; items in the index become out of date, comparisons are being made with a far distant point in time, and eventually the index becomes very large and unwieldy for calculation purposes. This was actually the situation when in 1987 the base of the index was changed. At the time of the change the 'old' index series, based on January 1974, stood at 394.5. When the change was made, the government took the opportunity also to make some changes in the calculation of the index, including a number of items and categories of expenditure which had not appeared in the index hitherto, such as expenditure on leisure activities.

The changes naturally led to some criticism, particularly with regard to the applicability of the new index to the 'average' or 'typical' household. In fact, whenever the base year of the index is changed, political capital can be made of the decision, particularly now that regular announcements in the news media of the monthly values of the index have made the public more 'index-conscious'. The suggestion can be made that the party in power hopes to make the rate of inflation look better by exploiting the public's erroneous view that an RPI of 102 is 'better' than one of 302. In practice, however, though it is a government minister who actually takes decisions regarding the RPI, he or she is strongly influenced by the views of the non-party advisory panel already mentioned, so it is unlikely that such a decision could be taken on purely political grounds.

Other kinds of index

We have concentrated so far almost entirely on price indices and on the RPI in particular, because these are the ones you are most likely to encounter, and which have the most obviously useful applications. You have probably heard of the Financial Times – Stock Exchange 100 Share Index (FTSE 100, or 'Footsie') which measures price movements on the Stock Exchange in London, and the Dow Jones index which does the same sort of thing for the New York stock market – this last was mentioned in one of the quotes at the start of the chapter.

But there are many other index numbers which are not price indices, as a glance at the contents page of any issue of the *Monthly Digest of Statistics* will show you. Index numbers of output, index numbers of retail sales and index numbers of basic wage rates of manual workers are just three examples. These all have their individual mode of calculation, details of which you can find, should you need to know, in the specialised government publications dealing with these topics, but all have in common with the price indices we have looked at the fact that they are designed to examine how a situation has *changed* when referred to some base period in the past, and that they consist of some form of *weighted average* over a whole collection of different items.

A final example

To obtain some insight into the construction of just one of the many other types of index apart from price indices, consider the following situation. Let us suppose that, in 2008, exports to the UK from Country Y consisted of 25 000 tins of creamed bananas at a cost of 43 pence per tin, 11 500 boxes of frozen squid at £3.20 per box, and 600 sheets of copper plate at £15 per sheet. The same three commodities were imported in 2009, but both prices and quantities had changed: 21 000 tins of creamed bananas at 52 pence, 12 000 boxes of squid at £4.00, and 620 sheets of copper plate at £18 were involved.

Country Y's trade mission to the UK now wants to compute an index that will measure the change in the *value* of its exports to the UK in 2009 as compared with 2008. We begin by computing the value of the exports in each separate year:

in 2008, value was $25\ 000 \times 0.43 + 11\ 500 \times 3.2 + 600 \times 15 = £56\ 550$;
in 2009 it was $21\ 000 \times 0.52 + 12\ 000 \times 4 + 620 \times 18 = £70\ 080$.

So the index measuring the change in value will quite simply be the ratio of these two figures:

value index for 2009 based on $2008 = 70\ 080/56\ 550 = 1.239$.

This indicates that the value of the exports increased by nearly 24 per cent over the year. This change in value is, of course, partly due to the changes in the quantities exported and partly due to changes in prices – both have been taken into account in calculating the index. Notice that there was no problem here about base- or current-weighting, since we actually wanted to take into account changes in both price and quantity.

EXERCISES

*Further examples on the work of this chapter can be found on the **Companion Website**.*

1 Customers of the *Statisticians Arms* have a rather limited choice of beverages, being restricted to beer, whisky or tomato juice. The prices of these items, and the consumption by customers, for 2009 and 2010 are as follows:

	2009		2010	
	Price	Quantity	Price	Quantity
Beer (pint)	180	60 000	190	55 000
Whisky (single)	250	20 000	270	21 000
Tomato juice (small)	90	15 000	110	18 000

Calculate a base-weighted and a current-weighted price index for the data in 2010, using 2009 as base year. (Use INDEX.XLS if you wish.)

2 A firm quoted turnover figures of £16 000 000, £18 000 000 and £22 000 000 for the three years 2007, 2008 and 2009. Use the values of the Retail Prices Index given in the section 'Advising the investor', p. 133, to deflate these turnovers to constant 2007 values, and hence find out if they kept pace with inflation.

3 'The Retail Prices Index went up from 245 to 265 over the last six months, but we have not had a 20 per cent rise to keep up with it, so we are worse off now.' Criticise and correct this statement.

4 Get hold of an annual report and accounts for a large public company, which usually includes a summary for the past five years of key figures such as turnovers and profits. By finding the values of the Retail Prices Index for the corresponding period from the *Monthly Digest* or via the Companion Website deflate the five-year series of profits or turnovers, and deduce whether the company's performance is actually improving or not. You might also like to compare the performance of two companies in the same industrial sector on this basis.

5 By keeping a record of your expenditure, and noting the prices of 'typical' items which you buy, you can construct your own personal 'cost of living index'. Ideally you need to carry out the exercise over a period of about three months. The procedure would be as follows:

(a) Choose two or three items for each of the eleven major categories in the RPI which you feel are 'representative' items for you, and make a note of their prices on a single fixed date at the beginning of your three-month period.

(b) Keep a record of *all* your spending over a period of about a fortnight. If there are some items, such as rent, which happen not to be included during your chosen fortnight, you should add in an appropriate proportion to the fortnight's budget. From this expenditure record you can find what percentage of your budget goes on food, alcoholic drink, and the rest of the eleven RPI categories – in other words, the *weighting* of each of these categories within your personal 'basket' of goods and services.

(c) At the end of your three-month period, collect the new prices of your selected items. Many of them may not have altered – do not worry!

(d) The easiest way to calculate your index from the data is by means of a *weighted average of price relatives*, which is effectively identical with the kinds of indices we have discussed in the chapter, but avoids your having to collect information about the quantities you use. The method is best shown with some simple figures. Suppose your chosen items are only three: a small tin of baked beans, representing food, which has increased in price from 23 pence to 24 pence over the period; a return bus-ticket to college, representing transport, which has stayed the same at 90 pence; and a pair of jeans, representing clothing, which have gone up from £19.95 to £21.45. Suppose too that your expenditure record shows that you spend 60 per cent of your budget on food, 30 per cent on transport and 10 per cent on clothing. Then you would calculate your index by:

(i) finding the price relative for each of the three items:

Food 24/23 = 104.3

Transport 90/90 = 100

Clothing $\frac{21.45}{19.95}$ = 107.5

(ii) finding the appropriate weighted average of these:

60% × 104.3 + 30% × 100 + 10% × 107.5 = 103.3.

Your personal index would therefore be 103.3.

(e) Having calculated your index, you might like to consider these further points.

(i) How does it compare with the official RPI for the same period? (You will have to wait for a few weeks to find this.)

(ii) What sort of difficulties have you come across in constructing the index? Do you think the producers of the RPI have the same difficulties and, if so, how do they resolve them?

(iii) If your 'personal inflation rate' as measured by your index continued at the same level for the next year, how much would you need to receive for the corresponding period next year?

6 Very different impressions of the performance of organisations can be conveyed, depending on whether actual figures or some type of index are used to report the data, and whether or not monetary figures are deflated. To obtain more insight into the use of the different types of index, consider the following situation.

Two companies, A and B, are competing in the same market, though at present B has a much larger turnover than A. Their respective after-tax profits over the past eight years are shown below, together with the corresponding values of a relevant price index (profit figures have been divided by £10 000 for convenience):

Year	A	B	RPI
2002	23	82	176.2
2003	25	85	181.3
2004	28	91	186.7
2005	31	94	192.0
2006	35	99	196.1
2007	39	102	206.6
2008	44	108	214.8
2009	50	114	213.7

(a) Taking the 2002 profit figure as 100, compute a simple index series for the profits of Company A.

(b) Do the same for Company B.

(c) Now compute a series of indices for the profits of A, but in each case taking the previous year's profit as 100 (e.g. the index for 2005 on this system would be 31/28, and so on – this is sometimes known as a *chain-based* index series). Do the same for B.

(d) Use the given RPI figures to deflate the profits for both companies, and then carry out steps (a)–(c) again using the deflated figures.

(e) Discuss the information conveyed by each of the series you have calculated, and the use to which they might be put in examining the performance of the companies, individually and comparatively. You may find it helpful to plot the series against time – preferably not all on a single graph!

7 A retired person receives an index-linked pension. The pension paid in 2004 was £9000. Use the values of the Retail Prices Index given in Exercise 6 to calculate how much the pensioner should have received in 2005 and 2006 taking the index-linking into account.

8 An engineering company uses about 200 000 screws, 150 000 washers and 100 000 clips per year. Last year the price of screws was £2.50 per 100, washers were £3.50 per 100 and clips were £1.20 per 100. This year, the prices have increased by 10 per cent, 4 per cent and 5 per cent respectively. Calculate an index for this year's cost of these items based on last year, using the annual usages as weights.

9 In Utopia, the cost of living is always falling, so the Utopian price index for 2010 was 93, whereas in 2009 it was 97, both figures being based on 2008. What would you pay in 2010 for goods which cost 100 Utopian pounds in 2009?

10 If you had purchased £1000 worth of index-linked bonds in 2002, use the values of the RPI given in Exercise 6 to work out what they would have been worth in 2009. Would you be any better off in real terms?

Case Study

National Express

The table below shows the revenues of the National Express group of transport companies for the five years from 2005 to 2009:

Year ended 31 December	2009 (£m)	2008 (£m)	2007 (£m)	2006 (£m)	2005 (£m)
Revenue	2711.1	2767.0	2612.3	2525.5	2216.0

Source: National Express Annual Report and Accounts 2009, available online at http://www.nationalexpressgroup.com/ar2009/

As a shareholder, you are interested in the growth or otherwise of the company in real terms. Visit the Hub for National Statistics at **http://www.statistics.gov.uk/hub/** and locate the Consumer Prices Index (CPI) for Transport. Use this to deflate the National Express revenue figures to constant 2005 values. Plot a graph to show the original and deflated figures over the period 2005–9, and comment on the results from the shareholder's point of view.

Further reading

I will not suggest any specific additional reading for this chapter; most texts on introductory business statistics cover price indices from a technical point of view. However, if you are interested more in their construction and application, try some of the publications of the United Nations Statistical Office such as *Methods Used in Compiling UN Price Indices and Retail Price Comparisons*.

If your home is not in the UK, you might like to try to find out something about how your country calculates its equivalent of the RPI. There is an interesting article on updates to the US Consumer Price Index, accessible via a link on the **Companion Website**, Chapter 5.

Also take a look at the website of the Office for National Statistics at www.statistics.gov.uk, where you will find values for many published index series together with useful explanatory material.

Part 3

NUMBERS –
A BASIS FOR DEDUCTION

Throughout Part 2 we have been concerned only with *descriptive statistics* – we have presented information in tables and diagrams, we have summarised it with the aid of means, standard deviations, index numbers and so forth, but we have always confined our attention to the sample of data actually available.

In many situations, however, what we wish to do is go *beyond* the available sample of data, and use the data as a basis for making deductions about the entire population from which the sample was drawn. This is the case, for example, in a market research enquiry where having discovered that 60 per cent of a sample of 500 people will purchase our product, we want to find out what this implies about the percentage of the entire buying population who will buy the product. It is the case in controlling the quality of output from a production line: if a machine is producing 5000 screws a minute, it is clearly impossible to inspect every single one, so only a sample will be inspected and deductions about the quality of the whole production will be made on the basis of the sample.

We could, of course, content ourselves with saying 'Well, the figure for the whole population buying our product will be near enough 60 per cent too', or 'This sample of screws is OK – I expect the rest are as well'. But 'near enough' is not good enough in many such cases; we want to know just how near – and how likely we are to be wrong in our estimate. It is that word 'likely', in fact, that gives the clue as to how we should proceed. What we need to deal with such problems effectively is a proper mathematically based theory with which we can pin down statements of the 'likely' or 'near enough' kind. So we start our work in this part, the rest of which will be concerned with the drawing of conclusions from statistical information, with a discussion of probability theory.

Chapter 6

A FIRM FOUNDATION:
ELEMENTARY PROBABILITY

Chapter prerequisites

Before starting work on this chapter make sure you are happy with:

1 addition, subtraction and multiplication of fractions (see Chapter 1, pp. 11–14);

2 conversion of fractions to decimals or percentages and vice versa (see Chapter 1, pp. 13–15);

3 calculation of the arithmetic mean (see Chapter 4, pp. 99–103).

Learning outcomes

By the end of your work on this chapter you should be able to:

1 define probability in a given situation using *a priori* or empirical methods as appropriate;

2 solve problems involving the calculation of simple probabilities and their combination in 'or' and 'and' situations;

3 say what is meant by the expected value of a process, and calculate expected values for simple processes;

4 construct decision tables and trees, and make use of expected values to arrive at decisions;

5 explain the limitations of this approach to decision-making.

Quantitative methods in practice

ACNielsen is one of the largest consumer research companies in the world. Among a wide portfolio of activities, it provides advice and support to companies intending to launch new products and services onto the market. Here is what one ACNielsen website has to say about the process of product launch (**www.acnielsen.co.nz**):

Getting New Product Launches Right

The key to the success of any product marketing company is largely dependent on the success of its brand portfolio. Over recent years brands have been introduced to some companies' balance sheets as a financial asset. At the same time, there have been countless seminars and books on how to effectively manage brands, and innovations in the measurement of brand equity and brand health.

Yet 70 per cent of all new product introductions still fail! (Source: ACNielsen BASES).

There are numerous reasons for this poor success rate. Some global companies simply throw onto the market their global products with a foreign ad. Others spend a fortune on product development but bypass consumer research. Some conduct exhaustive consumer research and product testing and then decide that despite poor results their gut feeling says it's going to be a winner. The reason for failure in all of these cases is a failure to understand or listen to the consumer.

Companies have to innovate and develop new products to survive, but new product development is expensive and risky and increasingly companies are looking to minimise risk by conducting thorough consumer research at the pre-launch and post-launch phase.

Let's focus on a few specific points from this quote. We're told that 'new product development is expensive and risky', so clearly an important task for a company embarking on this process is to try to estimate the costs and the risks, in order to take decisions based on the fullest possible information. We have ways of measuring costs – it may not be easy to get agreement on actual figures, but we know that the resulting measurements will be in units of euros, dollars, rupees or another currency. But how can we measure *risk*? Does it even make sense to talk about 'measuring' it, or are we stuck with qualitative expressions such as 'very unlikely', 'almost certain' and so on?

There's a clue to how this question might be answered earlier in the quote: '70 per cent of new product introductions still fail'. Another way of interpreting this might be that 'there's a 70 per cent chance that a new product will fail on introduction'. Of course, that is a simple-minded way of looking at things – the chance of a *particular* product failing will depend on a whole bunch of other factors – but it suggests a possible way of measuring, or quantifying, the risk of failure.

The last significant phrase is the reference to those who, despite poor results from consumer research, trust their 'gut feeling' that the product will nevertheless be a winner – and generally come to grief as a consequence. There is nothing wrong with judgements based on informed management experience, but isn't there a better way to make decisions than on the basis of 'gut feeling' alone?

In this chapter, we will look at a number of ways in which the concept of 'chance' or 'risk' in the colloquial sense may be quantified or measured. The statistician's word for this quantification is 'probability', and so what we are really doing is laying the basis of probability theory, on which the next few chapters will build. We will also see how measurements of probability can be linked to costs and profits to produce a rational approach to decision-making.

The product development manager's problem

Let's stick with the product launch situation discussed by ACNielsen. Harold Black is responsible for the development of new product lines for Potters Toys Ltd, an old-established firm which manufactures dolls and other small plastic toys. He has recently been working on the development and promotion of a line of Asteroid Wars toys, which will be marketed to coincide with the UK opening in six months' time of a film of that name. However, he has recently heard a worrying rumour that the film has 'bombed' with preview audiences in the United States.

Although he reckons that this rumour only has about a 40 per cent chance of being true, it presents him with a difficult choice. If the product is launched to coincide with the film opening, then sales during the first month on the market had been expected to generate a profit of £120 000. However, if the film is not a success this could fall to as little as £20 000.

The alternative is to launch the product immediately rather than waiting for the film opening. In that case, he is fairly sure that a profit of £65 000 will result.

To make matters worse, there is a possibility that if the film succeeds, then a rival company, ToonToys, will enter the market with a very similar product, reducing Potters' profits to £60 000. Admittedly, the chances of ToonToys doing this are only believed to be about 50 per cent, but the possibility still has to be considered. Potters thus has to choose between delaying the product launch or going ahead now, taking into account both the doubts over the film's performance and the possible competition from ToonToys.

There are two clear requirements if Harold Black is to be able to tackle his problem logically. First, he needs to understand precisely what statements like 'a 50 per cent chance' and 'a 40 per cent chance' mean, and to be able to find the chances of the various sequences of events occurring. Second, he needs to have a way to link together the *chance* of something happening with the *financial outcome* if it does happen.

Reckoning the chances

Whether wittingly or unwittingly, we are making assessments of chances, or *probabilities* as statisticians prefer to call them, all the time. For example, when you look out of the window in the morning and decide not to wear a raincoat to go out, you are making a decision based on your estimate of the chance of rain during the day; if you learn that in past years 95 per cent of students on your course have passed the first-year examination, and accordingly feel somewhat encouraged, it is because you recognise that your chance of passing is presumably about the same; and of course, if you place bets on horses, you are making assessments of the chance that a particular horse will be successful.

Probably, in these cases, you would not like to be pinned down to an actual numerical statement of the chance involved, but in order to make use of probabilities in dealing with problems such as that outlined in the section above, that is just what we need to do. We will therefore begin by looking at the various ways in which a quantified probability might be defined.

Working it out in advance

Imagine that the Queen is coming to open a new factory for a firm with 600 employees, and that one employee is to be chosen to present her with a souvenir book. So that the selection of the lucky employee is done fairly, 600 pieces of paper, of which 599 are blank and one marked with a cross, are put into a hat, and each employee is invited to take one (you may be reminded of what we said about simple random samples in Chapter 2). Then I think you will agree that, if the hat is well shaken and all the pieces of paper are indistinguishable, the chances of any one individual, say Fred Smith, being chosen are 1 in 600 or 1/600.

In other words, we have found the probability of the event 'Fred Smith is chosen' by taking the number of ways this may happen – just one – as a fraction of the total number of possible events. We often denote the probability of an event occurring by writing p(event); so here we would say

$$p(\text{Fred Smith chosen}) = 1/600.$$

We call this an *a priori* method of finding the probability, because we are able to assess the probability of the event *prior* to its actual occurrence simply by using our knowledge of the situation. Before generalising this definition to any event, however, we should look again at the assumptions we made in reaching our figure of 1/600. We said: 'the hat is well shaken and all the pieces of paper are indistinguishable'; in other words, the chances of each person being chosen are exactly the same, or, in statistical terms, all the outcomes are equally likely. Of course, if this were not the case – if the piece of paper bearing the cross were blue, say, so that the first person offered the hat could be sure of taking it – then, far from having a 1 in 600 chance of selection, poor old Fred, unless *he* were the lucky first, would have no chance at all!

With the provision, then, that all outcomes *are* equally likely, we can define a probability *a priori* as follows:

$$p(\text{event}) = \frac{\text{number of ways that event can occur}}{\text{total number of possible outcomes}}.$$

So if we know that out of the 600 employees, 250 are women, we can say that the chance of the chosen individual being a woman is given by

$$p(\text{woman}) = \frac{250}{600},$$

since there are 250 ways in which the selected person could be a woman.

Doing an experiment

Unfortunately, there are many situations in which we just do not have the requisite prior knowledge to calculate probabilities in this way. Suppose, for example, that a firm wants to know what the probability is of an item produced by a particular automatic machine being defective. It is a perfectly reasonable question to ask: presumably a small proportion of defective items is unavoidable, whereas a large proportion would need to be remedied; but there is no way in which we can find this probability by *a priori* means. To ask 'How many ways can an acceptable item occur?' is a question no more meaningful than 'How long is a piece of string?' – the item either is defective or it is not, so the whole basis of the *a priori* method breaks down.

The obvious course to adopt here is to monitor the output of the machine over a reasonable period of time and actually find out how often it produces a defective item. Note that proviso 'over a reasonable period of time' – it is clearly no good just looking at two or three items; a sample of a few hundred items will give a much clearer picture of what is going on. If among 200 items, say, we found 12 defectives, then we might estimate the probability of a defective item being produced by the machine as 12/200. This is the experimental or *empirical* approach to probability, based on looking at what actually happens in practice rather than theorising ahead of the event. We might define probability in this way as

$$p(\text{event}) = \frac{\text{number of times that event occurs}}{\text{total number of experiments}},$$

where we are using 'experiment' in a rather loose sense to mean the occasions on which the event *might* have occurred.

It might well happen, of course, that if we were to take a second sample of 200 items we would find 14 defectives, or perhaps only 11; for this reason a probability arrived at in this way can really only be regarded as an estimate. However, the larger the number of experiments, the more accurate we should expect the estimate to be. There are cases where we can actually verify this expectation by finding out how closely the experimental probability agrees with an *a priori* figure. For instance, we know that the chance of obtaining a six on a single throw of an unbiased dice* is theoretically 1/6. If we perform the experiment of actually throwing the dice a number of times, we do not expect to get exactly 1/6 of the throws producing sixes, but the greater the number of throws, the nearer the proportion should get to the theoretical figure of 1/6. For this reason we say:

Experimental probability approaches theoretical probability as the number of experiments becomes very large.

Trusting to instinct

If you think back for a moment to the problem posed at the start of this chapter, you will realise that neither of the two definitions of probability given so far is likely to be the basis for a statement such as 'the chance of ToonToys getting away with piracy is 50–50'. A probability of this kind is almost certainly the product of someone's intuition – hopefully backed by experience and information – and in many business situations it is this third, *intuitive*, method of quantifying probabilities that we have to fall back on.

* Strictly, the singular term is die: one die, two dice; but I will adopt the popular usage of 'dice' for both singular and plural.

By whatever means we arrive at a probability figure, we will end up with something that is a fraction, either expressed as such (Fred Smith's chance of selection is 1/600), or as a percentage (like ToonToys 50–50 chance of getting away with piracy). Probabilities are thus measured on a scale from zero – representing, in terms of our three definitions, an event which cannot occur in any way, which has never been known to occur, or which we feel is impossible – to one – representing an event that is bound to occur, which has always happened so far, or which we feel to be inevitable.

This fact gives us a useful check on the correctness of our arguments in future, more complex probability calculations. An answer which is supposed to be a probability, and which is greater than 1, must be wrong!

Before we go on to consider how these definitions of probability apply to more complicated problems, let us apply them in a few simple cases. (You will often receive the impression in studying basic probability that statisticians are obsessed with gambling – all the problems seem to be about dice, cards and roulette wheels – but that is mainly because these are easy problems to consider.)

Some easy examples

Suppose first that you have a dice which, instead of the usual numbered faces, has two green, two red and two yellow. What is the chance that, when it is thrown at random, a yellow face will show? The *a priori* definition gives two yellow faces out of six faces altogether, or 2/6. Notice, incidentally, that it often is not worth cancelling probability fractions like this one, particularly if you need to combine them later; you will often find yourself cancelling and then putting them over a common denominator, thus going round in circles!

If we had two such dice, and tossed them simultaneously, what would be the chance of obtaining one yellow and one green face? There are altogether 36 combinations, since any of the six faces of the first dice can be combined with any of the six faces of the second. Of these, how many fall into the category we are interested in? Either of the two yellow faces on the first dice could be combined with either of the two green ones on the second, so there are four possibilities there; or we could have either green face of the first dice combined with either yellow face of the second – another four possibilities. Altogether, then, there are eight possibilities in the category we are looking for, out of 36 possibilities in all, giving a probability of 8/36.

Now consider how you would determine the probability that it will be a wet day tomorrow. This is one which we need to approach via the experimental method, since there is no way we can count 'how many ways it might rain tomorrow'. If tomorrow is 28 February, then one way of approaching the problem would be to look up the weather records over the past, say, ten years, and find out, among all the February days in the ten-year period, what proportion have been wet. This will then give at least an approximate idea of the figure, though of course there is always the possibility that *this* year is exceptionally wet – or exceptionally dry!

Finally, what happens if someone asks you what you reckon to be the chance that you will pass the assessment at the end of your course? How would you reply? You *could* adopt an experimental approach, and look up the percentage of students on your course who have passed the assessment over the past few years; but ultimately only you know whether you have done sufficient work, written good lecture notes and so on, so your best bet is probably to give some kind of intuitive assessment of the probability based on that knowledge.

Quick check questions

1 A class contains 43 male and 27 female British students, plus 16 males and 24 females of other nationalities. What is the probability that if you pick a student at random from the class it will be a British male? A female student? Which definition of probability are you using here?

2 If you were asked to estimate the chance that you will be earning more than £40 000 per year within ten years of your graduation, how would you proceed? Which definition of probability would you be using?

3 The probability that it will rain tomorrow is estimated by forecasters to be 45 per cent. What is the probability that it will not rain? What fact about probability did you make use of in reaching your answer?

Answers:

1 p(British male) = 43/110; p(female) = 51/110. This uses the *a priori* definition of probability, because we know the composition of the class.

2 Although you could try to find out what proportion of people who obtain degrees in your subject earn more than £40 000 within ten years of graduating, this would not necessarily give you a good idea of the position in relation to yourself. You would probably be better off simply making an informed estimate – using the intuitive approach.

3 Probability of no rain = 1 – probability of rain = 55 per cent. Here we are using the fact that the probability of a certainty is 1. Since 'it will either rain or not rain' amounts to a certainty, we can say that the probability of no rain is 1 – probability of rain. We will look at this kind of calculation in more detail below.

Putting probabilities together

If you glance again through our solution of the problem above concerning the two coloured dice tossed simultaneously, your reaction may well be 'There must be an easier way!' The business of counting the number of ways the thing we are interested in might happen is certainly very tedious. The problem is really a combination of two separate problems – throwing the first dice, and throwing the second – each of which is very easy on its own. So is there some way we can combine what we know about the two separate problems to give us the answer to the combined one?

There are actually *two* ways in which separate events may be combined in order to give a composite event, and fortunately there are ways of dealing with both forms of combination. If we refer to the two separate events as A and B, then we may ask what is the probability of either A *or* B happening, or alternatively what is the probability of A *and* B happening at once?

The 'or' rule

Taking the first of these forms of combination, let us ask what would be the probability, in throwing just one of our coloured dice, that we get either a yellow or a red face showing? The probability of a yellow face is 2/6, and that of a red one is 2/6 also, and since it is easy to see that all together four faces fall into the category of 'yellow or red', the probability of this latter event is clearly 4/6. It looks, then, as if we have combined the separate probabilities in this case by adding them. In fact, it would appear that this is a general rule, for if we return to the *a priori* definition of probability, then:

Probability of A or B happening

$= \dfrac{\text{number of ways A or B can happen}}{\text{total number of possibilities}}$

$= \dfrac{\text{number of ways A can happen} + \text{number of ways B can happen}}{\text{total number of possibilities}}$

$= \dfrac{\text{number of ways A can happen}}{\text{total number of possibilities}} + \dfrac{\text{number of ways B can happen}}{\text{total number of possibilities}}$

$=$ probability of A happening + probability of B happening.

However, we must be a little careful when applying this result. The step we have taken in saying that the number of ways A or B can happen is the sum of the ways A can happen and the ways B can happen is only true if A and B cannot both happen at once – if, in statistical jargon, they are *mutually exclusive*. If A and B *can* occur simultaneously, then we will, in adding up the two sets of cases like this, be counting twice over those occasions on which both A and B happen.

This will be clear if we consider another example. If we throw an ordinary dice and ask what the probability is that an even number or one divisible by three will show, the addition rule in its simple form would suggest that the answer should be $p(\text{even}) + p(\text{divisible by 3}) = 3/6 + 2/6 = 5/6$. In fact, of course, the answer should be 4/6: one of the even numbers, 6, is also divisible by 3, and so the events 'even' and 'divisible by 3' are not mutually exclusive. The simple rule fails because it causes us to count 6 twice over.

There *are* ways of dealing with 'or' problems when the events are *not* mutually exclusive, as we will see later. For the time being, we state the rule in its simple form:

When A and B are mutually exclusive events
$$p(\text{A or B}) = p(\text{A}) + p(\text{B}).$$

The 'and' rule

Now consider the other type of combination, where we wish to find the probability of A *and* B happening at once. The problem discussed on p. 148 of throwing the two coloured dice so as to obtain a combination of one yellow and one green face can be broken down into the probability of getting a yellow on the first dice *and* a green on the second, *or* vice versa. The first of these, a yellow on the first and a green on the second, we saw could occur in four ways, giving a probability of 4/36. Now the chance of a yellow on the first is 2/6, as is the chance of a green on the second, so it looks as if what we have done here is to *multiply* the two separate probabilities to get the combined one:

Probability of A and B happening = probability of A × probability of B.

But once again, there is a cautionary note to be sounded in the application of this result. In the example we have just looked at, the colour that showed on the second dice was clearly independent of what showed on the first; the fact that the first produced a yellow face did not make it any more, or any less, likely that the second would show a green one.

But situations arise quite frequently in which the outcome of the second event does depend on what has happened on the first attempt – where, in other words, the events are *dependent*. This, while it does not actually alter the form of the 'and' rule, does mean that we have to be careful to take into account the event which has already occurred in finding the probability of the other event.

Imagine, for example, that in a certain firm 40 per cent of the workforce are women – in other words, the probability that a worker chosen at random is a woman is 2/5. Only 25 per cent of the female workforce are management grade, whereas for male workers the figure is 30 per cent. What is the probability that a worker selected at random is both female *and* management grade? Here the probability of selecting a management grade worker varies according to whether the worker is male or female, so we must modify the 'and' rule slightly and say

$$p(\text{female and management}) = p(\text{worker is female}) \times p(\text{worker is management}$$
$$\textit{given that} \text{ worker is female})$$
$$= \frac{2}{5} \times \frac{1}{4} = \frac{2}{20} \text{ or } \frac{1}{10}.$$

With this reservation we can write the 'and' rule for combining probabilities as

$$p(\text{A } \textit{and} \text{ B}) = p(\text{A}) \times p(\text{B}).$$

These two rules are really all one needs to know in order to solve quite a wide range of probability problems. If you find it difficult to remember '*and* means multiply and *or* means add', which may seem a bit back to front at first – after all, it is usually 'and' that means add – ask yourself how big you would expect your combined probability to be, relative to the two separate probabilities. If we insist on two things happening at once – the 'and' case – this is surely less likely to occur than either of the separate events alone, so multiplying the two (fractional) probabilities gives an answer that is *smaller* than either of the figures being multiplied. If on the other hand we want one or another of two events to occur, and we are not fussy which it is, this is *more* likely to happen than either of the events alone, so adding the two separate probabilities gives an answer that is *bigger* than either of the individual figures.

Before we go on to solve some problems using our two rules, there is one useful consequence of the 'or' rule which should be pointed out: if we have a set of mutually exclusive events which between them cover all possible outcomes of a situation – let us call them A, B, C, . . . – then the probabilities of all these events together must add up to 1, for one or another of them is *bound* to occur – in other words it is a certainty, with probability 1. The probability of A or B or C or . . . happening is $p(\text{A}) + p(\text{B}) + p(\text{C}) + \ldots$, so this must be equal to 1. We call such events exhaustive, because between them they exhaust all the possible results of a process.

This fact can save a lot of arithmetic if recalled at the appropriate time. It is particularly useful if we want to find the chance of something *not* happening. Between them 'A happens' and 'A does not happen' are exhaustive events, and so

$$p(\text{A happens}) + p(\text{A does not happen}) = 1,$$
$$\text{whence } p(\text{A does not happen}) = 1 - p(\text{A happens}).$$

Thus, for example, if the probability that you will pass the examination at the end of your course is reckoned at 9/10, then the probability that you will fail (i.e. *not* pass) must be 1/10.

Tackling problems

Although the definitions of probability, and the two basic rules for combining probabilities, are very simple, it is only fair to recognise that many students find it quite difficult at first to deal with problems involving them. The English language is, I think, at least partly to blame for this difficulty. There are many different ways in which, for instance, an 'and' type of combination may be expressed – as 'both', 'neither' or 'also', to name but three possibilities. Unfortunately there is really no foolproof 'method' for tackling such problems – practice is the only way to acquire facility. So, here are a few illustrations to get you into the right frame of mind.

Example I

A production line involves the use of three machines consecutively. The chance that the first machine will break down in any one week is 1/10, for the second the chance is 1/20 and for the third 1/40. What is the probability that at least one of the machines breaks down in a certain week?

Here is a case where it pays to recall that exhaustive probabilities add up to 1. To count the number of ways in which at least one of the machines may break down is very time-consuming; it might be the first which breaks down, while the second and third are working; or the second could break down while one and three are working, or the third break down while one and two are working. But 'at least one' also includes the possibility that any *two* of the machines are broken down and only one is working – or, for that matter, that all three machines are broken down. So there are, in fact, seven different possibilities to examine. However, the *opposite* of at least one being out of action is that all three are working, in other words

$$p(\text{at least one not working}) + p(\text{all three working}) = 1$$

so that

$$p(\text{at least one not working}) = 1 - p(\text{all three working}).$$

Now the chance that all three are working is easily found, for this means that the first is working and the second is working *and* the third is working:

$$p(\text{all three working}) = p(\text{1st working}) \times p(\text{2nd working}) \times p(\text{3rd working}).$$

If the chance that the first is *not* working, as given in the statement of the problem, is 1/10, then the chance that it *is* working will, of course, be 9/10. Applying a similar argument to the other two machines, we have

$$p(\text{all three working}) = \frac{9}{10} \times \frac{19}{20} \times \frac{39}{40} = \frac{6669}{8000},$$

so

$$p(\text{at least one not working}) = 1 - \frac{6669}{8000} = \frac{1331}{8000}.$$

Of course, the solution could be written down in a much more abbreviated way; we have dotted the i's and crossed the t's rather laboriously here for the sake of illustrating the method.

Example 2

In a certain firm, when an employee arrives late there is a one in four chance that she will be caught by her manager. On the first occasion she is caught, she is given a warning; the second time she is dismissed. What is the probability that a worker who is late three times is not dismissed?

Here we have a situation involving conditional probabilities: what happens to the employee on the second and third occasions she is late depends on what happened the previous time. Such problems can often be presented most simply by means of a *probability tree*, as shown in Figure 6.1. The extreme left-hand branch of the tree stops after two stages because, since this corresponds to the case when the employee is caught on the first two occasions, she will then be dismissed and so the possibility of her being caught a third time does not arise.

The tree makes it easier for us to see the ways in which the case we are interested in – when the employee is late three times but caught at most once – may arise. There are in fact four possibilities: she may be caught just once, either on the first, second or third occasions, or she may not be caught at all. Each of these cases involves an 'and' combination of probabilities; for example,

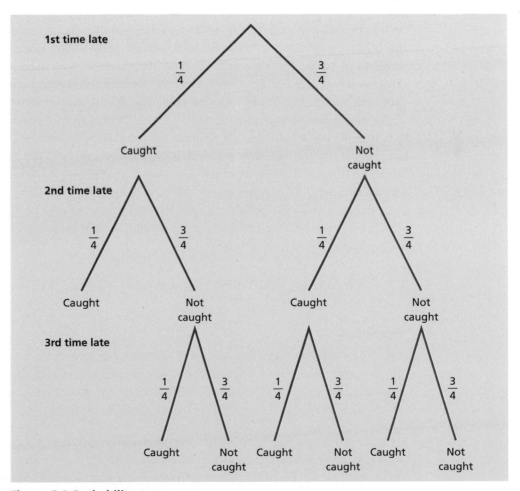

Figure 6.1 Probability tree

$$p(\text{caught the first time but not the second or third}) = \frac{1}{4} \times \frac{3}{4} \times \frac{3}{4} = \frac{9}{64}.$$

You should check that p(caught only on second occasion) and p(caught only on third occasion) are also equal to 9/64, while p(not caught at all) = 3/4 × 3/4 × 3/4 = 27/64. The four cases are linked together in an 'or' combination to give the answer we require:

$$p(\text{late three times but not dismissed}) = 9/64 + 9/64 + 9/64 + 27/64 = 54/64.$$

It might actually have been slightly quicker here to have worked from the opposite end, that is find the probability that she *is* dismissed, and take that away from 1 to find the probability that she is not – but there is little saving of effort.

Example 3

Two building contractors compete for contracts, and on past performance firm A has a probability of 3/4 of obtaining any one contract, while firm B has probability of 1/4 (there are no other firms bidding). What is the probability that, when they bid for two contracts, firm A will obtain either the first or the second?

At first sight this looks like a straightforward 'or' combination:

$$p(\text{A gets first or A gets second}) = 3/4 + 3/4 = 6/4$$

which immediately tells us that something has gone wrong, because we cannot have a probability greater than 1. What has gone wrong is that we have ignored the restriction in using the 'or' rule – the events must be mutually exclusive – and of course in this case they are not. There is nothing to stop A getting the first *and* second contract. Our wrong 'method' has resulted in our counting twice over the occasions when this happens.

So what argument will give the correct answer? There are various possibilities: we may say, since we are looking for the probability that A gains the first or the second, *or both*, the only case we are *not* interested in is that in which B gets both the contracts. The probability of this is p(B gets first) × p(B gets second) = 1/4 × 1/4 = 1/16 (assuming that bids are independent). So p(A gets one or the other or both) = 1 − 1/16 = 15/16.

Alternatively, we can split up 'A gets the first or the second or both' into the three separate cases 'A gets the first but not the second' or 'A gets the second but not the first' or 'A gets both', which gives as before

$$p(\text{A gets first or second or both}) = \left(\frac{3}{4} \times \frac{1}{4} \right) + \left(\frac{1}{4} \times \frac{3}{4} \right) + \left(\frac{3}{4} \times \frac{3}{4} \right) = \frac{15}{16}.$$

Example 4

Refer to the firm we discussed on p. 151 where 40 per cent of the workforce are female, 25 per cent of the female workers are management grade and 30 per cent of the male workers are management grade. If a management-grade worker is selected at random from this firm what is the probability that she will be a female?

The first point to note here is that we are *not* asking 'What is the probability that a worker is a female management grade'; we are saying 'We *know* this worker is management; what's the probability that she is female?' In other words, rather than selecting our sample workers from the entire workforce, we are restricting ourselves to look at the management-grade workers only. The safest way of dealing with this situation is to draw up a table, with two dimensions representing the two quite separate divisions of the workers into male/female and management/non-management:

	Male	Female	Total
Management	18	10	28
Non-management	42	30	72
Total	60	40	100

In drawing up this table we have assumed for simplicity that the total workforce is 100 people, since this makes the calculations a bit easier. As we are only concerned with probabilities – that is, with proportions – it really does not matter what size workforce we assume.

It is now a simple matter to pick out of the table the figures we need: there are altogether 10 female management workers out of 28 management workers, so the probability that a management-grade worker is female is 10/28.

This tabular arrangement of the data is the one safe way of obtaining probabilities in this type of situation where we are looking, not at the entire population, but at a restricted group within it. The key point to look for is that we are *given* some additional piece of information about the cases we are looking for, which enables us to narrow down our interest from the whole population to one of its subgroups – in this case, the management-grade workers.

Before reading the remainder of this chapter, you are strongly recommended to try Exercises 1–5 in order to practise handling probabilities. Although these examples may appear simple, probabilities for complex real-life scenarios can be built up using the principles we have established.

Quick check questions

1 A private equity company is bidding to purchase two businesses. The chance that the first bid will be successful is reckoned by analysts to be 1/4, while the chance that the second is successful is estimated at 1/5. The probability that neither bid is successful is (a) 3/5, (b) 1/20, (c) 9/20?

2 A bag of mixed fruitdrops contains 20 sweets, 6 of which are raspberry flavoured. If you select two sweets at random, the chance of getting two raspberry ones is (a) 6/20 × 6/20, (b) 6/20 × 5/19?

3 A company is running a promotion in which one packet in eight of the biscuits which it sells contains a token for a second free packet. The probability that if I buy two packets, neither will contain a token is (a) 1/4, (b) 63/64, (c) 49/64?

Answers:
1 (a) is correct – probability that neither is successful means probability that first is unsuccessful *and* second is unsuccessful = 3/4 × 4/5 = 3/5.
2 (b) is correct – if the first one you select is raspberry, then there are only 5 raspberry ones left out of the 19 remaining when you make the second selection.
3 (c) is correct – the chance that each individual packet does not contain a token is 7/8, so the chance that both packets do not contain a token = 7/8 × 7/8 = 49/64.

Giving probabilities a cash value

If you go back and reread the problem posed at the beginning of this chapter, you will realise that, although we would now be in a position to advise Mr Black as to the probability of various combinations of events in which he might be interested, we still have no way of linking the probabilities of events with the financial results of those events. It is to this problem that we now turn our attention.

Let us begin with a very simple problem. A vendor sells cups of tea on a railway station at 35 pence per cup, and by keeping records of his sales over several weeks finds that they vary as follows in convenient multiples of 10:

No. of cups sold	Percentage of days
40	20
50	20
60	30
70	20
80	10

What can he expect his average takings per day to be, assuming that this pattern persists? He brews the cups of tea separately on demand, so that there is no problem of trying to predict the sales in advance of each day's business.

Clearly we can calculate his average takings per day by considering the distribution of takings over a period of, say, 100 days, and calculating the mean as in Chapter 4:

Takings (£) (x)	No. of days (f)	fx
14	20	280
17.50	20	350
21	30	630
24.50	20	490
28	10	280
		2030

So mean takings per day = 2030/100 = £20.30.

We call this the *expected value* of his daily takings, sometimes also called expected monetary value or EMV. Of course, he does not expect to get this precise amount on any one day – he gets either £14, or £17.50, or £21, or £24.50, or £28. But this is what he would expect, *in the long term*, his average daily takings to work out to.

Now we would have got exactly the same figure of £20.30 if, rather than taking an imaginary sample of 100 days as our averaging period, we had simply said that there is a 20 per cent chance that on any given day he will take £14, a 20 per cent chance that he will make £17.50, and so on. In other words, his expected average daily takings would be

$$0.2 \times 14 + 0.2 \times 17.5 + 0.3 \times 21 + 0.2 \times 24.5 + 0.1 \times 28 = £20.30.$$

So the expected value of his daily takings can be calculated as

Probability of selling 40 cups × financial result of selling 40 cups + probability of selling 50 cups × financial result of selling 50 cups + . . .

and we can generalise this to define the expected value of any process as follows:

$$\text{EMV} = \sum(\text{probability of outcome} \times \text{financial result of outcome})$$

where the $\sum$ sign means 'added up over all the possible outcomes of the process'.

Before going on to apply this idea to decision-making problems, let us see how it can be used in a couple of simple cases.

Example 1

Suppose an insurance company finds, by examining its past records, that on 80 per cent of its policies there is no claim, on 15 per cent there is a small claim, typically £50, and on the remaining 5 per cent there is a large claim, typically £500. In order to make a profit, it must make the premium per policy larger than the expected value of the claim per policy; but this, using the theory just developed, will be $0.8 \times 0 + 0.15 \times 50 + 0.05 \times 500 = £32.50$. It is really a much elaborated version of this calculation that insurance companies actually use in deciding how much their premiums should be.

Example 2

Imagine that you have watched people playing a fruit machine in a certain pub, and have noticed that over a long period it gave a £1.00 payout on average every 20 turns. Is it worth your while playing the machine, if the charge per turn is 10 pence?

Your expected winning per turn is

$$p(\text{winning}) \times \text{gain if you win} + p(\text{losing}) \times \text{loss if you lose} = 1/20 \times 90 + 19/20 \times (-10)$$
$$= 4.5 - 9.5 = -5.$$

So on the average, you stand to make a loss of 5 pence per turn, and therefore it is not worth playing.

Really, without saying so explicitly, we have moved here into the realm of decision-making, for you have to make a decision – to play or not to play – and on the basis of your expected winnings, the sensible decision would be not to play. The problem also highlights one of the defects of this approach to decision-making, in that someone with a well-developed gambling instinct would probably argue that it is worth something to them simply to have the *chance* of winning £1.00. The rather detached way in which we have looked at the decision takes no account of this; nor, being essentially a 'long-term' view of things, can it allow for the possibility that the machine will pay out on your very first turn, and you will have the strength of mind to quit at that point! Fortunately for the promoters of lotteries, very few people think in this way when deciding whether to gamble.

Decision tables

When we have a large number of possible courses of action among which a decision has to be made, and a large number of possible consequences to consider, the process can be made more systematic by drawing up a *decision table* (sometimes given the more technical-sounding name of decision *matrix*). To illustrate how it works, let us return to the problem of our railway-station tea vendor, and imagine that he has decided to diversify his business by also selling fruit pies. Unlike the cups of tea, however, these cannot be prepared on demand as each customer arrives; they have to be ordered in advance, and the supplier does not like the size of order changing from day to day – it will only accept orders for a week at a time. In other words, if our vendor decides to order 40 pies a day this week, he will be stuck with 40 per day for the whole week, and cannot change the number until next week.

Once again, the vendor begins by keeping a record of demand for the pies over a period of a few weeks and finds that it is as follows:

No. of pies demanded	Percentage of occasions
25	10
30	20
35	25
40	20
45	15
50	10

Of course, in practice there would probably be some kind of pattern of variation discernible from one day of the week to the next which might help him to plan his supplies. But for the moment, let us suppose that there is no such pattern and furthermore that the supplier insists that for the good of its reputation only fresh pies are sold; any left at the end of a day are to be returned to the bakery for a nominal refund of 5 pence. The vendor buys the pies from the supplier at 15 pence each, and sells them at 25 pence; thus every pie sold represents a profit of 10 pence, while every unsold pie represents a loss of 10 pence.

The vendor's problem is an example of decision-making *under uncertainty*; if he *knew* what the demand for pies each day would be, then he could buy just the right number and maximise his profits, but he does not have that knowledge. How then can he decide the 'best' number of pies per day to order?

The decision table for the vendor's problem is shown below: the possible decisions are at the left-hand side, and the uncontrollable factor – in this case, the demand for pies – across the columns of the table, the probability of each demand also being shown. There is clearly no point in considering buying fewer than 25 pies, since this number can *always* be sold; by the same token, as more than 50 are never required, to order such quantities would be pointless. So only the quantities actually demanded will be considered.

		Demand						Expected value
		25(0.1)	30(0.2)	35(0.25)	40(0.2)	45(0.15)	50(0.1)	
	25	2.5	2.5	2.5	2.5	2.5	2.5	2.5
	30	2.0	3.0	3.0	3.0	3.0	3.0	2.9
	35	1.5	2.5	3.5	3.5	3.5	3.5	3.1
Buy	40	1.0	2.0	3.0	4.0	4.0	4.0	3.05
	45	0.5	1.5	2.5	3.5	4.5	4.5	2.8
	50	0.0	1.0	2.0	3.0	4.0	4.0	2.4

The figures in the body of the table are arrived at as follows. Consider the occasions when 35 pies are demanded and only 25 have been bought; obviously in this case only 25 can be sold, which at a profit of 10 pence per pie will give a total profit of £2.50. The same will apply, in fact, to all other combinations in the top row (we are ignoring any question of the cost of lost goodwill through turning customers away). If, however, 35 pies are demanded and 40 have been bought, then although the sale of the 35 will produce £3.50 profit, we must offset against this the 5 pies that have to be returned at a loss of 10 pence per pie – a total loss of 50 pence. Thus the actual profit resulting from the '40 bought, 35 demanded' combination is only £3.00. You should verify in a similar way the calculation of the rest of the figures in the table.

The table, once completed like this, provides us with all the information we need to calculate the *expected value* of the vendor's profits resulting from each possible decision. For example, if he decides to buy 30 pies then his expected profit will be, using the method developed above,

$$0.1 \times 2 + 0.2 \times 3 + 0.25 \times 3 + 0.2 \times 3 + 0.15 \times 3 + 0.1 \times 3 = £2.90.$$

You can see the expected values of the remaining decisions in the right-hand column of the table.

Thus, if the vendor wishes to maximise his expected profits, he should choose to buy 35 pies per day. What this means is that if he persists in this strategy and the pattern of demand also remains as established, then in the long run this will give him an average profit of £3.10 a day – better than that achieved by any other choice.

This basis for decision-making is sometimes known as the *expected monetary value*, or EMV, decision criterion; we will return to a discussion of its suitability in particular cases, and alternative criteria that might be adopted, below.

Decision trees

We were able to deal with the problem in the last section by means of a simple decision table, because it involved only one set of 'uncontrollable circumstances' which applied with the same probabilities whatever the decision selected. Where there are different sets of consequences, with different probabilities, dependent upon which decision is made, such a method will not do and we must resort to drawing a decision *tree*. This, as its name suggests, is somewhat akin to a probability tree, with the incorporation of the financial outcomes which will result from each set of circumstances.

We will at last return to the problem posed at the start of the chapter to see how the decision tree method works. You will recall the choice faced by Harold Black at Potters Toys: whether to delay the launch of his new range of toys to coincide with the opening of the associated film, thus gaining profits of £120 000 if the film is a success but only £20 000 if it turns out to be a 'turkey', or to go ahead with the launch immediately and gain a definite £65 000. The probability that the film is a success was estimated at 60 per cent. He also has to deal with the possibility that, if the film does succeed, a rival company will enter the market and so reduce his profits to £60 000. The chance of this happening is 50 per cent.

In Figure 6.2 you can see the probability tree representing the various decisions and their consequence, without as yet the inclusion of any of the profits or costs. Notice that the tree *begins* with the decision to be made – this is the general rule – and that this *decision node*, as it is often called, is represented by a square box. This is in contrast to *chance nodes*, shown as circles. Of course, the decisions 'market now' and 'wait' do not

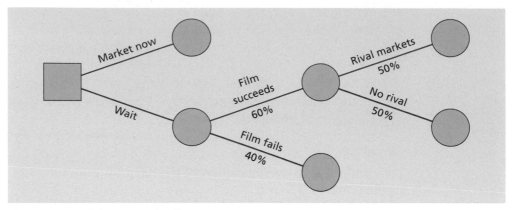

Figure 6.2 Decision tree: the first stage

have probabilities associated with them like the other branches of the tree, because unlike 'rival markets' or 'film succeeds' they are not subject to uncontrollable, probabilistic forces; one of them definitely *will* happen, and the other definitely will not, depending upon what choice is made.

We now begin to insert the profit figures into the tree, always starting from the *endpoints* of the branches, since it is these final consequences whose effects have been estimated. For example, the profit resulting from 'film succeeds, rival markets' will be £60 000. In the same way, 'film succeeds, no rival' yields £120 000, while 'film fails' gives £20 000. The result of the decision 'market now' is simply £65 000, since this is not associated with any further events.

We now use our definition of expected value to find the expected results of the various chains of events. First let's consider the expected value associated with the 'rival/no rival' chance node. This will be

$$\begin{array}{cc} \text{chance of rival} \\ \text{marketing} \end{array} \times \begin{array}{cc} \text{profit if} \\ \text{rival markets} \end{array} + \begin{array}{cc} \text{chance that rival} \\ \text{doesn't market} \end{array} \times \begin{array}{cc} \text{profit if} \\ \text{no rival} \end{array}$$

$$= 0.5 \times 60 + 0.5 \times 120$$
$$= 90 \text{ (using profits in £000s for simplicity).}$$

So the expected result of the event 'film succeeds', taking into account what the rival company might do, is £90 000. Now we work back once more, to find the expected value associated with the decision 'wait': this will be $0.6 \times 90 + 0.4 \times 20 = 62$ (make sure you can see where this calculation comes from).

Taking into account all the possible circumstances, then, we would advise Harold Black to market his product now, since the expected profit in that case, £65 000, is a little higher than the expected result from waiting. The completed tree is shown in Figure 6.3. The decision in this case is quite marginal, since the profits associated with the two decisions are very close.

To summarise the process for constructing a decision tree:

● draw the tree representing the logical sequence of events, always beginning with the decision to be made;
● insert the financial result of each sequence of events at the corresponding terminal node of the tree;
● work back towards the decision node, using the expected value.

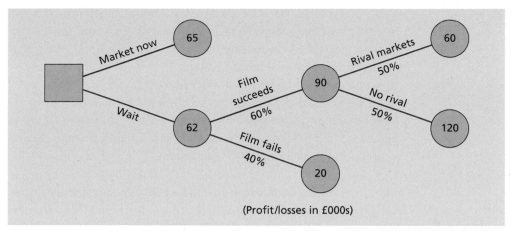

(Profit/losses in £000s)

Figure 6.3 The completed decision tree

Example

We will finish this section with another example of a decision tree. I am about to buy a new calculator, and have the choice of a cheap unbranded model at £4.50, or a well-known make at £7.50. There is no guarantee with the cheap model, so if it breaks down during the first year of use I will simply have to buy another, at the same price. Friends who have similar calculators tell me this happens with about 1 in 5 of them. The more expensive calculator is much less likely to break down – the manufacturer states that the proportion which do so is only about 1 in 50 – and if it does, the guarantee means that I will only have to pay the 50 pence postage to return it to the factory. Is it worth buying the dearer machine?

The tree for this problem is shown in Figure 6.4, starting at the left with the decision 'dearer' versus 'cheaper' machine. The total cost to me of having a cheap machine which

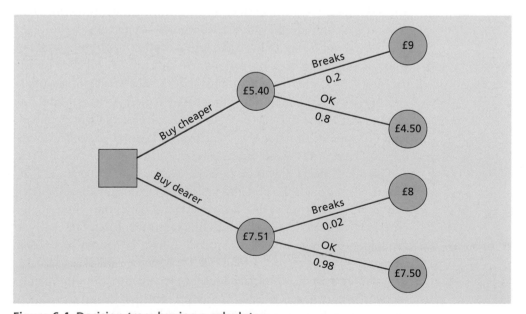

Figure 6.4 Decision tree: buying a calculator

breaks down is £9, since I have no choice but to buy another at £4.50. The cost of an expensive machine which breaks down is only £8 – the initial cost of £7.50 plus the 50 pence postage. If the machine does *not* break down, of course, then in either case the cost is merely the initial purchase price.

As you can see, the expected cost of buying a cheap machine is $0.2 \times 9 + 0.8 \times 4.5 = £5.40$, whereas for the dearer machine it is $0.02 \times 8 + 0.98 \times 7.5 = £7.51$. So it would appear that the cheaper machine is the better bet – though of course you might ask, since the chance of a breakdown is so high in this case, what is the chance that your replacement machine will break down – and so on!

Both the examples we have considered here involve only a single decision. However, many real decision problems involve sequences of decisions; they can be tackled in the same way as our simpler examples. When the decision tree becomes very large and complex, it is often necessary to use computer software for the analysis; this will generally speaking be a 'dedicated' package specifically designed for decision analysis, rather than an application of a multi-purpose package such as Excel.

Such packages often offer additional facilities to the user. They may allow a manager to give a range of options, such as 'most likely, pessimistic, optimistic', rather than a single figure as the financial consequence of a decision. They may also help to answer questions such as 'How much should I be prepared to pay for further information about this situation which will help to improve my decision-making?'

Drawbacks of the method

Strictly speaking, decision theory belongs in a later section of this book, since it is definitely 'a tool of planning', and a very important one at that. However, we have really only scratched the surface of the topic here, to illustrate how probability theory can be applied to some very real problems. In practice, problems would rarely be as simple as the ones we have solved, and would often involve not just one decision but a whole sequence.

It would not be fair to leave this topic without mentioning some of the defects of this whole approach to decision-making. We have already touched on this in the section on decision tables, where we mentioned that the EMV as a decision criterion is really most appropriate in a situation where the process is going to be repeated numerous times, since it is in such a case that the EMV can guarantee us the best possible overall return. In a 'one-off' type of situation – such as the marketing decision discussed in the section on decision trees – it is by no means clear that EMV will give the 'best' solution.

The other major drawback to using EMV as our criterion is that it requires at least estimated values for the probabilities of the various uncontrollable circumstances which may arise. Where no such estimates are available, the whole method fails, and other criteria have been developed for coping with such cases. For example, in the case of the vendor's problem examined on pp. 156–7, had the vendor had no idea of the pattern of demand for fruit pies, other than that the most he would ever be asked for was 50 in one day, and the least 25, he might adopt the pessimistic viewpoint that, if the worst comes to the worst, he will sell 25 pies in a day. From that standpoint, his best decision would clearly be to buy 25 only, as this gives him the maximum possible profit if 25 are demanded. This 'pessimistic' strategy is sometimes referred to as 'maximin', since it maximises his profits in, as it were, the 'minimum' circumstances.

An optimistic vendor, on the other hand, would hope that he might sell 50 pies – the maximum that has ever been demanded of him in one day. His choice therefore would be to buy 50, since that will give him the maximum profit under the circumstance he is hoping for. The 'optimist's' strategy is often called 'maximax', since it maximises profits under the 'maximum' circumstances that may arise.

This by no means exhausts the possible choices of decision criteria, but unfortunately, in the absence of any idea what the probabilities of various contingencies may be, some of them are little more than shots in the dark. A further defect of the method as a whole is that we need to be able to put at least an approximate cash figure on the outcome of various sequences of events, but some of the figures used may be no more than inspired guesses. How, for instance, does Mr Black of Potters Toys *know* that his profit will be £65 000 if he markets now? And if he has got his estimates wrong, will he end up by making a disastrously wrong decision? It is easy to visualise a situation in which the expected results of two or more possible decisions could be so finely balanced that just a small change to one of the profit estimates – or, for that matter, to one of the probabilities – would completely alter the decision. You will have a chance to think about this question of the *sensitivity* of the decision to changes in the figures a bit more in some of the exercises at the end of the chapter, and this whole topic of how small errors in the data of a problem may alter the solution is one that will become familiar as you read Part 4.

Finally, as pointed out earlier, we have taken a very cold-bloodedly financial point of view throughout our decision-making. But frequently where business decisions are concerned, there are other, less quantifiable, but equally important, factors to be considered. Suppose a firm is considering resiting its plant on a green-belt industrial estate; how can it measure in cash terms the benefits to its workers of a healthier working environment, or the inconvenience of being more distant from a railway station, or the effect on production of workers having much longer journeys to reach the plant? And yet these are precisely the kinds of questions the firm *should* be considering when trying to decide whether to make the move. There are ways of attempting to attach nominal cash values to factors of this kind, but naturally the subject is much less cut and dried, and much more open to controversy than anything we have considered in this chapter.

EXERCISES

*Further examples on the work of this chapter can be found on the **Companion Website**.*

1 A public health inspector is visiting the PQR supermarket, and inspects the staff washroom. The manager knows that one day on average out of every three the sink is blocked, and two days out of five there is no towel available. If the inspector will only pass the premises if the sink is clear and a towel is available, what is the chance that he will do so?

2 Half the workers in a certain factory are women, but among part-time workers they represent a much higher proportion, in fact four-fifths. A quarter of the overall workforce consists of part-timers. What is the probability (a) that a worker is male; (b) that a part-time worker is male; (c) that a male worker is a part-timer?

3 The probability that Martin Moribund will die during the ten-year term of a life insurance policy is assessed by the insurance company at 1/5. Arthur Average's probability of living to the end of the ten-year period is reckoned at 95 per cent. What is the probability that at the end of the ten years (a) both and (b) one or the other, but not both, is living?

4 As part of a very strict auditing procedure, every audit document is examined first by an articled junior accountant, then by a qualified accountant, and finally by one of the partners in the accounting firm. If there is an error in the document, the chance that the junior will detect it is 4/5: if he finds the error, he will not bother passing on the document to his senior. The chance of the qualified accountant detecting an error in the documents he examines is 3/5, and once again he passes on only those documents that appear to him to be correct. Finally, when the partner examines the documents that reach him, his chance of detecting an error is 1/2.

(a) What is the probability that an erroneous document will be detected by one or other of the three examiners?

(b) Do the three probabilities for the three personnel quoted suggest that the junior is better at detecting errors than the partner?

5 An unscrupulous tradesman knows that in a box of a dozen lightbulbs which he is selling to a customer, four are in fact not working. He watches nervously as the customer insists on removing three and testing them. What is the probability that only one of the three tested fails to work?

6 I am trying to decide whether to move house or stay in my present one. I must decide immediately, but unfortunately there is an element of uncertainty in the situation, as my firm is in the middle of reorganisation, and may shortly move me to another site, closer to my present home than to the house I am considering buying. I reckon the chances of my being moved are about 40 per cent. If I am moved, I estimate that annual fares from my present home would cost £200, as opposed to £250 from the new house. To reach the site where I work at present, on the other hand, currently costs me £300 per year from my present house, but would cost only £200 a year from the new house. If there is no price difference between the two houses, so that I make neither a profit nor a loss on the transaction, what would you advise?

7 If I do not put any money in a parking meter when I park, there is a one-in-ten chance that a warden will notice, and I will be fined £25. If I pay now, it will cost me 20 pence. Is it worth trying to get away without paying?

8 I have an old tea set inherited from my great-aunt. At the moment I would get £50 for it if I sold it, which can be invested to give me £65 in a year's time. If I hang on to the tea set for a year, an antique dealer friend tells me there is a 1/5 chance that this particular type of pottery will become fashionable and I will be able to sell the tea set for £125. Otherwise the value will remain the same, though my cleaning lady is very clumsy and there is always the chance, if I do decide to keep the tea set for another year, that she will smash it during that year. On past performance I assess the chance of this happening at 10 per cent. What should I do?

9 Discuss how you would assess the probability that:

(a) a candidate of a given party, standing in a by-election in a given constituency, will be elected;

(b) the baby your elder sister is expecting will be a girl;

(c) a consumer, presented with two otherwise identical packages, will take the red one in preference to the blue;

(d) the aeroplane on which you are flying to Majorca for your holidays will crash on the way.

10 Demonstrate for yourself how the probability given by the experimental approach becomes closer to that given by the *a priori* approach as the number of experiments becomes larger. You can do this by tossing a coin over and over, keeping a running record of the cumulative number of heads obtained, and the cumulative probability, and seeing how the latter figure approaches 0.5 (assuming, of course, that the coin is fair!).

As an example, suppose your first ten tosses gave H, H, T, H, T, T, H, T, H, H. Then your running total of heads would be 1, 2, 2, 3, 3, 3, 4, 4, 5, 6, and the cumulative probabilities would be as follows:

$$1/1 = 1, \ 2/2 = 1, \ 2/3 = 0.67, \ 3/4 = 0.75, \ 3/5 = 0.6,$$
$$3/6 = 0.5, \ 4/7 = 0.57, \ 4/8 = 0.5, \ 5/9 = 0.55, \ 6/10 = 0.6.$$

If you choose to plot the cumulative probabilities on a graph against the number of experiments, you will see in an even more striking way how, as the number of experiments becomes larger, the probability tends to 'home in' upon 0.5.

11 Referring to the problem posed on p. 145 and the decision tree in Figure 6.3, all other things being equal, how small would the chance of the rival marketing have to be before it would be worthwhile abandoning the project?

12 In Exercise 7 what chance of discovery by the traffic warden would make it worth your while trying to get away without paying the meter? Given the probabilities as in the question, what increase in the standard charge for the meter would convince you that it is worthwhile not to pay?

(In Exercises 11 and 12 we are investigating the sensitivity of our decision to changes – a topic to which we will be returning in later chapters.)

13 At the moment there is much discussion in the serious media about the wisdom and efficacy of 'screening' programmes for various potentially fatal diseases. At first sight the issues seem clear cut: if there is a test which can tell you whether or not you have a disease at an early stage, so that if you have, you can be given treatment, surely that is a good thing?

That would certainly be true if such tests were infallible, but unfortunately that is rarely the case: they can wrongly return negative results for a person who actually has the disease, and sometimes also register as positive someone who does not have it. Suppose, for example, that historic data suggests one person in 200 000 suffers from Gauss's Disease, and that a new test has just been developed that can detect this unpleasant complaint before any symptoms appear. However, early results indicate that the test returns a false positive (i.e. it indicates someone has the disease when they have not) in 2 per cent of cases, and also that it gives a false negative (indicating that someone is free of the disease when they actually have it) in 5 per cent of cases.

(a) If you have just been tested for Gauss's Disease and given a positive result, what is the chance that you actually have the disease?

(b) What is the implication of your answer to (a) for the introduction of widespread screening for the disease?

(c) What assumptions are being made in your approach to this problem, and to what extent do you think they are realistic?

Case Study

Credit scoring

You work for a large business consultancy which offers, among other services, quick creditworthiness checks for British companies. The major indicators of potential financial difficulty within the next year have been established on the basis of a large sample of evidence as:

(a) consistent late payment of invoices
(b) one or more adverse accounting ratios in the past year
(c) more than five adverse County Court judgments in the past year
(d) adverse economic conditions in the relevant sector

If two or more of these indicators are present, the company is classed as 'medium risk'; if three or four are present, the classification is 'high risk'; in all other cases, the company is classified as 'low risk'.

The probabilities associated with the four indicators are estimated for the entire population of businesses as follows:

$$p(a) = 0.2$$
$$p(b) = 0.1$$
$$p(c) = 0.05$$
$$p(d) = 0.3.$$

These probabilities are regarded as independent. Calculate the probability, for a randomly chosen company, that it will be classed as 'medium risk'; do the same for 'high risk'. What 'health warnings' would you wish to add to your answers?

Further reading

For further reading on the topic of probability and decision making, the following book may be useful:

Goodwin, P. and Wright, G. (2009), *Decision Analysis for Management Judgment*, 4th edn, Wiley.

Chapter 7

PATTERNS OF PROBABILITY:
SOME DISTRIBUTIONS

Chapter prerequisites

Before starting work on this chapter make sure you are happy with:

1 the definitions of probability and the rules for combining elementary probabilities (see Chapter 6, p. 149);

2 the ideas of frequency distributions and histograms (see Chapter 3, p. 77);

3 the definition and meaning of mean and standard deviation (see Chapter 4, pp. 99 and 109);

4 the conversion of decimals to percentages and vice versa (see Chapter 1, pp. 15–16).

Learning outcomes

By the end of your work on this chapter you should be able to:

1 recognise problems that can be modelled by the binomial, Poisson and normal distributions;

2 solve such problems with the use of the appropriate tables;

3 recognise when the use of these distributions involves approximations in the original problem;

4 outline the connections between these three distributions.

Quantitative methods in practice

The *Risks Digest*, subtitled 'Forum on Risks to the Public in Computers and Related Systems', is an electronic journal published by the Association for Computing Machinery's Committee on Computers and Public Policy (you can find its website at **http://catless.ncl.ac.uk/Risks/**). A sample from the contents list of the October 2010 editions will give you an idea of the flavour of the journal:

- Aptly-Named HMS Astute Nuclear Submarine Runs Aground
- Washington D.C. Internet voting experiment risks
- Cross-site scripting bug leads to massive Twitter worm attacks
- Facebook outage blamed on handling of error condition

In other words, tales of computer disasters. Actually, when you consider the extent to which every aspect of our lives today depends on computer-based systems, the proportion of failures is remarkably small – but of course, the consequences can be enormously inconvenient or even disastrous when a system does fail.

After our discussion in the previous chapter, you may find yourself wondering how the risks of such failures are assessed. Given the complexity of the systems involved, the 'first principles' approach adopted in Chapter 6 is clearly not a realistic option – when a computer program may contain thousands of lines of code, and may have been written by a team involving many people, we can hardly ask 'how many ways might an error occur?'! And yet it is essential to be able to assess the chances that various kinds of system failure may occur.

In this situation, rather than working 'from scratch', we generally resort to using well-established patterns of probability which can be shown to model the problem effectively. These patterns have a theoretical basis; they have been studied and tabulated; and their behaviour is well understood. The technical name for these models is probability distributions (for reasons that we will explore later). Dozens of theoretical distributions exist; in this chapter we will look at three of the most important.

The quality manager's problem

Bennetts is a small firm which manufactures 'wholefood' cakes and confectionery. Originally something of a 'cottage industry', started in the premises behind a wholefood retail store by the proprietor, the business has expanded rapidly in line with the entire wholefood business, and now employs some 30 people manufacturing around two dozen product lines and distributing to wholefood and healthfood stores over quite a large area.

When the business was started, the control of the quality of the product presented no problems, as output was so small that every item could be individually checked. With expansion, however, it has been increasingly difficult to maintain this standard of checking, particularly since some automatic packing machinery has been purchased. Moreover, the requirements of trading standards in relation to weights and measures need to be considered. One of the staff has therefore been designated – along with his several other job functions – 'Quality Manager', and has been given overall responsibility for ensuring that products generally come up to scratch, that the packing machines are not producing large numbers of underweight packs, and so on.

We will concentrate on just three of the problems he has encountered in his new role. First, there is the Crunchy Flapjack situation: these rather fragile biscuits are packed by machine in boxes of half a dozen; in the interests of customer goodwill, Bennetts will replace any box in which more than half of the biscuits are broken. The quality manager has monitored the machine and found that it tends to break, on average, 1 biscuit in every 20. So what sort of proportion of returned boxes is Bennetts likely to have to deal with? He is assuming, of course, that the biscuits are so well packed that once they get inside the box, no more will be broken – in other words, all breakages can be ascribed to the packing machine.

The second problem concerns the Natural Molasses Coated Toffee Apples. These are supplied to retailers packed in boxes, but as the boxes are filled by weight, and of course the weight of individual apples varies, there is no knowing exactly how many are in a given box (though it is a pretty large number – around 144). Inevitably, now that the apples are produced in large numbers, the occasional one is not properly dipped in the toffee. One important customer has suggested that, if as the apples are being unpacked in his shop there appear to be an exceptionally large number with faulty toffee coatings, he should have the option of returning the whole box for replacement. While Bennetts agrees to this in principle, the quality manager would like to know just what should be agreed on as 'an exceptionally large number'. He knows that the average number of faulty apples per box is 6, and he would like to fix the agreement in such a way that he will only need to replace one box in 100.

Finally, the machine that fills bags of Carrot Candy has been causing problems. The nominal weight of these bags is 500 g, but of course in practice there is a certain variation in the exact weights produced by the machine. The current procedure is to set the machine to an average weight slightly higher than 500 g – at present 510 g – and then check-weigh the bags and refill by hand any which are underweight. However, this is wasting a great deal of time as it turns out that about 20 per cent of all the bags have to be manually refilled. So the quality manager would like to know what setting he should use for the average weight on the packing machine if he wants to cut this proportion down to 5 per cent.

You will not be surprised to learn that all three of these problems are connected with probability. The manager wants to know, for example, what is the probability that a box of Crunchy Flapjacks will contain more than three broken out of six; he wants to know what the probability is of various numbers of faulty toffee apples per box, so that he can make an informed decision about the agreed number for an automatic replacement of the consignment; and if he knew the probability, for a given setting of the packing machine, that a bag of Carrot Candy weighing less than 500 g will be produced, then he could adjust the setting to give the required proportion of underweight bags.

But, like the computer problems mentioned in the introduction to this chapter, these are not the sort of probability questions with which we have dealt in Chapter 6. The first one *could* be dealt with 'from scratch', as it were, since we know the probability of a single biscuit being broken, and want to find the probability that more than three biscuits out of six will be broken. Even this, however, would be very tedious, since we would have to work out all the different ways in which four biscuits out of six might be broken (there are in fact 15 of them!), or five out of the six might be broken, or all six might be broken

– rather a daunting task. And when it comes to the remaining two problems the methods we have used so far fail completely.

However, what these three problems have in common is that each belongs to a well-established *pattern* of problem – patterns that recur so often and in so many different situations that to save our having to develop the theory for such a problem every time it is encountered, the required probabilities have been calculated once for all, and provided in the form of tables. Thus all that you, the user of the established theory, need to be able to do is, first, to recognise *which* of the established patterns your problem conforms to – or can be made to conform to, since sometimes a bit of approximation is needed – and second to make use of the appropriate set of tables in the context of your problem to obtain the probability you need.

These standard patterns of probability are called *probability distributions*, which may ring a bell in your mind; we have already come across that word 'distribution', though in a different context, in Chapter 4. There we were discussing frequency distributions; is this one of those confusing cases where the same word is used to mean different things in two different contexts?

There is actually a very close link between the idea of a probability distribution, which will form the main topic of this chapter, and the familiar frequency distribution; but in order to establish this link, we will have to abandon for a moment the *theoretical* probability distributions – the standard patterns of probability which we have just been talking about – and take a look at a more practical example.

The idea of a probability distribution

We will return, for this section, to the frequency distribution which became very familiar in Chapter 4 – the wage distribution of the Grimchester workers, which for convenience is repeated here:

Weekly take-home pay (£)	No. of Grimchester workers
300 but under 310	3
310 but under 320	7
320 but under 330	33
330 but under 340	26
340 but under 350	24
350 but under 360	20
360 but under 370	18
370 but under 380	15
380 but under 400	4

Suppose we now ask, not how many of the workers in this sample earn between £300 and £310 per week, but what is the *probability* of a Grimchester worker earning between £300 and £310 per week? Then, assuming this sample of workers is representative, we can easily calculate the required probability using the familiar definition:

$$\frac{\text{number of workers in the £300–£310 bracket}}{\text{total number of workers in the sample}} = 3/150 = 0.02.$$

In the same way we could convert all the other frequencies to probabilities simply by dividing by 150, and so convert our frequency distribution into a probability distribution – a table which tells us how the probabilities are distributed between the various wage-groups:

Weekly take-home pay (£)	Probability
300 but under 310	0.02
310 but under 320	0.047
320 but under 330	0.22
330 but under 340	0.173
340 but under 350	0.16
350 but under 360	0.133
360 but under 370	0.12
370 but under 380	0.1
380 but under 400	0.027

This is an example of an *experimental* probability distribution, since it was obtained by actually taking a sample of workers and noting their wages. Many of the features with which we are familiar in the frequency distribution carry over into the probability distribution. It will, for instance, have a mean and a standard deviation, which are identical to those we calculated in Chapter 4 (can you see why?). Just as the frequencies in the original distribution added up to 150, the total number of workers in the sample, so the probabilities in the new distribution add up to 1; between them they cover all the possible wages for the sample.

We can also convert the diagram that represented the frequency distribution – the histogram – into one which represents the probability distribution. You can see this in Figure 7.1 – apart from the vertical scale, the diagram is identical to Figure 4.1(a). But whereas in the ordinary histogram the area of each block represented the frequency of

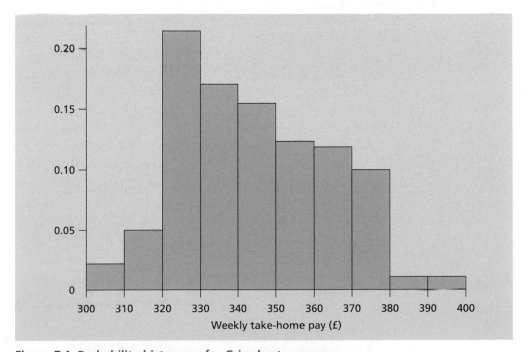

Figure 7.1 Probability histogram for Grimchester wages

the corresponding class, in what we might call the probability histogram the area of the blocks represents the probability that a value falls in the corresponding class. It follows from this that the overall area under the probability histogram must add up to 1, the sum of the probabilities. This is a point we shall be returning to later.

Although this experimental probability distribution serves quite well as an introduction to the idea of a probability distribution, it is not very useful in terms of working out probabilities, since it applies only to the particular sample of 150 workers included in the survey (although if the survey was well designed it presumably has some degree of applicability to the population from which the sample was taken). But far more useful in general terms are the *theoretical* probability distributions which relate to the kind of experimental distribution we have just looked at rather as the *a priori* definition of probability relates to the experimental definition. They are distributions worked out on general, theoretical grounds, which retain many of the features we have observed in the experimental distribution, but which are applicable to a much wider class of problems.

The binomial distribution

Recognising the pattern

The first of the quality manager's problems was, you will recall, concerned with the fragile Crunchy Flapjacks. He has determined that the packing machine breaks, on average, 1 biscuit in 20 – which is another way of saying that the probability of a biscuit being broken is one-twentieth or 0.05. What he needs to know is the proportion of boxes which will contain more than three broken biscuits; this is, again, equivalent to knowing the probability that a box of six biscuits will contain more than three broken.

Let us try to summarise the things we know about this problem. The most obvious, perhaps, is that we are concerned with a situation in which there are only a finite, discrete number of possibilities: there could be 0, 1, 2 . . . up to 6 broken biscuits in a box, but it does not make any sense to think of the probability that there are, say two-and-a-half broken ones! Furthermore, we are in an either/or situation: either a biscuit is broken or it isn't – there is no such thing as a partly broken biscuit. The remaining information with which we are supplied is: first the number of biscuits in a box, which is known and fixed; and second the probability of an individual biscuit being broken by the machine, which presumably if the machine is warmed up and running steadily will again be fixed.

The facts about this problem which we have just summarised make it a typical example of a *binomial* probability situation, which can be tackled with the aid of the binomial distribution. The name *binomial* gives a clue as to one major feature of this distribution: it applies in cases where there are just two possible outcomes to a process – here, the individual biscuit is broken or it isn't. We could summarise the requirements for a problem to fit this binomial pattern as follows:

> Conditions for a binomial problem:
> 1 either/or situation;
> 2 number of trials (usually called n) is known and fixed;
> 3 probability of success on each trial (usually called p) is known and fixed.

We are using the terms 'trials' and 'success' fairly loosely here, to mean respectively the number of times a thing might have a chance of occurring, and the times when it actually *does* occur. This means that, in the problem of the biscuits, a 'success' consists of a biscuit being broken by the machine!

Before looking at the actual probabilities obtained in binomial situations, it is a good idea to practise recognising a binomial problem when you see one. We will look at three further examples.

Problem 1

Five coins are tossed simultaneously; what is the chance of obtaining three heads?

The either/or requirement is clearly met here, since each coin must come down showing either heads or tails. The number of 'trials' is the number of coins being tossed, so $n = 5$; and if the coins are all fair ones, then the probability of 'success' (i.e. getting a head) each time is 0.5. All the requirements for a binomial problem are thus present.

Problem 2

By looking up weather records for the past ten years I have discovered that the proportion of wet days in the current month of the year has been 60 per cent. What is the probability that next week there will be five or more wet days?

If a day is defined as wet (it rains sometime during the day) or dry (it doesn't), then we have our either/or situation. We can use the 60 per cent figure to give an approximate value of 0.6 for p, the probability of 'success' (a wet day), but there is a certain amount of approximation here in assuming that p is fixed; wet days, corresponding to periods of atmospheric low pressure, tend to come in twos and threes, so you might argue that if it rained today the probability of rain tomorrow is higher than if it had been dry today. However, we will not be making too serious an error if we treat p as having a fixed value of 0.6. Of course, n will be 7, the number of days in the week.

Problem 3

An unscrupulous shopkeeper has packed lightbulbs into crates of 144 and is selling them at a bargain price; what his customers do not know is that in each box, 24 are in fact faulty bulbs which will not work. A customer insists on trying a sample of six bulbs before she buys; what is the probability that they will all work?

Here the either/or corresponds to the bulbs working/not working, and n is 6, the number being tried. As for p, it is clearly 24/144 – or is it? When the first bulb is taken, there are altogether 24 ways of picking a dud bulb out of 144 bulbs. But presumably the customer will not replace the first bulb before taking a second one, so that on her second choice the chance of getting a dud is either 23/143 – if the first was a dud – or 24/143 if the first was working. So the requirement that p is known *and fixed* appears to break down again. However, the difference between 24/144, which as a decimal is 0.167, and 23/143 (0.161) or 24/143 (0.168), is so small that in practice we would not be making too sweeping an approximation if we took $p = 24/144$ and used the binomial distribution.

This is only the case, however, because the 'population' of bulbs from which we are sampling is relatively large (144). If the whole case of bulbs contained only, say, 30 bulbs, then the differences between the values of p as successive bulbs were taken would be a good deal greater, as you can easily verify, and the use of the binomial distribution would hardly be justified; see also Exercise 5, Chapter 6.

From this it should be clear that frequently, in 'squeezing' our practical problem slightly to fit the binomial pattern, we are using the theoretical distribution as a reasonably good but easier-to-handle imitation of the real-life situation. We are in fact using the binomial to *model* the practical problem, a process with which you will become increasingly familiar as you read later sections of this book.

Using the tables

As mentioned earlier, we could in principle solve problems of the binomial pattern by means of the basic rules for combining probabilities introduced in Chapter 6. To see how this can be done, and also how much simpler the process is with the aid of the tables of the distribution, let us return to the first of the problems examined above. If five coins are tossed simultaneously, what is the probability of obtaining three heads? We can, somewhat laboriously, write down all the different ways in which three heads out of five coins might occur:

HHHTT	HHTHT	HHTTH	HTHHT	HTHTH
HTTHH	THHHT	THHTH	THTHH	TTHHH

In other words, there are ten different ways in which the case we are interested in might arise. The probability of any one of these will be 1/32; for example, $p(\text{HHHTT}) = \frac{1}{2} \times \frac{1}{2} \times \frac{1}{2} \times \frac{1}{2} \times \frac{1}{2}$, and so on. So the probability we are looking for will be $10 \times 1/32$ or 10/32, which as a decimal is 0.3125.

In fact, we could say that in general for a binomial problem, the chance of getting r successes out of n trials will be given by the following formula:

> $p(r$ successes in n trials$) = $
> probability of r successes × probability of the remaining $(n - r)$ failures × the number of ways in which r successes out of n trials can happen.

However, as you can see, the process of working out binomial probabilities in this way, particularly the business of determining the number of different ways in which a certain number of successes can occur, is quite complicated, even though there are short-cut methods which can help. We will therefore rely for our solution of binomial problems on the tables in Appendix 3.

You will find the tables headed '*Cumulative* binomial probabilities' – in other words, they give the probability of getting r *or more* successes out of n trials in a binomial situation. The values of n – from 1 to 10 – correspond to the main blocks of the table, while the values of p – from 0.05 to 0.5 – are to be found at the heads of the columns. Where there are blanks in the table, for instance for $n = 5$ with $r = 4$ and $p = 0.05$, this simply means that the probability is so small that it would not show up in these tables (which are given only to four decimal places).

To see how the tables are to be used, let us first deal with the coin-tossing problem we have just been looking at 'by hand'. We had $n = 5$ and $p = 0.5$, and we were interested in the chance of getting three heads. Now if we look in the block $n = 5$ of the tables, under the column $p = 0.5$ and in the row $r = 3$, what we find – namely 0.5000 – is the probability of getting three or more heads. This, of course, is not exactly what we want. However, the figure opposite $r = 4$ – namely 0.1874 – is the probability of getting four or more heads. Now 'four or more' heads out of five means four heads or five heads, whereas 'three or more' means three or four or five. So the difference between these two figures must give the probability of getting *exactly* three heads.

Thus p(three heads in five throws) $= 0.5000 - 0.1874 = 0.3126$, just as we calculated at the beginning of this section.

You may wonder *why* the tables are arranged in this way, which means we have to perform subtraction sums to find the probability of getting an exact number of successes. But in practical situations it is often more useful to answer such questions as 'What's the chance of more than three eggs being smashed?' or 'What's the probability this sales representative will make at least six sales?', so on balance, I think this cumulative method of presenting the tables is preferable.

Another example

Let us now solve problem 2 posed on p. 000, where the probability of rain on a particular day is 60 per cent, giving $p = 0.6$, and we wish to know the probability of five or more wet days next week, so $n = 7$. It is easy enough to find the block of tables headed $n = 7$, but where is $p = 0.6$? The values of p at the heads of the columns only go as far as $p = 0.5$ so how are we to deal with the remaining values between 0.5 and 1? The answer is by turning the problem on its head and asking not what the probability is of five or more wet days if p(wet day) $= 0.6$, but rather what the probability is of two *or fewer* dry days if p(dry day) $= 0.4$ – which of course amounts to exactly the same thing. Because of the either/or nature of binomial problems, a problem involving a value of p greater than 0.5 can always be re-expressed in terms of the *opposite* situation, for which p is less than 0.5. That is why the tables need only go as far as $p = 0.5$.

To solve this problem, then, we want p(2 or less dry days out of 7) with p(dry day) $= 0.4$; we are still not quite home, however, for the tables are arranged to give the probability of r or more events, not r or less. But here the fact that probabilities add up to 1 comes to our rescue:

$$p(2 \text{ or less dry days}) + p(3 \text{ or more dry days}) = 1$$

because between them the two situations cover all possibilities, so we have

$$p(2 \text{ or less dry days}) = 1 - p(3 \text{ or more dry days}).$$

If we look in the $n = 7$ block of the tables, under $p = 0.4$ and opposite $r = 3$, what we find is the probability of three or more dry days, which turns out to be 0.5800. So p(2 or less dry days) $= 1 - 0.5800 = 0.4200$, which is therefore also the chance of five or more wet days in the week.

You will realise by now that one often has to do a certain amount of juggling with a problem before it appears in the right form for use with the tables. Here again, as with the elementary probability problems in Chapter 6, I am afraid the English language is very much to blame. It is worth spending a little time looking at the various ways in which questions of this kind can be posed, and how they relate to each other. For this purpose it is useful to make use once more of the 'number line' which we encountered in Chapter 1 and which is repeated below:

The probabilities given directly by the tables are, as we have seen, of the 'or more' variety – for example, five or more wet days out of seven. The *opposite* of this can be found from the number line by drawing a division which cuts off the '5 or more' cases from the rest, as shown; then it is clear that the remaining possibilities are '4 or less'. (The precise position of the division does not matter since we are dealing with a discrete situation where values between 4 and 5 cannot occur.) But there are other ways of expressing these two fundamental cases: '5 or more' is the same as 'more than 4', or 'not less than 5', or 'at least 5', while '4 or less' can also be stated as 'less than 5', 'not more than 4' and 'at most 4'. So you really need your wits about you in untangling this sort of problem, and the use of the number line, though it may seem a bit infantile, can be a great help. You can always write it on a scrap of paper and throw it away afterwards, so no one need know you resorted to such basic methods!

Some general features of the tables

There are two other points about the binomial tables worth noting. First, you have probably observed that the figures in the $r = 0$ row for every block of the tables are all 1.0000. This is not surprising, if you recall that these figures represent the probability of 0 or more successes out of n; there are *bound* to be 0 or more successes, so this probability corresponds to a certainty, whatever the value of n. Hence it is always equal to 1.

The second fact is that the set of tables provided in Appendix 3 is very limited. There are larger sets of published tables, but most people now would make use of Excel or a similar computer-based resource to give them the necessary values; we will look at how this works later in the chapter. Meanwhile, here are two more examples to help familiarise you with the use of the tables.

Example 1

Information is transmitted electronically in the form of *bits*. Suppose that a message consisting of eight bits is to be transmitted, and that the chance of any one bit being transmitted erroneously is 0.1. What is the chance that the entire message is transmitted correctly?

Here we have $n = 8$, $p(\text{error}) = 0.1$, and we want to find $p(\text{exactly 0 errors})$. This will be

$$p(0 \text{ or more errors}) - (1 \text{ or more errors}) = 1 - 0.5695$$
$$= 0.4305,$$

that is about a 43 per cent chance, which is not very satisfactory. Of course, in practice the chance of an error in one bit would be very much smaller – perhaps of the order of 10^{-10} or 0.000 000 000 1!

We have assumed here that the errors occur randomly, which is an important assumption not always met in practice. For example, if the information were being transmitted over a telephone line which was subject during the transmission to a burst of electronic 'noise', then it is likely that several consecutive bits would be corrupted; in this case, the binomial model would not apply.

Example 2

A certain type of orthopaedic surgery works successfully for about 75 per cent of patients with a particular condition. What is the probability that in a randomly selected group of nine patients with the condition who have this type of surgery, it is successful in at least seven cases?

Here $n = 9$ and p(success) = 0.75. However, because this is greater than 0.5 it does not appear among the tabulated p-values, so we need to turn the problem round and express it in terms of the number of failures, noting that p(failure) = 0.25.

We are interested in at least seven successes – that is 7, 8 or 9 successes, which is the same as 2, 1 or 0 failures. Thus in terms of failures we want p(2 or less). But the tables are not arranged to give probabilities of this kind – instead we need to note that p(2 or less failures) = $1 - p$(3 or more failures). Now the tables show that p(3 or more) with $n = 9$ and $p = 0.25$ is 0.3993. So finally we can say

$$p\text{(at least 7 successes)} = p\text{(2 or less failures)}$$
$$= 1 - p\text{(3 or more failures)}$$
$$= 1 - 0.3993 = 0.6007 \text{ or about 60 per cent.}$$

This may seem a long and convoluted process; it will be easier to follow if you try to think your way through it step by step, rather than attempting to turn it into some system of 'rules'. It is always safer to *understand* what you are doing!

We will now conclude our use of the binomial tables by returning to the quality manager's problem with the Crunchy Flapjacks: given $n = 6$ and $p = 0.05$, what is the probability of more than three broken biscuits in a box? Now p(more than 3) = p(4 or more), so we should be looking up the block $n = 6$, the column $p = 0.05$ and the row $r = 4$; the probability then turns out to be 0.0001 within the accuracy of the tables, so apparently the proportion of replacements demanded will be only 1 in 10 000. This is not too surprising if you ask what would be the average number of broken biscuits you would expect to find in a box; if the proportion of broken ones is 1 in 20, and boxes contain six, then the average proportion broken per box will be one-twentieth of six, which is 0.3. So the chance of getting a box with more than three broken biscuits will indeed be very small.

Quick check questions

1 One in three shops in a particular area of a city is unoccupied at any given time. You need to find the probability that in a row of ten shops, only one is unoccupied. Identify n and p assuming that you want to solve this problem using the binomial distribution. Do you think the distribution is a good model in this case?

2 In a group of 12 people, saying 'at least 3 are female' is the same as saying (a) 'at least 9 are male'; (b) 'no more than 9 are male'; (c) 'less than 9 are male'?

3 Work out from first principles (i.e. without using the tables) the probability that two students in a randomly selected group of three at Stratford University are Business Studies students, if the proportion of Business Studies students in the (large) student population of the university is 20 per cent.

Answers:
1 $n = 10$, $p = 1/3$ or 0.33. The distribution probably isn't a very good model in this case, because it's likely that groups of unoccupied shops might occur together – thus the distribution is not random.
2 The correct answer is (b) – if you can't see why this is, try using the number line to display the situation.
3 The probability is $0.2 \times 0.2 \times 0.8 \times 3 = 0.096$ – there are three different ways in which the situation could arise, since it could be any one of the three students who is the non-Business Studies student.

The Poisson distribution

Recognising the pattern

If you were approaching the second of the quality manager's problems from scratch, you might well, armed with your new knowledge of the binomial distribution, try to fit it into that pattern. Remember that the difficulty with the toffee apples was that small number with faulty toffee coating – an average of three per box. The number of apples in a box was not known exactly, since they are packed by weight, but it is fairly large.

We certainly have the binomial-type either/or situation here: either an apple has a faulty coating or it hasn't. But we look in vain for the other two requirements, *n* and *p*: we do not know *n*, as we have just observed; nor do we know what the probability of an individual apple being faulty may be. All we have is the average or *mean* number of faulty apples per box. What we can say, however, is that the faulty ones are pretty unusual – there are only six of them in a box containing round about 144 – so the value of *p*, whatever it may be, must be quite small.

The information which we have here characterises a *Poisson* problem, for which probabilities are given by the Poisson distribution (called after its French discoverer). These characteristics may be summarised as follows:

> For a Poisson problem we require
>
> 1 either/or situation;
> 2 mean number of successes per unit, *m*, known and fixed;
> 3 *p*, chance of success, unknown but small (the event is 'unusual').

As with the binomial problems, we will begin our study of Poisson problems by learning to recognise this pattern in particular cases.

Problem 1

Attendance records at a large factory show that on average there are seven absentees on any day. What is the probability that on a certain day there will be more than eight people absent?

Here the either/or situation is provided by absent/present. The mean to be used is clearly seven, and if the factory is large and only seven people per day on average are absent, the chance of an individual being absent is clearly small. The only assumption we need to make is that the average number of absences is fixed, in other words it does not vary with, for instance, the day of the week or the time of year. This might lead to slight inaccuracies if we are actually interested in a day in February which falls in the middle of a flu epidemic, or the day after a public holiday when some workers may decide unofficially to extend their time off.

Problem 2

An automated production line breaks down on average once in every two hours. A certain special production run requires uninterrupted running of the line for eight hours. What is the probability that this can be achieved?

Our two-way outcome here is breakdown/no breakdown, but when we come to identify the mean we have to be a bit careful about the relevant unit over which to average. As stated in the problem, there is a breakdown every two hours; that is, an average of 0.5 breakdowns per hour. But we are actually interested in the numbers of breakdowns over an *eight*-hour period, so the mean relevant to this period will be *four* breakdowns. At this rate, the chance of the machine breaking down at any particular point in time is pretty small, so we have the 'unusual event' requirement.

Problem 3

It is known that an automatic packing machine produces, on average, 1 in 100 bags that is underweight. What is the probability that a case of 500 bags filled by the machine will contain fewer than 3 underweight?

Although the magic word 'average' occurs in this problem, it is, strictly speaking, a binomial problem. We have the bags classified as either underweight or not; we know *n*, which is the 500 bags per box; and *p*, the probability that a bag is underweight, is 1/100 or 0.01. However, we certainly cannot use the tables in Appendix 3 to solve the problem since they do not go anywhere near $n = 500$.

What we *can* do, though, is to make use of the Poisson distribution as an approximation to the binomial. As $p = 0.01$ is certainly small, the 'unusual event' requirement is satisfied, and the mean number of underweight bags per crate is easily calculated as 5 (1 in 100 is underweight, and there are 500 in the crate). So we have the necessary conditions for using the Poisson distribution.

You may say 'Well, in that case where does the approximation come in?' It arises from the fact that, in a binomial problem, there is an *upper limit* to the number of successes that can occur; there is no way we could have 501 underweight boxes if the crate only contains 500. But strictly speaking, in a Poisson situation, as we do not know *n* there is *no* upper limit to the number of successes which might occur. It is pretty unlikely, in problem 2, that the machine would break down 20 times, or even 100 times, over the eight-hour period; nevertheless, it just *might* happen and the Poisson distribution takes account of this.

However, in a case like the present one, where *n* is very big and *p* is very small, these probabilities at the 'top end' of the range of possibilities are going to be so tiny that the difference between the two distributions, over the range of practical interest, is not important.

From what has been said it will be clear that in many cases, as with the binomial problems, we are using the Poisson pattern as a model, which *may* fit our problem exactly, or may involve a certain amount of approximation.

Using the tables

Tables of the probabilities which apply to problems of the Poisson pattern are given in Appendix 4. In many respects these resemble the binomial tables: they are cumulative, giving the probability of *r or more* successes; the probabilities are quoted to four decimal places, so that a blank does not indicate that something is impossible, merely that the chance of its occurrence is too small to show up in the tables; and all the entries for $r = 0$ are 1.0000, since '0 or more successes' is an event that is bound to occur. The tables are, however, simpler in that, as the Poisson pattern only requires the knowledge of a single quantity m, they are arranged throughout in columns corresponding to the various values of m.

You can see, too, how the point made above about the absence of an upper limit to the number of successes shows up in the tables. The column of the table with $m = 2.0$, for instance, stops at $r = 9$ only because that is where the probabilities cease to show up in four-figure tables. There is no reason why, given more accurate tables, the possibility of $r = 10$ or higher values should not be considered.

So much for the theoretical aspects of the tables; we can now make use of them to solve the problems posed in the preceding section. Let us start with problem 1 where we had $m = 7$, and wished to know p(more than 8 people absent). Before the tables can be used, 'more than 8' has to be rephrased as '9 or more'; then all we need do is look in the column $m = 7$ and the row $r = 9$ to obtain a probability of 0.2709.

For problem 2, we found that the relevant mean, the number of breakdowns per eight-hour period, was equal to 4, and we were interested in the chance of obtaining such a period with no breakdowns. We can find this in a manner similar to the one we used on p. 174 with reference to the binomial tables:

$$p(\text{no breakdowns}) = p(0 \text{ or more breakdowns}) - p(1 \text{ or more})$$
$$= 1.000 - 0.9817, \text{ looking under } m = 4$$
$$= 0.0183.$$

Finally, problem 3 had $m = 5$, and we need the chance of fewer than three underweight bags: p(less than 3 underweight) + p(3 or more underweight) = 1, so p(less than 3 underweight) = $1 - p$(3 or more underweight). Looking in the tables under $m = 5$ and $r = 3$ we find the figure 0.8753, so

$$p(\text{less than 3 underweight}) = 1 - 0.8753 = 0.1247.$$

Having practised the use of the tables with these examples you will realise that many of the points raised in connection with the binomial tables – particularly the way in which the wording of a question may need adjustment to the precise form given in the tables – apply equally well here.

Let us now return to the quality manager's second problem which concerned the faulty toffee apples. These were averaging out at six per box – in other words $m = 6$. But he does not want to know a probability; rather he has *decided* what probability he is interested in – the 1-in-a-100 replacement rate which he is prepared to accept – and needs to know what number of faulty apples that probability corresponds to. That is, he wishes to find the value of r, with an m of 6, such that the probability of r or more 'successes' (i.e. faulty apples) is 1/100 or 0.01.

We are, in effect, using the tables 'backwards' here; we look under $m = 6$ and run down the column of probabilities until we meet 0.01. Actually that precise value does not occur; the probability of 12 or more 'successes' is 0.0201, while that of 13 or more is 0.0088. Thus if the quality manager agrees to replace the entire box if 13 or more badly coated apples are encountered, he can be confident that he will have to do this with a probability of only 0.0088, which represents fewer than 1 box in 100.

As with problems 1 and 3 above, strictly speaking the Poisson is only an approximation here, since there is an upper limit to the possible number of 'successes'. However, since this limit is large, the approximation will be good.

Quick check questions

1 Name two differences between a problem which could be modelled by the binomial distribution and one which would require the Poisson distribution to be used.

2 The mean number of customers per week at a travel agent who book Business Class flights is 15. The agent is open five days per week. What value of *m* would you use to find the probability that on a particular day five passengers book Business Class? What would you be assuming in using the Poisson model here?

3 In the tables of Appendix 4, when $m = 2$, what numbers of occurrences have a probability of less than 20 per cent?

Answers:

1 For the Poisson, we don't know *n* and *p* separately, and there is no upper limit to the number of possible 'successes'.

2 We should use $m = 3$; 15 Business Class travellers over a five-day week averages to 3 per day. It might, however, be the case that Business Class travellers are more likely to book on certain days of the week, in which case the distribution is not random and the Poisson might not be a good model.

3 Four or more occurrences (because the probability falls below 0.2000 between $r = 3$ and $r = 4$).

The normal distribution

Spotting the pattern

When we turn from the two distributions we have looked at so far in this chapter to consider the quality manager's last problem concerning the weight of bags of Carrot Candy, one major difference should strike you immediately. Whereas with both binomial and Poisson problems we were talking about either/or situations where the number of times a thing occurred could be *counted*, in the Carrot Candy problem we are talking about something – weight – which is not being counted but *measured*. The distinction is more or less the same as the one made in Chapter 2 between discrete and continuous variables, and so the binomial and Poisson distributions are referred to as *discrete* probability distributions. What we need to deal with the Carrot Candy problem is a *continuous* probability distribution – one that will tell us (given of course a certain amount of data) what the probability is that a continuous variable, such as the weight of a bag of Carrot Candy, will take certain values.

We approached the idea of a probability distribution in the section 'The idea of a probability distribution', p. 170, by way of frequency distributions, so let us try to shed some light on the current problem by doing the same thing. If the quality manager were to take a sample of 100 bags filled by an automatic machine (assume it is a different one from the one causing his problems), he might get the following frequency table:

Weight of bag (g)	No. of bags
503 but under 505	2
505 but under 507	12
507 but under 509	21
509 but under 511	29
511 but under 513	23
513 but under 515	11
515 but under 517	2

This could, of course, be turned into an experimental probability distribution by dividing all the frequencies by 100. The probability histogram for this distribution is shown in Figure 7.2(a). It shows a certain degree of symmetry, as we might expect, the machine apparently producing roughly equal proportions of bags above and below the average weight. It is also clear that weights a very long way from the centre of the distribution occur much less often than those close to the central value.

This histogram, however, is not likely to be very representative of the entire output of the machine since it applies only to one particular sample of 100 bags. Were the sample to consist of 1000 rather than 100 bags, we could expect to find a good deal more regularity in the behaviour of the distribution, resulting in something like the histogram in Figure 7.2(b). You can see that as there is so much more data, it has been possible to subdivide it into classes with a width of only 0.5 g rather than the 2 g interval used in Figure 7.2(a). All together the histogram exhibits a much smoother appearance, though the feature of symmetry about a central peak value is still noticeable.

By now you should find it quite easy to imagine that, were we to take more and more bags in the sample and subdivide the intervals of the histogram with increasing precision, we would ultimately obtain a histogram with steps so small and so close together as to be almost indistinguishable from the smooth curve shown in Figure 7.3. This is what is known as the *normal distribution* curve, and it will become very familiar to you in the course of the next few chapters.

How the normal distribution works

Before proceeding to ask how the normal distribution can help us in calculating probabilities, we should take note of some of its important features. The symmetry which we noticed in the histograms is apparent also here; if the curve were folded down the centre the two halves would lie exactly on top of each other. The curve is often described as 'bell-shaped', expressing the fact that it drops on either side of a central peak. But it never actually touches the horizontal axis, though it gets closer and closer to it the further away from the peak we go. And here is where the element of 'modelling' comes in again – the normal distribution is a *theoretical* distribution, so we cannot expect that our real-life distributions will conform to it exactly. The weight distribution, for example, will have a lower limit; the samples of 100 and 1000 bags contained no bags weighing less than 500 g, and even if we admit the possibility that the machine may occasionally omit to fill a bag at all, thus producing an item with zero weight, it certainly cannot produce negative weights. Yet the theoretical distribution carries on, in principle, indefinitely to the left as well as to the right, so clearly it does not fit our real-life situation very well at these extremes. However, over the part that matters – the bit between about 500 and 520 g – it fits very

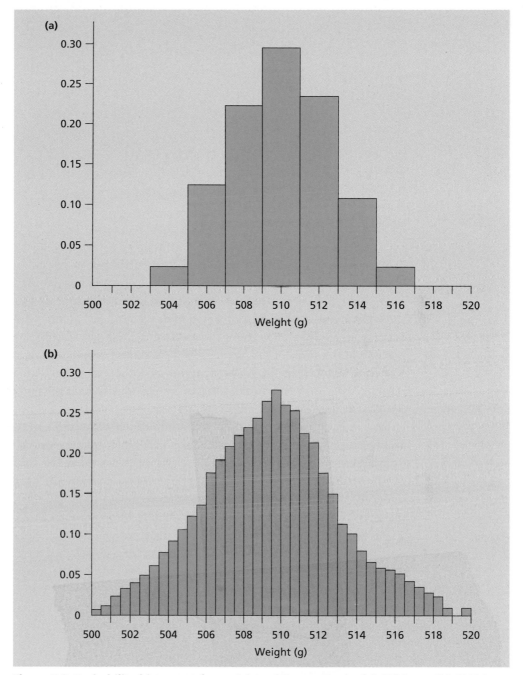

Figure 7.2 Probability histogram for weights of Carrot Candy: (a) 100 bags; (b) 1000 bags

well, and the part of the distribution in the region where it *does not* fit is so tiny that it is not very important. We will be returning later on to this question of how well a particular practical case fits the theoretical normal curve.

Two very important facts about the probability histogram which were noted in the section 'The idea of a probability distribution', p. 170, apply equally well to the smoothed-off histogram which gives the normal curve. First, the *area* occupied by the histogram represented probability; so it is for the areas under the normal curve. Second, the total area of the histogram was 1; similarly with the total area under the normal curve.

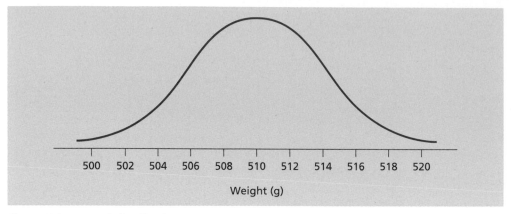

Figure 7.3 Normal distribution curve

We are happily talking about 'the' normal curve, but of course what we have got in Figure 7.3 is only one of an infinite number of possible normal curves, all basically the same shape, but varying in their position and amount of spread; several such curves are shown in Figure 7.4. So what information do we need in order to distinguish one normal curve from another? If we know the *mean* of the relevant distribution we will know the position of the 'peak' of the curve, while the standard deviation is the easiest way of characterising how spread out the distribution is. For the weight distribution in Figure 7.3 the mean is 510 g as shown, and the standard deviation, as you can check from the distribution for 100 bags, is about 2.5 g.

Now that we know how the normal distribution behaves and have the mean and standard deviation to describe our particular normal distribution, we can begin to ask questions about probabilities. Suppose, for example, that we want to know what proportion of these bags weighs more than 515 g; this will be given by the proportion of the area under the curve to the right of 515 g, as shown in Figure 7.5(a). (You are strongly recommended always to draw such a diagram when tackling normal distribution problems.)

But how are we to determine this area? True, we know that the total area is 1, but that does not help us to find exactly what fraction of the area falls to the right of 515. We could try plotting the curve accurately on graph paper and finding the area by counting squares, but apart from being very slow, that would require a knowledge of the equation of the curve, which is so unpleasant that I will not alarm you by writing it down. Anyway, such an answer would not be very accurate. So we resort to the expedient which has come to

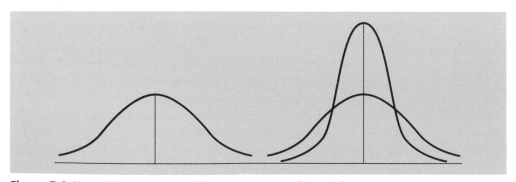

Figure 7.4 Normal curves with different means and spreads

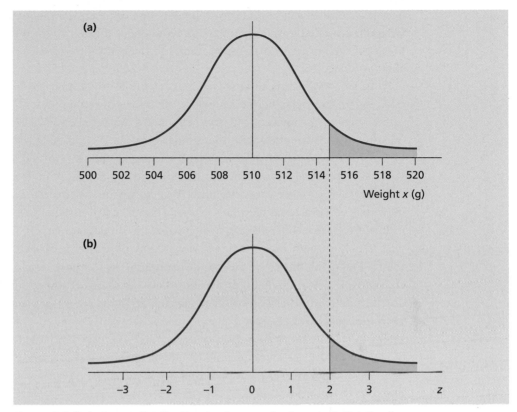

Figure 7.5 Relating a distribution to the standard normal distribution

our aid with the previous two distributions: we make use of a set of tables of the areas under the normal curve, which have already been computed accurately by someone else. All we need know, once again, is how to use them.

Using the tables

That insidious phrase '*the* normal curve' has slipped in again in the last paragraph, but we now know that there are any number of normal curves with different means and different standard deviations. This is rather a depressing thought: does it mean we need an infinite, or at least a very large, set of tables to cope with all the different combinations of mean and standard deviation which we might come across? Happily the answer is no. Since all these different normal curves are the same fundamental *shape*, tables are provided for just one such curve, called the *standard* normal distribution, and all other normal distributions are then related to that.

You will find a table of areas under the standard normal curve in Appendix 5. It really is the simplest normal distribution that one could have since its mean is 0, as shown in the sketch at the top of the tables, and its standard deviation is 1. The table, as its heading tells us, gives the areas in the 'tail' of the distribution – the bit to the right of a given value. The horizontal axis is called the *z*-axis, and *z* is often referred to as the *standard normal variable*. So, the tables work like this: to find the probability, say, that *z* is greater than 2 – perhaps more meaningfully interpreted as finding the proportion of the values in the standard distribution which are bigger than 2 – we simply look down the left-hand side of the tables until we find *z* = 2, and then read off the probability under the column headed 0.00. This tells us that the probability of a value greater than 2.00 is 0.022 75. Had we wanted a value greater than 2.05 we would have located 2.0 in the left-hand column first, and then proceeded across the tables to the column headed 0.05 to obtain a probability of 0.020 18.

This, you may say, is all very well, but how does this highly theoretical distribution, referring to nothing in particular, help us to answer questions about the weight distribution of bags with a mean of 510 g and a standard deviation of 2.5 g? How can we connect our practical distribution with the standard one in the tables? The clue is provided in Figure 7.5(a) and (b). Remember that the *shape* of the two normal distributions is the same; all that varies are their means and standard deviations. So the necessary connection will be provided if we can determine what points in the theoretical distribution – on the z-axis – correspond to what points in the practical distribution on the x-axis. For instance, to take a concrete case, what z-value lies directly under $x = 515$?

It is easy enough to see that $z = 0$ will coincide with $x = 510$, these being the peak values, that is the means, of the two distributions. As we move out from the means, it is the standard deviation that indicates how far from the mean the rest of the values in the distribution tend to be. By the time we reach $x = 515$, we are two standard deviations away from the mean of the weight distribution (the standard deviation was 2.5 g, remember). Thus $x = 515$ must correspond to a point on the z-axis two standard deviations away from the mean. But the standard deviation of this distribution is 1; so $x = 515$ will correspond to $z = 2$. In other words, z tells us *how many standard deviations away from the mean* the point we are interested in lies.

If you like formulae rather than words, we can translate this fact as follows: the distance from the mean, 510 g, to the value we are interested in, 515 g, is $515 - 510$; then z is the number of standard deviations in this distance, so

$$z = \frac{515 - 510}{2.5} = 2$$

as before. In fact for *any* point x in a distribution with a mean m and a standard deviation s, we can define the corresponding standard normal variable z thus:

$$z = \frac{x - m}{s}. \quad *$$

The process of calculating z from x is sometimes called *standardisation*.

Once we have made this transition from x to z, the rest is easy. We set out to find the proportion of the bags which have weight in excess of 515 g, represented by the area under the standard curve to the right of $z = 2$, which we have already looked up in the tables and found to be 0.022 75. Because five-figure decimals do not say much to most people, I prefer to convert this to a percentage and say that 2.275 per cent of all bags filled by this machine will weigh more than 515 g.

Using the normal distribution in practice

Setting up the machinery for using the normal tables has taken rather a long time, but really the process is quite simple: we sketched the normal distribution for our problem,

---

* You will also encounter this formula with the Greek letters μ and σ used in place of m and s in other textbooks and sets of statistical tables.

and identified on it the mean and the particular value we are interested in. Then we made the transition from our x-distribution to the standard z-distribution by using the fact that z is the number of standard deviations from the mean up to our x-value. Finally, we used the tables to tell us the required probability. When we apply this process to a few more sample problems you will see how quick it is. For simplicity we will stay with the weight distribution, mean 510 and standard deviation 2.5 g.

Problem 1

What percentage of the bags filled by the machine will weigh less than 507.5 g?

The area we require is shown in Figure 7.6(a); it is the shaded area beyond one standard deviation to the *left* of the mean, so that it corresponds, as the sketch at the top of Appendix 5 shows, to a *negative* value of z. (You should find the same thing if you use the formula for calculating z.) But there are no negative values of z given in the tables, and a minute's thought should suggest why not. The symmetry of the distribution means that if the areas at the left-hand end of the distribution, where z is negative, *were* tabulated, they would be exactly the same as those at the right-hand end, so the exercise would be a bit of a waste of time.

We can, then, find the area we are interested in, to the left of $z = -1$, by ignoring the fact that z is negative and looking up the area to the *right* of $z = +1$, which is 0.1587. So 15.87 per cent of bags weigh less than 507.5 g.

Problem 2

What is the probability that a bag filled by the machine weighs less than 512 g?

As you can see from Figure 7.6(b), the area we want here is not the right shape for looking up directly in the tables. What we *can* find directly, though, is the probability that a bag weighs *more* than 512 g. The z-value corresponding to $x = 512$ is

$$\frac{512 - 510}{2.5}$$

or 0.8, and the tables give the area to the right of 0.8 as 0.2119.

So p(bag weighs more than 512 g) = 0.2119. But of course p(bag weighs more than 512 g) + p(bag weighs less than 512 g) = 1, so p(bag weighs less than 512 g) = 1 − 0.2119 = 0.7881.

At this point you may feel a bit worried about the bags that weigh *exactly* 512 g, which seem to have got left out of our analysis. In fact the normal distribution cannot deal with the probability of obtaining a single exact value, as for instance $p(x = 512$ g). In terms of the diagram it is not too difficult to see why this is: the 'area' corresponding to a single value such as this is zero. In practical terms this can be interpreted by saying that, when there is an infinite range of possible weights for the bags, as there is with any continuous distribution, the chance of any one precise value occurring is so small as to be effectively zero; we might get a bag which we think weighs 512 g, but no doubt if we weighed it more accurately we would find it actually weighed 511.97 g, or 512.01 g. So whether we write p(bag weighs less than 512 g) or p(bag weighs less than or equal to 512 g) is really immaterial.

Problem 3

What percentage of the bags will weigh between 512 and 515 g?

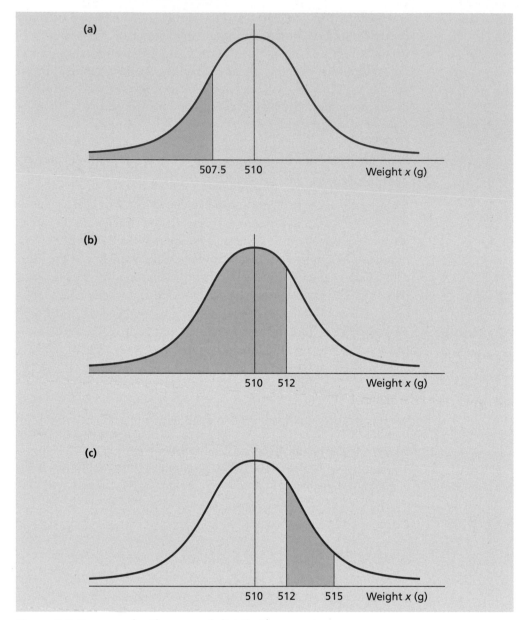

Figure 7.6 Areas under the normal distribution curve

Again, the area as illustrated in Figure 7.6(c) cannot be looked up directly. What we have to do in this case is express the required area as the difference of two areas which *can* be looked up: namely, the area to the right of 512 and that to the right of 515. We have just found, under 2, that the area to the right of 512 is 0.2119, and earlier in this section we determined the area to the right of 515 as 0.022 75. So p(bag weighs between 512 and 515 g) = 0.2119 − 0.022 75 = 0.189 15, which means nearly 19 per cent of bags fall between these two limits.

These examples do not cover all the possible types of area which may arise, but by now you should realise that the way to tackle any area which is not suitable for direct use with the tables is to split it into several that *are* suitable, not forgetting the useful facts that the total area under the curve is 1 and the areas on either side of the mean are each 0.5.

Quick check questions

1 In a normal distribution with a mean of 12 and standard deviation 1.5, what is the probability of the value of the variable being more than 15? Less than 9.5?

2 What z-value cuts off the top 2 per cent of values in the standard normal distribution?

3 A normally distributed variable has a mean of 20 mm, and 5 per cent of its values are above 24 mm. What is its standard deviation?

Answers:
1 When $x = 15$, $z = (15 - 12)/1.5 = 2$, so tables give the probability as 0.022 75 or 2.275 per cent. When $x = 9.5$, $z = (9.5 - 12)/1.5 = 1.66$, so the probability is 0.0485 or 4.85 per cent.
2 Look for a value as near as you can find to 2 per cent or 0.02 in the main body of the normal tables. The nearest is 0.020 18, corresponding to a z-value of 2.07.
3 The z-value which cuts off the top 5 per cent of the normal distribution is about 1.65. Thus $1.65 = (x - \text{mean})/\text{s.d.} = (24 - 20)/\text{s.d.}$. This can be solved to give s.d. $= 4/1.65 = 2.42$ mm.

Some general points about the normal distribution

Before returning to and solving the quality manager's third problem, there are a few more general points worth making about the normal distribution. The first takes us back to Chapter 4, where in our efforts to get a 'feel' for the meaning of the standard deviation, we noted that most of the values in a fairly symmetric distribution will lie within three standard deviations either side of the mean. The reason for this becomes clear if we now interpret 'reasonably symmetric' as meaning 'approximately normal', and examine the normal tables. Three standard deviations away from the mean gives $z = 3$, and sure enough the tables show that only 0.135 per cent of the distribution lies beyond this point. At the same time, you can verify the statement made earlier in this chapter that the normal curve never actually hits the z-axis. By the time we get out to $z = 4$, only 0.003 per cent of the distribution is excluded, but no matter how large the value of z, we would find, given sufficiently accurate tables, that there would always be a tiny bit 'left over'.

Another question which may have occurred to you is 'How do we know that the normal distribution is a good model for a given problem?' After all, we have been careful to note, in our study of the binomial and Poisson distributions, where we have had to make assumptions in order to use the distributions. The fact is that we rather tend to *assume* that distributions of continuous variables such as weights, people's heights, IQs and so on will be normal. The very name of the distribution reflects this assumption: it is what we 'normally' expect to occur; and in most of these cases the assumption is fairly well justified, as long as we are talking about a pretty big population. Take IQs, for example. The majority of people have IQs somewhere near the mean; the further away from the mean an IQ is, the less likely one is to encounter someone with that IQ, and the proportions of the population with IQs above and below the average are, in principle, roughly the same, the numbers of Einsteins being balanced by people at the other end of the distribution. Thus we would expect the shape of this distribution to be something close to the normal. The same will apply to *any* variable that is the result of the accumulative effect of a large number of random influences (this can actually be demonstrated mathematically).

Nevertheless, there *are* other continuous distributions of importance – we will encounter one of these in Chapter 9. There are even other symmetrical distributions with infinite tails on either side, looking to the naked eye indistinguishable from normal curves. So it does not do to be *too* ready to assume that a variable is normally distributed, but a method of deciding whether this is the case or not will have to wait until Chapter 9.

Solving the original problem

As the grand finale to our discussion of the normal distribution, we will now tackle the quality manager's third problem. The machine filling bags of Carrot Candy is set to a mean weight of 510 g, but this setting is producing rejects – bags weighing under 500 g – at a rate of 20 per cent of total production, which is unacceptably high. So what should the new average setting of the machine be if the rate of rejects is to be cut to 5 per cent?

We will assume that the weights of bags as filled by the machine are normally distributed with a mean of 510 g. A sketch of the distribution is given in Figure 7.7. But this problem differs from all those we have solved so far in that we are not trying to find a probability, or percentage, or whatever one likes to call it. Instead we are *given* the proportion of bags weighing less than 500 g – in other words, we are told that the shaded area in Figure 7.7 is 20 per cent of the whole or 0.2. So what *do* we need to find?

What we do not know at this point is the variability of the weights being produced by this machine as measured by the standard deviation. However, we can deduce this via the known proportion of rejects being produced. The problem is the reverse of the ones solved earlier, in that we know the area and want to work backwards from there. So when we consult the tables, we look among the areas – the figures in the body of the table – for something as near as possible to 0.2000. The nearest is 0.2005, corresponding to a z of 0.84 (you should be following this in the tables).

Recalling that z tells us 'how many standard deviations from x to the mean', we can therefore deduce that from 500 to 510 is 0.84 standard deviations. That means 10 g is $0.84 \times s$, so that s must be 10/0.84 or 11.9 g. (If you find this hard to follow, try asking yourself how you would work out s if 10 g had turned out to be two standard deviations.)

This is a rather high value for the standard deviation. However, it is generally much more difficult – and expensive – to adjust the variability than the mean. So we therefore ask: given this degree of variability, what should the mean setting on the machine be if only 5 per cent of the bags are to fall below 500 g?

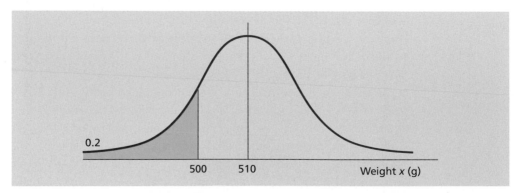

Figure 7.7 Present distribution of weights

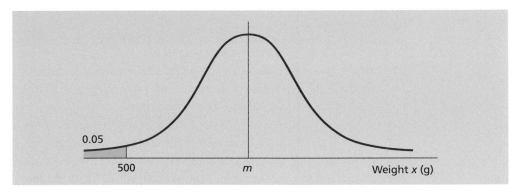

Figure 7.8 Required distribution of weights

A new sketch is required, since the distribution produced by the adjusted machine will centre on the new, unknown mean, m, as shown in Figure 7.8. Again, what we know is the area to the left of 500 g, but now this area is reduced to 5 per cent or 0.05. The same 'backward' use of the tables as before shows that such an area is cut off by the value $z = 1.65$ (this actually gives an area of 0.0495, but that is the nearest we can get within the accuracy of these tables). So the distance from 500 to the mean must be 1.65 standard deviations, hence the mean is 1.65 standard deviations above 500:

$$m = 500 + 1.65 \times 11.9 = 519.64 \text{ g}$$

This is therefore the average weight to which the machine would have to be set to give only 5 per cent of bags below 500 g, with its existing variability.

One final point about all these problems. You will find that many textbooks and sets of tables use notation in such situations which bristles with Greek letters, brackets, < and > signs. It is quite unnecessary for you to try to use such notation; as long as you explain what you are doing clearly, and do not just produce numbers like rabbits out of a hat with no indication as to whether they are areas, standard deviations or what, there is no one 'right' way of writing out these problems.

Quick check questions

1 What is the probability that a normally distributed quantity will be more than 1.2 standard deviations above the mean?

2 In the tables of Appendix 5, what value of z is exceeded in only 5 per cent of cases?

3 The amounts of petrol purchased by customers of a filling station are normally distributed with a mean of 40 litres and a standard deviation of 8 litres. What value of z would you use to find the probability that a customer purchases less than 26 litres?

Answers:
1 0.1151 or about 11.5 per cent.
2 Between $z = 1.64$ and $z = 1.65$.
3 $z = (26 - 40)/8 = -1.75$. We would actually look up $z = 1.75$ in the tables, using the fact that they are symmetric.

Some further points

The distributions – two discrete and one continuous – that we have studied in this chapter are only three, though arguably the three most important, out of the large number of probability distributions which have been investigated and tabulated. As already mentioned, we will be coming across two other continuous distributions, called the *chi-squared* distribution and the *t*-distribution, in Chapter 9, and a glance through a book of statistical tables will show several others. With all of them, however, the same two-stage process is needed: first the recognition of the type of situation to which the distribution in question applies, and second the use of the tabulated probabilities associated with the distribution.

The normal as an approximation to the binomial and Poisson

Although we have made the distinction between the continuous normal distribution and the discrete binomial and Poisson, there are in fact links between them. We have already seen how the Poisson can be used as an approximation to the binomial, but both of these can be approximated by the normal under certain circumstances. If you recall how we approached the normal curve in the first place by taking histograms with larger amounts of data and smaller class intervals, you should not be surprised to learn that when n becomes large and p is not too far from 0.5 the binomial is approximated quite well by the normal; the requirement that n should be large means that 'smoothing off' the histogram does not introduce too much inaccuracy, while the need for p to be near to 0.5 is occasioned by the symmetry of the normal curve. It is impossible to lay down hard and fast rules as to how large is large, but roughly speaking if p is between 0.1 and 0.9, and $n \times p > 5$, the approximation is a reasonable one. Figure 7.9 shows a binomial distribution histogram resulting from tossing 20 coins together 1000 times and recording the number of heads (so $n = 20$, $p = 0.5$). You can see from the superimposed normal curve how closely the approximation works.

Normal approximation to the binomial

A sample of 400 adults is randomly chosen by a market researcher from a large population; members of the sample are asked to give their views on the taste of a new minced

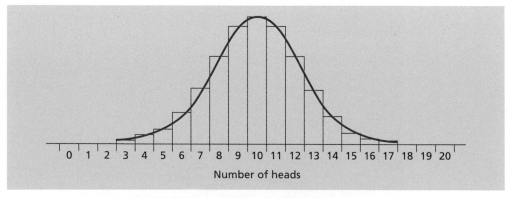

Figure 7.9 Normal approximation to a binomial situation

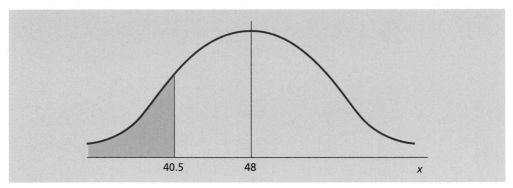

Figure 7.10

chicken product. However, 12 per cent of the population is vegetarian, though the researcher cannot identify the vegetarians in advance. What is the chance that at least 360 of the sample will agree to taste the product? (We have to assume that the only people who will refuse are the vegetarians.)

Here we have a binomial problem with $n = 400$ and $p = 0.12$, but this value of n is far too big to allow us to use binomial tables. Fortunately, $p > 0.1$ and $np = 48$, so we can use the normal approximation instead. The mean will be 48 (this is just the average number of vegetarians we would expect to find in the sample of 400 people), and the standard deviation is given by

$$\sqrt{np(1 - p)} = \sqrt{(400 \times 0.12 \times 0.88)} = 6.5.$$

Before we can use the normal distribution to work out the required probability, we need to decide precisely what value of x we are interested in. We are using a continuous normal curve here to approximate a discrete binomial situation, and so we need to think rather carefully about the appropriate value of x to use. If we want to find the chance that 40 or fewer people agree to taste the product, then we need to ask 'What value of a continuous variable would be rounded off to 40 as the nearest discrete value?' The answer is, of course, 40.5; so the probability we are looking for is $p(x < 40.5)$, not $p(x < 41)$ as you might think. The process we have gone through here is called a *continuity correction*, and it should always be used when approximating a discrete variable with a continuous one.

Having decided on the value of x, we can plot the relevant normal curve as shown in Figure 7.10, where the required probability is represented by the shaded area:

$$p(40 \text{ or less}) = p(x < 40.5) = p\left(z < \frac{40.5 - 48}{6.5}\right) = p(z < -1.15) = 0.1243,$$

from normal tables.

So the researcher has about a 12.5 per cent chance of getting at least 360 non-vegetarians in her sample. And in case you are interested, the 'true' answer calculated using the binomial formula (rather a tedious process!) would be 0.1227, so the approximation is quite good in this case.

Normal approximation to the Poisson

The Poisson, too, can be approximated by a normal curve if m, the average number of successes, is large (bigger than about 30); Figure 7.11 shows how well the normal curve fits

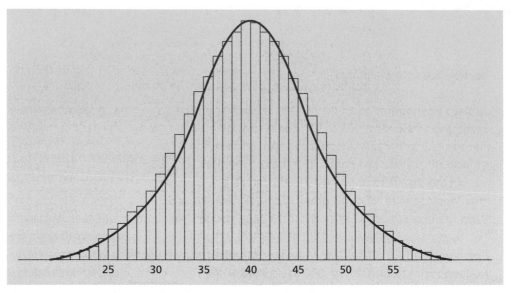

Figure 7.11 Normal approximation to a Poisson situation

a Poisson probability histogram with $m = 40$. This is why most tables of binomial and Poisson probabilities do not cover a very wide range; over a large part of the range the normal approximation is quite adequate. This tendency of other distributions to become normal when large amounts of data are involved is one reason why the normal is so important, and explains why it crops up again and again in more advanced statistical work.

To see how the normal approximation to a Poisson distribution works, consider the following situation. An environmental scientist is studying a plant whose presence in an area indicates that the area is free of certain pollutants (this is one way in which the recovery of industrially polluted land can be studied). He divides up the area of interest into a large number of squares, each 10 m × 10 m, and counts the number of specimens of the plant in each square; the average turns out to be 52. If the distribution were random, what proportion of the squares would you expect to contain more than 60 specimens?

On the assumption that the distribution is random, we can use a Poisson distribution to model this situation. However, because the mean is large – 52 – we cannot use the tables in the appendix; instead we have to use the normal approximation, with mean = 52. It can be shown mathematically that the standard deviation of a Poisson distribution is always equal to the square root of its mean, so in this case it will be $\sqrt{52}$ or 7.21. Just as with the normal approximation to the binomial, we need to use a continuity correction here when choosing the value of x; in this case, we are interested in all discrete values over 60, so we choose $x = 60.5$ (because all values above this would round up to 61 or more). Thus the probability we want is given by the shaded area in Figure 7.12, and can be calculated as

$$p(x > 60.5) = p\left(z > \frac{60.5 - 52}{7.21}\right) = p(z > 1.18) = 0.1192,$$

so that nearly 12 per cent of squares would be expected to contain more than 60 plants. Since the exact answer, using the Poisson distribution formula, would be 0.1208, the approximation here is quite good.

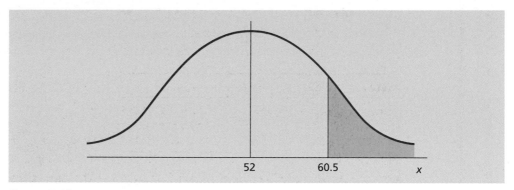

Figure 7.12

Which distribution should I use?

The major problem which most students have when tackling probability distribution problems for the first time is deciding on the appropriate distribution to use in a given situation. The critical question is 'What information do I have?', since this will generally determine the distribution to be used, even if some approximation is called for. You may find the diagram in Figure 7.13 helpful in dealing with this difficulty.

Probabilities from the computer

Excel has a large number of statistical functions, a list of which can be obtained by searching for HELP on STATISTICAL FUNCTIONS. For example, the function =NORMDIST(16.7, 15, 0.8, TRUE) will give the cumulative normal probability for a value of 16.7 in a normal distribution with a mean of 15 and a standard deviation of 0.8 – in other words, the probability of getting a value less than or equal to 16.7 from this distribution, which turns out to be 0.983 207. The role of the TRUE parameter in this function is to indicate that we want the cumulative probability – if any other value is entered, Excel returns instead the probability density function, whose use need not concern us.

In a similar way, =NORMINV(0.92, 15, 0.8) gives us the inverse distribution, equivalent to looking up the normal tables 'backwards' as described earlier in this chapter. The value returned is 16.124 06, indicating that 92 per cent of values in a normal distribution with mean 15 and standard deviation 0.8 are less than 16.12.

The function =BINOMDIST(2, 10, 0.2, TRUE) will give the cumulative probability of up to two successes in a binomial situation with $n = 10$ and $p = 2$ (which is 0.6778), while =BINOMDIST(2, 10, 0.2, FALSE) gives the probability of *exactly* two successes. However, Excel will not give the inverse for a discrete distribution.

Likewise the function POISSON(4, 2, TRUE) gives the probability of up to four occurrences of an event, where the mean number of occurrences is two; the value returned by Excel is 0.947 347. As with the binomial, POISSON (4, 2, FALSE) gives the probability of *exactly* four occurrences.

Try experimenting with these functions in Excel, and check your results against the tables in the appendices.

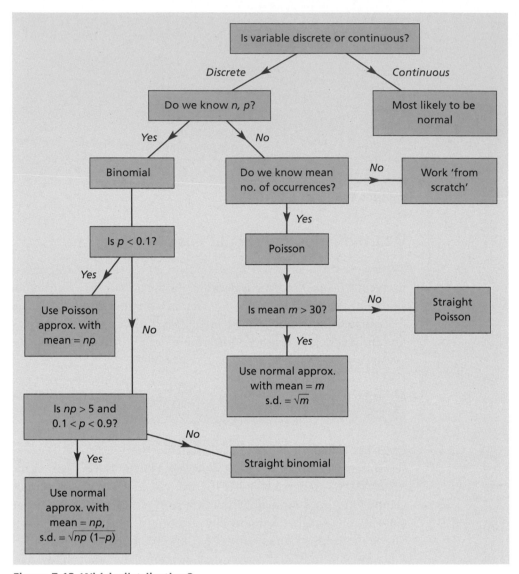

Figure 7.13 Which distribution?

Thinking again about computer failures

We began this chapter by considering the question 'How do people assess the risks of computer failure?' We will end by examining one aspect of this question which can be tackled with the aid of the distributions we've been studying.

When a computer reads data from a disk or CD – or for that matter, when you listen to music on a CD, download music to your iPod or watch a DVD – millions of 'bits' of encoded information are being individually read. An error in reading any one of those bits may result in a problem – a 'glitch' in the sound you're hearing, a wrong figure in a bank's records, or something more serious. So it's vital for manufacturers of computer hardware and other electronic equipment to be able to guarantee a very low error rate.

Let's suppose that a particular computer storage device has a stated error rate of 1 error in every 20 000 bits read, and that a particular set of data involves reading 100 000 bits (in reality the error rate would be much lower and the volume of data much higher, but we will use these figures so as to get manageable calculations). The question 'What is the chance that all the data is read without any errors?' is clearly an important one. But can we model this, and obtain an estimate of the probability, by using the distributions we've looked at in this chapter?

As usual, we start by identifying what information we've got. We know the number of bits being read is 100 000 – that's the value of n, the number of 'opportunities for an error'. We know the chance of an error in reading any one bit – it's 1 in 20 000 or 0.000 05, and it's what we have called p earlier in the chapter. If we are prepared to assume that errors occur randomly and independently (which in practice may not always be the case), then we have an example of a binomial situation:

$$n = 100\ 000,\ p(\text{error}) = 0.000\ 05,\ \text{and we want } p(\text{zero errors}),\ \text{so } k = 0.$$

However, we certainly can't use the tables provided in the appendix to solve the problem, since the value of n is far too big, and p too small. But this is exactly the case where the Poisson approximation to the binomial becomes applicable. The *mean* number of errors in reading 100 000 bits will be 100 000 × 0.000 05 or 5; another way of looking at this is to say that if there is, on average, one error in every 20 000 bits read, then in 100 000 there will be five errors.

So we use the Poisson tables with mean = 5 to find $p(\text{exactly zero errors})$:

$$p(\text{exactly zero errors}) = p(0 \text{ or more}) - p(1 \text{ or more})$$
$$= 1 - 0.9933 = 0.0067.$$

Thus there is only a small chance of reading the 100 000 bits without any errors occurring. With a more realistic probability of error – say, one in a million or 0.000 001 – it can be shown mathematically, using the formula for the Poisson distribution, that the chance goes up to over 90 per cent, and of course the lower the chance of an error, the bigger the probability of reading the data without any errors at all.

EXERCISES

*Further examples on the work of this chapter can be found on the **Companion Website**.*

Here is a hotch-potch of problems of all three types, so that you get used to recognising each distribution.

1 A greengrocer has checked six trays of tomatoes and found that they contain respectively 2, 0, 1, 4, 3 and 2 bad fruit. What is the probability that a tray will contain (a) 2 or more; (b) no bad fruit?

2 A manufacturer of Christmas crackers knows that 3 crackers in every 20 do not contain a paper hat and a customer complains that his box of 10 crackers contained 3 without paper hats. What is the probability of this occurrence?

3 A machine produces small metal components whose lengths are normally distributed with a mean of 5 cm and a standard deviation of 0.2 cm. What is the probability that a component will have a length (a) less than 4.7 cm; (b) more than 4.8 cm; (c) between 4.6 and 5.3 cm?

→

4 A worker is late, on average, one morning in four. If he works a five-day week, what is the probability that he will be late less than three times next week? What is the most likely number of times he will be late?

5 A work-study engineer times a certain operation, and discovers that the average time it takes is 10 minutes, but on 15 per cent of occasions it takes more than 13 minutes. Assuming that times for the operation follow a normal distribution, what is its standard deviation?

6 Nine times out of ten a quotation made by a firm to a customer leads to a definite order. What is the probability that a batch of five quotations leads to four definite orders?

7 A small internal switchboard can cope with up to six incoming calls per minute. The average number of incoming calls received is 12 every five minutes. What is the probability that in a two-minute interval the switchboard receives more calls than it can cope with?

8 An automatic packing machine is filling bags of sugar to a nominal weight of 1 kg. Fifty thousand bags per week are produced by the machine, which at present is set to a mean of 1005 g. All bags below the nominal weight are rejected, this policy resulting at present in a reject rate of 1500 bags per week. (a) What is the standard deviation of the bags filled by the machine? (b) To what mean should the machine be reset if the standard deviation cannot be changed, if each rejected bag costs the company 8p, and a saving of £40 per week is to be made?

9 Ten coins are tossed together and the number of heads is counted.

(a) Using the binomial distribution, find the probability of getting six or more heads.
(b) Now see how close to this figure the normal approximation comes. The appropriate mean to use will be 5, since that is the average number of heads we would expect to get in ten tosses of a fair coin. It can be proved that the standard deviation of a binomial distribution is $\sqrt{np(1-p)}$, so here it will be $\sqrt{10 \times 0.5 \times 0.5}$ which is 1.58. You need to be careful, too, as to what '6 or more' means in terms of a continuous distribution like the normal. Everything from 5.5 upwards has to be included, since 5.5, 5.6, etc., would all be rounded off to 6 when treated as discrete; this is the 'continuity correction', mentioned earlier in the chapter.

10 Now try the same sort of thing with the Poisson as an approximation to the binomial. Suppose 5 per cent of items produced by a machine are defective in some way, and a sample of ten items is taken.

(a) Use the binomial to work out the probability that at least one of the ten is defective.
(b) Now use the Poisson to work out the same thing. The mean to use is, of course, 0.5, since if 5 per cent of the items are faulty, the number of defectives to be expected out of ten would, on average, be 5 per cent of ten.

11 Very large reels of electrical cable may have quite large numbers of small flaws without their usefulness being seriously impaired. Suppose the average number of such flaws per 2000 metre reel is 36. What is the probability that if you purchase such a reel it will have fewer than 30 flaws? This is strictly a Poisson problem, but since the mean is large (36) we can use the normal as an approximation. It can be proved that the standard deviation of the Poisson is the square root of its mean, so that here standard deviation $= \sqrt{36} = 6$. Use normal tables to solve the problem (remember that, as in Exercise 9, we are approximating a discrete situation by a continuous one).

12 Companies that rely on external suppliers to provide essential components often operate what is called Sampling Inspection. Under this system, a sample is taken from every batch which arrives

from the supplier, and tested. If the sample meets certain acceptance criteria, the whole batch is accepted; if not, the whole batch is sent back to the supplier.

For example, a company that retails fizzy drinks in plastic bottles obtains the bottles from an external supplier. In the past, the quality of bottles sent by this supplier has not been entirely satisfactory, with an average of 5 per cent of bottles sent being faulty and likely to explode when subjected to the pressure of gas in the drink. To avoid problems that will occur if faulty bottles get through to the filling line, it has been agreed that the following sampling scheme will operate: from every batch of 500 bottles received from the supplier, a sample of 10 will be selected at random, and put through a pressure-testing procedure. If any bottles in the sample fail the test, this will be regarded as a signal of unsatisfactory quality, and the whole batch will be returned to the supplier.

(a) If in fact 5 per cent of the batch is faulty, what will be the chance that the sample contains no defectives, and therefore the batch will be accepted?

(b) What is the chance of accepting the batch if 10 per cent of the batch is faulty?

(c) Repeat the calculation above for defective rates 15 per cent and 20 per cent. Hence sketch a graph of the probability of accepting the batch against the percentage of defective items in the batch, and comment on your results. (This graph is called an *operating characteristic* for the sampling scheme; we will be returning to the topic of operating characteristics and sampling in Chapter 10.)

Case Study

Orbital Engineering

Orbital Engineering is a company which manufactures precision components for the petrochemical industry, including drill bits. The useful lifetime of a bit, before it has to be replaced with consequent costly downtime, is of key importance. Orbital has tested a sample of bits and found their lifetimes to be normally distributed with a mean of 240 operating hours and a standard deviation of 20 operating hours. You have been asked to provide recommendations as to whether the process for producing the bits requires improvement.

(a) At present the guaranteed lifetime of a bit is stated as 200 hours. What proportion of bits will need to be replaced under guarantee?

(b) This proportion is considered to be too high. Orbital has the option of purchasing improved raw materials, which will increase the mean lifetime to 246 hours while leaving the standard deviation unchanged. Alternatively, it can purchase a new machine for producing the bits; this will leave the mean unchanged at 240 hours, but reduce the standard deviation to 18 hours. On the basis of the proportion of bits which need to be replaced, which course of action would you recommend, and why?

(c) What further information would you wish to have in order to make a better business decision in this situation?

Chapter 8

ESTIMATING FROM SAMPLES:
INFERENCE

Chapter prerequisites

Before starting work on this chapter make sure you are happy with:

1   simple random samples (see Chapter 2, p. 44);

2   the binomial distribution (see Chapter 7, p. 172);

3   the normal distribution (see Chapter 7, p. 181);

4   solution of equations (see Chapter 1, p. 19).

Learning outcomes

By the end of your work on this chapter you should be able to:

1   estimate a population mean or percentage from the mean or percentage in a large simple random sample taken from the population, to any required level of confidence;

2   determine the minimum sample size needed to estimate a population percentage or mean to a given level of accuracy with a prescribed level of confidence;

3   find the probability that a sample of a given size from a known population will have a certain mean or percentage;

4   state the conditions under which the above processes are valid.

Quantitative methods in practice

The website of the polling organisation Ipsos MORI carried the following item shortly after the May 2010 British general election:

Most prediction polls were very accurate

	Conservatives	Labour	Lib Dems	Other	Average error
Actual Result	37	30	24	10	
ICM	36	28	26	10	1.25
Harris	35	29	27	10	1.5
Ipsos MORI	36	29	27	8	1.75
Populus	37	28	27	8	1.75
Com Res	37	28	28	7	2.25
YouGov	35	28	28	9	2.25
Opinium	35	27	26	12	2.25
Angus Reid	36	24	29	11	3.25
TNS BMRB	33	27	29	11	3.25

Source: British Polling Council

Ipsos MORI

As the headline says, all the polls did pretty well at predicting the percentage of the vote going to each party. There is a tendency for the polls to underestimate the Conservative and Labour votes and overestimate support for the Lib Dems, but overall the average errors in the predicted percentages are, as indicated in the table, all less than 4 per cent. And yet if you look on the website at the description of how the polls were carried out, you'll find that for Ipsos MORI, as for the other organisations, typically some 1000–1500 people of voting age, spread geographically around the country, were questioned – a tiny proportion of the overall electorate.

So how is it possible to predict the vote in the actual election from such a small sample? And why are the variations between the samples taken by different organisations so small, when they are questioning completely different groups of people?

This chapter will examine the theory of sampling, which enables us to answer these questions. We will see that the variability among samples of a given size is in fact quite predictable, and that we can actually give a 'margin of error' around the percentage estimates to indicate how reliable they are (some reporting of opinion polls in the media now includes these error margins). And of course, this theory is not just applicable to political polls – it applies also to market research, to sampling of manufactured items for quality checking, indeed to almost any situation where we need to draw conclusions about a population when we've looked only at a sample.

The dissatisfied customer's problem

Radio Supplies (To You) Ltd is a firm which supplies small components to the electronics industry. A particular type of connection is normally dispatched in boxes of 500, and as a small number of faulty items are unavoidable with this type of component, customers have agreed that a rate of 2 per cent defectives is acceptable. However, Radio Supplies has recently received a complaint from one of its major customers, suggesting that as a recent consignment of 500 of these connections contained 25 which were faulty, the quality of the product must be deteriorating, and threatening cancellation of future orders unless the previous quality can be maintained. Naturally Radio Supplies' management is very concerned that this should not happen, and wishes to investigate the contention that quality is deteriorating.

If you recall what was said about sampling methods in Chapter 2, you should realise that the first question to be asked is 'Was this box of 500 representative of production as a whole?' Perhaps the batch all came from one machine which was causing problems at the time; perhaps they were produced after a weekend or a holiday period when machines had not warmed up or workers were not operating at maximum efficiency. It may not be very easy, several weeks or even months after the event, to discover the answers to these questions, but if a valuable order depends on obtaining the information it is clearly worth making the effort.

However, even if all these possibilities can be ruled out, and the batch genuinely appears to be a random sample of the entire output of the connections, it does not necessarily follow that the quality is deteriorating. The box of 500, after all, only constitutes a *sample* from the whole output, and we have already seen that samples, even random ones, can be very unrepresentative of the populations from which they are taken. Maybe another lucky customer has received a box with no defective items at all – but it would be foolish to deduce that Radio Supplies has managed to produce a 100 per cent perfect product.

These *sampling variations* are to be expected. It would be naive to imagine that every sample will reflect the proportion of defective items in the population exactly. The relevant question is, if the overall proportion of defective items *has not* increased, just how likely is it that a box of 500 with 25 defectives will occur – or, to look at the problem another way, what proportion of all the boxes of 500 sent out will contain as many as 25 defectives, or maybe even more? These are clearly questions which should vitally concern the management of Radio Supplies, and, as you will have realised by now, they are questions concerned once again with *probabilities*.

A simple example

To be able to answer questions of the kind posed in the previous section we need to know quite a lot about how samples of a particular size taken from a given population may vary. (We say 'of a particular size' because it is intuitively clear to most people that a big sample is 'more reliable' or 'more representative' than a small one, so the size of the sample should be an important factor.) We can get some useful preliminary ideas about this if we begin by considering a very simple situation in which the entire population contains only six members.

Let us suppose, then, that a market researcher is carrying out a survey on a small Hebridean island with only six households, in order to determine which of them consume that staple Scottish breakfast-food, porridge. Of course, in this situation he could easily carry out a census (a survey of the entire population) but instead he has decided to take a sample of three of the six households. We will further suppose that we already have, from some other source, perfect information as to the diets of the six families, which reveals the following facts:

$$\left.\begin{array}{l}\text{Adams}\\\text{Brown}\\\text{Carter}\\\text{Davies}\end{array}\right\} \textit{do} \text{ breakfast on porridge} \qquad \left.\begin{array}{l}\text{Evans}\\\text{Finch}\end{array}\right\} \text{do not}$$

Now, because the population is so small, we can actually list all the possible samples which the researcher might obtain, and thus find the percentage of each sample possessing the required characteristic – in this case, porridge consumption. The samples are listed below, together with the percentage for each, using A, B, C . . . to denote the six families:

Sample	Percentage eating porridge	Sample	Percentage eating porridge
ABC	100	BCD	100
ABD	100	BCE	67
ABE	67	BCF	67
ABF	67	BDE	67
ACD	100	BDF	67
ACE	67	BEF	33
ACF	67	CDE	67
ADE	67	CDF	67
ADF	67	CEF	33
AEF	33	DEF	33

So, out of the 20 possible samples, 4 contain 100 per cent, 12 contain 67 per cent and 4 contain 33 per cent with the required characteristic. Moreover, *if* the researcher chooses his sample randomly (in the technical sense in which we defined that term in Chapter 2), then each sample is equally likely to arise, and so we can say that the probability of his getting a sample with 100 per cent porridge-eaters is 4/20, for 67 per cent it is 12/20, and for 33 per cent, 4/20 again. We can summarise this in the table below:

Percentage in sample	Probability
100	4/20 or 0.2
67	12/20 or 0.6
33	4/20 or 0.2

What we have here is, of course, a *probability distribution* of the kind we discussed in Chapter 7. However, because this particular distribution refers specifically to the probability of obtaining various percentages in a sample, we give it the more descriptive name of a *sampling distribution* – the sampling distribution of percentages in samples of three items, in this case. In general, we can define the sampling distribution of percentages as follows:

> The sampling distribution of percentages is the distribution obtained by taking all possible samples of fixed size *n* from a population, noting the percentage in each sample with a certain characteristic, and classifying these percentages into a distribution.

Although this is such a simple example, there are certain features of the sampling distribution which are worth noticing because they will appear again later when we look at other, more realistic sampling situations. First, if we work out the *mean* of the distribution in the usual way, we have

$$\text{Mean} = 100\% \times 0.2 + 67\% \times 0.6 + 33\% \times 0.2 = 67\%.$$

In other words, the mean of the sampling distribution is the true percentage for the population as a whole. This seems intuitively reasonable; we would expect samples containing the population percentage to crop up more often than samples with any other percentage (unless, of course, the samples are deliberately biased).

Second, we can see that if the investigator were simply to assume that the percentage obtained in his sample automatically reflects that in the entire population, he might be led very seriously astray – depending on which sample he obtains, he could get the impression that as many as 100 per cent of the households, or as few as 33 per cent, consume porridge for breakfast. In order to get a fair impression of what the population figure might be, he obviously has to make some allowance for the variability of the samples.

You may like, before going further, to try constructing for yourself the distribution of percentages in samples of *four* households from this same population. There will be 15 possible samples and you should find that, while the mean is still 67 per cent, the sample percentages this time only vary between 50 and 100 per cent, reflecting the feeling we have that the bigger a sample is, the more 'reliable' – that is, the closer to the true population figure – it is likely to be.

The sampling distribution of percentages

In the example given above we could actually explicitly construct the sampling distribution because the number of possible samples was very small. Normally, however, we are going to be considering populations that are so large that we certainly will not be able to do this. In fact, we shall generally be able to assume that the population is so big in comparison with the size of the sample that removing the sample makes no effective difference to the population – that, for all practical purposes, the population is infinitely large.

This being so, it follows that when we start choosing our sample, the percentage of the population having the characteristic we are interested in will remain the same whether the items we remove have the characteristic or not; the probability of selecting an item with the required characteristic remains constant throughout the selection of the sample. So, in the process of selecting the sample, these three conditions apply:

1 the number of items in the sample, say n, is fixed and known in advance;
2 as each item of the sample is selected there are two possible outcomes – either it has, or does not have, the characteristic we are interested in;
3 the probability of selecting an item *with* the characteristic remains constant, and is known to be P per cent.

These three conditions should be familiar to you already; they are, of course, the conditions under which the binomial distribution is applicable (see Chapter 7, pp. 172–7, if you have forgotten this). The sampling distribution of percentages is, in fact, a binomial distribution, as long as the assumptions we have made – simple random samples, taken from a population which is effectively infinite – are satisfied.

We are not, however, going to use the binomial distribution directly in answering questions such as the one posed in the first section of this chapter. If we are prepared to make one further assumption, we can instead use the normal approximation to the binomial, which is a great deal more convenient. That assumption is that the sample is large – an assumption that is certainly likely to be justified in many of the applications of sampling, such as the analysis of market research surveys, that we will be looking at. We saw in Chapter 7 that if n is 'large', then the binomial is very well approximated by a normal distribution, though what exactly constitutes 'large' in this context depends on how symmetrical the binomial we are concerned with is; roughly speaking, the more *unsym*metrical the binomial, the bigger n needs to be before the normal approximation becomes valid. A sort of rule-of-thumb answer for the question 'How big is big?' in this context is that samples should contain 30 or more items, though for fairly symmetrical situations – that is, percentages near to 50 – we can often get away with a smaller sample, and occasionally we have to be rather careful with values of P near to 0 or 100 per cent.

Once we have accepted that the sampling distribution of percentages for large samples is more or less normal, there are two further things we need to know before we can begin to apply this fact to the solution of problems – namely the *mean* and *standard deviation* of this normal sampling distribution, which as we saw in Chapter 7 are the two *parameters* that define a normal distribution. If you did Exercise 9 in Chapter 7 you will know that the mean *number* of items with the characteristic we are interested in, in samples of n items chosen at random, will be np, where p is the probability of an item having the characteristic. In the same exercise we saw that the standard deviation of this number was $\sqrt{np(1-p)}$. This is not quite what we are after, however, because what we have been talking about so far is not the *number* of items per sample, but rather the *percentage*, which is usually a much more useful concept.

The transition from numbers to percentages is not difficult to make: if the mean number of items in a sample with our characteristic – let's call it characteristic X – is np, then the mean percentage is

$$\frac{np}{n} \times 100 = 100p = P,$$

where P is the percentage of the population with characteristic X. In the same way, the standard deviation expressed in percentage terms will be

$$\frac{\sqrt{np(1-p)}}{n} \times 100 = 100\sqrt{\frac{p(1-p)}{n}} = \sqrt{\frac{P(100-P)}{n}}.$$

This quantity – the standard deviation of the sampling distribution – is so important that it has been given a special name. Remember that the standard deviation measures how spread out around the mean the points of a distribution are. So this particular standard deviation will tell us, more or less, how the sample values differ from the mean P, which is the population value. It could therefore be thought of as giving an idea of the *error* we might be making if we were to use a sample value instead of the population value. For that reason it is called the *STandard Error of Percentages* – subsequently referred to in this book as STEP.

We now have all the information we need to begin applying sampling theory to practical problems, but as there has been quite a dose of theory to swallow in the last few pages, let us pause before we carry on to summarise what we have shown so far, and to see how it fits in with common sense.

We have seen that the sampling distribution of percentages in samples of n items ($n > 30$ approximately) taken at random from an infinite population in which P per cent of items have characteristic X, will be

a NORMAL distribution
with MEAN $P\%$
and STANDARD DEVIATION (STEP) $= \sqrt{\dfrac{P(100 - P)}{n}}\%$.

The % signs are put in here to remind you that, just as for a distribution of heights in centimetres the mean and standard deviation are in centimetres, so for this distribution of percentages the mean and standard deviation will also be percentages.

Now, how does this fit in with the intuitive feelings most of us have as to how samples 'ought' to behave? Let us think about the shape of the distribution first: the normal curve is symmetrical, so that there will be equal chances of obtaining samples with, say, over 30 per cent and under 20 per cent of 'characteristic X' items from a population where the actual figure is 25 per cent. This seems fair enough – we have no reason to suppose, unless the samples are chosen in a biased way, that they will have any tendency either to lower-than-average or to higher-than-average percentages.

In saying 'lower-than-*average*' here we are really making the second point – the average or mean percentage occurring in the samples will be P, the percentage that applies to the population as a whole. This again is reasonable – if we are going to use samples as a guide to the situation in the entire population, then although we have to realise that they *will* vary somewhat, it is reassuring to think that 'the average sample' will actually contain the same percentage as the population.

Finally, the standard deviation, which we have called STEP, depends *inversely* on the size of the sample – that is, as n increases, STEP will decrease, so that the distribution becomes more compact – in other words, all the sample values will tend to be closer to the population value. (You can see an illustration of this in Figure 8.1.)

This merely confirms what we already noted in relation to the porridge-eaters example above, namely that bigger samples are more reliable as a guide to the population than smaller ones. To put it another way: a small sample could be very misleading because just a few atypical items could give it a strong bias. This is much less likely to happen in a large sample.

We have gone into some detail over these points because they are probably some of the most subtle you will be required to deal with. However, if you have not followed all the

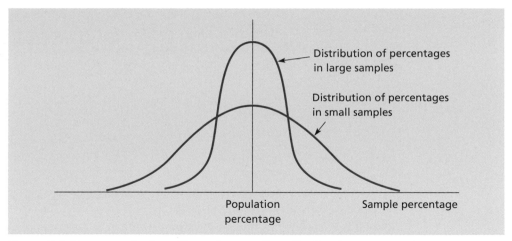

Figure 8.1 How sample size affects the sampling distribution

details, do not worry – they will probably begin to fall into place as we proceed with practical applications of the theory.

Applications of STEP

We are going to use the results of the preceding section to examine three categories of problem:

1 Those where a straightforward probability is required – we want to answer a question of the type 'What is the probability that such a sample will arise?'
2 Those where we wish to estimate the percentage P in the population from information obtained from a single sample.
3 Those where we want to know how large a sample would be required in order to estimate a population percentage with a given degree of accuracy.

There is a fourth type of problem, that in which we want to test some theory concerning a population by taking a sample from it, but this latter type is a topic of such importance that we have reserved Chapter 9 for its discussion.

Finding a probability

An example of the first type of problem described above might be the following. Suppose the personnel records of a firm show that a quarter of its workforce consists of women, and imagine that a random sample of 80 workers is to be selected to take part in a work-study exercise. How likely is it that this sample will contain 25 or more women?

We know that the distribution of percentages of women in these samples will be normal, with a mean of 25 per cent (one-quarter, the population value) and a standard deviation of STEP, where

$$\text{STEP} = \sqrt{\frac{25 \times 75}{80}} = 4.84\%.$$

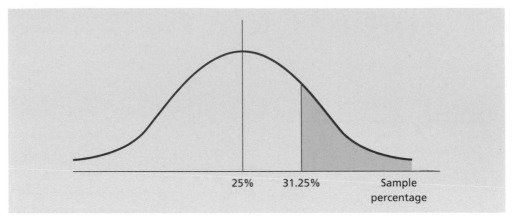

25%   31.25%   Sample
                           percentage

Figure 8.2 Probability of finding 25 or more women in a sample of 80

We want to find the probability that there will be 25 or more women in a sample, which means the sample contains 31.25 per cent or more of women (since 25/80 is 31.25 per cent). This will be represented by the area shaded in Figure 8.2, so we have exactly the same type of problem as we were solving when we discussed the normal distribution in Chapter 7, the only difference being that the standard deviation in this case is the special one we have called STEP. So, as usual, we begin by calculating z, the number of standard deviations from the mean to our figure of interest:

$$z = \frac{31.25 - 25}{4.84} = 1.29.$$

The normal tables in Appendix 5 then show that the probability we require is 0.0985. That is, nearly 10 per cent of all the possible samples of 80 workers will contain 25 or more women.

Of course, there are several unrealistic features to this problem. First of all, it is fairly unlikely that a sample, particularly in connection with a work-study exercise, would be selected completely randomly in this way – it is much more likely that it would be stratified in some way so as to reflect, among other factors, the male/female composition of the workforce. We have not, either, said anything about how big the workforce is all together, but to satisfy the assumptions we made in building up the theory, it must be very much larger than the 80 in the sample. Most seriously, perhaps, we have chosen here a rather unusual situation in which the population percentage P is actually known, but it is far more often the case that we are taking a sample precisely because we *cannot* find P for the whole population – either because it would take too long or cost too much, or because it simply is not worth the effort of getting an accurate answer. It is this sort of circumstance that is covered by the kind of problems outlined under point 2 above.

Estimating a percentage

Such a problem might be confronted by a market researcher who wishes to conduct a survey to determine what percentage of consumers purchase her company's products. If a sample of 400 consumers is selected at random, and 280 of them are found to be purchasers of the products, what can be concluded about the percentage of *all* consumers who buy them?

It is helpful to start by saying what the researcher definitely *cannot* conclude – namely, that the figure 280/400 or 70 per cent will be exactly representative of the population as a whole. We know from the example of the porridge-eaters how misleading *that* assumption might be. The figure will be somewhere *around* 70 per cent – but it would help to be a bit more precise as to how far away from 70 per cent 'around' might mean. We can get some ideas as to how we could achieve this precision by looking at some populations from which such a sample *could* have come.

First, could it have come from a population in which the actual percentage buying the products is 72 per cent? This is equivalent to asking what the probability is of obtaining a sample with a percentage of purchasers as low as 70 from a population with 72 per cent. This is, of course, just the type of problem we looked at under point 1 on p. 207. We therefore leave you to check that here, with $P = 72$ per cent and $n = 400$, STEP is 2.24. So $z = 0.89$, and the normal tables then tell us that the chance of getting a sample with a percentage as low as 70 per cent or even less is 0.1867 (represented by the shaded area in Figure 8.3(a)). So more than 18 per cent of all samples would contain a percentage as low as or lower than 70; such a sample would not be at all unusual, and therefore might well have come from a population for which the figure *is* 72 per cent.

If, on the other hand, we ask whether it could have come from a population with $P = 60$ per cent, the answer is certainly that it is most unlikely. STEP in this case would be

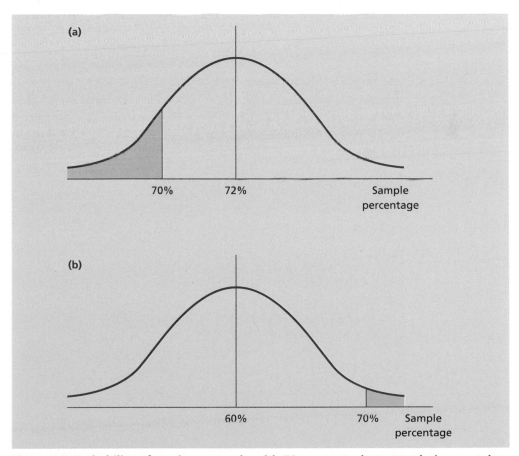

Figure 8.3 Probability of getting a sample with 70 per cent where population contains (a) 72 per cent; (b) 60 per cent

2.45, so that $z = 10/2.45$ (see Figure 8.3(b)), and this z-value is well beyond the range of our tables, showing that the chance of getting a sample with as high a percentage as 70 or more from a population which contains only 60 per cent is so small as to be virtually zero.

So, 72 is quite likely; 60 is very *un*likely. But we obviously cannot proceed in this haphazard manner; what we need are some limits between which we can be reasonably confident that the population value will lie.

It seems sensible, first of all, that these limits should be symmetrically placed on either side of the sample figure of 70, since we have no reason to assume that this sample is biased either upward or downward. So what we are looking for, as illustrated in Figure 8.4, are two possible population percentages, one on either side of 70, which represent the lowest and highest population percentages from which such a sample could reasonably be supposed to come. What we mean by reasonably, of course, will depend on the circumstances, but for many purposes a convention has grown up: that to demand that we can be '95 per cent confident' in our estimate is a reasonable requirement.

By 95 per cent confident we mean that in view of our symmetry requirement, the limits must be so arranged on either side of 70 as to exclude only $2\frac{1}{2}$ per cent in each 'tail' of the normal sampling distribution (see Figure 8.4). As a decimal $2\frac{1}{2}$ per cent is 0.025, and if we consult the normal tables again we find that a z-value of 1.96 will cut off an area of this size. Thus the two extreme values we are looking for will lie 1.96 standard deviations away on either side of 70. If, in other words, we give as the limits for our estimate points which are 1.96 standard deviations above and below 70, we can be 95 per cent confident in our estimate, since we have excluded only the extreme 5 per cent of possibilities.

There is one further slight complication: we know that the standard deviation in question is STEP, but how are we to find it? To do so, we need to know the population percentage, P, but this is precisely what we *do not* know at this stage, otherwise we would not be going to all this trouble! However, we do know the *sample* percentage, 70, and if we use that as an approximation to P in calculating STEP we shouldn't go far wrong. So we can say

$$\text{STEP} = \sqrt{\frac{70 \times 30}{400}} = 2.29\%$$

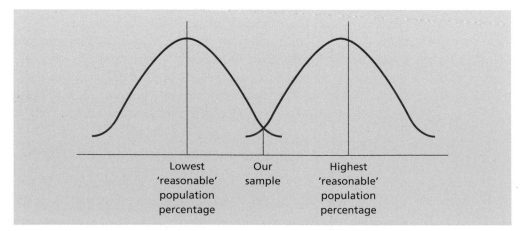

Figure 8.4 The idea of confidence limits

and thus we would give our estimate for the population percentage, with 95 per cent confidence, as $70 \pm 1.96 \times$ STEP or $70 \pm 1.96 \times 2.29$ (the $\pm$ indicating the two limits equal distances each side of 70). When we do the arithmetic this gives 65.51 per cent and 74.49 per cent as the two limits, and 65.51 to 74.49 is often referred to as the *95 per cent confidence interval*, though you may find it more helpful to think of allowing 1.96 standard deviations 'margin of error' around the sample value in estimating the population figure.

No doubt, at a first reading this seems a very involved process, but in fact, in practice it can be simplified in a number of ways. First of all, having once established the fact that for 95 per cent confidence one must go 1.96 standard deviations either side of the mean for the normal distribution, we can simply quote this in future – there is no need to go to the normal tables every time. Second, for many purposes it is sufficiently accurate to round off 1.96 to 2. With these two assumptions, we can state very succinctly that if a sample of n items contains P per cent with characteristic X, then with 95 per cent confidence we estimate the population percentage with that characteristic as lying in the interval $P \pm 2$ STEP. For instance, if a sample of 60 students contained 12 who were left-handed (i.e. 20 per cent) then we could estimate with 95 per cent confidence that the percentage of left-handers in the student population as a whole will be in the range

$$20 \pm 2 \times \text{STEP} = 20 \pm 2 \times \sqrt{\frac{20 \times 80}{60}}$$

or between 9.67 per cent and 30.33 per cent. So the actual mechanics of the estimation process are quite simple, and could be summed up as follows:

1 Identify n and P (the sample size and the percentage in the sample).
2 Calculate STEP using these values.
3 The 95 per cent confidence interval is approximately $P \pm 2$ STEP.

Of course, there is nothing sacrosanct about 95 per cent confidence; we could in theory use any level we wished, but there are a few others which are generally used, of which 99 per cent is perhaps the next most common. If we think of the confidence interval as a sort of 'margin of error' around the sample value, then it is clear that in order to have greater confidence in our estimate, we must allow a wider margin of error – the interval for 99 per cent confidence will be bigger than for 95 per cent. By using the normal tables as before, but now looking for the z-value which cuts off only $\frac{1}{2}$ per cent in each tail (see Figure 8.5), we find that in this case we need to go $2.58 \times$ STEP either side of P. Conversely, a lower confidence level will result in a narrower interval – though this *is not* a good way of achieving what might at first sight seem a more precise, because a smaller, range in our estimate. If we need a smaller interval, the correct way to achieve it would be to take a bigger sample, thus reducing the size of STEP.

Incidentally, although we can increase the confidence level to 99.9 per cent or even 99.99 per cent if we so wish, we cannot ever achieve 100 per cent confidence in our estimate – or at least, only if we are prepared to accept the rather obvious estimate of the population percentage as somewhere between 0 and 100! The point is that when we quote a confidence level, we are not saying 'The probability that the population percentage is in this interval is 95 per cent' – or whatever confidence level we are using. The percentage

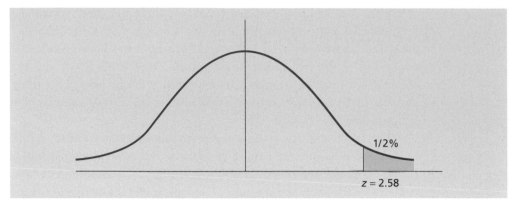

Figure 8.5 Looking for 99 per cent confidence

for the population either *is* in the interval or it *is not*. What we *are* saying is that if we make a habit of estimating population figures from sample figures in this way, then 95 per cent of the time we are going to be right, in the sense that our confidence interval will contain the true population figure. This may seem like playing with words, but it is the misunderstanding of points like this which causes statements such as 'You can prove anything with statistics' to be made!

Finding a sample size

Finally in this section on the uses to which sampling of percentages may be put, we examine the question posed in point 3 on p. 207, which is of very real practical importance to market researchers designing sample surveys: how large a sample is needed to estimate a population percentage to some predetermined degree of accuracy? Sampling costs money and takes time, so clearly it is pointless to interview 6000 people if 600 would have been enough to give us a sufficiently accurate figure; equally, however, it is no good interviewing 600, processing all the results and then finding that the answers are not accurate enough. Fortunately, with the aid of STEP both these dangers can be avoided.

Imagine, then, that you have been asked to conduct a survey to determine the percentage of full-time students who own cars. How many students must you interview? This will naturally depend on (a) how accurate you want your answer to be, and (b) how confident you want to be in that answer. Let us be fairly generous and say that a figure within 5 per cent either way from the true percentage will do, and as usual let us take a 95 per cent confidence level. Furthermore, suppose that a rough pilot survey suggests the figure is somewhere around the 30 per cent mark. Then, referring to Figure 8.6, it becomes apparent that we have two quite separate expressions representing the distance *d*. First, in order to satisfy the 95 per cent confidence requirement, it must be equal to $2 \times \text{STEP}$; second, to achieve the desired accuracy it must also be no more than 5 per cent. So, at worst, these two things must be equal to each other: $2 \times \text{STEP} = 5$, whence $\text{STEP} = 2.5$. Using the rough value for P obtained in the pilot survey, we can now say

$$\text{STEP} = \sqrt{\frac{30 \times 70}{n}}$$

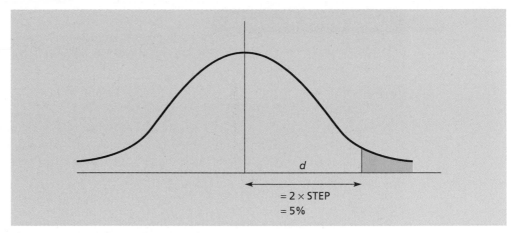

Figure 8.6 Two ways of expressing the distance *d*

where *n* is, of course, unknown – the sample size is what we are trying to find. So we have an equation for *n*, namely

$$\sqrt{\frac{30 \times 70}{n}} = 2.5.$$

The details of how this can be inverted to find *n* should not cause you any problems if you revise the solution of equations in Chapter 1 (as a hint, begin by squaring each side of the equation). The final result is *n* = 336. That is, we must interview 336 people to be 95 per cent confident that our estimate is within 5 per cent of the true answer.

This process can easily be adapted to deal with other levels of confidence and/or other required accuracies. The only small defect in the method is that we had to have a rough idea what *P* was likely to be – in the example above, obtained from a pilot survey. This is not generally too difficult to arrange, but if you *should* be in the position of trying to find out what size sample you need without any idea at all of what you expect the answer to be, then you must, as it were, assume the worst. The 'worst', in this case, is the value of *P* which, should it occur, would give rise to the largest error, and you can easily verify by calculating STEP for, say, samples of 100 items with *P* = 10 per cent, 20 per cent, etc., that STEP has a maximum when *P* = 50. This is true for any sample size, in fact, and so, if you have no prior information as to roughly what *P* might be, assuming it is 50 per cent will give you a sample that is more than big enough to cope with any other value of *P*.

We have now covered the three types of problem mentioned at the start of this section. One final word of warning before we leave the topic of sampling percentages: you will have noticed that we have worked throughout with *percentages*, even when the original information was perhaps given in terms of actual *numbers* in a sample. Where necessary, we converted to percentage terms at the start of the problem and converted back at the end. There *are* alternative versions of the theory designed to deal with numbers or proportions in a sample, but by far the safest principle is always to use figures in percentage form, thus avoiding confusion; then the only point in the theory at which an actual *number* occurs is the sample size *n* in the denominator of the STEP formula.

Quick check questions

1 Calculate STEP when the sample size is 400 and the percentage of the population with the characteristic of interest is 50.

2 Explain in your own words why it is better to give an estimate in the form of a confidence interval rather than as a single value.

3 One quality assurance inspector takes samples of 500 items regularly from a production line and records what proportion are underweight; another inspector on the same line takes samples of 100 items. Which inspector would expect greater variation in the proportions recorded?

Answers:
1 STEP = 2.5 per cent.
2 By quoting a confidence interval in association with an estimate, we are allowing for sampling variability, and can attach a specific level of confidence to our estimate.
3 Greater variability would be expected in the smaller samples than in the larger ones – this is reflected in the fact that STEP is inversely proportional to sample size.

The sampling distribution of means

Although we have chosen to discuss the sampling of percentages in order to introduce you to the theory of sampling, *every* statistic calculated from a sample will have its own sampling distribution. So, for example, we could talk about the sampling distribution for standard deviations or for quartiles, or indeed for any of the measurements we discussed in Chapter 4. The trouble with many of these situations, however, is that they do not follow simple distributions such as the normal, and are therefore difficult to examine theoretically, though we could of course build them up experimentally by actually taking lots of samples from a known population and using them to calculate the measurement we are interested in.

One measurement that fortunately *does* follow a straightforward pattern is the *mean*. (Remember from Chapter 4 that the mean is what is colloquially called the 'average'.) We could define the sampling distribution of means in much the same way as we defined that for percentages, as the distribution we would get if we were able to take all possible random samples of a given size from a particular population and calculate their means. It would seem that the resulting distribution is bound to depend on what the population we are sampling looks like. After all, surely a population in which all values occur the same number of times (a *uniform* distribution of values) is going to give us very different-looking samples from, say, a normal population where some values are much more likely to arise than others.

The extraordinary thing is, however, that although this is undoubtedly true if the samples are small, if the samples are big enough the distribution of their means turns out to be near enough normal *regardless of what kind of population they are taken from*! (You can see an illustration of this in Figure 8.7.) This remarkable fact is a consequence of a result called the Central Limit Theorem, the proof of which need not concern us; what we are going to concentrate on is the use of the result.

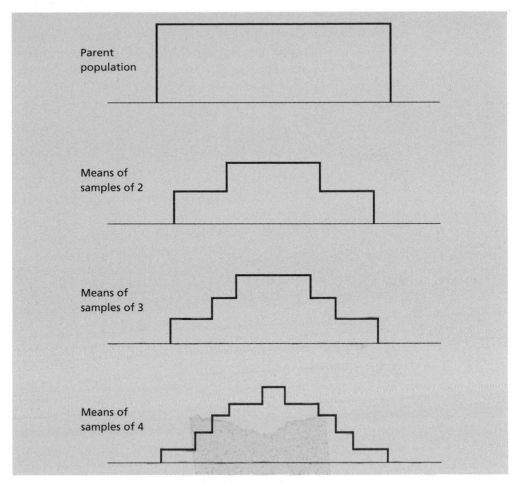

Figure 8.7 The Central Limit Theorem in operation

So, if we accept that for large enough samples – and again, as with sampling percent-ages, 30 is generally considered to be 'large' – the distribution of sample means is normal, then we also need to know its mean and standard deviation. The fact that the mean of the sampling distribution is equal to the overall population mean does not take much swal-lowing; it seems reasonable that there should be more samples with the same mean as the whole population than with any other mean. (This is a point at which newcomers to this topic often get a sort of mental indigestion due to the multitude of 'means' encountered. However, if you remind yourself that we are talking about a distribution all of whose members are means, so that the mean of *this* distribution is a mean of means, you should not be confused.)

As for the standard deviation, it will come as no surprise to you to learn that it is called the *ST*andard *E*rror of the *M*ean, which we will abbreviate to STEM. Once again, as with the Central Limit Theorem, we are not going to give a proof but simply state that

$$STEM = \frac{s.d.}{\sqrt{n}}$$

where s.d. denotes the standard deviation of the population and n is, as usual, the size of the sample. Like STEP, and for the same common-sense reason, STEM decreases as the samples get bigger. The fact that it gets larger as the population s.d. gets larger is also in accordance with common sense, for clearly the more variation in the population, the more varied will be the samples taken from it, and hence their means.

Armed with a knowledge of the shape, mean and standard deviation of the sampling distribution of means, we can now use it to solve all the types of problem considered in the previous section on the application of STEP in relation to percentages. We give just two examples below.

Example 1

What is the probability that if we take a random sample of 64 children from a population whose mean IQ is 100 with a standard deviation of 15, the mean IQ of the sample will be below 95?

Here, $s = 15$, $n = 64$ and population mean $= 100$, so

$$\text{STEM} = \frac{15}{\sqrt{64}} = \frac{15}{8} = 1.875.$$

In Figure 8.8 the probability we want is represented by the shaded area, and by calculating

$$z = \frac{100 - 95}{\text{STEM}} = \frac{5}{1.875} = 2.67$$

and then using the normal tables, we find that the required probability is 0.0038. So the chance that the average IQ of our sample is below 95 is very small indeed. Note that this is a fact about the *average* IQ of the sample – it does not say anything about the individual children who make up the sample.

Example 2

The problem in Example 1 was a bit unrealistic in that we actually *knew* the population mean and standard deviation. In many situations we will be taking a sample precisely because we *do not* have that information, and trying to estimate the population figures from the sample as we did with percentages in the preceding section. Exactly the same argument we went through there tells us that we can estimate with 95 per cent confidence that the population mean will lie in the interval: sample mean $\pm 2 \times \text{STEM}$.

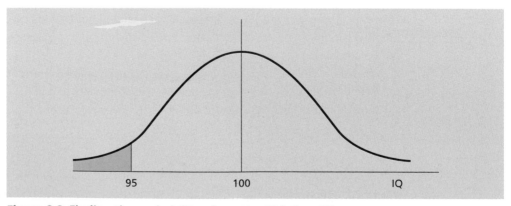

Figure 8.8 Finding the probability of a mean IQ below 95

For example, suppose that an inspector, wishing to check the weight of tins of baked beans but unable to weigh every single one that comes off the production line, contents himself with weighing a random sample of 100 tins. He finds that the sample mean weight is 225 g with a standard deviation of 5 g. Now to calculate STEM we really need to know the *population* standard deviation, but in the absence of that information we can use the sample value, 5 g, instead without serious error (again, as long as n is large). If we do this then STEM $= 5/\sqrt{100} = 0.5$, and so our 95 per cent confidence interval for the mean of the whole population will be $225 \pm 2 \times 0.5$, or from 224 to 226 g.

The problem revisited

If you now go back and reread the section at the beginning of this chapter on the dissatisfied customer's problem you will realise that Radio Supplies' problem is connected with sampling of percentages; it wants to know how likely it is that a box of 500 connections would contain 25 – that is, 5 per cent – faulty items if overall only 2 per cent faulty were being produced. Has the customer just been unlucky? Here we have $P = 2$ per cent, $n = 500$, so STEP $= \sqrt{2 \times 98/500} = 0.626$. To find the probability that the sample percentage is 5 per cent or over, we need to find the area shown in Figure 8.9. Thus we have $z = (5 - 2)/\text{STEP} = 3/0.626 = 4.79$. Now the normal tables show that the area to the right of $z = 4.79$ is negligible, so the chance of such a sample occurring if the population contains only 2 per cent defectives as claimed is very small indeed. It would be hard for Radio Supplies to convince the customer that he has just been unfortunate – particularly if he knows any statistics!

What are we assuming?

We ought to think for a moment here about the effect on this 'solution' to Radio Supplies' problem of the assumptions we have made in the process of deriving the theory. We saw earlier that the more unsymmetrical the binomial – that is, the further away P is

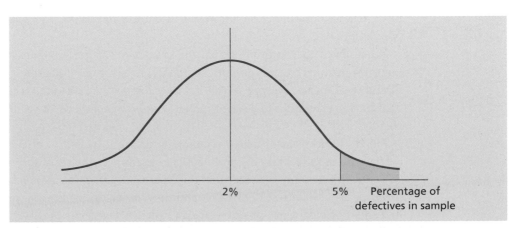

Figure 8.9 Finding the probability that a sample will contain over 5 per cent defectives

from 50 per cent – the bigger the sample needs to be before the normal becomes an adequate approximation. Now, here we have $P = 2$ per cent, which is certainly a long way from 50 per cent by any standards. However, the fact that we have such a very large sample should ensure that, even so, we are safe with the normal approximation.

More serious, not just for this particular problem but in general terms, is the assumption that the sample is a simple random one. We discussed briefly in the first section of this chapter why it might be hard, particularly investigating the customer's complaint in retrospect, to ascertain whether the 'sample' represented by the box of 500 connections really was random, and in Chapter 2 we noted a number of very good reasons why it might be impossible or undesirable to take a simple random sample. In most market research enquiries, for example, some kind of stratified sample is preferred because it ensures adequate and representative coverage of the population in a way that a simple random sample does not.

So have we wasted our time in discussing STEP and STEM? Are they just elegant pieces of theory with no real application in practice? Well, of course the answer is no. Sampling theory such as we have examined in this chapter is the basis for the theory of obtaining estimates and so on from samples of more complicated structures. For stratified samples, for instance, it is often a question simply of modifying our version of the estimation procedure slightly to make allowance for the effect of the stratification (students of marketing may recall the term 'design factor'). Equipped with your knowledge of STEM and STEP, you are in a good position, should the need arise, to understand the theory dealing with more complex types of samples.

The assumption that the population from which we are sampling is infinite (or at least very large compared with the sample size) is also easily overcome, by the insertion of what is called a *finite population correction factor*. If your sample constitutes more than about 10 per cent of the population, then STEM and STEP should be multiplied by

$$\sqrt{1 - \frac{n}{N}}$$

where N is the size of the population. You can check that if n is less than $0.1N$ this factor will not make much difference. When it *is* used, it has the effect of reducing the standard error; this is sensible, since a sample that constitutes a large portion of the population is more reliable, and hence should result in a lower degree of uncertainty about the true population.

What about the assumption that the sample size is greater than 30? If we are sampling proportions, we can go back to the exact binomial if sample sizes are small. For sampling of means, we will see in the next chapter that a modification to our sampling distribution enables us to deal with small samples by methods very similar to those of this chapter.

Finally, let us return briefly to Radio Supplies and its faulty connections. In fact what we have done in tackling this problem is to examine a theory about the population – in this case, the customer's theory that the 2 per cent defective rate is not being maintained – and decide, with the aid of STEP and our knowledge of normal probability, whether that theory holds water or not – in this case, the customer may well be right. We have really been testing a *hypothesis* about the population – and a more detailed examination of such *hypothesis tests* forms the subject of the next chapter.

So how reliable are opinion polls?

At the beginning of this chapter we looked at the results of some political opinion polls, and saw that there was quite a bit of variability between them. You should now have a better insight into why this should be; so let's look in more detail at what can, and what cannot, be deduced from the poll figures.

We will use a rather more up-to-date poll as an example. The following extract is taken from the Ipsos MORI website at **www.mori.com**:

Ipsos MORI July Political Monitor for Reuters

FINAL RESULTS
Fieldwork: 23–25 July 2010
CON 40(+1); LAB 38(+7); LIB DEM 14(−5)

Technical Details
Ipsos MORI interviewed a representative sample of 1,009 adults aged 18+ across Great Britain. Interviews were conducted by telephone 23–25 July 2010. Data are weighted to match the profile of the population.

Q1a   How would you vote if there were a General Election tomorrow?
IF UNDECIDED OR REFUSED AT Q1a

Q1b   Which party are you most inclined to support?
Base: All absolutely certain to vote (589) Q1a/b

	%
Conservative	40
Labour	38
Liberal Democrats (Lib Dem)	14
Scottish/Welsh Nationalist	2
Green Party	3
UK Independence Party	2
British National Party	2
Other*	
Conservative lead (+%) +2	
Would not vote	1
Undecided	5
Refused	2

* Less than 0.6%.

So it looks like the Lib Dems would get 14 per cent of the vote. However, we can now put a confidence interval around that figure, since we are given the information about sample size (this is always given by reputable polling organisations).

If we treat the sample as a simple random sample (actually, as indicated above, the sample is very carefully structured to match the known population profile, but that's too complex a process for us at this stage) then we can say

$$n = 589$$
$$P = 14\% \text{ (for Lib Dems)}$$

so

$$STEP = \sqrt{14 \times 86/589} = 1.43,$$

and the 95 per cent confidence interval for the Lib Dem vote is $14 \pm 1.96 \times 1.43$ or 11.20 per cent to 16.80 per cent.

EXERCISES

*Further examples on the work of this chapter can be found on the **Companion Website**.*

1 A survey of 400 voters contains 208 who will vote for the Regressive candidate at the next election. Estimate with 95 per cent confidence the percentage of the total vote that the candidate is likely to receive in the actual election. What additional information would you like to have about the sample of 400 to ensure that your conclusion is justified?

2 A quick count in the college car park tells me that out of 40 cars parked there, 15 are hatchbacks. Assuming that these cars are representative of the entire population of vehicles on the road, estimate the percentage of that population which are hatchbacks (a) with 95 per cent, and (b) with 99 per cent confidence.

3 An advertiser claims 'Eight out of every ten housewives can't tell Albatross margarine from butter!' A consumers' group sets out to test this claim, and finds that among 75 of their members, 21 *can* distinguish between Albatross and butter. Would this cause you to doubt the advertiser's claim?

4 An Office Efficiency expert times 60 people typing a page of text and finds that the average time for the task is 5.5 minutes with a standard deviation of 0.4 minutes. Estimate the average time taken by all similarly qualified secretaries to type a comparable page of text. (Use 95 per cent confidence.)

5 Your managing director demands that you determine, with 99 per cent confidence and to an accuracy of 1 per cent either way, the percentage of bills sent out by your firm which are in error. At present no one has any idea what this figure may be. How many bills would you need to examine?

6 A survey of the amount spent on a package holiday by a random sample of 65 customers of a travel agency shows that the average expenditure is £423 with a standard deviation of £115.

   (a) Estimate the mean amount spent by all customers, with 99 per cent confidence.
   (b) If you wanted to obtain an estimate with a margin of error of no more than £25, how many more people would you need to question?

7 (a) In a sample of 100 people from a population, you find that the percentage of them with a certain characteristic is 10 per cent. What would be the value of STEP and the width of the 95 per cent confidence interval in this case?
   (b) Now suppose that you obtain the same figure of 10 per cent, but from samples with 400, 900 and 1600 people. What are the corresponding values of STEP?
   (c) Using the values you have calculated, sketch a graph to show how STEP varies with sample size. What do you notice?
   (d) In the light of your graph, comment on the fact that many market research and political opinion surveys contain 500 to 1000 respondents.

8   Carry out a small survey to estimate a percentage such as, for example, the percentage of shoppers at a local supermarket who are male. This is information that might be of interest if, say, the supermarket were considering stocking a new line of male toiletries. There will be problems as to how you get a representative sample. What time of day should you collect your data? What day of the week? And how big should your sample be?

9   Construct a population with a known mean and standard deviation by writing numbers on identical slips of paper. For instance, use a uniform distribution by writing twenty 1s, twenty 2s and so on up to 9. Put the slips in a bag and use the population to build up a sampling distribution of means by taking, perhaps, samples of 9 and 16 slips at a time and finding their means. Strictly speaking, these samples are too small for the theory to apply exactly, but nevertheless if you take a reasonable number of samples – say 50 to 100 of each size – you should get distributions with means close to the population mean, and standard deviations not too different from the values given by the STEM formula.

10 Look out for advertisers' claims based on samples in newspaper articles, etc., and get into the habit of being sceptical about them. Ask 'How big was the sample? Was it really random? What confidence level might they have been using?'

11 Look up in some source of published statistics a figure such as the percentage of imported cars in the UK (you can find this in the *Motor Industry of Great Britain*) and then compare this with the percentage from a sample you yourself have taken. How consistent are the two figures?

12 Build up an experimental sampling distribution of percentages by taking a large number of identical slips of paper, say about 300, and marking 75 per cent of them with a cross, so that $P = 75$ per cent. Shake them up in a bag and then remove samples of perhaps 20 or 30 at a time. Count the number of crossed slips in each sample, and thus build up the sampling distribution. Or you can do it more conveniently with dried butter beans, some of which are marked with a spot of paint. Although, again, the sample size is a bit on the small side, the salient features of the distribution as discussed in 'The sampling distribution of percentages', on p. 204, should emerge. Put the slips/beans back between samples! You can think of this experiment as *simulating* a market research enquiry if, instead of marking a known percentage of the population, you mark an arbitrary number and then try to deduce what percentage they represent by taking samples.

   You will find a computer-based version of this simulation on the student area of the Companion Website.

13 Using the dataset STUD.XLS, and assuming that the students whose details are given constitute a random sample of all students on similar courses, estimate (a) the average age of all male students on such courses, and (b) the proportion of all such students who are from overseas.

Case Study

The Subrose survey revisited

Take another look at the results of the survey described in the case study at the end of Chapter 3 (these are on the website in the file SUBROSE.XLS).

Use the data from the survey to estimate with 95 per cent confidence:

(a) The mean distance travelled to the store by customers.
(b) The proportion of customers who travelled to the supermarket by car.
(c) The proportion of customers who would definitely use the free bus service.
(d) The average age of the customers.

If approximately 3000 customers use the store each day, estimate with 95 per cent confidence the number who would definitely use the free bus service. What have you assumed in reaching your conclusion? How would you answer a manager who suggests that the bus service should only be introduced if there is a guaranteed demand from at least 1000 customers per day?

Further reading

If you are interested in seeing derivations of the formulae for STEM and STEP (which are not very difficult), then a good starting-point is:

Clarke, G.M. and Cooke, D. (2004), *A Basic Course in Statistics*, 5th edn, Hodder Headline.

Chapter 9

CHECKING A THEORY:
HYPOTHESIS TESTING

Chapter prerequisites Before starting work on this chapter, make sure you are happy with all the material on sampling distributions covered in Chapter 8.

Learning outcomes By the end of your work on this chapter you should be able to:

1 formulate and test an appropriate null hypothesis in situations involving percentages in large samples, means and differences of means in large or small samples;

2 recognise situations in which a chi-squared test can be applied, and carry out the test.

Quantitative methods in practice

Boys educated at single-sex schools 'more likely to divorce by early 40s'

'When we examined the risk of divorce or separation by age 42 for those who had ever been married, there was a statistically significant increased risk of divorce or separation for men from single-sex schools,' IoE emeritus professor Diana Leonard said.

www.telegraph.co.uk, 2 December 2009

Man-made climate change blamed for 'significant' rise in ocean temperature

Peter Challenor, of the National Oceanography Centre in Southampton, said the overall picture is clear – the oceans are warming up. 'I'm convinced of that. Everything is consistent with it. The slope [of the graph of ocean temperature against time] is statistically significant, whereas the levelling off in recent years isn't statistically significant,' he said. 'This study has removed many of the nagging doubts about the details. It shows the warming is real.'

www.independent.co.uk, 20 May 2010

The phrase 'statistically significant', as used in the two quotes above, is becoming a familiar one in news reports. We hear that there is (or is not, depending on who is speaking) a 'statistically significant' link between the measles/mumps/rubella (MMR) vaccination of children and the occurrence of various serious disabilities; some scientists warn against 'statistically significant' relationships between mobile phone use and the development of various cancers; and so on.

In business and management, too, the expression raises its head. To mention just three examples: service providers want to know whether increases or decreases in the rate of complaints they receive are 'statistically significant' or just 'blips'; manufacturers need to ask whether quality improvement campaigns have produced a 'significant' reduction in the proportion of poor-quality products; and hospital managers would like to be able to claim 'statistically significant reductions' in patients' waiting times for surgery.

What does the phrase convey to you? One of the self-inflicted problems which statisticians have to grapple with is the fact that we use ordinary, everyday words to convey statistical ideas – but not with their ordinary, everyday meanings. So most people, hearing the phrase 'statistically significant', would probably think that it means 'really big' or 'important' or 'definite'. The true meaning is a good deal more complex, as you might guess from the controversial nature of the examples I have mentioned. It is related to the business of weighing evidence from a sample and deciding whether or not it supports a theory or *hypothesis*. In this chapter we use the concepts of sampling set up in Chapter 8 to explore this process of *hypothesis testing*.

The training manager's problem

Elizabeth Field is the training manager of a light engineering firm which employs a considerable number of skilled machine operators. The firm is constantly making efforts to improve the quality of its product, and so recently Elizabeth has introduced a new 'refresher' training course for workers who have been on the same machines for a long time. The first group has now completed the course and returned to normal work, and Elizabeth would like to assess the effect, if any, that the retraining has had upon the standard of the group's work so that she can decide whether to make such courses a regular event.

There are three particular questions which she would like to answer:

1 Is the *quality* of the product produced by the retrained workers, as measured by the proportion of reject items they produce, better than that produced *before* retraining?
2 Has the *speed* at which they operate their machines increased?
3 Do some classes of workers respond better to retraining than others – for example, younger workers, or female operatives?

In each of these cases, Elizabeth is not, of course, asking the question in a vacuum. She has some idea what was going on before the training course, and she wants to compare the new situation with that established position. Moreover, she clearly hopes that the course *will* have produced improvements all round. She wants, in fact, to test a theory or *hypothesis* about the effect of the course.

Testing hypotheses about percentages

Pinning down the problem

Take first the question regarding the proportion of defective items which the workers produced before and after the course. As far as the position *before* the course is concerned, there will undoubtedly be records available which show what percentage of reject items had been produced over a period by each worker. The amount of data available is probably so large that we can regard this as giving the percentage of defective items among the entire *population* of items produced by the worker in question.

But when it comes to the position *after* the course, there will not be nearly such a large amount of data available – or at least, not if Elizabeth wants to make her assessment fairly soon. She will have to rely on taking just a *sample* of items produced by a retrained worker, and base her assessment of the efficacy of the course on that sample. Suppose, for instance, that worker X, before the course, had been producing 4 per cent of reject items; after the course, his performance is monitored during the production of 400 items, and 14 of them are found to be defective. This represents a rate of only 3.5 per cent, which is certainly an improvement. So Elizabeth can congratulate herself that the course seems to have worked. Or *can* she?

We know from our work on sampling distributions in the last chapter that, just because the *population* percentage of reject items was 4 per cent, it does not follow that every single sample of 400 items taken from that population would also contain exactly 4 per cent rejects; there would be quite a bit of variation among the samples. So perhaps the 3.5 per cent figure does not demonstrate an improvement at all, but is simply the product of a random sampling variation. Maybe, in fact, if we continued to monitor this worker's output, we would find that he is still producing 4 per cent rejects overall – or even, perhaps, that having been away from the job during the retraining, he has deteriorated in efficiency and is now producing *more* than 4 per cent rejects!

In order to draw a sound conclusion on the basis of the sample evidence, then, we have to take sampling variations into account. It is also important that we do not begin by assuming what we are trying to prove. Elizabeth obviously hopes that her course will have produced an improvement, but to convince her sceptical manager she must begin with the assumption that it has not produced any change at all. This initial assumption is called the *null hypothesis*, often abbreviated to NH; you may find it helpful to think of it as the 'boring hypothesis' – everything's the same, nothing's changed, the population is just as it always was.

The implication of the null hypothesis is that the sample of 400 items taken after the course has been drawn from a population in which the percentage of reject items is still 4 per cent, so using the notation of Chapter 8, $P = 4$. From this point of view, the null hypothesis is the only logical assumption we *can* make, since the 4 per cent figure is the only one we are sure about. (If the figure is not 4 per cent, then what on earth is it? Not 3.5 per cent – that only applies to a sample, which may turn out to be an atypical one.)

With this value of P, and knowing that $n = 400$, we can proceed to calculate STEP:

$$\text{STEP} = \sqrt{\frac{4 \times 96}{400}} = 0.98\%.$$

We could now go ahead and calculate the probability that a sample such as we have got – with 3.5 per cent of rejects or even less – could arise from a population in which the proportion of rejects is 4 per cent. This is very much the sort of thing we did in Chapter 8, and in many ways it has a lot to recommend it. But a rather more systematic procedure has grown up for deciding whether or not the sample is consistent with the truth of the null hypothesis.

Setting out the procedure

Remember that we found in Chapter 8 that 95 per cent of all the possible samples from a population with 4 per cent defective items will be contained within two standard deviations – $2 \times \text{STEP}$ – either side of 4 per cent. So the great majority – 95 per cent or 19 out of 20 – of all the samples of 400 items which we might get if the population percentage were 4 per cent will contain percentages of rejects in the range $4 \pm 2 \times 0.98$; that's between 2.04 per cent and 5.96 per cent. You can see this illustrated in Figure 9.1.

This suggests that the sample taken after the course, containing 3.5 per cent rejects, is not at all inconsistent with the assumption that overall the worker is still producing 4 per cent rejects. In fact, quite often before the course he would have been producing samples

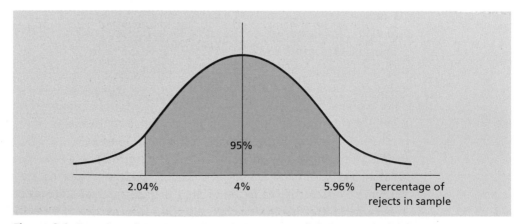

Figure 9.1 Samples of 400 items from a 4 per cent defective population

as good as this or even better. So really we have no grounds, at least from this sample, for deciding that the percentage of defective items he is producing has changed at all. However, being naturally cautious, statisticians do not say anything so definite as 'The null hypothesis is correct', or 'We've proved that the worker hasn't improved'. All that can be fairly claimed is that, on the strength of this sample, we have no grounds for rejecting the null hypothesis.

Of course, as always in sampling situations, we have to accept the fact that this conclusion *may* be incorrect. The usual way of expressing the conclusion is to say that the difference between the sample and the population percentage is 'not significant at the 5 per cent level'; the 5 per cent refers to the leftover portion of the sampling distribution, the 'odd 5 per cent of samples', as it were, among which our sample would have to fall before we would be justified in rejecting the null hypothesis.

It is easier to understand why the conclusion is expressed in this way if we take another example.

A second example

Suppose that a second worker had been producing 5 per cent reject items before the course, and afterwards his sample of 400 items contains only 10 rejects – that is, 2.5 per cent. Has *this* worker changed?

In this case the null hypothesis is that $P = 5$ (i.e. there has been no change). So

$$\text{STEP} = \sqrt{\frac{5 \times 95}{400}} = 1.09$$

and 95 per cent of all samples of 400 would fall in the interval $5 \pm 2 \times 1.09$, or 2.82 per cent to 7.18 per cent. However, this time when we compare the sample taken after the course with this interval, we find that it lies outside the limits; in other words, if it *does* come from this population, it is a pretty unusual sample – one of only 5 per cent that differ from the mean by more than 2.18 per cent. So we would be quite justified here in concluding that the sample is so different from what we would expect to get most of the time, were the null hypothesis true, as to cast doubt on that hypothesis.

We would therefore conclude that the null hypothesis should be *rejected*. Again, note the word 'used' – we do not say 'The null hypothesis must be wrong' – and we must qualify our statement, as usual, according to the particular interval we used to make the decision. We would say in this case that the difference between the sample and the population is 'significant' at the 5 per cent level; there probably *has* been a change in the proportion of rejects being produced by this worker.

Interpreting the result

It is important to realise that we have *not* proved at the 5 per cent level that the worker has improved. By taking a symmetrical confidence interval, and dividing the 'leftover' 5 per cent equally between the two tails of the sampling distribution, we have considered the possibility of either an improvement *or* a deterioration in the quality of the worker's output. This is sometimes expressed by saying that our *alternative hypothesis* is $P \neq 5$ per cent. So all we have shown is that there is a difference since the worker went on the course. We will be returning to this point in the next section.

As always, setting up the procedure for carrying out a hypothesis test has made it appear much more lengthy than it really is. The process can be summarised as shown below.

If you find it difficult to remember which way the decision rule works, remember that the bigger the difference between the sample and the population percentages, the less likely the population percentage is to be applicable; when the difference gets so big that the sample actually falls outside the 95 per cent interval, then we are forced to conclude that the population percentage cannot be applicable, so the null hypothesis must be rejected. If, on the other hand, the sample is one of the 'majority' – the 95 per cent of samples that fall within the limits – then there are no grounds for doubting the null hypothesis.

Procedure for testing a hypothesis about a percentage:

1 Formulate a null hypothesis, which will give you the value of P, and an alternative hypothesis.
2 Calculate STEP, and hence the appropriate interval (2 STEP on either side of P if you are using a 5 per cent significance level).
3 Compare the sample percentage with this interval to see whether it is inside or outside.
4 If the sample value falls *outside* the interval, reject the null hypothesis – the sample differs significantly from the population percentage (at the 5 per cent level if you have used the 95 per cent interval).

If the sample value lies *inside* the interval, do *not* reject the null hypothesis – the difference is not significant at the 5 per cent level.*

Quick check questions

1 The records of a train operating company show that, over a long period, about 10 per cent of trains have arrived at their destination more than 15 minutes late. The new managing director of the company has now instituted a punctuality drive, and last month only 8 per cent of trains were more than 15 minutes late. What null hypothesis would you test in this situation?

2 When you carry out the test in the above situation, you find that your sample falls within the extreme 5 per cent of the sampling distribution. Would you reject the null hypothesis or not?

3 Which of the following statements would be correct as the conclusion of a hypothesis testing procedure? (a) We reject the null hypothesis with 95 per cent confidence. (b) We reject the null hypothesis at the 5 per cent significance level.

Answers:
1 The null hypothesis would be that the proportion late is still 10 per cent.
2 The conclusion here would be to reject the null hypothesis.
3 Statement (b) is correct – a hypothesis test is associated with a significance level (confidence levels are associated with estimates, as in Chapter 8).

* It has probably struck you that embedded in this process for testing hypotheses is the construction of what looks very much like a 95 per cent confidence interval. It is *not*, however, a confidence interval – we are *not* trying to estimate anything – and so the word 'confidence' is strictly barred from our discussion. We are *not*, for instance, 'rejecting or accepting a null hypothesis with 95 per cent confidence', but at a certain *significance* level. To avoid the possibility of confusion, the interval in a hypothesis test is sometimes called the 'acceptance region', and the part outside the interval the 'rejection region', since we reject the null hypothesis for a sample in this region.

Further points about hypothesis testing

This section contains some rather more theoretical considerations. Do not skip over it, but do not, either, worry too much if you do not grasp all the details; they will probably fall into place later.

Changing the significance level

Just as there was nothing special about the 95 per cent confidence level, merely conventional popularity, so there is nothing sacred about the corresponding 5 per cent significance level. By using a 99 per cent interval when carrying out the test (which, you will recall, requires an interval of 2.58 STEP either side of the population percentage), we could obtain conclusions at the 1 per cent level of significance instead. Of course, the 99 per cent interval is wider than the 95 per cent one, so we would be less likely to conclude that a result is significant. In that sense, it is 'harder' to prove something significant at the 1 per cent than at the 5 per cent level – the lower the significance level, the less likely we are to conclude that something is significant when it is not.

Statistical significance

We can now give a better interpretation of the concept of statistical significance mentioned in the introduction to this chapter. In carrying out our tests above, we have used a threshold of 5 per cent – a 1 in 20 chance, if you like – as our dividing line between events that are 'not unusual' and those that are 'unusual', where 'usual' means 'consistent with the null hypothesis'. So a statistically significant result is one that falls in the 'unusual' range – it's unlikely to have occurred by chance if the null hypothesis is true, and is therefore regarded as significant.

You may begin to see why the interpretation of results in terms of statistical significance can give rise to controversy. After all, there is nothing special about 5 per cent. But someone who used a different significance level – say, 1 per cent – might come to the conclusion that a result is not statistically significant when the analyst using a 5 per cent significance level says that it is (think about where the 1 and 5 per cent limits fall on the normal curve to see how this could occur).

It might really be better, as we hinted earlier, to find the exact probability associated with our sample data, rather than relying on the 'in or out' approach of conventional hypothesis testing. However, the method has been around for many years and is not going to disappear in a hurry; and as long as it is used honestly – for example, by clearly stating the sample size and the significance level used in a test – someone who really understands the concepts should not be misled.

The risks of being wrong

Perhaps the best way to understand what these significance levels mean is to think about the times when we will make a *wrong* decision in a hypothesis test. There are two ways we might do this: we might conclude that there *is* a significant difference when there is not, or we might decide that there is *no* significant difference when in fact one does exist. The table shows the situation schematically:

	True situation	
Decision	Null hypothesis true	Null hypothesis false
Reject null hypothesis	Type 1 error	✓
Do not reject null hypothesis	✓	Type 2 error

The first of these possibilities is by far the easier to consider – we conclude that something is significant at, say, the 5 per cent level if our sample falls outside the 95 per cent interval. But 5 per cent of the perfectly respectable samples from the null hypothesis population will be outside this interval anyway; how do we know that the sample we have got does not just happen to be one of those 5 per cent? The answer is, of course, that we *do not* know that, so the chance of making a mistake of this kind is precisely 5 per cent: in 5 per cent of the cases when the null hypothesis is true, we will reject it. A mistake of this kind is known technically as a Type 1 error, so the significance level with which we make our decision is just the chance of making this kind of error – concluding that something is significant when it is not.

The second kind of mistake is much more difficult to think about. The chance that we will fail to spot a real difference between the null hypothesis and the true situation depends on a lot of factors. For example, it is clear that a big difference is much easier to spot than a small difference, so that the chance of making this kind of error – called Type 2 – will depend on how close the true population is to the null hypothesis population. But of course, we do not *know* about the true situation; if we did we would not be doing the test in the first place!

That is only one of the problems in considering the second sort of error – an error we risk making, remember, every time we fail to reject a null hypothesis. It is partly because of the difficulty in assessing the chance of being wrong in this situation that we are only prepared to make the very cautious statement 'No grounds for rejecting null hypothesis'.

One tail or two?

When we conclude, on the basis of a test of the kind we did in the section on testing hypotheses about percentages, that there *is* a significant difference between the sample and the null hypothesis population, we cannot, as indicated already, draw any *statistical* conclusions as to which direction the difference is in, since we have apportioned the 'left-over' 5 per cent of the sampling distribution equally between the two tails. So it would be wrong, in the second case above, to say that 'There has been a significant improvement at the 5 per cent level'; although common sense suggests that an improvement is more likely than a deterioration under the circumstances, all we have actually shown is that there is a difference, one way or the other, which is significant at the 5 per cent level.

It *is* possible to test for a difference in a predetermined direction, by using an unsymmetrical interval. For example, in the case we have just been considering we could refuse to contemplate the possibility that the course has caused a decline in the quality of the workers' efforts, and look only for differences in the direction of an improvement. In practice that would mean putting all the 'leftover' 5 per cent of the sampling distribution under the left-hand tail of the distribution, where the percentages are lower than average, and forgetting all about the higher-than-average end. In this case, we would be carrying out what is known as a *one-tailed test*, because we are considering only the cases in one

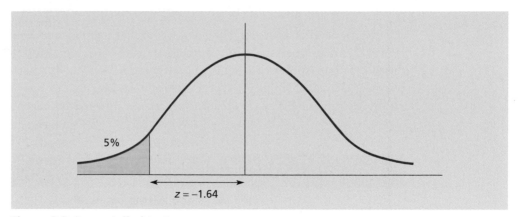

Figure 9.2 A one-tailed test

tail of the sampling distribution. In contrast, the type of test we developed earlier is known as a two-tailed test.

In the case of the one-tailed test, the actual statements of the hypotheses are slightly different from those for a two-tailed test. Because we are not concerned with detecting changes at the upper end of the distribution, we are now testing the null hypothesis: $P \geqslant 4$ per cent against the alternative $P < 4$ per cent.

If we want to complete the one-tailed test then we need to know how many standard deviations from the mean will cut off 5 per cent under one tail of the sampling distribution (see Figure 9.2). If you consult the tables of the normal distribution to find what value of z corresponds to an area of 5 per cent (0.05) you should discover that the relevant z is about 1.64. Since we are concerned with the lower tail of the distribution in this case, we therefore need to be 1.64 STEP below the mean. For the first worker, whose mean before the course was 4 per cent, a figure of $4 - 1.64 \times$ STEP or 2.39 per cent is obtained (STEP, of course, still has the value of 0.98 which we computed earlier). So the acceptance region in this case becomes *all* sample percentages bigger than 2.39 per cent. Since the worker's new figure is 3.5 per cent, we come to the same conclusion as before – that is, there is no reason to conclude that things have improved.

You may have noticed that the rejection region in the one-tailed case consists of all sample percentages less than 2.39 per cent, whereas for the two-tailed test it was all sample percentages less than 2.04 per cent. Thus by deciding to carry out a one-tailed rather than a two-tailed test, we are in a way making it 'easier' to conclude that there has been a change – a consequence of the fact that we are choosing to ignore the possibility of a deterioration, and focusing on the 'improvement' end of the scale. For this reason, you need to have pretty strong grounds for carrying out a one-tailed test; if you are in any doubt, it is probably preferable to use two tails.

For easy reference in carrying out one- and two-tailed tests at 5 per cent and 1 per cent levels of significance, the z-values cutting off 5 per cent and 1 per cent under 1 and 2 tails are shown in the table below:

	5%	1%
One tail	1.64	2.33
Two tails	1.96	2.58

It may have struck you that, by juggling about with the number of tails and the significance level of your tests, it is possible to make almost any result look significant. However, this is *not* a respectable way to use statistical argument! You should decide *before* carrying out a test how many tails you are going to use, and at what significance level – that is, what risk of making a Type 1 error you are prepared to accept. This is what was meant when we said on p. 229 that the process must be used honestly.

Testing hypotheses about means of large samples

Having established the routine for hypothesis testing on percentages, we can apply it also to tests on means of samples, just as we were able to adapt the inference procedures of Chapter 8 quite easily to this situation. So, we have really got two types of test for the price of one.

As an example, take Mrs Field's second requirement: she wants to test whether the average time taken by the workers to produce items has been reduced since they went on the course. As with the percentage of rejects, there should be plenty of pre-course data to give us a population figure for the mean time taken, and the standard deviation of the times (presumably each worker does not always take exactly the same time). But for the post-course information, she will have to rely on a sample only.

Worker X took a mean of 2.5 minutes to produce one item before the course, and the standard deviation of his times was 0.5 minutes. After the course, he is timed over the production of 64 items, which take him 2 hours 45 minutes to make; that is, a mean of 2.58 minutes – actually slower than before. But again, this may not be indicative of any change; it may simply be the result of sampling variations, which if we took another sample of 64 items might produce a value *better* than 2.58 minutes.

In order to decide whether this is the explanation, we begin with the null hypothesis that there has been no change in the mean time taken by the worker for the job. So we are assuming that the population mean is 2.5 minutes just as it always was. We will carry out a two-tailed test, since we are open to the possibility that the time might have increased or decreased. So the alternative hypothesis is mean ≠ 2.5 minutes. The distribution of means of samples of 64 items taken from this population would then, as we saw in Chapter 8, be normal, with a mean of 2.5 minutes and a standard deviation of STEM, where

$$\text{STEM} = \frac{\text{population standard deviation}}{\sqrt{n}}$$

$$= \frac{0.5}{\sqrt{64}} = 0.0625 \text{ minutes.}$$

Ninety-five per cent of all the random samples of 64 items taken out of this population would then fall in the range $2.5 \pm 2 \times 0.0625$ minutes, that is, between 2.375 and 2.625 minutes. The worker's mean after the course – 2.58 minutes – falls within this range; thus such a value could well arise even if there has been no change in his overall rate of working. We therefore have no grounds for rejecting the null hypothesis – there is no change significant at the 5 per cent level.

An alternative way of carrying out hypothesis tests

In our tests with both STEM and STEP, we have chosen to calculate an acceptance region and see whether or not our sample value (mean or percentage) falls within this region. There is another, completely equivalent way of carrying out the test which is widely used; I mention it here because you may well come across it in other books.

Suppose, to make things definite, that we are going to repeat the test on p. 225, where we wanted to know whether a sample of 400 items with 14 rejects produced by a worker after a training course enabled us to conclude that there had been a change from his previous rate of 4 per cent defectives. In this case our null hypothesis was that overall there had been no change, so the population percentage of defectives P was still 4 per cent. Then with $n = 400$, STEP turned out to be 0.98 per cent.

When we dealt with this problem earlier, we then worked out the interval $4 \pm 2 \times 0.98\%$, and found that 3.5 per cent lay inside this interval, furnishing no grounds for rejecting the null hypothesis. However, we can instead calculate a z-value based on our sample, exactly as we would if we were going to work out the probability of such a sample occurring using the normal tables. We would get

$$z = \frac{\text{our value} - \text{mean}}{\text{standard deviation}}$$

$$= \frac{\text{sample percentage} - \text{population percentage}}{\text{STEP}}$$

$$= \frac{3.5 - 4}{0.98} = -0.51.$$

We then compare this with the z-value which would be needed to ensure that our sample falls in the 5 per cent 'tails' of the distribution; by now you will be very familiar with the fact that this critical z, as it is often called, is 1.96 or roughly 2. As our z is much less than this, we can conclude that the probability of getting by random chance a sample which differs from the mean of 4 per cent as much as ours does, or even more, is quite high – certainly greater than the 5 per cent significance we are looking for. So, as before, the conclusion is that our sample is quite consistent with the null hypothesis, which should therefore not be rejected.

Had we been using a 1 per cent level of significance, the critical z-value would be 2.58. The process for doing the test in this way can be summed up as follows:

1 State null hypothesis and alternative (one-tailed or two-tailed).
2 Decide on significance level to be used and find corresponding critical value of z.
3 Calculate sample z as (sample value – population value) standard error (STEM or STEP as appropriate).
4 Compare sample z with the critical z. If it is smaller, do not reject the null hypothesis; if greater, the sample provides grounds for rejecting the null hypothesis.

Because of the use of the letter z to represent the standard normal variable, this type of hypothesis test has come to be known as a z-test. There is an increasing move among statisticians to encourage people to go further, and actually calculate the probability that the null hypothesis population could give a sample such as the one obtained. This probability is referred to as a *p*-value, and the point about insisting that it should be calculated is that this prevents the user of the test from blindly using a conventional figure such as 5 per cent or 1 per cent without thinking about the meaning of his or her results. You will therefore sometimes see statements like 'the result was significant ($p < 0.01$)', which is really just an alternative way of saying 'significant at the 1 per cent level'. And if you carry out hypothesis tests using a statistical computer package, you will find that the relevant *p*-value is given automatically (see the section 'Hypothesis testing with Excel', p. 252, and the corresponding chapter of the MyMathLab Excel supplement).

Testing hypotheses about the means of small samples

The theory

As we noted when first encountering the sampling distribution of the mean in Chapter 8, this distribution will be normal only if the samples are large – 30 was mentioned as the conventional threshold size. But of course, people need to test hypotheses based on much smaller samples, because in many situations they only have a small amount of data to go on.

For instance, suppose that Elizabeth Field, the training manager of the company introduced earlier in this chapter, wishes to determine whether the time needed to train workers who are recruited to a particular job is different for women. The mean training time required for a large number of men trained in the past was ten days, but the only information she has about women recruits is based on a group of just eight women trained in the last six months. They took an average of nine days to train, so it looks at first sight as if they were quicker.

What we must remember, however, is that the variation might have been caused merely by sampling variations. After all, eight is a very small sample indeed. So we need to know what the sampling distribution for the means of small samples looks like, before we can properly assess the implications of Elizabeth's data.

You may have noticed that we do not yet have the complete picture: there has been no mention of the standard deviation of the training times, or of what type of distribution the times might be expected to follow. This is absolutely crucial information. You will recall that, on p. 214, we met the Central Limit Theorem, which assured us that what-ever the form of the underlying distribution the means of *large* samples will be normally distributed. But this does *not* apply for *small* samples. We can only carry out tests of the kind we are studying here for small samples *if the underlying distribution is known to be normal*. (If it is not, there are other methods outside the scope of this book that can be resorted to.)

Even if we are sure that the underlying population *is* normal (and we will assume that that is the case here) there is still another complication. If we know the standard deviation of the underlying distribution, then the sampling distribution of the means is still normal, and everything proceeds as in the section earlier in the chapter on testing hypotheses about means, with STEM calculated in the usual way. But if we only know the standard deviation of the sample, and have to use that to approximate the population standard deviation, then more uncertainty creeps in. In this case the normal distribution

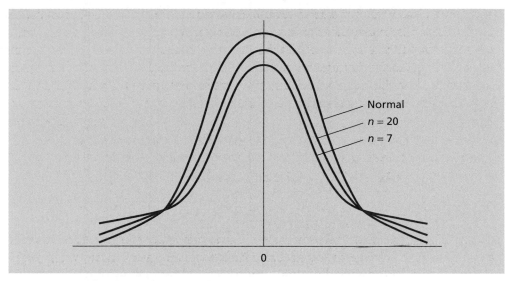

Figure 9.3 Student's *t*-distribution

of sample means will not apply, and instead we have to use a different distribution, called Student's *t*-distribution.

This curiously named distribution (named after its inventor, an employee of Guinness Breweries by the name of Gosset who used 'Student' as a pseudonym when writing statistical papers) looks very much like a normal distribution, in that it is symmetric and bell-shaped. However, it is in a way a mistake to talk about 'it' when referring to the *t*-distribution – we should really say 'them', because there is actually a whole family of *t*-distributions, their precise shape varying with the sample size we are using.

Some of these are sketched in Figure 9.3. You can see that as *n* gets bigger, the *t*-distribution looks more and more like the normal curve, until by the time *n* = 30 or so, the two are pretty indistinguishable. That is why, for samples of size bigger than this, we can use the normal quite safely. For smaller samples, the distribution is wider than the normal, so that a 95 per cent confidence interval based on it would be correspondingly wider also; this reflects the greater degree of uncertainty in having to approximate the population standard deviation by that of the sample.

The process

To get a clearer idea precisely how the *t*-distribution is used, let us go back to Elizabeth Field's problem where the mean training time for the population is ten days, the sample mean for eight women is nine days, and let us further assume that we only know the sample standard deviation which is two days. First of all, we need to recall what was said in Chapter 4 about approximating a population standard deviation (s.d.) by a sample – really we get a better idea of the population figure if we divide the sum of the squared deviations in the s.d. calculation by $n - 1$ instead of n, before taking the square root. This did not matter with large samples, but here it does make a difference. So we will assume that the $n - 1$ divisor was used in arriving at the sample s.d. of 2.

We can now say that STEM = $2/\sqrt{8}$ = 0.71, and formulate our null hypothesis: there is no difference in overall mean training time between men and women. Instead of calculating a z-value, however, as we did on p. 233, we calculate a t-value in exactly the same way:

$$t = \frac{\text{sample mean} - \text{population mean}}{\text{STEM}} = \frac{9 - 10}{0.71} = -1.41.$$

The final stage of the process should be to compare this with a 'critical value' of t, to find whether or not it is significant. The critical values of t, like those of z, have to come from a table.

You will find the table of the t-distribution in Appendix 8. As you can see, it differs from the normal tables; because we need a lot of different values for different sample sizes, we cannot have each distribution tabulated in such detail, otherwise the tables would be very bulky. Instead, we just have the t-values for a selection of the usual significance levels (across the table) and a variety of sample sizes (down the table).

Just to make life even more interesting, for reasons you do not need to go into, the rows of the table are labelled not according to sample size n but according to $n - 1$, called the *degrees of freedom* of the distribution and often denoted by the Greek letter ν (*nu*, pronounced 'new'). Note also that the significance levels at the tops of the columns refer to the area under one tail of the distribution, so to do our usual type of two-tailed test we need to multiply them by 2.

Our sample with $n = 8$ means therefore that we should look in the row where $\nu = 8 - 1 = 7$. If we want a significance level of 5 per cent or 0.05, then as explained above we look in the 0.025 column and find that the critical t is 2.365. What we calculated above was $t = 1.41$, which is smaller than this, so our decision would be *not* to reject the null hypothesis.

There are a few other things to notice while you are looking at the tables of the t-distribution. First, the t-value for a given significance level is always greater than the z-value would be, regardless of the value of n – the z-value for 5 per cent significance, for example, would be the familiar 1.96 or roughly 2 – which confirms what was said earlier about the t-distribution being wider. Second, you can see the t-values getting closer to the normal or z-values as n, and hence ν, gets bigger. The tables indicate this by saying that the normal values apply to a t-distribution with 'infinite degrees of freedom' (bottom row of the table). Hence we can use the normal instead of t with reasonable accuracy as long as the sample is not too small.

By now you have had to absorb quite a lot of information about testing hypotheses on sample means, so we will pause for a summary of the situation:

1 If the underlying population is normal and we know its standard deviation, then the distribution of sample means is normal with standard deviation = STEM = population s.d./$\sqrt{n}$, whatever the value of n, and we can use a z-test.

2 If the underlying population is unknown but the sample size is large, the distribution of the sample means is approximately normal with standard deviation = STEM = population (or sample) s.d./n, and again a z-test can be used.

3 If the underlying population is normal, but we do not know its standard deviation, and we have data about a small sample, then we can use the sample s.d. to approximate that of the population (remembering to use the $n - 1$ divisor in the calculation of the s.d.). The distribution of sample means is then a t-distribution with $n - 1$ degrees of freedom, and standard deviation STEM = sample s.d./$\sqrt{n}$. So a t-test can be used.

4   If the underlying population is not normal and we only have a small sample, none of the hypothesis testing procedures we have discussed can be safely used.

Of course, the use of the t-distribution is not confined to hypothesis testing; you can use it also to get confidence intervals. The process is no different from that using the normal distribution, except that t-values rather than z-values are used in the construction of the interval.

Testing the difference between two sample means

You may have felt a certain sinking of the heart when reading the title of this section – not another hypothesis testing procedure! But one of the better things about hypothesis testing is that once you have the basic routine clear in your mind, many different types of test can be carried out with relatively few new ideas to grasp.

Suppose, for example, that we need to test, not the mean of a single sample against a hypothesised population value, but whether there is a significant difference between two sample means. To be definite, imagine that the overworked Elizabeth Field has data on the wages of two groups of workers, both taken from large populations: a group of 30 taken from Production had a mean weekly wage of £360 after deductions, with a standard deviation of £25, while 50 workers from Maintenance had a mean of £380 with standard deviation £30. Does this evidence suggest that there is a difference in wages between workers in these two areas?

If we proceed in the usual way, the first step is to formulate the null hypothesis: here it will be 'There is no difference between the wages of workers in Production and Maintenance'. In other words, the two samples are effectively taken from the *same* population.

Second, we need to calculate the appropriate standard error, and it is here that the only real difference arises. The standard error we want here is that of the *difference* of two sample means, and it is calculated as

$$s\sqrt{\frac{1}{n_1} + \frac{1}{n_2}},$$

where s is the standard deviation of the common population from which the samples are taken, and n_1 and n_2 are their respective sizes.

So here $n_1 = 30$, $n_2 = 50$ (it does not matter which way round we number the samples). However, there is a bit of a problem when it comes to the population standard deviation – namely, we do not know what it is. Instead, since the null hypothesis tells us that both samples came from the same population, we can estimate it by combining the information from the two samples (rather in the manner of a weighted average) according to the formula

$$s = \sqrt{\frac{n_1 s_1^2 + n_2 s_2^2}{n_1 + n_2}}.$$

s_1 and s_2 here are the sample standard deviations, and so we find

$$s = \sqrt{\frac{30 \times 625 + 50 \times 900}{30 + 50}} = 28.23.$$

You can see that this estimate is nearer to the standard deviation of the larger sample than that of the smaller, just as we expect with a weighted average.

We can now proceed to calculate the standard error:

$$\text{Standard Error of Difference in Sample Means}_{\text{(unpronounceably shortened to STEDM)}} = 28.23\sqrt{\frac{1}{30} + \frac{1}{50}} = 6.52.$$

Third, we need to know the relevant sampling distribution. For the difference of two large samples, just as with a single large sample, the distribution is normal. Its standard deviation is STEDM as calculated above, and of course its mean is zero, because if the null hypothesis is true there is *no* difference between the populations from which the samples come. All this enables us to calculate

$$z = \frac{\text{difference in sample means} - 0}{\text{STEDM}}$$

$$= \frac{360 - 380}{6.52}$$

$$= -3.07.$$

This is well outside the critical z for 5 per cent significance, which would be -1.96, so we have grounds for rejecting the null hypothesis, and concluding that there is a difference in wages between the two populations of workers.

Had we had small samples from normal populations instead, then as with a single sample we would have to replace the z-test by a t-test, this time with $n_1 + n_2 - 2$ degrees of freedom (the sum of the degrees of freedom for each sample separately). In this case too, we need to put in the correction factors for using sample standard deviations to estimate a population s.d., and remember to divide by $n - 1$ rather than n when calculating the standard deviations. The formula for pooling the standard deviations then becomes

$$s = \sqrt{\frac{(n_1 - 1)s_1^2 + (n_2 - 1)s_2^2}{n_1 + n_2 - 2}}$$

The STEDM formula remains unaltered and the process for completing the test is exactly as before with z replaced by t.

By now you should be able to see that, whatever the context of your hypothesis test, the procedure can be summarised as follows:

1 State null hypothesis and decide significance level to be used.
2 Identify information given (number of samples, large or small, mean or proportion, etc.) and decide what standard error and what distribution are required.
3 Calculate required standard error.
4 Calculate z or t as difference between sample and population values divided by standard error.
5 Compare your z or t with the critical value from tables for the significance level you are using; if your z or t is greater than the critical value, reject the null hypothesis.

We will see in the next section, concerned with testing hypotheses about more than one proportion, how this procedure actually extends to further cases where neither z- nor t-tests apply, but the basic routine is still the same. Before going on to that, however, it would be a good idea to tackle the quick check questions below, and perhaps to work through some of the exercises at the end of the chapter to make sure you have your ideas straight so far!

Quick check questions

1 We carry out a t-test when (a) we have a small sample from a normal population, or (b) we have a sample of any size from a population which is not normal?

2 We have a sample of 50 items with standard deviation 9 units, and a sample of 80 items with standard deviation 12 units. Estimate the standard deviation of the population from which both these samples were drawn.

3 The smaller the p-value of a test, the more likely we are to reject the null hypothesis. True or false?

Answers:
1 Correct answer is (a).
2 Estimated standard deviation of the population is

$$s = \sqrt{\frac{n_1 s_1^2 + n_2 s_2^2}{n_1 + n_2}} = \sqrt{\frac{50 \times 81 + 80 \times 144}{50 + 80}} = 10.94.$$

3 The statement is true.

Testing hypotheses about more than one proportion

Elizabeth Field's third problem, about the relative effects of the course on different groups of workers, could be expressed in terms of the difference between the proportions of various groups who have, or have not, improved. If she has collected some data broken down according to age, for example, she might be faced with something like the table below:

Age group	Improved	Did not improve
Under 35	17	4
35–50	17	7
Over 50	6	9

What she needs to test here is whether the proportion (or percentage) improving is consistent across all the age groups, or varies significantly from one to another. But the sort of test carried out on p. 225 is no use to her here, since it dealt with just *one* sample percentage at a time. Even the tests of the last section for the difference of two samples are no good, since we have more than two. What we must develop is a method of testing the various categories simultaneously.

We begin, as always, by formulating a null hypothesis. In this case, the 'no difference' hypothesis takes the form of the assumption that the figures given are consistent with an improvement rate which is the same for all age groups; the variations that occur in practice between one age group and another are merely chance sampling fluctuations and not indicative of any real difference. This hypothesis can be expressed very succinctly by saying that there is *no association* between age group and improvement.

If this hypothesis were true, then we would expect the same rate of improvement to be found in all three age groups. Our best guide to what that overall rate may be is given by the combined rate for all groups together, and so we start by finding the totals for the various categories, as shown in the table below:

Age group	Improved		Did not improve		Total
Under 35	17	(14)	4	(7)	21
35–50	17	(16)	7	(8)	24
Over 50	6	(10)	9	(5)	15
	40		20		60

Thus overall, 40 out of 60 people improved – two-thirds. Now, *if* the null hypothesis is true, then this rate applies equally to all three age groups. So we would have expected two-thirds of each age group to improve. We can therefore insert the *expected* numbers of people in each category into the table; these are the bracketed figures in the table above. They are easily calculated from the two-thirds improvement rate. For example, there were 21 people in the 'Under 35' age group; two-thirds of these would be expected to improve – that is, 14. Similarly, in the '35–50' group, two-thirds of 24 people would be expected to show an improvement, whence we get the figure of 16. If you like formulae, you can express this calculation as follows:

$$E_{ij} = T_i T_j / N$$

where E_{ij} is the expected figure in the ith row and jth column, T_i and T_j are respectively the totals of the frequencies in the ith row and the jth column, and N is the total of all the frequencies. For example, for the '35–50, improved' cell we have $i = 2, j = 1$ (second row, first column), and

$$E_{21} = \frac{40 \times 24}{60} = 16 \text{ as before.}$$

The two 'expected' figures that we have calculated are the only ones that need to be calculated explicitly in this way. Once they are written into the table, the other 'expected' numbers can all be found using the known totals in each group. For instance, if the number of under-35s expected to improve was 14, and there were 21 altogether, then naturally 7 must be expected not to improve. We will be returning to this question of how many 'expected' figures must actually be calculated later on.

It is now clear that *more* of the two younger age groups have improved than the null hypothesis would suggest, while for the 50+ group the figure is lower than expected. But are these differences significant? What we need is some way of measuring the disagreement between what actually happened (the 'observed' figures as they are usually called) and what the null hypothesis leads us to expect should happen. If we write O to denote the observed numbers and E for the expected numbers, then the obvious way to measure how much disagreement there is between them is to look at $O - E$ for each category in the table. It is more convenient for this purpose to rewrite the data in columns – making sure we keep the pairs of Os and Es together correctly:

O	E	$O - E$
17	14	3
17	16	1
6	10	−4
4	7	−3
7	8	−1
9	5	4

(Some of the $(O - E)$s are negative since E is bigger than O.)

Now, if we want a measure of the *overall* amount of disagreement for the entire table, between O and E, the sensible thing would seem to be to add up the $O - E$ column. But unfortunately, if you try this you will find the column totals to zero. This is no freak of the figures just for this set of data – the same thing will occur with *any* set of Os and Es worked out according to a null hypothesis. So this so-called 'measure of total disagreement' is not much use.

Haven't we seen something like this before, though? In Chapter 4, when we were developing the method for calculating standard deviation, our first effort at a measurement of the spread of the points in a distribution around the mean broke down for exactly the same reason – the cancellation of positive and negative differences. The trick which solved the problem there was, you will recall, to *square* the troublesome differences, thereby getting rid of the awkward minus signs without altering the relationship between the distances. Perhaps something similar is worth trying in this case.

Accordingly, we add a column for $(O - E)^2$ to our table:

O	E	$(O - E)$	$(O - E)^2$
17	14	3	9
17	16	1	1
6	10	−4	16
4	7	−3	9
7	8	−1	1
9	8	4	16

The sum of the $(O - E)^2$ column should then give us a measure of the total amount of disagreement between O and E.

But is it really this *absolute* disagreement that is of interest? Suppose we had two sets of Os and Es, and worked out the corresponding values of $(O - E)^2$, as follows:

O	E	$(O - E)^2$		O	E	$(O - E)^2$
1	2	1		101	102	1
2	2	0		102	102	0
3	2	1		103	102	1

The total of the $(O - E)^2$ column is the same in each case, but you will probably agree that the discrepancy between the Os and the Es is not nearly as serious in the second case. This, of course, is because it is not so much the actual *size* of the disagreement that matters, as the size of that disagreement *relative* to the figure that was expected. A disagreement of 1 on an expected figure of 2 represents a 50 per cent error, whereas the same disagreement on an expected figure of 102 is an error of only 0.98 per cent.

What we need, therefore, is a further column in our calculation giving the value of $(O - E)^2/E$, the size of the squared disagreement relative to the corresponding expected figure:

O	E	$(O - E)$	$(O - E)^2$	$(O - E)^2/E$
17	14	3	9	$9/14 = 0.643$
17	16	1	1	$1/16 = 0.0625$
6	10	−4	16	$16/10 = 1.6$
4	7	−3	9	$9/7 = 1.286$
7	8	−1	1	$1/8 = 0.125$
9	5	4	16	$16/5 = \underline{3.2}$
				6.92

The final measurement of the overall disagreement in the table between the Os and the Es is given by the sum of the last column (which can be calculated as the individual divisions are performed by using the memory on your calculator). Incidentally, it was not strictly necessary to bother putting in the minus signs in the third column, since they will disappear when the quantities are squared; however, the fact that this column should add up to zero provides a useful check on the accuracy with which you have calculated the Es and the differences.

The measurement of disagreement which we have now constructed is known as chi-squared (pronounced 'ki-squared' and denoted by the Greek letter χ^2). We can define it, according to the way we have worked it out, as

$$\chi^2 = \sum \frac{(O - E)^2}{E}$$

where the $\sum$ sign indicates that we are to add up the values over all the categories in the table. By the way, χ on its own, without the square, means nothing and is not used.

However, although we now have a way of measuring how well – or how badly – the Os and Es agree, we are not yet in a position to say anything about the null hypothesis. We need some standard of comparison from which to judge whether a value of χ^2 such as we have obtained is 'large' – indicating a lot of disagreement and therefore casting doubt on the null hypothesis – or 'small' – suggesting that the discrepancies noticed between O and E are merely the result of minor sampling variations. We want, in other words, to know what sampling distribution χ^2 should follow.

Using the χ^2-distribution

The distribution, not surprisingly, is known as the χ^2-distribution. Like the normal distribution, it is continuous, though unlike the normal it is not symmetric. We will look at its precise shape in a minute; first, turn to Appendix 6 where you will find this distribution tabulated.

The tables are arranged in a different manner from the ones for the normal distribution you are used to using and are similar to those for the t-distribution. They are, as it were, the 'opposite' of the normal tables in that, whereas with the normal tables the figures in the body of the table gave the probability associated with the z-value at the head of the column, in the χ^2 tables the probabilities are given at the heads of the columns and the corresponding values of χ^2 in the body of the table. The sketch at the top of the tables indicates just what is being tabulated: the table shows the value of χ^2 which cuts off an area α under the right-hand tail of the distribution. We are always carrying out a one-tailed test with χ^2, since it is always *big* discrepancies between O and E that are of interest.

However, that is not all we need to know to look up the tables; if you glance at the right-hand edge of the tables you will find the letter ν again. It tells you how the values of χ^2 relate to the amount of data that we begin with. Our argument so far has gone something like this: χ^2 measures the disagreement between O and E, so if χ^2 is big, there is a lot of disagreement and the null hypothesis, from which the Es were calculated, must be wrong. But, of course, χ^2 might also be big simply because we are adding up a lot of figures – because we had a big table to begin with. So the definition of what we mean by a 'big' value of χ^2 must be related in some way to the size of the table.

The table we began with, before we added on the row and column totals, had six categories altogether – three for age and two for improvement/no improvement. But when we calculated the expected frequencies we found we could not just play around with these categories at will – once two of the Es were calculated, the rest were automatically fixed because of the totals in each class. We say that only two of the categories are *free*, or that the number of *degrees of freedom*, ν, is 2 in this case. (You may recall this term from our work on t-tests in the section 'Testing hypotheses about the means of small samples', p. 234.)

You may feel that this is a rather hit-and-miss way of calculating the number of degrees of freedom. After all, if you picked the wrong categories you might find you had to calculate three of the expected figures before you could insert the rest, so you might wrongly conclude that $\nu = 3$. Fortunately, there is a more systematic way of working out ν; if the original table had r rows and c columns, then once all expected values except those in the last row and the last column have been calculated, these could be filled in automatically. As shown in Figure 9.4 then, only the categories in the top left-hand part of the table are 'free' in the sense described above, and so there are $(r - 1) \times (c - 1)$ degrees of freedom. In words, ν = number of rows minus one multiplied by number of columns minus one. (Alternatively, you may like to obtain the number of degrees of freedom by crossing out one row and one column in the table, and then counting the remaining figures.)

Whichever way we look at it, then, ν is 2 in the present case, and so we should be consulting the second row of the table. Remembering that the α-value tells us what area is left over in the tail of the χ^2-distribution, we find that a χ^2 of 5.991 will leave an area of only 5 per cent or 0.05 in the tail.

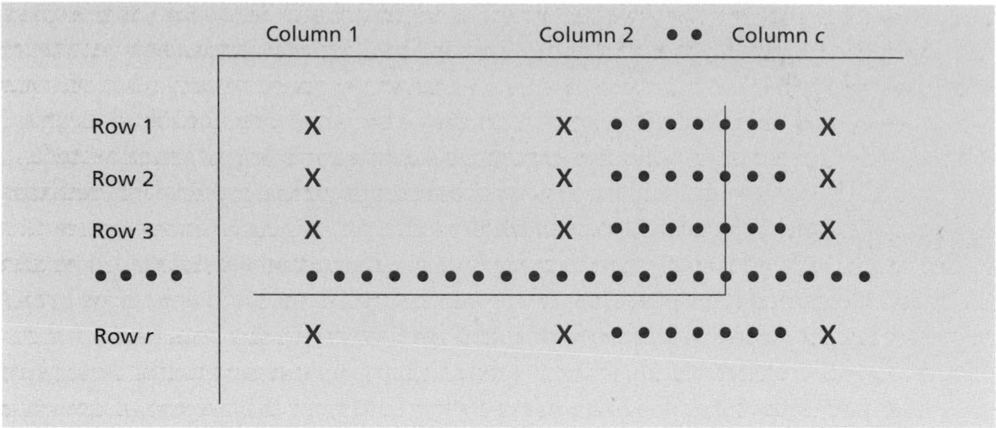

Figure 9.4 The number of degrees of freedom

This fact can be interpreted as follows: if the null hypothesis were correct, and the variations between the O and E figures were merely due to chance, then we could expect 95 per cent of samples to yield a χ^2 which is less than 5.991 and only the odd 5 per cent of samples to fall above that value. A sample yielding a χ^2 less than 5.991 is therefore not unusual, and furnishes no evidence for disbelieving the null hypothesis. If, on the other hand, our sample produces a χ^2 greater than 5.991, it is unlikely to have come from a population for which the null hypothesis holds good.

Because the χ^2-value obtained from the tables (5.991 in this case) is the one that decides whether we are going to reject the null hypothesis or not, it is often referred to as the *critical* value of χ^2, and denoted by χ_c^2. We can interpret the meaning of all this in a way exactly analogous to our decision rule for other hypothesis tests, if we understand the interval from $\chi^2 = 0$ to $\chi^2 = 5.991$ as simply a 95 per cent interval – a one-sided interval, since we are not interested in the left-hand tail where χ^2 is small, showing that the agreement between O and E is good. With this understanding, the rule becomes as before: a sample value of χ^2 *inside* the interval does not cause us to reject the null hypothesis – the differences between O and E are small enough to be accounted for by chance variations. If, however, the sample value of χ^2 falls *outside* the interval, then the differences between O and E, as measured by χ^2, are so large that the null hypothesis must be rejected. If we have used, in constructing the confidence interval, the α corresponding to a 'tail' area of 5 per cent, then of course these decisions will be made 'at the 5 per cent significance level'.

What then, after all this theory, is the implication of the value of χ^2 we have obtained? Our sample χ^2 there turned out to be 6.92, whereas the value of χ^2 obtained from the tables was 5.99. So our sample falls outside the 95 per cent interval and we conclude that the null hypothesis should be rejected. There is an association between the age of workers and the improvement rate which is significant at the 5 per cent level.

Once again, this apparently lengthy process can be summed up in a few simple steps, now the method has been established:

1 Formulate the null hypothesis (which, in this case, will always be of the 'no association' form).
2 On the basis of this hypothesis, calculate the expected frequencies.
3 Hence calculate χ^2.

4 Work out the number of degrees of freedom, ν, as (rows minus one) $\times$ (columns minus one), and look up the critical χ_c^2 in the tables under the selected significance level.

5 Compare the value of χ^2 calculated from your sample with χ_c^2. If the sample χ^2 is smaller (*inside* the interval) *do not* reject the null hypothesis, if it is bigger (*outside*) the null hypothesis can be rejected.

More about χ^2

To demonstrate how easy the process is to apply, we will examine a second lot of data produced by Elizabeth Field. She suspects that whether workers show an improvement as a result of retraining may be connected with the length of time for which they have been doing the job. Accordingly she draws up the table below:

Length of time on this job (months)	Improved	Did not improve	Total
6 and under 12	6 (8)	6 (4)	12
12 and under 18	9 (10)	6 (5)	15
18 and under 24	13 (12)	5 (6)	18
24 and over	12 (10)	3 (5)	15
	40	20	60

We have put the marginal totals in already, and as before the overall improvement rate is two-thirds. The null hypothesis here will be: there is no association between improvement rate and length of time on the job. That being so, we would expect the two-thirds improvement rate to apply equally to all four groups, for example we would expect two-thirds of the 12 people who have done the job for 6–12 months to improve, which gives $E = 8$ for the top left-hand category. You should verify for yourself the remaining E values; they are all shown in brackets in the table above.

As you can see, some of these Es are rather small. You should be accustomed by now to the idea that very small amounts of data cannot be relied on to give a fair picture of a situation, so perhaps you will not be surprised to learn that we should really have Es which are all at least 5 before we can safely use χ^2. However, that does not mean we have to give up in the present case. We can easily get round the difficulty by combining the two groups '6–12' and '12–18' into one group '6–18'. The new, contracted table is then as shown:

Length of time on this job (months)	Improved	Did not improve	Total
6 and under 18	15 (18)	12 (9)	27
18 and under 24	13 (12)	5 (6)	18
24 and over	12 (10)	3 (5)	15
	40	20	60

We can now go ahead and calculate χ^2 as before. You should check that the value obtained is 2.95. The number of degrees of freedom (*after* we have done the necessary combining of classes) is $(3-1) \times (2-1) = 2$, so if we stick to the usual 5 per cent significance level, then χ_c^2 is 5.991 as before. This time our χ^2 is within the interval, being less then χ_c^2, and so there is no reason to reject the null hypothesis; there is no evidence of an association between time on the job and improvement rate significant at the 5 per cent level.

Finally, let us test whether there is any evidence that men and women respond differently to the retraining, using the following data:

	Improved	Did not improve	Total
Male	21 (24)	15 (12)	36
Female	19 (16)	5 (8)	24
	40	20	60

The null hypothesis here will be: no association between sex of worker and improvement rate. Although in the previous two cases we worked out the *E*s using the fact that the overall improvement rate is two-thirds, there is no reason why we should not use instead the fact that here 36/60, or 60 per cent, of the workers are male, so we would expect 60 per cent of the improved workers – that is, 60 per cent of 40 or 24 – to be males. In general, there is no rule as to whether one should use the column or the row totals to calculate the expected figures – pick whichever makes the calculation easier.

What we have here is a 2-by-2 table – two categories in each direction – which is, of course, the smallest table that can occur. With a table that *is* so small, a point becomes important which, for larger tables, we could afford to slide over. The χ^2-distribution is, as we have already mentioned, a continuous distribution – but all the problems we have solved with its aid are discrete problems, involving as they do *counting* the number of items in each category of the table. So there is a certain amount of approximation involved in using χ^2 – an approximation which fortunately is only really serious in this 2-by-2 case. We allow for it by making use of an adjustment to the value of χ^2 known as *Yates's correction*, the application of which is very easy: reduce each $O - E$ (ignoring the sign) by 0.5. If this is applied correctly, all the resulting figures should be the same, as indicated in the table below.

There is $(2-1) \times (2-1) = 1$ degree of freedom here, so the critical value, χ_c^2, at the 5 per cent level is 3.84. As our sample χ^2 is less than this, we have no grounds for rejecting the null hypothesis – women do not appear to respond to the course any better or worse than men. You may like to check that the *uncorrected* version of χ^2 would be 2.81, so actually in this case the correction does not make any difference to the conclusion, but it is easy to envisage cases where it might.

O	E	O – E	Corrected	$\dfrac{(Corrected\ difference)^2}{E}$
21	24	(–)3	2.5	0.26
19	16	3	2.5	0.39
15	12	3	2.5	0.52
5	8	(–)3	2.5	0.78
				1.95

Single-row tables

It was remarked towards the end of the last section that a 2-by-2 table is the smallest that can arise, but in some ways that is not strictly true – the table might only have a single row. For example, if a firm wished to test whether numbers of absentees varied significantly from one day of the week to another, the data might be collected in the following way:

Day of week	Mon	Tues	Wed	Thur	Fri
Number of absentees	17	12	11	12	18

Here we have a perfectly respectable set of observed frequencies; the null hypothesis will state that the numbers *do not* vary significantly from day to day (the usual 'no difference' hypothesis) and so we can work out the expected frequencies. There were 70 people absent altogether during the week, so if the null hypothesis were true we would expect to get the same number – one-fifth of 70, or 14 – absent each day. All the *E*s are therefore 14, and without going through the intermediate calculation, which you can check, we find that χ^2 is exactly 3.

So far, apart from a slight difference in the method of obtaining the expected frequencies, there has been no difference between the method for this single-row table and the bigger tables we had in previous examples. However, when you come to find the number of degrees of freedom, the formula we have used so far gives a silly answer in this case: (rows minus one) × (columns minus one) is zero, since the number of rows is only 1 to start off with. We therefore have to go back to the *meaning* of the number of degrees of freedom – how many of the daily frequencies are 'free'? The total number of absentees during the week is known to be 70, which means we can write down any old frequencies for Monday to Thursday, but then we have to give Friday a frequency which makes the whole lot add up to 70. So only four of the frequencies are 'free' in this sense; and more generally, for a single-row table of this kind with n categories, there will be $n - 1$ degrees of freedom.

The χ^2 tables, with $v = 4$, then tell us that χ^2_c is 9.488 at the 5 per cent level, which suggests, our sample χ^2 of 3 being much less than this, that the null hypothesis should not be rejected: the sample provides no evidence that the number of absentees varies significantly from day to day.

What we have been doing here, in effect, is testing how well the observed frequencies fit a *uniform distribution* – one in which the frequencies of each category are expected to be the same. In a similar sort of way, χ^2 can be used to test the *goodness of fit* of a set of observed frequencies to *any* theoretical distribution; in particular, it can help to answer the question, left unresolved in Chapter 7, 'How do we know when a distribution is normal?'

The process in detail, however, is quite complicated, involving as it does first calculating the mean and standard deviation of the observed frequencies, then using the normal tables to calculate the frequencies we would *expect* to get from a normal distribution with that mean and standard deviation – all this before we even start on the χ^2 calculation! Then the question of degrees of freedom is not straightforward; in fact, it is an altogether messy business which we will not pursue further.

Quick check questions

1 Find the expected frequencies for the following contingency table, which refers to the recovery rates of patients after a routine operation:

	Rapid recovery	Slow recovery
Smoker	12	28
Non-smoker	33	57

2 How many degrees of freedom are there in a contingency table with three rows and four columns?

3 Use the tables in Appendix 6 to find the critical value of χ^2 for a 1 per cent level of significance and 8 degrees of freedom.

Answers:

1 Expected frequencies are as shown, correct to two decimal places:

	Rapid recovery	Slow recovery
Smoker	13.85	26.15
Non-smoker	31.15	58.85

The expected frequency for the 'rapid recovery, smoker' cell is calculated as $45 \times 40/130$, using the row, column and overall totals; the other expected figures are calculated in a similar way.

2 There are $(3 - 1) \times (4 - 1) = 6$ degrees of freedom.

3 The value is 20.090.

A cautionary note

Obviously χ^2 provides an extremely useful and versatile kind of hypothesis test which is also relatively easy to apply. If I were going to be cast away on a desert island and could only take one set of statistical tables with me, I would certainly choose to take χ^2! In the contingency table context, the test is useful in analysing the results of surveys, in assessing the efficacy of new manufacturing processes, in comparing the performance of different machines, to name but three areas. The single-row table, as we have seen, can be used to assess how well a set of observed data fits a theoretical distribution. And there are other uses of the tables, too, which we have not even touched on. For example, you may have wondered why there are so many significance levels given in the tables; we might want to use 1 per cent or even 10 per cent, but why bother giving an α of 0.99 which corresponds to a significance level of 99 per cent?

The point of these very high significance levels is to enable χ^2 to be used to test for 'fiddling' of results. A *very small* value of χ^2 – less than the 99 per cent significance level critical value for the number of degrees of freedom in question – indicates an extraordinarily good agreement between O and E – an agreement *better* than would be found in 99 per cent of cases. Such *very* good agreement might, if we had suspicious minds, cause us to wonder about the Os involved – how come they are so good? Are these really random results? The high significance level values of χ^2 help us to decide.

But just because χ^2 is such a simple quantity to calculate, we must beware of using it *too* readily, perhaps in circumstances where it is not really applicable. We have already seen that it will not do if some of the *E*s are below 5; it cannot be used either if there is overlapping between some of the categories so that items may be counted more than once and the totals of rows and columns are meaningless.

Nor will χ^2 tell us the *direction* of an association. In the example on p. 244, we decided that there was evidence of an association between age and response to the retraining, but we have to look back at the data and use common sense to discover that it is the younger people who responded better. As far as the calculated value of χ^2 is concerned, we could have obtained the same value from another set of data in which the situation was completely reversed and the *older* people were doing better. All χ^2 tells us is that there is some kind of connection.

A mixed batch of examples

Many people coming to sampling theory for the first time find that, although they can follow the arguments when someone else sets them out, it is a different matter when they are required to decide what kind of hypothesis test to use in a given situation and carry it out for themselves. There seem to be too many to choose from – one sample, two samples, z and t, χ^2 – the list goes on and on! But by taking a step-by-step approach, it is possible to find one's way through the apparent maze. To get a better insight into how it is done, consider the following results from a survey of small businesses:

	Retail sector	Manufacturing sector	Financial services sector
Mean number of employees	4.1	11.7	7.2
Standard deviation	3.3	3.9	3.7
No. of businesses with cash flow problems	17	32	11
No. with no cash flow problems	13	18	9
Total no. in sample	30	50	20

Here are some questions we might want to ask in connection with the data:

1 Does the proportion of businesses having cash flow problems vary from one sector to another?
2 Is there a significant difference between the average numbers of employees in the retail and manufacturing sectors?
3 Given that this is quite a small sample, what would you expect the average number of employees over all small businesses in the manufacturing sector to be?
4 In a survey of retail businesses done last year, about 50 per cent admitted to having experienced cash flow problems. Has this proportion increased significantly?

None of these questions is expressed in terms of testing hypotheses, constructing confidence intervals and so on. However, in order to answer the questions using only a sample of data, we need to carry out such operations.

One pointer to the need for some kind of hypothesis test in connection with sample data is a question which looks as if it could be answered by a simple 'yes' or 'no'. That would apply to questions 1, 2 and 4 here. Question 3 is slightly different – it requires us to estimate a parameter (the mean) for a *population* of small businesses using sample data. For this we need to construct a confidence interval.

Question 1

Even when we have decided that a hypothesis test of some kind is needed, there are still a number of further choices to be made. Take question 1: it clearly concerns proportions, so you might think first of a test using STEP. However, we are dealing here not with a single sample, but with a comparison between proportions in three different sector samples. Extracting the relevant data in the format below makes it clear that what is needed here is a χ^2-test – the question can be recast as 'Is there an association between sector and cash flow problems?'

	Retail	Manufacturing	Financial services
No. of businesses with cash flow problems	17	32	11
No. with no cash flow problems	13	18	9

The null hypothesis as usual is that there is *no* association between the two dimensions of the data. On this assumption, the expected frequencies are as follows (check that you could calculate these correctly):

	Retail	Manufacturing	Financial services
No. of businesses with cash flow problems	18	30	12
No. with no cash flow problems	12	20	8

Then, by hand-calculation or using a computer (see p. 252) we find that $\chi^2 = 0.681$. There are 2 degrees of freedom here, since $(\text{rows} - 1)(\text{columns} - 1) = 1 \times 2 = 2$. The critical value of χ^2 at the 5 per cent level is thus 5.99, and since our value is much smaller than this, we have no grounds for rejecting the null hypothesis – there does not seem to be any variation in the proportion of businesses with cash flow problems between different sectors.

Question 2

Here we are being asked to look at the difference between the means in two samples, so we need a test based on STEDM. As we are asked simply to look for a difference, we choose to carry out a two-tailed test, using a significance level of 5 per cent. We begin by identifying the information we are given:

$$n_1 = 30, n_2 = 50 \qquad x_1 = 4.1, x_2 = 11.7 \qquad s_1 = 3.3, s_2 = 3.9.$$

Since the sample sizes are large enough, we can use a test based on the normal distribution. The null hypothesis (NH) will be

NH: the mean numbers of employees in the two populations are equal.

The alternative hypothesis (AH) will be

AH: the mean numbers of employees in the two populations are different.

We choose to assume that the two populations also have the same s.d., and therefore to pool the s.d.s of the two samples to get a better estimate of the population s.d.:

$$s = \sqrt{\dfrac{n_1 s_1^2 + n_2 s_2^2}{n_1 + n_2}} = \sqrt{\dfrac{30 \times 3.3^2 + 50 \times 3.9^2}{80}} = 3.69.$$

Then we can find STEDM:

$$\text{STEDM} = s\sqrt{1/n_1 + 1/n_2} = 3.69\sqrt{1/30 + 1/50} = 0.852.$$

So for a two-tailed test at the 5 per cent level, the acceptance region will be $0 \pm 2 \times \text{STEDM}$ (0 because the null hypothesis tells us that the difference in the means in zero), that is

$$0 \pm 2 \times 0.852 = \pm 1.704.$$

However, the actual difference in means is $4.1 - 11.7 = -7.6$, which is well outside the acceptance region. We therefore reject the null hypothesis, and conclude that the mean numbers of employees in the two populations are different.

Question 3

We see that what is required here is not a hypothesis test, but rather a confidence interval for the mean in the manufacturing sector. Since this will be based on the mean of a single sample, we use STEM; and in the absence of any other indication we choose to use a 95 per cent level of confidence.

We can identify $n = 50$, $x = 11.7$ and $s = 3.9$. STEM is thus $s/\sqrt{n} = 3.9/\sqrt{50} = 0.55$, and so the 95 per cent confidence interval is sample value ± 2 STEM $= 11.7 \pm 2 \times 0.55$. We are therefore 95 per cent confident that the mean number of employees for the population in the manufacturing sector lies in the range 10.6–12.8. This is quite a narrow range, partly because the standard deviation is not very big and partly because n is fairly large.

Question 4

Here we want to compare data from a single sample – this year's survey – with a population figure from last year, so we need to carry out a single sample test. The sample size – 30 respondents from the retail sector – is just big enough to allow us to use a test based on the normal distribution rather than t. Because we are discussing the *proportion* of businesses with cash flow problems, the correct standard error to use is STEP. Because we are specifically asked to test whether this has increased, we choose to carry out a one-tailed test, and so our two hypotheses are

NH: Proportion is still 50 per cent or maybe even lower, i.e. $P \leq 50$.
AH: Proportion is now greater than 50 per cent, i.e. $P > 50$.

The value of P to use in computing STEP is thus 50, and the sample size $n = 30$. So

$$\text{STEP} = \sqrt{(50 \times 50/30)} = 9.13\%.$$

For a one-tailed test at the 5 per cent level, the relevant z-value is 1.64, as seen from the table on p. 231. Since we are interested in the upper tail in this case, the limit of the acceptance region becomes $50 + 1.64$ STEP $= 64.97\%$. Anything above this limit would cause us to reject the null hypothesis.

Now actually in our sample we found 17/30 with cash flow problems – that is, 56.67 per cent. This lies comfortably within the acceptance region, so there is no reason to reject the hypothesis that overall the figure is still 50 per cent.

Had we wanted to use the alternative method of calculating a z-value here, we would have $z = (56.67 - 50)/\text{STEP} = 0.73$, much less than the critical value of 1.64, so we would come to the same conclusion.

In all these examples, by identifying the information we are given (n, P, s, etc.), whether we want to carry out a test or estimate something, deciding how many samples are involved and whether the situation requires STEM, STEP, STEDM or χ^2, we are able to focus on the precise method needed in each case. You should apply the same kind of thinking when dealing with your own problems.

Hypothesis testing with Excel

In Excel, there are automated procedures for carrying out a hypothesis test on the difference of two sample means, though not, curiously, for comparing a single sample mean with a population. To illustrate how the procedures work, load the EMP.XLS data into Excel; we are going to test for a significant difference in mean age between male and female workers, as we did earlier by hand. First you need to sort the data by SEX so that the female ages occupy rows 2–25 and the male ages rows 26–61.

You can find the relevant command by selecting the DATA tab, then DATA ANALYSIS. The list of data analysis topics shows quite a few related to hypothesis testing; to reproduce the calculation we did by hand, the one we need is 't-test: two sample assuming equal variances'. This carries out the test using an estimate of the variance obtained by pooling the two samples, just as we did earlier. On selecting this command, you will be presented with a dialogue window which requires you to enter the range of data for each of the samples (this is why we need to have all the data for each gender together). You also need to specify the hypothesised mean difference, which will generally be 0 (i.e. no difference in the mean age of males and females), and a destination for the output – the default is a new ply of the worksheet. The default significance level used is 5 per cent (denoted by alpha = 0.05), though this can be overwritten.

The results of the procedure are shown below:

t-Test: Two Sample Assuming Equal Variances

	Variable 1	Variable 2
Mean	36.25	38.80555556
Variance	58.10869565	56.27539683
Observations	24	36
Pooled Variance	57.00239464	
Hypothesized Mean Difference		0
df	58	
t Stat	−1.28445834	
$P(T <= t)$ one-tail	0.10204418	
t Critical one-tail	1.671553491	
$P(T <= t)$ two-tail	0.20408836	
t Critical two-tail	2.001715984	

Thus we see that there are two samples, with means respectively 36.25 and 38.81, and variances (squared s.d.s) 58.11 and 56.28, based on 24 and 36 observations. The variance obtained by pooling the two samples is 57.00, and we hypothesise that there is no difference between the means of the populations. There are 58 degrees of freedom $(24 + 36 - 2)$, and the calculated value of t (actual difference in means/STEDM) is 1.28 – the minus sign can be ignored, since it just indicates that sample 2 has the bigger mean.

The printout gives us results for both one- and two-tailed tests. In our case, since we want to test simply whether there is a difference in the age of the two groups, without specifying the direction of the difference, it is the two-tailed result which is of interest. For the two-tailed test, at the 5 per cent significance level, the critical t is 2.00 (a bit different from the 1.96 we used in our hand-calculation, since the program is using the more accurate t-distribution whereas we used the normal, though with such large samples there is little difference between the two). This is greater than the calculated t, so our decision would be that there are no grounds for rejecting the null hypothesis – apparently the difference between male and female ages is not significant. The p-value confirms this conclusion, since it is 0.20 or 20 per cent – much higher than the 5 per cent significance level. The chances of getting a difference as big as this, even were there no difference between the populations of males and females, are more than 20 per cent.

The other versions of hypothesis tests provided by Excel are applicable in different situations. The paired two-sample t-test is needed when we have two samples of equal size which are matched in some way (e.g. if the samples consist of the weights of a group of people before and after trying a certain diet). The t-test assuming unequal variances does not pool the two samples in order to estimate the overall variance, but uses two separate estimates, one for each population. Finally, the z-test requires that the variances of the populations are provided as input, rather than computing them from the sample data.

The χ^2-test is not found under the DATA ANALYSIS menu, since it is merely a simple function. Excel does not do all the work for you – you need to calculate the expected frequencies by hand before invoking the formula. For example, suppose we want to carry out a χ^2-test on the example from the section 'More about χ^2' on p. 245:

Time on this job (months)	Improved	Did not improve
6 and under 18	15	12
18 and under 24	13	5
24 and over	12	3

First we need to enter the figures into the spreadsheet, in this tabular layout – say, into cells A1 to B3 (there is no need to input the headings unless you want to). Then we must compute the corresponding expected frequencies, as explained earlier in the chapter; these can be entered thus, into cells A4 to B6,

$$18 \quad 9$$
$$12 \quad 6$$
$$10 \quad 5$$

Then, in an empty cell of the spreadsheet, we enter the formula

$$=CHITEST(A1.B3, A4.B6)$$

where the first range specified is that for Observed frequencies, the second for the Expecteds. Excel returns a value of 0.228 779 for the function, which is the *p*-value associated with the computed χ^2, taking into account the degrees of freedom of the table. So in this case the probability of obtaining a χ^2-value as great as, or even greater than, the one generated by the table, even if there is no association, is about 23 per cent – much higher than the 5 per cent significance threshold. We would thus conclude that there is no evidence to support an association between improvement and time in the job.

If you want to compute the actual value of χ^2 for yourself, the spreadsheet format is well suited to doing so: a table can be set up with columns for O, E and $(O - E)^2/E$, and then the calculation is very easily performed by copying the formulae down the necessary number of rows, and using the =SUM function to add the $(O - E)^2/E$ column. You will find that a spreadsheet for doing this is stored as CHI.XLS on the Companion Website.

Conclusion

From a theoretical point of view, the last two chapters have probably been the toughest in the book, but the actual application of the hypothesis testing procedure, once you are used to it, is something of a sausage-machine – turn the handle, go through the appropriate steps and out pops the conclusion. Try *not* to apply *your* hypothesis tests in this way. A great help in thinking clearly about what you are proving is to write down a proper null hypothesis at the start of every test, and to draw your conclusion in terms of the particular problem you are dealing with. Do not, in other words, just write '. . . significant' or 'there is no association'. Write: 'this sample probably did not come from such-and-such a population', or 'Gender of worker is not associated with response to retraining'. And do not get so accustomed to using 95 per cent intervals/5 per cent significance that you forget to state what level you are using. *Think* about the level used, and if necessary use something different. After all, if you were going to fly in an aeroplane, the engine of which had been tested to see whether it was substandard, I think you might not be very happy to be told it had been passed as OK with 95 per cent confidence!

EXERCISES

*Further examples on the work of this chapter can be found on the **Companion Website**.*

(Use 5 per cent significance unless otherwise indicated.)

1 The mean wage of workers in a certain industry over the whole country is £310 per week, with a standard deviation of £7.50. A sample of 100 workers from one large factory is found to have a mean wage of £308 per week. Are the workers in this factory different from the rest of the industry?

2 It is known that 40 per cent of retail outlets in a certain area stock your product. An intensive marketing campaign is carried out, after which a survey of 80 outlets shows 41 stocking the product. Does this indicate a change significant at the 1 per cent level?

3 It has been suggested that women are less willing to join a trade union than men. A survey of 200 workers in a factory showed that, of 80 women, 53 belonged to the appropriate union; for men the figure was 97 out of 120. Is the suggestion supported by these figures?

4 A factory employs three quality control inspectors, each of whom is asked to keep a record of the number of items he tests, and those he rejects, in the course of a day. The results are as follows:

	Accepted	Rejected
Inspector A	75	15
Inspector B	83	19
Inspector C	92	16

Do the inspectors differ significantly in the proportion of items they reject?

5 An anthropologist is researching into hereditary factors in a certain country, and has formulated a theory that, overall, 40 per cent of the population is fair-haired, 10 per cent is red-haired and the remainder is dark-haired. A sample from one particular tribe, however, contains 65 fair-haired, 19 red-haired and 66 dark-haired. Are these proportions consistent with the theory?

6 Examine the following data which forms part of the results of a survey of 83 passengers on the services of a city bus company, and then use it to answer the questions below:

How many bus journeys have you made during the past month?

The mean number was 14, with a standard deviation of 5.2.

Do you use the bus service for (a) travel to work only; (b) leisure purpose only; (c) both?

37 answered (a), 16 (b) and the remainder (c).

Are you satisfied with the frequency of the service you use?

	Yes	No
Travel to work only	11	26
Leisure only	11	5
Both	15	15

(a) Estimate the mean number of journeys made by all passengers during the past month.
(b) In a much larger survey carried out two years ago, 48 per cent of customers said they used the bus service for travel to work only. Has this proportion altered significantly?
(c) Do customers' levels of satisfaction vary according to their reason for using the service?

In each case, you should explain your results in terms which would be comprehensible to a manager with little knowledge of statistics.

7 Test a dice to see whether it is fair: throw it 120 times and keep a record of the number of times each face occurs. Then test these observed values against the expected frequency of 20 for each face, by using χ^2.

8 Collect some data to enable you to formulate and carry out a hypothesis test about proportions. For instance, you might be able to find out from your university registry what percentage of students in your institution are female. Then you could take a sample in, say, the bar, or the library, and test the hypothesis that the percentage of women using these facilities is the same as the percentage in the population as a whole.

Alternatively, you can find out from the *Motor Industry of Great Britain* what percentage of the cars registered in the UK are from a Japanese manufacturer, and then test a sample of cars from your university car park to see if it is consistent with this percentage. Again, you can probably think of other interesting hypotheses to test.

9 Use the data file STUD.XLS to test whether the age of the male students differs significantly from that of the females.

10 You are monitoring the time taken to process orders in your organisation, and have found from examining a long run of historical data that the average time to process a certain type of order is 5.2 working days, with a standard deviation of 0.8 working days. This is regarded as acceptable, but you are anxious to make sure standards do not decline, so you examine a sample of 40 orders once a month. How high would the mean of such a sample need to be before you felt justified in concluding that standards are declining?

(The reasoning behind this question is an example of the ideas of *statistical process control*, which have made a considerable contribution to the total quality movement. We will examine these ideas in more detail in Chapter 10.)

Case Study

Subrose yet again

Using the data from the case study at the end of Chapter 3, prepare to answer the following questions as part of your presentation of the survey data to management:

1 Is there an association between the type of transport used and the distance travelled to the supermarket? If so, explain what form this association takes, using appropriate diagrams.
2 Is there a significant difference in age between those who use a car and those who use other forms of transport? Does this justify the statement 'older people are more likely to drive to the supermarket'? Again, use a diagram to illustrate your answer.

Chapter 10

MAKING IT BETTER:
STATISTICS AND QUALITY IMPROVEMENT

Quantitative methods in practice

Improving quality at Ford Motor Company

> statistical science . . . is necessary to achieve what is demanded from us by our customers – a consistent level of superlative performance.

So said Richard Parry-Jones, Group Vice-President for Global Product Development and Quality, in a speech at Northwestern University, in the United States, in May 2001. Why should this be the case? After all, Ford makes cars, so it clearly needs good engineers – but statistics? And surely the performance of a car is related to its engine, the shape of the bodywork, and so on – again, where does statistics come in?

Parry-Jones provided a very simple example to illustrate why statistical methods are vital to Ford's success – controlling the thickness of the film of paint sprayed onto car bodywork. 'One key paint attribute necessary to deliver high quality is film thickness – too much and the paint will sag and run, too little and it will be too thin.' He then went on to explain how taking regular measurements of the paint thickness, plotting them on simple graphs so that everyone can see what is happening, and using a few simple statistical tools to investigate the causes of excessive variations in the thickness, enabled Ford to significantly improve its control over paint thickness. Not only does this deliver better quality for the customer, but it also avoids wasting paint by using too much, and so impacts directly on costs.

In this chapter, we will look at some of the techniques, based on statistical ideas which we've already encountered such as normal distributions and bar charts, which are being used by major companies such as Ford to constantly improve the quality of their products and services.

(You can find the Parry-Jones lecture at **http://media.ford.com** – there is a link from the **Companion Website** associated with this book.)

The pizza manufacturer's problem

Agnelli's Bakery is a manufacturer of ready-prepared part-baked pizza bases, which are supplied to a number of pizza restaurants throughout the north of England. The business has expanded rapidly since it was started by Mr Agnelli in the early 1990s, and now produces hundreds of pizza bases per day in a range of sizes. However, recently an increasing number of complaints relating to the quality of the pizza bases have been received from restaurants, and now one major chain has threatened to take its business elsewhere unless Agnelli's can remedy the problems within a short time.

But this is not a simple matter. The manufacturing process for the pizza bases can be outlined as follows:

1 A bakery worker starts a batch of dough by measuring pre-set quantities of flour, salt, yeast, water and oil into an electric mixer.
2 The dough is kneaded automatically by the mixer for a predetermined time.
3 The kneaded dough is left to rise in a warm room.

4 When the baker judges that the dough has risen sufficiently, he or she 'knocks it back' by hand and passes it through a machine which divides it into pieces of a certain weight, the exact weight depending on the size of pizza to be made.

5 The pieces of dough are shaped by the baker and placed on trays.

6 They are then left in a warm room to rise a second time.

7 When they are judged to be ready, they are placed in the oven and baked for a short time.

8 After baking they are removed from the oven, left to cool for ten minutes on the trays, then removed from the trays, cooled rapidly by a blast of cold air, and vacuum-packed into plastic bags ready for delivery.

There is, initially, no way of knowing at what stage of this process the problems leading to poor quality are arising. However, Mr Agnelli realises that the viability of his company will be jeopardised if his customers start going elsewhere, and since he believes in getting expert help when necessary, he has engaged the services of a quality consultant, Dr Khan, to try to sort out the situation.

The importance of quality

In a simple case such as the one described above, it is clear that producing products which are of a quality deemed by customers to be unsatisfactory is very damaging to a business. If poor-quality products are allowed to reach the customers then, at best, there will be many complaints, demands for refunds, and so on; at worst, the customers may simply switch to a competing product, and may advise their friends and business contacts to do likewise, thus further damaging the company's market.

If you were trying to advise Agnelli's as to how to tackle its current difficulty you might suggest that it should adopt a strategy of inspecting the pizza bases carefully before they leave the bakery, to ensure that they are of an acceptable quality. This inspection could be done either on a sampling basis (as discussed briefly in Chapter 7) or on 100 per cent of the products. But, while such a policy may result in fewer complaints from customers, it could be almost equally disastrous from a financial point of view. The time and effort occupied by inspection of 100 per cent of the products, or even of substantial samples at regular intervals, would be enormous, while a great deal of waste would be generated if the unsatisfactory bases were simply scrapped. Even if they can be reused – for example, by cutting them down to size if they are found to be too large – additional time will be required to rework them.

The real problem with this strategy is that it only addresses the symptom of the problem – the fact that some unsatisfactory bases are being produced – instead of trying to determine the cause of the problem, and eliminate it. Poor-quality pizza bases are still being produced at the same rate; the bad ones are simply being weeded out more effectively. A better approach would be to develop a technique enabling the people responsible for producing the pizza bases to become aware as quickly as possible when large quantities of poor-quality product begin to occur, to identify the reason for the problem and to take prompt remedial action.

Even this second approach, however, may not be sufficient to enable Agnelli's to survive in an increasingly competitive environment. Simply maintaining the status quo will not retain the company's share of the market; what is needed is constant improvement in a product or service, so that it continually surprises and delights customers by actually turning out to be better than they had expected. If what they want is ever-crunchier pizza bases, then ways to improve the crunchiness have to be found. Thus the emphasis should not be merely on the negative aspects of quality – trouble-shooting problems as they arise – but on the positive aspects – discovering ways to achieve continuous improvement.

Total quality management

The three approaches to the question of quality outlined in the last section – from inspection to weed out poor-quality product, through control of processes to prevent production of poor-quality items, to efforts to achieve constant quality improvement – roughly mirror the development of the quality movement in Western industry. The inspection-based approach to maintaining quality was prevalent in many Western industries until the beginning of the 1980s, even though experts as far back as the 1930s had been pointing out that it is preferable to try to prevent problems arising in the first place. Indeed, simple and effective methods, some of which we are going to examine later in this chapter, had been developed to help in controlling processes and making sure that large quantities of substandard products did not get produced without anyone noticing. These methods had been taken up with enthusiasm in Japan, and subsequently in other Pacific Rim countries, and had made a major contribution to the success of the products of those nations in world markets. However, it was only when Western managers visited Japanese organisations and saw for themselves how well the methods worked that they began to be introduced into European and American companies.

More recently, approaches to quality problems were broadened further, to create a philosophy of quality improvement, known as Total Quality Management (TQM), which pervades the entire organisation and embraces behavioural and managerial as well as more technical issues. This broader perspective, while essential to a full appreciation of the importance of quality in the running of a modern business, cannot be addressed within the confines of this book. In the rest of the chapter we will therefore restrict ourselves to discussing the purely statistical techniques involved. However, I would strongly advise you, if you wish to view these techniques in context, to read one of the many texts now published on the subject of TQM; some suggestions are given at the end of this chapter.

The most recent major development in the area is the growth in popularity of a set of methods known under the generic label of 'Six Sigma'. These methods, pioneered and trademarked by the Motorola company in the United States, began with the use of statistical approaches not dissimilar to those introduced in this chapter, but have now expanded to include more general approaches to problem-solving. An elaborate – and profitable! – structure of training has also grown up around the methods. Again, the references at the end of the chapter provide a starting point if you wish to pursue this methodology.

One final word of warning: the whole area of quality bristles with jargon, with acronyms and with the names of 'gurus' associated with particular techniques. Different authorities hold different, and sometimes opposing, points of view. Often, essentially the same technique is used under totally different names in different organisations. Thus it is important, in your reading, not to become confused, and to examine the substance of a technique or approach rather than simply the label attached to it.

How can statistics help?

By now you may be wondering what all this – whether the philosophical definition of 'quality', or the practicality of trying to make better pizzas – has to do with statistics. The answer is quite simple: before we can solve a quality problem, or decide how to produce an improved product or service, we need accurate information about the current situation – and the best way to provide that information is in the form of statistical data. Then we can make use of all the statistical techniques developed in the book thus far to analyse the data. We can make informed decisions on the basis of that analysis, and we can gather further data to help us decide whether our decisions have led to improvements.

Many of the examples studied in earlier chapters have, of course, had a quality dimension. For example, when in Chapter 7 we used a normal distribution to model the weights of bags of sweets, or a binomial distribution to look at the probability of getting broken biscuits in a packet, we were really addressing quality problems. In this chapter, our objective is to look as some techniques which have been developed more specifically to deal with issues of quality improvement.

Tracking down the problem

When a serious quality problem arises in an organisation it can be quite difficult to persuade people to sit down and discuss what the cause may be – there is a strong instinct to be seen to be rushing about and 'doing something'. However, unless action is driven by information, it may turn out to be worse than useless, so the first step should always be an attempt to find out what is *really* going wrong, and why. The application of some very simple statistical tools, often associated with the name of the Japanese quality expert Ishikawa and referred to as 'Ishikawa's Seven Tools', can be of considerable assistance in this problem-chasing process.

The seven tools are generally listed as follows (though you may find slight variations):

1 Checksheets (or tally sheets).
2 Pareto charts.
3 Cause-and-effect (or Ishikawa) diagrams.
4 Stratification.
5 Histograms.
6 Scatterplots.
7 Control charts.

We will examine the use of each as applied to Agnelli's problems with the pizza bases.

Checksheets

Before any action to deal with the problem can be planned, more information needs to be gathered as to why the customers are complaining. Dr Khan, the quality consultant, suggests that a simple tally of the reasons for complaint is kept over the next few weeks, leading to a table like this:

Base too hard	⊞Ⅰ
Base undercooked in centre	ⅠⅠⅠ
Base too thin	⊞Ⅰ ⊞Ⅰ ⊞Ⅰ ⅠⅠⅠ
Base burned underneath	ⅠⅠⅠⅠ
Base cracks when lifted	ⅠⅠ

This immediately makes it clear that the majority of complaints arise from bases which are too thin, closely followed by those which are deemed to be too hard. The checksheet is, of course, just an easy way of constructing a frequency table for categoric data; it can be built up very quickly by whoever handles the complaints, or perhaps by an inspector who examines products returned by customers.

Pareto chart

The data gathered via the checksheet can be displayed graphically by means of a Pareto chart (so called after the distinguished economist). At its simplest, this is no more than an ordered bar chart in which the categories are arranged in order of descending frequency. Often it is enhanced by the addition of a cumulative percentage frequency curve, as shown in Figure 10.1. Excel does not offer Pareto charts among its charting options, though you can use the Bar Chart option to produce the bars without the cumulative frequency line (remember to sort them into descending order by frequency before plotting).

The idea behind the Pareto chart is what is sometimes referred to as the 80–20 rule, or the Pareto principle: 80 per cent of problems are produced by 20 per cent of causes. The figures 80 and 20 are not meant to be taken too literally, but the general idea is that the great majority of problems are produced by a small proportion of causes. Thus

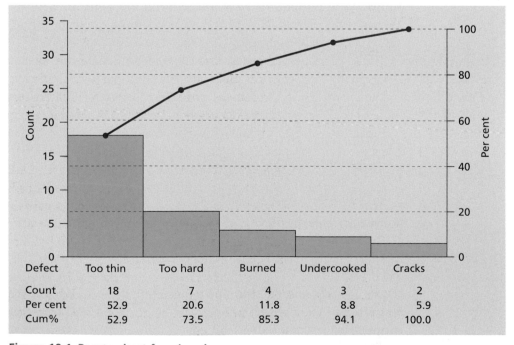

Defect	Too thin	Too hard	Burned	Undercooked	Cracks
Count	18	7	4	3	2
Per cent	52.9	20.6	11.8	8.8	5.9
Cum%	52.9	73.5	85.3	94.1	100.0

Figure 10.1 Pareto chart for pizza bases

in the example above, 73.5 per cent of complaints were accounted for by bases which were too thin or too hard. If Agnelli's can sort out those two problems, the number of complaints would be reduced substantially. If, on the other hand, Agnelli's focuses on the bases which are undercooked in the centre, a lot of time and effort may be spent to very little effect, since the proportion of customers complaining about undercooked bases is very small.

The American quality expert Juran coined a good phrase to describe the objectives of a Pareto analysis: he pointed out that it was important to separate the 'vital few' causes of quality problems from the 'trivial many'. The Pareto chart is a tool to help us do this.

In Agnelli's case, it was sensible merely to plot the frequency of occurrence of each type of complaint. Sometimes, however, the vertical axis of the Pareto may more usefully relate to some monetary measure, such as cost or value, rather than frequency. For example, consider the case of a hotel manager who wishes to analyse the reasons for customer complaints. There may be some complaints which arise frequently, but which are very easy to put right, and cause little loss of customer goodwill – for example, a missing towel in a bathroom can easily be replaced. However, other problems, such as difficulties in making a reservation, may occur much less commonly but have a potentially much more serious impact on revenue when they do.

In such a situation a Pareto which showed only the frequency of each type of complaint would be misleading, since it might encourage the manager to pursue common but trivial faults instead of trying to get to the bottom of the infrequent but serious failures. In contrast, a Pareto showing the total cost of each type of complaint (i.e. the estimated cost incurred due to the occurrence of each type of fault multiplied by its frequency of occurrence) would be a much more effective tool for helping the manager decide which areas to tackle first. Figure 10.2 shows the differing impressions which are given depending on whether the frequency of faults (a), or their potential cost (b), is plotted.

Cause-and-effect diagrams

Once Agnelli's has determined that the major problems with the pizza bases are 'too thin' and 'too hard', Dr Khan sits down with the entire production team to try to discover the cause of these problems. It is important at this stage that he does not just talk to management, since the shop-floor staff may well be aware of facts about the process of which management is ignorant. Nor should he be too ready to listen to 'received wisdom' about the causes of problems – 'everyone knows that it's the ovens which cause the hardness'. Instead, he will probably organise a *brainstorming* session, in which everyone is invited to contribute possible reasons for the problem under consideration, and no suggestion, however apparently silly, is ruled out.

The first point to emerge from the discussion is that in fact the two problems 'too thin' and 'too hard' are really one and the same problem. If the bases are too thin, then they will dry out more in the baking process, and thus become hard. So both difficulties can and should be dealt with together – solve one and you have solved the other. If the hardness problem had been tackled in isolation, the team would have been dealing with a symptom rather than the real underlying difficulty. This can often happen in handling quality problems, unless we are very careful to ask the right questions.

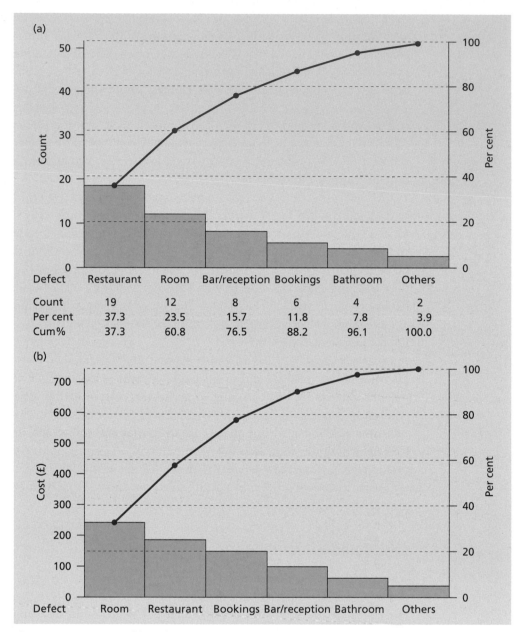

Defect	Restaurant	Room	Bar/reception	Bookings	Bathroom	Others
Count	19	12	8	6	4	2
Per cent	37.3	23.5	15.7	11.8	7.8	3.9
Cum%	37.3	60.8	76.5	88.2	96.1	100.0

Figure 10.2 Pareto of hotel complaints by (a) frequency and (b) cost

The suggested causes of the problem will, to begin with, just be noted in order as they arise, so we might end up with a list like the following:

1 poor-quality flour being supplied
2 dough is allowed to prove for too long
3 too much water added
4 mixing is not thorough enough
5 oven is too hot
6 oven is too cool

and so on.

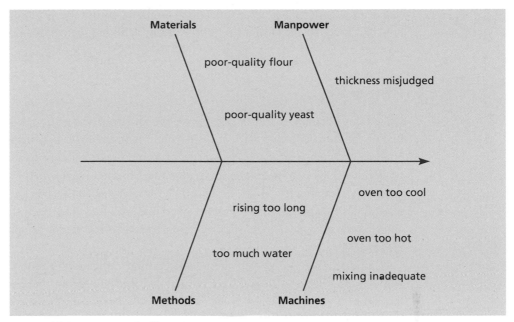

Figure 10.3 Cause-and-effect diagram

Once the team has run out of suggested reasons for the excessive thinness of the bases, Dr Khan needs to put some sort of structure on their suggestions. This is where the cause-and-effect diagram proves useful. This diagram, also called an Ishikawa diagram after its inventor, or a fishbone diagram because of its shape, is simply a way of structuring the list of potential causes which has emerged from the brainstorm. At the head of the 'fish' we have the 'effect' which we are trying to cure – in this case, the thin bases. The major 'bones' of the fish are often structured around four Ms – materials, methods, machines and manpower (the terminology pre-dates equal opportunities legislation!). Sometimes a fifth, rather desperate, category called 'environment' is added to capture any potential causes which cannot be neatly placed in any of the other four categories.

The cause-and-effect diagram for the thin pizza bases is shown in Figure 10.3. Only a selection of the suggested causes is illustrated; many more could be added.

Stratification

Once the potential causes of a quality problem have been structured in this way, some data needs to be collected to try to narrow the area of investigation. It is no good simply theorising in the abstract about possible causes of problems – we need evidence to give us a better idea as to what is actually going on. But it is important, as with all data collection, that the data gathered is appropriate, and in particular that important trends are not obscured by lumping together data that should be kept separate. For example, if Agnelli's regularly uses three different machines to divide the risen dough into pieces, and Dr Khan recommends that the weights of the pieces of dough should be checked to see if this is where the problem arises, it is pointless to mix the output of the three machines before the weighing is done. Instead, the samples of weights from the three machines should be kept separate, so that if just one of them is the source of the difficulty, this fact will become evident.

This is what is meant by stratification – dividing output into suitable subgroups before any data is collected, so that the source of problems can be pinned down as precisely as possible.

Histograms

Once the information about, say, the weights of the pieces of dough has been collected, one of the most effective ways of displaying it is in the form of a histogram. We spent a good deal of time discussing the construction and use of histograms in Chapter 3, so here we will just look at a few examples to illustrate how, to an informed eye, a histogram can tell a very clear story.

Suppose that the pizza bases are weighed just after they have been shaped by the baker, and that those made using dough from machine A give a weight distribution as shown in Figure 10.4.

A quick glance shows that there is something rather odd about this distribution. It would approximate quite well to a normal distribution, except that the upper end of the distribution appears to have been 'chopped off', or *truncated*, to use the technical term. We know from our discussion of the normal distribution in Chapter 7 that we might well expect the dough-cutting machine, left to itself, to produce weights which are normally distributed – so what has happened?

Dr Khan discusses the histogram with the bakery worker responsible for handling the output of this machine – the histogram provides a good basis for discussion, since it gives a simple yet vivid picture of the weight distribution. It soon becomes apparent that when the worker starts to shape a piece of dough which she feels is 'too big', she has been putting it back through the machine again. So the 'natural' distribution of weights has been interfered with – a fact which might not have been discovered without the aid of the histogram.

For the bases from machine B, the picture is somewhat different (see Figure 10.5). As you can see, the weights have been recorded to the nearest 5 g, but a curious pattern has emerged. Apparently there are far more bases with weights ending in 0 than there are ending in 5.

This puzzle is easily solved. Dr Khan examines the rather old-fashioned spring-balance which was used to weigh the bases, and notes that the divisions on the scale for 220, 230,

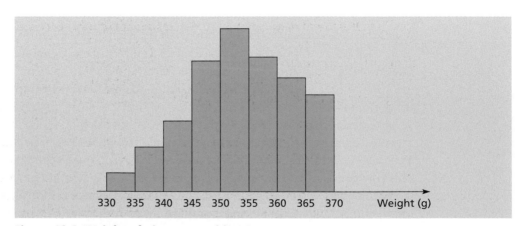

Figure 10.4 Weight of pizzas – machine A

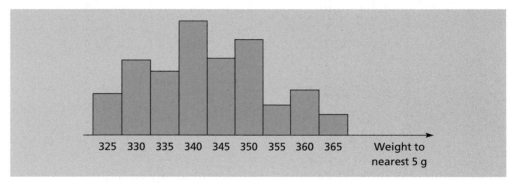

Figure 10.5 Weight of pizzas – machine B

etc., are much clearer than those in between. The person reading the weights has therefore tended to gravitate towards the clearer divisions, and thus produced the 'peaks' seen on the histogram. This kind of peculiarity in a set of measurements is sometimes known as a *measurement artefact* – it tells us something about the nature of the measurement process, rather than a genuine fact about the underlying data.

From these two examples, we can see how plotting histograms of data not only shows basic information about the distribution of variables, but may provide valuable clues as to the process generating the data.

Scatterplots

In the process of looking for causes of undesirable effects, a question that often arises is 'I wonder whether these two variables are connected?' For example, Mr Agnelli might surmise, based on his knowledge of the dough-making process, that the longer a batch of pizza bases is left for its second rising, the more likely it is that some of the bases will turn out to be too thin.

One way to begin investigating this conjecture would be to carry out an experiment, leaving standard-sized batches of bases to rise for varying lengths of time, and monitoring the proportion of 'too thin' bases produced in each batch. We might find something like the following:

Rising time (minutes)	% too thin
10	6
10	8
12	5
12	9
15	9
15	10

The data could then be plotted on a scattergraph, as discussed in Chapter 3. The result would look something like Figure 10.6.

The plot certainly seems to give some support to Mr Agnelli's conjecture, though of course much more thorough investigation would need to be done before any definite conclusions could be drawn. The business of designing experiments to investigate cause-and-effect relationships of this kind is a major statistical topic in its own right, called

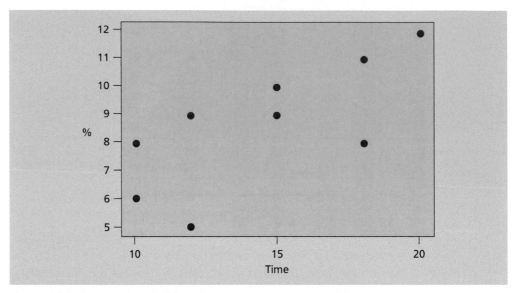

Figure 10.6 Scatterplot of rising time vs percentage too thin

Design of Experiments or DoE. A statistical quality consultant like Dr Khan would probably spend a good deal of his or her time designing such experiments and analysing their results. We will return briefly to this topic at the end of the chapter.

Control charts

As a result of all the investigations described above, Dr Khan and Mr Agnelli's team finally come to the conclusion that the source of the problems with the pizza bases lies primarily in the weights of the pieces of dough produced by the dough-cutting machines. When the machines are left to operate without interference, and the difficulties in recording measurements are sorted out, the distributions from the three machines are as shown in Figure 10.7.

The nominal setting of all three machines, for producing 30 cm bases, should be 350 g. Furthermore, by experimentation Dr Khan has determined that as long as the weight lies between 330 and 370 g, the bases will be neither too thin nor too thick. Below 330 g, they will be thin and hard; above 370 g, they will be too thick and tend to be undercooked in the centre. This information is often summarised by saying that the weights must be in the range 350 ± 20 g, and the limits 330 and 370 are referred to as *tolerance limits*. Tolerances of this kind commonly arise in manufacturing; thus a bolt that is to fit into a nut must not be too large, otherwise the fit will be too tight, nor too small giving too loose a fit, and so on. Sometimes tolerances may be one-sided: for example, in setting waiting-time targets for patients at a dental surgery, 30 minutes may be regarded as the maximum acceptable time, but there is no sensible lower limit – the shorter the time, the happier everyone will be.

The mean of the distribution from machine A does indeed seem to be close to the target value, and the standard deviation is quite small so that, assuming a normal distribution, a very small proportion of the weights will fall outside the tolerance limits.

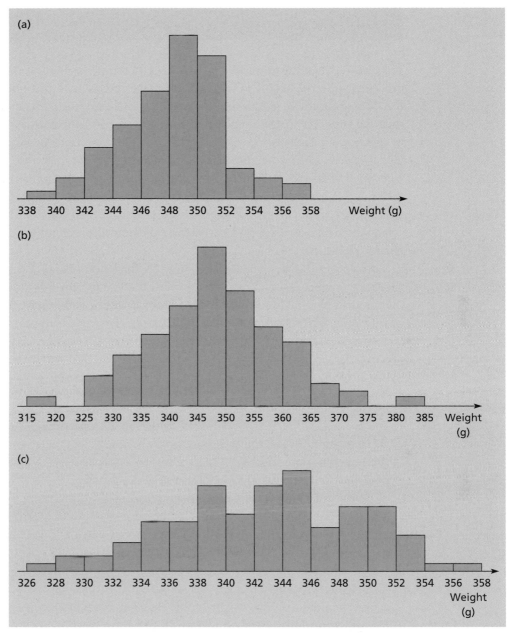

Figure 10.7 Weight distribution from (a) machine A; (b) machine B; (c) machine C

With the other two machines, however, the picture looks very different. Machine C is clearly set to a mean value which is too low, while machine B produces weights which are excessively variable. What can be done to remedy this situation, and to make sure that it does not occur again?

The idea of a *control chart* provides at least a partial answer to this question, but because the concepts underlying this seventh of Ishikawa's tools are rather more complex than those behind the first six, we need to step back and think in a bit more detail about just what is causing the problems.

The effect of variability on processes

The real source of the difficulty with the dough-cutting machines is the *variability* of the process. If it were possible to target the machines precisely to the desired weight, and if they were to continue to produce that weight, with no variation whatsoever, *ad infinitum*, then the problem would simply disappear. But of course that is not how things work in practice. No matter how expensive the machines, and how accurately set up, there will always be some inherent variability in the weights they produce. The same will be true of any process, whether it be the answering of telephones by a switchboard, the processing of invoices by an accounts department, or the assembly of complex electronic components by a computer manufacturer: total consistency is impossible to achieve, and it is variability – particularly uncontrolled variability – that gives rise to quality problems.

However, this is not an excuse simply to throw our hands up and say 'Well, it's variability – what can you expect?' We can get some insight into how we might tackle the problem by thinking about the nature of variability, and in particular by adopting a classification introduced by the late W Edwards Deming, an important pioneer of the quality movement both in Japan and the United States. He suggested that variability in a process arises in two ways:

1 Variation due to *special causes* – these are one-off occurrences which can generally be easily identified and corrected by the people directly involved with the process. For example, if in the operation of filling up the machine with dough, a worker accidentally knocked the weight-setting off target, so that all the bases produced subsequently were too heavy, that would be a special cause. Once it is noticed, the machine can be reset and the problem should not recur.

   If there are many special causes influencing a process, the resulting variability will mean that the behaviour of the process is totally unpredictable, as illustrated in Figure 10.8.

   So we need a method that will warn us quickly when a special cause has occurred, so that steps can be taken to bring the process back into line.

2 Variation due to *common causes* – even if we are very careful so that no special causes disturb the process, there will be all sorts of features of the process itself which generate variations. The weights produced by the dough-cutting machine, for example, will vary despite our best efforts: an expensive machine may have low variability (indicated by a small standard deviation among the weights), a cheaper one will probably exhibit much greater variations in weights (large standard deviation). If only common causes of variation are present, the process will certainly be more predictable, as shown in Figure 10.9(a); but if the common cause variations are too big, then some products that are outside the acceptable tolerances are inevitable, as Figure 10.9(b) shows.

   Generally speaking, it is much more difficult to reduce common cause variation, since such a reduction is likely to require management action – for example, to purchase a more accurate machine, to start ordering higher-quality raw materials, or to change operational systems within the organisation. Nevertheless, the reduction of these variations forms a vital part of the process of continuous improvement which many companies are now undertaking.

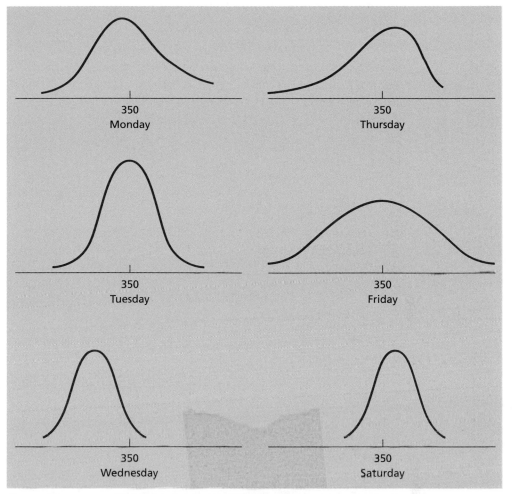

Figure 10.8 Unpredictable behaviour of weight distribution due to special causes

Can our machines meet the tolerances?

A process such as that shown in Figure 10.9(b), in which items outside the acceptable range are bound to occur, is said not to be *capable* of meeting the tolerances set. In this case, no matter how carefully we monitor the process, we are not going to avoid problems. Thus the question of *process capability* is a very important one, and we should make sure our processes are capable before trying to control them.

For example, the sample output from machine A, as shown in Figure 10.7, has a mean of 349.53 g and a standard deviation of 4.08 g. Normal distribution theory then tells us that almost all values in this distribution will lie in the range mean $\pm$ 3 $\times$ s.d., or 349.53 $\pm$ 3 $\times$ 4.08, which is 337.29 to 361.77 g. This is comfortably within the required limits of 330 to 370 g. (The actual proportion within this range will be 99.73 per cent as you can verify from normal tables.) So machine A is capable of meeting the specification.

On the other hand, the output from machine B has a mean of 348.56 g and a standard deviation of 11.15 g. This means, following the argument used above, that the range of

271

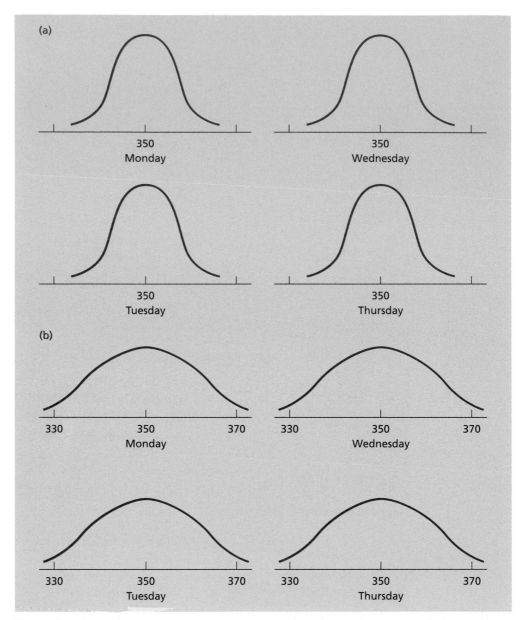

Figure 10.9 Variations due to common causes only: (a) capable process; (b) incapable process

the entire population will be about 315.11 to 382.01 g, and so quite a large proportion of the items produced will be outside the required range 330–370 g. You can use normal tables to verify that the exact proportions are 4.8 per cent at the bottom of the distribution and 2.7 per cent at the top, 7.5 per cent altogether. This may not sound much, but if, say, 1000 pizza bases are produced by this machine each day, then 75 rejects may be expected, and if these are all sold to one customer, there could be considerable problems. Machine B is therefore not capable of meeting the specification. The main reason for this is its excessive variability, though its mean is also rather low.

Machine C has a different problem: the expected range here is 323.57 to 362.09 g, and the problem is not excessive variability but the fact that the mean is 342.83 g – a long way below the nominal mean of 350 g. The machine seems to have wandered off its setting – or to have been wrongly set in the first place – and so reject items at the lower end of the weight range are inevitable.

Some simple measures have been devised to indicate whether or not a process is capable of meeting a specification. One such measure is based on the notion that the expected range of the distribution is 6 × s.d., so if six standard deviations are less than the distance between the tolerance limits, then the process is capable. The measure actually uses the ratio (UTL − LTL)/(6 × s.d.), where UTL and LTL are the upper and lower tolerance limits. This quantity is called the *process capability index*, generally written as C_p, so

$$C_p = \frac{\text{UTL} - \text{LTL}}{6 \times \text{s.d.}}.$$

If C_p is greater than 1, we can therefore say that the process is capable. In fact many companies are now looking for much higher values of C_p to give correspondingly lower reject rates; in engineering situations, where thousands of items may be produced daily, target reject rates of just a few parts per million are not uncommon.

For machine A, the calculation is

$$C_p = \frac{370 - 330}{6 \times 4.08} = 1.63,$$

so this machine is, as we had already concluded, easily capable of meeting the specification. For machine B, you can verify that $C_p = 0.60$, confirming our conclusion that the variability of the pizzas produced by this machine is far too great.

Machine C is an interesting case. Here $C_p = 1.04$, which is just about OK – so in terms of the variability, this machine should not be giving any problems. The trouble is that C_p does not take any account of the centring of the process – and that, as we know, is where the problem lies with this machine. So a second capability measure has been devised to take this into account. Called C_{pk}, it is designed to tell us whether the distance from the process mean to the nearest tolerance limit is less than 3 standard deviations; if it is, then rejects are again inevitable. Symbolically this may be expressed as

$$C_{pk} = \min\left\{\left(\frac{\text{UTL} - \text{process mean}}{3 \times \text{s.d.}}\right), \left(\frac{\text{process mean} - \text{LTL}}{3 \times \text{s.d.}}\right)\right\}.$$

This definition means that, as for C_p, a value of C_{pk} less than 1 means there is a problem. Using the machine C data, we can calculate that

$$C_{pk} = \min\left\{\left(\frac{370 - 342.83}{3 \times 6.42}\right), \left(\frac{342.83 - 330}{3 \times 6.42}\right)\right\} = \min\{1.41, 0.67\} = 0.67.$$

The fact that C_{pk} is less than 1 shows that there will be difficulties, and we can see from the calculation that it is, as we already knew, the lower limit that is too close to the mean.

Figure 10.10 illustrates the general idea behind the two capability indices we have considered. Many more such indices have been devised to deal with other types of process problem, but the two we have discussed are by far the most widely used.

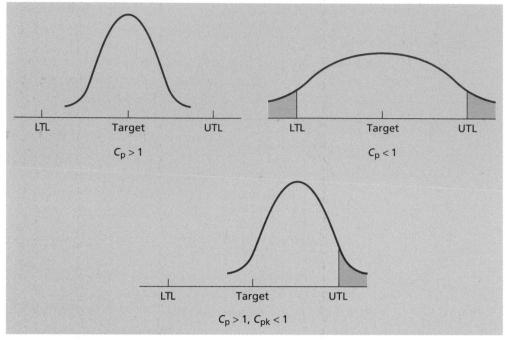

Figure 10.10 Process capability: in each case, shaded area represents rejects

Quick check questions

1 You want to discover if there is a link between the number of complaints received per day by a hotel and the number of customers who are checked in. Which of Ishikawa's seven tools would you use?

2 If the lids of food cans are to fit the body of the can, they must have a diameter between 98 and 102 mm. Checks on a sample of lids show that their mean diameter is 99 mm with a standard deviation of 0.4 mm. Are the lids capable of meeting the tolerance requirements?

3 Which of the following correctly expresses the principle behind a Pareto chart? (a) 20 per cent of problems are created by 80 per cent of causes; (b) 80 per cent of problems are created by 20 per cent of causes; (c) we can ignore 80 per cent of problems.

Answers:

1 Use a scatterplot to look for a connection between two sets of measurements.

2 The capability index $C_p = (102 - 98)/(6 \times 0.4) = 4/2.4 = 1.67$, which is greater than 1, so the process would be deemed to be capable. However, $C_{pk} = 0.83$, so the mean needs adjustment.

3 Answer (b) is correct – a small proportion of causes generate a high proportion of problems.

Controlling the mean of a capable process

A process in which only common cause variations are operating is said to be *in control*; it will go *out of control* if a special cause intervenes. *Statistical process control*, or SPC for short, applies statistical concepts to ensure that processes do not go drastically wrong because of special causes. The idea of a control chart is to enable us to monitor a process, identify the occurrence of special causes quickly, and take action to bring the process back into control. The monitoring must be easy to carry out, so that it can be done by workers as part of their regular routine without the need for a great deal of specialist training; and it must be done by using samples – ideally small ones – since the testing required might, in some cases, destroy the product.

In the case of Agnelli's monitoring of the weights of pizza bases, you might suggest weighing just one base chosen randomly, say, every 15 minutes during the working day. This would certainly give you an idea whether the target weight was being met; but a single item can give no idea at all about the all-important variability of the process. To obtain a picture of that, we must use a sample of at least two items and preferably more. Let us suppose, then, that having taken into account the time it will take to check the weights, and the availability of the workforce, Dr Khan recommends taking a random sample of four bases from each machine every 30 minutes. The size and frequency of the samples to be taken are, in practice, often determined in this way by non-statistical considerations such as the budget for inspection and the nature of the process in question.

Suppose that this has been done for the output of machine A, which as we know is capable of meeting the specification, and that the results from 25 samples of four items each are as shown in Table 10.1. The table also shows, for each sample of four values, the mean and the range (difference between largest and smallest values).

The target weight, you will recall, was 350 g for a 30 cm base, with a tolerance range of 330 to 370 g. The mean of the sample means in Table 10.1 gives an estimate of the over-all process mean, in this case 349.53 g; this is written as $\bar{\bar{x}}$, and pronounced 'x-double-bar'. The standard deviation of all 100 items in the 25 samples is 4.08 g. Thus, as we have already seen, machine A is capable. But suppose that the next sample examined has a mean of 347.28 g: does this give us cause for concern that the process mean is becoming too low?

One way to answer this question, of course, would be to carry out a hypothesis test on the sample mean, in the way we did in Chapter 9. However, if you have grappled with the examples in that chapter you will appreciate that the workers in the bakery would not enjoy having to go through the hypothesis testing process every 15 minutes! What is needed is a simple routine which will provide the same information as the hypothesis test, but without all the computation. This is what the control chart sets out to provide, as we will see.

The thinking behind a hypothesis test can be illustrated as in Figure 10.11(a); sample means falling within the limits cause us to decide that there has been no change in the process, while those falling outside suggest that something has changed. The *control chart* simply turns this diagram on its side, as shown in Figure 10.11(b): the sample means are plotted as they arise, and as long as they remain within the limits, there is probably no cause for concern.

The sensitivity of the chart to changes in the process naturally depends on the arrangement of the limits. In a conventional hypothesis test, we tended to use 5 per cent or 1 per cent significance, so that the risk of a Type 1 error (a 'false alarm' suggesting there has been a change when there has not) is either 0.05 or 0.01. But in the present situation, this would result in far too many false alarms, with changes to the process being made quite unnecessarily. Thus in constructing control charts, the limits are generally placed at three standard errors above and below the mean, giving a 'false alarm' risk of only about 0.17 per cent,

Table 10.1

Item no.	Sample no.								
	1	2	3	4	5	6	7	8	9
1	345.78	347.63	358.93	341.33	351.07	351.71	355.88	348.13	349.78
2	345.54	346.45	347.34	348.85	347.12	352.64	352.96	349.33	349.38
3	353.78	351.92	352.25	346.02	343.96	349.54	343.42	345.40	356.18
4	351.18	344.04	352.74	342.90	345.62	352.23	351.43	348.63	355.37
Mean $\bar{x}$	349.07	347.51	352.81	344.77	346.94	351.53	350.92	347.87	352.68
Range R	8.24	7.88	11.58	7.52	7.10	3.11	12.46	3.93	6.80

Item no.	Sample no.							
	10	11	12	13	14	15	16	17
1	353.33	350.70	350.10	348.09	352.19	348.13	345.93	352.62
2	343.97	351.49	350.48	353.62	345.23	351.12	351.09	350.63
3	351.09	353.35	352.32	347.32	351.69	344.56	346.19	351.45
4	355.66	350.36	346.19	352.45	352.65	352.54	342.90	352.28
Mean $\bar{x}$	351.01	351.48	349.77	350.37	350.44	349.09	346.53	351.74
Range R	11.69	2.99	6.12	6.30	7.42	7.98	8.19	1.99

Item no.	Sample no.							
	18	19	20	21	22	23	24	25
1	354.06	338.54	342.88	349.20	341.83	348.80	346.23	350.92
2	350.54	351.74	351.24	353.16	344.64	349.09	347.82	346.52
3	345.95	346.37	358.41	353.76	348.48	340.84	353.96	357.95
4	349.07	356.03	348.02	350.58	350.99	342.31	352.87	351.87
Mean $\bar{x}$	349.91	348.17	350.14	351.67	346.49	345.26	350.22	351.81
Range R	8.11	17.49	15.54	4.56	9.16	8.26	7.73	11.43

Slight discrepancies in calculations depend on how figures are rounded.

as you can check from normal tables. (With a sample size of four, we should strictly speaking be using a t- rather than a normal distribution, but in practice control chart theory is generally based on normal distributions, even when the samples are small.)

So in the present case the limits would be placed at $349.53 \pm 3 \times 4.08/\sqrt{4}$ (using the usual formula for the standard error of a mean). A little arithmetic gives the limits as 343.41 to 355.65. Should the mean of a sample of four items fall outside this range, we can be pretty sure something has gone wrong with the process, and so suitable action should be taken. The exact nature of the action will depend on the process in question; with the dough-cutting machine we might halt the process while investigating the cause of the problem.

In practice, the upper and lower control limits (UCL and LCL) are not usually calculated in this way, because having to know the standard deviation of the population is not very convenient. Instead, they are computed using the *mean range $\bar{R}$* as a measure of spread. For the 25 samples above, the mean range will be 8.14 (obtained in the standard way, by adding the 25 sample ranges and dividing by 25). There is then a numerical relationship between range and standard deviation which enables the control limits to be expressed in terms of the mean range. Tables based on this relationship are available; an extract from one of these is shown in Table 10.2.

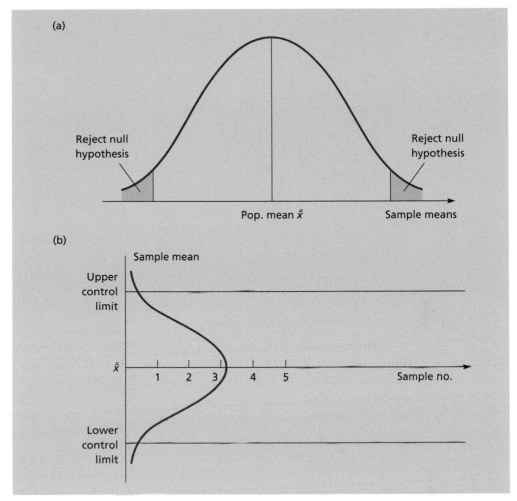

Figure 10.11

The table is used as follows: find the row giving the sample size you are using – here, that is 4. Then the constant A_2 tells us that the control limits will be $\bar{\bar{x}} \pm 0.73 \times \bar{R}$, which as you can verify gives us pretty much the same limits as before.

Because the conventional notation for the mean of a sample is $\bar{x}$ (x-bar), the control chart shown in Figure 10.11 is usually referred to as an x-bar chart. The completed x-bar chart for the data in Table 10.1, with the means of the 25 samples plotted, is shown in Figure 10.12. This chart would not merely be used to plot the 25 samples from which it is calculated; samples would continue to be plotted on it until there is some major change in the process which requires the limits to be recalculated.

Table 10.2

Sample size	A_2 (factor for means chart)	D_3 (factor for lower limit of range chart)	D_4 (factor for upper limit of range chart)
2	1.88	0	3.27
3	1.02	0	2.57
4	0.73	0	2.28
5	0.58	0	2.11

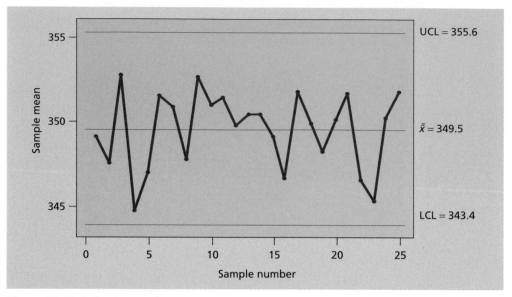

Figure 10.12 $\bar{x}$ chart

To someone experienced in their use, control charts can convey a great deal more than simply the bald information that the process has gone out of control. For example, if the points are steadily drifting towards one of the limits, as shown in Figure 10.13, then perhaps a problem such as wear on a tool needs investigating; if points appear to be more tightly bunched around the mean than expected, there may again be something worth investigating – perhaps the standard deviation of the process has reduced, in which case we would like to know why. A number of rules for interpreting the charts, based on the probabilities of certain patterns arising, have been formulated, such as the 'eight in a row' rule. We will not give all the rules here; you can find details in some of the references given at the end of the chapter, and many software packages for process control also incorporate these rules (see the section 'Software for SPC' on p. 285).

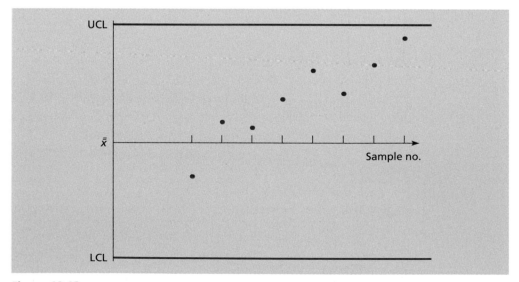

Figure 10.13

Controlling the range

It is possible that a process may appear to be in control according to the mean chart, but is in fact exhibiting excessive variability. Thus to get a complete picture of how the process is behaving, we need also to monitor the range R. Because the sampling distribution of ranges is not normal, however (as a little thought will demonstrate – for one thing, the range must always be positive), we have to resort to the use of Table 10.2 again. This time, we obtain the upper control limit for the range by taking the value of D_4 corresponding to our sample size, and multiplying it by the mean range:

$$\text{Upper control limit for range} = 2.28 \times \bar{R} = 2.28 \times 8.14 = 18.56.$$

Strictly speaking, we do not need a lower control limit, since small ranges are not a worry – the lower the range, the happier we are. However, to alert the user to possibly significant *improvements* in the process, a lower limit is sometimes plotted, in which case we use D_3 from the table:

$$\text{Lower control limit for range} = 0.$$

The completed range chart for our 25 samples, with the 25 points plotted, is shown in Figure 10.14.

The interpretation of the chart is very similar to that of the means chart. Often the two charts are combined into one, as in the example in Figure 10.15, and much background information may also be included – the date and time of each sample, the name or number of the operator, and so on. To this is added information about any process adjustments made when the charts detect a potential problem. In this way, the charts build up to give a valuable record of the history of the process, as well as providing rapid warning when things may be going wrong.

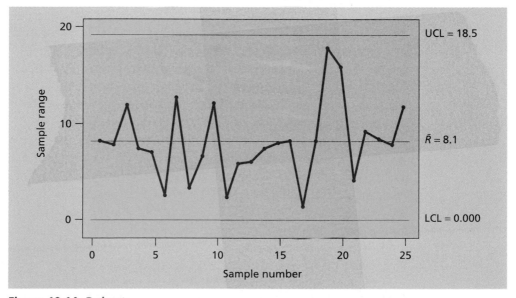

Figure 10.14 *R*-chart

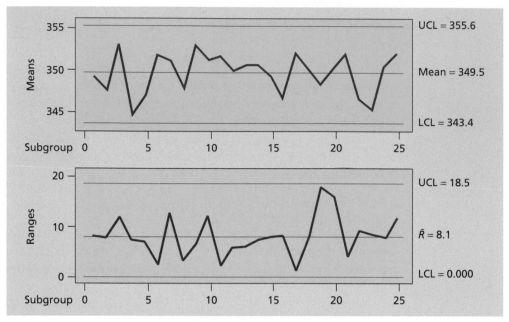

Figure 10.15 $\bar{x}$–R chart

Controlling other aspects of a process

The proportion of defectives

When we are dealing with a situation where items produced by a process are simply classified as 'OK' or 'Not OK', rather than being measured, the $\bar{x}$–R charts described above are of little use. Instead, a similar chart based on STEP rather than STEM is used. Since the theory is very similar to that discussed above, an example will suffice to illustrate the construction of such a chart.

Suppose that one of the critical quality parameters for a mail-order company is the percentage of deliveries which are received by the customer within 14 days of placing an order. The target for this percentage, set by management, is 85 per cent, and at present this is being met. The company wishes to set up a chart to monitor this percentage over time, so that should the standard start to slide, management will be alerted.

Generally speaking, charts based on percentages require larger sample sizes than those based on means – often in the hundreds – since accurate estimates of percentages are difficult to obtain from small samples. We will suppose here that the company has decided to monitor a sample of 200 orders once a month. If the target were being met, then STEP would be $\sqrt{(85 \times 15/200)} = 2.52$ per cent and so the limits would be placed at $85 \pm 3 \times 2.52$ or 77.44 per cent and 92.56 per cent. Strictly speaking, as with the ranges chart above, we do not need the upper limit since we are concerned to monitor only *deteriorations* in quality, but we include it to help the company detect significant improvements.

The chart, which is often referred to as a p-chart (p standing for proportion or percentage), is shown in Figure 10.16, with a number of sample points plotted.

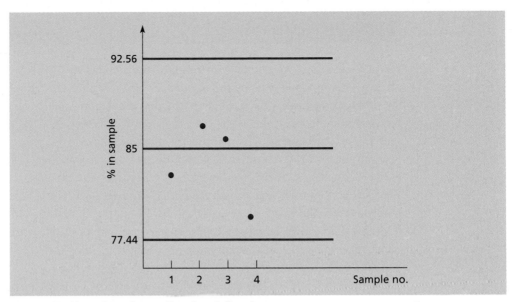

Figure 10.16 *p*-chart for mail-order deliveries

The number of defectives in a sample

Sometimes it is more convenient to plot the actual number of defectives per sample of 200, rather than the percentage. In this case, we have an *np*-chart (can you see why it is given this name?), which really amounts to no more than a rescaling of the axis of the *p*-chart.

The number of defects per item

Yet another situation arises when we wish to monitor the number of defects per unit in a process. For example, a manufacturer of refrigerators might wish to control the total number of small defects (scratches, bubbles in paint and so on) on a finished item. The historic data available here is likely to consist of the average number of defects per fridge worked out over a fairly large sample. Suppose this is calculated as 3.4 defects per item.

Mention of the average per unit should remind you of our discussion of the Poisson distribution in Chapter 7, and, indeed, the charts for this situation are based on Poisson probabilities. For example, to find an upper control limit which will be exceeded only one time in 500 when the mean is 3.4, we need to look at the Poisson probabilities for $m = 3.4$, and find what value is exceeded with a probability of $1/500 = 0.002$ or less. Of course, we cannot expect to find a probability of *precisely* 0.002 in the tables, since we are dealing with a discrete situation, but examination of the numbers in Appendix 4 shows that if the limit is placed between 10 and 11, then the probability that it will be exceeded will be less than 0.002 (because the probability of 11 or more occurrences is only 0.0008). Limits for any required probability level can be worked out in the same way, using the tables 'back-wards' to determine where the limit should fall. The resulting chart is called a *c*-chart.

The types of control charts which we have examined here, though probably the most widely used, only represent the tip of a very large iceberg; many more have been developed for use in specific circumstances. Descriptions of these can be found in a number of the references given at the end of the chapter. However, the basic principles of construction and interpretation remain the same.

Sampling inspection

We have seen how Mr Agnelli can monitor the weights of his pizza bases – and many other process parameters – by the use of suitable control charts. However, it may be that the problems he has experienced are partly due to the poor quality of incoming materials sent by his suppliers. If this is the case, then he should clearly try to take steps to prevent such material getting into his manufacturing process.

In an ideal world, of course, this should not happen: suppliers should send only the required quality to their customers, and customers should have confidence in their suppliers so that only very occasional checks are necessary. Some areas of industry have indeed established this level of trust within the supply chain, but sadly, many have not. For those where poor-quality incoming material remains a problem, and where incoming items can be classified as 'acceptable' or 'not acceptable', *sampling inspection* often provides at least a partial solution.

We have touched on this topic already when discussing the binomial distribution in Chapter 7. The fundamental idea is that, when a large batch of items is received from a supplier, a small sample taken from the batch is tested. If the sample proves satisfactory according to some predetermined criterion (e.g. containing no more than one defective item), then the whole batch is accepted. If the sample fails to reach the criterion, the entire batch is returned to the supplier.

Suppose, for instance, that Mr Agnelli's bakery regularly takes delivery of large batches of heavy-duty plastic bags, in which part-baked pizza bases can be vacuum-sealed before distribution to restaurants. If these bags have any perforations or weaknesses, however small, then they are liable to fail to maintain the necessary vacuum, thus leading to a risk that the pizza bases will deteriorate in transit. Agnelli's therefore wishes to test a sample from each batch of bags as it arrives, to ensure that the quality is as required.

Because the bags are a fairly cheap, high-volume item, Agnelli's has accepted that a small proportion of reject-quality bags is inevitable; the figure agreed with the bag supplier is presently 4 per cent. Ideally, batches with up to 4 per cent would therefore be accepted; those with more than 4 per cent would be rejected. If we were to plot the probability of accepting a batch against the proportion of defectives in the batch, the graph would thus resemble Figure 10.17.

This graph is called the *operating characteristic* of the inspection scheme. The version of the operating characteristic in Figure 10.17 can be achieved only by 100 per cent inspection, which is hardly going to be cost-effective for small items such as bags. Besides, the test, which consists of blowing air at increasing pressure into a bag until it bursts, actually destroys the bags, so testing all of them would be rather impractical!

Instead, Dr Khan, the quality consultant, devises the following inspection scheme: from each batch of 10 000 bags which is received, take a sample of 10. If no more than 1 defective is found, accept the batch; if more than 1 is found, reject the batch. The number 1 is called the acceptance number for the scheme.

The crucial question about such a scheme is how good it is at distinguishing good batches from bad ones. In this case, imagine first that the supplier is maintaining the agreed standard and sending batches which are 4 per cent defective. What is then the probability of a batch being accepted – that is, the probability that it will contain no more than one defective?

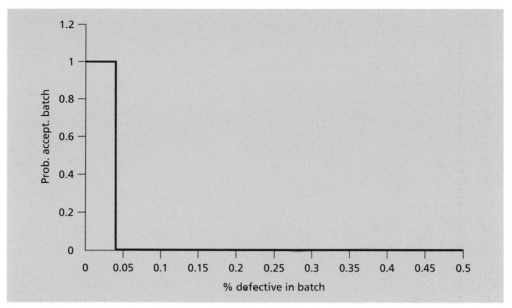

Figure 10.17 Ideal operating characteristic

To answer this question, we need (as you should already have realised) to use the binomial distribution. We have a sample size of 10, $p = 0.04$ (the quality of the batch), and we want to find p(0 or 1 defectives). This value of p does not actually occur in the tables in Appendix 3, but by consulting a larger set of tables (or by using the probability distribution functions in Excel), we can find that the probability in question is 0.94. There is thus a 94 per cent chance that with this scheme a batch which is 4 per cent defective is accepted.

Now consider the other extreme, where the supplier is sending very poor-quality material – say, 20 per cent defective. n remains at 10, and the scheme remains as before, but now $p = 0.2$. The probability of accepting the batch is now reduced to 0.38 (this one can be checked using Appendix 3). So there is still quite a high chance of accepting a really unsatisfactory batch; this inspection scheme is not very discriminating.

If we sketch the operating characteristic in this case, it looks something like Figure 10.18. Comparing this with the ideal case in Figure 10.17, you can see that the slope – the reduction in the probability of acceptance as the quality deteriorates – is much too gradual. What Dr Khan will need to do is to vary the size of the sample and the acceptance number to bring the graph more into line with the ideal – which, in general, will mean taking bigger samples.

In practice schemes are not designed in this slightly haphazard way. Instead, supplier and customer will together decide what levels of risk they are prepared to take: the customer needs to decide what risk he or she will run of accepting 'really awful quality' (which of course must be defined); the supplier must agree what risk he or she can tolerate of having 'perfectly OK quality' (again, something that needs defining) sent back. Armed with these figures, the consultant can then resort to tables which will give an indication of suitable sample sizes and acceptance numbers.

The scheme we have outlined here is just the simplest in a large range of possible inspection schemes. Some involve taking not one, but two samples; others involve sampling continuously until a certain level of defectives is reached, so the 'sample size' is not

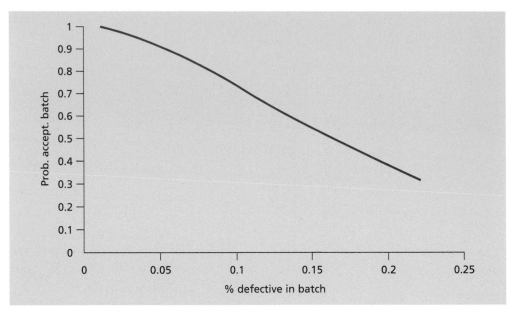

Figure 10.18 Actual operating characteristic

predetermined. However, the underlying idea – that we make a judgement on the quality of the batch by examining a sample – remains the same.

The whole concept of acceptance sampling is open to the criticism that it encourages both customer and supplier to think in terms of an unavoidable, acceptable level of defectives, instead of striving to achieve zero defects. However, in cases where large volumes of relatively low-value items are concerned, where testing is quick and simple, and where the consequences of poor-quality material reaching the process are not disastrous, acceptance sampling is still widely used.

Quick check questions

1 'Using control charts will prevent any faulty material from being produced.' Is this true?

2 You want to use a control chart to track the number of pulled threads per garment in samples of cardigans arriving from an overseas supplier. Which type of chart would you use?

3 Why are control chart limits for the mean conventionally placed three standard deviations above and below the overall mean?

Answers:

1 No control system will totally prevent the production of faulty material, but a control chart used effectively can alert the user quickly to changes in the process which may lead to faulty material being produced.

2 In this case you need an *np*-chart, based on the Poisson distribution.

3 Three standard deviations either side of the overall mean give limits which will only be breached on a very small proportion of occasions when the process is in control, thus giving only a low proportion of 'false alarms'.

More advanced applications of statistics in quality improvement

There are many other ways in which statistical techniques can play a part in the quality improvement process. One area where major achievements have been made is the design of systematic experimentation on industrial processes, which was touched on briefly earlier in this chapter. If Agnelli's wish to experiment to determine what combination of rising time, rising temperature, flour type, oven temperature and yeast quantity produces the best results in terms of pizza thickness, then many decisions will need to be made: what range of values of each parameter should be tested, how these should be combined, and so on. With five factors to be examined here, a very large amount of experimentation could be involved. Even if only two levels of each factor are tested, 2^5 or 32 experiments will be needed to cover all possible combinations just once in a systematic way – and since many of the experiments could produce totally unusable pizzas, the costs of the experimentation could become quite high. If a more haphazard approach is used – as is often the case in practice – the whole thing could become a financial disaster.

Fortunately there is a set of techniques, generally known as statistical design of experiments, which enable investigations of this kind to be carried out in an organised way so as to provide the maximum amount of information. Since the 1980s the term 'Taguchi methods' has come to be used loosely to cover this area; Genichi Taguchi is a Japanese engineer who has done much to popularise the use of these methods in Japanese industry and elsewhere. However, strictly speaking this term should be reserved for a subset of the methods, together with an accompanying structure of quality costs and methods of analysis which has been developed by Dr Taguchi.

Yet another area where statistical techniques can be usefully applied to quality improvement is the analysis of lifetime and reliability data. Manufacturers of items such as cars and computers are very anxious to know how long is likely to elapse before certain components will fail and need replacement – in particular, if failure occurs during the period of warranty of the product, the resulting costs to the manufacturer can be considerable. By examining historic failure data, suitable probability distributions can be fitted so that predictions of likely failure times can be made. This enables manufacturers to budget for the expected volume of claims under warranty, and to look for significant improvements in performance resulting from process changes.

Software for SPC

There are many dedicated software packages for constructing control charts, helping to design and analyse experiments, and so on. The choice of a particular package may well be determined by the extent to which it interfaces with other software in use in the organisation, and can capture data gathered by computers controlling processes.

Excel does not provide any statistical process control routines as such, though with a bit of ingenuity some of the standard diagrams provided by ChartWizard can be adapted to produce Pareto plots, control charts, and so on. The diagrams in this chapter, however – the Pareto and fishbone in Figures 10.2 and 10.3, and the control chart in Figure 10.12 – were generated using a multi-purpose statistical package called Minitab, which incorporates a wide variety of SPC routines.

You will find some more examples of the various quality plots on the Companion Website.

How did it work for Ford?

Now think back to the problem with paint thickness described at the start of this chapter. You should be able to see how some of the methods we've been discussing could be used in overcoming this problem – for example, simple histograms of the thickness of paint samples could be used to examine averages and variability; cause-and-effect analysis could be used to determine the potential causes of excessive variation, and so on. If you read the rest of Richard Parry-Jones's lecture (there is a web link to the text from the Companion Website) you will see that the flow of air in the paint sprayer was discovered to have a major impact on the paint thickness (possibly by means of some scatterplots, and certainly using designed experimentation as described above); once the thickness was brought under control, plotting control charts enabled it to be effectively monitored in case further problems arose.

So you can see that the statistical tools you have been learning about are being used every day, all over the world, to help leading companies to maintain and improve their quality, and hence to retain their existing customers and attract new ones.

EXERCISES

*Further examples on the work of this chapter can be found on the **Companion Website**.*

1 A Pareto analysis is to be carried out on the reasons for the return of electric toasters to a manufacturer during the guarantee period. The reasons identified from a large sample of returns, together with the estimated cost to the company of repairing each type of fault, are shown below. Use the data to construct Pareto charts (a) by frequency and (b) by value, and compare the two.

Reason	Frequency %	Cost
Total failure to function	10	£40
Too hot – burning toast	40	£9
Too cool – toast undercooked	15	£8
Ejector mechanism fails	30	£5
Other minor faults	5	£2

2 A police force is concerned that its officers are not responding quickly enough when members of the public telephone to request assistance in non-emergency situations – for example, to report an attempted burglary or a stolen vehicle. Accordingly, senior management has decided that each month a sample of 50 such calls will be monitored, and a chart plotted to show the number within the sample where an officer responded to the call within 30 minutes.

(a) At present the percentage of calls meeting this criterion is 60 per cent. Where would you place the limits on a control chart if the chart is required to detect departures from the existing position, both improvements and deteriorations?

(b) Senior management sets a target for the percentage at 80 per cent. Where would the limits be placed if the chart were based on this target?

(c) Compare the two sets of limits found in (a) and (b), and comment on the results.

3 Many British children learn to play the recorder (a simple wind instrument) at school, and there is consequently a big market for cheap recorders. These are made in two pieces, the 'head' and 'foot', which must fit together neatly when the instrument is played – the head fits inside the foot. There is thus a fairly tight tolerance on the diameter of the head – if it is too large, the fit will be too tight and it will be difficult to put the instrument together and take it apart; too small, and the fit will be loose, resulting in air leaking out or perhaps the instrument coming apart in use.

Economic Instruments manufactures wooden recorders, and specifies the diameter of the head pieces as 23 mm ± 1.5 mm. Data based on a sample of 100 head pieces as currently produced by the wood-turning machine shows that the mean is 22.88 mm with a standard deviation of 0.52 mm. What does this suggest about the capability of the process? Estimate the proportion of out-of-specification head pieces which will be produced, assuming a normal distribution.

4 In the situation described in Exercise 3 above, you have also been given the diameters of 40 samples of five foot pieces (nominal diameter 27 mm). The data is shown below. Use the first 20 samples to plot control charts for the mean and the sample range, and then plot the values for the remaining 20 samples on your charts. Comment on the results. (The data is also on the website in the file FOOT.XLS.)

26.1728	26.8443	27.7552	25.9497	27.395	27.5711	26.7029	27.4253	26.6858	26.7324
28.2255	27.1743	26.4524	26.5755	26.9776	27.0643	26.9556	27.4765	26.8256	27.4129
27.6594	27.3276	26.8992	26.7479	27.0602	27.1227	27.1334	26.8653	27.3327	27.0699
26.4802	26.6011	27.3206	27.0986	27.2925	26.9075	25.7242	26.4866	28.5835	26.5064
26.4975	27.6313	25.6521	28.4448	27.9713	26.4661	28.2806	27.3542	27.7705	26.6301
26.9066	26.8787	26.3823	26.7083	26.7281	26.5569	26.0158	26.9938	27.8594	27.13
25.886	27.1686	26.2042	28.4803	27.0307	27.6613	27.2197	28.1235	26.6009	26.2304
27.2329	28.2648	27.3721	26.9698	26.7696	26.9993	27.4889	26.7297	27.2716	27.1226
26.414	26.8341	26.7614	26.9749	27.1549	27.231	27.1865	25.7169	26.6528	27.467
26.8613	26.4757	26.4045	27.1268	26.6565	27.5811	26.3508	27.3762	26.6236	26.6097
27.5882	27.5118	26.4437	27.0492	27.2587	26.8167	25.8931	27.6046	27.0209	27.4002
26.1144	27.1023	27.3204	26.2615	25.7789	27.3241	25.8884	26.8567	26.831	27.2281
27.1033	27.5569	26.9442	27.1858	28.6311	27.0558	27.239	27.2713	26.7208	27.1227
26.4791	26.3917	27.3545	27.6973	27.2903	27.9399	27.2704	27.6477	27.3986	26.7766
26.9789	25.9811	26.9683	26.8837	27.4292	26.9505	26.4634	27.2015	27.1874	26.6633
27.0749	27.0408	27.121	26.6748	26.223	26.185	28.0721	26.6259	27.058	25.3268
26.7626	26.4645	27.0625	27.8542	27.0181	27.1121	27.0446	26.3684	26.5681	25.7445
26.3536	26.9854	26.9878	26.902	26.7589	27.176	27.4878	27.0125	26.6066	26.6272
26.328	26.8866	26.2293	27.0877	27.165	27.0152	27.929	26.2021	26.7606	26.3522
27.1563	27.5799	26.5208	27.3913	26.5654	27.6086	26.5054	27.4606	26.9081	27.8621

5 You have been asked to construct a chart to control the number of shut-downs per week on an assembly line in a computer manufacturing plant (the line is shut down when a serious quality problem has been discovered). Over the past two years the average number of shut-downs per week has been 5.2.

(a) Where would you place the limit on the chart to detect an increase in the number of shut-downs, if the company requires the limit to be exceeded only once in 100 weeks when the process is stable?

(b) If you wished to include a lower limit on the chart to detect significant improvements, and again a level of 1 in 100 is to be used to determine the position of the limit, where would it be placed?

6 A clothing manufacturer regularly takes delivery of batches of zip-fasteners from a supplier in another EU country. In the past there have been problems with some of these zips jamming in use, resulting in complaints from customers and the need to replace the zip, or sometimes an entire garment. A policy of sampling inspection has therefore been introduced: from each batch of 5000 zips received, 10 will be taken, and subjected to a standard test in which they are mechanically fastened and unfastened 200 times. Any zips which jam during this test are classed as failures, and if one or more zips in the sample fail the test, the whole batch is rejected.

(a) What is the probability of rejecting a batch in which (i) 5 per cent, (ii) 10 per cent and (iii) 20 per cent of zips are defective?

(b) Sketch the operating characteristic for the scheme and comment on what it reveals.

(c) If the supplier sends 100 batches per year, all with 5 per cent defective, and this scheme is in operation, what is the average number of batches that will be rejected per year? On average, how many satisfactory zips will therefore be sent back?

7 A process manufacturing plumbing pipes is known to be in control, with the pipes having a mean diameter of 20 mm with a mean range of 0.8 mm. Where would the upper and lower limits be placed on a chart to control the mean of this process, using a sample size of 4?

8 In a call centre, the management's target is that no telephone call should last more than 3 minutes. Monitoring of calls over a long period reveals that the mean length of a call is 2.6 minutes, with a standard deviation of 0.2 minutes. Assuming that the lengths of calls are normally distributed, can the target be met? How does this example relate to the ideas of process capability discussed in this chapter? Do you think the normal distribution is likely to be a good model in this case?

9 If a control chart were plotted with limits at the overall mean plus and minus two standard errors, what proportion of 'false alarms' would you expect to get from an in-control process? Can you imagine any possible use for limits of this kind?

10 In an acceptance sampling scheme used by a manufacturer of paper cups, samples of ten cups are to be examined from each hour's output, and if any of the cups leak then the whole hour's production is scrapped. Assuming that the underlying rate of leaky cups is 1 per cent, use the binomial probabilities provided by Excel to find the probability that a sample of ten cups will contain at least one which leaks. Comment on the scheme in the light of your answer.

Case Study

Sorting out slow service at the *Poppleton Arms*

As a business consultant, you have been engaged by the management of the *Poppleton Arms*, a popular hotel and conference venue, to try to find out why the numbers of complaints from customers in the restaurant have been increasing over recent months.

(a) By examining records and interviewing staff, you establish the following list of types of complaint, together with the rough percentage of occasions when each occurred:

Slow service	35%
Food not as ordered	23%
Food not hot	18%
Dirty crockery	9%
Temperature of room too hot	4%
Temperature of room too cold	4%
Poor value for money	3%
Piped music too loud	2%
Others	2%

Prepare a Pareto chart for the hotel management, and indicate where you would concentrate your problem-solving efforts.

(b) You decide to investigate the slow service first, and after discussion with staff, you develop a hypothesis that service becomes slower when the restaurant is crowded. You therefore collect some data over the course of a week, and discover the following:

No. of guests in restaurant	Average time from arrival to receiving first course (minutes)
21–30	14
31–40	15
41–50	23
51–60	19
61–70	27

The maximum capacity of the restaurant is 70. Construct a scatterplot to help you explain the link between number of guests and waiting time to the hotel manager.

(c) As a result of your investigations, workflow in the kitchen is improved, and an additional waiter is made available when bookings rise above 40. How might you go about controlling the situation to ensure that any deterioration is detected and remedied quickly? (Hint: what would be a suitable measure to use, and how could it be controlled?)

Further reading

If you wish to read more about the role of statistics in quality improvement, you may find the following books provide a useful starting-point:

Owen, M. and Morgan, J. (2000), *SPC in the Office: A Practical Guide to Continuous Improvement*, Greenfield Publishing.

Hayler, R. and Nichols, M. (2005), *What is Six Sigma Process Management?*, McGraw-Hill.

Slack, N. *et al.* (2009), *Operations Management*, 6th edn, FT Prentice Hall. (Although this is primarily an operations management text, Chapters 17, 19 and 20 cover much material which is relevant to the content of this chapter.)

Chapter 11

LOOKING FOR CONNECTIONS:
CORRELATION

Chapter prerequisites   Before starting work on this chapter make sure you are happy with:

1 the idea of a scattergraph (see Chapter 3, p. 85);

2 calculation and interpretation of mean and standard deviation (see Chapter 4);

3 the concept of ranking (see Chapter 2).

Learning outcomes   By the end of your work on this chapter you should be able to:

1 recognise when a scattergraph suggests a relationship between two variables;

2 realise when the elimination of an outlier would make such a relationship more apparent;

3 calculate and interpret the rank correlation coefficient;

4 calculate and interpret Pearson's product–moment correlation coefficient.

Quantitative methods in practice

We thought the internet was killing print. But it isn't

A fascinating new piece of research this week looks in detail at the success of newspaper websites and attempts to find statistical correlations with sliding print copy sales. As one goes up, the other must go down, surely? These are the underpinnings of transition.

But 'in the UK at least, there is no such correlation', reports the number-crunching analyst Jim Chisholm.

(www.guardian.co.uk, from *The Observer*, 17 October 2010)

The example cited above suggests that the relationship between print media and news provision over the Internet might be expected to follow the same pattern as often happens when technical innovations occur in an industry. For example, when DVDs were introduced, sales of video cassettes declined, eventually to pretty well zero. However, in the case of newspapers and the Web, when the figures over time are examined using the proper statistical methods, that turns out not to be the case. But what are the proper methods?

The analysis cannot be done using the tools we have studied thus far: means and standard deviations, hypothesis tests and confidence intervals – all the methods we have covered up to now involve focusing on just one variable at a time, whereas investigating the claim made above requires us to examine the relationship between two variables. (The one exception to this was the chi-squared test – do you think that could be used in this case?)

This is, of course, a very common situation: establishing whether or not relationships exist between quantities is an essential step in dealing with many problems, both in science and in business. For example, a fertiliser manufacturer might want to examine the link between the amount of fertiliser used on a crop and the weight of crop achieved; a maintenance engineer would be interested in knowing whether the speed at which a drill is operated has something to do with the frequency with which it needs to be replaced; and the proprietor of a British seaside hotel might wonder whether the number of rooms that are booked is in some way related to the weather. You can probably think of many other examples of this kind.

Our exploration of these problems will extend over the next three chapters. First we will look at the idea of *correlation* mentioned in the article above. Correlation is one of the many statistical terms which tend to be used somewhat loosely in everyday conversation, to indicate any kind of connection – thus someone might say 'There's no necessary correlation between having a white van and being a bad driver'. However, we will see that in its proper sense the term means something much more specific, and provides a useful way of assessing not only the existence, but the strength of a relationship between variables.

The sales manager's problem

Tim Newton is the sales manager of a firm which manufactures meat products (pies, sausages, etc.) and markets them directly to retail food stores via a large force of sales representatives. Recently, as the recession has begun to affect the business, Mr Newton has become aware of the need to monitor representatives' performance more closely, but the trouble is that he does not have very much idea what factors may influence that performance. He feels, for example, that it would not be fair to classify a representative as inefficient on the basis of the comparatively low sales revenue he or she generates, if that particular representative happens to cover a very sparsely populated area, in which he or she cannot be expected to do as well as a colleague who has been allocated to a well-populated urban sales region.

As a preliminary step, to help clarify his ideas, Mr Newton has collected some information relating to a random sample of ten representatives. This information is shown in the table below.

Rep. no.	Value of last quarter's sales (£000s)	Number of retail outlets visited regularly	Population of sales area (000s)	Area covered (square miles)
1	2	63	200	450
2	5	42	40	500
3	9	47	40	350
4	11	51	90	250
5	11	56	70	150
6	12	64	100	420
7	14	60	140	275
8	15	68	200	200
9	17	75	160	400
10	17	81	240	300

But this mass of figures, as it stands, does not convey much information to Mr Newton. He really has a twofold objective:

1 *Control*: if he can demonstrate that there is a close connection between the value of the sales which a representative generates – a variable that is not directly within his control – and, for example, the number of retail outlets visited regularly by the representative – something that he *can* directly influence – then he can attempt to alter the sales revenue by making sure his representatives visit more outlets in future. So he would like a way of measuring how close a relationship there is between variables.

2 *Estimation/prediction*: if he can go one step further and actually specify what the relationship between variables is, rather than merely stating that there is such a relationship, then he will be able to predict, with at least some degree of accuracy, what value of sales will be generated by, for example, a representative who visits 80 retail outlets regularly. A knowledge of what the relationship *ought* to be will also help him to spot a representative who seems to be 'the exception to the rule' – who, for instance, is failing to generate the appropriate sales volume considering the number of outlets he or she claims to visit. Such a representative would merit further investigation to see if he or she is very inefficient for some reason, or perhaps 'on the fiddle' and not actually visiting all the outlets claimed. Conversely, if a representative seems to be unusually successful when compared with the general pattern as established, it might pay dividends to follow him or her up and find out why this should be: has the representative got a new and more effective line of approach, perhaps?

As we saw at the start of the chapter, the ability to spot a relationship between two quantities, to measure how close it is, and if possible to state explicitly what the relationship is, opens up all sorts of useful consequences, not just in this problem but in a more general context. In a sense, though, we have been begging the question by talking vaguely about 'a relationship' without defining what exactly is meant by that. So before we go any further into investigating the closeness of relationships, let us try to be a bit more precise as to the meaning of the expression.

What kind of relationship?

It should already be clear to you from the examples mentioned at the end of the last section that we are not talking about *exact* relationships any more. By 'exact' I mean the sort of relationship which applies if you buy 5 kilos of bananas at £3.50 per kilo; you can be quite certain that the price you have to pay will be $5 \times £3.50 = £17.50$, unless you are being overcharged! There is an exact relationship of the form: price = number of kilos bought $\times$ price per kilo, which enables you to predict with complete accuracy what the price will be for any number of kilos purchased. No other factors, such as how tall the greengrocer is, or the temperature on the day you buy the bananas, will make any difference to this.

In the case of predicting your examination mark from your assessment mark, however, we have a completely different sort of problem. Presumably there *is* a link between the two marks – people with higher marks in assessment will probably get higher exam marks too – but there are many other factors that will also have an influence on your examination performance: your basic ability in the subject, perhaps as measured by your A-level performance; your innate intelligence, maybe given by your IQ; the percentage of lectures you have missed during the year; and so on.

So there is no way in which you could establish a 'rule' for calculating the examination mark given the assessment marks in the way that we calculated the price of the bananas given the number of kilos bought. The problem is too complex and too full of imponderable factors for that, and the same goes for all the other examples mentioned above.

The banana problem can, however, give us some idea how we can start to tackle these more complex relationships. One good way to show the connection between the quantity of bananas bought and the price paid would be to draw a graph, with the number of kilos bought on the horizontal axis and the price paid on the vertical axis. This would, of course, be a straight line as shown in Figure 11.1. The three points marked are those which are used to plot the line, and represent the cost of 0, 5 and 10 kg. Naturally, since the relationship is an exact one, the line passes precisely through all three points.

If we try doing the same thing for some of the sales data in the section on the sales manager's problem, we will not get a straight line, certainly, or even any kind of smooth curve; but if we plot, as an example, the sales value for each representative (on the vertical axis) against the number of retail outlets he or she visits regularly (on the horizontal axis), the points *do* seem to cluster fairly near to a line, even though they are not all exactly on it. The graph is shown in Figure 11.2 and it should not be completely strange to you. It is a *scattergraph*, which we looked at briefly in Chapter 3.

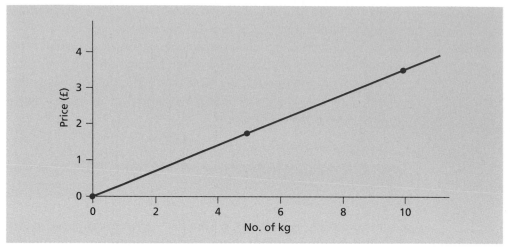

Figure 11.1 An exact linear relationship

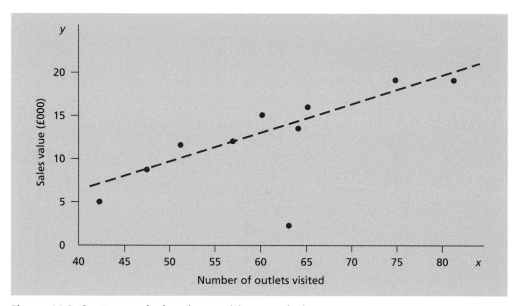

Figure 11.2 Scattergraph showing positive correlation

Using the scattergraph

Scattergraphs can be very useful as a preliminary step in investigating the existence of a relationship between two quantities. The kind of situation demonstrated by Figure 11.2, where the points appear to cluster near to an upward-sloping straight line, is referred to as a *positive correlation*: as x (the horizontal variable) increases, so does y (the vertical one). So we expect to get such a relationship in situations where the two variables in question are rising or falling together: the more shops a salesman visits, the more sales he can hope to make, for example.

The converse situation, not surprisingly, is called *negative correlation*: one variable gets bigger as the other gets smaller. This produces a scattergraph in which the points are again

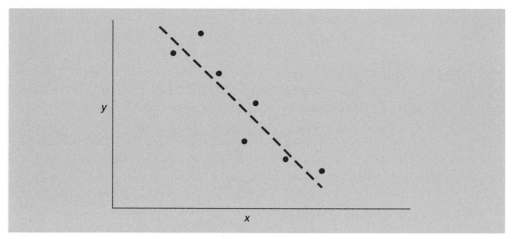

Figure 11.3 Scattergraph showing negative correlation

near to a straight line, but this time one which slopes downhill from left to right. For instance, the more lectures you miss, the worse (I hope) your exam mark will be, producing a scattergraph resembling Figure 11.3.

Of course, there is no reason why a relationship of this kind *must* be a straight line; in fact, if the data for sales value is plotted against the population of the representative's region, the scattergraph produced (Figure 11.4) suggests the existence of a curved relationship, as shown roughly by the dashed line. And it may turn out that our suspicions were wrong, and there is actually no relationship of any kind between two quantities: in this case the points of the scattergraph are indeed scattered, with no discernible pattern at all, like Figure 11.5 which indicates the apparent absence of a link between the value of the sales generated by each representative and the size of his or her sales region. (A bit of thought suggests that this is what we really ought to have expected: the area covered on its own is not a significant factor; a representative could cover hundreds of square miles,

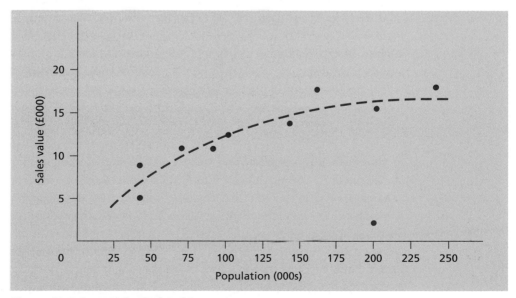

Figure 11.4 A curved relationship

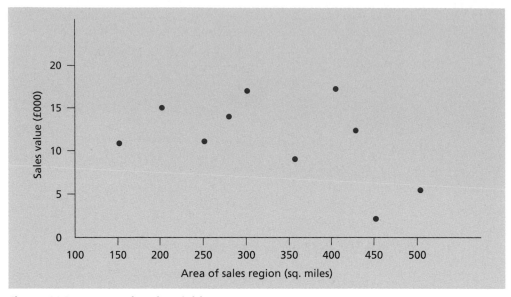

Figure 11.5 Two unrelated variables

but if they were in the middle of the Scottish Highlands where very few people live to buy the products, this would not yield much in the way of sales revenue.)

Exact relationships, like the banana example we looked at earlier, can be tidily included among all the other types we have mentioned, if we regard them as cases of *perfect correlation*. The banana example gives a perfect positive correlation between price paid and number of kilos bought, and the resulting 'scattergraph', as we have seen, shows all the points lying exactly on the straight line.

Although it is easy enough to spot relationships of a curved type, like that in Figure 11.4, by examining the scattergraph, curved graphs are, as we saw in Chapter 1, a much more complicated proposition than straight lines. A straight line graph is really the only kind one can be sure of plotting correctly, simply by using a ruler. From now on, therefore, we are going to limit our discussion to relationships like those shown in Figures 11.2 and 11.3, where the points seem to be near to a line. As far as all our future analysis in this chapter is concerned, a relationship like that shown in Figure 11.4 is, almost as much as that shown in Figure 11.5, an example of *zero correlation*.

The moral of all this is that, in investigating a suspected link between any two variables, your best bet to begin with is to draw a scattergraph. It will indicate whether there is a correlation worth pursuing by more complex methods; if the relationship happens to be curved, it will indicate that too, and should that be the case your only course of action is to put in a freehand approximation to the relationship on the graph, trying to make your curve pass fairly 'through the middle' of the set of points.

There is a further piece of information which can be obtained from the scattergraph, as we can see by examining Figures 11.2 and 11.4 again. On each of these diagrams, there is one point that does not seem to conform to the general pattern. A point like this is often called an *outlier*, and if we go back to the original data in this case we find that the outliers in both diagrams are the points corresponding to representative number 1. A closer look at his figures suggests that there is indeed something funny going on: he covers a well-populated area, seems to be visiting a fair number of outlets, yet his sales are lower than anyone else's. Maybe he is only *claiming* to have visited 63 outlets; maybe he *did* visit them but is simply very poor at the job; but in either case, the question needs investigating. And this representative should not be included in any further analysis of the problem; whatever relationship may apply to the other representatives in Figure 11.2, it certainly does not apply to this one, and his presence in our calculations will tend to make the relationship seem less clearcut than it really is. We will return to this point later in the chapter.

For all these reasons, then, a scattergraph is a good start. Why, you may ask, do we need to go further? Can't we spot the relationship, if one exists, on the scattergraph and put in a reasonably good freehand line? For that matter, why do we need the line at all when we can *see* that there's a relationship, without having to specify exactly what it looks like?

There are two major drawbacks to this totally graphical approach. First, it is very hard to judge 'by eye' just how close a relationship is – the scale on which you choose to draw the scattergraph can make a lot of difference to the appearance of a relationship, as you will discover if you try plotting Figure 11.2 twice over, the second time with scales on both axes twice as big as the first time. So we could do with a proper numerical *measurement* of the closeness of the relationship.

Second, where exactly are we going to draw the freehand line on the graph? We must have such a line if we are to achieve the second objective mentioned on p. 292, the prediction of one variable given a value of the other. But if you make several copies of Figure 11.2, and get different people to put in what *they* consider to be the line that fits the points best, you will probably find you get some very varied results. Again, a proper systematic method of working out where the line should go is needed.

The second of these requirements we will defer until Chapter 12; the first will occupy us for the rest of this chapter.

Measuring the strength of a relationship: the correlation coefficient

We have actually already looked at one way in which we could assess the strength of the relationship between sales and number of outlets visited. Perhaps if that is rephrased as 'assess the association between sales and number of outlets visited' you will spot that we could use χ^2. Sales could be classified as 'high', 'medium' or 'low', as could the number of outlets visited, and then χ^2 could be used to determine whether the association between the two is significant. But this is unsatisfactory in the present situation for a number of reasons: it involves throwing away quite a lot of information, since at present we have actual measurements for the two variables, which would not be used if we simply lumped the items together into three broad categories. Nor would this method give us any idea whether the correlation is positive or negative. χ^2, as we noted in Chapter 9, does not tell us anything about the direction of an association. Finally, we are now specifically interested in looking for *straight line* relationships, which χ^2 certainly cannot help with.

So we need a new way of measuring the strength of the relationship between two variables, in the specific sense of the closeness of points on the scattergraph to a straight line. Before actually calculating such a measurement, however, let us think about the characteristics we would like it to have. It would be sensible if it gave a positive value when there is a positive correlation, and a negative value for a negative one, and if it were zero when there is no correlation. It should have a rather special value when there is a perfect correlation, either positive or negative, and obviously it should not depend on anything subjective such as the scale or units of measurement being used.

To illustrate the calculation of such a measurement, we will start off with some figures which are rather simpler than those in the section on the sales manager's problem. The figures shown below represent a company's expenditure on advertising a certain product, and the sales revenue generated by that product, for five years:

Year	Advertising expenditure, x (£000s)	Sales revenue, y (£000s)
1997	2	60
1998	5	100
1999	4	70
2000	6	90
2001	3	80

We would expect to find some degree of positive correlation here, since presumably the more one advertises a product, the more of it one will sell, at least within certain limits. This expectation is confirmed by the scattergraph of these figures (Figure 11.6a) – higher values of x, the advertising expenditure, correspond to higher values of y, the sales revenue.

We can actually note something further from the scattergraph, which gives us a clue as to how we could devise a measure of the 'strength of relationship' between advertising and sales. The point $(\bar{x}, \bar{y})$ will, in some sense, be 'in the middle' of the cloud of points on the scattergraph; so if we define new variables $(x - \bar{x}, y - \bar{y})$, then that will be equivalent to moving the axes of the graph to have their origin at $(\bar{x}, \bar{y})$, as shown by the coloured axes in Figure 11.6(a).

Notice now how the points are placed in relation to the new axes: nearly all of them are either in the top-right or bottom-left quarters of the graph (or *quadrants*, to give them their technical name). In the top-right quadrant, both $x - \bar{x}$ and $y - \bar{y}$ will be positive, while in the bottom-left quadrant, both will be negative. The products $(x - \bar{x})(y - \bar{y})$ will therefore nearly all be positive, as will the sum $\Sigma(x - \bar{x})(y - \bar{y})$ over all the points.

If we had had a negative correlation, the reverse would have been true, as you can see by looking at Figure 11.6(b). Here nearly all the points are concentrated in the top-left quadrant, where $x - \bar{x}$ is negative and $y - \bar{y}$ is positive, or in the bottom-right quadrant where $x - \bar{x}$ is positive and $y - \bar{y}$ is negative. So the product $(x - \bar{x})(y - \bar{y})$, and the sum $\Sigma(x - \bar{x})(y - \bar{y})$, will be negative also.

Finally, consider what happens when there is virtually no correlation, as in Figure 11.6(c): here the points are pretty uniformly scattered throughout all four quadrants, so the products $(x - \bar{x})(y - \bar{y})$ will be fairly evenly balanced between positive and negative. Thus, when we sum them, the positives and negatives will tend to balance out, so that the total will be close to zero.

The covariance

It looks as though the expression $\Sigma(x - \bar{x})(y - \bar{y})$ thus has at least one of the character-istics which we identified as being desirable in a measure of correlation: its sign follows the

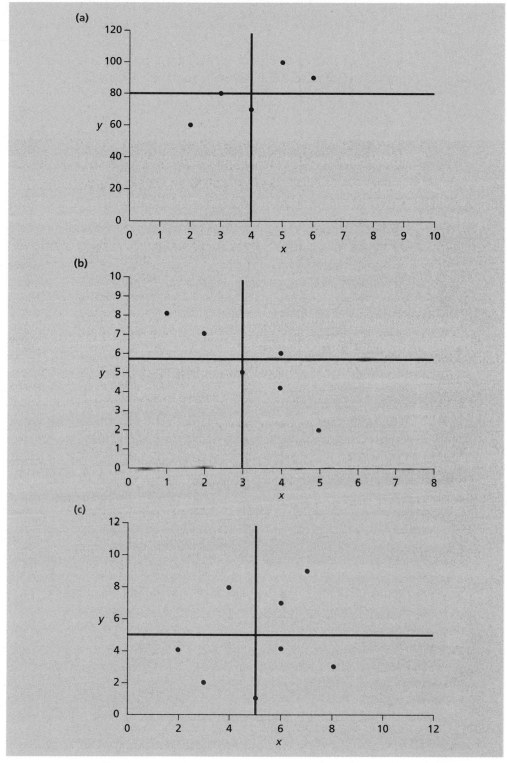

Figure 11.6

sign of the correlation. However, it does not do so well on the other criteria: its size will depend first on the number of points, and second on the actual size of the measurements involved in the calculation, so interpretation will not be easy. We can get around the first difficulty simply by averaging out over the number of points in our sample; the resulting measure is called the *covariance* of x and y:

$$\text{Covariance}(x, y) = \Sigma(x - \bar{x})(y - \bar{y})/n$$

where n is the sample size. You can see how this quantity obtained its name of covariance if you compare the formula with that for the variance of a single variable (which, as you will recall, is the square of the standard deviation):

$$\text{Variance of } x = \Sigma(x - \bar{x})^2/n = \Sigma(x - \bar{x})(x - \bar{x})/n.$$

So the variance of a single variable is its covariance with itself – or, looked at another way, whereas the variance of one variable indicates the degree of scatter of the distribution of that variable about its mean, the covariance gives us a measure of the variability in two dimensions of the points (x, y) around their mean $(\bar{x}, \bar{y})$.

The correlation coefficient

We still have the problem that the covariance depends on the sizes of the variables involved – we say that it is *scale-dependent*. In order to get a measure that is simple to interpret and not scale-dependent, what we do is to standardise the measure by dividing by the product of the two separate standard deviations of x and y; the resulting measure is called Pearson's Product–Moment Correlation Coefficient (often simply referred to as 'the correlation coefficient'), and is generally written as r or R:

$$r = \frac{\text{covariance}(x, y)}{s_x s_y} = \frac{\Sigma(x - \bar{x})(y - \bar{y})/n}{s_x s_y}$$

where s_x and s_y denote the respective standard deviations of x and y.

It can be shown that r always has a value between −1 and 1, with −1 corresponding to a perfect negative correlation and +1 to a perfect positive correlation. We will not prove the result here, but you can check by working out the formula using points which you know to be exactly on a straight line – for example, the points (2, 5), (3, 7), (4, 9), (5, 11) and (7, 15) lie on the line y = 2x + 1, and should therefore give you r = +1.

As with the formula for standard deviation, this definition of the covariance is not very convenient for computational purposes. Generally we would be using a computer package to do the calculation (see the later section on the use of Excel for details), but if we want to do it by hand, the formula for covariance can be manipulated into the form

$$\text{Covariance}(x, y) = \frac{\Sigma xy}{n} - \bar{x}\bar{y}.$$

Let us now calculate the correlation coefficient for the advertising and sales data which formed the starting-point for this discussion. Looking at the formula, you can see that we will need to compute Σx, Σy, Σx^2, Σy^2 and Σxy, so we can set out the computation as shown below, which makes it very convenient for spreadsheet calculation:

x	y	x^2	y^2	xy
2	60	4	3 600	120
5	100	25	10 000	500
4	70	16	4 900	280
6	90	36	8 100	540
3	80	9	6 400	240
20	400	90	33 000	1680

If we plug the totals into the various formulae, we find that

$$\bar{x} = 20/5 = 4,\ \bar{y} = 400/5 = 80,$$
$$\text{Covariance}(x, y) = 1680/5 - 4 \times 80 = 16,$$
$$s_x = \sqrt{90/5 - 16} = \sqrt{2},\ s_y = \sqrt{33\ 000/5 - 6400} = \sqrt{200},$$

and thus

$$r = 16/\sqrt{2 \times 200} = 16/20 = 0.8.$$

You may have wondered why we took advertising as x and sales as y, and not the other way round. In fact if you look at the formula for r you can see that it is completely symmetric in x and y; so had we chosen to reverse the variables, the result would have been exactly the same. (It is worth noting, however, that if you are going to proceed to a *regression* calculation, as discussed in the next chapter, then the choice of x and y *does* make a difference.)

Interpreting the correlation coefficient

We can begin to get a feel for the meaning of the correlation coefficient which we have calculated by considering Figure 11.7. The two ends of the scale represent respectively perfect negative and positive correlation; the closer we are to the ends, the higher the degree of correlation between x and y.

But by now I hope you will be a little uneasy with a subjective statement like 'the nearer to +1 or −1, the better'. Just how close is close enough? And remembering that our correlation is only computed from a sample of five years' data, how reliable is the figure we have calculated anyway? We can easily see that the size of sample has an important impact on the interpretation of correlations by considering the extreme case where we have only two points. In this situation, whatever the variables, the correlation coefficient will always be either +1 or −1 (depending on the relative position of the points), but all this shows is that it is always possible to put a straight line through two points.

It is actually possible to construct a sampling distribution for r in a similar fashion to that used for the sampling distributions of means and percentages in Chapter 9. To make

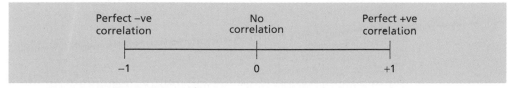

Figure 11.7 Scale for interpretation of r

life easier for you, a table based on this distribution is given in Appendix 7. This table tells us the minimum value of r (ignoring the sign) for a given sample size, in order to demonstrate a significant non-zero correlation at various significance levels. Because the table can be used for correlations of more than two variables (which we will not be discussing here), it is arranged not in terms of the sample size n, but the degrees of freedom, ν, which for a correlation with two variables is equal to $n - 2$.

In our example, there were five pairs of values, so that $\nu = 5 - 2 = 3$. Our null hypothesis in tests of this kind is always that $r = 0$ in the population. The calculated correlation coefficient was 0.8, and we will test the significance of this value at the 5 per cent level. This means that in Appendix 7 we should look in the row with $\nu = 3$, and in the column headed 0.05; we find the tabulated value to be 0.8783. Since our sample value is less than this, we conclude that the correlation is not significantly different from zero at the 5 per cent level; even though 0.8 looks quite a high value, because it is based on only five points it is not big enough to indicate significance. A value of r as high as this, or even higher, would occur quite frequently in samples of five pairs even if the underlying variables in the population were not correlated at all.

Because the sign of r is ignored when using the table, had we found a value of $r = -0.95$ with the same sample size, we would conclude that this correlation *is* significantly different from zero at the 5 per cent level.

The significance values given in the table are for two-tailed tests, so we are effectively testing for significant positive *or* negative correlation; if we wanted to test explicitly for a positive relationship (or a negative one), the significances would need to be halved, to give the area under a single tail.

Quick check questions

1 Which of the following statements is correct? (a) A value of the correlation coefficient near to –1 means that x and y are not connected. (b) A value of the correlation coefficient near to –1 means that increasing x causes y to decrease. (c) A value of the correlation coefficient near to –1 means that as x increases, y tends to decrease.

2 For a sample of eight British cities, a correlation has been carried out between the mean price of a ticket for bus travel within the city boundaries last year and the numbers of journeys made by bus during the year. The correlation coefficient is –0.72. What can you conclude?

3 You have found the following values for a pair of variables x and y, based on seven pairs of values:

$\sum x = 119$, $\sum y = 1190$, $\sum x^2 = 2139$, $\sum y^2 = 205\,092$, $\sum xy = 20\,775$.

Calculate the correlation coefficient between x and y.

Answers:
1 The correct statement is (c) – x and y are negatively associated, but we can't say that the relationship is one of causation just on the basis of the correlation coefficient.
2 A correlation coefficient of –0.72 from eight points is significant at the 5 per cent level (using the table in Appendix 7, with 6 degrees of freedom – the threshold value for 5 per cent significance is 0.7067). This suggests that there is a significant negative association between bus fares and bus travel – the lower the average fare, the more people travel by bus, as one would expect.
3 Substituting the values given into the formula for r gives $r = 0.958$.

The sales data revisited

We will complete our practice in handling the correlation coefficient by calculating its value for the sales/number of outlets data on p. 292.

With the elimination of the 'outlying' representative number 1, the calculation is as follows:

Rep. no.	Value of sales (y)	No. of outlets visited (x)	y^2	x^2	xy
2	5	42	25	1 764	210
3	9	47	81	2 209	423
4	11	51	121	2 601	561
5	11	56	121	3 136	616
6	12	64	144	4 096	768
7	14	60	196	3 600	840
8	15	68	225	4 624	1020
9	17	75	289	5 625	1275
10	17	81	289	6 561	1377
	111	544	1491	34 216	7090

Then:

$$\bar{y} = 111/9, \bar{x} = 544/9,$$

$$\text{Covariance} = \frac{7090}{9} - \frac{111}{9} \times \frac{544}{9} = 42.296,$$

$$s_y = \sqrt{\frac{1491}{9} \times \left(\frac{111}{9}\right)^2} = 3.682,$$

$$s_x = \sqrt{\frac{34\,216}{9} \times \left(\frac{544}{9}\right)^2} = 12.176,$$

and finally,

$$r = \frac{\text{covariance}}{s_x \times s_y} = \frac{42.296}{3.682 \times 12.176} = 0.94.$$

Consultation of Appendix 7 shows that a value of 0.6664 would be significant at the 5 per cent level in a sample of nine pairs such as we have here; so there is evidence of a significant correlation between sales value and number of outlets visited. In fact, inspection of the second column of the table shows that our value of r is sufficiently large to be significant at the 1 per cent level.

What we have – and have not – proved

The cautionary note sounded at the end of our work on χ^2 needs repeating even more forcefully with regard to correlation: because so many problems boil down to the question 'Is x connected with y?', and because the technique is relatively simple to apply (particularly now that computers and many scientific calculators give the correlation coefficient practically at the touch of a button), it is very much open to abuse. The main source of this abuse is, I think, a misunderstanding of the fundamental fact that *correlation does not mean causation* – in other words, just because x correlates well with y, we cannot necessarily deduce that x *causes* y, or vice versa.

The sillier examples of this fact – so-called 'spurious correlations' – are not hard to spot. Many totally unconnected quantities which show an increasing behaviour will produce quite respectable-looking correlation coefficients, and, of course, once the 'connection' has been 'proved' it is usually possible to find some kind of explanation for it. For example, students of mine produced a very high correlation between the numbers of divorces and the numbers of women in higher education in the UK over the past ten years: they then theorised that educated women do not make good wives, so their husbands divorce them! (Needless to say, these were male students.)

More difficult to detect are the correlations which are created by some 'hidden third factor'. If one were to correlate the numbers of deaths from, say, typhoid, over a few years towards the end of the nineteenth century with the numbers of children attending school over the same period, the resulting negative correlation coefficient would probably be quite significant; but this would not prove that school attendance confers a degree of immunity to typhoid! Rather, both figures are indicative of an underlying trend of improvement in living standards from which hygiene and educational opportunities both benefited.

This problem in interpreting the correlation coefficient makes it very difficult, except in strictly controlled scientific experiments, to rule out the possibility that an apparent correlation is actually being caused by some unsuspected factor. To take a classic example: there is, as everyone knows by now, a very high correlation between the number of cigarettes a person smokes each day and their chance of dying of lung cancer. But opponents of the 'smoking causes cancer' theory could suggest that there is something which renders certain individuals more likely to smoke, and also more likely to contract lung cancer – perhaps, for instance, they are people who react to stress in a certain way. Although this particular case is now fairly conclusively sewn up, you can see how difficult such a suggestion might be, in general, to disprove.

If you really feel you have strong grounds for expecting a correlation to exist between two variables, yet find that r does not appear significant when calculated in the usual way, there are two expedients open to you. One is, as we have indicated earlier, to try the elimination of dubious or outlying values. This has to be done with discretion, however. It is no good whittling down your data until there is so little left as to be meaningless; only those points that are genuinely outside the predominant pattern (preferably for some identifiable reason) should be discarded.

The other possibility only applies if you are correlating figures over a period of time. Suppose, for instance, that you have data referring to a large supermarket chain showing capital investment in opening new branches and total takings of all branches for a period of several years. Probably the effect of new premises on takings will not be apparent until some time, a year or maybe even two years, after the capital investment in those premises is made. Thus a direct correlation of capital investment with takings in the same year might not be very useful, whereas a correlation in which the investment figures were 'lagged' (displaced) by a year or two years to match up with the relevant takings might look very much more convincing. Another possibility is that the *change* in takings correlates with the *change* in investment, year on year – this can be a good way of dealing with the correlation of data taken over time, where otherwise trends in the data may lead to spurious correlations.

We have taken a rather narrow-minded view in restricting our investigation to connections between *two* variables. We have already acknowledged, for example, that it is the factors neglected in our analysis which cause correlations to be less than perfect. The variations in sales revenue are not by any means solely related to the advertising budget; they are influenced by what competitors are doing, by the stage which the product's life cycle has reached, by the rate of inflation, even perhaps by the weather if we are selling umbrellas or ice-cream. So it might be sensible, rather than investigating these connections one at a time, to try to evaluate the effect of all these things *simultaneously* on sales.

This can be done by means of measuring, not how close points on a graph are to a straight line, but how close points in umpteen-dimensional space are to the umpteen-dimensional equivalent of a straight line! Actually, although this sounds horrific, technically it is not much worse than the two-variable case we have looked at – at least with the aid of a computer. We will come across this idea again in Chapter 13.

The rank correlation

Very often, particularly when dealing with data in the social sciences, it is impossible to measure the quantities we are interested in on a genuine measurement scale. However, it may be possible to give ranks to the individual items – that is, to order them in ascending or descending value. We came across this idea in Chapter 2. For example, suppose that eight students have been ranked by their tutors on two aspects of their work – 'ability to work in groups' and 'ability to communicate orally'. The resulting ranks are as follows:

Student's name	Groupwork rank	Oral communication rank
Maria	1	2
Harjit	3	1
Peter	2	4
Suzanne	5	3
Giovanni	4	5
Michael	6	7
Tang	8	6
Paul	7	8

Here a 1 denotes the most able student and an 8 the least able.

It is then natural to pose the question: is there a relationship between abilities in the two areas? We could go ahead and compute Pearson's correlation coefficient as we did in earlier sections, but there is something special about the data here which makes the computation particularly simple – namely, the ranks are just the numbers 1 to 8 arranged in two different orders. For that reason, the formula for Pearson's coefficient can be very much simplified. The resulting formula, which applies only to ranked data, is known as Spearman's rank correlation coefficient; we will not go through the details of the algebra, but the final result is as follows:

$$r_{\text{rank}} = 1 - \frac{6 \sum d^2}{n(n^2 - 1)},$$

where d is the difference between the ranks for the two variables, and n is the number of pairs in our data. Here, for example, n would be 8, and we could calculate the ds as follows:

Groupwork rank	Oral communication rank	d	d^2
1	2	−1	1
3	1	2	4
2	4	−2	4
5	3	2	4
4	5	−1	1
6	7	−1	1
8	6	2	4
7	8	−1	1
			$\sum d^2 = 20$

Thus

$$r_{\text{rank}} = 1 - \frac{6 \times 20}{8 \times 63} = 0.76.$$

So there is a positive correlation between the ranks in the two subjects. Notice that it does not matter which way round we take the differences d here: because they are squared in the final formula, taking oral minus groupwork or the other way round would give the same result.

The rank correlation should only be used when you do not have access to proper measured data from which Pearson's coefficient could be calculated. This is because the rank coefficient is less accurate than Pearson's coefficient, based as it is simply on rankings rather than exact measurements. It may thus give a false impression of the extent of a correlation as you can see by first calculating the full Pearson coefficient for the data:

x	1	2	4	5	7
y	3	5	8	11	16

and then ranking the figures and calculating the rank correlation coefficient. You will find that r_{rank} turns out to be +1, although Pearson's coefficient is only 0.992 and the points certainly don't lie exactly on a straight line.

Correlation with Excel

Excel has a built-in correlation function: simply choose an empty cell, enter the function =CORREL(var 1, var 2), where var 1 and var 2 are the ranges containing the two variables, and Excel will return the value of the correlation coefficient.

To plot a scattergraph with Excel, enter the values of y and x into two adjacent columns (you need to put y – the values which are to be plotted on the vertical axis – to the left of x). Then highlight both columns, select the ChartWizard, and click on the 'XY scatter' option. A variety of formats is available – for a scattergraph you want the version which only shows the points, without any attempt to join them. You can then customise the graph by giving labels to the axes, changing the scales, adding a title, and so on. The scatterplots in this chapter were produced by using Excel in this way.

EXERCISES

*Further examples on the work of this chapter can be found on the **Companion Website**.*

1 A rank correlation coefficient can be used as a measure of the consistency of judgement between two people. For example, a trainee wine-taster and a Master of Wine together try ten sample vintages, and then each ranks them in order of his opinion of their quality. The rankings are as follows:

Sample	1	2	3	4	5	6	7	8	9	10
Master	5	3	7	2	10	9	1	4	8	6
Trainee	4	1	7	3	8	9	2	5	10	6

How consistent does the trainee's judgement appear to be with the Master's?

2 Eight samples of low-fat spread are ranked according to flavour by a panel of testers. Their consensus is:

Sample	A	B	C	D	E	F	G	H
Rank	8	6	1	3	7	4	5	2

The measurements of a certain vegetable oil in the samples are known to be:

Sample	A	B	C	D	E	F	G	H
Per cent	12	18	32	28	10	22	25	32

(a) By ranking the samples on oil content from highest to lowest, decide what you would say to the statement 'This oil imparts a better flavour'.
(b) Try ranking the samples the other way round, and see what difference it makes to your result.

3 The manufacturers of Happihog pigfood have compiled the following table after studies at their test-farm:

Age of pig (months)	Weight of Happihog consumed per week (kg)
4	2
6	3
6	4
9	6
10	8
12	9
15	10
18	9
24	11

Calculate Pearson's correlation coefficient:

(a) for the first six pairs of data;

(b) for all the data, and using a scattergraph explain the difference between the two figures.

4 Calculate *r* for the following two sets of data:

x	4	10	8	12	6
y	180	300	210	270	240

Compare this with the correlation coefficient obtained for the advertising/sales figures on p. 298. What do you notice?

5 Do the same with the following data:

x	14	20	18	22	16
y	80	200	110	170	140

What can you deduce? By examining scattergraphs of the three sets of data, suggest why your deduction applies. How could this fact be used to simplify calculations?

6 The figures shown below give the annual salary (in £000s) and the age of a sample of employees in an organisation:

Salary	18	11	12	17	28	15	13	23	11	18
Age last birthday	32	39	48	26	37	50	45	35	42	27

(a) Calculate the correlation coefficient for all ten employees. Comment on the result.

(b) Plot a scattergraph of the data. What do you notice? What light does this shed on the correlation coefficient you calculated in (a)? What advice would you offer to someone trying to analyse this data?

7 Look at the government statistics website **www.statistics.gov.uk** for two variables which you think may be correlated. If you enjoy economics you could try Retail Prices Index/unemployment or inflation/money supply; if you are ecologically minded, amount of carbon monoxide in the air/deaths from lung complaints; for something sociological, unemployment/crime rate or numbers of divorces – the scope is endless. If the figures are complicated you may need either to use a rank correlation, or to round them off fairly drastically, before calculating *r*.

Try to interpret your result, bearing in mind the dangers of spurious correlation and seeking other factors which may be influencing your data. Remember, too, to look for outliers. Interpretation may be simpler if you select 'cross-sectional' data taken at the same point in time (e.g. regional figures) rather than 'longitudinal' data taken over a period of time.

8 Use the data in the Excel worksheet QUAL.XLS to compute the correlation coefficient between takings of branches and floorspace for (a) the entire group of stores, and (b) the shopping precinct and street branches separately. Plot the relevant scattergraphs, and comment on your results.

9 Consider the following quote:

> The Turn-Off lobby continues to maintain that TV causes obesity – yet a recent Harvard study of 10 000 US children aged 10 to 15 found no correlation between restricted TV viewing and increased physical activity. (James Donaghy, *Guardian*, 23 April 2007)

(a) What data would you need to gather in order to replicate the results of this study?
(b) What possible problems might arise in carrying out and interpreting the analysis?
(c) See if you can find relevant data, via published statistical sources, from the Internet or by collecting primary data, to enable you to carry out the analysis.

10 Another quote:

> There is no correlation between increasing rates of incarceration and reduced crime rates; during the 1990s Texas increased incarceration levels by 144 per cent while New York's rate only grew by 24 per cent, yet both experienced similar reductions in crime.
> (from the website of the organisation 'Justice behind the walls' at
> **http://www.justicebehindthewalls.net**)

(a) What data would you need to gather in order to replicate the results of this study for the UK (or for your own country of residence if you live outside the UK)?
(b) What possible problems might arise in carrying out and interpreting the analysis?
(c) See if you can find relevant data, from either published statistical sources or the Internet, to enable you to carry out the analysis.

Case Study

Interpreting a correlation matrix

A company which manufactures household cleaning materials has been conducting some market research on its aerosol cleaner for all kitchen surfaces. A questionnaire was given to 500 customers at three major supermarkets who indicated that they bought the product regularly, and 392 replies were received. The questionnaire asked respondents to use a five-point scale (where 1 = strongly disagree, 5 = strongly agree) to answer the following questions:

1 The product has a pleasant smell
2 The product is effective at removing stubborn stains
3 The product represents good value for money
4 The product is easy to use
5 The product performs as indicated on the label
6 The instructions for using the product are clear
7 The packaging of the product is attractive
8 The product leaves worktops looking clean and shiny
9 The product is effective on cooker hobs
10 The product is effective on sinks

When the results of the survey are processed, the following table is generated showing all the correlation coefficients between the answers to these ten questions. (This table is called a *correlation matrix* – can you see why we only need to fill in half the table, and why all the figures on the diagonal are 1?)

309

	1	2	3	4	5	6	7	8	9	10
1	1	0.14	0.09	0.67	−0.03	0.54	0.88	0.43	0.26	0.11
2		1	0.17	0.22	0.61	0.22	0.08	0.89	0.91	0.79
3			1	0.19	0.36	0.17	0.23	0.37	0.39	0.22
4				1	0.55	0.64	0.48	0.27	0.31	0.24
5					1	0.53	0.33	0.51	0.43	0.36
6						1	−0.04	0.10	0.14	0.21
7							1	−0.02	0.06	0.03
8								1	0.87	0.74
9									1	0.90
10										1

Investigate what this matrix tells you about consumers' responses to the product. Why are some of the correlations negative? Can the questions be grouped into subsets where correlations within the subset are strong, but those with variables outside the subset are weaker? If so, can you attach an overall 'label' to each subset?

(Correlation matrices like this are the basis for a more advanced technique called *factor analysis*, which enables highly correlated subgroups to be identified in a more systematic way.)

Further reading for this chapter is given at the end of Chapter 13.

Chapter 12

SPOTTING THE RELATIONSHIP: LINE FITTING

Chapter prerequisites Before starting work on this chapter make sure you are happy with:

1 the material on correlation in Chapter 11;

2 the equation of a straight line (see Chapter 1, pp. 25–7);

3 the basic ideas of graph plotting (see Chapter 1, pp. 25–8).

Learning outcomes By the end of your work on this chapter you should be able to:

1 calculate the equation of a regression line, say for what purposes it is the 'best' line through a set of points, and make sensible use of it to obtain forecasts;

2 use suitable software to perform regression calculations, and interpret the output.

Quantitative methods in practice

UK heatwave boosts sales of air-con and fans

Sales of air-conditioning units and desk fans surged this weekend as sun-basking Britons sought to cool down in the sweltering dry heat.

After weekend temperatures hit as high as 35°C in some areas of the UK during the hottest weekend of the year, retailers also reported buoyant sales of barbecues, sun cream, parasols and sun hats.

Rebecca Smithers, guardian.co.uk, 28 June 2010

It's not surprising that, as reported in the above quote, when the weather gets hotter more people buy fans and air-conditioners. If you wanted to investigate the truth of the statement, you might, following our study of correlation in the previous chapter, try to correlate monthly sales of fans with the average daytime temperature for the month – you would expect to obtain a positive correlation.

However, if you are a manufacturer of fans, this information alone isn't very useful. You need to know what sort of demand you are going to face in a particular month, so that you can ensure that you have the necessary goods in stock. One way to approach this question would be to try to build a model which enables the demand for fans to be predicted from the temperature – in other words, to answer questions like 'If forecasters say the average temperature next month will be 27°C, how many fans are we likely to sell?'

In order to do this, we need to address the second issue mentioned on p. 292 – how to estimate or predict the value of one variable given the value of another, when the two variables are correlated. The methods used to enable us to do this come under the general heading of regression analysis.

More problems for the sales manager!

We have already encountered Tim Newton and his difficulties with sales representatives in Chapter 11. But that was just a sample of the variety of headaches he encounters in trying to plan a rational sales policy. Many of these problems are connected with the fact that, if he is to get anywhere at all in planning sales targets and so on, he has to attempt to predict or forecast values of variables which are essentially out of his control. The more accurate his predictions, the better his planning can be.

We have seen one example of this in his need to determine the relationship between sales revenue brought in by the representatives and the number of retail outlets they visit regularly. With a knowledge of this relationship he can decide what number of outlets they should be aiming at. The existence of the relationship was demonstrated, with the aid of a correlation coefficient, in Chapter 11; as yet, however, we have not tackled the second objective mentioned in Chapter 11 – the determination of the *form* of that relationship, so that it can be used to give estimates of sales if we know how many outlets a representative visits, or vice versa.

In the case of the sales/outlets data, we are seeking a relationship between two variables. A large number of Mr Newton's planning problems involve the rather special situation where one of the two variables we are trying to relate is *time*. This is what we usually understand by 'forecasting' or 'prediction' in its narrower sense. Although relationship problems of this kind *can* be treated just like questions of relationship between any two variables, there are a number of methods which are especially designed for the analysis of a series of figures over a period of time – a *time series*, as it is often called. We will be looking at some of these methods later in this chapter, and in Chapter 15.

However, to begin with we return to the question of the relationship linking sales and number of outlets visited.

What is a 'well-fitting line'?

The scattergraph of the sales/number of outlets data is repeated in Figure 12.1, which shows a straight line apparently fitting the set of points fairly well. But at this point we have to face the fact that, so far, we have not really been precise about what a 'well-fitting' line is. I suppose the natural answer would be 'one that goes as near as possible to all the points', so let us begin from that idea.

Consider for a moment the question of the distance of one single point from the line. Figure 12.2 shows that, out of the infinite number of directions in which this distance might be measured, there are at least three that have some claim to consideration. Normally we understand 'the distance of a point from a line' to mean the perpendicular distance, but we could also choose to measure the distance parallel to the *x*-axis (which we could regard as the amount of error in the value of *x* between the line and the actual point) or parallel to the *y*-axis (which would give the corresponding error in the value of *y* as given by the line).

Which of these three ways of measuring the distance is most suitable? The answer depends very much on what we want to *use* the line for. The perpendicular distance can be disregarded, as it is never of much use; but if we want to use the line to predict *y* from

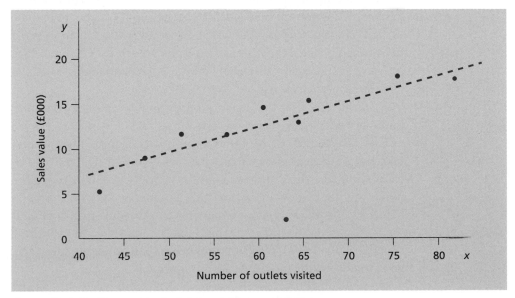

Figure 12.1 Scattergraph showing positive correlation

313

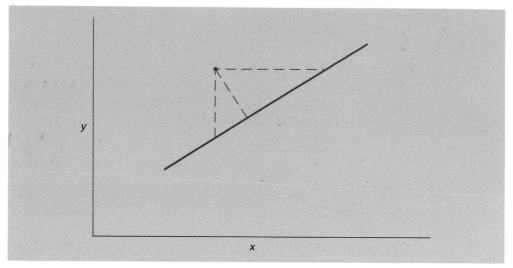

Figure 12.2 The distance of a point from a line

a given x-value, then presumably we would like the 'error' in the estimate of y as given by the line to be as small as possible; so the appropriate procedure would be to choose the line in such a way that the *vertical* distances of the points from the line are minimised.

If, however, our objective was to estimate x given y, then we would wish to minimise the disagreement between the x-value as given by the line and the actual x-value of the points, so the horizontal measurement would be better. These two ways of measuring the distance of points from the line give, in general, two completely different lines (the only exception being the case of perfect correlation when all the distances are zero), and it is very important that you choose the right line for the kind of estimation you want to do. You can, in fact, get away with always using the *same* line – the one that cuts down on the vertical, or y, errors – *if* you are careful always to make the 'given' quantity x, and the 'thing to be estimated' y. In the case of the sales outlets data, for example, if Mr Newton is interested in finding out how much revenue is likely to be brought in by a representative who has, say, 50 outlets on his regular 'beat', he should make the number of outlets his x-variable and the sales revenue his y. The straight line equation which then needs to be determined is called the *regression equation of y on x*. (The line which would be defined by using the horizontal distances between points and line is called the *regression line of x on y*, but is not widely used.)

Even when we have decided how we are going to measure distance of points from the line, our problems are not at an end.

If we take 'as near as possible to all the points' to mean that the total of the vertical distances of all the points from the line chosen is smaller than it would be for any other line, we are immediately up against a difficulty. Do we take note of which side of the line the points are on, or not? If the answer is no, then we get the curious situation shown in Figure 12.3(a) where line A is apparently a 'better' line than B, since the total distance of the three points from A is certainly smaller than that from B; most people, however, would feel that B fits the set of points better than A. So this attempted definition of 'best' gives results which run counter to our intuition.

If, on the other hand, we decide to say that points below the line are a negative distance from it, and those above a positive distance, then we get some very ambiguous cases. In

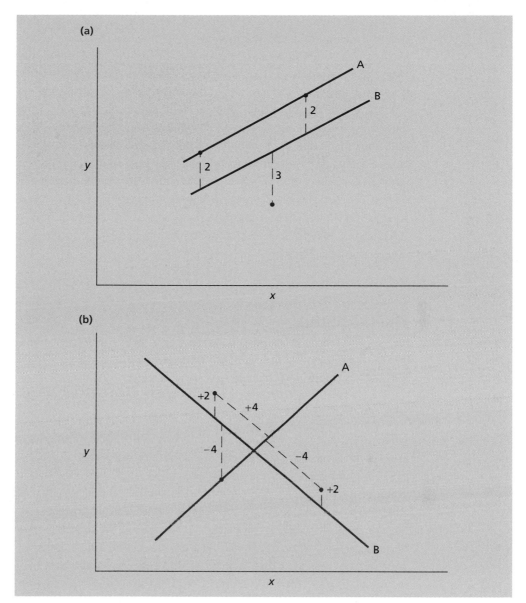

Figure 12.3 Lines of 'best' fit

Figure 12.3(b), for instance, both lines give a total distance that is zero, yet they are completely different and even slope in opposite directions. So this definition of 'best', too, is a non-starter.

The next step may not come as too much of a surprise to you, after your experience with the standard deviation and χ^2. We had difficulties with points above and below the mean in constructing the standard deviation, and difficulties with frequencies higher and lower than expected when constructing χ^2. In both cases, the way out of our difficulty was to square the distances; and that is exactly what is done in this case, too. The 'line of best fit' is defined to be the one that makes the sum of the squares of the distance of the points from the line as small as possible.

This line is often called, for obvious reasons, the 'least-squares' regression line, and the definition certainly gives one unambiguous line, which, as we will see when we plot it, accords well with our ideas of what a 'well-fitting' line should look like. Working out just what the equation of such a best-fitting line will be for a given set of data is, however, by no means simple.

The determination of the values of slope and intercept, which, for a particular set of data, minimise the sum of squared deviations from the line, involves the use of calculus, and since many of you probably have not studied maths to that level, I will not give the general derivation of the regression equation. Instead I will simply present you with the relevant formulae, and then demonstrate how they work in practice. As with so many of the techniques we have studied, you are unlikely to need to use the formulae 'from scratch' very often, since computer packages such as Excel now perform regression calculations. We will have a look at the results of regression using Excel in the section 'Regression with Excel', p. 325.

Calculating the regression line

The equation of the least-squares regression line of y on x is

$$y - \bar{y} = \frac{r \times s_y}{s_x}(x - \bar{x}),$$

where as usual $\bar{x}$ and $\bar{y}$ denote the means of x and y, the s-values the standard deviations, and r is the correlation coefficient. You should recognise this as the equation of a straight line, containing as it does just a single x and a single y. It may look at first as if you are going to have to go yet again through the painful process of calculating the means and standard deviations, but if you think for a minute you will realise that you should already have done all the work in the process of finding the value of r – because you should not be going to the trouble of calculating a regression line unless first your scattergraph, then your value of r, suggest that the relationship between x and y is sufficiently close to make the calculation worthwhile. Of course, you can go through the motions of the calculation no matter *what* the amount of correlation, but the line you end up with will not tell you anything useful.

We will use the formula to calculate two regression lines: first, the one for the simple set of advertising/sales data on p. 298. In the process of calculating r for the data we found that $\bar{x} = 4$, $\bar{y} = 80$, $s_x = \sqrt{2}$, $s_y = \sqrt{200}$ and r itself was 0.8, so the equation of the regression line of y on x for the data is

$$y - 80 = \frac{0.8 \times \sqrt{200}}{\sqrt{2}}(x - 4),$$

giving

$$y - 80 = 8(x - 4)$$
$$= 8x - 32$$
$$y = 8x - 32 + 80$$
$$= 8x + 48.$$

This equation could now be used to give us an estimate of y for any value of x – at least, with certain reservations we will come to later. Remember, x was the advertising expenditure and y the sales revenue; the equation therefore shows that when the advertising expenditure is £7000, so that $x = 7$, we have $y = 8 \times 7 + 48 = 104$, giving the predicted sales revenue as £104 000. What we could *not* do with this 'y on x' equation is answer the question 'How much would we need to spend on advertising to get sales of £110 000?' For that we would have to calculate a new equation with x and y interchanged, since the 'y on x' equation is only suited to finding y given x.

The predictions obtained from this line cannot be expected to be very reliable, since the correlation coefficient was not significant, so although the example has served to illustrate the method, in practice in this case one probably would not bother calculating the equation. In the case of Mr Newton's sales/outlets data, however, the correlation *was* significant, so a regression line can give us some useful information. Remember that the x here was the number of outlets visited, while y was the sales revenue generated by each representative. Our 'y on x' regression line will therefore be suitable for estimating sales revenue given the number of outlets a representative visits.

After the elimination of the 'outlier representative', number 1, we found (p. 303)

$$\bar{x} = 60.44, \bar{y} = 12.33, s_x = 12.18, s_y = 3.68 \text{ and } r = 0.94$$

so the equation of the regression line required is

$$y - 12.33 = \frac{0.94 \times 3.68}{12.18}(x - 60.44)$$
$$= 0.28(x - 60.44)$$
$$= 0.28x - 16.92$$
$$y = 0.28x - 16.92 + 12.33$$
$$= 0.28x - 4.59.$$

If you feel that this method of calculating the regression equation is rather messy, there is an alternative version which you may find easier, as long as you are comfortable with solving simultaneous equations. If we write the equation of the regression line as $y = a + bx$, so that a is the intercept and b the slope, then a and b can be found by solving the pair of equations

$$\Sigma y = na + b\Sigma x$$
$$\Sigma xy = a\Sigma x + b\Sigma x^2$$

where n is the number of points for which we have data. For instance, with the sales/outlets data, substituting the values of x, y, etc., which we have already computed in the process of finding the correlation coefficient gives the equations

$$111 = 9a + 544b$$
$$7090 = 544a + 3421b.$$

You can verify that solving these equations leads to the same values of a and b as before; the numbers involved are large, but if you keep your head there are no real problems. So for hand-calculation of regression lines, choose whichever of the two methods you prefer. The second method is particularly convenient if you have not previously calculated r.

What does this equation mean?

We can get a better feel for what the line is telling us if instead of x and y we use the actual names of the variables:

$$\text{Sales} = 0.28 \times \text{number of outlets visited} - 4.59.$$

The numbers in the regression equation – the slope and the intercept of the line – generally have a useful meaning, and should not just be regarded as mysterious figures. For example, here the sales revenue increases by 0.28 units for every extra outlet visited. If we recall that the units of sales revenue were £000s, that means that each extra outlet visited regularly generates on average extra sales revenue of £280 per quarter. As for the intercept, that is not terribly useful here – it indicates that if no outlets are visited, sales revenue will be negative – a pretty silly result. Since in fact the smallest number of outlets visited in our sample was 42, this represents a wild extrapolation and it is not surprising that it does not give a sensible answer. In other cases, however, the intercept can be informative – for example, with the advertising/sales data used earlier in the chapter, the intercept represents the base level of sales when nothing is spent on advertising – a perfectly reasonable concept.

Getting predictions from the line

This line can easily be plotted on the scattergraph, using the point $x = 0$, $y = -4.59$ as one extreme, and perhaps $x = 80$, $y = 17.81$ as the other. A useful check on the accuracy of your plotting of the line is provided by the fact that, since it passes, as it were, through the 'middle' of the set of points, the means of the two sets of data should lie exactly on it. In this case, the point represented by the two means is $(\bar{x}, \bar{y}) = (60.44, 12.33)$, and inspection of Figure 12.4 shows that this point is indeed on the line.

Having plotted the line, we can use it to give predictions of the value of y for a given value of x, simply by reading off the required values from the graph. However, there are

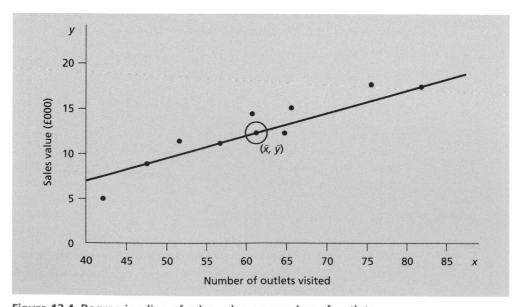

Figure 12.4 Regression line of sales value on number of outlets

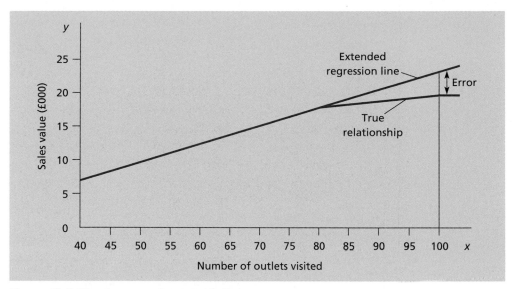

Figure 12.5 The dangers of extrapolation

important limitations to be borne in mind when doing this. We have fitted the line to the set of points, which in this case have x-values ranging from about 40 to 80, and certainly in this region the line fits the points very well; we are quite justified in using it to estimate y for, say, an x of 50 or 70. But *outside* that region we cannot be sure that the line will continue to give us reliable estimates.

It could be, for example, that if we had data available for higher values of x, and plotted the corresponding points on the scattergraph, they would indicate that the straight line relationship between x and y does not persist, but begins to level off as shown in Figure 12.5. Indeed, this is what we might expect to happen in practice; after a certain number of outlets have been visited, the market is saturated, and so further increases in the number of outlets visited does not produce a corresponding increase in sales. In these circumstances, if we were to use the straight line to estimate sales when, say, 100 outlets are visited, we would end up with a figure of about £23 400 – a serious overestimate, since Figure 12.5 shows that the true figure is more likely to be in the region of £20 000.

This process of estimating y for values of x beyond the original range of the data is called *extrapolation*, and although it is sometimes necessary (and, for values of x fairly close to the original figures, will not give rise to too much inaccuracy), it should always be used with great caution. This becomes even clearer if we recognise that, as our regression line is based only on a sample of data, it is subject to sampling error, and therefore we should really consider where the 95 per cent confidence limits around the line might be.

Figure 12.6 shows roughly the shape of these confidence limits. Within the range of the original data, they are pretty well parallel to the line, so that the margin of error around estimates obtained from the line is reasonably narrow, at least if the correlation between x and y was significant to begin with.

As we go further and further away from the original data in either direction the confidence limits become further and further apart, showing that an estimate of y obtained from a value $x = 100$, such as we considered above, will be subject to a very wide margin of error, and could prove to be 'out', with respect to the true value of y, by more than 100 per cent.

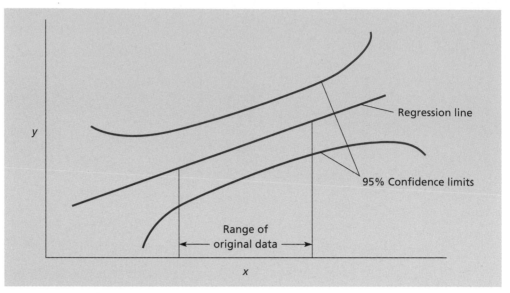

Figure 12.6 Confidence limits on a regression line

Quick check questions

1 Calculate the equation of the regression line of y on x, when the following information is given, based on seven data points:

$\Sigma x = 119$, $\Sigma y = 1190$, $\Sigma x^2 = 2139$, $\Sigma y^2 = 205\ 092$, $\Sigma xy = 20\ 775$

2 Under what circumstances would the regression line of y on x and the regression line of x on y be the same?

3 Regressing the annual before-tax profit of a company (in £000s) on the number of employees in the company gives the equation: profit = 572 + 23.4 × number of employees. What does the 23.4 represent in practical terms?

Answers:
1 By substituting into the formulae for slope and intercept, you should find that $y = 90.13 + 4.70x$.
2 The two regression lines would be the same only when the correlation is perfect, so that all points lie exactly on the line.
3 The 23.4 is the slope, and represents the fact that each additional employee generates on average an additional profit of 23.4 × £1000 or £23 400.

Some additional points

Before leaving the subject of regression lines, there are one or two further points that are worth noting. It is important not to go on using a regression line for prediction purposes after the circumstances in which it was constructed have altered. For example, in the case of the sales/outlets data above, a substantial change in marketing strategy, or a retraining course for the representatives, would alter the situation considerably, and a new regression line would need to be computed (if a straight line relationship still applied) using data collected subsequent to the change.

Both the examples we have looked at have involved positive correlations. If a negative correlation were involved then of course we would expect the number multiplying x

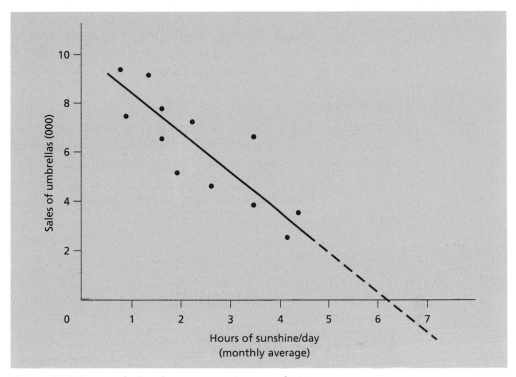

Figure 12.7 Extrapolation from a negative correlation

in the regression equation to be a negative one, since this number represents the slope of the line, which will be negative. The regression line in this case also provides a vivid illustration of the folly of unthinking extrapolation. Figure 12.7, for instance, shows the approximate position of the regression line representing the negative correlation between sales of umbrellas over 12 months and average hours of sunshine per day in the same 12 months. The more the sun shines, the less likely people are to buy umbrellas, which is perfectly reasonable. But if we continue the regression line and attempt to predict what umbrella sales will be in a month when there are seven hours of sunshine a day, we find that the line has fallen below the horizontal axis – sales of umbrellas are negative, so presumably people are deciding that they have no further use for them and are selling them back to the manufacturer!

Finally, we return to the question of relationships between more than two variables which was mentioned briefly in the last chapter. It is, of course, very limiting to consider the effect of only one independent quantity on a dependent quantity; in most practical situations a whole host of variables may have an influence. The price of a house, for example, will depend on the number of bedrooms it has, whether it has a garden, where it is situated, what state of repair it is in – you can continue the list almost indefinitely.

It is possible to determine a linear relationship between a dependent quantity and many independent ones, in much the same way as we have fitted a regression line. The 'line' will be replaced by a plane if we are looking at the effect of two independent variables – in this case the 'scattergraph' could be drawn in three-dimensional space. If there are more than two independent variables the equivalent of our line is a *hyperplane* – hard to visualise, but easy to express as an equation of the form $y = a_0 + a_1x_1 + a_2x_2 + \ldots$ The 'best' values for the *a*s in this equation can be determined, for a given set of data, by the same kind of least-squares fitting we used to determine the best line in two dimensions. In this case, however, you would certainly need to use a computer package.

We will therefore be looking in more depth at the ideas of multiple regression in the next chapter. But first, here is another example of correlation and regression analysis.

Another example

A car manufacturer is carrying out some tests on a new type of engine to examine the impact of speed on petrol consumption. The following data is obtained, under laboratory conditions where the engine can be run at a constant speed:

Speed (miles per hour)	Miles per gallon of petrol
20	52
24	50
30	47
40	42
50	40
60	38

The manufacturer is interested in being able to predict consumption at a given speed, so speed should be the independent variable x, and consumption should be y. (If the intention was to try to recommend a driving speed at which a consumption of, say, 45 miles per gallon could be obtained, then x and y would need to be interchanged.)

We therefore set up the usual table:

	x	y	x^2	y^2	xy
	20	52	400	2 704	1040
	25	50	625	2 500	1250
	30	47	900	2 209	1410
	40	42	1600	1 764	1680
	50	40	2500	1 600	2000
	60	38	3600	1 444	2280
Σ	225	269	9625	12 221	9660

Then we have

$$\bar{x} = 225/6 = 37.5,$$
$$\bar{y} = 269/6 = 44.833,$$
$$s_x = \sqrt{9625/6 - (225/6)^2} = 14.068,$$
$$s_y = \sqrt{12\,221/6 - (269/6)^2}\ 5.177,$$
$$\mathrm{cov}(x,y) = 9660/6 - (225/6)(269/6) = -71.25,$$

and overall

$$r = \frac{-71.25}{14.068 \times 5.117} = -0.98$$

(you should check all this arithmetic to make sure you can follow the process).

Thus there is a strong negative correlation between speed and consumption, as we might expect – the faster you drive, the more petrol the engine consumes.

We can then find the regression equation:

$$y - \bar{y} = \frac{rs_y}{s_x}(x - \bar{x}),$$

that is

$$y - 44.833 = \frac{-0.98 \times 5.117}{14.068}(x - 37.5)$$

giving

$$y = 58.33 - 0.36x,$$

or more meaningfully

$$\text{Consumption} = 58.33 - 0.36 \times \text{speed}.$$

Thus for every mile per hour increase in speed, the number of miles to the gallon decreases by 0.36. In the present case, the constant term has little meaning – it seems to suggest that at a speed of zero, you would get 58.33 miles to the gallon, which is not very sensible!

In order to give a fuller interpretation of the regression equation, and particularly to examine the significance of the coefficients – which, after all, are only based on sample data – it is really essential to have access to a suitable computer package, and you are recommended to read the section on pp. 325–6 for more information.

Using straight lines to forecast over time

One special case of forecasting using regression lines deserves our consideration. This is when we want to 'forecast' in the usual sense of the word – to obtain an estimate of a quantity at some point in the future. Chapter 15 will explore this topic more fully, but while we are on the topic of regression it is worth examining the simple situation where we expect the growth (or decline) of a quantity to behave linearly with time.

For example, consider the following figures which show the numbers of students in higher education institutions in the UK for the last five academic years (data from the Higher Education Statistics Agency's website at **www.HESA.ac.uk**):

Year	Number of students (000s)
2004–5	2236
2005–6	2281
2006–7	2305
2007–8	2306
2008–9	2396

Plotting this data suggests that the growth is not too far from a straight line pattern, as Figure 12.8 shows. We will therefore fit a regression line to get a forecast of the total

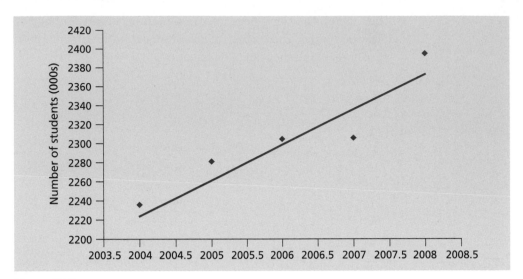

Figure 12.8

for, say, 2011–12. The number of students is 'to be predicted', and thus becomes the *y*-variable.

This means that the year should be *x*. However, there is no need to use the four-digit year number – things are considerably simplified if we just number the years as 1, 2, 3, 4, 5. We thus have the following data from which to compute the regression line:

Year, x	Number of students (000s), y
1	2236
2	2281
3	2305
4	2306
5	2396

We will not go through the calculation in detail, but you should verify that the equation turns out to be

$$\text{Number of students} = 2186.30 + \text{year} \times 37.50.$$

So the number appears to be increasing by about 37 500 students per year. In order to get a forecast of the figure for 2011–12, we need to note that, starting numbering the years from 2004–5 as we have, 2011–12 becomes year 8. The forecast is therefore

$$\text{Number of students in 2011–12} = 2186.30 + 8 \times 37.50 = 2486.30 \text{ thousands,}$$

or 2 486 300 students.

The plot in Figure 12.8 shows the fitted line as well as the original data. You can see that the line appears to be a good fit. However, forecasting for 2011–12 is, of course, extrapolation, and so we should be cautious about the reliability of the forecast. This is where knowledge of the practical situation becomes important: the proposed introduction of much higher fees for students from 2012–13 is likely to have an effect on the numbers of students going into higher education in 2011–12, and so our forecast is quite likely to be incorrect. A good forecaster will always combine statistical proficiency with in-depth understanding of the real-world context within which the data is obtained.

Regression with Excel

Regression can be carried out in Excel in a number of ways. If all you want are the values of the intercept and slope in the regression equation, then there are standard functions to compute these. To find the intercept, choose an empty cell and enter =INTERCEPT(y-range, x-range), where y-range is the range of cells containing the y-values and x-range that for the x-values. It is important to get these the right way round – y must come first. To find the slope, do the same using the function =SLOPE(y-range, x-range).

To obtain rather more information, select DATA ANALYSIS on the DATA tab followed by REGRESSION. The Regression window then requires you to select the y- and x-ranges, as well as allowing you to select a number of options some of which we will mention later. You also need to decide where you would like the results to be printed – the default is a new ply of the worksheet.

If we carry out this process using the sales/outlets data, the resulting output is as follows:

SUMMARY OUTPUT						
Regression Statistics						
Multiple R	0.943 519 43					
R Square	0.890 228 92					
Adjusted R Square	0.874 547 34					
Standard Error	1.383 167 79					
Observations	9					
ANOVA						
	df	*SS*	*MS*	*F*	*Significance F*	
Regression	1	108.607 928	108.607 9	56.769 07	0.000 133 38	
Residual	7	13.392 071 95	1.913 153			
Total	8	122				
	Coefficients	*Standard Error*	*t Stat*	*P-value*	*Lower 95%*	*Upper 95%*
Intercept	−4.912 058 6	2.334 823 985	−2.103 82	0.073 455	−10.433 036 1	0.608 918 8
X Variable 1	0.285 309 79	0.037 866 99	7.534 525	0.000 133	0.195 768 655	0.374 850 9

The important bit here is at the bottom of the output: the column headed 'Coefficients' gives us the information from which the regression equation can be constructed. Here the intercept – the constant term in the regression equation – is about −4.91, agreeing with our hand-computations, while the coefficient for 'X Variable 1' – the slope – is 0.29. So we can write the equation as $y = 0.29x - 4.91$, as before.

We also get a lot of additional information. At the top of the results you can see the 'Multiple R' – in our case with just two variables, this is the familiar correlation coefficient. Just below it is R Square, the percentage of variation in y explained by x.

The quantities Adjusted R Square and Standard Error we will not discuss; at this price the number of observations is, of course, 9.

The ANOVA part of the results stands for Analysis of Variance, another method of testing the linear regression which we will discuss in Chapter 13. At the bottom next to the values of the Intercept and X-coefficient we get some further information which enables us to test whether the coefficients are significantly different from zero, in the following way.

Consider the X-coefficient – that is, the slope. If its value were zero, then the regression line would be parallel to the x-axis, indicating that x has no association with y; thus testing slope = 0 is a useful thing to do, equivalent to testing for a significant association between x and y. As with any other hypothesis test, we first compute the test statistic – a t-statistic in this case because the sample size is below 30. The value of t will be

$$\frac{\text{sample slope} - \text{population slope}}{\text{standard error}} = \frac{0.2853 - 0}{0.0379} = 7.53,$$

and if you look at the value in the t column, this is the value you will find. So Excel has actually computed the test statistic for us. But it has gone further than that – it has done the equivalent of looking up the tables for us. The P-value given next is precisely the probability of getting a sample slope as high as 0.29 if the population slope were in fact zero. So the smaller the P-value, the more significant the result. In this case, the P-value is 0.0001, indicating that the slope is very significantly different from zero – that is, x and y are strongly associated.

If, on the other hand, we test the hypothesis that the intercept is zero (the line passes through the origin), we see that the P-value is 0.07, so if we adopt the usual 5 per cent significance criterion, this indicates that the population intercept could well be zero – not a surprising result, since we expect that if no outlets are visited, no sales will result.

Finally, the Lower and Upper 95% values give the range within which we can be 95 per cent confident that the population values of the coefficients will lie – for example, we can be 95 per cent confident that the true slope lies between 0.196 and 0.375. Notice that the interval for the Intercept contains zero, confirming our conclusion in the last paragraph that the line could well pass through the origin.

This is a very rapid run through the main features of the Excel results; for more details about the interpretation and use of the results you are advised to consult one of the more advanced texts mentioned at the end of the next chapter. Excel also has other methods for obtaining a least-squares trend line to a series of data, and for fitting such a trend line directly onto a graph, but these methods do not provide so much statistical information, so you are recommended to stick with the method described above.

We will discuss the use of Excel for multiple regression, and the interpretation of the resulting output, in the next chapter.

EXERCISES

*Further examples on the work of this chapter can be found on the **Companion Website**.*

1 Refer to the data about age of pigs/consumption of Happihog in Chapter 11, Exercise 3. From the data, obtain a regression equation suitable for predicting how much Happihog a five-month-old pig will eat in a week, and hence calculate the predicted value.

2 You receive the following memo from your sales manager:

> I got the quarterly figures of representatives' performance through yesterday and I thought I'd see if there's any connection between how far they travel and how many sales they make, so I put the data through our computer package that does correlations and works out regression lines. While I was at it, I thought I'd see if there's any evidence that they get better at making sales the longer they've been with us, so I tried that too. I must say I was pleased with that bit – apparently if they stay with us for six years they should be making about 51 sales a month! But I can't make sense of the other bits at all – could you interpret, please!

Representative	Mileage per month	No. of sales made	Time with company (months)
Smith	256	27	32
Adams	462	8	6
Williams	322	34	36
Green	211	25	28
Murphy	153	18	8
Evans	186	23	12
Newton	372	38	50
Halliday	223	19	12

Correlation coefficient: time with company/no. of sales = 0.92. Regression equation for no. of sales on time with company is

$$y = 11.35 + 0.55x.$$

Correlation coefficient: mileage/no. of sales = −0.03. Regression equation for no. of sales on mileage is

$$y = 24.72 − 0.033x.$$

Write notes to guide you in explaining to the sales manager what this information means, and how it should be interpreted in the light of the data.

3 Return to the data which you correlated in Chapter 11, Exercise 7, and make use of your calculations from that problem to derive an appropriate regression equation. Use this equation to give a forecast which will be comparable with an actual published figure (one which was not used in your calculations). How much disagreement is there between the two, and what factors, neglected in your analysis, do you think might have caused the difference?

4 Use the data in the file QUAL.XLS/QUAL.DAT to examine the relationships between (a) gross takings and floorspace; (b) gross takings and number of sales staff. What can you conclude from your results?

5 If you gathered data for either Exercise 9 or 10 of Chapter 11, carry out an appropriate regression analysis and interpret your results (preferably using Excel).

→

6   A direct sales company operates from a large warehouse, where staff pick the items for each order and pack them for despatch. The warehouse manager has collected the following data by tracking a number of orders:

Number of items in order	Time to complete order (minute)
1	5
1	7
2	6
4	8
5	8
6	10

Calculate a regression equation suitable for predicting the time required to complete an order of a given size. How confident would you feel in using this equation to predict the time required to complete an order for three items? For ten items?

7   In the equation you calculated for Exercise 6, give a practical interpretation of the constant term and of the slope.

8   A company recently launched a new type of chocolate bar onto the market, and has found that sales (in thousands of bars) over the first eight weeks on the market have been as follows:

Week number	Sales
1	4.8
2	4.6
3	4.9
4	5.1
5	5.2
6	5.5
7	5.4
8	6

Is there evidence that these sales are growing linearly? If so, calculate the equation of a regression line to predict sales for the next month. Do you think that the linear model is likely to be a good one in this situation?

9   Below is some of the output from an Excel regression which relates the speed at which a piece of drilling machinery is operated to the length of time between replacements of the drill bit:

	Coefficients	Standard Error	t Stat	P-value	Lower 95%	Upper 95%
Intercept	12.78	0.29	44.56	0.00	12.04	13.51
speed (rpm)	−0.03	0.00	−10.26	0.00	−0.03	−0.02

Multiple R	0.98

Draft a short report for the company operating the machinery, explaining the meaning of this information, and its practical implications.

10   What would happen if you tried to use the equation derived in Exercise 9 to predict the time between replacements when the drill is operated at 500 rpm? What can you conclude?

Case Study

What determines vehicle ownership?

(Use Excel for this question if possible. The data can be found on the Companion Website in the file CARS.XLS.)

You are working in sales for a firm of car distributors, who are thinking of expanding into a new market. You have been asked to investigate the factors which determine vehicle ownership in various European countries; the most recent data you can find is for 2002, and is as shown below:

	Per capita income, ($000s)	Vehicles per 1000 population	Total vehicles (millions)	Population (millions)	Population density per km^2	% of population in urban areas
Austria	26.3	629	5.1	8	97	68
Belgium	24.7	520	5.3	10	315	97
Switzerland	27.7	559	4	7	184	67
Czech Republic	13.6	390	4	10	133	75
Germany	23.5	586	48.3	83	236	88
Denmark	25.9	430	2.3	5	127	85
Spain	19.3	564	22.9	41	82	78
Finland	24.3	488	2.5	5	17	59
France	23.7	576	35.3	61	108	76
Great Britain	23.6	515	30.6	59	246	90
Greece	16.1	422	4.6	11	82	61
Hungary	12.3	306	3	10	110	65
Ireland	29.8	472	1.9	4	57	60
Iceland	26.7	672	0.2	0.3	3	93
Italy	23.3	656	37.7	57	196	67
Luxembourg	42.6	716	0.3	0.4	173	92
Netherlands	25.3	477	7.7	16	477	90
Norway	28.1	521	2.4	5	15	75
Poland	9.6	370	14.4	39	127	63
Sweden	25.4	500	4.5	9	22	83

Source: *The Energy Journal*, 28(4), pp. 163–190 (Dargay, J., Gately, O. and Sommer, M. 2007). Reprinted with permission from The Energy Journal.

To prepare for a presentation to management about opportunities for sales in Turkey, carry out the following steps:

(a) Plot scattergraphs of vehicles per thousand population against two other variables in the table with which you believe there might be a correlation. What do your results suggest?
(b) For the variable which is more closely correlated to vehicles per thousand population, calculate the equation of the regression line, and interpret the results.
(c) Plot scattergraphs of total vehicle ownership against two other variables. What do these graphs suggest?
(d) For the variable which is more closely correlated to total vehicle ownership, calculate the equation of the regression line, and interpret the results.
(e) Which of the two regression equations do you think will be more useful to the company?

(f) Data for Turkey is as follows:

Income	Population	Population density	% urban
6.1	67	90	67

Use this data and the regression equations calculated in (b) and (d) above to predict the total number of vehicles and number of vehicles per 1000 population for Turkey. The actual figures are 6.4 million and 96 per 1000 population. Explain why your predictions differ from these values.

For further reading please see the end of Chapter 13.

Chapter 13

MORE COMPLEX RELATIONSHIPS:
MULTIPLE REGRESSION

Chapter prerequisites   Before starting work on this chapter make sure you are happy with all the material on correlation and regression in Chapters 11 and 12.

Learning outcomes   By the end of your work on this chapter you should be able to:

1 use Excel to obtain the regression equation of a dependent variable y on a set of predictors $x_1, x_2, \ldots$;

2 interpret the results of a multiple regression analysis in practical terms;

3 assess the significance of the individual regression coefficients and of the overall linear relationship;

4 use dummy variables to represent qualitative factors in a regression;

5 use multiple regression to fit quadratics and other curves to data;

6 recognise the difficulties which may arise in carrying out and interpreting a multiple regression analysis.

Quantitative methods in practice

Economic recovery 'losing momentum'

The likelihood of a double-dip recession in the UK has been 'exaggerated' but the pace of recovery is losing momentum, an economic forecaster has said.

The Ernst & Young ITEM Club predicts GDP growth of 1.4% this year and 2.2% in 2011, but said the recovery will face a 'soft patch' in the months ahead.

The group, which bases its forecasts on the Treasury's economic model, said it was 'hardly surprising' that policymakers at the Bank of England were considering pumping more cash into the economy in the wake of Chancellor George Osborne's spending review, to be revealed later this week.

www.shropshirestar.com, Monday 18 October 2010

You may have come across other references to the Treasury Economic Model mentioned in the above quote. It is used by the government and by others who are interested in forecasting how various economic parameters important to business and commerce, such as inflation and employment, are going to behave in the future.

Of course, this is a very complex situation, so the model that is used, unlike the regression models we looked at in the previous chapter, does not simply look at how one single variable influences another. For this type of situation, and in particular when we want to examine how one *dependent* variable – here, the rate of growth of the economy – is influenced by a whole set of independent variables rather than just one, we need to extend the *bivariate* (involving two variables) regression models we have already encountered, and look at *multiple regression* models, where we have more than one independent variable.

The advertising manager's problem

Amira Shah works as an advertising manager for a company which markets do-it-yourself products through a nationwide chain of retail outlets. The company advertises mainly on a local basis, via newspapers, hoardings and the exterior of buses. Amira has been asked to assess the relationship between the amount spent on advertising per quarter and the corresponding level of sales achieved.

She has decided to focus for the moment on the data from the last complete quarter, breaking the information down according to the company's ten sales regions. However, when she gives some thought to the situation she realises that many other factors will affect the sales – even the weather in the region may have an impact on do-it-yourself activity! Clearly it is impossible to include every variable which may show some relationship with sales, so she decides as a starting-point to include just one – the number of households in each region – arguing that higher sales are likely to be achieved in areas where there are more households. (Why do you think she selected households in this case rather than total population?)

The data she has collected is shown below:

Region	Sales (£00 000s)	Advertising expenditure (£00 000s)	Number of households (000s)
A	20	0.2	515
B	25	0.2	542
C	24	0.2	576
D	30	0.3	617
E	32	0.3	683
F	40	0.4	707
G	28	0.3	500
H	50	0.5	742
I	40	0.4	747
J	50	0.5	770

Amira decides to use regression analysis to examine the data; it is obvious that the dependent variable should be the sales, but there are now two independent or predictor variables rather than one – the advertising expenditure (adexp) and the number of households – so a multiple regression, taking account of both predictors, is called for. In other words, instead of fitting an equation of the form $y = a + bx$ as in the previous chapter, we need to fit the equation $y = b_0 + b_1 x_1 + b_2 x_2$, where we are using the bs to represent numerical coefficients and the xs to represent our two predictor variables.

The 'best' equation can be calculated according to exactly the same definition as in the previous chapter – that is, in such a way as to minimise the sum of the squared disagreements between the actual y-values and those predicted by the equation. But it is not so easy to see exactly what the equation represents in geometric terms. Whereas before we found the equation of a line, we now have what is actually the equation of a plane in three dimensions. The concept of the slope of the line, and of a positive or negative relationship, therefore no longer holds; it is possible that the coefficient b_1 is positive, while b_2 is negative, indicating that y has a positive relationship with one variable and a negative relationship with the other.

When we have more than two predictors – say p of them – the equation looks like

$$y = b_0 + b_1 x_1 + b_2 x_2 + b_3 x_3 + \ldots + b_p x_p$$

This represents a *hyperplane* in $(p + 1)$-dimensional space (!), but the interpretation of the results remains the same.

Carrying out the multiple regression

If you worked through the examples in the previous chapter, you will be aware that calculating the regression equation by hand, even when there is only one predictor, involves a lot of messy arithmetic, and to do so with two or more predictors is simply not practical. It is therefore essential to have access to a suitable computer package if you wish to use multiple regression. We will focus on Excel's regression routine, but the output from other packages should look sufficiently similar for you to be able to interpret the main features.

If you have not read the section on regression with Excel at the end of the previous chapter, go back and do so now. The procedure for a multiple regression is exactly the same, except that, where you are asked to specify the x-range, you need to highlight all the columns containing predictors. Here there are two, and it is easiest if they are placed in adjacent columns in the spreadsheet. Once the data ranges have been identified, click on OK, and the results will appear.

Interpreting the results

The output from analysis of the sales/advertising/households data is as shown:

Regression statistics	
Multiple R	0.99
R Square	0.98
Adjusted R Square	0.98
Standard Error	1.62
Observations	10.00

ANOVA

	df	SS	MS	F	Significance F
Regression	2.00	998.49	499.25	189.83	0.00
Residual	7.00	18.41	2.63		
Total	9.00	1016.90			

	Coefficients	Standard Error	t Stat	p-value	Lower 95%	Upper 95%
Intercept	−4.31	4.39	−0.98	0.36	−14.68	6.06
X Variable 1	73.75	9.29	7.93	0.00	51.78	95.73
X Variable 2	0.02	0.01	2.06	0.08	0.00	0.05

If your results do not look quite the same, it is probably because those given here have been formatted to show only two decimal places.

What useful information can Amira obtain from these results? To answer this question, we need to look at them section by section. The Multiple R value of 0.99, and the R Square of 0.98 or 98 per cent, both indicate that the linear model with two predictors fits the data very well. R^2 tells us that 98 per cent of the variation in the sales figures is associated with variations in the advertising spend and numbers of households.

However, we need to be careful here. The addition of *any* variable to the regression equation (even a completely irrelevant one) will, because of the way R^2 is calculated, result in an increase in its value. So you could boost the value of R^2 simply by sticking more and more variables into the equation – not a very sensible strategy. This is where the adjusted

R^2 comes into play; without going into the mathematical details, the 'adjustment' takes account of the number of variables in the equation, in such a way as to produce an unbiased figure. Thus, when looking at multiple regression results, it is preferable to use the adjusted R^2 to assess how well the model fits the data; here they are the same, so there is no problem.

Jumping down now to the bottom set of results, we see that the intercept is given as −4.31, the coefficient of x-variable 1 as 73.75, and that of x-variable 2 as 0.02. This means that we can construct the regression equation thus:

$$\text{Sales} = -4.31 + 73.75 \times \text{adexp} + 0.02 \times \text{households}.$$

What do the coefficients tell us? We have to be a little careful in how we word our conclusions here: for every unit increase in the advertising expenditure, *if the number of households remains constant*, the sales will increase by 73.75 units. Likewise when advertising spend remains constant, each unit increase in the number of households will be associated with an increase of 0.02 units in sales.

The constant term here is negative, which seems a bit odd — it suggests that with no advertising in a region with no households, sales would be negative! However, as we will see below, there is a simple explanation for this.

If we look at the significance of the coefficients, as indicated by the p-values, we see that the p-value for x-variable 1 is zero, indicating that this variable in the population is very unlikely to be zero (remember that the smaller p is, the greater the significance). The upper and lower 95% confidence limits confirm this, showing we can be 95 per cent confident that the true value of this coefficient is between 51.78 and 95.73.

However, for the second x-variable, and for the constant term, the p-values are much higher — in fact, if we adopt the usual convention of 5 per cent significance, then both coefficients would be regarded as 'not significantly different from zero'. Again, this is confirmed by the confidence intervals, both of which contain zero as a possible value for the coefficient. So the equation could, after all, indicate that sales are zero for a region with no households and no advertising — a much more sensible conclusion.

Does this mean that we could leave households out of the equation on the grounds that they are not significantly related to sales? The answer is no, not necessarily: even though the coefficient of households appears 'not significant' in the presence of adexp, its removal would alter the coefficient of adexp. By including households in the equation, we are getting an estimate of the effect of adexp which is not muddled up, or 'confounded' to use the technical term, with possible effects of the number of households. So it is better on the whole if households stays in — dropping variables just because their coefficients do not appear significant is a dangerous strategy.

Look now at the middle part of the results, headed ANOVA. We can use the figure headed 'Significance F' here to assess the overall strength of the linear regression equation. Here the figure — which is really another p-value — is 0.00, so we can say that there is a highly significant linear relationship between sales and the two variables adexp and households taken together. This is in contrast to the p-values for the individual coefficients, which indicate the significance of each variable taken separately.

Overall, then, it appears that there is a strong relationship between sales and the two predictor variables chosen, and the equation could reasonably be used to obtain predictions for sales in other regions given information about advertising spend and numbers of households.

Qualitative variables in a regression equation

So far all our regressions have involved only measured variables, but it is quite possible that we might want to examine the impact of a qualitative variable such as gender on some dependent quantity. There is a very simple and useful way in which this can be done.

Suppose we are carrying out a study of the relationship between engine size in cc and petrol consumption in miles per gallon (mpg) for a sample of small family cars, but we notice when the data has been collected that some of the cars in our sample have catalytic converters, while others do not. The presence or absence of a converter will have an impact on the performance of the car, and should be taken into account when looking at the mpg/cc relationship; if not, it may obscure the effects which we are trying to identify – another possible case of confounding.

We therefore need to build the variable 'presence/absence of a converter' into our equation as a variable. However, this variable only takes two (non-numerical) values. We therefore use what is known as a *dummy variable* to represent the two qualitative values; if we call the dummy variable CAT, then CAT = 1 for cars with a converter, and CAT = 0 for those without.

Once we have created a column to represent this variable, alongside the variables cc and mpg, we can use Excel to carry out the regression in the usual way. The results will be identical in format to those we discussed above, and the regression equation can be constructed from the information relating to coefficients in the following form:

$$mpg = 58 - 0.013cc - 7.8CAT.$$

How can we interpret this equation? Since CAT can take one of only two values, it is easy to examine the effect of each of these on the equation. When CAT = 0 we have

$$mpg = 58 - 0.013cc,$$

while with CAT = 1, the equation becomes

$$mpg = 58 - 0.013cc - 7.8 = 50.2 - 0.013cc.$$

So we have effectively got two equations for the price of one! They represent two straight lines, both with the same slope of -0.013 (the negative sign indicates that mpg goes down as engine capacity increases, which of course is what we would expect), but with different intercepts. The two lines are shown on Figure 13.1. Furthermore, if the p-value for the coefficient of CAT shows it to be significantly different from zero, we can conclude that CAT does have a significant effect on the mpg/engine capacity relationship.

You might ask why using the dummy variable in this way is better than the alternative approach of simply splitting the sample into two groups, with and without converter, and carrying out the regression for each group separately. The answer is twofold: first, by retaining all the cars in a single sample, we get a larger sample size, which will give us more reliable results (narrower confidence intervals, better estimates). Second, as we have seen, by testing the coefficient of CAT we can actually state whether or not that variable has a significant effect – something that would be much more difficult to do if we kept the two equations separate.

Figure 13.1 shows that, with the equation in its present form, it is only the intercepts of the two lines that may differ – the slope is bound to be the same, so that the rate at

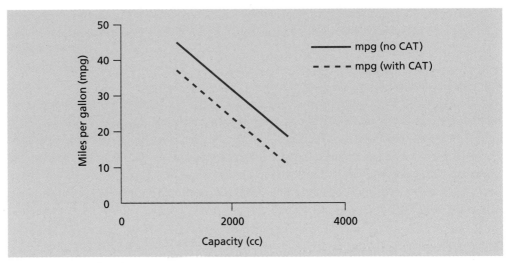

Figure 13.1 Use of dummy variable in regression

which mpg declines as cc increases is the same whether or not a converter is present. You may feel that this is not very realistic, and that the converter might also change this rate. We can easily allow for this by introducing what is called an *interaction term* into the equation. We want to allow CAT and cc to interact, and so we add a term which is the product of these two variables; thus we are looking for an equation of the form

$$\text{mpg} = b_0 + b_1 \times \text{cc} + b_2 \times \text{CAT} + b_3 \times \text{cc} \times \text{CAT}.$$

We need to add a further column to our spreadsheet, containing the values of cc × CAT for each car. Then we carry out the regression in the usual way, obtaining the result

$$\text{mpg} = 60.2 - 0.011\text{cc} - 8.1\text{CAT} - 0.003\text{cc} \times \text{CAT}.$$

Now when CAT = 0 (no converter) the equation becomes

$$\text{mpg} = 60.2 - 0.011\text{cc},$$

while with CAT = 1 it is

$$\text{mpg} = 52.1 - 0.014\text{cc}.$$

So both the intercept and the slope now change between the two equations, and we can say that the rate of decline of mpg with increasing engine capacity is greater for cars with a converter than for those without. Figure 13.2 illustrates this fact. Again, looking at the *p*-value for the product term will tell us whether the difference in slopes is significant.

This was a particularly simple situation because our qualitative variable was *binary* – it could take only two possible values. When a qualitative variable has more than two values, we have to be a bit more careful. For example, suppose we are carrying out a regression of 'value of annual sales' on a number of predictors, one of which is 'location of customer' which can take the three values UK, continental Europe, Rest of World. We might be tempted to introduce a dummy variable LOC, and to say LOC is 1 for UK, 2 for Europe and 3 for Rest of World.

However, if we do that we will have difficulty in interpreting the resulting equation; the particularly simple interpretation above was due to the fact that the dummy variable could only have the value 0 or 1. Fortunately there is an easy way around the

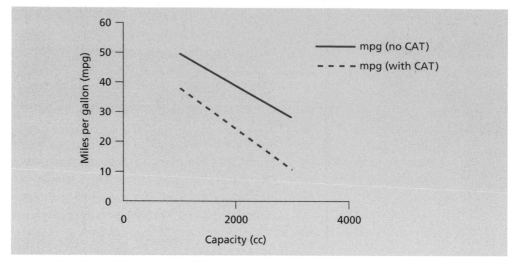

Figure 13.2 Use of dummy variable with an interaction term

problem – we introduce not one, but *two* dummy variables. Let us just call them $x1$ and $x2$. We then arrange that $x1$ is 1 for UK customers, and 0 for all others, while $x2$ is 1 for continental European customers, 0 for the remainder. Thus we have:

	x1	*x2*
UK	1	0
Continental Europe	0	1
Rest of World	0	0

Now we have no problem in interpreting the coefficients of $x1$ and $x2$: $x1$ tells us the overall difference in the value of sales between UK and Rest of World, while $x2$ does the same for continental Europe. Notice that we are using Rest of World here as the basis for comparison, but we would get essentially the same results if we rearranged the dummy variables so that, say, it was continental Europe that had zero values for the dummies.

In general, for a qualitative variable with n categories, we will need to introduce $n - 1$ dummy variables, so multi-category qualitative variables can give rise to rather long equations. Nevertheless, the dummy variable is a powerful way of incorporating both measured and qualitative data into a single model.

Quick check questions

1 A regression has been carried out using a dummy variable to represent educational status in a regression of annual income (£000s) on age and education. The coding used was graduate = 0, non-graduate = 1. The coefficient of the dummy variable turns out to be –2.6. How could this be interpreted?

2 You have carried out a regression using Excel and found that the *p*-value associated with the ANOVA part of the results is 0.23. Which is true: (a) the dependent variable has a significant linear relationship to the set of independent variables, or (b) the dependent variable does not have a significant linear relationship to the set of independent variables?

3 Is it possible for each of the individual coefficients in the regression not to be significant, but the overall regression to be significant nevertheless?

Answers:
1 The coefficient of the dummy variable tells us that for two people of the same age, one of whom is a graduate and the other not, the non-graduate's income will on average be lower by £2600 (lower because the coefficient is negative).
2 This *p*-value is 'large', and so the relationship is not significant – it would need to be smaller than 0.05 for the relationship to be significant at the 5 per cent level.
3 Yes, it is perfectly possible to have a regression where no individual coefficient is significant, and yet where the overall linear relationship is significant – the set of independent variables when taken together has a significant linear relationship with the dependent variable.

Using multiple regression to fit curves

Sometimes when a scattergraph of bivariate data has been drawn, it becomes clear that while a definite relationship between x and y exists, it is not linear in form. When this happens, we may wish to fit some form of curve, such as a quadratic. This is easily done using Excel multiple regression, as an example will show.

Consider the following set of data (we will not worry here about what x and y may represent):

x	1	2	3	4	5	6	7	8
y	7	10	12	18	22	32	45	60

When these points are plotted, the scattergraph is as in Figure 13.3.

It is clear that, while we could try to put a straight line through these points, some kind of curve would probably be a much better fit. So we will try a quadratic – an equation of

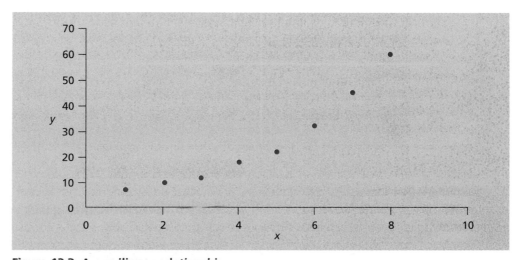

Figure 13.3 A curvilinear relationship

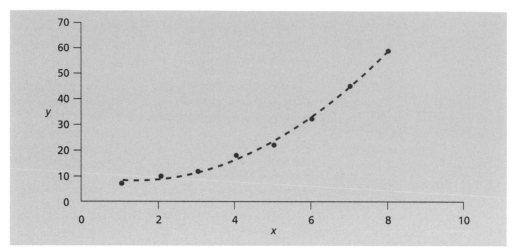

Figure 13.4 The points of Figure 13.3 with fitted curve

the form $y = b_0 + b_1x + b_2x^2$, as you should recall from Chapter 1! We need to set up in the spreadsheet, next to our columns of y- and x-values, a column containing the values of x^2. Then we carry out a regression using both x and x^2 as predictors. The results, in part, are as follows:

	Coefficients	Standard Error	t Stat	p-value
Intercept	10.30	1.95	5.29	0.00
X Variable 1	−3.09	0.99	−3.11	0.03
X Variable 2	1.15	0.11	10.68	0.00

'X Variable 2' here is the squared term, and as you can see by looking at the p-value, it is significantly different from zero – in other words, the quadratic term has a significant association with y (as does the x term in this case). The adjusted R^2 is 0.99, which confirms that the quadratic $y = 10.30 − 3.09x + 1.15x^2$ is a very good fit, as we can see when it is superimposed on the data as in Figure 13.4.

More complicated curves, involving log functions, higher powers of x and so on, can be fitted in a similar way. Of course, the more complicated the equation, the more difficult it is to interpret, so one should resist the temptation to put in more and more terms in an effort to boost the value of R^2.

Some points to watch for when using regression

We have not said much about the statistical theory underlying regression; it is a very large topic, and indeed whole texts are written on the subject. While packages such as Excel make it unnecessary for you to be familiar with all the details, it is important that you are aware of certain assumptions which must be met if conclusions drawn from the regression output are to be valid. There are also a number of practical difficulties which can arise in a regression analysis, for which you need to be prepared.

Assumptions

It is simplest to discuss these in terms of a bivariate relationship, though they apply also to equations with more than two variables. The theory requires, roughly speaking, that the data points should be scattered round the linear equation according to a normal distribution, and that the 'width' of the scatter should be the same throughout. Thus data as shown in Figure 13.5(a) would conform to the requirement, while data shown in Figure 13.5(b) would not, since the width of the scatter becomes greater for greater values of x.

The values of y for different values of x should also be independent of each other. This means that it is often not a good idea to use time-series data, such as monthly sales figures as predictor variables in a regression – the tendency for one period of high sales to be followed by another, and similarly for low sales, violates the independence requirement. A good way to get round this is to use, not absolute values of sales, but the actual or percentage *change* in sales from one period to another.

There are various tests which can be carried out to determine to what extent the regression assumptions are met by a real set of data. You can read more about these in the texts given in the Further reading list at the end of the chapter. However, generally speaking it

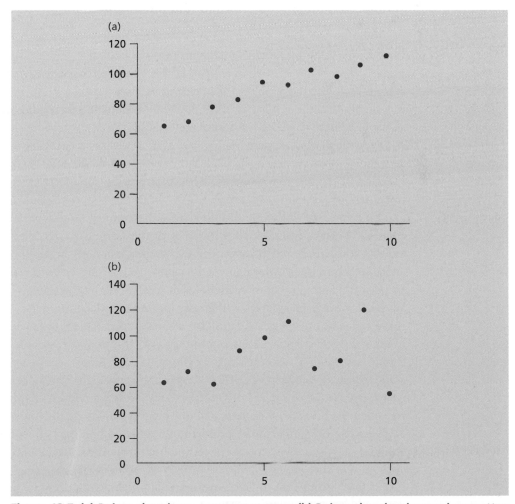

Figure 13.5 **(a) Points showing a constant scatter. (b) Points showing increasing scatter as *x* increases**

is the validity of the significance tests and confidence intervals that is called into question if the assumptions are not met, rather than the computation of the regression relationship and R^2, so you need not feel too anxious.

Practical difficulties

Amount of data available

Just as you will always obtain a perfect regression relationship between two variables if you use only two points – because you can always put a straight line exactly through them! – so the same will be true in three dimensions if you have three points, and so on. The moral of this is that you need 'enough' data to give you a reliable analysis. Of course, there is no strict definite of 'enough', but an often-used rule of thumb is that you should have at least five data points for each predictor in the equation. This means that in the example above concerning sales data, we had just enough data – ten points for two predictor variables.

Choosing which variables to include

The number of variables to go into the equation will be determined, as we have just seen, partly by the amount of data available. But the actual choice as to what the variables should be can be more problematic. A knowledge of the practicalities of the situation under investigation is, of course, vital, as this will suggest some obvious candidate variables. The ability to get hold of the relevant data may also be a limiting factor.

One important point is that it is not a good idea to choose predictors that may themselves be closely correlated. An extreme example of this would be the inclusion, in an equation to predict student performance, of assessment and examination marks and also the combined final mark. The point here is that the combined mark is simply a function of the other two, and so its inclusion in the equation does not add any useful information.

This is obviously silly (and would give rise to technical problems in the regression calculation which cause Excel to return an error message). However, even when there is not a direct relationship like this between two predictors, they can still be very closely correlated. For example, in Amira Shah's data at the start of this chapter, it is likely that advertising spend and number of households in an area will be correlated – it is worthwhile to advertise more in an area where there are lots of potential customers. (You can check that this is in fact the case by calculating the correlation coefficient between adexp and households.) Thus we are not 'getting our money's worth' out of the variable 'households', since it may not be telling us much that we did not already know via the variable 'adexp'. This could explain why adexp has a high p-value and is not significant. The effect of including correlated predictors such as this is often to give wide confidence intervals for coefficients, reflecting the uncertainty as to which one is actually making the impact on y.

The technical name for the problem of correlated predictors is 'collinearity', and you will find more discussion of its effects and how it may be detected in the references given at the end of the chapter.

You might think that when trying to decide which predictors to include in a regression, you could try experimenting with different regression equations to see which one is 'best' in the sense of giving the largest adjusted R^2. However, this is not always a good idea (though there are computer routines that will allow you to do it in an automated way). The point is that, if you thrash around for long enough and try enough different combinations of variables, you are very likely to come up, just by pure chance, with one that looks highly significant. Whether or not it has any real practical meaning is, however, a very different matter. So there is no substitute for thought and a good knowledge of your subject area.

Choosing how to measure variables

Even when you have decided which predictors to include, there will very often be a number of ways in which a possible predictor could be measured. For example, if you are interested in 'education expenditure' in a variety of countries, this could be given as expenditure per head of population, percentage of total government expenditure devoted to education, percentage of gross domestic product (GDP) spent on education and so on. Only careful thought and some experimentation will tell you which is the best version to use.

Dealing with outliers

We came across the term *outlier* in Chapter 11; we use it to refer to a data point that does not seem to conform to the overall pattern of the data. The point for representative number 1 in Figure 11.2 was an example of an outlier. The inclusion of such points in the regression calculations may 'mess up' an otherwise close relationship, resulting in a lower adjusted R^2 than we might have hoped for.

However, deciding arbitrarily to omit such points from the computation simply *because* they spoil the results is a very doubtful business – it is all too easy to 'whittle down' the data by leaving out points until you have a really good value of R^2. You should not leave out a point unless you have a good argument as to why it does not fit the overall pattern – perhaps simply because of an error in recording the figure, perhaps because the sample is not sufficiently homogeneous. For example, if you were looking at the relationship between dollar exchange rates and volume of imports for various countries, and your sample included the member states of the EU together with one developing country in South America, you might well expect the 'odd one out' to show up as an outlier, and the fact that it is not comparable with the rest of the data, and cannot be expected to conform to the same pattern, would be a good reason for leaving it out.

Research is still going on into some of the problem areas outlined above, so you can see that we are quite close to the frontiers of the subject here. However, do not let this rather long cautionary list make you feel that regression is too risky a method to be used in practice – unless your data is very odd, sound common sense and an awareness of the possible difficulties should prevent your going seriously astray.

Back to the Treasury Economic Model

We have now seen how flexible multiple regression models can be, allowing us to deal with qualitative as well as quantitative variables, to fit some types of non-linear as well as linear behaviour, and to isolate the effects of individual independent variables while taking the presence of other factors into account. Of course, the government's economic models are several orders of magnitude more complex than anything we have dealt with, but you should now have more insight into the power and usefulness of this kind of modelling. And you should realise that the forecasts quoted in the article at the start of the chapter will, like all regression-based forecasts, be subject to a degree of uncertainty.

EXERCISES

*Further examples on the work of this chapter can be found on the **Companion Website**.*

1 An insurance company is studying the factors that influence the amount of life insurance held by managers in private sector companies. The variables it is using are as follows:

   ins = amount of insurance cover held (in £000s).

   inc = a dummy variable which is 0 for annual incomes up to £35 000, 1 for those above this limit.

   kids = number of children under 21.

   age = age in years at last birthday.

   When ins is regressed on the other three variables, using data for a random sample of 15 managers, part of the results is as shown:

   Adjusted $R^2 = 0.671$

	Coefficient	p-value
Intercept	29.05	0.034
X variable 1	34.507	0.004
X variable 2	−1.691	0.711
X variable 3	−0.082	0.830

   (a) Write down the equation for predicting ins given the other three variables.
   (b) What does the adjusted R^2 tell us?
   (c) How would you explain the results in practical terms to an executive of the insurance company?

2 A supplier of personal computers offers an after-sales maintenance service to customers, and has been monitoring the time taken by its engineers to carry out routine six-monthly maintenance on customers' machines. The variable 'time' gives the time in minutes to complete the service, and this has been related to two other variables: 'exp', indicating the number of years of experience of the engineer carrying out the maintenance, and 'num' indicating the number of machines to be serviced.

   The resulting regression equation, based on the returns of 30 engineers, is

   Time = −179 + 10.2exp + 33.0num.

The *p*-values for the three coefficients are respectively 0.16, 0.44 and 0.00.

(a) What would you say to someone who pointed out that the positive coefficient for exp is rather odd, since it suggests that engineers with more experience take longer to carry out maintenance?

(b) What other information would you like to have been able to include in the equation?

3 Two service stations belonging to the same company, one in a town-centre location and one on an outer ring-road, have been examining the relationship between petrol sales and traffic flow. They have recorded data for 100 one-hour periods, and have regressed sales value in £00s during that hour (sales) on the number of cars passing (flow, measured in hundreds of cars). Also included was a dummy variable 'loc' representing the location of the service station, with loc = 1 for the town centre and loc = 0 for the ring-road.

The equation calculated is

$$\text{Sales} = 1.41 + 0.36\text{flow} + 4.6\text{loc},$$

and the *p*-value for 'loc' is 0.02.

(a) Does the location of the service station make a significant difference to sales?

(b) Does the fact that the coefficient of 'flow' is much smaller than that of 'loc' suggest that flow is a less important variable in determining sales? Explain your answer.

4 (a) Use the data in the file QUAL.XLS to examine the relationship between gross takings and the two variables number of sales staff and floorspace. Interpret your results, and compare them with those you obtained in Exercise 4 of Chapter 12.

(b) Create a dummy variable to represent store location (street/precinct), and incorporate this into your regression. What effect does this have?

5 The following data has been gathered from a group of male students:

Height (cm)	Hours of exercise per week	Weight (kg)
178	4	72
180	1	80
175	6	65
188	3	85
184	3	76
168	5	58
181	1	92
180	2	74

Carry out a regression of weight on height and hours of exercise, and give a full interpretation of the results.

6 In Exercise 5, why was it important that all the students were male? If you wished to incorporate data about females, how could this be done, and how would you interpret the coefficient of the 'male/female' variable?

7 A company which has been operating for 12 years has experienced very rapid growth. Numbers of employees over that period have been as follows:

Year	*Employees*
1	87
2	253
3	286
4	370
5	392
6	450
7	584
8	520
9	611
10	641
11	636
12	580

Use Excel to compute the regression of the number of employees on the year, and thus predict the number who will be employed in year 14.

8 Now add a column for the square of the year number to your spreadsheet, and by regressing the number of employees on the two independent variables year number and (year number)^2, fit a quadratic expression to the data. Use your quadratic to predict the number of employees in year 14. How much does this prediction differ from that obtained in Exercise 7? Which would you regard as more reliable, and why?

9 Carry out a regression using Excel with the following values of x and y:

x	y
1	2.4
3	7.2
4	9.6
6	14.4
7	16.8
9	21.6
12	28.8
15	36

What do you notice about the results, and why is this the case?

10 An organisation which carries out telephone contacting of potential charity donors has gathered data relating to the success of its contacts. The data was collected as follows: 20 telephone operatives were monitored over a randomly selected sample of 100 calls, and the percentage of calls which led to a donation was recorded. The number of months' experience of the operative, and the time of day at which the call was made, were also noted. The resulting data was as follows:

Percentage successful	Experience (months)	Time of day
15	3	Morning
9	2	Evening
17	11	Morning
8	7	Evening
13	5	Afternoon
11	3	Morning
12	8	Afternoon
19	16	Morning
23	22	Afternoon
4	1	Evening
8	14	Evening
10	4	Afternoon
20	11	Morning
13	5	Afternoon
4	7	Evening
9	19	Evening
21	13	Afternoon
11	16	Evening
14	3	Morning

(a) Create a dummy variable or variables to represent 'time of day'.
(b) Carry out a regression of the percentage of successful calls on the other variables, and interpret your results.

(The data for this question is also available from the **Companion Website**.)

Case Study

Selling wind turbines to China

(Use Excel for this case.)

   You work for a company which manufactures and repairs wind turbines for the generation of 'clean' energy. The company is considering opening a sales operation in China, since it is aware of the rapid growth of demand for energy in that country. You have therefore been asked to analyse some relevant data.

   You find the following figures for cumulative installed wind turbine capacity in China (units not stated) on the website of the oil company BP.

Year	Capacity
2003	571
2004	769
2005	1264
2006	2588
2007	5875
2008	12 121
2009	25 853

(a) Plot this data on a graph. What do you notice about the growth of the wind turbine capacity? Do you think that a straight line will be a good fit to this data?

(b) Calculate the regression line which best fits the data (number off the years 1, 2, etc., to make figures more manageable). Add the regression line to your graph, and comment on the result.

(c) Now add a column to your spreadsheet showing the values of x^2, where x is the year number. Carry out a multiple regression using both x and x^2 as predictors. Write down the resulting equation, and confirm that it is a quadratic. Add the resulting curve to your graph.

(d) Use your graphs, and the values of R^2 provided by Excel, to determine whether the line or the quadratic is the better fit, explaining the reasons for your choice.

(e) How confident would you be in using your chosen model to predict the installed capacity in 2012, and why?

Further reading

To learn more about multiple regression, try:

Hair, J., Tatham, R. and Anderson, R. (2002), *Multivariate Data Analysis with Reading*, 6th edn, Prentice Hall.

Wonnacott, R.J. and Wonnacott, T.H. (1990), *Introductory Statistics for Business and Economics*, 4th edn, Wiley.

Part 4

NUMBERS –
A TOOL OF PLANNING

In this section we shall see how, by constructing a *mathematical model* of a practical problem, we can make decisions on a more sound and logical basis than if we were simply to rely on a subjective approach. You have in fact already encountered some mathematical models, though they were not specifically described as such. For instance, in Chapter 7 we used the theoretical probability distributions – binomial, normal and Poisson – as models for real-life situations which, while they might not fit the patterns of the theoretical distribution exactly, were adequately represented by them for many purposes. However, as the process of constructing a mathematical model will occur repeatedly in the following chapters, it is worthwhile to look briefly at the essential features of the process.

In most cases, the initial step will be the recognition that a problem exists – not always such an obvious step as it may sound. Even when the problem has been recognised, defining it precisely and deciding just what our objective should be in attempting to reach a solution can also be a lengthy process. To take an example which will be looked at in more detail in the next chapter: if we are trying to decide what is the best level of stocks for a retailer to hold, we may have to keep records for many months before we have sufficient information about the demand for each product, how that demand varies in the course of time, how serious the effects of running out of a particular product may be, and so on – all of which information must be known before we can begin building our model. Then, when we come to specify the objective we are aiming to achieve, we are faced with several possibilities: do we want to find the policy which will minimise the total cost of stock-holding; do we want to minimise the risk of being out of stock; or do we perhaps want to cut down on administrative nuisance by placing standing orders for deliveries of stock which will only need to be changed at infrequent intervals?

Only after these questions have been answered can we proceed to build up a model for the problem, from which we hope to obtain a solution. The kinds of mathematical model we are going to use will take a variety of forms: algebraic equations, graphs, diagrams and charts, and so forth; but there is one major feature that will apply to some extent, no matter what kind of model we are using. That is, that some degree of simplification will be required before we can construct, and certainly before we can solve, our model. It is most important that we should be aware of the assumptions that we have had to make in simplifying the problem, as of course these will have a bearing on the validity of the solution we obtain, and the extent to which we can expect it to work in practice.

In many of the cases we are going to look at, actually obtaining the solution is a relatively simple matter once the model has been set up; but the process does not end there. The solution must be implemented – that is, applied in practice – and its validity checked against what happens in the real-life situation. Often at this stage it may become apparent that our problem was too simplified, or that circumstances have altered in the meantime and rendered some of our data obsolete, so that we then have to return to the stage of formulating the problem and repeat the whole process with the appropriate modifications. In other words, generally speaking the cycle is a dynamic, not a static, one, because real-world situations are constantly altering. When mathematical methods are given a bad press by businesspeople and other 'lay' people, quite often it is because this point has not been appreciated, so that solutions which are long out of date are still being blindly applied – which is naturally not a recipe for success!

We will try to emphasise these various stages of the modelling process in the ensuing chapters, and hopefully by doing so will avoid giving the impression that you are being armed with a mathematical 'box of tricks' for the solution to all the ills of business.

Many of the techniques covered in this part of the book fall into the general area known as operational research. For further reading on the material of Chapters 14–18, a good starting-point is D. Anderson, D. Sweeney and T. Williams (2006), *Quantitative Methods for Business*, 10th edn, West Publishing.

Operational research is now a very large field, and new approaches to the kinds of problems considered in Chapters 14–18 are being developed all the time. Very often these depend on the use of specialised software to deal with complex real-life problems. In a book of this size, and without using more advanced mathematics, it is not possible to cover the topics in depth; instead, each chapter will give you an introduction to a class of problems and the ways in which they can be solved, which should provide a good basis for going into greater depth should you need to. You will find more suggested reading at the end of each chapter to help you in doing this.

Chapter 14

PLANNING AN INVENTORY POLICY:
STOCK CONTROL AND SIMULATION

Chapter prerequisites   Before starting work on this chapter make sure you are happy with the following topics:

1 construction of equations (see Chapter 1, p. 21);

2 plotting graphs from algebraic expressions (see Chapter 1, pp. 25–9);

3 the basic ideas of modelling (see Part 4, pp. 349–50).

4 the idea of a probability distribution (Chapter 7).

Learning outcomes   By the end of your work on this chapter you should be able to:

1 construct an algebraic model for a simple inventory system involving replenishment costs and stock-holding costs;

2 determine the cost-minimising solution graphically;

3 state the simplifying assumptions involved in constructing your model;

4 compare specific inventory policies involving stock-outs;

5 examine the effect on our solution of small changes in the quantities involved;

6 discuss the limitations of this approach;

7 construct a random number distribution which models the behaviour of a given experimental distribution;

8 use random number tables in conjunction with your distribution to simulate a given process;

9 set out the simulation in a meaningful way;

10 draw conclusions from the results of your simulation.

Quantitative methods in practice

> Dear Customer,
>
> We are sorry to report that the following item has been delayed.
>
> . . .
>
> Our current estimate is that it will take an additional 3–5 weeks to obtain this item for you.
>
> . . .

I received the message above from a well-known company a few days before writing this. I'm sure we have all had similar experiences – going to the supermarket and finding that our favourite brand of breakfast cereal is out of stock, hoping to purchase a piece of furniture or a carpet only to discover that we will have to wait 8–12 weeks for it to arrive, and so on.

To be fair to the various companies involved, they face an increasingly difficult problem. Consumers are evermore demanding, expecting any one of thousands of products to be available all the time. So how does the company go about ensuring that, within reason, this demand is met?

In fact, the question is not only applicable to the retailing area. Manufacturing companies – whether they are making cars or mobile phones, equipment for oil rigs or cutlery – need supplies of components and raw materials in order to keep up with production. And whereas it may be annoying to a consumer not to be able to purchase the preferred variety of sugar-free muesli, for a manufacturer it can be disastrous, and cost huge sums of money, to run out of some vital item.

The methods by which organisations maintain and control their stocks form the subject variously known as stock control or inventory theory. It would not be an exaggeration to say that something of a revolution has been going on in this area over the past 10–15 years, prompted partly by improving technological support and partly by pressures on companies to reduce the amount of capital tied up in stock. You may have heard the phrase 'just-in-time manufacturing', which refers to the situation where manufacturers obtain supplies of raw materials and use them immediately, rather than holding stocks for any length of time.

So the method described in this chapter, which assumes that stock will be ordered at regular intervals and held until needed, is not so widely applicable as it once was. Nevertheless, it is worth examining, partly because it is still used in some businesses, partly because it features on many examination syllabuses, and partly because it provides a good and relatively straightforward introduction to the topic of model building as outlined on pp. 349–50.

The small business's problem

John and Mary Williams have just set up a two-person picture-framing business. They offer three basic styles of frame – a plastic and a metal frame, both of which they purchase ready-made in various standard sizes, and a wooden frame which they make themselves from lengths of wooden framing supplied by a wholesaler. They have plenty of customers, and there are no cash flow problems so far, but they are finding it very difficult to manage the ordering of the ready-made frames and the lengths of wooden framing. Because their premises only have a very limited amount of storage space, they do not want to have too much stock at any one time, but several times in recent weeks they have lost a customer because they did not have the required type of frame in stock.

Up to now they have been reordering on a rather haphazard basis, simply taking a look at the stocks of the various types of frame on Monday morning and ringing the supplier to order items which seem to be getting low. However, they now feel that this *ad hoc* approach is not very successful and may be costing them money, so they are hoping to establish a reordering policy on a more rational basis.

The information needed

Obviously one major requirement in this situation is that the firm should be able to satisfy demand as it arises. This suggests that a knowledge of the likely demand, with any regular patterns of variation therein, is a prerequisite for further progress with the problem. It also suggests that one should try to keep as large stocks as one can, so as to be able to satisfy any unusually high demands which may arise. Failure to do this may result in delays to production due to lack of raw materials, or, as the picture-framers have found, in loss of business and customer goodwill.

There are other reasons, too, why it might be a good idea to keep stocks as high as possible. If we order large quantities at a time, we may well be entitled to bulk discounts from suppliers. And there will probably be charges associated with obtaining further supplies from outside the business – at least the cost of the telephone call or letter by which we place the order, and very likely a charge for delivering the goods or going to collect them. In a large organisation, the overheads associated with running a purchasing department will probably also be apportioned as cost associated with ordering. Order costs are thus in the nature of a 'fixed cost' – they do not vary significantly with the size of orders. If we order large stocks at a time, then, to satisfy a given level of demand we will need to re-order less frequently than we would if we ordered only a few items at once, thus cutting costs. We will need to know exactly what the ordering costs, discounts and so on are in order to be more precise about this.

But there is another side to the coin. Even given unlimited amounts of storage space, it can be very expensive to hold large quantities of stock at a time. Capital will be tied up in the stock, which could otherwise be earning interest; stock will need to be insured in case anything happens to it before we have time to use it up; and we will probably have to employ someone to spend at least part of their time looking after stocks, perhaps carrying out maintenance if items are held for a very long time. If our stocks are perishables like foodstuffs we may even find that if they are held for too long they become unusable and have to be wastefully discarded. So now it is beginning to look as if it might be cheaper in the long run to hold only a small amount of stock. This is why, as mentioned at the start of the chapter, many firms have moved to a 'just-in-time' approach to inventory in which little or no stock is held for any length of time. Even if we *do* decide to hold stock, we would want to know what the various costs associated with holding items in stock – the *stock-holding costs* – are before deciding on a policy. Notice that, as the major contribution to these costs is the loss of interest on tied-up capital, stock-holding costs will vary with the amount of stock ordered.

As with many of the problems we have looked at earlier in the book, what we are trying to do here is arrange a compromise. *Large* orders mean infrequent orders, therefore low ordering costs but high holding costs. *Small* orders mean frequent orders, increasing ordering costs but cutting down on stock-holding costs. So we can now be much more precise and say that the objective of a good stock-holding policy (or *inventory* policy, as it is often called) is to determine the size of order which will give us the best trade-off between these two extremes, and result in *minimum total cost*. We have also identified the information that we will need to gather in order to try to determine this best policy – we need to know the demand, the ordering costs* and the stock-holding costs.

Simplifying the problem

The graph in Figure 14.1 shows what our picture-framers might discover if they keep a count of their stocks of one item over a period of several months. The graph shows stocks held on the vertical axis against time on the horizontal axis, and as you can see it has a markedly 'stepped' appearance. This is the appropriate way to draw it, because on some days, when there is a demand for several of the items, stocks will drop suddenly; then perhaps for several days no one will want that particular item, so the stock will remain steady. When a delivery of the items is received, the stock level will increase sharply – this happens

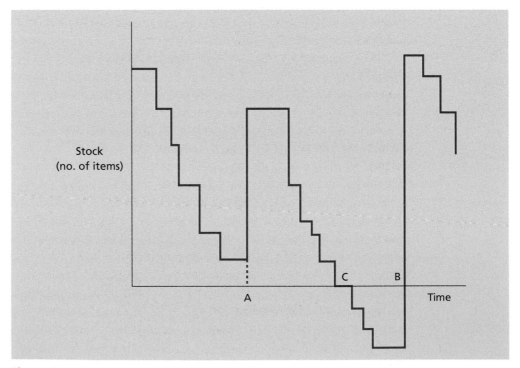

Figure 14.1 A realistic stock graph

* Ordering costs are sometimes alternatively referred to as replenishment costs. This is perhaps a slightly better name, as it covers also the situation where we are replenishing stocks from within the firm, rather than ordering them from outside.

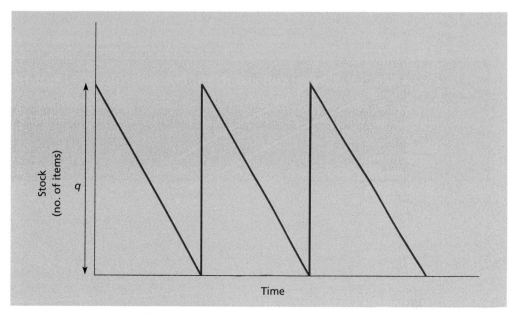

Figure 14.2 An idealised stock graph

at A and B on the graph, though the deliveries are of different amounts. At C there is a period when the items are out of stock, and a backlog of orders is building up, and so on.

At first sight the graph looks so irregular as to be very difficult to analyse, and certainly we would expect all stock control problems to have this element of irregularity to a greater or lesser extent, since demand for an item is bound to be subject to some unpredictable fluctuations. However, a second look at Figure 14.1 shows that there are discernible patterns among the irregularities, notably a repeating pattern of sudden increases in stock followed by gradual drops. We call this pattern the *stock cycle*.

In order to make the problem simpler, we are going to take this essential element from the realistic stock cycle and idealise it somewhat by assuming five things. First, we will assume that demand is *steady*, so that we can replace the irregular 'steps' in Figure 14.1 with a smoothly declining line, as shown in Figure 14.2. This, in many cases, is not such a sweeping assumption as it seems. If the items are used in very large numbers and at frequent intervals, the 'steps' in the first graph would be so small that they almost lie on a straight line.

Second, we will assume that all deliveries are of the same size – in other words, all the upward 'steps' are of the same height. This again is moderately realistic, at least in many situations. For example, the proprietor of a retail newsagency is not going to telephone his wholesaler every night and say 'I think I'll take 40 *Telegraph*s tomorrow'; he will put in an order for a fixed number of each paper to be delivered daily, at least for a month or two ahead.

Third, we will assume that the suppliers can deliver the goods immediately we order them, and that therefore we can afford to let stocks run right down to zero before ordering more, secure in the knowledge that as soon as we sell the last item, further supplies will be rushed round! This is obviously a less realistic assumption, but as we will see later it is one that is quite easy to eliminate.

Our last two assumptions will be that we refuse to allow stock-outs (i.e. what happened at C in Figure 14.1) and that the situation has already arrived at a steady state – that is, we are not looking at the initial period when word of the new business or product might be getting around to potential customers, so creating a rising demand, but at the time when the business is established and has a regular pattern of demand.

There is in fact one more assumption which we will have to make in the course of our analysis of the problem, but these five are sufficient to enable us to draw the version of the stock cycle shown in Figure 14.2.

Solving the simplified problem

As stated earlier, our objective is to determine what size of order will minimise the total cost of our stock policy. Let us call this order size q (as indicated in Figure 14.2). Then with our simplified version of the problem, the contributions to the total cost will come from just two sources – the ordering costs and the stock-holding costs. We will look at each of these separately.

Taking the ordering costs first, suppose that our picture-framing friends have kept a record of the demand for ready-made metal frames over the past six months, and have discovered that they sold 1200 of them over that period. That means, on our assumption that demand is steady, that there is a demand for 200 per month. So if they were to order 50 at a time, they would have to put in four orders a month; if they ordered only 25 at a time, they would need eight orders. In other words, to find out how many orders are placed in a month we divide the size of each order into the total quantity demanded during the month. Thus if they order some unknown amount q at a time, then they will need to place $200/q$ orders per month. To find out how much this will cost, they will need information as to the costs involved in placing an order – and this is where our last assumption comes in. We are going to assume that each order placed costs £2, *irrespective* of the size of the order. As mentioned earlier in the chapter, this is a reasonably sensible assumption, since the major part of this cost probably arises from administrative charges. If we accept this assumption, then the ordering costs will be $(200/q) \times$ £2, which comes to £400/q per month.

Now for the stock-holding costs. If a quantity q is delivered and used up at a steady rate until none remains, then the average amount in stock will be $\frac{1}{2}q$; this, of course, would not be the case if the demand were erratic, which is why we needed our 'steady demand' assumption. If this *is* so, then supposing that the overall cost of holding stock has been found to work out at $\frac{1}{2}$ pence per item for each month the item is held, we can say that the total stock-holding cost per month will be equal to the average stock held during the month multiplied by the cost of holding one item for a month – that is $\frac{1}{2}q \times \frac{1}{2}$ pence.

We can now write down what the total cost per month is going to be, but we have to be rather careful about units here. Our ordering cost was 400/q *pounds* per month, our stock-holding cost $\frac{1}{2}q$ *pence* per month, so before we can add them together to give the total cost, we need to express them in the same units. Let us take pence as the unit, and write the ordering cost as 40 000/q pence per month; then the total cost will be T, where

$$T = \frac{40\ 000}{q} + \frac{q}{4} \text{ pence per month}$$

Our objective, you will recall, was to find what value of q will give T its minimum value, and we are going to determine this by plotting the relationship between T and q on a graph. As a preliminary step we draw up the following table:

Order size, q	No. of orders per month	Order cost	Average stock	Stock-holding cost	Total cost, T
50	4	800	25	12.5	812.5
100	2	400	50	25	425
200	1	200	100	50	250
400	0.5	100	200	100	200
500	0.4	80	250	125	205

In the table all the costs are in pence. We chose to start at $q = 50$ fairly arbitrarily, simply because it is pretty clear that if something is being used up at a rate of 200 a month, we are hardly likely to be ordering it in quantities of one or two at a time. Having found that at $q = 50$ the order cost far exceeds the stock-holding cost, we need to consider larger (and less frequent) orders; the actual numbers used are chosen for convenience in arithmetic. There is no need to go beyond $q = 500$ because you can see that the total cost, having decreased to $q = 400$, has started to increase again, so we must already have passed its minimum.

Before plotting these figures on a graph, it is as well to check that they fit in with common sense. We expected big orders to give lower ordering costs, because we will not need to order as often, but higher stock-holding costs because there will be more stock to be held. This is what the figures seem to confirm, which, while it does not *prove* our analysis correct, is certainly encouraging.

Figure 14.3 shows the costs graphed against q. We have put in not just the total cost, but also the two components, order cost and stock-holding cost, which go to make it up.

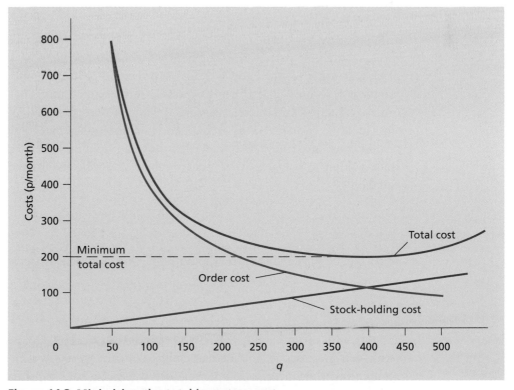

Figure 14.3 Minimising the total inventory cost

As you can see, the total cost reaches its minimum precisely where the two contributory costs are equal – at $q = 400$, as you may check from the table above.

Roughly speaking, total cost is minimised where the increasing stock-holding cost and the decreasing order cost 'balance out'. Now, this is a very useful fact to know, because it gives us the key to a method of finding the best stock policy without having to plot a graph. Of course, we have not actually proved that the minimum total cost will *always* occur where order cost is equal to stock-holding cost, but this *can* be proved mathematically. If we accept this as fact, then we can say that the value of q which minimises total cost will be given by the equation

$$\text{Order cost} = \text{stock-holding cost, or } \frac{40\,000}{q} = \frac{q}{4}.$$

Solving this equation (some of the intermediate steps are left out, but you can check the algebra for yourself) we get $q^2 = 160\,000$, or $q = 400$, which agrees with our graphical solution. So the best policy will be to order 400 frames at a time. From this we can calculate other useful things, such as the time between orders – two months – or the fact that there will be six orders placed every year.

We can repeat this argument using letters to represent arbitrary values of the various contributory costs, instead of the specific values 200 items demanded per month, order cost £2, and so on. This in fact gives a well-known formula which is often referred to as the Economic Batch Quantity (EBQ) or Economic Order Quantity (EOQ) formula. By this stage in the book you are probably well aware of the author's attitude to formulae, and certainly I would say that the present case is no exception to the rule that it is a good deal safer to work from scratch using the figures concerned than substitute blindly – and possibly wrongly! – into a formula. However, as this one is very widely used, it *is* interesting to see how it is obtained.

Suppose there is a demand for a quantity D of some commodity per month (or week, or year – the time periods involved need not concern us). Suppose also that the cost of placing an order for the items is C, and that the cost of holding one item in stock for a month is H, both C and H being expressed in the same units. Then there will be D/q orders placed per month, at a cost of $C \times D/q$ or CD/q per month altogether, while the stock-holding cost will be the average stock, $\frac{1}{2}q$, multiplied by H, giving $\frac{1}{2}qH$. Using the fact demonstrated above, that total cost will be a minimum when order cost is equal to stock-holding cost, we may say that the best value of q will be the solution of the equation

$$\frac{CD}{q} = \frac{qH}{2}$$

which can be solved (again, you should supply the intermediate steps) to give

$$q = \sqrt{\frac{2CD}{H}}$$

and this, with various alternative notations, is the EBQ formula. It is easy to see from this result that increases in holding costs will result in a smaller quantity being the most economical, while increases in ordering costs will mean that it is preferable to order larger quantities at a time – all of which accords with common sense.

It is worth noting that if you know some calculus, the EBQ formula can also be arrived at by minimising the total inventory cost

$$T = \frac{CD}{q} + \frac{qH}{2}$$

with respect to q.

The table of ordering, stock-holding and total costs drawn up above is very well suited to computation using a spreadsheet. You will find an Excel worksheet for the table, together with the associated graph, stored as INV.XLS on the Companion Website. The figures in this worksheet can be overwritten for solution of other inventory problems, and you will find it helps your understanding of the method to play around with the figures and watch the corresponding changes on the graph.

Quick check questions

1 A retailer sells 1600 of a particular item per year. If the items are ordered in batches of n items at a time, how many orders will need to be placed in a year?

2 The stock policy of the retailer in question 1 is to order a batch, use the items up at a steady rate, then order another batch. If items cost 2p per calendar month to keep in stock, what will be the stock-holding cost over a year, in £?

3 Orders of the items in question 1 cost £12 per delivery, irrespective of order size. Use the information given in questions 1 and 2, and the EBQ formula given above, to determine the size of order which will minimise costs.

Answers:
1 1600/n orders.
2 $0.5n \times 0.02 \times 12$ or £0.12n.
3 Using annual figures, we have C = £12, D = 1600, H = 0.24, so

$$q = \sqrt{\frac{2 \times 12 \times 1600}{0.24}} = 400$$

Thus 400 items at a time should be ordered, giving four orders per year, or an order every three months.

Eliminating some assumptions

The easiest of our simplifying assumptions to get rid of is the one concerning instant replenishment of stocks. If instead of obtaining immediate delivery when they reorder, our picture-framers have discovered that they generally have to wait a week for the supplier to send the goods, then if they wish to avoid running out of stock they will have to allow for this in their reordering policy. In one week they will need 50 frames (if we take it that there are four weeks in a month) and so they should allow for the *lead time*, as it is known, of one week on deliveries by reordering when their stock falls, not to zero but to 50 items. This sort of policy is easily implemented in practice by, for instance, inserting a reorder reminder into a stack of goods on top of the 50th item from the bottom of the

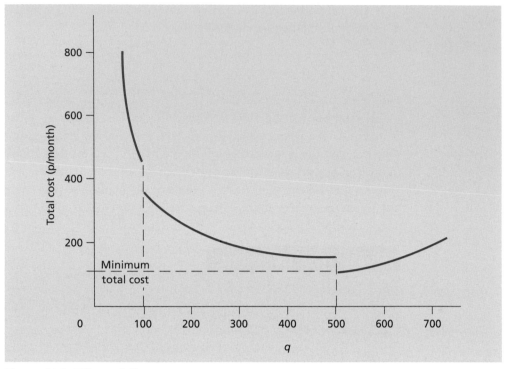

Figure 14.4 Effect of discounts

stack, so that on reaching that item the person in charge of issuing stock is alerted to the need to place an order.

Another popular method is the three-bin system where most of the stock is in a first 'bin', the 50 items needed during the lead time are in a second, and a certain amount of 'buffer stock' for emergency use in a third. When the first bin is empty, it is time to reorder. Of course, this requires careful attention to stock rotation.

It is also fairly easy to see the effect on our 'best' solution of discounts offered by a supplier for larger orders. If the supplier of picture frames offers, say, a certain discount on orders for more than 100 items, and an even larger discount for orders for 500 items or more, it could be more economical to order 500 at a time, as can be seen by looking at Figure 14.4. In such a situation the best policy is most easily seen from a graph, and to apply the EBQ formula blindly could result in quite the wrong policy being chosen.

Making and using

You may recall from the information given in the first section of this chapter that the wooden picture frames used by the Williams's business are not purchased ready-made from the supplier, but are made-to-measure from the lengths of framing. The control of stocks of this type of frame, therefore, constitutes a rather different problem from the one we have just looked at. If we imagine that John wants to spend a few days from time to time making these frames down to the finishing stage, rather than making them one at a time when the demand arises, then we have a situation where, instead of the stocks

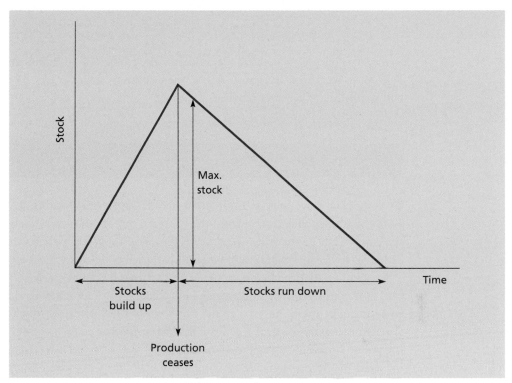

Figure 14.5 Stock cycle in a 'making and using' situation

suddenly increasing sharply when a delivery is received, they will build up gradually over the period when he is making them. At the same time, some of the ones he has just made may be sold immediately, so that he will never actually have the entire quantity that he has made in stock at one time. All this results in a stock cycle which looks like Figure 14.5.

To find out what effect this modification to the stock cycle has on the solution, we need some figures to work with. Let us suppose that John can produce frames at a rate of 15 per day, and that a demand for them exists at the rate of 5 per day. The costs associated with producing a batch of frames (equivalent to the ordering costs in the previous case) have been calculated at £3, and because the frames are more fragile than the metal ones the cost of storing them is much greater – say, 5p per frame per day.

If we take the stock-holding cost first, then in order to find the average stock held we need to know what is the maximum amount ever held in stock at one time. If John decides to produce a batch of q frames at once, it will take him $q/15$ days to make them (e.g. 45 frames would take 3 days). But during those $q/15$ days, there would also be a demand for 5 frames per day, so during this 'producing' part of the cycle $5 \times q/15$, or $q/3$, frames altogether would be used up; so the most that will ever be in stock will be $2q/3$. Thus the average stock held is a half of this, which is $q/3$. The stock-holding cost will therefore be $5 \times q/3$ pence per day.

As for the production costs, the batch of q frames will last $q/5$ days, so if we average out the £3 cost associated with producing a batch of frames over this period we have a cost per day of $£3/(q/5) = 300/(q/5)$ pence $= 1500/q$ pence per day.

From here on the solution proceeds in exactly the same way as for our earlier problem with the minimum total cost again being reached when ordering cost (or, in this case, the cost of setting up production of a batch) is equal to stock-holding cost. At this point,

$$\frac{1500}{q} = \frac{5q}{3}, \text{ which gives } q^2 = \frac{1500 \times 3}{5} = 900,$$

so $q = 30$. This means that John should produce a batch of 30 frames at a time, taking two days to do so. These 30 frames will be used up in six days, so that he will wait four days before producing another batch.

Allowing stock-outs

Up to now we have been assuming that the Williamses have unlimited space in which to store the frames they receive from the supplier, but of course in practice this may not be the case. What happens if, when we recommend the 'best' policy worked out earlier of ordering 400 ready-made frames at a time, they reply 'But we have room for only 350'?

In such a situation, it may actually be worthwhile deliberately allowing stock to run out, thus causing a stock cycle which looks like Figure 14.6. Of course, there will be some costs associated with the part of the cycle where they are out of stock – owing to loss of goodwill when customers' orders are held up and other such factors – but whether or not the policy is worthwhile will depend on how these *stock-out costs* relate to the other costs involved in the problem. What is happening is that while there is no stock, orders are building up, so that when new stocks eventually arrive some of them – the amount q_2 in Figure 14.6 – are sent out immediately to fulfil this backlog of orders. Thus the greatest quantity which actually has to be stored at one time is only q_1 and not the entire batch q.

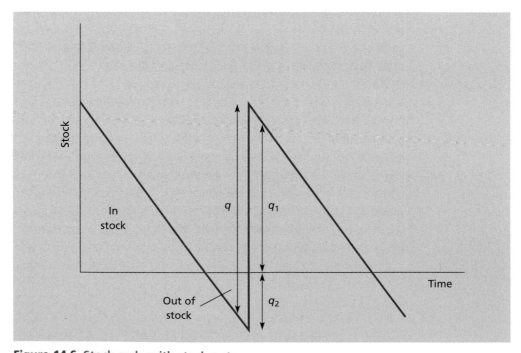

Figure 14.6 Stock cycle with stock-outs

To examine this problem in complete generality is complicated, firstly because we no longer have only two contributions to the total cost – the stock-out cost now also contributes – and so we do not get the simple result order cost = stock-holding cost for minimum total cost. Second, and a more serious blow to our previous method of solution, there are now not two but *three* variable quantities in the problem – the total cost T is related both to q_1 and to q_2. So we certainly cannot resort to drawing a graph any more – unless a three-dimensional one!

What we will do here, rather than solve the general problem, is compare certain specific policies involving stock-outs. As we have been told that only 350 frames can be stored, we will take as our *Policy 1* the case where the batch size ordered is reduced to 350 frames, and no stock-outs arise. In this case with a demand, as before, for 200 frames per month, we will need to order rather more often than every two months – in fact, there will be 200/350 orders per month, at a cost of £2 an order as already stated. The ordering cost will therefore be (200/350) × 200, or (4000/35) pence per month.

The maximum stock now held at one time is 350, so that the average stock will be half of this, costing $\frac{1}{2}$p per month each to store; thus the stock-holding cost is (350/2) × $\frac{1}{2}$, or $87\frac{1}{2}$p a month. To find the total cost of operating Policy 1, we add this to the order cost already worked out:

$$\text{Total cost of Policy 1} = \frac{4000}{35} + 87.5$$

$$= 202\text{p per month approximately.}$$

Policy 2 attempts to overcome the limited amount of storage space in a different way. Rather than reduce the size of the orders to the amount which can be stored, we advise continuing to order 400 frames at a time, but allow stock-outs in such a way as to ensure that no more than 350 frames ever need to be stored at one time. What will occur is easily seen by referring to Figure 14.6. During the 'out-of-stock' part of the cycle, orders to the amount of 50 frames are allowed to accumulate, so that when the new delivery of 400 frames eventually arrives, 50 of them will be needed straight away to satisfy this accumulated demand, and only the remaining 350 will need to be stored.

What effect will this have on our total cost? The order cost will, of course, decrease, since we are now placing larger orders at less frequent intervals; it will in fact be (200/400) × 200 or 100 pence per month. Stock-holding costs will also be reduced, since although our maximum stock held is still 350 frames, as it was under Policy 1, there is now a period of the cycle when we do not *have* any stocks, and so do not incur any stock-holding costs (i.e. if we ignore things such as rent and rates on warehouses which have to be paid whether they are full or empty). We take this into account by saying that the average stock held is 350 × $\frac{1}{2}$ or 175 frames, at a cost of $\frac{1}{2}$p per frame per month, but held for only $\frac{7}{8}$ of the cycle. You can see why the fraction is $\frac{7}{8}$ by looking at Figure 14.6. We therefore have a stock-holding cost of

$$175 \times \frac{1}{2} \times \frac{7}{8} = 76.5\text{p per month approximately.}$$

Finally, there is a third contribution to the total cost from the costs of being out of stock. If we suppose that John Williams has estimated the cost of being out of stock at 5p per frame per month, then we can work out what this will contribute to the total cost in much the same way as we have found the stock-holding cost. The average amount by which stocks run out is half of the maximum stock-out, which means $\frac{1}{2} \times 50$ or 25 frames; each costs 5p per month, but the out-of-stock situation actually arises for only $\frac{1}{8}$ of the cycle, so that the stock-out cost altogether will be $25 \times 5 \times \frac{1}{8}$ or about $15\frac{1}{2}$ pence.

Policy 2 therefore has a total cost of $15.5 + 76.5 + 100 = 192$ pence per month, as opposed to the 202 pence per month for Policy 1; so in this case it would be slightly cheaper to run out of stock by 50 frames, rather than reduce the size of orders. In another case, where the balance between the various components of the total cost was different, we might come to a different conclusion. There is no easy way of deciding in advance which policy would be best, other than to work out the total cost of each.

Quick check questions

1 Why does the graph of the stock cycle in Figure 14.2 involve vertical components where q increases suddenly, while that in Figure 14.5 has a more gradual upward slope?

2 Look back at question 3 of the 'Quick check questions' on p. 359. What will be the total annual cost of the policy of ordering 400 items at a time?

3 Now using the data provided in the earlier questions, find the total cost if 500 items rather than 400 were ordered at a time. What do you notice?

Answers:
1 In a situation where replacement stock is being delivered in a single order, the stock will increase suddenly – hence the vertical segments in Figure 14.2. Where items are being manufactured and used at the same time, the build-up of stock will be more gradual, giving a graph like that in Figure 14.5.
2 When 400 items are ordered, the ordering cost per year is $£12 \times 1600/400 = £48$ per year. The stock-holding cost is $0.5 \times 400 \times 0.24 = £48$ per year also (why are the two costs equal?). So total cost of this policy is £96 per year.
3 If 500 items are ordered at a time, then ordering cost $= £12 \times 1600/500 = £38.40$, while stock-holding cost $= 0.5 \times 500 \times 0.24 = £60$ per year, giving a total cost of £98.40. So even though the order size has been increased by 100 items or 25 per cent, the total cost has only increased by £2.40, indicating the stability of the solution, or its lack of *sensitivity* to changes in the order size. This point is discussed further in the next section.

The effect of errors in estimates

You may have noticed that a good deal of 'supposing' has gone on in the preceding sections. We 'supposed' that the stock-holding costs had been worked out to be $\frac{1}{2}$p per frame per month, we 'supposed' that the charge for placing an order was £3, and so on. Now, in practice, some of these suppositions may well turn out to be wide of the mark. Certainly if we are planning a stock policy for the whole of next year, it is quite likely that the order cost *will not* stay put at £3, but will increase during the year. Similarly, the demand, which we need to know in order to solve the problem, will certainly vary and the same could well apply to all the other quantities required in the solution of the problem.

So a point that might justifiably worry John Williams when we present him with our recommendations as to his 'best' stock policy is: 'What happens if some of these figures change? Will just a small error in one of my cost estimates result in your so-called "best" policy being wildly wrong, giving me a lot of unnecessary expense? Or can I be fairly confident that, even if I do go somewhat astray in my estimates, the solution you have come up with will still be pretty close to the cheapest?'

From a practical point of view, we might agree with John that a *good* solution is one that is *stable* – that is, it stays near to the real 'best' solution even in the face of minor errors in some of the data which has gone into its calculation. Another way of putting this would be to say that the solution must not be too *sensitive* to minor errors in the data, and we will come across this idea of *sensitivity analysis*, as it is called, again in later chapters. In any problem where the solution relies heavily on data that may not be completely accurate, it is vital that we should have some idea whether such inaccuracies are going to be disastrous to our solution, or just have minor effects.

In this particular case, the easiest way of examining the results of an error in, say, one of the cost figures which appear in the solution, is to use the EBQ result found on p. 359. We have already seen that if all the demands and cost estimates for the problem on p. 360 are accepted, then the total cost will be at a minimum if 400 frames are ordered at a time. But now imagine that in fact the estimated cost of placing an order, £2, turns out to be an underestimate – that the cost in practice is £2.50. This is really, in percentage terms, quite a serious error; our original figure has been increased by 25 per cent. What will be the effect on the total cost?

To find out what the correct EBQ should have been, we will, for once, make use of the formula. We have $C = 250$ pence, and if we take it that all the other quantities were estimated correctly, then $D = 200$ and $H = 0.5$ pence. So

$$q = \sqrt{\frac{2 \times 250 \times 200}{0.5}}$$

which comes to about 447 frames, instead of our previous value of 400. This is certainly quite a difference, but the crucial question is: if we persist in ordering 400 at a time, not realising that in fact the 'best' policy in the changed circumstances would be to order 447, how serious an effect will our error have on our total costs?

To answer this question, we need to work out the costs of the two policies. If we carry on ordering 400 at a time, the order cost will be $(200/400) \times 250 = 125$ pence per month, while the stock-holding cost will still be 100 pence per month, as we worked out earlier. So the total cost will be 225 pence per month.

If we were, as we should be, now ordering 447 in a batch, then the ordering cost would only be $(200/447) \times 250 = 112$ pence per month, but the stock-holding cost would increase to $1/2 \times 447 \times 1/2 = 112$ pence per month also – the two amounts are of course equal, because this is our 'best' solution now. So the minimum total cost would be $112 + 112 = 224$ pence per month. In other words, even though we have made a 25 per cent error in the estimate of the ordering cost, the error in the total cost – that is, the unnecessary extra cost we are incurring by sticking to our original 'best' policy – is only 1p per month, which percentage-wise over the total cost is less than 0.5 per cent.

You can check that this is not just a cooked-up example by trying out the effect of errors in the other quantities – the demand, for instance, or the stock-holding cost – on the solution. In all cases, you will find that the solution is not very *sensitive* at all. This relates to the fact that the total cost graph is pretty flat near to its minimum, as you can see by looking back at Figure 14.3. So we can reassure John Williams that even if he is slightly askew in his estimates of the data needed to get a solution, he can be fairly confident that he is not going to be paying out much more than he needs to pay.

Alternative approaches

As indicated at the start of this chapter, the method described in the preceding sections is not nearly so widely used as it once was, though the EBQ formula remains at the heart of some widely used stock control software.

A fundamental criticism of the EBQ method is that it militates against the flexibility that is increasingly crucial to the survival of companies in a competitive marketplace. Many world-class organisations now hold stock only for a matter of hours rather than days, weeks or months – the idea of 'just-in-time' manufacturing, mentioned in the opening section of the chapter, is exactly what it says: that parts, raw materials and so on should be delivered just in time to be used in the manufacturing process, and so should not go into long-term storage at all. This avoids waste, and prevents large amounts of capital being tied up in an unproductive way.

The moves towards manufacturing systems in which production is 'pulled' through the system by the demands of customers will render the EBQ idea still less relevant. Goods such as cars now incorporate so many optional extras that it is not economic to produce large numbers of models with each combination of features – and indeed some combinations may never be demanded by customers. Rather, when Mrs Lee orders a red GT model with electric windows, a heated driving seat and go-faster stripes, this sets in train a process whereby the necessary components are obtained from the supplier and assembled immediately. Of course, this method presupposes a very efficient system, otherwise Mrs Lee will have an unacceptably long wait for her car.

Yet another nail in the coffin of the EBQ approach is provided by the increasing numbers of products on the market that have a very short life cycle – sometimes less than a year. Consider the rate at which the mobile phone market has grown, for example, and the way in which ever-smaller models kept appearing: in this situation, concepts such as 'annual demand' become fairly meaningless, and certainly impossible to work out.

A further problem with the approach we have adopted is that it is totally deterministic – that is, it does not take into account any of the unpredictable elements that actually affect the control of stocks, such as erratic variations in demand, or variable delivery times from suppliers. If there are major unpredictable elements in the process, then a completely different approach, called *simulation*, is often used, as outlined in the next section.

Simulating an inventory process

Simulation offers a completely different approach to the modelling process. Instead of making a lot of simplifying assumptions about a situation in order to be able to build up an algebraic model (as we did earlier in this chapter), we aim at reproducing the complex random variations inherent in the real situation.

Just as with any other modelling process, we need to gather some data before we can start to set up a simulation. Suppose, for example, that John Williams wishes to simulate the rather unpredictable demand for a particular small size of picture frame, which is only sold in small quantities. By looking at sales records for this item over the past few months, he might find that weekly sales of this frame have been as follows: 8, 9, 7, 9, 6, 8, 11, 8, 9, 5 . . . This data can then be organised into a frequency table, of the kind we encountered in Chapter 3:

Number of frames sold	Number of weeks
5	2
6	5
7	8
8	11
9	10
10	8
11	5
12	1
Total	50

We can now calculate the probability of each level of demand, based on this data, very much as we did in Chapter 7. For example, the probability that five frames will be demanded in a week is 2/50 or 0.04 or 4 per cent; the probability of a demand for six frames in a week is 5/50 or 0.1 or 10 per cent, and so on. This gives us a set of probabilities as follows:

Number of frames sold	Probability
5	0.04 or 4%
6	0.1 or 10%
7	0.16 or 16%
8	0.22 or 22%
9	0.20 or 20%
10	0.16 or 16%
11	0.1 or 10%
12	0.02 or 2%
Total	1 or 100%

What we are now going to do is to use tables of random numbers to help us generate a series of weekly demands which are individually unpredictable, and yet, at the same time, will follow the established distribution. We have already had a brief encounter with random number tables in our Chapter 2 discussion of sampling methods. A page from a set of these tables is reproduced as Appendix 2. You can see, if you refer to that page, that the numbers are arranged in two-digit pairs, and although this is only done for ease of reading, it is very convenient for our present purposes. There are 100 possible two-digit pairs of this kind, running 01, 02, 03 . . . , and so on up to 98, 99, 00. We want to distribute these pairs in such a way that they mirror the behaviour of the demand distribution shown above.

Now there are eight possible levels of demand in this distribution, so we could assign the numbers 01 to 12 to represent the first of these levels (five frames per week), 13 to 24 to represent the second, and so on down to 85 to 96 representing the last; we would agree to ignore the leftover four numbers 97, 98, 99, 00. Then, if we chose a figure from the random number tables which turned out to be 16, we would say that this would correspond to a week when six frames were demanded.

But there is a defect in this system. We have assigned equal numbers of figures to each class, and since all the figures occur with equal frequency in the random number tables, overall we will end up with an equal probability for each level of demand – which is very far from being the case in practice. Our system of assigning the numbers to represent the demands has failed to reflect the *frequency* with which each level of demand occurs.

So what we need to do, rather than dividing up the numbers equally among the times, is to divide them up in proportion to the percentage of occasions on which each demand occurs. We therefore assign the numbers 01, 02, 03, 04 – that is, 4 per cent of the total set of numbers – to represent the occasions when five frames are demanded in a week, 05 to 14 to represent the weeks with a demand for six frames, and so on. With this arrangement, we have a 4 per cent chance, when we select a number from the random number tables, of obtaining one corresponding to a demand for five frames, a 10 per cent chance of selecting one which represents a demand for six frames, etc. – exactly as in the real-life situation.

Working in this way, we arrive at the complete distribution of the two-digit numbers as shown:

Number of frames sold	Corresponding numbers
5	01–04
6	05–14
7	15–30
8	31–52
9	53–72
10	73–88
11	89–98
12	99–00

We can check that we have allocated the numbers correctly by noting that we end up, correctly, at 00.

Thus far, all we have done is to reproduce the demand distribution using the paired digits. However, when this distribution is used in conjunction with a table of random numbers, it enables us to simulate a series of weekly demand figures which, while individually unpredictable, will in the long run reproduce the real-life pattern.

To see how this works, we will simulate the demand over ten weeks by using the random numbers in the third row of the table in Appendix 2, starting at the left-hand end: 32, 78, 14, 47, 01, 55, 10, 91, 83, 21. Referring to the table above, we can translate these into weekly demands for 8, 10, 6, 8, 5, 9, 6, 11, 10, and 7 frames.

These simulated demands can now be used to help John Williams examine the effect of various inventory policies. For example, suppose he has decided to order eight of these frames at the start of each week; that is, the weekly demand which occurs most frequently, so this seems a sensible policy. Any unsold stock from the previous week is carried forward. Suppose further that each frame sold generates £1.20 profit, and that each occasion on which a frame is requested but is not available costs the company 20p in lost goodwill. Then we could tabulate the financial impact of the simulated demands thus:

Week no.	Initial stock	Demand	Sales (£)	Profit	Lost sales	Cost	Final stock
1	8	8	8	9.60	0	0.00	0
2	8	10	8	9.60	2	0.40	0
3	8	6	6	7.20	0	0.00	2
4	10	8	8	9.60	0	0.00	2
5	10	5	5	6.00	0	0.00	5
6	13	9	9	10.80	0	0.00	4
7	12	6	6	7.20	0	0.00	6
8	14	11	11	13.20	0	0.00	3
9	11	10	10	12.00	0	0.00	1
10	9	7	7	8.40	0	0.00	2

(A table like this is easy to construct using Excel. Make sure that you can follow how the figures in the table were calculated.)

Over this period, you can see that there were few lost sales, but it looks as though the amount of stock may be building up. Of course, one would need to simulate a much longer period in order to get reliable information. The simulated data can then be used to examine the effect of different inventory policies; so we could generate a new table on the assumption that seven, rather than eight, frames are obtained at the start of each week; we could calculate the overall income from each policy; and so on. All of this can be done without any impact on the real situation, whereas carrying out such experiments in real life might have a disastrous impact on the firm's profitability.

Simulation is an approach to modelling which is very widely used in business, wherever there are situations of which the random aspect is an essential element. These include:

(i) queuing problems, which cover both physical queues of people (as at banks, supermarket checkouts, airport check-ins, etc.) and queues of objects (such as items waiting to be packed in a factory). The unpredictable elements here are the rate at which people or items join the queue, and the length of time taken to deal with them.

(ii) timetabling problems, such as scheduling appointments for a GP's surgery, or scheduling landing slots for aircraft. Unpredictable elements in the GP's case are the length of time taken by each consultation, and the possibility of missed appointments.

In practice, dedicated software is generally used to carry out simulations, though simple models can be carried out with Excel using its built-in facility to generate random numbers (see Exercise 8 at the end of the chapter). Computer simulation languages enable very large-scale simulation models to be constructed – for example, a simulation of the entire road network of a region in order to examine the impact of building a new bypass. Such simulations do not always use empirical probability distributions (distributions derived from real data, like the demand distribution used here) – very often they simulate values of variables using standard distributions such as the normal and Poisson.

One point worth noting, however, is that simulation does not provide the user with 'an answer' in the same way that, for example, the EBQ formula developed earlier in this chapter provides the 'best' order quantity. Simulation enables experimentation, and provides useful summary information about the results of that experimentation, such as the overall costs of various inventory policies; but it is up to the user to take this information and use it, together perhaps with other, non-numerical information, to reach a rational business decision.

EXERCISES

*Further examples on the work of this chapter can be found on the **Companion Website**.*

1 Complete the 'stock in hand' column of the following extract from the stock book of a do-it-yourself supplier, and use the information in the table to calculate the average weekly demand for the item concerned over the two weeks 4–16 March:

Item – wood screws ref. S101/3

Date	No. of boxes received from suppliers	No. of boxes sold to customers	Stock in hand (no. of boxes)
1 March	–	–	35
4 March	20	8	47
5 March	–	6	
6 March	–	7	
7 March	–	3	
8 March	–	9	
9 March	–	11	
11 March	40	5	
12 March	–	7	
13 March	–	7	
14 March	–	5	
15 March	–	10	
16 March	–	12	

2 Plot a graph to show the stock position of the firm in Exercise 1 over the period shown.

3 If the cost to this firm of raising an order is 50p, and the stock-holding cost is reckoned to be 5p per box per week, advise the firm as to its most economic order policy.

4 Should the storage space available for the boxes of screws become limited to 20 boxes, would the firm do better to reduce the size of its orders to 20 boxes also, or continue to order 30 and allow stock-outs? Assume the cost of being out of stock is 5p per box per week.

5 If typically two days elapse between placing an order with the supplier and receiving the boxes of screws, what modification would you make to the inventory policy discussed in Exercise 3 above?

6 A small electronics assembly company produces its goods in two stages: the interior electronics of the item are assembled first, and then inserted into a plastic casing, finished and packed. The interiors are produced on a batch basis, at a rate of 3000 items per day; the final stage goes on continuously, with 1000 items per day being completed. The cost of setting up a production run for the interiors is £200, while the cost of holding one interior in stock for one day is 0.2p. Over how many days should the production part of the cycle last to give the most economic policy?

7 Construct the distribution of two-digit numbers corresponding to the following:

Queuing time (minutes)	Percentage of customers
0	6
1	11
2	18
3	25
4	21
5	14
6	5

8 The spreadsheet SIM.XLS (available via the Companion Website) is an Excel simulation of the inventory problem which was simulated by hand in this chapter. Use the simulation to examine the impact of inventory policies which restock with 7, 8 or 9 frames at the start of each week. In each case simulate 100 weeks of operation of the policy; examine the average net weekly profit and the extent to which unsold stock is building up, and outline the recommendations you might make as a result of the simulation.

9 A sociological investigator wishes to interview a large number of unemployed persons, and is wondering how best to schedule the interviews. By keeping careful records over the first few days of interviewing, he finds that the times occupied by interviews are distributed as follows:

8 minutes	8 per cent of interviews
9 minutes	14 per cent of interviews
10 minutes	23 per cent of interviews
11 minutes	30 per cent of interviews
12 minutes	18 per cent of interviews
13 minutes	7 per cent of interviews

He schedules interviews at ten-minute intervals, but finds that only 40 per cent of interviewees arrive on time. Twenty per cent are one minute early and 12 per cent are two minutes early, while 16 per cent are one minute late and 12 per cent are two minutes late. Simulate a three-hour interviewing session, and suggest whether the ten-minute schedule will be adequate.

Note that this simulation will require you to generate two distributions, one for the lengths of the interviews and one for the arrival times of the interviewees. You may find it helpful to arrange your simulation under headings as shown below:

Interview due to start	Interviewee arrives	Interview starts	Interview lasts	Interview ends

10 A small electrical repair business at present employs just one skilled repair worker, who is having difficulty coping with the volume of work. The length of time taken by repairs is distributed as follows (rounded to the nearest 15 minutes):

Time for repair	Percentage of repairs
15 minutes	10
30 minutes	27
1 hour	35
2 hours	17
3 hours	11

The intervals between the arrivals of repair jobs are as shown:

Intervals between arrival of jobs (hours)	Percentage of occasions
1/4	25
1/2	30
1	20
2	15
3	10

By simulating an eight-hour working day, investigate whether the repair worker is justified in claiming that it is difficult to keep up with the volume of jobs.

Case Study

Is a single server best?

Many post offices, airline check-ins and other places where customers queue for service have introduced a 'single queue, multiple server' queuing model – that is, customers all join one queue, and then go to the next available service point. On the other hand, supermarket checkouts, garage forecourts, etc., operate a 'multiple queue, multiple server' model, where each service point has its own queue. Which of these is best? In this case we will use simulation to investigate the operation of a small sub-post office, with only two service points.

The distribution of service times for both points is as follows:

Time in minutes	% of occasions
1	5
2	11
3	35
4	28
5	14
6 or more	7

The arrival rate of customers follows the distribution below:

Time between arrivals (minutes)	% of occasions
1	12
2	19
3	29
4	22
5	10
6 or more	8

Either by using tables of random numbers, or by using Excel's random number generation facility, generate a series of 20 interarrival times and service times (treat the highest value in the distributions as 6). Use these to simulate the service process (a) assuming a single queue and (b) assuming that there are two queues and customers join whichever queue is shortest when they arrive. If both queues are the same length, then they select one randomly.

   Write a short report explaining the findings of your simulations, and the implications for queuing policy.

Further reading

If you would like to read more about modern inventory systems – a topic that is really the province of operations management rather than quantitative methods – you will find the topic well covered in the book *Operations Management*, by Slack *et al.*, of which details were given on p. 289.

Chapter 13 of Anderson, Sweeney and Williams (referenced on p. 350) covers inventory models.

Chapter 15

FORECASTING:
TIME-SERIES, SEMI-LOG GRAPHS AND EXPONENTIAL SMOOTHING

Chapter prerequisites Before starting work on this chapter make sure you are happy with the basic ideas of graph plotting (Chapter 1, pp. 25–8).

Learning outcomes By the end of your work on this chapter you should be able to:

1. recognise situations in which a semi-log graph might suitably be used to obtain forecasts, and plot and interpret such graphs;

2. recognise and define components which may be present in a time-series;

3. recognise a situation in which a moving average could be used to isolate the trend of a time-series, and calculate a moving average of suitable period;

4. distinguish, by examining the graph of a time-series, when an additive or percentage-based approach to seasonal variations would be more suitable, and calculate the variations according to the method selected;

5. make use of your analysis of a time-series to obtain a forecast, and be aware of the considerations to be borne in mind when assessing the likely accuracy of such a forecast;

6. recognise situations in which exponential smoothing would be a suitable forecasting method;

7. carry out exponential smoothing calculations;

8. suggest a suitable value of the smoothing constant for a given set of data;

9. use the mean square error as a measure of the quality of forecasts.

Quantitative methods in practice

Career interview: sales forecasting

by Kona Macphee

At Drury House on the banks of the Thames, Helen Thompson works for Sainsbury's as a Sales Forecasting Manager. Trained in maths and statistics, she uses a variety of tools and techniques to predict what customers will be buying in Sainsbury's vast network of shops.

. . .

Helen was soon promoted to Senior Statistician, and was promoted again to Forecasting Manager nine months before our interview. She said that a variety of sales forecasts need to be produced during the year. 'Twice-yearly forecasts are produced for each of our four hundred stores, projecting weekly sales for around a year out. Each store's forecast is based on its own history, using its own data. There's *lots* of data! Our forecasts are used by other areas of the business, such as logistics, finance and retail, to plan ahead and so need to be reasonably accurate, but of course they can never be one hundred percent correct.'

Source: http://plus.maths.org

I chose this quote to start the chapter for two reasons. First, it makes very clear the important role that forecasting – using quantitative techniques – plays in planning the operations of a business as large as Sainsbury's; and second, it gives an excellent summary in simple terms of the way that short-term forecasting works, and of its shortcomings.

The first point is perhaps not too surprising. After all, we saw in the previous chapter that goods need to be ordered in the right quantities, and at the right times, if the shelves are to be kept replenished. That has, as the Sales Forecasting Manager indicates, implications for budgeting – goods need to be paid for; for logistics – products have to be delivered from warehouses, or directly from suppliers, to the stores; and ultimately for the long-term financial health of the company.

The second point is worth looking at in a bit more detail. Helen Thompson talks about 'projecting weekly sales . . . each store's forecast is based on its own history, using its own data'. In other words, this kind of forecasting is about projecting into the future the patterns and trends which have been seen in the recent past. She also says, 'forecasts . . . need to be reasonably accurate, but of course they can never be one hundred percent correct'. So we are aiming to get forecasts of future sales patterns which are sufficiently accurate to be useful – certainly better than using 'gut feel' or 'managerial instinct', but which will always be subject to some unpredictable variation.

Many of the techniques used for this kind of forecasting are not mathematically complex (if you read the rest of the interview with Ms Thompson on the website you will find that she says much the same thing). We are going to examine several methods in this chapter, none of which requires more than ordinary arithmetical calculations. However, it is important to realise that we are talking here about *short-term* forecasting – for 'around a year out' as the interview says. Long-term forecasts, for things like economic variables, require different approaches, often based on the kind of regression models we studied earlier, but such applications are beyond the scope of this book.

The airline manager's problem

In Chapter 14 we saw how regression could be used to forecast from a linear growth pattern. However, there are many situations in which fitting a line will not tell us the whole story, and forecasting on the basis of such a fit might actually be downright misleading.

Consider, for example, the case of an airline which wishes to forecast demand for its flights over the four quarters of next year. If we have, say, four or five years' data on which to base our conclusions, we might well be able to see a linear trend in the figures, and we could fit a line by regression methods just as described in Chapter 14.

But what if the airline is expanding so rapidly that the trend is not a straight line, but some other kind of curve? What if the airline deals with many flights to holiday destinations, so that it is concerned not only to know the average amount by which demand for its flights is rising or falling in the long term – which might be done by fitting a straight line – but also how much higher demand is in summer than in winter? What if there are other flights – perhaps to capital city destinations – for which demand does not show any particular seasonal behaviour, but moves up and down in a fairly haphazard sort of way?

None of these situations can be tackled by the methods of Chapter 14, and yet accurate forecasts will obviously be very important to a firm such as our airline. In this chapter we look at three further methods of forecasting which go some way towards coping with such problems.

Forecasting: when can we do it?

At first sight, any attempt at forecasting – whether the quantity in question is demand for airline flights, population of a country, unemployment levels, sales of breakfast cereal or whatever variable you care to name – seems a fairly doubtful exercise. We cannot see into the future, so how can we possibly know what economic, political and social factors may affect a variable over the next four months, four years or forty years?

However, a little thought suggests that there is a big difference between trying to forecast sales of breakfast cereal or demand for holiday flights on the one hand and unemployment levels or population on the other. The difference rests on two facts:

1 For things such as sales of cereal, we are likely to be interested mainly in short-term forecasts – a supermarket manager might like to know how much cereal he can expect to sell in the next week or month, but will probably not need to plan much further ahead than one year. For quantities such as population, on the other hand, forecasts for years or even decades ahead are needed, in order that governments can plan aspects of policy such as healthcare, education and services for the elderly. So there is a distinction here between short-term and long-term forecasting.

2 With a quantity such as the demand for flights to holiday destinations, there is likely to be a well-established pattern over time which is not going to change drastically in the short term. Most people tend to take their main holiday during the summer months (for reasons related to the weather, timing of school vacations, and so on), and it is unlikely that their behaviour will suddenly change. But a variable such as

unemployment rate is influenced in a complex way by many economic and political issues, and thus will not follow a predictable pattern – indeed, in today's global economy, events on the other side of the world can have a significant impact on a country's employment patterns, as the redundancies in the Western European airline industry after 11 September 2001 demonstrated only too clearly.

It follows that short-term forecasting of quantities which follow some regular pattern, for which there is a clear reason, is a much easier process than long-term forecasting of less predictable variables or those which exhibit a more complex behaviour. In this chapter, we will confine our discussion to three types of short-term pattern:

1 steady percentage rates of growth;
2 short-term seasonal patterns;
3 random variations around an established level.

Forecasting a steady percentage growth

Consider an item whose price is being increased by a constant 10 per cent per annum. If the item costs £1 in 2005, then its price over the next five years will be as follows:

2005	100p
2006	110p
2007	121p
2008	133.1p = 133p approx.
2009	146.41p = 146p approx.
2010	161.051p = 161p approx.

Although the *rate* of increase is a steady 10 per cent per year, the *amounts* of the increase are larger each year, and the same would apply no matter what the rate of increase we assume. (This, as we will see in Chapter 16, is the basic principle of compound interest.) So if the prices were plotted against time on a graph, the result would be a curve which climbs more and more steeply as time goes on, as you can see in Figure 15.1.

It is not easy to continue the line of this curve in order to obtain a forecast of the price of the item in 2011. Of course, in the present example that does not matter too much, since we know the percentage rate of increase is 10 per cent per year, and so we could go ahead and calculate the price in 2011 without reference to the graph. But now suppose we have a situation where we *suspect* a steady, or approximately steady, percentage rate of increase, but do not know exactly what that rate is. How, then, could we first confirm our suspicion and then obtain a reasonably accurate forecast?

As we have just seen, plotting the figures on an ordinary graph will not be much help, since it is practically impossible to distinguish by eye a curve showing a steady percentage growth from any other type of curve. If, however, we could somehow arrange a type of graph in which steady growth, and no other kind of increase, gave a straight line, we would be in a much more hopeful position, straight lines being, as we know, really the only shape of graph which can be recognised with certainty.

At the mention of the word 'logarithm' you may blench; perhaps you thought that logarithms had been rendered obsolete by the advent of calculators. But don't worry –

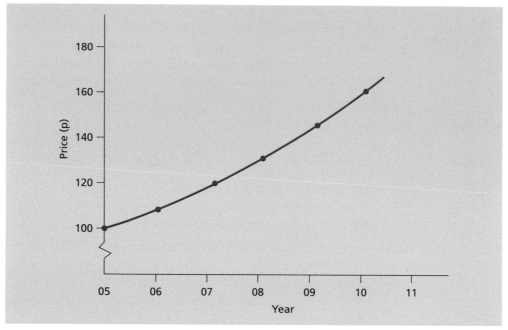

Figure 15.1 Steady 10 per cent growth

you don't need to remember anything about them to understand what follows, and even if you have never used them you should not have any problem following the argument.

If, then, we take the logarithms of the prices of the item mentioned above, whose cost is going up by 10 per cent a year, the result is as follows:

Year	Price (p)	Logarithm of price	Increase in logarithm
2005	100	2.0000	–
2006	110	2.0414	0.0414
2007	121	2.0828	0.0414
2008	133	2.1239	0.0411
2009	146	2.1644	0.0405
2010	161	2.2068	0.0424

(You can check this using a calculator with a log key, or the LOG function in Excel.)

So apparently when the price increases by a constant *percentage* each year, the logarithm of the price increases by a constant *amount* (the slight variations above are caused by a rounding off of the prices). For those of you who remember something about logarithms, the reason for this is that a rate of increase of 10 per cent per year corresponds to multiplication of the previous year's price by 110 per cent, and as multiplication of numbers means addition of their logs, we are simply adding the log of 110/100 each year.

Thus, if the logs of the prices were to be plotted on a graph, the result would be a straight line, rising by equal amounts as it does each year. The prospect of plotting such a graph is not, however, very appealing, since it would involve first looking up the logs, then plotting nasty four-figure decimals, which would be difficult to do accurately.

Fortunately, it is possible to plot such a graph without going to so much trouble, by using Excel. Start by plotting the graph in the usual way: enter your y- and x-values into two adjacent columns of the spreadsheet, making sure that the *y*-values are to the left of the *x*s. Then highlight the two columns, click on the Insert tab and then on 'scatter' in the Charts group. You will see various formats illustrated; select the version where both the points and the lines joining them are shown. This will give you a graph, which at this point will have normal *linear* scales – that is, equal intervals on the graph correspond to equal increments in the corresponding variable.

Now focus on the vertical axis and right-click. In the resulting dialogue box, click on 'Format axis'. Now check the 'Logarithmic scale' box and then click on 'close'. You should find that the graph which results looks something like the one in Figure 15.2. Instead of equal distances on the vertical axis representing equal amounts of increase in the price, they represent equal *factors* of increase – thus the distances from 10 to 100 and from 100 to 1000 are equal, since they both represent an increase by a factor of 10. This kind of scale is called *logarithmic*, and has the consequence that the line showing the prices which increase at a constant rate is now straight.

Incidentally, the reason why we must ensure that the vertical scale of the original graph doesn't start at zero is that the logarithm of zero does not exist – so if you try to change to a log scale when the axis includes zero (or any negative values) you will simply get an error message.

This type of graph, where the vertical axis has a log scale but the horizontal axis, representing time, has a normal linear scale, is sometimes called a semi-log graph. We can therefore say that data which gives a straight line when plotted in semi-log format

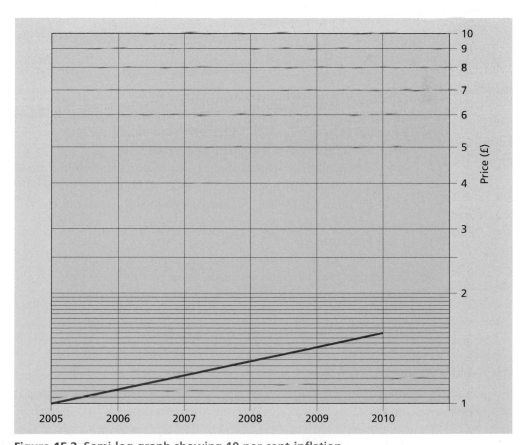

Figure 15.2 Semi-log graph showing 10 per cent inflation

represents a steady rate of increase or decrease, depending on whether the graph has a positive or negative slope.

Special graph-paper is also available which enables such graphs to be plotted by hand, but this is not much used now that software makes computer plotting so much easier.

More uses for semi-log graphs

The great strength of this type of graph is that it enables us to recognise whether a times-series of figures exhibits an approximately steady rate of increase, simply by plotting the data on a semi-log graph and seeing if it is an approximate straight line. If it is, then, without working out just *what* the rate of increase may be, we can obtain a forecast by continuing the straight line with a ruler.

For example, suppose that our old acquaintance Mr Newton has the following data relating to sales of a new line of fruit pies during the first few months on the market:

Month	Sales volume (100s of pies)
May	50
June	54
July	57
August	61
September	66
October	70

If he wants to check that sales are increasing at a steady rate, all he need do is plot them on a graph like that in Figure 15.3 and see that a straight line fits them well. Then, to get a forecast of sales volume in December, he continues the line for two more time periods and reads off the figure of approximately 8000 sold.

Of course, all the warnings about extrapolation sounded in the section on calculating the regression line also apply here. The sales of this product are not going to go on climbing at the same rate for ever. Sooner or later they will level off, and at that stage the semi-log graph will cease to be a straight line. Until that happens, however, it is very useful as a tool for planning.

Semi-log graphs can also be used to compare two or more rates of change. This is particularly useful if the figures involved are of very different sizes. For example, suppose the turnovers of two competing firms, one large and one small, are as follows:

Year	Megalithic (£ millions)	Minimal (£000s)
2005	2.4	80
2006	2.7	92
2007	2.95	106
2008	3.28	122
2009	3.64	140

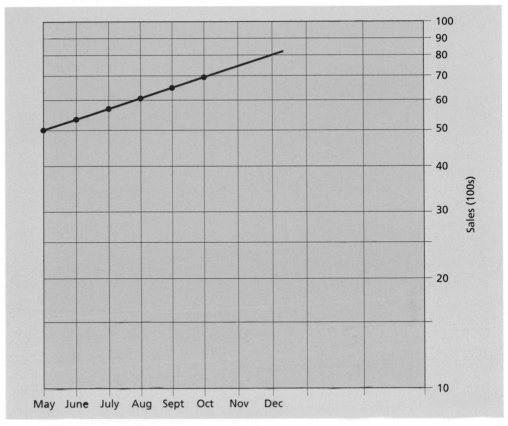

Figure 15.3 Semi-log graph for sales forecast

The fact that Megalithic's turnover is in millions of pounds, whereas Minimal's is only in thousands, makes direct comparison difficult, and plotting the two sets of figures on a single ordinary-scale graph would be awkward, since a scale which could accommodate Megalithic's figures would show Minimal's only in a very compressed form (see Figure 15.4(a)). If, on the other hand, a semi-log graph like Figure 15.4(b) is constructed, not only are the two sets of figures easy to accommodate but it becomes clear that, in spite of its smaller size, Minimal is actually expanding at a more rapid rate.

If we need to find the actual *rates* of expansion, the easiest way is simply to calculate the percentage change from year to year for each firm. This shows a rate of expansion of about 11 per cent a year for Megalithic and 15 per cent a year for Minimal:

Year	Megalithic	Minimal
2006	$\dfrac{2.7}{2.4} \times 100 = 112.5\%$	$\dfrac{92}{80} \times 100 = 115\%$
2007	$\dfrac{2.95}{2.7} \times 100 = 109.2\%$	$\dfrac{106}{92} \times 100 = 115\%$
2008	111%	115%
2009	111%	114.8%

You will find that logarithmic scales are quite often used in government-published statistics, not necessarily because a straight line graph results, but simply because a very

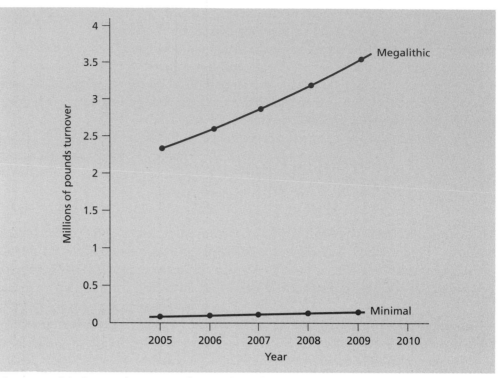

Figure 15.4(a) Comparing rates of growth: ordinary scales

wide range of figures have to be accommodated. Watch out for this kind of use, and do not fall into the trap of misinterpreting the graph because you have not noticed the scale!

Quick check questions

1 On a logarithmic scale, which of the following distances would be equal: (a) the distances from 1 to 10 and from 10 to 100; (b) the distances from 0 to 10 and from 10 to 100; (c) the distances from 2 to 4 and from 4 to 6; (d) the distances from 2 to 4 and from 4 to 8?

2 Which of the following sets of data, both of which represent sales of a product over a five-year period, would give a straight line when plotted on a logarithmic scale?

(a) 20, 40, 60, 80, 100   (b) 20, 22, 24.2, 26.62, 29.28

3 Data for the annual profits of a company which gives a straight line sloping downwards when plotted on a semi-log graph shows (a) a decreasing rate of growth; (b) a constant rate of decrease; (c) that the company is making losses?

Answers:
1 (a) and (d) -- in each case the ratio of the two pairs of values is the same.
2 The second set of data would give a straight line on a log scale, since the sales increase by a steady 10 per cent each year.
3 The correct answer is (b) – any straight line on a log scale shows a steady rate of change; if the slope of the line is negative, then the change is a decrease.

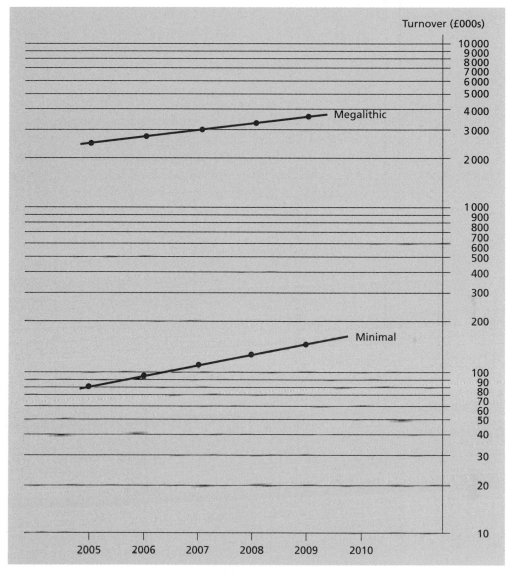

Figure 15.4(b) Comparing rates of growth: semi-log scale

Forecasting from a short-term pattern

Mr Newton, our friend from Chapter 12, finds that sales of fruit pies tend to be higher in winter, when customers feel the need for more substantial puddings than in summer. Accordingly, the sales of such products show quite a marked pattern of fluctuation from season to season. This pattern is particularly noticeable if the sales figures are plotted on a graph.

For one particular variety of pie, sales records broken down by quarters are as shown:

Year	Quarter	Number sold (00s)
2008	Spring	142
	Summer	54
	Autumn	162
	Winter	206
2009	Spring	130
	Summer	50
	Autumn	174
	Winter	198
2010	Spring	126
	Summer	42
	Autumn	162
	Winter	186

We have already considered the graphs of such data briefly in Chapter 3, where we decided that the appropriate way to join the points of the graph is by straight lines, which bring out the pattern of the data. Figure 15.5 shows the graph of the time-series above, and reveals the pattern we might have expected to find given the information about low summer sales.

But a closer examination of the graph tells us more than this. The most obvious feature is that, although the ups and downs from one quarter to the next tend to obscure the fact to some extent, there is a definite downward movement apparent when the figures are

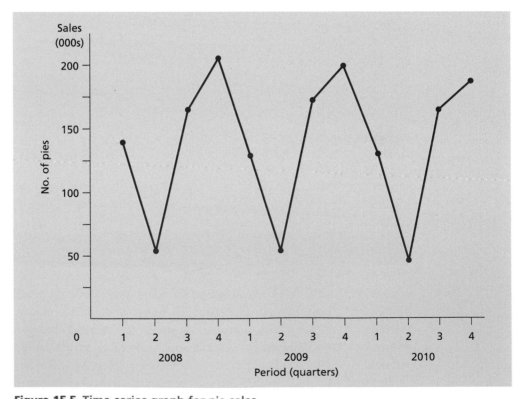

Figure 15.5 Time-series graph for pie sales

considered overall. This general downward – or upward, or steady – behaviour of the figures is called their *trend*.

Superimposed on the trend is, of course, the seasonal behaviour already noted, which repeats itself in a regular way from year to year. Variations of this kind in a time series, which repeat themselves regularly over a fairly short term – less than a year, generally speaking – are called *seasonal variations*, though the name is perhaps unfortunate, as the pattern may repeat itself over a period much shorter than a year. The takings of a super-market, for example, will probably show a 'seasonal' pattern which repeats from one week to the next – higher on Friday and Saturday, lower perhaps on Monday and Wednesday, average on the remaining two days. It is the repeating and predictable pattern which is important in deciding what we may call a 'seasonal' variation.

The seasonal pattern in Figure 15.5 does *not*, however, continue entirely undisturbed; sales for the autumn quarter of 2008 do not pick up to the same extent as those for 2009 and 2010. This variation of the pattern is probably due to some *random* effect, such as sudden competition from a rival product. Other sources of random variation, in general, might be government intervention in an industry, a strike by workers or a shortage of raw materials. Such variations are, of their very nature, unpredictable and may completely upset a carefully calculated forecast.

Conventionally, a fourth type of variation, called *cyclical*, is believed to influence many time-series. This is a tendency, only apparent when the figures for quite a long period of time are examined, for an alternation of upward and downward movements to appear, roughly connected with periods of expansion and contraction in the economy. Although these cycles are a well-established fact in certain industries, in most circumstances it is not easy to establish their existence, let alone allow for them in forecasts. In any case, as they are a long-term phenomenon and we are only going to be making short-term forecasts, neglecting them should not lead to any serious errors. So we will simply regard them, if they exist at all in a particular case, as being included with the random variations. The term 'residual variations' is often used to refer to the combination of cyclical and random variations.

Extracting the trend

The two components of the time-series which we can hope to identify and predict for the future are, then, the trend and the seasonal variation. We will look at the trend first and will begin with a slightly smaller set of figures than the sales data above, and one that does not have the added complication of the large random variation noticed in the sales figure for the autumn quarter of 2004.

If you were simply presented with the data we are going to use as follows:

$$170, 140, 230, 176, 152, 233, 182, 161, 242$$

with no explanation as to what it represents or what the time periods involved are, your first step might well be to plot the figures on a graph (labelling the horizontal axis 'Period 1', 'Period 2', etc.) which would bring out clearly the fact you may already have noticed when examining the figures that there is a marked pattern which repeats itself every three periods. The data may be taken to refer to the takings in some suitable units of a filling station during the three periods 8–12 noon, 12–4 p.m. and 4–8 p.m. over three days, with a tendency for higher takings during the morning and evening rush-hours than in the quieter midday period.

If we wish to start by extracting the trend of the figures, there are several ways we might go about it. If the trend on the graph appears to be reasonably close to a straight line, we could try fitting a regression line to the points. If it seems to be some sort of recognisable curve, then we could do worse than sketch it in by eye. But there is one well-established method for extracting the trend from a set of data like this with a strong repeating pattern, based on the following idea. One period of the data tends to be somewhat higher than average – in this case, the evening period. The afternoon period is lower than average, and the morning period is somewhere in between. If we take an average over three periods at a time, then the higher-than-average and lower-than-average figures should, roughly speaking, cancel each other, leaving an average for the three periods which is somewhere in between. This smoothing out of the 'seasonal' ups and downs is, of course, just what we require of a trend.

We *could* just take one average for each day's takings, which would give us the figures shown below:

				Average
Day 1	Morning	170		
	Afternoon	140		540/3 = 180
	Evening	230		
Day 2	Morning	176		
	Afternoon	152		561/3 = 187
	Evening	233		
Day 3	Morning	182		
	Afternoon	161		585/3 = 195
	Evening	242		

Notice that the average for each day has been placed opposite the mid-point of that day – the afternoon period.

This is all very well, but ideally we need a trend figure for *every* period, not just the afternoons, so that we have a basis for comparison from which we can say things like 'The morning of day 2 was so many units higher than average'. We can fill in the gaps in the set of averages above if we use not just one average for each day, but what is called a *moving average*. The idea is very simple: we begin by working out the first average as shown in the calculation above – that is, the average for the morning, afternoon and evening of day 1. But as soon as the figure for the morning of day 2 becomes available, we work out a *new* average which is obtained from the afternoon and evening of day 1 and the morning of day 2: $(140 + 230 + 176)/3 = 546/3 = 182$. And we continue in this way through the set of figures, so the next average would be $(230 + 176 + 152)/3 = 186$, and so on, always using the three most up-to-date figures.

Thus at each stage we are taking the average of a morning, an afternoon and an evening figure, but not always in that order. There is a quick way of doing this which may already have struck you, too. The first average was 180. To get the next one we dropped the 170 from the morning of day 1, and added the 176 from the morning of day 2. The total will therefore go up by 6, and the average (when we divide by 3) by 2; so the next average should be 182, as indeed it is. (The only trouble with this method is that, if you make a mistake near the beginning of the column, it will affect all the subsequent figures, so it is as well to check at least the last average by straightforward addition and division.)

When this process is completed we have the set of moving averages shown below, which will provide our estimate of the trend of the data. Notice the gaps opposite the first and last figures of the actual data; these are inevitable, for unless we have data for day 0 and day 4, there is no way of calculating the averages at those points in time.

		Actual	*Moving average = Trend*
Day 1	M	170	
	A	140	180
	E	230	182
Day 2	M	176	186
	A	152	187
	E	233	189
Day 3	M	182	192
	A	161	195
	E	242	

If you look at Figure 15.6 you can see how well this method of calculating the trend smooths out the peaks and troughs in the original data. The trend line is reasonably straight, too, certainly towards the later periods, so that continuing it to obtain some kind of forecast for the next few periods would not be too risky a process.

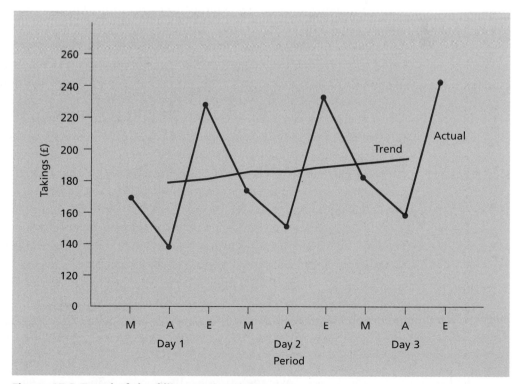

Figure 15.6 Trend of the filling station data

But the trend alone will not give us a very good forecast, since we have already seen that individual periods vary considerably around it. We need, therefore, to analyse the 'seasonal' fluctuations as well, in order to make allowance for them in our forecasts.

Analysing the seasonal variations

As a preliminary step towards finding the seasonal variation for each of our three daily periods, we find out how much each period differs from the trend. In other words, we calculate Actual minus Trend for each period (except, of course, the first and last where we do not have a trend figure). The resulting figures are as follows:

		Actual – Trend
Day 1	M	–
	A	–40
	E	48
Day 2	M	–10
	A	–35
	E	44
Day 3	M	–10
	A	–34
	E	–

If the process were not subject to any random influences, then we would expect the Actual – Trend figures for, say, all the afternoon periods to be the same. But because there *are* random effects at work, they are not quite the same, though they *are* similar in size and sign (–40, –35 and –34). The same applies to the evening figures of 48 and 44; as it happens, in this case the morning figures actually are the same, both being –10. Although of course we only have a small set of data here, and in practice one would need to use far more, you can already see the beginning of a regular pattern of signs in these Actual – Trend figures (morning and afternoon negative, evening positive). This reflects the pattern we observed in the original data, and if when you reach this stage in the analysis of a time-series you find that more than a couple of figures fail to conform to this sign pattern you should rethink your calculations carefully – it may be that you have made an arithmetical error, or perhaps you have picked the wrong number of periods over which to average in the first place.

In order to eliminate as far as possible the random effects, what we do next is collect together the Actual – Trend figure corresponding to each period of the day and thus find out what the average variation is for each period:

	M	*A*	*E*
Day 1	–	–40	48
Day 2	–10	–35	44
Day 3	–10	–34	–
Total	–20	–109	92
Average	–10	–36	46

In the averaging, we had to divide the middle total by 3, since three afternoon figures were available, but the morning and afternoon totals are for only two figures, so need only be divided by 2. Notice, too, that the middle average should really be 36.33, but to avoid fractions it has been rounded to 36. This makes the total of the average variations $-10 - 36 + 46 = 0$, which is what we would expect if the trend really does pass 'through the middle' of the figures: variations above and below the trend cancel out. If by any chance this total differs slightly from zero, judicious rounding of the averages will usually adjust it sufficiently, as it has here. If the total is *very* different from zero, however, it may be another warning sign of faulty arithmetic or a bad choice of moving average.

We call the figures −10, −36 and 46 the *seasonal variations* for the morning, afternoon and evening periods. So we have now achieved our objective of isolating the trend and seasonal effects present in the time-series. A knowledge of these seasonal effects is useful not only in forecasting, but in removing strong seasonal effects which may obscure other important movements in a set of data; see, for example, the government's 'de-seasonalised' unemployment figures.

Calculating random variations

Although a knowledge of the random variations is of no use in forecasting, these variations being essentially unpredictable, it is useful as a guide to the reliability of a forecast; a process on which, in the past, the random influences have been very small is likely to produce a reasonably reliable forecast. If, however, the time-series is habitually subject to large random fluctuations, then our carefully calculated forecast may be completely upset by such a fluctuation.

So our final step in analysing the series, prior to obtaining a forecast, is to extract the random variations from the figures. Now a random variation is anything which is not accounted for either by trend or by seasonal effects. So we start by working out what the figures would have been, if the trend and seasonal effects had operated in the absence of random influences. For the afternoon of day 1, we had a trend figure of 180; afternoons tend, however, to be 36 lower, on the whole, than the trend, which would reduce our figure to 144. What *actually* occurred was a value of 140, so some random effect reduced what we might have expected to occur by four units. We therefore say that the random variation in this period was −4.

Proceeding in a similar way with the rest of the figures, we find the following:

Actual	140	230	176	152	233	182	161
Expected (trend + seasonal)	144	228	176	151	235	182	159
Random (actual − expected)	−4	2	0	1	−2	0	2

So the random variations here are very small, the largest, −4, being only 4/180 or about 2 per cent of the corresponding trend figure. In other words, any forecast obtained from this analysis may be expected to be reasonably reliable. The data fits the 'pattern' of trend + seasonal variation pretty well.

Getting a forecast

You may have lost sight in all this arithmetic of what we originally set out to do – obtain a forecast for a few periods into the future. Suppose we specifically require a forecast of the figure for the afternoon of day 4. It will consist of two parts:

Forecast = trend for afternoon of day 4 + 'seasonal' adjustment for afternoon period.

How we extend the trend for a day beyond our original data depends very much on what it looks like when plotted on a graph. Had it shown a pronounced curve, we might do better by continuing the curve approximately and simply reading off the figure for the afternoon of day 4 from the graph; this would then have to be reduced by 36, the typical amount by which the afternoon period falls below the trend.

In the present case, however, inspection of the trend figures shows that, between the afternoon of day 1 and the afternoon of day 3, the trend here rose from 180 to 195. That is, during a lapse of six time periods (*not* seven – it is the gaps we need to count), the trend has increased by 15. So on average, the increase has been 2.5 units per period, and we will assume that this rate is going to continue to apply, at least over the next few periods. This gives 197.5 as the trend figure for the evening of day 3, 200 for the morning of day 4, and 202.5 for the afternoon of day 4. When adjusted downwards by the seasonal variation of 36, this produces a final forecast of 166.5, or 167 to the nearest unit, and inspection of the actual data shows that at least this is a credible figure, fitting in as it does with the general pattern.

Naturally, the further ahead we are forecasting, the less reliable will our forecasts be, based as they are upon the assumption that present trends will continue. But for a few periods ahead this assumption should be reasonably safe. As a rough rule of thumb, this method could be used to give figures for about one seasonal cycle ahead – for example, three periods in the case of the above data – with reasonable confidence.

Other patterns of variation

The seasonal variations in the example given in the previous section were analysed by regarding them simply as a constant amount added to or subtracted from the trend. Inspection of the graph of the original data (Figure 15.6) shows that this is a reasonable assumption, since the seasonal peaks and troughs are indeed of roughly constant size.

It is quite conceivable, however – in fact, in many ways it is more likely in practice – that seasonal variations will *not* be constant, but will themselves vary as the trend increases or decreases, the seasonal peak above a high trend value being greater than that above a low one. Such a situation is illustrated in Figure 15.7, where it is clear that the peaks and troughs are becoming less pronounced as the value of the trend declines. In this case it is probable that, rather than the seasonal variations being constant *amounts added* to the trend, they are constant *percentages multiplying* the trend. For this reason,

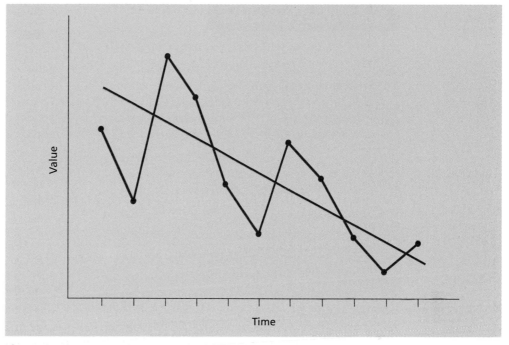

Figure 15.7 A multiplicative pattern of seasonal variations

the type of situation shown in Figure 15.7 is often referred to as a *multiplicative model* time-series, that in Figure 15.6 and the corresponding analysis being known as an *additive model series*.

The only way to decide to which, if either, of these patterns a set of real-life data conforms, is to plot it on a graph and examine the seasonal variations. If this appears to be inconclusive, analysing the series by both methods and inspecting the resulting random variations may help. Remember that the smaller the random variations, the more closely the series conforms to the chosen pattern.

The actual analysis of a multiplicative model series does not differ greatly from that of the additive model discussed in the earlier section on analysing the seasonal variations, except that the seasonal variations are expressed as percentages of the trend figure for the period rather than as simple *differences* between actual and trend. Rather than go into the details of the analysis here I will guide those who need it through the process in Exercise 4 at the end of the chapter.

Another problem which may have occurred to you is how we might decide what moving average to use in a case which was less cut and dried than the ones we have looked at – as most real-life examples would tend to be. One possibility is to try calculating several different moving averages, using perhaps three, four and five periods at a time, and choose the one which appears to 'smooth' the ups and downs of the data best. However, if it is really so difficult to decide what you should be doing because of the absence of any noticeable pattern in the data, it may be that the moving average method is not the best way of trying to get a forecast, and you should have resort either to a freehand graph or to another technique, such as *exponential smoothing*, described later in this chapter.

Quick check questions

1 How many periods would you use in a moving average to smooth the following sets of data? Would you need to centre the average?

(a) Numbers of complaints received per day by a hotel
(b) Monthly takings of a local newsagent
(c) Daily output of a product by a factory which works Monday–Friday
(d) The series 12, 20, 25, 4, 14, 19, 26, 6, 15, 23, 27, 7

2 You would use a multiplicative time-series model when (a) seasonal figures differ by a constant amount from the trend, or (b) seasonal figures are a constant proportion of the trend?

3 A friend says 'I can't see the point of calculating these random variations – after all, if they're random, there's no knowing what the next one might be'. How would you convince her that calculating random variations is a useful exercise?

Answers:
1 (a) 7, because we may expect a seven-day cycle. An odd number of periods means the average does not need centring. (b) 12, since there may be an annual cycle to the monthly data. Needs centring. (c) 5, given the five-day week; does not need centring. (d) This series shows a four-period cycle (sketch the graph if you can't see this from the figures) so use a four-period average, which will need centring.
2 (b) – the multiplicative method looks at seasonal variations as a proportion.
3 The random variations can tell us a number of useful things: if they are large, the model isn't a very good fit, and any forecasts will be unpredictable; and if they show some kind of pattern, then there is periodic behaviour in the data which has not been picked up – perhaps because the wrong number of periods has been used for the moving average.

Forecasting the pie sales figures

Now that we have set up all the machinery for analysing a time-series with a definite repeating seasonal pattern, let us go back to the data on pie sales mentioned earlier in this chapter and carry out a complete analysis and forecast, using the additive model.

Figure 15.6 shows the series to be of the additive pattern, since the summer 'low' and winter 'high' are roughly constant deviations from the trend, even though the trend itself is declining. The appropriate number of periods for the moving average is clearly four, and so the first moving average figure would be calculated as

$$\frac{142 + 54 + 162 + 206}{4} = 141.$$

When we come to write this figure down, however, we have a slight problem. It obviously belongs in the middle of the first year – but the middle of the first year comes half-way in between the summer and autumn quarters; the same thing will occur with all the other moving averages too. This means that they are not directly comparable with the original figures, which is a nuisance when it comes to calculating the seasonal variations. So we have to insert an additional step, called *centring* the moving averages. Since the moving average 141 applies to a point half-way between the summer and autumn quarters of 2008, while the figure 138 applies midway between the autumn and winter quarters, we can obtain a moving average directly comparable with the autumn quarter by taking the mean of 141 and 138 – that is, 139.5. It is these *centred moving averages* which will represent the trend in this case and, of course, a similar procedure will be needed whenever we average over an even number of periods.

First we calculate the trend and the quarterly variations for each quarter:

Quarter	Actual	Moving average	Centred moving average (trend)	Actual minus trend
1.00	142.00			
2.00	54.00			
3.00	162.00	141.00	139.50	22.50
4.00	206.00	138.00	137.50	68.50
1.00	130.00	137.00	138.50	−8.50
2.00	50.00	140.00	139.00	−89.00
3.00	174.00	138.00	137.50	36.50
4.00	198.00	137.00	136.00	62.00
1.00	126.00	135.00	133.50	−7.50
2.00	42.00	132.00	130.50	−88.50
3.00	162.00	129.00		
4.00	186.00			

Next we average the quarterly variations and round them so that they sum to zero:

	Spring	Summer	Autumn	Winter
2008	–	–	22.5	68.5
2009	−8.5	−89.0	36.5	62.0
2010	−7.5	−88.5	–	–
Total	−16	−177.5	59	130.5
Average	−8	−88.75	29.5	65.25
Rounded so as to add to zero	−8	−88	30	66

We can then complete the table thus:

Quarter	Actual	Moving average	Centred moving average (trend)	Actual minus trend	Expected (trend in quarterly variation as calculated above)	Random (actual minus expected)
1.00	142.00					
2.00	54.00					
3.00	162.00	141.00	139.50	22.50	169.5	−7.5
4.00	206.00	138.00	137.50	68.50	203.5	2.5
1.00	130.00	137.00	138.50	−8.50	130.5	−0.5
2.00	50.00	140.00	139.00	−89.00	51	−1.0
3.00	174.00	138.00	137.50	36.50	167.5	6.5
4.00	198.00	137.00	136.00	62.00	202	−4.0
1.00	126.00	135.00	133.50	−7.50	125.5	0.5
2.00	42.00	132.00	130.50	−88.50	42.5	−0.5
3.00	162.00	129.00				
4.00	186.00					

The greatest random variation is thus 7.5, which is only about 5 per cent of the corresponding trend value of 139.5, so the data fits our model pretty well, and would in fact be an even better fit if it were not slightly distorted by the presence of the exceptionally low figure of 162 for autumn 2008.

This 'odd' figure has caused the slight ups and downs apparent when the trend is plotted on Figure 15.8. From summer 2009, however, there has been a steady downward trend. In making a forecast from this trend, we adopt a slightly different approach from that used in the earlier section on analysing the seasonal variations, since there is no steady decrease evident from one period to another. We say that over the time from summer 2009 to the latest trend figure available – summer 2010 – the trend declined from 139 to 130.5; that is, over four quarters or one year its decrease was 8.5. Now in spring 2010 the trend value was 133.5, so if we assume that the annual decrease of 8.5 is going to persist at least for a while then we would expect the trend in spring 2011 to be 133.5 − 8.5, or 125. We must adjust this to allow for the fact that the spring quarter is, on average, 8 below trend, giving a final forecast of 125 − 8 = 117 for spring 2011.

How reliable is this figure likely to be? The method we have used to obtain it is based on the assumption that the trend and the seasonal pattern will persist – an assumption which clearly becomes less likely to be valid the further ahead we forecast. However, the small random variations evident here suggest that in the short term the forecasts should be quite close to what actually occurs.

You may feel that all this is a great deal of work to arrive at a figure which, when all is said and done, can be little more than a hopeful approximation to what will actually happen. But the forecasts are not the only use of our analysis. The knowledge of seasonal variations in particular can be a very useful tool of control for the sales manager. In the

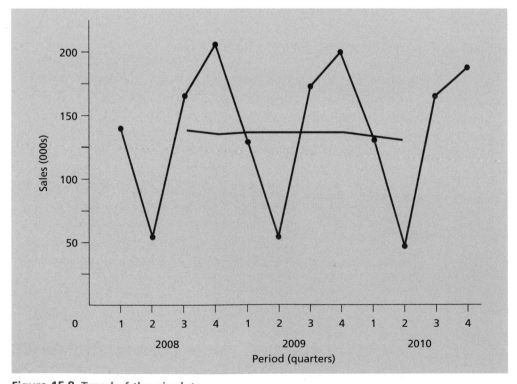

Figure 15.8 Trend of the pie data

absence of such knowledge, he might feel suicidal when the sales figure drops from 142 in spring 2008 to only 54 in summer 2008, not realising that this is a well-established yearly event. Equally, he might feel he could rest on his laurels when the figure leaps up to 206 in winter of that year, in blissful ignorance of the fact that this is only a temporary, seasonal reversal of a dangerous downward trend in the sales of his product which, to project our trend to its ultimate point, will become negative by about 2019.

Forecasting in an unpredictable situation

The two methods we have looked at so far for obtaining short-term forecasts have both depended on certain features being evident in the recent data on which our forecast is to be based. In the case of semi-log graphs, we needed to have a roughly steady rate of increase in the data, while to use time-series analysis, there had to be a repeating pattern of seasonal variations so that we could decide what moving average to use.

There are, however, many cases which do not conform to either of these patterns. Consider, for example, the following sales figures for another of our pie-producer's products, a high-quality cheese tart, which are given weekly over an eight-week period:

Week no.	Sales (hundreds of kilograms weight)
1	45
2	40
3	38
4	46
5	46
6	42
7	36
8	41

You can see that here there is no obvious trend, no short-term pattern – in fact the best we can say is that the sales hover around the 4200 mark, making unpredictable excursions to either side of this figure but not by very large amounts. Either of our previous methods is useless, and yet it is perfectly reasonable to ask how one might try to get a useful forecast of week 9 sales in week 8.

The method developed for use in such circumstances is very much in accordance with what you might do faced with this situation and armed only with your intuition. Suppose you, in the position of the sales manager of this company, were trying to make a forecast of week 2 sales at the point in time where all you know is that week 1 sales were 4500. In the absence of any other information, your best guess would have to be that the sales will stay the same; so your week 2 forecast would be 4500 also. The position so far is therefore:

Week no.	Actual sales	Forecast
1	4500	–
2	4000	4500

You now wait until the actual sales figures for week 2 come in. These were, as we know from the table above, only 4000, so your forecast of 4500 has turned out to be 500 too high. Now most people's reaction to this would be to say, 'Ah, I overestimated last week, so this time I will compensate for that overestimate in making my forecast, and therefore reduce it somewhat from last week's level of 4500.'

However, to compensate by the entire error you made last time – 500 in this case – is a little drastic; if you do that, you will end up with every week's forecast being merely the previous week's actual sales. Instead, what we do is allow for a *proportion* of the error we made last time. Expressed formally what we are saying is that

New forecast = old forecast + proportion of error

or

New forecast = old forecast + $\alpha \times$ (old actual – old forecast),

where the Greek letter α (alpha) is used to represent the proportion of error we allow for. Of course, the choice of a value of α to use is very important, and we will look later at criteria for making this choice. For the time being, we choose fairly arbitrarily to use $\alpha = 0.3$; that is, we are allowing for 30 per cent of the error. Our week 3 forecast will then be

$$4500(\text{week 2 forecast}) + 0.3 \times (4000 - 4500) = 4500 - 0.3 \times 500 = 4350.$$

So the effect of this method of reaching the forecast is that, having overestimated on our last forecast by 500, we reduce the next one somewhat, but not by the full 500 – only by 30 per cent of it.

As usual there is no need to go into this detail once you have the idea of the method. The best way to lay out the calculation is in a table, as follows:

Week no.	Actual	Forecast	Error (actual – forecast)	$\alpha \times$ error
1	4500	–	–	–
2	4000	4500	–500	–150
3	3800	4350	–550	–165
4	4600	4185	415	124.5
5	4600	4309.5	290.5	87.2
6	4200	4396.7	–196.7	–59
7	3600	4337.7	–737.7	–221.3
8	4100	4116.4	–16.4	–4.92
9	–	4111.4		

There are a number of points to note here. Whenever our last forecast was too high, the next one should be lower; whenever it was too low, the next one should be higher.

Remembering this should make sure you get the signs the right way around: the error is always Actual – Forecast. Another point on which newcomers to the technique are often confused is that the correction – the '$\alpha \times$ error' term – is always added to the last forecast, not to the actual figure. Finally, as you will discover when you try to follow through the steps of the construction of this table for yourself, decimal places proliferate at an alarming rate in this type of calculation, and you should round off to just a couple more figures than were in the original data to keep things under control.

The method of forecasting we have developed here is known as *exponential smoothing*, and the constant α is called the *smoothing constant*. The 'smoothing' part of this name is easy to understand, as a glance at the forecasts above will show – they are smoother than the actual figures, in the sense that they do not fluctuate by such large amounts. The 'exponential' bit is not quite so obvious; I will explain it here for those who are interested, but do not worry if you do not follow all the details of the argument.

We write A_t to denote the Actual figure in period t, and similarly F_t, E_t, for that period's Forecast and Error. We then use A_{t-1}, A_{t-2}, and so on to denote the figures from one period back, two periods back, etc. Thus we can express the rule for obtaining a forecast in the form

$$F_t = F_{t-1} + \alpha(A_{t-1} - F_{t-1}) = \alpha A_{t-1} + (1 - \alpha)F_{t-1}.$$

However, since $F_{t-1} = \alpha A_{t-2} + (1 - \alpha)F_{t-2}$, we can substitute this to get

$$F = \alpha A_{t-1} + (1 - \alpha)[\alpha A_{t-2} + (1 - \alpha)F_{t-2}]$$
$$= \alpha[A_{t-1} + (1 - \alpha)A_{t-2}] + (1 - \alpha)^2 F_{t-2}.$$

You may like to do the next step, replacing F_{t-2} by $A_{t-3} + (1 - \alpha)F_{t-3}$ and rearranging to get

$$F_t = \alpha[A_{t-1} + (1 - \alpha)A_{t-2} + (1 - \alpha)^2 A_{t-3}] + (1 - \alpha)F_{t-3}.$$

If we carry on like this, we find that all previous Actual values of the data are included in the forecast for time period t, but multiplied by higher powers of $(1 - \alpha)$ the further back we go. Since we are using an α between 0 and 1, $1 - \alpha$ will also be between 0 and 1, and so its powers get smaller and smaller (e.g. with $\alpha = 0.3$, $\alpha^2 = 0.09$, $\alpha^3 = 0.027$, and so on).

The upshot of all this (and this is the part you should remember even if the previous discussion has left you behind) is that the importance, or *weight*, given to old Actual data gets smaller and smaller the older the data gets. This, of course, is entirely sensible – up-to-date figures are surely more relevant, and should be given a bigger importance, than more out-of-date ones. The weights actually get exponentially smaller (they behave like powers of $(1 - \alpha)$), and it is from this that the technique gets the other half of its name. You can also see from this that the smaller the value of α, the greater the weight given to older data, since the weights decrease like powers of $(1 - \alpha)$. We will be coming back to this point later.

You will also find this method referred to in some books as *exponentially weighted moving averages*, which ties it in with the last method we looked at. In the 'ordinary' moving average over, say, four quarters, each of the last four quarters' data is given a 'weight' of $\frac{1}{4}$, while anything before then is completely ignored. So in some respects the present method is an improvement.

We still have to consider under what circumstances this method would be a suitable one to use, but before we address that question in the next section, you should try working through the exponential smoothing process described above using a value of α equal to 0.1, to make sure you have the basic idea clear.

Features of exponential smoothing

We began our discussion of this method with a set of data which varied apparently in a random way around a steady value – there was no trend and no apparent 'seasonal' pattern to the variations. The forecasts obtained by exponential smoothing with $\alpha = 0.3$ were certainly smoother than the actual data, and this smoothness is often a desirable feature in a set of forecasts. In the present case, by passing more or less through the 'middle' of the data, the forecasts ensure that overestimates in one week will be compensated by underestimates in another (though this is, perhaps, not very reassuring in the case of a highly perishable product where stocks not needed in one week cannot be carried forward to the next).

If you have performed the calculations with $\alpha = 0.1$ you will notice that the forecasts are even smoother. But we do not always want forecasts to exhibit this kind of smoothness. Suppose, for example, that owing to a health scare about unpasteurised cheese, there is a sudden drop in the market for our product, so that sales are reduced to exactly 2000 in each of weeks 9, 10 and 11.

If you continue the series of forecasts started above, you should find that the forecasts for these three weeks would be, using our two values of 0.3 and 0.1, as shown:

Week no.	Actual	$\alpha = 0.3$	$\alpha = 0.1$
9	2000	4111.4	4300.6
10	2000	3478.0	4070.5
11	2000	3034.6	3863.5
12	–	2724.2	3677.2

You can see that at this rate it will take the $\alpha = 0.1$ a lot longer to catch up with the drop in sales than the $\alpha = 0.3$ forecast – though even that is not brilliant. This is because with a higher value of α, as explained in the last section, old data is given less weight, and therefore the new, changed situation carries proportionately more importance. The two extremes are, of course, $\alpha = 1$ where the next forecast is simply the last period's Actual figure, and $\alpha = 0$ where our initial forecast will never change at all. It seems, therefore, that in a situation where sudden changes of this kind are the norm, a higher value of α might be preferable.

Now imagine that later in the year, sales pick up again in such a way that a steady trend appears – say the sales for weeks 22–26 are 2200, 2400, 2600, 2800, 3000. How will each of our values respond to this new factor? For simplicity we will assume that in each case we start with a totally accurate forecast.

Again, you should verify for yourself that the position will be:

Week no.	Actual	$\alpha = 0.3$	$\alpha = 0.1$
22	2200	2200	2200
23	2400	2200	2200
24	2600	2260	2220
25	2800	2362	2258
26	3000	2493.4	2312.2

It is easy to see here that in both cases the forecasts are falling further and further behind the actual figures. It looks as if exponential smoothing, at least in this form, is not a suitable method to use when there is evidence of a trend in the actual figures.

You may be feeling that we are taking a rather piecemeal approach to the connected questions (a) what kind of situations can exponential smoothing cope with and (b) what are 'good' values of α to use in given circumstances? Would it not be better to establish a definite criterion for deciding when an α-value is 'good'?

This criterion is provided by the *mean square error* (MSE), which is calculated in a way which may remind you of the standard deviation. We have already defined the error at any point in our forecasting exercise as Actual – Forecast. We find the mean square error at that point by squaring all the errors up to and including the present one, and dividing by the number of periods we have included in the adding-up process. For example, using weeks 22–26 and the $\alpha = 0.3$ forecasts worked out above:

Week	Actual	Forecast	Error	0.3 × error	Error²	MSE
22	2200	2200	0	0	0	0
23	2400	2200	200	60	40 000	20 000
24	2600	2260	340	102	115 600	51 867
25	2800	2362	438	131.4	191 844	86 861
26	3000	2493.4	506.6	152.0	256 643.56	120 817.5

Here the week 24 MSE is arrived at by taking $(0 + 40\ 000 + 115\ 600)/3$, and similarly for the others. You can see how the MSE confirms what, in this case, we had already noted – that the forecasts get worse as time goes on. The sign of good forecasts would be an MSE that stabilises as the forecasting proceeds. Roughly speaking it has been found that α values of between 0.1 and 0.3 generally perform best.

One final point: when starting our forecasting process in the present example, we chose to wait for a week and then use the first week's sales as the forecast for week 2. An alternative method of getting started is to use some *ad hoc* method to get a forecast for week 1 – perhaps by looking at advance orders, or by asking the salesforce to give estimates based on their experience – and begin the forecasting process in the first week instead.

Software for forecasting

People who are seriously interested in forecasting tend to use software specifically designed for that purpose, but general-purpose packages such as Excel can also help. In fact both the decomposition method and exponential smoothing are well suited to spreadsheet implementation, since both involve repetitive calculations which can easily be carried out by copying suitable formulae down the necessary number of rows of the spreadsheet. Moreover, in exponential smoothing different values of α can be tried very quickly simply by changing the contents of one cell.

As an example, you will find a spreadsheet for the analysis of the fruit pie sales data stored under the name TS.XLS on the Companion Website, and another which analyses the cheese tart sales via exponential smoothing stored as ES.XLS. Explanatory notes about the contents of the cells are given with each spreadsheet; you should examine the various formulae carefully and ensure you follow what is going on. You can then modify the spreadsheets to tackle the exercises below.

Excel in particular provides methods for adding trendlines to plotted data series, and for computing moving averages (the latter is part of the Analysis Tools add-in). If you wish to learn more about these features, the easiest way is simply to enter some data of a suitable kind and then experiment with the commands using HELP if necessary to guide you, or to consult the MyMathLab Excel guide.

The story continues . . .

You will have realised by now that exponential smoothing requires a good deal of tedious arithmetic – not difficult to carry out, but perhaps difficult to carry out accurately. It is, of course, an ideal candidate for computer implementation, and indeed there are many packages available which not only do the basic forecasting and enable the user to try different α-values, but give the MSE and often incorporate more sophisticated versions of the method. Forecasting is a very large subject, and the simple methods we have looked at are merely a selection from an extensive range. However, if you have cause to use a package based on more advanced techniques, the work of this and the previous chapter should enable you to do so in an informed way.

At the start of this chapter we looked at the work of the Sales Forecasting Manager for Sainsbury's. We have now examined a number of methods which would help her to analyse different types of data, and to produce forecasts based on this analysis. However, forecasting is always going to be a complex and risky matter; the development of new forecasting models is an ongoing area of research, and it may well be that some of those currently being developed will be of assistance to Sainsbury's in the future.

EXERCISES

*Further examples on the work of this chapter can be found on the **Companion Website**.*

You can also use the website to access the data for most of these exercises.

1 Sketch (do not plot accurately) a graph to represent the following data, which shows the daily record of numbers of defective items produced by a factory. Use a suitable moving average (centred if necessary) to smooth the series, and plot the moving averages to confirm that they do indeed smooth the peaks and troughs of the data. Why do you think the observed pattern might occur?

Day	Defectives
M	32
T	27
W	30
Th	38
F	48
M	31
T	28
W	29
Th	35
F	50
M	34
T	25
W	31
Th	40
F	47

2 Sales of a particular type of babyfood at one branch of a chain of chemists' shops have been as follows over the past 12 months:

Month no.	Sales (packs)	Month no.	Sales (packs)
1	117	10	109
2	115	11	112
3	110	12	116
4	123	13	114
5	120	14	120
6	116	15	115
7	114	16	115
8	119	17	111
9	119	18	118

(a) Carry out exponential smoothing on this data using $\alpha = 0.3$, and thus obtain a forecast for month 19.

(b) At the end of month 18 there is a scare about possible contamination of this type of baby-food, and sales plummet to only 57 packs in month 19. They gradually recover, with sales of 78, 84 and 95 packs over months 20–22. Extend your exponential smoothing table to cover months 19–22, and comment on the results.

3 Use Excel to plot the following data using a log scale for the vertical axis. What do you notice and why?

Period	1	2	3	4	5	6
Series 1	0.01	0.1	1	10	100	1000
Series 2	1	2	4	8	16	32

4 Plot the following figures on a graph and confirm that they appear to fit the 'multiplicative' model of a time-series:

$$22, 70, 40, 121, 196, 85, 220, 322, 130.$$

Calculate a three-period moving average in the usual way, and complete the analysis of the series by filling in columns under the following headings:

Moving average (trend)	Actual minus trend	(Actual minus trend) as % of trend

Hence confirm that the seasonal variations for the three periods are roughly 3 per cent above trend, 50 per cent above trend and 49 per cent below trend.

Can you see why the seasonal variations in this model total about 300 per cent?

Also confirm by carrying out the ordinary 'additive' analysis that the additive model is not a good fit to the data, as it leads to very large random variations.

5 The following figures show the numbers of new car registrations in Great Britain (in thousands) on a monthly basis for the years 2008–10:

$\rightarrow$

Month	2008	2009	2010
January	158.4	108.8	138.9
February	67.8	52.8	65.2
March	449.0	310.7	393.4
April	173.4	132.0	145.3
May	176.5	132.9	150.6
June	206.6	173.1	190.8
July	151.1	154.7	133.6
August	62.5	65.3	53.7
September	328.6	364.9	331.8
October	127.5	166.5	130.1
November	101.2	156.5	139.0
December	109.5	150.1	123.9

Source: UK National Statistics Hub at http://www.statistics.gov.uk/hub/index.html

(a) Plot a time-series graph of this data and comment on the seasonal pattern you observe. Can you suggest reasons for your observations? Does the graph appear to suggest an additive or a multiplicative model?

(b) What is the appropriate number of periods to include in a moving average to find the trend of this data?

(c) Calculate the trend, and the monthly variations, using both additive and multiplicative models.

(d) Which model do you think will give the more accurate forecasts?

(e) Why is the model calculated here not appropriate to today's situation?

6 The figures below show the weekly demand at an electrical repair workshop for a certain type of connector over a ten-week period:

Week no.	1	2	3	4	5	6	7	8	9	10
No. demanded	27	23	23	25	26	29	25	21	22	24

(a) Use exponential smoothing with α-values of 0.2, 0.3 and 0.4 to smooth the data and obtain a forecast for week 11.

(b) Using the MSE criterion, which value of α gives the best results?

7 More published statistics! Lots of the data in the *Monthly Digest* are given quarterly, and some of these sets of data are suitable for analysis by moving average methods (e.g. domestic gas or electricity consumption, production of home-grown cereals, passenger movements into the UK). Choose such a set of data and analyse it by the moving average method, rounding the figures if necessary to simplify calculations. Try to compare a forecast given by your analysis with what happened to the real figure at the same period. (You may be surprised to find that numbers of live births have a strongly seasonal behaviour, at least for England and Wales. Try them and see!)

8 A firm has costs and revenues as follows:

Year	1	2	3	4	5	6	
Costs	70	74	79	83	88	94	(£000s)
Revenues	90	94	97	101	105	109	(£000s)

Use Excel to plot semi-log graphs to confirm that, though both costs and revenues are increasing at an approximately steady rate, revenues will not keep pace with costs if the present trend continues, and estimate the year in which a loss will first be made. Do you think such a situation could arise in practice?

9 Look up population figures for the past ten years or so for two developed countries (e.g. the UK and the United States) and two developing countries (e.g. India and Brazil). Plot all the figures on a single semi-log graph, and hence compare the rates of growth of population in your chosen countries. Suggest methods in each case for estimating the population of the country by 2020.

10 Which of the following sets of data would you expect to exhibit a strong seasonal behaviour? In those cases where you expect seasonality, indicate what the pattern is likely to be, and why this pattern is expected.

(a) Numbers of people taking annual holiday entitlement in a large organisation, recorded monthly.
(b) Quarterly sales of electric heaters.
(c) Quarterly sales of paper tissues.
(d) Monthly sales of furniture.
(e) Numbers of logins to the website of a direct sales company.
(f) Numbers of people joining a motorists' breakdown and rescue service.

Case Study

House price movements

(Use Excel for this case if possible. If carrying out calculations by hand, round data to the nearest £1000 before starting the calculations.)

You are working for a large estate agency, and have been asked to analyse the movements in house prices since the start of 2001. You obtain historic quarterly data for average house prices over the UK as follows from the website of the Nationwide Building Society (http://www.nationwide.co.uk/hpi/historical.htm). This data is also available at the Companion Website.

Q1 2001	£83 976
Q2 2001	£87 638
Q3 2001	£91 049
Q4 2001	£92 533
Q1 2002	£95 356
Q2 2002	£103 501
Q3 2002	£110 830
Q4 2002	£115 940
Q1 2003	£119 938
Q2 2003	£125 382
Q3 2003	£129 761
Q4 2003	£133 903
Q1 2004	£139 027
Q2 2004	£148 462
Q3 2004	£153 482

Q4 2004	£152 464
Q1 2005	£152 790
Q2 2005	£157 494
Q3 2005	£157 627
Q4 2005	£157 387
Q1 2006	£160 319
Q2 2006	£165 035
Q3 2006	£168 460
Q4 2006	£172 065
Q1 2007	£175 554
Q2 2007	£181 810
Q3 2007	£184 131
Q4 2007	£183 959

(a) Using an additive time-series model, calculate the four-quarter moving average over this period, and the quarterly and random variations. Comment on the patterns revealed by your calculation. If you had been asked to obtain a forecast at the end of 2007 for prices in the fourth quarter of 2009, how might you have proceeded? (Do not calculate the forecast.)

(b) You now obtain more recent data from the same site, as follows:

Q1 2008	£179 363
Q2 2008	£174 514
Q3 2008	£165 188
Q4 2008	£156 828
Q1 2009	£149 709
Q2 2009	£154 066
Q3 2009	£160 159
Q4 2009	£162 116
Q1 2010	£162 887
Q2 2010	£168 719
Q3 2010	£167 354
Q4 2010	£163 244

Plot the whole data series from 2001 to 2010. What can you say about the accuracy of the forecast you would have obtained in 2007 for the fourth quarter of 2009? What does this suggest about the process of forecasting in general?

Further reading

Forecasting is a major topic with a large literature of its own; it is also an active field for research. It is therefore not a good idea simply to pick a book with the word 'Forecasting' in the title off the shelf in your university library. If your course requires you to go into more detail on the topic, your lecturer will recommend suitable reading. If you would like to read a little more around the subject, then the first few chapters of the following book are a good starting-point:

Makridakis, S.G., Wheelwright, S.C. and Hyndman, R.J. (1998), *Forecasting*, 3rd edn, Wiley.

Chapter 16

ALLOWING FOR INTEREST:
FINANCIAL MATHEMATICS

Chapter prerequisites

Before starting work on this chapter make sure you are happy with the following topics:

1 the meaning of the notations x^n and x^{-n} (see Chapter 1, p. 17);

2 the method of working out powers of numbers on your calculator (refer to the instruction booklet if necessary);

3 calculation of percentages (see Chapter 1, p. 15).

Learning outcomes

By the end of your work on this chapter you should be able to:

1 apply the compound interest method to problems such as the establishment of sinking funds;

2 use discounting tables to solve problems involving annuities, hire purchase and mortgage repayments, etc.;

3 compare and choose between different capital investment projects using discounting methods.

Quantitative methods in practice

UK inflation rate in surprise October increase

BBC News website, 16 November 2010

Don't cut interest rates, building societies tell Bank of England

www.telegraph.co.uk, 3 February 2009

Zimbabwe's inflation rate surges to 231,000,000%

The Guardian, 9 October 2008, Chris McGreal. Copyright Guardian News and Media Ltd. 2008.

How often have you read headlines like these in the newspapers? Have you ever wondered why interest rates are so important for business and the economy, or how managers can take interest and inflation into account in their planning? On a more personal level, are you really clear about how to compare the deals offered by different credit-card providers or building societies?

Most people will have an idea that when we borrow money, interest is the charge we pay for the privilege, while if we lend money – as we do, in effect, when we invest in a bank or building society – interest is the fee we are paid for the use of our funds. But in order to be able properly to allow for the effects of interest on business decisions, managers need to have a much more detailed understanding of the processes behind interest calculations. That's what this chapter sets out to provide.

The management accountant's problem

The Panamount Manufacturing Company last year achieved a very satisfactory level of profits, and the Board has decided to retain part of these in order to finance the purchase of new machinery. There are two machines, only one of which is to be purchased; one costs £3900 and the other £4000. At first sight, it would seem clear that the Board should, all other things being equal, buy the cheaper of the two – but *are* all other things equal? For instance, do the two machines operate at the same rate, and, if not, what difference is there in the revenues which they may be expected to generate? To enable Panamount to make a more informed decision, the Board has asked the firm's management accountant to carry out a detailed analysis of the results to be expected from the two machines.

His first step is to obtain an estimate of the amounts of saleable goods which will be produced by each of the machines – let us for convenience refer to them as Machine A, the dearer of the two, and Machine B. He then decides how much revenue is likely to be generated by the sale of these goods, and also, by talking to the firm's production engineers and others who have experience of the performance of similar machines, finds out what the running costs and the likely lifetimes of the two will be. Finally, he investigates the market for second-hand models of each machine.

His analysis is simplified by the discovery that both machines will only be used by the firm for three years. However, Machine A could then be resold for £500, whereas Machine B would simply be scrapped at no return to the company.

When running costs are taken into account, he finds that the revenues generated by the two are as follows:

	Machine A	Machine B
Year 1	2000	1500
Year 2	2500	2500
Year 3	1000	2000

So if we include the £500 resale value of Machine A, then the returns for the two machines are exactly the same, both being equal to £6000. Surely the management accountant should therefore recommend the purchase of the cheaper machine?

This conclusion would be quite reasonable if he knew that the purchase price of the machine would simply be taken out of an old tin trunk under the managing director's bed, to which the profits would in due course be returned. But this is most unlikely to be the case. Much of the capital required to finance the purchase of the machine may need to be borrowed, in which case interest will certainly be charged on the loan by the lender. Even if the firm can finance the purchase from existing capital such as retained profits, it must consider the possibility that the money could be put to better use elsewhere – for example, left to earn interest in a bank deposit or other investment account, rather than used to buy either of the machines.

It therefore becomes clear that to make a fair comparison of two capital projects such as these at a less than superficial level, a knowledge of the workings of interest is required. So, leaving Panamount Manufacturing's problems to be re-examined later in the chapter, we will begin with the basics.

The fundamentals of compound interest

Many readers will already be familiar with the difference between simple and compound interest, but for those who are not we will give a brief definition of the two. Interest is said to be *simple* if it is withdrawn at the end of each interest period – that is, monthly, annually or whatever – so that the value of the investment remains the same no matter how long the period for which it is invested. With *compound* interest, on the other hand, the interest is added to the investment at the end of each period – that is, is *compounded* – so that the value of the investment increases steadily. Suppose, for example, that £100 is invested at a rate of 10 per cent per annum* for five years. By the end of the first year it will have attracted £10 in interest, so that the initial investment for year 2 is £110. The

---

* Of course, 10 per cent is very much higher than today's interest rates, but as it makes the arithmetic much easier we will use it as a hypothetical figure, here and in other places throughout the chapter.

interest for the second year will therefore be 10 per cent of £110, which is £11, giving a balance of £121 at the start of year 3. If you continue the process you will find that by the end of year 3 the amount will be £133.10, increasing to £146.41 by the end of year 4 and £161.05 by the end of year 5.

The actual amounts by which the total increases are, of course, getting larger as time goes on. In fact, those of you who have read Chapter 12 will probably recognise this as a situation in which year-end totals, if plotted against time on a semi-logarithmic graph, would give a straight line. But although it was easy enough to work year by year in this particular case, because the percentage chosen was an easy one, in general the year-by-year approach will be very inefficient. Imagine, for instance, trying to work in this way if we wanted to find how much an investment of £2427 would amount to if invested for 25 years at an annual rate of $17\frac{1}{2}$ per cent! As we are not interested in the intermediate figures for each year, but only in the final amount, and as $17\frac{1}{2}$ per cent is not a particularly nice quantity to calculate 25 times over, what we need is a way of going direct to the final figure without having to do the calculations for all the in-between years.

To discover what this direct route to the answer is, let us return to our easy problem of £100 invested at 10 per cent per annum for five years and redo it in what will undoubtedly seem a very long-winded manner, for which, however, a reason will become apparent. By the end of the first year our original £100 has increased to

$$£100 + 10\% \text{ of } £100$$
or £100 + 0.1 × £100, since 10 per cent as a decimal is 0.1,
or £100(1 + 0.1), taking out the £100 as a common factor.

This is the amount with which we start the second year of the investment, so by the end of that year we have

$$£100(1 + 0.1) + 10\% \text{ of } £100(1 + 0.1)$$
or £100(1 + 0.1) + 0.1 × £100(1 + 0.1)
or £100(1 + 0.1)(1 + 0.1), taking out £100(1 + 0.1) as a common factor
or $£100(1 + 0.1)^2$.

Similarly, by the end of year 3 we will have

$$£100(1 + 0.1)^2 + 10\% \text{ of } £100(1 + 0.1)^2$$
or $£100(1 + 0.1)^2 + 0.1 × £100(1 + 0.1)^2$
or $£100(1 + 0.1)^2(1 + 0.1)$
or $£100(1 + 0.1)^3$.

You should now be able to see a pattern emerging. Every year the starting amount gets multiplied by another factor of (1 + 0.1), the 1 corresponding to the fact that the initial amount is still there at the end of the year, and the 0.1 to the 10 per cent interest which has been added during the year. So by the time our money has been invested for five years, the original £100 will have been multiplied by this factor five times, and the final amount in the account will therefore be $£100(1 + 0.1)^5$. It is not too difficult to work this out with a calculator, making use of the 'constant multiplier' facility to save putting the factor (1 + 0.1) in via the keyboard five times, or using the x^n key if your calculator has one. The final amount at the end of the five years is £161.05, just as we already found using step-by-step methods.

We can generalise this to apply to any starting amount, invested for any number of years at any rate of interest, if we introduce a bit of notation. The usual name for the starting sum is the *principal*, written P; we will call the percentage rate r per time period (month, half-year, etc.), and suppose that the investment is left for n time periods. Then, the final sum in the investment is called the *amount*, written A, and since the initial amount will be multiplied by a factor of $(1 + r/100)$ for each time period which elapses, the final value of the investment will be given by the formula

$$A = P(1 + r/100)^n.$$

This is the basic compound interest formula, which enables us to calculate the value of an investment at any time in the future if we know the rate of interest earned; I would advise you to commit it to memory. (You will sometimes find it written on the assumption that the rate is already expressed as a decimal R, in the form $A = P(1 + R)^n$.)

Applications of the compound interest formula

We will now examine some of the uses to which the basic result derived in the previous section can be put. You may encounter in other textbooks a variety of formulae obtained from that fundamental result, for applications such as sinking funds, regular savings and so on; but as the 'formula' approach means that you have not only to commit the various formulae themselves to memory, but also to remember in what context each is applicable, I would recommend just learning the basic result, and then applying that from first principles in each case, as will be illustrated in the following examples.

Example 1

Your parents invest £200 in your name on your 18th birthday, to be paid to you on your 21st birthday, together with interest earned at 5 per cent per annum. How much will you receive?

In the notation of the previous section, $P = £200$, $r = 5$ and $n = 3$, so the amount at the end of the three years will be

$$A = 200(1 + 5/100)^3$$
$$= 200(1 + 0.05)^3$$
$$= 200 \times 1.05^3 = £231.52.$$

Example 2

You decide not to withdraw the money from the account described in Example 1, but to leave it there and to add £50 per year to the investment, making the first payment on your 21st birthday. How much will there be in the account by the eve of your 25th birthday, assuming that the rate of interest remains the same?

There are two ways we could proceed with this calculation, and not a great deal to choose between them. We could operate on a year-by-year basis, saying

Amount invested on 21st birthday	= £231.52 + £50
	= £281.52
Interest for year 21–22	= £14.07 (5% of £281.52)
Payment on 22nd birthday	= £50.00
Amount invested on 22nd birthday	= £345.59
Interest for year 22–23	= £17.28
Payment on 23rd birthday	= £50.00
Amount invested on 23rd birthday	= £412.87
Interest for year 23–24	= £20.64
Payment on 24th birthday	= £50.00
Amount invested on 24th birthday	= £483.51
Interest for year 24–25	= £24.18
Amount invested on eve of 25th birthday	= £507.69

Alternatively, we could deal with each year's investment separately, and make use of the formula again, thus. From 21st to 25th birthday is four years, so the £231.52 already in the account will be there for another four years, together with the £50 you put in on your 21st birthday. That is, we have a principal of £281.52 invested for four years at 5 per cent per annum giving

$$\text{Amount} = £281.52(1 + 5/100)^4$$
$$= £281.52 \times 1.05^4$$
$$= £342.19.$$

The £50 you invest on your 22nd birthday will only be invested for three years, so that will amount to

$$£50 \times 1.05^3 = £57.88.$$

Similarly for the payment made on your 23rd birthday we have

$$\text{Amount after two years} = £50 \times 1.05^2 = £55.13$$

and for the last payment, made on your 24th birthday, which will only be invested for one year, we have

$$\text{Amount after one year} = £50 \times 1.05$$
$$= £52.50.$$

All together, then, there will be the sum of these four amounts, which is £507.70 – in agreement, apart from a discrepancy of 1p caused by rounding, with the figure obtained before.

Of course many of these steps would not need to be written down in practice, especially if you are using a calculator with a memory; the total could then be calculated as you go along by adding each separate amount into the memory as soon as it is calculated.

Example 3

The term *sinking fund* is usually understood as describing the situation that arises when a firm wishes to purchase some piece of capital equipment at a future date, and decides to make regular savings to finance the purchase. Nearly always, these savings will be in the form of equal instalments, invested annually, monthly or whatever. So the problem, given the price of the piece of equipment, is to determine what the instalments should be. Suppose, for example, that it has been estimated that a certain machine costing £3000 will have to be purchased in three years' time, and that provision for this purchase is to be made by three equal investments, the first to be made now, the second in one year's time and the third in two years – that is, one year before the purchase. If no interest were going to be earned by the investment, then obviously the annual amount to be saved would be £1000, but if, as is much more likely, the investments *will* earn interest – let us say, for simplicity, at 10 per cent per annum – then part of the £3000 will be provided by that interest, so that the actual amount put away each year will be somewhat less than £1000.

To find out just how much less, call the annual instalment £x. Then, using our compound interest formula, we can see that the first payment of £x, which will be in the account for the full three years before it is withdrawn to pay for the machine, will by then amount to £$x(1 + 0.1)^3$. The second payment, being in the account for only two years, will have increased to £$x(1 + 0.1)^2$, and the third, which is invested for only one year, will by the time it is withdrawn amount to £$x(1 + 0.1)$. All together, then, there will be £$x(1 + 0.1)^3 + £x(1 + 0.1)^2 + £x(1 + 0.1)$ in the account, which can be written more simply as £$x(1.1^3 + 1.1^2 + 1.1)$.

But this has to be just sufficient to pay for the £3000 machine. So we have an equation

$$x(1.1^3 + 1.1^2 + 1.1) = 3000,$$

from which we can determine x:

$$x = \frac{3000}{1.1^3 + 1.1^2 + 1.1} = £823.95.$$

(See 'Computational note' on p. 422 for advice on calculating this.)

This confirms what we have already stated on common-sense grounds – that the amount to be saved is less than the £1000 a year we would need if no interest were being earned.

It is instructive, though not something one would want to do in every such problem, to work through the calculation 'backwards', as it were, to follow the progress of the account as it would accumulate in practice:

1st instalment	823.95
1st year's interest	82.40
2nd instalment	823.95
Amount in a/c at start year 2	1730.30
2nd year's interest	173.03
3rd instalment	823.95
Amount in a/c at start year 3	2727.28
3rd year's interest	272.73
Total by end of year 3	3000.01

Thus the amount saved by the end of the third year will just cover the purchase of the new machine, as required. (The 1p discrepancy is due to rounding off of figures.)

Be careful, when tackling problems of this kind, about the date of the final instalment: sometimes, as here, it is invested one year before the purchase, but alternatively it may be paid in immediately before the purchase is made.

Quick check questions

1 What will a sum of £500 invested at 4.5 per cent per annum compound interest amount to after five years?

2 You borrow £2000 from a bank which will charge you 1.25 per cent per month interest. If you pay off the loan after six months, how much interest will you pay? What is this as a percentage of the amount borrowed? Comment on the result.

3 £120 per year is paid into an account which offers 3.2 per cent per annum compound interest. How much will be in the account after three years?

Answers:
1 The compound interest formula with $P = $ £500, $r = 4.5\% = 0.045$, and $n = 5$, gives $A = 500 \times (1 + 0.045)^5 = $ £623.09.
2 The total you will owe after six months can be obtained from the compound interest formula with $P = $ £2000, $n = 6$ and $r = 1.25\% = 0.0125$. Thus the amount owed is £2000 $\times$ $1.0125^6 = $ £2154.77. The interest paid is therefore £154.77, which as a percentage of £2000 is $154.77/2000 \times 100 = 7.74$ per cent to two decimal places. This rate for six months does not sound nearly so good as the monthly rate quoted! (Why isn't the rate for six months equal to six times the rate per month?)
3 We can use the formula to say that the first deposit of £120 will be in the account for three years, and thus amount to $120 \times 1.032^3 = $ £131.89. In the same way, the second deposit will amount to £127.80, and the third, which is only in the account for one year, to £123.84. The total at the end of three years is thus £383.53.

The idea of present value

One of the characteristics which is said to distinguish adults from small children (and animals) is that adults will frequently defer gratifications – for instance, save half of a bar of chocolate until tomorrow – whereas your average baby will almost certainly eat the lot now, even if it does not *really* want it. There are circumstances, though, in which the baby's 'grab it now' instinct is actually sounder than the adult's willingness to wait – though not for reasons that the baby could appreciate!

Consider, for example, the decision you would have to make if offered the choice of £100 now or £100 in a year's time. Setting aside the possibility that you might want to spend the money, we will suppose that you are going to invest it, whenever you get it. Now, if you have it in your hand today, you can have it in your building society account, or wherever you keep your savings, by tomorrow, and in a year's time it will have increased, if the going rate of interest is, say, 4 per cent, to £104 – rather better than the alternative of £100 in a year's time. We say that the *present value* of the £100 which you are going to get in a year's time is less than the value to you of £100 now.

That is pretty easy to see. It is not quite so obvious if the choice is between £100 in a year's time or £90 now; but again, if the interest rate stays at 4 per cent, we can expect our

£90 to have increased to £93.60 in a year, so in this case the £100 received a year hence is preferable. (It is important here, and in what follows, to realise that we are concentrating on the effects of *interest* – nowhere are we considering the effects of *inflation*, which of course might well have chewed away at the value of money in the interim. Try, if you can, to forget inflation for the rest of this chapter!)

An alternative way of making the comparison between £100 now and £100 in a year's time, rather than looking at the increased value of the 'now' amount in a year, is to ask 'How much would we need to be given now in order to have the £100 a year from now?' In other words, what amount must be invested – let us stick with our rate of 4 per cent for the moment – in order to accumulate to £100 in one year?

This is the reverse of the question we were answering in the section on the fundamentals of compound interest, where we *knew* the initial sum invested and wanted to know what it would amount to in the future. Now we know the final amount, and want to find out what we should have started with.

However, we can still make use of the basic formula derived in that earlier section, setting $n = 1$ (since we are only interested at present in a single year), $r = 4$ per cent and $A = 100$. If we put these into the formula we have

$$100 = P(1 + 4/100)^1$$

where P is the unknown starting investment.

Solving for P we find

$$P = \frac{100}{(1 + 4/100)^1}$$

$$\text{or } P = 100(1 + 4/100)^{-1} \qquad (a)$$

recalling the definition of a negative power which we made in the section 'Powers and roots' in Chapter 1.

We define this value of P as the *present value* of £100 payable one year from now at 4 per cent per annum interest. It is the amount we would need to invest for one year at 4 per cent interest in order to get £100 at the end of the year.

Similarly we could say that the present value of £600 in four years' time at 10 per cent per annum will be P, where P is given by

$$600 = P(1 + 10/100)^4,$$

$$\text{so } P = \frac{600}{(1 + 10/100)^4} \text{ or } 600(1 + 10/100)^{-4}. \qquad (b)$$

We can generalise this to get an expression for the present value of an amount A payable in n interest periods from now at a rate of r per cent per period, simply by inverting the formula on p. 409:

$$P = A(1 + r/100)^{-n}.$$

This is the *present value* formula (from now on we will often write PV for present value), which as you can see involves a negative power. Of course, we know that this simply means that we have to *divide* A by $(1 + r/100)^n$, but that still leaves us with some quite messy calculations to do. So it has become the standard practice, particularly among actuaries and other people who are doing such calculations all the time, not to do them from first principles, but to use tables of the quantities $(1 + r/100)^{-n}$ which someone has

Table 16.1 Discount factors

n	1	2	3	4	5	6	7	8	9	10
1	0.990	0.980	0.971	0.962	0.952	0.943	0.935	0.926	0.917	0.909
2	0.980	0.961	0.943	0.925	0.907	0.890	0.873	0.857	0.842	0.826
3	0.971	0.942	0.915	0.889	0.864	0.840	0.816	0.794	0.772	0.751
4	0.961	0.924	0.888	0.855	0.823	0.792	0.763	0.735	0.708	0.683
5	0.951	0.906	0.863	0.822	0.784	0.747	0.713	0.681	0.650	0.621
6	0.942	0.888	0.837	0.790	0.746	0.705	0.666	0.630	0.596	0.564
7	0.933	0.871	0.813	0.760	0.711	0.665	0.623	0.583	0.547	0.513
8	0.923	0.853	0.789	0.731	0.677	0.627	0.582	0.540	0.502	0.467
9	0.914	0.837	0.766	0.703	0.645	0.592	0.544	0.500	0.460	0.424
10	0.905	0.820	0.744	0.676	0.614	0.558	0.508	0.463	0.422	0.386

obligingly worked out for a whole range of different values of r and n – with the aid of a computer, of course!

The sets of tables which professionals in the field use are arranged with the rate increasing in steps of $\frac{1}{2}$ per cent, or even $\frac{1}{4}$ at a time, and run up to times of 25 years or longer, as they must if they are to be used for calculations connected with, for instance, mortgage repayments, which rarely run for less than ten years. However, we will use a much simpler table, which you will find in Table 16.1. Just ten integer rates – from 1 to 10 per cent – are shown, and the table runs for only ten years. The numbers in the body of the table are simply the values of $(1 + r/100)^{-n}$ worked out for the various combinations of r and n.

Using the table is therefore very easy. To find the present value of any given amount at a known rate, payable a known number of years from now, all we have to do is to look up the figure for the appropriate combination of r and n in the table, and multiply the amount by that figure. It is really the same sort of calculation as in equations (a) and (b) above, except that the hard part of the calculations has already been done for us by the compiler of the tables – in this case, me!

For instance, to work out the example of equation (b) using the tables, we look up the figure in the 10 per cent column and the four-year row, which is 0.683. What this is telling us is the value of the $(1 + 10/100)^{-4}$ part of equation (b). So all we need do is multiply that by the 600 to get the present value of £600 in four years' time at 10 per cent per annum as £409.81. You can check by working forwards, if you like, that £409.81 invested at 10 per cent for four years really does come to £600, give or take a penny.

Tables such as 16.1 are called *discount tables*, the numbers in the body of the table are called *discount factors*, and the process of finding present values is called *discounting*. The whole area of problem-solving using these ideas is often referred to as *discounted cash flow*, or DCF for short.

Before we go on to look at applications of present values and discounting, let us quickly recap on the differences between the two processes we have looked at so far in this chapter. They might be summarised as follows:

Compound interest	moves *forward* in time; values are *increasing*
Discounting:	moves *backward* in time; values are *decreasing*

If you get confused as to which process you should be using in a particular situation, going back to these two basic definitions should help you to decide.

Applications of discounting

Again, there are a variety of more complicated results derived from the fundamental discounting formula, and corresponding sets of tables to simplify the calculation of such things as mortgage or hire purchase repayments. However, the fairly straightforward applications which we shall examine can all be tackled merely with the aid of Table 16.1.

Calculating annuities

People who are self-employed, or for some other reason will have no pension over and above the state retirement pension, often purchase an *annuity* to provide them with additional income when they are no longer working. What happens is that the purchaser pays, to an insurance company or similar organisation, a lump sum, in return for which he or she receives a guaranteed income of a fixed amount per year for a fixed number of years. Imagine, for instance, that you wish to purchase an annuity that will pay you £1000 per year for five years. How much would you expect to have to pay for it, assuming that investments earn interest at 5 per cent per annum?

Clearly, if no interest were being paid, you would have to pay £5000. The process then would simply be that someone would hold the money on your behalf and return it to you in five payments of £1000 each. But what will happen in practice is that the organiser of the annuity will not just, as it were, keep the money in a piggy-bank; he or she will invest it on your behalf. So you would expect to pay *less* than £5000 for it, since some of each year's payment will be provided for by the interest which the money has been earning.

Although you would really only make *one* payment at the start of the period, the calculation is simplified if you think of that payment as made up of five separate bits: the amount which will give you £1000 in one year's time, the amount which will give you £1000 in two years' time, and so on. From what we have said in the previous section about present values, you should recognise 'the amount that will give you £1000 in one year's time' as being the present value of £1000 payable in a year's time at 5 per cent. All together, then, we will have

$$\text{PV of £1000 in 1 year from now} = 1000 \times 0.952$$
$$\text{PV of £1000 in 2 years from now} = 1000 \times 0.907$$
$$\text{PV of £1000 in 3 years from now} = 1000 \times 0.864$$
$$\text{PV of £1000 in 4 years from now} = 1000 \times 0.823$$
$$\text{PV of £1000 in 5 years from now} = 1000 \times \underline{0.784}$$

$$4.329$$

So total PV of the five payments,
which is the minimum you could
expect to pay for the annuity $= 1000 \times 4.329$
$$= £4329$$

It is much more efficient, of course, to add up the discount factors and then multiply the total by 1000, rather than to do the multiplications first and then the addition. This would be all the more true if the annual payment were not a nice tidy amount like £1000 but something more complicated. The total amount to be paid is considerably less than £5000, just as we expected. We have said that £4329 is the *minimum* you could expect to pay, because the insurance company organising the annuity will presumably want to make some profit out of the whole operation.

Once again, we can check by working through the five years step by step that this solution gives just enough for five payments of £1000, with nothing left over at the end, though you would not wish to do the check every time. At the start, the £4329 is paid into the account:

Amount in account at start yr 1	4329.00
Interest earned during yr 1	216.45
Amount in account at end yr 1	4545.45
First payment made	1000.00
Amount in account at start yr 2	3545.45
Interest earned during yr 2	177.27
Amount in account at end yr 2	3722.72
Second payment made	1000.00
Amount in account at start yr 3	2722.72
Interest earned during yr 3	136.14
Amount in account at end yr 3	2858.86
Third payment made	1000.00
Amount in account at start yr 4	1858.86
Interest earned during yr 4	92.94
Amount in account at end yr 4	1951.80
Fourth payment made	1000.00
Amount in account at start yr 5	951.80
Interest earned during yr 5	47.59
Amount in account at end yr 5	999.39

The slight shortfall on the final payment is due to the fact that we are using discount tables which only give three decimal places, so that by the time the discount factors are multiplied by 1000 there is some doubt as to the last digit. However, this is easily overcome by using more accurate tables, and in fact insurance professionals use tables which give seven or more decimal places.

One can also pose a slightly different annuity problem by asking how much annual income could be generated by a given initial investment over a fixed period of time. For example, if you have a lump sum of £4000 to invest, and would like to receive your return in the form of ten equal annual payments, how much will you get each year?

Denoting the annual payment by £*x*, what we are saying is that the present value of the ten annual payments together must be equal to the £4000 which is being invested. So, assuming as before that the rate of interest is 5 per cent per annum and that the first payment is to be made one year after the initial investment, we have

PV of £x in one year's time + PV of £x in two years' time + ... + PV of £x in ten years' time = £4000.

Using Table 16.1 then gives

$$0.952x + 0.907x + 0.864x + 0.823x + 0.784x + 0.746x + 0.711x + 0.677x$$
$$+ 0.645x + 0.614x = 4000,$$

whence $\qquad\qquad 7.722x = 4000,$

so that $\qquad\qquad x = 4000/7.722 = £518.00.$

Again, this is a good deal more than the £400 per year which is all we could expect to get if no interest were being earned. You might like to do the 'check' calculation here, and convince yourself that, apart from small errors due to the rounding-off of figures, the £4000 plus its interest will just provide the ten annual payments of £518.00.

Calculating mortgage and hire purchase repayments

We can make use of the discount table to work out what the annual or monthly repayments on a mortgage or hire purchase will be. If you buy, say, a three-piece suite costing £800 under a hire purchase agreement which requires you to pay a deposit of 20 per cent now and the balance in six equal monthly payments, how much can you expect to pay each month if you are being charged interest at the rate of 5 per cent per month?

If we call the monthly repayment £x, and assume that you are required to make the first repayment one month after purchase, then the balance after the deposit has been paid – 80 per cent of £800, or £640 – must be equal to the present value of £x paid in one month's time, plus the present value of £x paid in two months' time, and so on up to six months. Referring again to Table 16.1, but now using the 5 per cent column, we have

$$640 = 0.952x + 0.907x + 0.864x + 0.823x + 0.784x + 0.746x,$$
so $640 = 5.076x$, which means $x = £126.08.$

You will therefore actually pay the deposit of £160, plus £126.08 × 6, for the furniture – that is, £916.51, a good deal more than the cash price of £800. The additional cost, of course, is really the price you are being charged for the convenience of deferring part of the payment, which effectively gives you the use of someone else's money – or of the furniture, whichever way you like to look at it – for six months.

You will see, if you compare this with the second annuity example above, that this is essentially the same calculation. It is interesting to carry out the check calculation for the first few months at least, because this demonstrates a fact of which anyone who is buying a house with a mortgage will be only too well aware: at the start of your repayments you are paying off only a very small amount of the capital each month – by far the greater part of each month's repayment is interest. However, as time goes on the ratio of capital to interest in each month's payment increases, until by the time the mortgage is paid off, only a very small element of each month's payment is taken up by interest. The working goes as follows:

Amount borrowed initially (after paying deposit)	640.00
Interest incurred during month 1	32.00
Total owed by end of month 1	672.00
First payment made at end of month 1	126.08
Total owed at start of month 2	545.92
Interest incurred during month 2	27.30
Total owed by end of month 2	573.22
Second payment made at end of month 2	126.08
Total owed at start of month 3	447.14

and so on. You can finish the checking if you like, but the point we are making is that, out of the first repayment of £126.08, £32.00 consists of the first month's interest, and only the remaining £94.08 is paid off the capital. In the second repayment, however, the balance has altered to £27.30 of interest and £98.78 of capital, and if you complete the calculation you will find that in the remaining four repayments, a larger and larger proportion is taken up by capital. With a house-purchase mortgage, which typically would run for some 20–30 years, and would involve a much larger amount borrowed, the effect is far more noticeable, so that at the start of the repayments one sometimes wonders if one is ever going to pay off all the capital!

Quick check questions

1 What is the present value of a sum of £1200 payable in four years' time, if the interest rate is assumed to be fixed at 3 per cent?

2 A company pays for a new piece of equipment in three equal instalments, the first made at the time of purchase and the other two at yearly intervals thereafter. If the purchase price is £15 000, and interest is charged at an annual rate of 2 per cent, what will be the value of each instalment?

3 A company wishes to buy an annuity for an employee who is retiring; the annuity is to pay her £2000 per year for four years, the first payment being made one year after purchase. Assuming an interest rate of 4 per cent, how much will the company need to invest?

Answers:
1 Using Table 16.1 with $n = 4$ and a rate of 3 per cent, the answer is $1200 \times 0.888 = £1065.60$.
2 Suppose that each instalment is £x. Then the present value of the three instalments together must be equal to the purchase price of £15 000. Using Table 16.1, this gives

$x + 0.980x + 0.961x = 15\,000$ (Note that we start with x here because the first payment is made immediately.)

$2.941x = 15\,000$

$x = £5100.31$.

3 We need to find the present value of the four payments. This will be

$2000(0.962 + 0.925 + 0.889 + 0.855) = 2000 \times 3.63 = £7260$.

Some further points

In all the problems we have looked at so far, whether of compound interest or discounting type, we have assumed that the interest rate was known. There are situations where this is not the case, and where one perhaps needs to work out the interest rate, given other information. For example, if you were offered a loan of £60, to be paid back in three monthly instalments each of £22, the first to be paid one month after the money was borrowed, then you might ask what interest rate per month this offer represents.

But solving problems of this kind is much more difficult than dealing with those where the interest rate is known. To solve this particular one exactly we would need to look at the equation which tells us that the present value of the three instalments of £22 is equal to £60, when discounted at the applicable rate of interest.

If we call the interest rate per month r per cent then this can be written as

$$22(1 + r/100)^{-1} + 22(1 + r/100)^{-2} + 22(1 + r/100)^{-3} = 60$$

which is a pretty nasty equation to have to solve for r. One way to go about solving it is to try putting in different values for r and see how close the two sides of the equation are to being equal. With a sufficiently detailed set of discount tables, this can lead to a reasonably accurate answer, but you can see that, particularly for a problem which involves not just 3 but 20 or 25 years, the process is going to be a slow one, and the assistance of a computer is required.

One point that should not need mentioning after our work on index numbers and semi-logarithmic graphs, but which often causes confusion, is that you cannot say '3 per cent interest per month – that means 36 per cent per year'. If you want to translate an interest rate of 3 per cent per month into an annual rate, then you must use the compound interest formula to tell you how large a year's increase would be. This gives an annual increase factor of $(1 + 0.03)^{12}$, which works out at about 1.42 – an increase of 42 per cent per year. The consequence of this is that you need to be very careful when comparing rates of interest which are quoted for different periods. What looks like a nice low monthly rate may well turn out, when calculated annually, to be quite astronomical. There are now legal requirements for loan companies and so on to quote their Annual Equivalent Rate (AER) – you may have seen this mentioned in advertisements.

Comparing investments

We now have the techniques at our disposal for making a comparison of the Panamount Manufacturing Company's two investment projects introduced in the first section of this chapter. You will recall that, including scrap value of Machine A, the costs and revenues for the two machines under consideration are as follows:

	Machine A	Machine B
Cost	4000	3900
Year 1 revenue	2000	1500
Year 2 revenue	2500	2500
Year 3 revenue	1500	2000

The units here are pounds.

We have seen that we cannot justifiably add together, say, the revenue of £2000 which Machine A earns in year 1 and that of £2500 which it earns in year 2, because the value of money payable in the future is not the same as that of money now. If we want to combine the revenues for the different years so that we can compare the two projects, then we must first find the present value of each year's revenue. We will then make our comparison on the basis of the total present value of the surplus (if any) produced by the projects, and will also be able to see whether we might do better not to invest in either of the projects, but to leave the money in the bank.

To find present values, of course, we need to know the appropriate discount rate to use. Let us suppose, without worrying too much about where the figure comes from for the moment, the firm knows that the rate to be used with investments of this kind is generally 10 per cent per year. If we assume that all the revenues are received at the *end* of the relevant year, and that the initial costs are incurred at the *start* of year 1, then we have the calculations below (once again expressed in pounds to the nearest whole pound):

	Machine A	Machine B
Cost	(4000)	(3900)
Year 1 revenue	2000 × 0.909 = 1818	1500 × 0.909 = 1364
Year 2 revenue	2500 × 0.826 = 2065	2500 × 0.826 = 2065
Year 3 revenue	1500 × 0.751 = 1127	2000 × 0.751 = 1502
Total PV of surplus	1010	1031

So both projects will produce a surplus, when the returns are discounted at 10 per cent. But what exactly does this mean? There are two useful ways of interpreting the fact. We can say that, since we have used a rate of 10 per cent in discounting, the surplus shows that both projects actually give a return *better* than 10 per cent – better, that is, than we would get by leaving the money in the bank or wherever at 10 per cent interest. Or we can say that, to achieve these returns from an investment giving 10 per cent interest, we would need to invest, in the case of Machine A, £5010, and for Machine B, £4931 – the cost of each machine plus the surplus it produces. This second way of looking at the result is perhaps the easier to grasp, since we can actually demonstrate what is happening.

Take Machine A as an example. We are claiming to have proved that, to get returns of £2000 in year 1, £2500 in year 2 and £1500 in year 3, an investment of £5010 would be required. How would that work? Well, we can follow the course of the investment over the three years for which it runs:

Start of year 1	5010.00
Year 1 interest	501.00
End of year 1	5511.00
Less year 1 revenue	2000.00
Start of year 2	3511.00
Year 2 interest	351.10
End of year 2	3862.10
Less year 2 revenue	2500.00
Start of year 3	1362.10
Year 3 interest	136.21
End of year 3	1498.31

Thus, apart from the slight discrepancy due to rounding, there is just sufficient at the end of year 3 to provide that year's revenue of £1500. This confirms that £5010 would have to be invested at 10 per cent to give these returns, so that we are doing rather better by buying Machine A, which gives us the same returns from an investment of only £4000, than we would by simply investing our money at 10 per cent. You might like to perform the same calculation for Machine B.

We now certainly have evidence that either machine is worth buying, but we do not as yet have enough information to enable us to make a choice between them. There is no doubt that A gives a slightly bigger profit than B, but then so it should – after all, it is costing more to begin with. What we need to look at is not the actual *size* of the surplus produced by each machine, but what kind of return this represents on the purchase price. For Machine A we have

$$\frac{1010}{4000} \times 100 = 25.25\%$$

while for B the calculation is

$$\frac{1031}{3900} \times 100 = 26.44\%.$$

So, viewing the surplus as a percentage of the initial cost, Machine B does very slightly better than Machine A, and would be the one recommended by Panamount's accountant – *if* he chose to adopt this method of *investment appraisal*, as it is called. For it would be misleading to give the impression that this is the only method in use; there are a number of assumptions which we have made in the course of the analysis, which render the whole process open to criticism.

What have we assumed?

First, we assumed that all the revenues were received tidily at the ends of the years, whereas in practice they are much more likely to come in during the year, maybe not even at a steady rate. We *could* work on a monthly rather than a yearly basis, or use even smaller time units, but then of course the amount of work involved would increase substantially.

Second, how do we *know* before either project has even started that the costs and revenues are going to be as stated? Our calculations could be totally invalidated if the machine purchased turns out to be the one-in-a-thousand which has serious running problems during its first year of operation, thus drastically raising overall costs and cutting away at our revenues.

Finally, and perhaps most seriously, how do we know that 10 per cent is the right discounting rate to use – and why, in any case, should we use the same rate over the whole lifetime of the projects? Again, an error in selecting the discounting rate could easily lead to a wrong decision.

Other methods for comparing investments

An alternative approach to the problem would be, rather than using some definite rate, to ask just *what* rate of return is represented by the revenue from each project. We went some way towards answering this question when we said earlier in this section that the existence of a surplus on a project when discounted at 15 per cent means that the rate of return from the project is better than 15 per cent, but finding out how much better is an example of one of those 'find the rate' problems we mentioned in the previous section as being somewhat awkward to solve. Generally a trial-and-error strategy is adopted, discounting the returns at various rates until the one is found that gives perfect balance between discounted revenues and costs, with neither a surplus nor a deficit. The rate that produces this effect is known as the *internal rate of return* of the project, but clearly for the trial-and-error method to be successful we would need to have tables of discount factors for rates increasing by steps of 1 per cent or even less.

Another criterion which we have not looked at so far is how quickly each project will give us our money back – an important consideration, particularly if the money had to be borrowed in the first place. In determining the so-called *pay-back* period we are really just finding out when the projects break even – a topic we have already discussed in Chapter 1. In the particular case of Panamount Manufacturing, you may like to verify that Machine A comes off slightly better, having paid for itself after 1.8 years, while Machine B does not do so until 1.95 years have elapsed (what has been assumed in reaching these figures?). In these calculations, of course, we have used the *non*-discounted revenues.

Perhaps the existence of so many methods, which can lead to quite different decisions, is an indication of the complexity of the problem. Ultimately, there is no 'right' method which will lead us inevitably to the best decision; there are too many imponderable factors in the problem for that. What the methods of this section *can* do, however, is to provide a spectrum of approaches from which the most suitable can be chosen as a back-up to sound judgement and experience.

Computational note

In calculations connected with sinking funds etc. one often has to deal with expressions such as

$$1.1^4 + 1.1^3 + 1.1^2 + 1.1.$$

Such expressions are well suited to the use of a spreadsheet. You will find sample spreadsheets for annuity and sinking fund calculations stored as ANN.XLS and SINK.XLS on the Companion Website, together with full explanations of the way they are constructed and used. These days any serious work involving mortgages, investment appraisal, etc., will be carried out with the aid of an appropriate computer package. Excel also provides a number of financial functions for calculating present values, internal rates of return, etc., which you may like to explore; the Excel supplement on the Companion Website would be a good starting point. There is also an entertaining 'calculator' provided by the Money Guardian, to which the Companion Website has a link. You can check your understanding of the methods of this chapter by using the 'calculator' to work out interest and then verifying the results by hand-calculation.

Worked examples

Before you begin to work some examples for yourself, here are a few more illustrations of the various types of problem discussed in this chapter.

Example 1

What is the minimum amount you would expect to pay in return for a guaranteed income of £5000 per year for ten years, the first payment made one year after investment? Assume an interest rate of 5 per cent.

This is an annuity problem. In order to have enough money to cover the first payment of £5000 made one year from now, we need to invest 5000×0.952 (using the discount factor for 1 period at 5 per cent from Table 16.1). We can deal similarly with the payments for years 2–10; the resulting calculation can be set out as follows:

For first payment, we need	5000×0.952
For second payment we need	5000×0.907
etc.	5000×0.864
	5000×0.823
	5000×0.784
	5000×0.746
	5000×0.711
	5000×0.677
	5000×0.645
	5000×0.614

Total required $= 5000 \times (0.952 + \ldots + 0.614) = 5000 \times 7.72 = £38\ 608.67$.

Example 2

A company has the choice of two investments, both costing an initial £30 000. The first will yield cash flows of £6000 per year for three years (the first payment receivable one year after investment), while the second will simply yield a lump sum of £20 000 at the end of the three-year period. Which investment should be chosen? Assume an interest rate of 5 per cent.

The present value of £20 000 in three years' time at five per cent is $20\ 000 \times 0.864$ (from Table 16.1) which is £17 280.

The present values of the three payments of £6000 are as follows:

After 1 year: $6000 \times 0.952 = 5712$
After 2 years: $6000 \times 0.907 = 5442$
After 3 years: $6000 \times 0.864 = 5184$.

Thus the total present value of the three payments is £16 338. So on a present value basis the lump sum investment would be selected.

Example 3

A sum of £200 is invested at 7 per cent per annum compound interest. How many years will it take for the total in the account to exceed £500?

Here we want to find the value of n for which $200 \times 1.07^n > 500$. The easiest way to do this is to try various values of n. Clearly n needs to be fairly large, since at 7 per cent per annum it is going to take a long time for the investment to more than double its value. If we try $n = 10$, we find the value of the investment to be $200 \times 1.07^{10} = £393$, so this is not long enough. $n = 15$, on the other hand, gives £552, so this is too big. A bit of further experimentation should show you that 14 years is the required time.

It is easy to tackle this problem with a calculator. Since $500/200 = 2.5$, we are looking for the value of n for which $1.07^n > 2.5$. If you set up the constant multiplier on your calculator so as to generate a series of powers of 1.07, and count how many times you need to press the '=' key before the display exceeds 2.5, you will have the answer – remembering, of course, that the first '=' already gives the square of 1.07, which is the total after 2 years.

EXERCISES

*Further examples on the work of this chapter can be found on the **Companion Website**.*

1 On 1 January 2007 you invested £1000 in a building society. Assuming a constant interest rate of 7 per cent per year, how much will be in the account by 1 January 2012?

2 You now decide to withdraw £50 a year from the account mentioned in Exercise 1 making the first withdrawal on 1 January 2012. Will this reduce the total investment if interest remains at 7 per cent?

3 A machine which currently costs £600 will increase in price by 20 per cent per year.
   (a) What will it cost in three years' time?
   (b) How much should be invested each year in a sinking fund earning interest at 15 per cent per annum to cover this purchase? (The first investment is to be made at once.)

4 Fred borrows £500 from Bill, and promises to pay it back in instalments of £100 monthly. If Bill charges interest at 5 per cent a month, how long will it take Fred to pay back the loan, and how much will the last payment be? The first payment is made one month after the money is borrowed.

5 'Brackley card' credit cards charge 4 per cent per month interest on debts; 'Excess' charge 25 per cent per half-year. Which represents the better value to the borrower?

6 When employees retire from a certain firm, they are given a lump sum of £5000 in lieu of pension. If the firm has worked its employees so hard that their life expectancy on retirement is only five years, how much per year will they have to live on if they invest the lump sum at 5 per cent? (Assume that the first withdrawal from the account is made one year after retirement.)

7 A man has an annuity which will pay him £500 a year for four years, the first payment to be made three years from now. However, he is short of cash and proposes to sell the annuity. What is the most he can expect to get for it? Use a discounting rate of 10 per cent.

8 The cost of an Eskimo deep-freeze is £150. It will last four years, and I estimate that the cost of servicing and repairs, including insurance, will be £20 for the first two years, £25 for the third year, and £40 for the fourth (assumed payable at the end of the year). At the end of the fourth year I expect to be able to sell the machine for £50.

   The rival brand, Polar Bear, costs £140, but I can get a discount of 10 per cent on this because my brother works for the firm. However, the cost of servicing, repairs and insurance for this model will be £25 per year for each of the four years that it lasts (again paid at the year-end), and I will have to pay the council £5 to take it away.

Assuming a discount rate of 15 per cent, which deep-freeze would you recommend me to buy?

9 A firm is considering the purchase of one of two machines. The first, costing £1700, is expected to bring in revenues of £1000, £800 and £500 respectively in the three years for which it will be operative, while the second, which costs £2000, produces revenues of £1200, £900 and £600, and has the same lifetime. Neither machine will have any appreciable scrap value at end of its life. A discount rate of 20 per cent has been suggested as appropriate.

Advise the firm as to the financial wisdom of purchasing one or the other of these machines.

10 The following is an extract from the cash book of a small business, relating to its investment account at the bank:

1/1/10	Balance in bank account	£11 252.73
5/1/10	Bank charges (December 09)	10.00
9/1/10	Deposit per J Smith	4 750.00
15/1/10	Transfer to current a/c	5 000.00
28/1/10	Deposit per N Jones	2 142.36
5/2/10	Bank charges (January 10)	7.50
12/2/10	Standing order no. 3136.	500.00
21/2/10	Deposit per R Brown	1 413.47
26/2/10	Transfer to current a/c	5 000.00

Assuming that interest at 0.4 per cent per month is added to the account on the last day of each month, and is calculated on the balance in the account at that date, compute the total in the account on 1/3/10. (This is, of course, not a very realistic assumption – in practice the interest would be computed on an average balance, and/or added more frequently than once a month.)

Case Study

Choosing a mortgage

You are working as a financial adviser, and have been asked by a client to help her decide which of a number of mortgages she should choose, in order to purchase a house costing £125 000 at the start of 2011. She can afford to put down a deposit of £20 000, and wishes to pay off the mortgage over 20 years. The mortgages on offer are as follows:

(a) Company A offers a fixed rate of 7 per cent per annum for five years, after which you estimate that the rate is likely to rise to 10 per cent for the remainder of the period. Calculate the annual payments for the first five years on the assumption that the rate will remain at 7 per cent over the whole period. Hence find the amount outstanding at the end of the five years, and from this work out the annual payments for the remainder of the period at an interest rate of 9 per cent per annum.

(b) Company B offers a fixed rate of 8.5 per cent per annum for the whole period. What will be the annual payments under this scheme?

Advise the client on her best option, mentioning any warnings which need to be borne in mind when making a decision.

Further reading

For a more detailed discussion of the methods referred to in this chapter, you should probably consult an accounting, rather than statistics, text, for example:

Wood, F. (2002), *Business Accounting 1*, 9th edn, FT Prentice Hall.

Introductory economics texts, such as the following, will give you an idea as to why interest rates loom so large in discussions of the general health of the economy:

Sloman, J. (2006), *Economics*, 6th edn, FT Prentice Hall.

Matthews, K., Parkin, M. and Powell, M. (2005), *Economics*, 6th edn, Addison-Wesley.

Chapter 17

PLANNING PRODUCTION LEVELS:
LINEAR PROGRAMMING

Chapter prerequisites

Before starting work on this chapter make sure you are happy with the following topics:

1 construction of equations and inequalities (see Chapter 1, p. 21–2);

2 plotting graphs from equations and inequalities (see Chapter 1, pp. 25–9);

3 slopes of straight line graphs (see Chapter 1, p. 26);

4 solution of simultaneous equations (see Chapter 1, pp. 22–4);

5 the basic ideas of modelling (see Part 4, p. 349).

Learning outcomes

By the end of your work on this chapter you should be able to:

1 recognise, and formulate an algebraic model of, a problem involving maximisation or minimisation of an objective function subject to a set of linear constraints;

2 in cases where the problem involves only two variables, plot the graph representing the problem, and hence determine the feasible and optimal solutions;

3 state which variables are slack in the optimal solution;

4 determine the scarcity values of the tight constraints, and the ranges over which they apply;

5 determine the range of profits or costs over which the solution remains valid.

Quantitative methods in practice

The London Ring Main

Thames Water inherited a water distribution network for London which was developed by the Victorians. This was based on trunk mains radiating from four main water treatment works. Some of the pipes were 100 years old and could no longer be relied upon to meet constantly rising demand. Rather than simply replacing pipes (which would have caused enormous disruption), Thames Water decided to build the London Ring Main, a 2.5 m diameter tunnel 80 km long running 45 m below London.

There are 5 locations where water can be poured into the Ring Main and 11 where it can be pumped out. Water flows around it under pressure and the only active components are the pumps on the output shafts. The problem which Thames Water faced was therefore to determine for each of the 5 input shafts how much water to pour into the Ring Main and when, and for each of the 11 output shafts how much to pump out and when.

. . .

From 'Simulation and optimisation join forces to schedule London's water', by Robert Simons, MP in Action, January 1996, www.eudoxus.com/mp-in-action (accessed 21 November 2010)

The problem above sounds – and is – very complicated, but it's an example of a type of situation which arises in many different contexts in business and industry. The task facing Thames Water, as explained in the quote, was to determine the values of the inputs to and outputs from the water system. But the whole operation was subject to a number of limitations – for example, because the pipes were old, they could not withstand too high a pressure; a certain level of demand had to be met; and so on. Moreover, as in any sensible business, one of Thames Water's objectives was to minimise costs of the process.

This kind of problem, where we want to determine the values of a set of variables which will optimise some target quantity (here, minimise the cost), subject to a set of limitations or *constraints*, is known in mathematics as an *optimisation* problem. Optimisation is now a huge subject, with much active research going on into new methods and improved computer applications; we are going to look at a very simple version of one particular method, called *linear programming*.

The production manager's problem

Jim Brown is the production manager of Apex Garden Tools, a small firm which specialises in the manufacture of high-quality tools for the amateur gardening market. The firm produces quite a wide range of items, but has a flexible workforce which can easily be switched from one production line to another. Much of the machinery is also used in the production of more than one type of tool, as are many of the raw materials – sheet and tubular metal, wood, paint and so on. The profits gained by Apex from the sale of different types of tools naturally vary widely – a wheelbarrow will generate a lot more profit than a trowel – as do the times taken to produce them, and the potential markets for them.

Jim Brown's problem is to decide how Apex ought to divide up its production among the various types of tools it manufactures in order to obtain the maximum possible profit, taking into account all the factors mentioned above. In other words, it is not sufficient for him simply to say 'Produce as many as you can of everything' – there will be many limitations or *constraints* within which the production must operate, such as limited quantities of raw materials available, limited amounts of machine time, a fixed number of hours per week for each type of worker – the list could be continued almost indefinitely. Moreover, because the profits generated by each type of tool vary, perhaps it would be better not to produce *any* of a less profitable line, but to concentrate all resources on producing the more profitable ones. But then again, maybe Apex will not be able to sell them because of limitations to the market . . .

You can see from this brief outline of the problem that the chances of arriving at the 'best' solution – the one giving maximum possible profits – by simply thinking about it are minimal. Mr Brown is more likely to obtain a nervous breakdown than an optimal solution! What he needs is a *systematic* way of tackling the problem – preferably a way that guarantees that he will end up with the most profitable solution, at the same time ensuring that the firm operates within all its limitations of materials, personnel, etc.

Although this is a much simpler problem than the one faced by Thames Water, it has essentially a similar structure, and can be dealt with using *linear programming*.

Setting up the model

We simplify Jim Brown's problem a bit further in order to illustrate the basics of the technique. Let us suppose that Apex has drastically rationalised its range of products, and decided to concentrate on producing just two: a single-wheeled barrow called the 'Workhorse', and a two-wheeled model called the 'Donkey'. We will find in the next section that this reduction to only two products means that the problem can be solved in a particularly simple way.

Let us cut down, too, on the number of limitations or constraints, and assume that there are just four that need to be allowed for: only 40 wheels (purchased ready-made from a supplier) can be obtained per week; not more than 24 barrows per week can be sold to wholesalers; the 'Workhorse' needs a rubber tyre, of which only 16 per week are available; and the skilled metalwork for the barrows, which takes three hours for a 'Workhorse' and two hours for a 'Donkey', has to be done by one of two men, each of whom works only a 30-hour week.

Our first step is to define some *variables*: what are the quantities which can be varied at will by the company? Obviously not the amounts of wheels, tyres and so on; they are all fixed by external circumstances beyond the company's control. The only things that it can determine at will – subject, of course, to the various constraints – are the numbers of each type of barrow which it chooses to make. It is those numbers that Mr Brown hopes to determine in such a way as to get the maximum possible profit. So, our variables are going to be:

- w, the number of 'Workhorse' barrows made per week; and
- d, the number of 'Donkey' barrows made per week.

Having defined these two variables, we can now translate the four constraints into inequalities involving the variables.

Consider the wheels constraint first. Each 'Workhorse' has one wheel, so producing, say, four 'Workhorses' would need four wheels, and more generally producing w of them will need w wheels. On top of that, we need two wheels for each 'Donkey' produced; thus six 'Donkeys' would need 12 wheels, eight would need 16 wheels, and in general d of them will need $d \times 2$ or $2d$ wheels. The total number of wheels used in making both w 'Workhorses' and d 'Donkeys', then, will be $w + 2d$. But we know this cannot be more than 40, because that is all the wheels available in one week. So we arrive at the inequality

$$w + 2d \leqslant 40 \tag{a}$$

representing the wheels constraint.

We can now obtain the other inequalities in a slightly less long-winded way. The total number of barrows made in a week is $w + d$, and it is no good letting this be more than 24 because that is the most the wholesalers will take. So

$$w + d \leqslant 24 \tag{b}$$

is the wholesaler constraint.

Three hours' metalworking time for a 'Workhorse' means that w of them will take $w \times 3$ or $3w$ hours; we also need $2d$ hours to make d 'Donkeys' at two hours each. So the total time needed is $3w + 2d$, and as the two people who can do the work only have 60 hours a week available between them, we have

$$3w + 2d \leqslant 60 \tag{c}$$

as the metalwork constraint.

Finally, since each 'Workhorse' has one tyre, and there are at most 16 available per week, we have

$$w \leqslant 16 \tag{d}$$

as the tyre constraint – this inequality only involves one of the variables, because clearly any limitation on the numbers of tyres available will not have any effect at all on how many 'Donkeys' we can produce, since they do not need tyres!

We have not yet introduced the question of profits, so let us now assume that we know each 'Workhorse' will give £4 profit when sold, and each 'Donkey' £3. Our objective is to maximise the total profit, and so we can write down the *objective function* to be maximised as

$$\text{Profit} = 4w + 3d.$$

The problem has now been reduced to the set of four inequalities (a)–(d)* plus the objective function. What is more, you should recognise that it involves only *linear* expressions – there are no w^2 or $1/d$ terms, for example – so that, if plotted on a graph, all would give straight lines. This explains why the technique is called linear programming – and it also gives the clue as to how we should proceed with trying to find the solution.

---

* Strictly speaking we should include the two 'non-negativity constraints' $w \geqslant 0$ and $d \geqslant 0$, expressing the fact that one cannot make a negative number of wheelbarrows!

Quick check questions

1 A company makes A4 and A5 size notebooks. An A4 notebook requires three staples and an A5 notebook requires two. If 1000 staples per hour are available, write down an inequality to show the constraint on the numbers of notebooks produced. Be sure to define your variables carefully.

2 A catfood manufacturer makes two types of tinned food, 'Tabby' and 'Kitty'. Each tin contains 300 g of food. 'Tabby' is composed of 60 per cent horsemeat, 20 per cent rusk and 20 per cent water, while 'Kitty' has 70 per cent horsemeat, 20 per cent rusk and 10 per cent water. If the quantities of horsemeat and rusk available per hour are 90 kg and 120 kg respectively (the supply of water is unlimited), write down the constraints which apply to the numbers of tins of the two types of food produced per hour.

3 In question 2 above, the profit on a tin of 'Tabby' is 4p, while on a tin of 'Kitty' it is 5p. Write down the profit function.

Answers:

1 Let the numbers of A4 and A5 notebooks respectively made per hour be x and y. Then the staples constraint is $3x + 2y \leq 1000$.

2 Let the number of tins of 'Tabby' and 'Kitty' produced per hour be T and K respectively. In a 300 g tin of 'Tabby' there will be 60 per cent of 300 g = 180 g of horsemeat and 20 per cent or 300 g = 60 g of rusk, while in a tin of 'Kitty' the quantities will be 210 g of horesemeat and 60 g of rusk. Working in grams, so that 90 kg becomes 90 000 g etc., we obtain the following constraints:

For the horsemeat: $180T + 210K \leq 90\ 000$
For the rusk: $\quad\quad 60T + 60K \leq 120\ 000$.

These can be simplified to give

Horsemeat constraint: $6T + 7K \leq 3000$
Rusk constraint: $\quad\quad T + K \leq 2000$.

3 Profit (in pence per hour) is $4T + 5K$.

Graphing the model

Because we have only two variables in this problem we are able to plot the constraints on a two-dimensional graph. There will be four lines on the graph, one for each constraint, and it is most important that you concentrate on plotting one at a time, without worrying about the effect of the others. To start trying to think about more than one constraint at a time is a recipe for disaster, and is in any case unnecessary since the graph itself is going to show us *how* they interact with each other.

Consider then, inequality (*a*), representing the wheels constraint. The easiest way of deciding where it should be plotted is to concentrate on the two extreme cases, supposing first that the entire supply of wheels is to be used up on making 'Workhorses', and no 'Donkeys' are to be made at all. Clearly this would mean that 40 'Workhorses' could be produced. So one point on the line bounding this constraint will be $w = 40$, $d = 0$. At the other extreme, we have the possibility of making 20 'Donkeys' if no 'Workhorses' are made, giving a second point at $w = 0$, $d = 20$. Thus the line bounding the constraint will

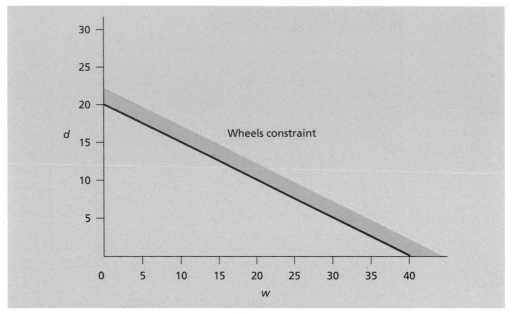

Figure 17.1 Beginning the linear programming graph

run from 40 on the w-axis to 20 on the d-axis, and all combinations of w and d using less than or equal to 40 wheels will fall in the region below this line, as indicated in Figure 17.1. Of course, in practice we could not actually make 40 'Workhorses' because we would not have enough tyres for them, but at the moment we are not considering that constraint. This is what was meant earlier by 'Concentrate on one constraint at a time'.

If we go on to inequality (b), and repeat the 'extremes' argument, you should be able to see that the line for this constraint will run from $w = 0$, $d = 24$, to $w = 24$, $d = 0$. Once again, all points below this line are possible as far as the wholesaler constraint is concerned. For inequality (c), the same process gives the two extremes of the line as $w = 0$, $d = 30$ and $w = 20$, $d = 0$. In other words, if the metalworkers spent all their time on making 'Workhorses', which take three hours apiece, and did not make any 'Donkeys' at all, they could in their 60 hours produce 20 'Workhorses'; or, alternatively, they could concentrate on 'Donkeys' and make 30, since they only take two hours each.

You can see these three constraints plotted and labelled in Figure 17.2. It is customary, as shown there, to shade the 'forbidden' side of the line – the side on which the constraint would be violated – as this avoids having lots of criss-crossing shading where the constraints interact. You can also see in the figure the slightly different sort of line which results from inequality (d). This told us that, regardless of how many 'Donkeys' are made, the number of 'Workhorses' can never exceed 16, and so is represented by a line that, however big d becomes, will restrict w to below 16 – in other words, a line parallel to the d-axis at $w = 16$. Incidentally, the choice of w as the horizontal and d as the vertical axis is quite arbitrary – there is no reason why you should not take them the other way round.

Having drawn all the constraints on the graph, we can now see the effect of their interaction: the possible combinations of 'Workhorses' and 'Donkeys' which can be made will be represented by the points inside the region ABCDEO which correspond to whole-number values of w and d, because only within that region are all the constraints satisfied. We call these points the *feasible solutions*, and the region ABCDEO is called the *feasible*

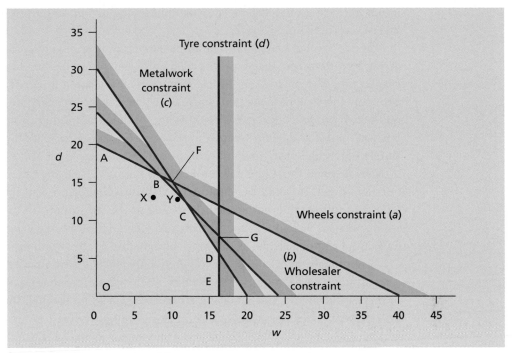

Figure 17.2 The completed linear programming graph

region. The reason for the restriction to whole-number values of *w* and *d* is, of course, that we are not interested in manufacturing fractions of a wheelbarrow!

Finding the best solution

Now that, in theory at least, we know what all the possible solutions are, we *could* go about trying to find which of them is the 'best' – in the sense of yielding maximum possible profit – by finding out what profit each of the possible solutions would give, and then choosing as our 'best' combination the one for which the profit is greatest. But even in such a simple problem as this, there are a great many possible solution points within the feasible region; even to write them all down would be a time-consuming process – and also an unnecessary one, as can easily be seen.

Consider, for example, the point X, at which 13 'Donkeys' and 8 'Workhorses' are being produced. This will yield a profit of $13 \times 3 + 8 \times 4 = £71$. But clearly we will get more profit from point Y, where the same number of 'Donkeys' but three more 'Workhorses' are being produced, or from point B, where the number of 'Workhorses' is the same as at X but three more 'Donkeys' are being made. This argument suggests that the 'best' solution is going to be a point on the edge of the feasible region rather than in the middle of it.

That still leaves us with quite a few points to look at. But fortunately there is a way we can narrow down the candidates for the 'best' solution still further. Imagine for a moment that we are interested, not in gaining the maximum possible profit, but simply in achieving a profit of, say £60. We could do that in a variety of ways: by making no 'Donkeys' at all and just 15 'Workhorses', or by making no 'Workhorses' and 20 'Donkeys', or by producing and selling 6 'Workhorses' and 12 'Donkeys', and so on. But there is one important fact about all these combinations giving us our £60 profit: they all lie on the line AQ, as shown in Figure 17.3.

This line is called a *profit line*. The particular one we have drawn represents combinations giving a profit of £60. Bigger profits will be shown by lines further away from the origin, smaller profits by lines closer to the origin, but all the profit lines will have one thing in common: they will have the same *slope*, since that is determined by the ratio of the profits on the two products. You can check this by working out another profit line, perhaps the one for a profit of £48. So what we are doing, as we try to increase the possible profit, is simply sliding the profit line outwards from O, while keeping it always parallel to AQ.

Now, as we do this, there will come a point at which, if we were to move the profit line out any further, it would cease to intersect the feasible region, and therefore profits any larger cannot be achieved in practice because of the constraints. In the present case that will happen, as you should test for yourself, when the profit line is just passing through C. So the point C will give us the 'best' combination of the two items to produce.

This probably seems rather a complicated process, and you may well be wondering if it might not have been quicker to examine all the whole-number points around the edge of the feasible region. But, in fact, it is not necessary to go through the whole process of drawing profit lines every time, for the following reason. The 'best' point we finally found, C, is at a corner of the feasible region, and if you try using profit lines of different slopes you will find that, in general, the furthest extreme to which the profit line can be moved – the point giving maximum possible profit – is *always at a corner* of the feasible region. (The only exception to this would be if the profit line happened to be parallel to one of the edges of the feasible region, in which case we would not get just one, but a whole set of 'best' solutions.)

Having once demonstrated this fact, we may quote it without proof in future, which gives us a very simple rule for finding the 'best' solution in any such problem: having drawn the graph, we now know that the maximum profit will occur at one of the corners

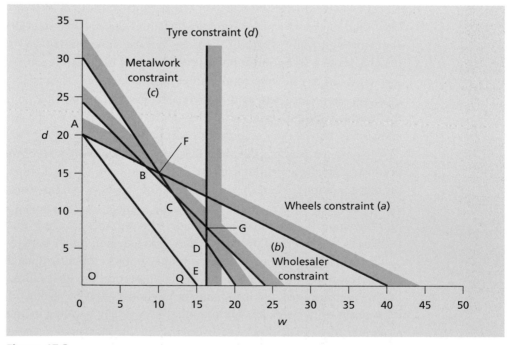

Figure 17.3

of the feasible region. So, all we need do is work out the profit at each of those corners – there will not usually be too many of them – and pick the one where the profit is greatest. It is easiest to do this systematically in the form of a table:

Corner	w	d	Profit (£)
A	0	20	60
B	8	16	80
C	12	12	84
D	16	6	82
E	16	0	64

This confirms what we already know from our study of the profit line in this case – that the maximum possible profit is obtained by producing 12 of each type of barrow. Notice that although strictly speaking O is also a corner of the feasible region, we did not bother to include it in the table because it obviously represents the point where zero profit is made. Actually we really did not need to put in E either. D is bound to give a bigger profit than E since it involves making the same number of 'Workhorses' as at E, and six 'Donkeys' as well.

We have now solved the problem posed in the earlier section 'Setting up the model', using a process which could be summarised in the four steps:

1 write down the algebraic model for the problem;
2 plot the graph representing this model;
3 identify the feasible region and its corners;
4 find the profit at each corner, and select the one for which this is greatest.

But, as you will have learned to expect by now, we have had to make quite a lot of assumptions to simplify the problem enough to solve it in this way. So we now need to ask just what those hidden assumptions were, and how disastrous an effect it will have on our 'best' solution if one or more of them turns out to be wrong. If you have read Chapter 14 you will recognise that what we are going to do is carry out a *sensitivity analysis* on the solution. First, however, here are some examples so that you can check your understanding thus far.

Quick check questions

1 You want to plot the constraint $3x + 2y \leq 1000$. Where will the constraint line meet the x- and y-axes?

2 On a graph involving two variables, A and B, you want to plot a constraint to show that $A \geq 10$. How would you show this?

3 You are plotting a profit function, in pence per hour, which has the form $4T + 5K$. Where would the line representing a profit of £10 per hour cross the T- and K-axes?

Answers:
1 The line meets the x-axis at $x = 1000/3$ or 333.3, and the y-axis at $y = 1000/2$ or 500.
2 The constraint would be a line through $A = 10$ parallel to the B-axis. The shading would be on the lower side of the line.
3 Remembering that we are working in pence, the line representing a profit of £10 per hour has the form $4T + 5K = 1000$. This crosses the T-axis at $T = 250$, and the K-axis at $K = 200$.

Varying the constraints

In setting up the model for our problem, we had to assume that we had adequate information about two sets of things: first of all the amounts of the various resources by which the production is constrained, and second, the profits that would be generated by the sale of the products. In practice, of course, these can be quite difficult to estimate, particularly if we are trying to plan production not just for a week or two, but for a whole year or more ahead. We may expect to receive deliveries of 4000 tonnes of raw materials from our suppliers, and plan our production accordingly, only to find that shortages cut down our deliveries to 3000 tonnes. We may expect to be able to use a certain machine for 50 hours a week, and then find that, owing to breakdowns, the figure is closer to 40 hours. Or we may hope to be able to sell a product at a price that will give us a profit of £6 per item, and then discover that a competitor has put a cheap new alternative product on the market and we must cut our profit margins if we are to maintain our market share.

All of these circumstances will result in our so-called 'best' solution, worked out for a set of assumptions which are no longer valid, failing to be the 'best' any more. However, to avoid being *too* pessimistic we will not assume that everything goes wrong at once! We will begin by supposing that the profits of £3 and £4 on our two products can actually be realised, but that some of our estimates as to the constraints are in doubt.

You will see if you refer again to Figure 17.2 that only two of the constraint lines actually pass through the solution point, C; these two are the metalwork constraint and the wholesaler constraint. We say that these two constraints are *tight* at C – in other words, *all* the available metalwork time, and *all* the wholesaler's purchasing capacity, are being used up when we produce the optimum quantities of 12 'Donkeys' and 12 'Workhorses'. The wheels constraint and the tyres constraint, however, are said to be *slack*, because there is some spare capacity in these two resources. Making 12 of each type of barrow will use up 36 wheels, and there were 40 available, so 4 will be spare per week. As for the tyres, although we could have had up to 16 a week, we will only in fact be using 12, so again there will be 4 left unused.

It is clear from this that as far as the slack constraints go, we could make a small error in estimating the amounts available without affecting the solution at all. For example, if we had *hoped* to get 16 tyres a week but in fact only 14 materialised next week, we would still be able to make our chosen quantities of 12 of each kind of barrow, and our profits would be unaffected. Equally, if our wheel supplier suddenly rang up and said 'You can have 50 wheels next week if you want', we would be rather silly to accept, because we would not be able to use them – there would not be enough metalworking time to make more barrows than our present 12 of each kind, nor would the wholesaler take them if we did make them.

It follows that we need only worry about the effect of errors in the *tight* constraints on our solution. And again, we will be optimistic and suppose that *one* of the tight constraints is definitely all right – let us say the metalwork constraint. We can then narrow down the problem to the question: what effect will an increase of one barrow in the number that the wholesaler is prepared to take have on our profits? (We could, of course, equally well have looked at the effect of a *decrease*, but that's rather depressing, and we get the same result in the end!)

An increase of 1 in the number of barrows the wholesaler will take means that inequality (b) changes to

$$w + d \leqslant 25$$

while the other tight constraint remains the same (inequality (c)):

$$3w + 2d \leqslant 60.$$

We *could* try to find the new position of our 'best' point C by moving the line (b) on the graph out by one unit, and watching what happens to C. This, however, is not easily done unless one has drawn the graph on a very big scale, so we choose instead to use an alternative method. You will recall from Chapter 1, in the section on making use of graphs, that the point of intersection of two lines on a graph represents the simultaneous solution of the equations of those lines. Now C is the point where the two lines (b) and (c) intersect, so if we solve the equations

$$w + d = 25 \text{ and } 3w + 2d = 60$$

simultaneously, we will find what the new value of C should be. If we multiply the first equation by 2, we get

$$2w + 2d = 50$$
$$3w + 2d = 60$$

and on subtracting the top equation from the bottom one, d will be eliminated:

$$w = 10.$$

Replacing this value of w in the first equation $w + d = 25$ gives us $10 + d = 25$, whence $d = 15$. So our new profit-maximising solution is to make 10 'Workhorses' and 15 'Donkeys'. What effect will this change have on the profit?

Well, the old maximum profit was £84, as we calculated in the previous section. We will now be making 10 'Workhorses' with a profit of £4 each – that is, £40 – and 15 'Donkeys' with a profit of £3 on each – that is, £45 – giving a total of £85 altogether. So the fact that the wholesaler is willing to take one more barrow enables us to obtain £1 more profit. We call this the *scarcity value* of the resource 'wholesaler's capacity', because it tells us how valuable, in terms of its effect on profits, this *scarce* resource is. By the same token, of course, every one barrow *reduction* in the number that the wholesaler is willing to take will cut down our profits by £1.

However, useful though this information is, it does not represent the whole story. We would be quite mistaken, for instance, if we proceeded to say 'Right, if we can persuade the wholesaler to take 60 more barrows a week, that will give us another £60 profit' – because there is no way in which we can produce a further 60 barrows per week – there would not be enough wheels for them, to name just one problem! The scarcity value only applies over a limited range of wholesaler capacities, and we need to know what that range is in order to have a complete picture of the situation.

To find the range, we need to return to Figure 17.2, and look at what happens to the solution point, C, as the wholesaler constraint is varied. When we move the constraint outwards, C will move *up* the metalwork line (you can easily see this by putting a ruler along the wholesaler line and then sliding it out), but it can only move as far as the point labelled F, since beyond that we would be violating the wheels limitation. So the greatest number of barrows which it would be useful to us to persuade the wholesaler to take is represented by point F, at which 10 'Workhorses' and 15 'Donkeys' – a total of 25 barrows – are being made. Conversely, when the wholesaler line is moved inwards, C will move *down* the metalwork line, until its progress is halted at D by the tyres constraint. In other words, the smallest number of barrows which the wholesaler can accept, without making our choice of C as the 'best' solution wrong, is represented by point D, at which 16 'Workhorses' and 6 'Donkeys' are being made – 22 barrows in total.

Thus the complete statement regarding alterations to the wholesaler constraint is that every extra barrow that the wholesaler is prepared to take will generate £1 extra profit, but only within the limits 22 to 25 barrows. Outside these limits, the problem is changed by the operation of the other constraints, and one can no longer rely on point C – the intersection of constraints (*b*) and (*c*) – to give the most profitable solution.

We must now repeat this process to see what will happen if it should turn out that our estimate of the wholesaler's capacity was correct, but the metalwork hours were wrong.

In that case, inequality (*b*) would stay the same

$$w + d \leqslant 24$$

but if (*c*) were in fact an underestimate by one hour, then we would have

$$3w + 2d \leqslant 61.$$

Solving these simultaneously as before to find the new position of C, we find that $w = 13$ and $d = 11$ are the new 'best' production levels. You can check that this solution, with w bigger than before and d smaller, is reasonable, by watching how C moves as the line (*c*) is moved out on the graph. The new profit will therefore be $4 \times 13 + 3 \times 11 = £85$, so once again we are gaining an extra £1 profit by increasing the metalwork hours by one hour.

To find the range over which this applies, we must move line (*c*) on the graph outwards and inwards, watching what happens to C when we do so. As the metalwork line is moved out, C slides down until it reaches G, where the tyres constraint prevents any further increase. At G, 16 'Workhorses' and 8 'Donkeys' are being made, which will use up $3 \times 16 + 2 \times 8 = 64$ hours of metalwork time; more hours than that will not be any use to us because there will be insufficient tyres. When we move the metalwork line inwards, C slides up until, at B, it comes up against the wheels constraint. So the minimum number of metalwork hours for which C represents the best solution will be the number used at B, where 8 'Workhorses' and 16 'Donkeys' are being produced. The metalwork hours requirement for these is $3 \times 8 + 2 \times 16 = 56$ hours.

We can therefore state that for every extra hour of metalworking time that can be gained, an extra profit of £1 will be made, but this only applies between 56 and 64 hours. Outside that range the problem becomes a completely different one, for which C may no longer be the best solution. Using the terminology introduced earlier, we say that the scarcity value of metalwork hours is £1 per hour. Of course, the larger the scarcity value of a resource, the more serious will be the effect on our profits of an error in estimating the amount of that resource we are going to be able to use.

Changes in the profits

The other kind of error in estimation which we might make is a wrong assessment of the profit resulting from the sale of each product. Suppose we were in fact only able to sell the 'Donkey' at a price that gave a profit of £2 per item; would our so-called 'best' policy of making 12 of each type of barrow still give us the biggest possible profit, or should we perhaps be operating at totally different production levels under these changed circumstances?

To answer this question we need to go back to the profit line which we drew on Figure 17.3. The point C turned out to be the most profitable in this case because it was the furthest limit to which the profit line could be moved without going outside the feasible region. But this will only be the case as long as the slope of the profit line lies between the slopes of the metalwork constraint and the wholesaler constraint. If the profits are such that the slope of the profit line becomes steeper than that of the metal-work line, then point D will be the furthest it can be moved, while if the profit line should become flatter than the wholesaler line, it can be moved up to B before going outside the feasible region. You can verify these statements by sliding rulers around the graph again.

So our best solution at C only remains valid as long as the profits are such that the slope of the profit line is between those of the two constraints passing through C. Now the slope of the wholesaler line is 24/24 = 1 (actually, according to the definition we had in Chapter 1, it is −1, since it is going downhill, but as the same applies to *all* the lines on the graph we will omit the minus signs). Similarly, the slope of the metalwork line is 30/20 = 1.5. Thus the slope of the profit line has to be between 1 and 1.5 if C is to be the best solution. But what is the slope of the profit line?

Well, recalling that we saw in the section 'Finding the best solution' that all the profit lines are going to be parallel and therefore have the same slope, it does not matter which of them we look at to work out the slope, so we might as well use the one plotted on Figure 17.3. The slope of that one is 20/15 or 4/3, and if you remember that the profit on a 'Workhorse' is £4 and that on a 'Donkey' is £3, you will realise that the slope of the profit line is just Profit on *w*/Profit on *d*. This may be the opposite way up from what you might have expected, if you are used to thinking of slope as vertical/horizontal. So, if you feel you are likely to get confused, it is always safer to draw in a typical profit line on the graph.

The result of all this is that we have shown that as long as the profits on the two products are such that

$$1 < \frac{\text{Profit on } w}{\text{Profit on } d} < 1.5$$

we are safe in using C as our best production level. But, to go back to the hypothetical case quoted at the start of this section, if the profits on each 'Donkey' fell to £2, we certainly could not use C any more to get the maximum profit, since the profit ratio would now be 4/2 = 2, which is outside the allowable range we have just calculated. On the other hand, in the problem as originally posed, the ratio is 4/3 which certainly lies inside the range we have calculated, just as it should. This in fact provides a useful check as to whether you have the profit ratio the right way up: if you have, the profit ratio as it exists in the original problem should lie within the calculated range.

A different type of problem

The problem we have been looking at so far has involved the maximising of a profit subject to various linear constraints. But the same approach can also be used to minimise costs, in a situation where that is a more appropriate objective (as, for instance, in the Thames Water case at the start of the chapter). We will illustrate this by the following example.

Suppose that our garden tool manufacturer produces, in addition to wheelbarrows, spades and forks. Both of these are made by the same workman, who takes one hour to make a spade but two to make a fork, and has been promised at least 48 hours of work a week. A wholesaler has a standing order for 10 forks per week, so at least that number of forks must be made, while a productivity agreement with the unions specifies a minimum production of 32 items per week altogether (forks and spades).

If we let s represent the number of spades made each week, and f represent the number of forks, then we can set up the algebraic model for the problem in the form of three inequalities. First, the workman's hours constraint: the time he takes to make s spades will be s hours, on top of which he takes $2f$ hours for the forks, so his total working time is $s + 2f$ hours per week. This must be at least 48 hours, so we have

$$s + 2f \geqslant 48. \qquad (a)$$

The wholesaler's constraint is easily written as

$$f \geqslant 10 \qquad (b)$$

while the total number of items made per week will be $s + f$, giving the union agreement constraint the form

$$s + f \geqslant 32. \qquad (c)$$

By looking at the extremes for each constraint – that is, the cases in which all the resource in question is used up on one type of product and none of the other is made – we can find where the 'ends' of the constraint lines must be plotted. The line for (a) will run from $s = 48$ to $f = 24$; that for (b) will, of course, simply be plotted at $f = 10$, parallel to the s-axis; and that for (c) will join $s = 32$ to $f = 32$. The resulting graph is shown in Figure 17.4, where as before the 'forbidden' side of each constraint – the side on which it is violated – has been shaded.

One difference between this graph and Figure 17.3 should strike you immediately – the fact that the feasible region in Figure 17.4, instead of being an enclosed area as it was in Figure 17.3, now consists of the whole unbounded area above the three constraint lines. However, we can still identify the three corners of the region, which have been labelled as A, B and C on the graph.

We have not yet got an objective function, so let us now suppose that we are interested in determining the combination of forks and spades that will incur the least total costs, and that we have already found out the costs associated with producing one spade and one fork, which are £4 and £6 respectively. We could now plot a cost line just as we plotted the profit line in the earlier section on graphing the model, but, of course, we are now interested in moving it *in* as close to the origin as possible, rather than out. Naturally

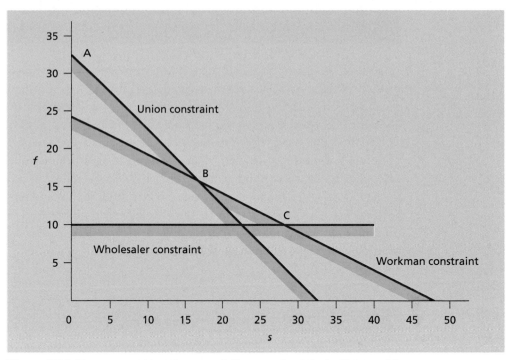

Figure 17.4 Linear programming graph for a cost minimisation problem

there is no limit to how far *out* it could be moved – we can incur costs as large as we choose, though to do so would not be very good business sense!

When it comes to moving the cost line *in*, however, the same arguments as used for the profit line will show that the smallest costs must arise at one of the three corners A, B or C. If we tabulate the costs at each of these points, we have:

Point	f	s	Cost (£)
A	32	0	192
B	16	16	160
C	10	28	172

So the objective (cost) function $6f + 4s$ is minimised when 16 forks and 16 spades are produced.

We could now proceed to a sensitivity analysis of this solution, asking what extra cost would be incurred if the workman wanted to work 49 hours a week instead of 48, or if the union raised its minimum production requirement to 33 items per week (the other 'wholesaler' constraint is slack by 6 forks per week at the solution point). However, we will leave it to you to verify, by the methods given in the previous two sections, that the extra cost of increasing the workman's hours by 1 would be £2 and that this would apply so long as his hours per week were between 42 and 64. As for the union's requirement, every extra item per week which the union demands will increase costs by £2 also, and this statement holds true for numbers of items from 24 to 38 per week. The solution we have found will remain the best so long as the ratio Cost of spade/Cost of fork falls between 0.5 and 1.

Problems where the solutions must be integers

In both of the examples above, the solution in practice had to consist of integer values of the variables – wheelbarrows and garden implements cannot be made in fractional quantities. Fortunately, with the given constraints, the optimal solution at one of the corners of the feasible region did indeed involve integer values in both cases.

Had this not been the case – in other words, had the theoretical 'mathematical' optimum *not* produced integer values – you might have been tempted simply to round off to the nearest whole number. However, this is *not* guaranteed to produce the optimum in such a case – depending on how you do the rounding, it may even lead to a 'solution' which is not feasible. There is in fact a rather different approach to the whole optimisation question, known *integer programming*, which is designed to deal specifically with problems where the solution must be integers.

Solving linear programming problems with Excel Solver

Although specialised computer packages are generally used in practice for handling very large linear programming problems, the Solver tool within Excel enables you to deal easily with the kind of problems we have examined in this chapter.

To illustrate the use of this tool, we will revisit the Apex production problem which was formulated and solved earlier in the chapter. This can be summarised as

$$\text{Maximise profit } 4w + 3d$$

$$\text{subject to constraints } w + 2d \leqslant 40$$
$$w + d \leqslant 24$$
$$3w + 2d \leqslant 60$$
$$w \leqslant 16$$
$$w \geqslant 0$$
$$d \geqslant 0$$

where w and d are respectively the numbers of Workhorses and Donkeys produced per week.

Before we can use Solver, we need to enter the constraints, and the function to be maximised, into cells of the spreadsheet. So, in a new sheet, we will use cells A1 and B1 to contain the values of w and d, and cell C1 to contain the objective function. There is nothing special about these cells – the values could be placed anywhere. Solver works by changing the values of the variables according to a certain rule, until it finds those that maximise the objective subject to the constraints.

We generally start by putting both variables equal to zero, so enter a zero into cells A1 (for w) and B1 (for d). Now enter the formula +4 * A1 + 3 * B1 into cell C1 – this is of course the profit function, and at the moment it will have the value 0.

Entering the constraints is a bit less obvious. What we do is place into a convenient cell – say, A2 – the left-hand side of the first constraint. In this case, the formula we enter will be +A1 + 2 * B1. Forget about the right-hand side for the time being. Do the same with the other constraints – put +A1 + B1 into A3, +3 * A1 + 2 * B1 into A4, +A1 into A5, +A1 again (for the positivity constraint) into A6, and +B1 into A7.

Now we have the data set up, we can call up the Solver routine. You will find it under the TOOLS menu, and when you click on Solver a dialogue window headed 'Solver Parameters' will appear (this will make a lot more sense if you read it while actually carrying out the operations at your computer). First we need to set what Solver calls the 'Target Cell' – this is the function we wish to optimise, and in our case it is C1. Then we have a choice of maximising (the default), minimising or achieving a particular value of the function, so check the appropriate box. We are going to do this by changing cells A1 and B1, so enter those into the next box.

Now come the constraints. If you click on 'Add' in the 'Subject to the constraints' box you get a new dialogue box called 'Add constraint'. We have already put the left-hand side of the first constraint into cell A2, so enter this into the box headed 'Cell Reference'. In the middle box, select the appropriate sign (here it is <=) and, in the last box, type the right-hand side of the constraint – 40 in this case. Now click on OK, and you will see that the constraint in its familiar form has been entered into the 'Subject to the constraints' box.

Click on 'Add' again, and you will be able to enter the other five constraints in the same way (do not forget that you need >= as the sign for the last two). By the end you should have all six constraints looking much as they did when we solved the problem by hand.

Now comes the exciting moment when you can click on 'Solve'. You should soon see a new dialogue box headed 'Solver results', which tells you (I hope!) that a solution has been found, and offers you various options as to the information displayed. Choose 'Keep Solver solution', ask for a Solution report, then click on OK.

The solution is now displayed. In cells A1 and B1 (which, you will recall, contain the values of w and d) you will see that we now have 12 and 12 respectively, indicating that the optimal solution is to make 12 of each type of product – exactly as we found by manual calculation. Cell C1 contains the value 84, which is the optimal value of the objective function – in other words, the profit generated by making 12 of each. Again, this is in agreement with previous calculations.

The remaining cells tell us the values of the various constraints at the solution point. Thus the 24 in A2 shows that for the constraint on $w + 2d$, the right-hand side is 36 at the solution, whereas it could have been as large as 40. This constraint is therefore slack at the solution point, and we have four units of spare capacity. If you look back to the original problem, you will see that this was the constraint on wheels, and that 12 Workhorses and 12 Donkeys do indeed require 36 wheels, so there are four left over. The other cells can be interpreted in the same way.

The other reports that are available – Sensitivity and Limits – provide the information that we obtained from our sensitivity analysis of the solution. However, the reports are not particularly easy to interpret, and are couched in unfamiliar terminology. I would recommend you to familiarise yourself thoroughly with the basics of using Solver before looking at these more advanced aspects. You might begin by using Solver to tackle the minimisation problem on p. 440.

Of course, the application of Solver is not limited to problems with just two variables; we can specify any number of cells whose values can be changed in seeking a solution. Exercises 5 and 6 on p. 446 give you some practice in handling three-variable problems, and once you are used to the procedure, larger numbers of variables should not present any difficulty.

You will find more information on Solver in the Excel supplement on the Companion Website, and there are more problems for you to practise on there too.

Reservations and conclusions

You will probably realise by now that linear programming, at least at this simple level, is a technique that can be carried out in a fairly 'handle-turning' manner, once you have got the basic ideas sorted out. This perhaps accounts for its strong 'student appeal' in examination questions! But the apparent simplicity of the technique should not be allowed to conceal its many limitations in practice, so it will be salutary to have a look at some of these.

The most obvious, if you glance back at the original problem of Apex Tools as posed at the beginning of this chapter, is that the method as we have studied it is restricted, by the graphical nature of the solution, to problems in which only two variables are involved. Had we had three products to consider in the section on setting up the model rather than two, we would have needed a three-dimensional graph, which is just about imaginable; but for a company with, say, 160 different lines, a 160-dimensional graph might be required, which certainly defies *my* imagination!

Fortunately there are other ways of arriving at the best solution without having recourse to graphs. There is a systematic algebraic technique known as the Simplex Method which enables us simultaneously to arrive at the optimum solution and to obtain useful information about sensitivity. But since this method involves quite heavy arithmetic we generally resort to the use of a computer package when dealing with realistic problems with many variables. The method has such wide practical application that there are many computer packages on the market which will produce the solution once the model has been properly specified, together with all the information obtained from a sensitivity analysis. We have seen above how Excel Solver can do this, though for really big problems most companies would probably use a specialised package. However, even setting up the model for input into the software (known as *formulation*) can be quite complicated if there are many variables and/or constraints, as you will see if you attempt Exercise 6 at the end of this chapter.

Once the solution has been found, by whatever means, more difficulties may arise when attempts are made to implement it. For instance, the theory may tell you that you should concentrate all your efforts on producing just one very profitable item, but if abandonment of other products would lead to redundancies among your workforce, then you may have difficulty convincing your union representatives that this really is the best solution! Moreover, the 'maximum profit' solution which we found earlier was based on the assumption that all the items made could be sold at the same profit; but in practice laws of supply and demand, economies of scale for higher production levels, and so on, might render this assumption very dubious.

So linear programming is not, after all, a cure for every industrial ill, but it *is* a very powerful technique with many applications in a much wider range of problems than we have been able to examine in this chapter. Other areas in which the method can be applied include transportation problems, where items have to be distributed according to demand from suppliers to customers and the objective is to determine the most economical way of achieving this; determination of minimum staffing levels needed to operate a factory or production line; and blending problems, where raw materials have to be mixed in specified proportions to produce a variety of products, and we seek the best usage for the materials available. The Exercises section illustrates some of these problems, together with further examples of a more elementary kind for you to practise on.

EXERCISES

Further examples on the work of this chapter can be found on the **Companion Website**.

1 An amateur gardener wants to use part of his allotment to grow cabbages and cauliflowers. Each cabbage takes an average of two minutes to plant (including preparing the soil etc.) and each cauliflower takes three minutes, and he has got only two hours to spare for planting them. He would have room for 72 cabbages if he did not grow any cauliflowers, but a cauliflower needs twice as much space as a cabbage. Moreover, his wife, who does not like cabbage, says she will not cook more than three dozen of them, whereas she insists that he grow at least ten cauliflowers.

   (a) If a cabbage, on average, gives four helpings and a cauliflower three, how many of each vegetable should the gardener plant to get the maximum number of helpings?

   (b) If the cauliflowers turn out to be very large, so that they give four helpings rather than the three he had reckoned on, would the solution you have recommended in (a) still give the most helpings?

   (c) What will be the effect on the number of helpings in part (a) if the gardener finds he only has an hour and three-quarters to spend on the planting?

2 You have been asked to help your managing director, Mr Green, to plan the transport for his daughter's forthcoming wedding. He has already decided to hire Silver Shadow and/or Princess cars; a Silver Shadow will hold six guests but a Princess only four. At present 36 guests must be accommodated. He insists that there must be at least two Silver Shadows, since the Joneses next door had two for *their* daughter's wedding last year. He has also promised the owner of the car-hire firm, in a rash moment while playing golf with him, that he will be hiring at least seven cars altogether. On the other hand, the church car park cannot hold more than 12 vehicles.

   (a) If the hire charges are £10 an hour for a Silver Shadow and £9 an hour for a Princess, how would you advise Mr Green to minimise his costs?

   (b) Mrs Green keeps inviting extra guests. By how much does the total cost increase for each extra guest, and over what range of numbers of guests will this apply?

   (c) Between what limits must the ratio of the costs of the two types of car fall, if the solution you have found is to remain valid?

3 What would happen to the optimum solution you found in Exercise 2 if both types of car cost £10 an hour to hire?

4 Why do the constraints need to be linear in form if this chapter's method is to work? (Try drawing a feasible region with non-linear edges and see what happens when you push a profit line around in it.)

5 The Foo-Ti Tea Company produces two grades of packaged tea, Puce Label and Olive Label, and teabags in a single grade. All three products are made by blending Indian, Ceylon and China teas in varying proportions: in Puce Label the ratio is 2:3:5, in Olive Label, 4:3:3, and in teabags, 2:6:2. Puce Label sells at £5 a kilo, Olive Label at £6 a kilo, and teabags at £6.50 a kilo, while the costs of the ingredients are £4 a kilo for China tea, £5 a kilo for Indian and £6 a kilo for Ceylon. The company wants to determine how much of each kind of product it should make each week in order to attain maximum possible profits, given that only 1600 kilos of Indian tea, 1200 kilos of Ceylon tea and 1000 kilos of China tea are available per week.

   Formulate the set of equations and inequalities describing this problem, calculate the profit per kilo for each type of tea, and write down the objective function. (You will not, of course, be able to solve the problem by hand, since it involves more than two variables. If, however, you have worked through the section 'Solving linear programming problems with Excel Solver' above, then you may be able to use your package to solve the problem once you have formulated the mathematical model.)

6 A small private hospital classifies patients into three categories: intensive care (IC), day-care (DC) and regular (R). All its beds are interchangeable between the three types, and it wishes to determine the best way to allocate them. Eighty beds are available in total; past experience indicates that no more than 15 IC beds will ever be required.

   One member of nursing staff is needed per two IC beds, per five R beds, and per ten DC beds, and the total number of staff who may be called on is 40. The medical director of the hospital has also requested that at least ten DC beds are available. Profit per bed per day is estimated as £80 for IC, £100 for R and £60 for DC, and the hospital's objective is to maximise daily profit.

   Formulate this situation as a linear programming problem, use Excel Solver to obtain a solution, and interpret your results.

7 A parent–teacher group is making items for a fund-raising fair. It has been decided that the group will concentrate on two types of item, aprons and cushions. These are made from the same fabric; an apron uses 1.5 m of fabric and a cushion uses 2 m, and 100 m of suitable fabric has been obtained. In addition, each cushion requires a pad, of which a maximum of 40 is available, while each apron requires 2 m of binding, and only 100 m of this can be procured. An apron will sell for £3.50, and a cushion for £3, all of which is profit since the materials have been donated. It has been suggested that since aprons are more profitable, no cushions should be produced. Draw a linear programming graph to represent this problem and comment on the suggestion.

8 A railway company has to make up its trains of two types of coaches: standard coaches which seat 120 people and business class coaches which seat 80. The power of the engine unit dictates that no more than ten coaches in total can be pulled, irrespective of their class. Furthermore, under the terms of the rail franchise, each train must be composed of at least 20 per cent but no more than 50 per cent business class coaches.

   (a) If the average profit per journey for a business class passenger is £25, and for a standard class passenger the figure is £15, plot a suitable graph to enable you to determine the most profitable make-up of the train, assuming that all seats are filled and no one is standing.
   (b) What is the maximum profit obtainable per journey?
   (c) By how much would the profit per passenger on a standard class seat need to change, assuming that the profit for business class passengers remains fixed, before the most profitable solution would change?

9   A telemarketing organisation employs two types of sales operatives, grades A and B. Grade A operatives are paid £7 per hour; they are able on average to handle 20 calls per hour. Grade B operatives are more experienced; they are paid £9 per hour, and on average deal with 30 calls per hour. The company wishes to have enough staff to deal with a call volume of at least 720 calls per hour. An agreement with the union specifies that at least 30 people in total must be employed, while there must be at least six grade B operatives in order to manage the process.

(a) Plot a suitable graph to show this information.

(b) Hence determine the combination of the two grades of operative which meets the constraints at minimum cost.

(c) What would be the impact of removing the requirement to employ a minimum of six grade B operatives?

10 Make up, and then solve, a linear programming problem involving two variables and three or four linear constraints. Try to draw on an area that you know something about (do not invent a problem about making two sorts of cakes if you never set foot in the kitchen!) and make the problem as realistic as possible. Think about the ways in which it can't be completely realistic.

   This problem will give you more insight into whether you really understand the technique than solving a dozen exercises set by someone else – and perhaps it will also give you a bit of sympathy for people who have to invent such problems all the time!

Case Study

Maximising profit from a craft business

You have been asked to advise a friend who has recently set up a one-person business making and selling hand-sewn children's clothing via a website. At the moment she is focusing on three products: dresses, dungarees and coats. Each garment uses 2 m of the same fabric, of which her supplier can provide 100 m per month.

   Your friend can devote up to 120 hours per month to the actual making of the garments; she can complete a dress in 2 hours, and the time is the same for a coat, but dungarees, being more complicated, take 4 hours.

   The dungarees and coats also require buttons – four on the coats and two on the dungarees; only 80 buttons per month can be supplied, as they are hand-made to order by another craftsperson.

   Hand-made goods such as these command high prices, so that selling a dress generates a profit of £20, dungarees make £25 profit, and coats £40.

(a) Develop a linear programming model from this problem, defining your variables carefully.

(b) Use Excel Solver to obtain a solution which generates maximum profit per month.

(c) Write a short report for your friend, outlining the main features of the solution, and mentioning any assumptions or unrealistic aspects of your approach.

Further reading

If you want to read more about linear programming, Chapters 7–9 of *Quantitative Methods for Business*, by Anderson, Sweeney and Williams (referenced on p. 350) give a comprehensive but accessible introduction.

Chapter 18

PLANNING A PROJECT:
NETWORK ANALYSIS

Chapter prerequisites Before starting work on this chapter make sure you are happy with the general principles of modelling (see Part 4, p. 349).

Learning outcomes By the end of your work on this chapter you should be able to:

1 draw up a dependence table for a set of activities;

2 construct a network from the dependence table;

3 find the earliest and latest starting and finishing times for the activities in your network, and hence determine the critical path and the shortest time in which the job can be completed;

4 draw up a Gantt chart from the network;

5 where appropriate, adjust the sequence of activities to make the best use of the available workforce.

Quantitative methods in practice

Olympic Park master plan submitted

Sports Management, 8 February 2007

The Olympic Delivery Authority (ODA) has submitted one of the largest planning applications in European history, detailing plans for the Olympic Park. The 15-volume, 10 000-page document outlines the plans for the construction of new venues, roads, drainage systems and power grids, including a wind turbine, on the east London site. Sebastian Coe, chair of LOCOG, said: 'This is one of the biggest and most complex planning applications ever prepared in this country, and is another key milestone for us on the road to 2012.'

The preparations for the London Olympics of 2012 will constitute one of the biggest construction and development projects ever undertaken in this country – and it's essential that the whole thing is completed exactly on schedule. Have you ever wondered how on earth huge projects like this are actually managed? Who keeps track of what is going on at each stage, makes sure that one job isn't held up because another has not been completed, and so on?

Even managing much smaller projects can be tricky, as any of you who have completed a piece of groupwork will know. The whole group's efforts can be brought to a standstill if the person who was given the task of looking up some essential data in the library has not done so.

In this chapter we are going to look at a method for scheduling and keeping track of projects, whether large or small. We will see how to identify those jobs where a bit of delay doesn't matter, and those which it's crucial to complete on time; and we will examine ways of juggling tasks to complete the project more efficiently.

As usual, we will start with something a little less ambitious than the London Olympics project – namely, getting the morning's urgent tasks completed in a busy office.

The office supervisor's problem

Mrs Holmes is in charge of the general office in a large firm of chartered surveyors, and it is her responsibility to divide the workload among the three administrators who work in the office. On this particular morning she is in something of a state; an important report *must* be delivered to clients as early in the day as possible, but its preparation is as yet far from complete. Her problem is to organise the tasks that remain to be done to complete the report in such a way as to have it ready at the earliest possible time.

She has made a start by drawing up a list of all the jobs that must be done before the report is ready, together with the number of administrators needed to do each job and the time it may be expected to take (rounded off to the nearest 15 minutes). The list looks like this:

A   Dictation to be taken from senior partner – 1 administrator $\frac{1}{2}$ hour.
B   Dictated notes to be typed – 1 administrator $\frac{1}{2}$ hour.
C   Notes already dictated yesterday to be typed – 1 administrator 45 minutes.

D   All typed notes to be combined and arranged in order – 2 administrators $\frac{1}{4}$ hour.

E   Results of typing to be checked through with senior partner – 1 administrator $\frac{1}{4}$ hour.

F   Plans, for inclusion in report, to be collected from drawing office – 1 administrator $\frac{1}{2}$ hour.

G   All typed material and plans to be photocopied – 1 administrator $\frac{1}{2}$ hour.

H   Report to be collated and stapled together – 2 administrators 45 minutes.

I   Report to be delivered by hand to client's head office – 1 administrator $\frac{1}{2}$ hour.

J   Copy of report to be delivered personally to client's managing director's home – 1 administrator 45 minutes.

After a little thought she adds three further activities:

K   Make and serve senior partner's morning coffee – 1 administrator $\frac{1}{4}$ hour.

L   Allow 15 minutes for senior partner to drink coffee.

M   Collect and wash coffee cup – 1 administrator $\frac{1}{4}$ hour.

It is immediately clear to Mrs Holmes that, although she has written down the various tasks in the order in which they occurred to her, they do not necessarily have to be carried out in this order. In fact, many of them can go on side by side so long as there are enough people available. So her next step is to try to differentiate between those jobs that can go on simultaneously and those that have to be completed before another task can begin. She can do this by means of a *precedence table*.

Drawing up a precedence table

The idea of a precedence table is to help identify which jobs precede others, so that the logical sequence of the process becomes clearer. Two columns are drawn up, under the headings 'Activity' and 'Preceding Activity'. Under 'Activity' the entire list of jobs noted in the previous section is written down, while under 'Preceding Activity' are written the activities (there may be just one or more than one) which *immediately* precede each of the jobs in the first column. By 'immediately' here we mean that the 'preceding' job or jobs lead directly into the following activity with nothing intervening, and that they must all be completed before the following activity can start. So, for example, we would say that activity L is the preceding activity for M. Although, of course, K – serving the coffee – also precedes M, it does not 'immediately' precede it in this sense.

Of course, there is a lot of scope for opinion in deciding what precedes what, even in such a simple problem as the one we are dealing with. In real-life project planning, this may be one of the major headaches. However, for the present we will abide by Mrs Holmes's experience and judgement in deciding precedence. Some are obvious: activity B (typing notes from this morning's dictation) cannot start until the notes have actually *been* dictated, so A must precede B. On the other hand, typing the notes from yesterday's dictation can start straight away, so that has *no* essential preceding activity. Some activities have two jobs immediately preceding them; for instance, the photocopying (activity G) cannot be done until the plans have been collected (activity F) *and* the typing checked (activity E).

When all these considerations are combined the following table results:

Activity	Preceding
A	–
B	A
C	–
D	B, C
E	D
F	–
G	E, F
H	G
I	H
J	H
K	E
L	K
M	L

You can see from this that Mrs Holmes has apparently decided that the senior partner will not get his coffee until after the checking of typing (activity E) has been done. This is a fairly arbitrary decision, but if you go through the precedence table you will find that most of the other precedences are a matter of common sense. Notice that although the typing must be done before the photocopying, we do not show B or C as preceding E – only D, which comes *immediately* before E. B and C have already been done before D. This is what was meant by 'immediately preceding'.

The precedence table is certainly a step towards sorting out a sequence of jobs to be done – for example, it indicates to Mrs Holmes that it is no good telling one of the administrators to do the photocopying unless the plans have already been brought from the drawing office – but it does not make clear which activities are going on simultaneously. To do that we need to construct a *network* from the table.

Constructing the network

The basic principle behind the construction of a network is very simple: each activity will be represented by a line; the starting-point of each line, marked by a circle, represents the stage of the process at which all preceding activities have been completed and the activity represented by that line can begin. The endpoint of a line, similarly marked, represents the stage of the process at which that activity has been completed. The lines are linked together in such a way as to follow the logical dependencies established in the precedence table.

Thus we express the dependence of activity B on A as in Figure 18.1. If we have two activities immediately preceding another, as is the case with E and F both preceding G, we show this as in Figure 18.2. The circle where the E and F lines meet then represents the stage at which both E and F have been completed, so that G may be started.

Note that the *length* of the lines in the network has absolutely no significance. It cannot, for example, be interpreted in terms of the duration of the activities, as newcomers to the technique often imagine. Note, too, the use of arrows to clarify the direction of flow through the network; the general convention is that it is read from left to right.

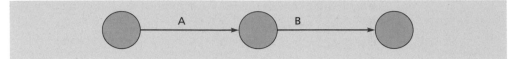

Figure 18.1

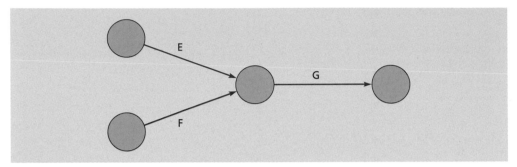

Figure 18.2

The major difficulty in actually drawing the network is the connecting together of all its component parts in such a way that the logic of the precedence table is followed, without accidentally introducing any further, unnecessary dependencies. To start off, we identify the initial activities by looking for those that have no preceding activity – in this case, A, C and F. We might then attempt to represent the beginning of the network as in Figure 18.3.

However, this would lead to a certain amount of ambiguity when we look for the point at which the whole process may be started. Is that point represented by the point marked 1, or by 2 or 3? Clearly we must avoid this ambiguity by having just one starting-point for all three initial activities, as in Figure 18.4.

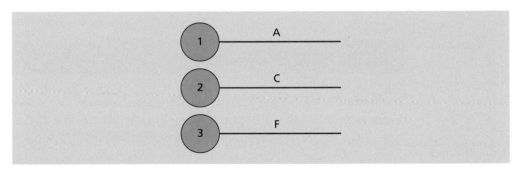

Figure 18.3

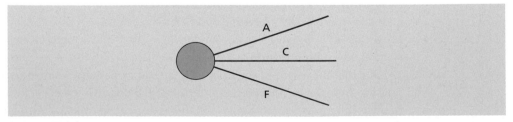

Figure 18.4

The same will apply at the end of the whole process: there must be a single point terminating all the final activities, to represent the point in time at which the whole process has been completed.

A similar situation arises when we have more than one preceding activity, as for example with B and C which both precede D. The only way this can be shown is by having B and C end at the same place, which is also the point at which D may start (see Figure 18.5).

After this it is not too hard to build up the network for all the activities except K, L and M – though it *is* a good idea to start off drawing it in pencil, since you will undoubtedly have to rub bits out! There is no one 'right' version either; there could be several equally correct networks looking quite different at first glance, though of course all would be logically equivalent. Anyway, my version for the network excluding K, L and M is as in Figure 18.6.

However, problems arise when we try to put in activity K. It follows E, certainly, but if we put it in starting at the endpoint of E, where F also terminates, that would suggest that F is a necessary prerequisite for K, which it is not. But what else can we do? F *has* to end on the beginning of G, so we cannot get round the difficulty that way.

In fact, the only way we *can* show the logic of this bit of the network is by making use of what is called a *logical dummy* – an activity that has no duration, occupies no people, and exists simply as a device to render the logic of the network correct. If, instead of attaching E directly to G, we introduce one of these dummy activities to connect E to G, the we can have K starting from the endpoint of E without implying any dependence of K and F. The dummy activity is generally indicated by a dashed line as in Figure 18.7.

A dummy of this kind will be needed whenever the same activity appears in more than one place in the 'preceding' column in combination with different activities; here E and F precede G, but E alone precedes K.

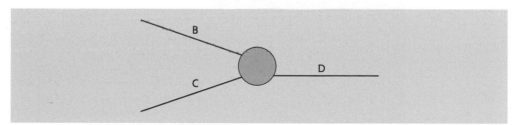

Figure 18.5

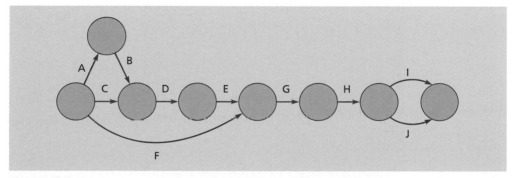

Figure 18.6

Figure 18.7

We can now complete the network without difficulty, to obtain the final version shown in Figure 18.8. You can now see how the network helps to clarify which activities are going on simultaneously. For instance, there appears to be no reason why A, C and F should not be going on at once, and the same is true of I and J, among others. Of course there may not be enough people to do these jobs all together; we have not yet bothered about that aspect of the problem.

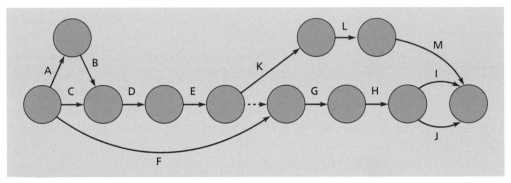

Figure 18.8 The completed network

Quick check questions

1 Draw the parts of networks which represent the following situations:
(a) activities A and B must be completed before C can start; (b) activity C is preceded by A and B; activity D is preceded by B only.

2 Sketch the network representing the following precedence table:

Activity	Preceding activity
A	None
B	A
C	A
D	B
E	C and D
F	None
G	E and F

3 How would you identify starting activities in a precedence table?

Answers:
1 See Figure 18.9(a).
2 See Figure 18.9(b).
3 Starting activities have no preceding activity.

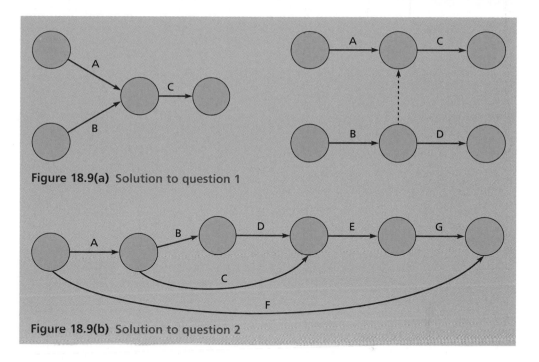

Figure 18.9(a) Solution to question 1

Figure 18.9(b) Solution to question 2

Numbering the network

When we were discussing where to introduce activity K, we had to keep referring to 'the endpoint of activity E' and 'the beginning of activity G'. This is really rather long-winded; what we need is a shorthand way of mentioning the beginnings and ends of the activities, and this shorthand is provided by *numbering* the starting/finishing points of the activity lines. There are lots of different ways this could be done, as long as two simple rules are borne in mind.

First, in line with common sense, the start of an activity should be given a lower number than the end of that activity – we do not, as it were, go 'backwards' with the numbering. Second, no two activities should have the same pair of numbers at start and finish. This again is based on common sense; if we *did* have two activities starting at the point labelled 3 and ending at 4, how would we know which one was meant if someone referred to activity 3–4? There would be an ambiguity.

This point is particularly pertinent when networks of a more complex character are being analysed by computer, since many computer packages for network analysis *do* identify activities by their starting and ending numbers in just this way.

Armed with these rules, let us return to Figure 18.8 and attempt to put some numbers in the circles. There is no real problem until we arrive at activities I and J, right at the end of the network, both of which start and end in the same place. How can we arrange a numbering which will not result in ambiguity? Once again, the dummy idea comes to the rescue. This time, by introducing a dummy activity after I (it could equally well be put after J) we can ensure that every activity has a *unique* pair of numbers associated with it. One possible numbering of the network is shown in Figure 18.10.

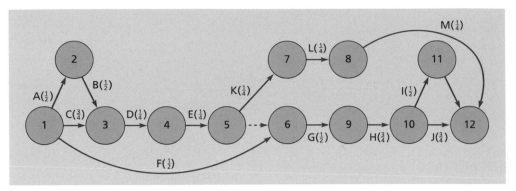

Figure 18.10 Numbering the network

An alternative way of drawing the network

In the section on constructing the network, we drew our network diagram according to what is called the 'activity-on-arrow' method – that is, the lines or arrows of the network were used to represent the activities, and their beginning and endpoints represented the points in time when an activity was begun or completed.

There is an alternative method of constructing the network, known as 'activity on node', in which the nodes or points (in practice drawn as circles) of the network represent the activities, and these are connected by arrows to show the logical flow of activities. In this method the arrows themselves have no real significance. It is easiest to see how the method works by looking at Figure 18.11, which shows the network for the office supervisor's problem drawn in the 'activity-on-node' format.

There are a few points worth noticing here. First, note how we use a 'dummy' starting and ending activity so as to get a single beginning and ending node for the network. If we

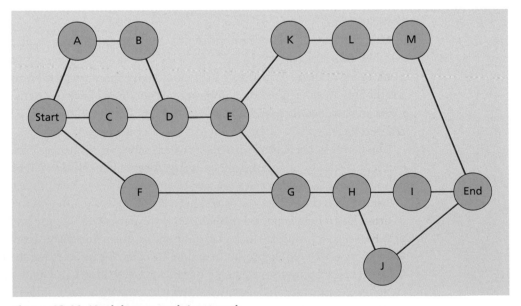

Figure 18.11 'Activity-on-node' network

allowed the network to have several starts and/or finishes it would be difficult to identify the shortest finishing time for the project, and to identify where the zero time point should be.

Second, you will probably have spotted that, unlike the 'activity-on-arrow' version of the network, this one does not require the use of any logical dummy activities – the fact that both E and F precede G whereas E alone precedes K can be quite easily shown simply by organising the connecting lines correctly. This is what many people would regard as one of the great strengths of the 'activity-on-node' method.

Both methods are widely used, and I would not particularly recommend the use of one rather than the other. What I would advise, however, is that you do not try to use them interchangeably – that can become very confusing. Choose one and stick to it. Most of what follows in this chapter applies equally whichever method you are using; where there is any difference, I will point it out.

The shortest time for the job

You will notice that the time each activity takes (in hours) has been put into the network in Figure 18.10 because one of the main objectives in drawing it was to try to find a way of organising the job to get the report completed in the shortest possible time. Now that we have the network to help us decide which activities may go on simultaneously, we are in a position to find this shortest possible time for the whole process.

If you examine Figure 18.10 or Figure 18.11 you will see that there are several ways of getting from the start of the network to the finish – that is, several different sequences of activities that must be completed. Identifying these 'routes' through the network by their numbers, we have eight possibilities:

1–2–3–4–5–7–8–12	1–2–3–4–5–6–9–10–11–12
1–3–4–5–7–8–12	1–3–4–5–6–9–10–11–12
1–2–3–4–5–6–9–10–12	1–6–9–10–11–12
1–3–4–5–6–9–10–12	1–6–9–10–12

Each of these eight sequences of activities must be completed before the whole job is finished, and each will take a different time to complete. If you add up the times encountered along each route you will find that, for the eight routes in order as listed above, the times required are $2\frac{1}{4}$, 2, $3\frac{1}{2}$, $3\frac{1}{4}$, $3\frac{1}{4}$, 3, $2\frac{1}{4}$ and $2\frac{1}{2}$ hours respectively.

Now comes the crucial point: the *shortest* time in which the whole job can be completed will be determined by the *longest* of these routes. It is easiest to see why this must be so if we examine a bit of the network at a time. Between 1 and 3, for instance, we have two possible routes, 1–2–3 or 1–3. Now, although 1–3 (activity C) can be accomplished in three-quarters of an hour, the next activity, D, cannot be started until route 1–2–3 (activities A and B) are also finished – and they will take an hour. So that will determine the earliest time at which D can begin; and the same will apply throughout the network. At each stage, it is the *slowest* activities that are going to determine how long the whole job takes.

So, looking back at the list of total times above, you can see that the shortest time in which the report can be completed is $3\frac{1}{2}$ hours. The route which gives this time

(1–2–3–4–5–6–9–10–12, or activities A, B, D, E, G, H, J) is called the *critical path*, and the activities on this route are said to be *critical*. This term expresses the fact that if any of these activities in practice turns out to take longer than had been estimated, the whole job will also take longer; if any of them can be speeded up, the job can be completed more quickly. So the time taken by those activities is critical to the completion of the job on schedule.

The remaining, non-critical activities, on the other hand, can be subject to a certain amount of variation in time without affecting the overall project duration. For example, if activity C took 50 minutes instead of 45, the start of the next activity, D, would not be affected because it would still have to wait on the completion of A and B, which together take an hour. Equally, it would be pointless trying to speed up activity F; it only takes half an hour anyway, whereas A, B, D and E, which are going on at the same time, take an hour and a half altogether, and until they are finished the next activity, G, cannot begin. We say that there is some leeway or *float* on the non-critical activities, and it is by playing around with this float that we can try to make best use of the available personnel.

However, it is by no means obvious from the network at present just how much float there is on any given activity. For that matter, the way we arrived at the critical path in the first place was rather hit-and-miss; even in this relatively simple case, there were eight possible routes to be considered, and it is easy to imagine that in a more complex network, listing all the possible routes would be a very slow process, in which some routes might well be overlooked. So we are going to develop an alternative, and more systematic, way of finding the critical path, based on the fact that critical activities have no float.

Finding the floats

We begin by working through the network from start to finish, finding the earliest times at which activities can be begun and completed. For example, if we call the start of the whole process time 0, then that is the earliest activities A, B and C can start. Now A takes half an hour, so the earliest it can finish is time $\frac{1}{2}$. This determines the earliest starting time for B, which therefore finishes, at the earliest, at time 1 hour. Meanwhile C, having also started at its earliest time of 0, can be finished by time $\frac{3}{4}$. Now comes the slightly tricky part. D follows on from both B and C, so both of these must be completed before it can start. This means that the earliest starting time for D is 1 hour; although C is finished by $\frac{3}{4}$ there is no way B can be finished before 1 hour.

All this is really just common sense, and takes much longer to explain than to do. There are two ways of setting out the results of the arguments – on the network, as shown in Figure 18.12 or in a table such as Table 18.1. You should follow through the calculation of all the earliest starting and finishing times either on the network or in the table; if you are using 'activity on node', the table may be easier to follow.

To determine the latest starting and finishing times for activities we begin at the *end* of the network, since the whole process has to be finished by time $3\frac{1}{2}$ hours. That means that the latest time by which activities I, J and M (the final activities in the network) must be completed is $3\frac{1}{2}$, otherwise the job will last longer than it need do. We then proceed backwards through the network, using the same kind of logic as we did in obtaining the earliest times. For example, M has to finish by time $3\frac{1}{2}$, so it must begin by time $3\frac{1}{4}$, since

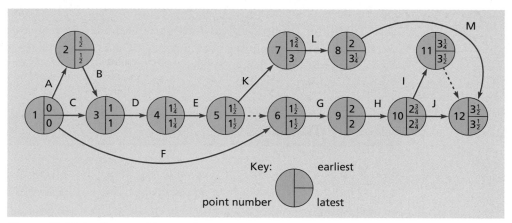

Figure 18.12 Earliest and latest times

Table 18.1 Starting and finishing times

Activity	Duration (hours)	Earliest start	Latest start	Earliest finish	Latest finish	Total float
A	$\frac{1}{2}$	0	0	$\frac{1}{2}$	$\frac{1}{2}$	0
B	$\frac{1}{2}$	$\frac{1}{2}$	$\frac{1}{2}$	1	1	0
C	$\frac{3}{4}$	0	$\frac{1}{4}$	$\frac{3}{4}$	1	$\frac{1}{4}$
D	$\frac{1}{4}$	1	1	$1\frac{1}{4}$	$1\frac{1}{4}$	0
E	$\frac{1}{4}$	$1\frac{1}{4}$	$1\frac{1}{4}$	$1\frac{1}{2}$	$1\frac{1}{2}$	0
F	$\frac{1}{2}$	0	1	$\frac{1}{2}$	$1\frac{1}{2}$	1
G	$\frac{1}{2}$	$1\frac{1}{2}$	$1\frac{1}{2}$	2	2	0
H	$\frac{3}{4}$	2	2	$2\frac{3}{4}$	$2\frac{3}{4}$	0
I	$\frac{1}{2}$	$2\frac{3}{4}$	3	$3\frac{1}{4}$	$3\frac{1}{2}$	$\frac{1}{4}$
J	$\frac{3}{4}$	$2\frac{3}{4}$	$2\frac{3}{4}$	$3\frac{1}{2}$	$3\frac{1}{2}$	0
K	$\frac{1}{4}$	$1\frac{1}{2}$	$2\frac{3}{4}$	$1\frac{3}{4}$	3	$1\frac{1}{4}$
L	$\frac{1}{4}$	$1\frac{3}{4}$	3	2	$3\frac{1}{4}$	$1\frac{1}{4}$
M	$\frac{1}{4}$	2	$3\frac{1}{4}$	$2\frac{1}{4}$	$3\frac{1}{2}$	$1\frac{1}{4}$

it takes a quarter of an hour. That means that L, its preceding activity, must be finished by $3\frac{1}{4}$ at the latest and so on.

Just as with the earliest times, the places to be careful are those where two or more activities are preceded by or precede a single one. H, for instance, precedes both I and J. I can be started as late as 3 hours without holding the job up, but J has to be under way by $2\frac{3}{4}$ hours to be completed at $3\frac{1}{2}$. Thus H needs to be completed by $2\frac{3}{4}$ at the latest.

Again, you should follow through the calculation of these latest times in Table 18.1 or on the network. Once the earliest and latest times have been calculated, it is a simple matter to find the float on each activity. Those activities which have no float, and are therefore critical, are the ones for which the earliest and latest starting times (and, of course, the finishing times also) are identical. If you compare the zero float activities in Table 18.1 with the critical activities we discovered in the earlier section on numbering the network, you will find that they are the same. On the remaining activities, the float is the difference between the earliest and latest starting (or finishing) times. Thus deferring the beginning of activity K, for example, by anything up to an hour and a quarter will not alter the overall time taken by the project – though it *will* affect some of the following activities. We will be returning to this point later.

Making the best of it

We still have not considered the possibility that three administrators may not be enough to carry out the job in the fashion represented by the network. Even if they are sufficient, we want them to make the best use of their time; it is more satisfactory to have a long spell at a job than to be doing it for a short time, go off and start something else, and then be called back to the original task. Perhaps by juggling around with the spare float time, we can free one of the administrators entirely to get on with other jobs. But it is not easy to see from the network whether this is the case, so we introduce a further diagram known as a *Gantt chart*, after its inventor.

Probably the best way to get to grips with the idea of a Gantt chart is to look at Figure 18.13. Each of the vertical columns in the chart represents a 15-minute period (if you are drawing such a chart on lined writing paper the easiest way to do it is to turn the paper sideways), and a horizontal line is drawn to represent each activity in the network, the number of columns occupied by the line corresponding to the duration of the activity. Conventionally the critical activities are put at the top of the chart. All activities are shown starting at their earliest possible starting times, while for the non-critical activities, the float is indicated by the dotted portion of the line. For example, activity F could finish any time up to $1\frac{1}{2}$, although at its earliest it will be completed by $\frac{1}{2}$.

You will notice that the beginnings and ends of the activities have been marked with their numbers as on the original network. This is particularly useful when we start pushing the non-critical activities around, as it helps us to distinguish between those activities that can be moved freely up to the full extent of their float, and those for which the full amount of float can be taken up only if some of the following activities are also moved.

This distinction becomes clear if we contrast activity F with K. Both have some float, but whereas F could be carried out between 1 and $1\frac{1}{2}$ hours without altering anything else, any postponement of K will immediately mean a corresponding postponement of L and M also. This is made evident by the numbering, the end of K being number 7, which is also the start of L, so that these two activities cannot overlap. The technical name for float which can be taken up without altering any following activities is *free float*; thus F has 1 hour of free float while none of the float on K is free. It is possible, although it does not happen in this particular network, to have an activity some, but not all, of whose float is free.

The advantage of the Gantt chart is that, by glancing down a column of the chart, we can see at once what activities are going on during that period. This in turn helps us to find out how many people are going to be occupied at any point in the process. To this end, the number of administrators required for each task has been noted at the side of the table, and at the bottom of each column is shown the number of administrators occupied during that period. To make the ups and downs in these totals even more obvious, they have also been translated into a histogram.

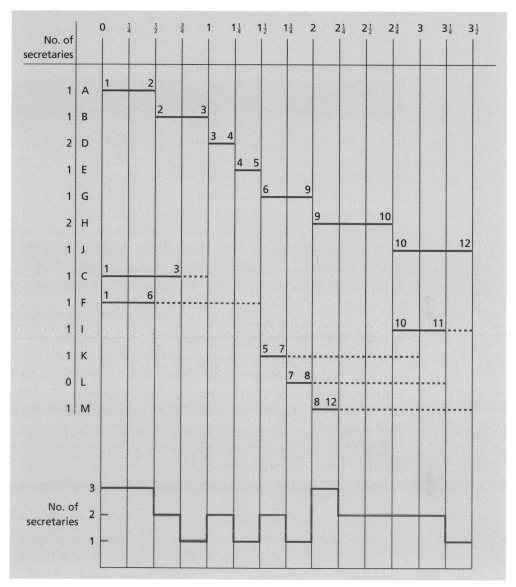

Figure 18.13 A Gantt chart

You can now appreciate how inconvenient the process as it stands is going to be from the point of view of Mrs Holmes, who is trying to organise the administrators' time. There are several slack times during the three-and-a-half hour duration of the job, when only one administrator is needed; but then the demand suddenly jumps up to three again, just for 15 minutes. This could be quite simply avoided if activity M – washing the senior partner's coffee cup – were deferred until the last 15-minute period.

The other irregularities are not so easy to get rid of. Even if it is permissible to split some activities into bits – for example, to do the first half-hour of C, then go away and do something else for 15 minutes before finishing C off – it does not appear possible to avoid the need for all three administrators at some stage. This could only be achieved by splitting F, which clearly cannot be done – F, you will recall, is the job of fetching the plans from the drawing office, which can hardly be done in two halves. So it looks as if

Mrs Holmes could be in trouble if one of her administrators is off work on this of all mornings!

Limitations of the method

By now you will probably agree that the construction and use of networks is as much of an art as a science. This is particularly true of the juggling around – or *smoothing*, to give it the technical name – of the profile of workers occupied. There is no guaranteed way of arriving at the 'best' use of personnel; it is merely a question of trial and error.

There are also a number of difficulties which we have quietly swept under the carpet in arriving at the network in the first place. The scope for differences of opinion about what precedes what was mentioned in the earlier section on drawing up a precedence table, but argument can arise at an even earlier stage, when the process is being broken down into individual activities. The durations of the activities were only estimates, too. What happens if a computer problem causes the typing of documents to take twice as long as expected? The effect on the overall project duration could be serious. And the same could be said of the estimated labour requirements; the final stages of the project would look quite different if the administrator assigned to deliver the report to the managing director's home insists on being accompanied by a colleague. We have also assumed that the administrators are interchangeable, but suppose the photocopier jams and only one of them knows how to unjam it? And we have not considered any questions of cost – for example, it would be possible to complete the project more quickly by hiring extra staff, but this would have to be offset against the penalty cost of being late, in order to decide whether it is worthwhile.

To allow for the fact that what happens in practice may not be quite the same as what was planned for in theory, the Gantt chart is often converted, once the project gets under way, into a progress chart. Such a chart for the project under consideration can be seen in Figure 18.14; it represents the situation at 10.15, the process having been started at 9 a.m. The dotted lines above each activity represent the portion of that activity that has been completed; in practice they would be coloured so as to stand out clearly. It seems that activity B has not finished yet, so D has been unable to start, which does not bode well for the completion of the project by 12.30 as scheduled, unless something else can be speeded up.

The technique in practice

Despite the issues mentioned in the previous section, network analysis remains a powerful tool for project planning and control, especially for large-scale projects such as the London Olympics development mentioned at the start of the chapter. In fact, in such cases its strength as a method of tracking progress, and helping project managers make adjustments as the project goes along to cope with the hold-ups and problems which will inevitably arise, probably exceeds its value as a tool for planning the project in the first place. If ever you have reason to visit a building site, you will often find rather scruffy and well-used Gantt charts pinned up around the walls of the site office.

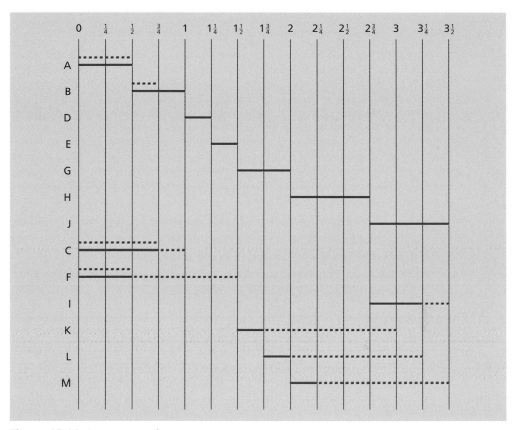

Figure 18.14 A progress chart

Naturally, when dealing with projects on a realistic scale, constructing the network by hand is not really an option. There are many packages on the market that enable the task to be carried out on a PC; most of these will also deal with the problems mentioned above, such as variable durations for activities, so that 'what if . . .' scenarios can be examined. Links to some further information about network packages are provided on the student side of the Companion Website for this chapter.

EXERCISES

*Further examples on the work of this chapter can be found on the **Companion Website**.*

(The first three exercises refer to the situation discussed in this chapter.)

1 What would be the shortest time in which the report could be ready if only two administrators were available that morning?

2 Would the time for the project be extended if the senior partner insisted on having his coffee before checking the typing (activity E)?

3 If the use of an automatic collator reduces the time for activity H to 15 minutes, what effect, if any, will this have on the critical path?

4 Consider the following report from a (purely imaginary!) newspaper:

> Three Mudport housewives claim to be operating Britain's fastest freshly-cooked takeaway pizza service. When our reporter visited *Casa Mudport* yesterday, it was the work of a minute for Mrs Carole Smith (37) to take his order. The team leapt into action immediately. Julie Jones had the dough out of the fridge, kneaded, rolled and into the tin in four minutes flat. Meanwhile, 56-year-old Iris Brown took only half a minute to get the frying pan on. At the same time, onions were being chopped for one minute, then they went into the pan while tomatoes and herbs were prepared; when the onions had fried for two minutes, in went the remaining ingredients, and the whole lot was simmered and stirred for three minutes. Then this filling was tipped onto the dough ready in its tin, and the pizza went into the microwave oven for five minutes, while Carole took five minutes to make out a bill and collect the payment. After the cooked pizza had been whizzed into a paper bag in under a minute, our reporter was able take his first bite less than ten minutes after placing his order. Ugh!

(a) Draw up a network for this process, on the assumption that all members of the team can carry out any of the tasks, and hence show that the claim to service in 'less than ten minutes' is not consistent with the information given in the article.

(b) If one of the team is ill and cannot work, what will be the shortest time in which the remaining two can complete the process as described?

5 Two motorway approach roads have to be constructed. The construction of each involves three separate stages: excavation, which takes three weeks; laying of the hardcore, which takes a fortnight; and laying and rolling of the top surface, which takes a week. Each job is done by a separate gang of workers, and each gang can work on only one road at a time.

(a) Draw a network to represent the task of constructing the two roads.

(b) Union agreements make it imperative that all three gangs should be on-site during the entire time the two construction jobs take. If each gang costs £400 a week when idle, and £800 a week when occupied, what will be the total cost of labour for the project?

6 A catering company has purchased a derelict building which is to be refurbished as a conference centre. The tasks to be carried out are as follows:

- Repairs to roof to make the building weather-proof – this will take four weeks, and must be done before any other work can be started.
- Structural alterations to interior – three weeks – can be started as soon as the roof is finished.
- Plumbing – two weeks – can be started as soon as the roof is finished.
- Installation of gas supply – one week – can be started as soon as the roof is finished.
- Decoration of conference room – two weeks – can be started as soon as structural alterations are finished.
- Decoration of cloakrooms – one week – must follow plumbing work.
- Fitting of catering area – six weeks – cannot be done until gas and plumbing are completed.
- Exterior landscaping – eight weeks – can be done as soon as roof repairs are complete.
- Furnishing and carpets – two weeks – after all other works are completed.

(a) Is it possible for this project to be completed in 12 weeks or less, assuming that all necessary personnel are available?

(b) What are the critical activities here?

(c) What will be the impact on the time taken to complete the project if (i) the plumbing work and gas supply cannot be carried out simultaneously and (ii) the decoration of the conference room cannot be started until eight weeks from commencement of the project?

7 Three students have to carry out a piece of groupwork. The tasks involved, with their preceding activities, duration, and the number of people required to carry them out, are as follows:

Task	Preceding	Duration (days)	Number of people
A Initial discussion	None	0.5	3
B Research in library	A	1	1
C Design survey	A	1	1
D Carry out survey	C	3	2
E Analyse survey	B, D	2	1
F Discuss presentation	B, E	0.5	3
G Prepare presentation	F	1	1
H Write handout	F	1	1
I Practice presentation	G, H	0.5	3

(a) Draw a network to represent this situation, and hence determine the shortest amount of time which the students should allow for completion of the task.

(b) Will the time for completion be extended if the best person to prepare the presentation is also the best to write the handout, and, if so, by how much?

8 Consider a simple task such as making a cup of coffee or changing a wheel on a car. Working either alone or with other students in your group, break the task down into its component activities. Then set up a precedence table, and construct a network to represent the task, assuming that an unlimited number of people are available to assist.

9 Visit http://www.thetimes100.co.uk/case-study--critical--path-analysis-at-network-rail--105-261-1.php to read an interesting case study showing how Network Rail uses critical path analysis in its planning. A link to this site is provided on the Companion Website.

10 From the network shown in Figure 18.15, construct the precedence table. What is the shortest time for completion of the task?

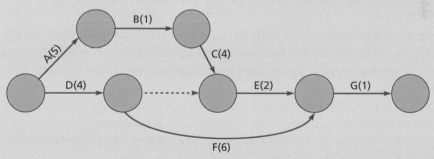

Figure 18.15

Case Study

Planning an office move

A few years after graduation, you are running your own business, importing herbs, spices and other ingredients from India and selling them to restaurants and shops in the UK. You now employ three staff (one warehouse supervisor, one accounts assistant and one marketing and sales assistant), and your current premises have become too small, so you are about to move into a building which offers larger office and storage space. However, you wish to plan the move with the minimum of disruption to business. You have identified the following activities which need to be carried out as part of the move:

A   Obtain keys to new premises. (1)
B   Shelving to be fitted in storage area of new building. (3)
C   Wiring for computer equipment to be installed in office area of new building. (2)
D   Crates to be delivered by removal company. (1)
E   Stock to be packed, transported to new building and unpacked. (5)
F   Two office staff to pack material from their individual offices (excluding computer equipment). (1)
G   Office material to be transported. (1)
H   Two office staff to unpack material at new location. (1)
I   Computer equipment to be packed, transported and installed at new location by specialist computer removals firm. (2)

The figures in brackets above are the times you have estimated for completion of each of the activities (in days).

One of your staff has drawn up the following network to represent this process:

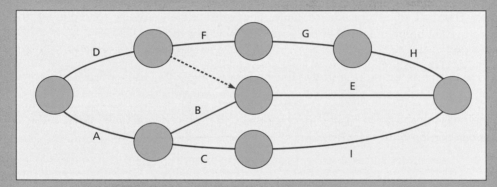

(a) Draw up the precedence table which the member of staff must have been using to construct the network. Do all the assumptions underpinning the table seem reasonable to you?
(b) Working from this network, determine the shortest possible period for completion of all stages of the move.
(c) What will be the effect on the timing for the move if (i) the crates are delivered a day late; (ii) it takes the carpenter a day longer than expected to fit the shelving?
(d) Examine the effect on the project of splitting activity E into three separate activities – pack stock (2 days), transport stock (1 day) and unpack stock (2 days).

Further reading

Chapter 12 of *Quantitative Methods in Business*, by Anderson, Sweeney and Williams (referenced on p. 350), covers this topic, though it is referred to by the alternative name of PERT (Project Evaluation and Review Technique).

Chapter 19

QUANTITATIVE METHODS IN THE
STUDENT RESEARCH PROJECT

Chapter prerequisites

This chapter will call upon a number of the techniques we have looked at in earlier chapters, particularly Chapters 2 to 12. You may find it necessary to go back and remind yourself of some of the details of specific methods while you are reading the chapter.

Learning outcomes

By the end of your work on this chapter you should be able to:

1 understand the general process of carrying out a business-related investigation involving quantitative data;

2 relate the research questions you are hoping to answer to the quantitative techniques at your disposal;

3 recognise the problems that may arise in the process of gathering and analysing quantitative data, and take steps to eliminate them or minimise their impact;

4 report your findings in practical terms and non-technical language.

The business student's problem

Many degrees in business involve the student in carrying out some kind of independent investigation, and reporting on this activity. Different titles are used for this aspect of the degree programme – very often the activity is referred to as a project, and the written report as a dissertation, though sometimes project is used for both. Projects may be based on a period of placement with a business organisation, or on a business-related problem provided by such an organisation, or they may involve more theoretical or desk-based work, using existing material – books, journals and so on. They may be very substantial, as is generally the case with MBA and other Masters-level projects, or quite small pieces of work equivalent to a 12- or 15-credit course, carried out at some point during your work for your degree.

However, irrespective of the precise nature of the project, the great majority involve the gathering and presentation of data in quantified form. Probably the most common source of the data is some kind of survey, but secondary sources – company accounts, business databases, government publications – may also be used.

Most students find this aspect of the project particularly daunting. I think that there are two reasons for this. First, work on the project often takes place near the end of the degree programme, whereas courses in quantitative methods are usually positioned in the earlier stages, and much of the material may have been forgotten in between. 'I think we did something like this in first-year quants, but I don't really remember!' is something which I often hear from those working on projects.

Second, it is one thing to apply a limited set of techniques to nice, neat tutorial problems or examination questions, quite another to be confronted by an untidy mass of data items, full of gaps and oddities, wondering which particular quantitative method may persuade the students to say what we would like them to say.

The major objective of this chapter, therefore, is to give you an overview of a methodology for carrying out the numerical part of a project, from the start – thinking about objectives and planning to get hold of the data – to the final stage of writing up the findings. In the process, we will have cause to revisit a number of the techniques examined earlier in the book. Finally, some examples of statistical project work actually carried out by students are given, to indicate the kind of thing that can be done using the techniques we have covered.

However, before looking in detail at the numerical aspects of the project, it is worth spending a little time examining where the idea for your project topic might come from.

What shall I write about?

Many students feel something akin to panic when faced with the selection of a project topic. If your project is linked to a placement, your choices will probably be more limited, and may be at least partly determined by the needs of the company for which you are working. Likewise, when the project is linked to a specific course within your programme, you will doubtless receive a detailed specification as to what the project is expected to cover. Even so, there will be choices to be made; and if the project is freestanding, you may well start out with an idea which is little more specific than 'find something interesting, vaguely related to business, and write 12 000 words about it'.

There are a number of purely common-sense considerations which should quickly give you a better focus on your options:

1   Choose something in which you are genuinely interested – if work on the project is going to take up a good deal of your time, you will enjoy it more if you find the topic stimulating. Some of the best student-defined projects I have read have been related to sport and other leisure activities. You will also find it easier to interpret your results if you have a thorough understanding of the context in which they apply. So if, for example, you are a student from another country studying in the UK, a comparison of some aspect of business in your home country with the way things are done in the UK will allow you to capitalise on your background.

2   Be realistic about what you can accomplish, in the time available, with the resources at your disposal, using the techniques with which you feel comfortable. To give an extreme example: if it were possible to produce a model for predicting share price movements with any degree of accuracy, it is likely that pension funds and other institutional investors, with all the information at their disposal, would have found a way of doing so. To my knowledge, they have not – so the chances that you will be able to do so, in six weeks, armed with the *Financial Times* and a knowledge of forecasting based on the contents of Chapter 15, are pretty remote.

3   Make sure you can get access to the necessary information. Your tutor, or your placement supervisor, may be able to help with this, by providing you with introductions to individuals or organisations. Many students find that companies are remarkably helpful when approached for assistance with project work. However, there are certain conventions about appropriate behaviour when carrying out this kind of research; your supervisor should be able to advise you, and your institution may also have an Ethics Policy which covers what is and is not possible. Many colleges and universities now require researchers – including students – to complete some kind of 'ethics clearance form' describing their proposed research, which must have institutional approval before the project goes ahead.

4   Do not underestimate the role of previous work; good research is never done in a vacuum, but always builds on other people's efforts. For most projects, a literature search – that is, a review of relevant work in the area – will constitute an important early chapter in the report. Such searches are very easily carried out using electronic databases. But even before you have selected your topic, doing some reading in the area in which you are interested can help to generate ideas. Papers in research journals are often not as daunting as you might think, and a comment in such a paper – for example, 'it seems likely that younger consumers are more receptive to this form of purchasing' in a paper on electronic commerce – can often spark an idea for a project investigation.

5   Finally, you need to strike a balance between defining the objectives of your project clearly and being prepared to be flexible. Large-scale projects in particular often take on a life of their own, and tend to expand in all directions as you discover interesting avenues for exploration. If you are not to run out of time, exceed your word-limit, or produce an amorphous and poorly structured report, you may need to sharpen your focus as you go along, and make a conscious decision not to pursue certain lines of investigation. This is where the advice of your supervisor can be invaluable – make use of it!

A general methodology for quantitative investigations

When should I use a quantitative approach?

There are a number of reasons why you might decide that you need to gather some quantitative data as part of your project. You may need some figures to back up a line of argument made on qualitative grounds; for example, if you are looking at the impact of different marketing strategies on the success of companies, it will be helpful to have some data about financial performance of the companies, as one aspect of the measurement of 'success'. You could probably obtain the necessary data from company reports, or more conveniently from a business database or from the Web.

Or you may be interested in investigating a hypothesis – that is, a theory about a situation, often based on previous work. For example, you might suspect that the strength of the pound sterling has a differential impact on exports in different business sectors, and want to verify whether the available data bears out this suspicion. In this case, published figures – on exchange rates, imports and exports in various industrial categories – may be helpful.

In both of these examples, the numerical part of the investigation will constitute only a part – perhaps a fairly minor part – of the overall project. If, however, you are setting out to investigate how people feel about shopping for books via the Internet, then you are likely to need to carry out some primary research – probably based on a survey of a sample of potential purchasers.

There are two features in particular which make these examples suitable candidates for quantitative methods of presentation and analysis. In each case, there will be quite a lot of data, much already quantified, the salient features of which need to be communicated effectively. Then, since the findings will almost certainly be based on only a sample of the data, there will be a need to assess the extent to which any 'interesting' features emerging from the analysis are simply due to 'chance effects', as distinct from demonstrating 'real' underlying phenomena. What we mean by interesting in this context, and how we judge when a feature which we note is 'real', will become apparent when we look at examples in more detail later in the chapter.

To put it in a nutshell, quantitative methods have something to offer when we are dealing with large amounts of data, and with situations where sampling is involved. There are types of study where they are less suitable – for example, certain types of case study. If your project consists of an in-depth investigation of aspects of two or three organisations, then it is more likely that, apart from reporting key individual figures such as numbers of employees or turnovers, you will adopt a qualitative or narrative approach for reporting your findings. Statistics, as we have said before, is concerned with data in bulk and not usually with one-off situations.

Carrying out a quantitative investigation

Although the examples we looked at in the last section differ widely, it is possible to identify a general approach using nine steps which is applicable in nearly every case:

1 Define objectives of enquiry and population of interest.
2 Decide on sources of data.

3 Design experiment or sampling enquiry.
4 Collect data.
5 Summarise data.
6 Draw conclusions from sample results about the population.
7 Qualify these conclusions with measures of significance/confidence.
8 Interpret results in terms of the practical situation you are examining.
9 Report on your findings.

We will look in detail at each of these steps in turn.

Define objectives of enquiry and population of interest

Many potentially excellent projects run into difficulties because the author has not been clear about his or her objectives from the start. Here are some of the questions you can usefully ask yourself at this stage:

- Is your enquiry exploratory, or is it designed to test a specific research hypothesis? In texts on research methods, there tends to be a lot of emphasis on the hypothesis testing kind of investigation – setting out to test a premise based on previous evidence, such as 'Employees' job satisfaction ratings are higher in companies with a participative management style'. But 'finding out more' is also a perfectly respectable research objective, as long as it is done in a systematic and focused manner. Thus, for example, you might set out to discover what factors influence a company's decision to enter into an overseas market. Often this kind of exploratory enquiry can lead on to testing of hypotheses at a later stage. And do not expect a hypothesis to present itself in a tidy manner like an example in a statistics text – very often it will be based on anecdotal evidence, a vague suspicion or an intuitive idea.
- What work has already been done in this area? Have you reviewed the existing litera-ture and taken on board the relevant findings of other authors? This may help in refining your objectives.
- What is your target population? You need to be precise about this – not 'students at the University of Rutland' but 'All full-time students at the University of Rutland registered on undergraduate degree programmes as at 1 November 2010'.
- Are there any subgroups within the target population that you will want to examine separately? If so, you need to ensure that you gather the right information to enable you to do this. So if you want to look at possible differences in the views of 'standard' or 'mature' students, you need to ascertain into which class each individual falls, and keep a record of this.
- How will you quantify the information obtained? Are you looking for categoric or measured data? How will this affect the analysis you can do? Some data clearly belong in the realm of measurements – financial information such as turnover or profit before tax, for example; other variables such as gender are obviously qualitative. But in many cases, we want to find out about less clearly defined matters such as attitudes or perceptions, which are not so easy to measure. Five- or seven-point rating scales of various kinds ('rate your satisfaction on a scale from 1 to 5, where 1 = very satisfied and 5 = very dissatisfied') are popular ways of handling this kind of data, but you must be clear that such ratings are not always going to have 'nice' statistical properties, and that the analysis you can carry out will be affected by your choice of measurement method.

Decide on sources of data

Once you have an idea of what information you would like to use, you can consider how to get hold of it. This is often a process that goes through several stages – you may discover that the information you want is not easily available, or not in the right format, and your initial objectives may have to be modified as a result. Ask yourself the following:

- Will you use primary (gathered yourself) or secondary data? As discussed in Chapter 2, a great deal of high-quality data is now available via both paper sources and newer media such as CD-ROMs and the Internet. Such data, however, may be of a purely factual nature, and be highly aggregated; so if you need more subjective information, or you want details relating to individuals, you will probably not find secondary data of much help.
- Where will you find secondary data, if needed? Are the data items in the format you want? Are they up to date and reliable?

Design experiment or sampling enquiry

The word 'experiment' is being used here in a rather loose sense. Most people gathering primary data in a business research context find that some kind of questionnaire is called for, though there are cases where you might need to set up an experiment – for example, if you want to look at the difference in recall rates for magazine advertisements depending on whether they are printed in colour or black and white. However, irrespective of whether you are doing an experiment or simply carrying out a survey, you will need to think about the following issues:

- How large a sample will you use? If doing a questionnaire, what response rate do you expect? Will this give you enough data? Will breaking down the data into a large number of categories mean that responses in each category are very few? How much time have you got? What is your budget?
- Will you use a formal questionnaire? Mailed, telephone or personal interview? Or will you use a less structured approach – for example, free-form interviews which are taped with the respondent's permission? If so, how will you summarise and report the findings?
- Is your questionnaire structured in a way that will enable you to carry out the analysis you wish to use? To carry out appropriate tests?
- How will you select a sample for your survey? Will it be structured (e.g. stratified) or will you opt for convenience (e.g. by using a quota)? (Have a look back to Chapter 2 if you do not recall the definitions of these terms – students often claim that they have stratified samples when in fact they are merely using quotas.) How easy will it be to obtain such a sample? Is there a sampling frame (a list of the population) from which you can select?
- If gathering secondary data (e.g. about companies), is the data available in the form in which you need it? Are different data sources compatible (e.g. in date, definitions of variables)?
- What further analysis are you going to undertake, and with what tools? Can the data you have gathered easily be put into a suitable format (e.g. for reading into a statistical package)? One thing to watch out for here when designing your questionnaire is what is called a multiple response question, where the respondent is allowed to choose as

many options as he or she wishes – for instance, 'What were your reasons for purchasing a Sunnitours holiday? Tick all that apply'. Some respondents may tick only one reason, others may tick all, or some number in between. This makes entry of the data into a spreadsheet more complicated; for each reason listed, you will need to allow for a yes/no or 0/1 coding, so to represent the answers to this one question in your spreadsheet will take as many columns as you have allowed choices. This can lead to very large spreadsheets rather quickly! So an easier option would be to say 'Tick the main reason' or 'rank the following reasons in order of importance'.

Collect data

In a way this is the easiest part. Although it may be time-consuming, there are few decisions to be made. You do, however, need to ensure that the quality of the data you gather is not compromised, perhaps by cutting corners in the interests of saving time. For example, if you have decided that you need to get the views of managing directors of small businesses on a particular issue, but for one or two organisations in your sample the managing director is unavailable, do not be tempted to take the views of the operations manager instead – these may differ in significant features from those of the managing director and including them could obscure interesting aspects of your results. Remember that if the data items you collect are of dubious quality, all your subsequent analysis may be invalidated.

If you have mailed questionnaires to your sample and are waiting for them to return, remember that a follow-up letter may be needed, to act as a reminder. Even with a reminder, you should be prepared for some lack of response – so remember to allow for this when deciding on your sample size.

Summarise data

Whatever more elaborate analysis you are planning on doing, the first priority when you have all your results should be to summarise them in such a way that you can begin to see what the interesting features of the data are. In this context, it will be helpful to revisit Chapters 3 and 4. Most of the following points are made in those chapters in more detail:

- For presenting results in a purely descriptive manner, tables and diagrams are best, but they invariably need referencing and explaining in accompanying text. Simple bar charts can be very effective; pie charts look pretty but are not so easy to read.
- Always go for simplicity and clarity, rather than ingenuity.
- Use additional measures (percentages, totals) to illuminate the important features of the raw data.
- Try lots of different formats for tables and charts – some will be more effective in getting your message over than others, and with suitable software it is very easy to try out your ideas quickly.
- With measured data, averages (means) can often usefully be quoted, but standard deviations are rarely helpful unless writing for a technical audience. Opt instead for easily interpretable measures such as quartiles ('25 per cent of people in our survey exercised more than three times a week'), percentiles ('The worst-off 10 per cent of the sample were earning under £6.00 an hour'), etc.
- To demonstrate links between variables, use cross-tabulations (for categoric data) or scatterplots (for measured data). However, cross-tabulations showing three or more

variables are often hard to interpret – it is better not to try to squeeze too much data onto one table.

Draw conclusions from sample results about the population

We are very rarely interested in the sample we have looked at for its own sake – usually it is only of interest insofar as it represents an underlying population of interest. And remember that, when you notice an apparently interesting aspect of sample data, the question to ask is always, 'Is this a real feature of the situation, or is it just an effect of chance sampling variations?' For this reason, you need to . . .

Qualify these conclusions with measures of significance/confidence

You may need to revisit Chapters 8 and 9 at this stage, to remind yourself of how samples behave and what conclusions we can legitimately draw from them. Generally speaking you should do the following:

- Modify statements about means, percentages, etc., that are based on sample data with confidence intervals to allow for sampling variation.
- Use suitable hypothesis tests to see whether differences between samples, correlations, etc., you have noted in your data are statistically significant, or could be simply the result of chance variation.
- Make sure that whatever statistical methods you use are suitable for your data. For example, do not fall into the trap of assuming that, just because data measured on a five-point scale (1 = very good, 2 = good, . . . , 5 = very bad) has a peak in the middle of the 1–5 range and tails off at the extremes, the figures must be normally distributed – they almost certainly will not be!
- Remember that the sampling theory we discussed in earlier chapters was based on the assumption that the data were a simple random sample from a large population. If the population is not large, you can apply a finite population correction; if the sample is not simple random but stratified or clustered, there are other ways of calculating standard errors, which you can read about in more advanced texts. However, if the sample is not random at all, but, say, a quota sample, or even a 'convenience sample' (which really means everyone you could get hold of), then strictly speaking you should not be using sampling theory or hypothesis tests at all. Having said this, it is the case that people *do* apply hypothesis testing and confidence intervals to such samples, but you should at least be aware that the results should be treated with a fair amount of caution, and mention this in your final report.
- Beware of carrying out dozens of hypothesis tests in succession – for example, performing a χ^2-test for differences in response between males and females on every question in a 40-question survey. Remember that if we use a 5 per cent significance level in the tests, then by definition 1 in every 20 tests, on average, will produce 'significant' results just by chance.

Students often find it difficult to decide just which bit of statistical theory to apply to their data in order to answer questions which are couched in non-statistical terms. As a rough guide the following apply:

- Estimated figures based on sample data (means, percentages) will need to be qualified by confidence intervals using STEM or STEP (see Chapter 8).

- Comparison of a sample mean or percentage with a hypothesised population figure will require a single-sample test, using STEP or STEM (see Chapter 9 for more details).
- Comparison of means in two samples may require either a paired two-sample test, or a test for the difference of means using STEDM, depending on the nature of your data.
- If you are looking for associations between measured variables, use a correlation coefficient – as long as you believe the association is likely to be linear. Do remember, however, that this is only a valid procedure if you have two sets of genuine measurements. If one of your 'numerical variables' is in fact just a set of arbitrary numerical codes (representing a qualitative variable such as 'region of residence') then you can go through the process of computing a so-called 'correlation coefficient', but it will of course be meaningless.
- In order to predict the value of one variable given values of one or more other variables, use regression, bivariate or multiple depending on the number of predictors; again, be aware that unless you explicitly include squared or other higher-power terms in the equation, a linear relationship will be fitted.
- If you are looking for an association between two categoric variables, set up a cross-tabulation and use χ^2.

These indications are neither watertight nor exhaustive – and remember, there are a great many more advanced statistical techniques which we have not covered, so do not imagine that every question should be answerable by using one of the methods in this book. Your project supervisor should be able to indicate when you have bitten off more than you can be expected to chew! Likewise, there is little point in carrying out an elaborate analysis involving hypothesis testing when the results are so clear as to be blindingly obvious, or when your data is of so doubtful a quality that the results of the tests will be meaningless.

Interpret results in terms of your practical situation

It is easy to lose sight, in the middle of a lot of statistical analysis, of the fact that you have carried out your survey or gathered your data for a practical purpose. It is at this stage that you need to revisit the practical problem with which you started, and see how far the analysis has got you. This is an aspect that many students find difficult – if you have worked through examples earlier in the book, which encouraged you to get into the habit of thinking 'What does this all *mean*?', you will have made a good start, but a few additional points are worth remembering:

- Be honest about problems with the data, data collection, etc., for example do not describe a sample as 'random' when it is not.
- Do not try to 'massage' the information to say what you want it to say – if it appears to contradict your initial assumptions about the situation, you will have to explain the fact, not explain it away!
- Do not confuse statistical significance with practical significance – a result can be highly statistically significant, and mean absolutely nothing in practice. For example, when sample sizes are very large, almost all hypothesis tests will give significant results, because standard errors will be very small (remember $s\sqrt{n}$?), but most will not be telling you anything important about the data.
- Do not try to use elaborate statistical methods as a substitute for thought.
- Be aware of the limitations and assumptions of the methods you have used.

- Do not overstate results – not for nothing do statisticians have a reputation for being cautious people. So a statement such as 'This sample does not appear to provide any evidence for the theory that older people have more days of absence due to sickness per year' is better than 'older people don't have any more days absent due to sickness than younger people'.
- Do not forget to use your common sense!

Report on your findings

The kind of report you write depends to some extent on the audience for which you are writing. For example, the extent to which it is appropriate to use technical language depends on how much statistics your readers will know. Even if you are writing for a readership that is very well informed statistically, it is important to remember that you know a great deal more about the project than any reader is likely to; do not fall into the trap of taking things for granted because you are very familiar with the situation. After working for weeks or perhaps months on your topic, you are probably the world expert!

It is difficult to give a general framework for a report of this kind, since the details will depend on whether your statistical work constitutes your entire project, or just a part of it, and on the nature of the topic you are investigating. However, a number of key points are worth remembering:

- Include an *executive summary* at the start of the project report. This is a short (certainly no more than two pages, and preferably less) summary which presents the main findings of your report without all the underpinning discussion and calculation. The idea is that a reader in a hurry could obtain a good idea of the results of your work, and whether they would be useful to him or her, without having to read the entire document.
- An *abstract*, which is an even shorter summary – no more than a paragraph – is sometimes included as well. You should ask your tutor or supervisor whether this is required in your case.
- Explain the background to the project. If you have been on placement, this will probably involve giving a short history of the organisation in which you were working, the nature of its business, and what your role was within the overall structure. For a project that is not externally based, you will need to explain how you became interested in the problem you have addressed, and why you believe it is worth tackling.
- Set out the objectives of your investigation. You will need to revisit these at the end of the report, in order to assess how successful you have been in meeting them, so make sure that they are clearly specified at the outset.
- Summarise the existing work on the topic, citing references to books and/or journal articles where you have found relevant material. This section is often known as a *literature review*.
- Outline the methodology you adopted, explaining why you proceeded as you did. If you had a choice of methods at any stage, you should indicate why you chose particular options.
- Present the data you collected, including the source if it is secondary data, or a description of the method of collection, questionnaire, sample, etc., if the data were collected first-hand. This need not necessarily include a listing of all the raw data – with a large amount of data, such a listing can be off-putting and take up too much space – but

should certainly cover presentation of the initial results using suitable descriptive methods, diagrams and summary statistics. Point out any interesting features that you notice; do not assume that the reader will spot them for him- or herself! However, there is no need to go to the other extreme and give tedious interpretations of perfectly clear tables and diagrams. Passages such as 'The number of employees went up to 510 in 2000, then it went down by 20 to 490, then up again in 2002 to 505' and so on do not make for interesting reading!

- Give details of the analysis you have carried out. Generally there is no need to explain the underlying statistical methods; so, for example, if you have used χ^2-tests on cross-tabulated data, you do not need to write 'The row and column totals were calculated, and then the expected frequencies were worked out using the formula . . .' Better simply to say that a χ^2-test was carried out; state the null hypothesis being tested, quote the calculated χ^2, and then indicate whether or not this indicates significance given the number of degrees of freedom and the level of significance you are using. If you are carrying out a great many similar tests, a tabular arrangement summarising the results can be useful.

- Discuss in plain English what your results imply for the practical situation under investigation. This does not mean writing 'This shows that the two variables are signi-ficantly correlated'. It means saying, for example, 'The results of the regression analysis show that there is a significant positive correlation between hours of sunshine and fishery catches, with catches increasing by 2000 tonnes for every additional hour of sunshine during the month'.

- Identify any limitations to what you have done, problems with the data, assumptions that may not be satisfied, etc. Be honest about this – for example, if you have used a t-test which requires normality, but the data is not really normal, then say so. Indicate as far as you can what impact these limitations may have on the validity of your results – though this can often be difficult to assess.

- Mention further work that could be done, or additional data that could be gathered, to improve the quality of the analysis and answer any outstanding questions. One of the features of a real-life study is that it is never really completed satisfactorily – there will always be other things you could have done, given more time, more data or a greater range of statistical techniques at your disposal. This section should mention those aspects.

- Revisit the objectives you set out at the start, and consider to what extent they have been met. What recommendations would you make as a result of your findings?

Finally, a few common-sense hints on the actual writing of the project report:

- Do use the spell-checker when you have finished your report – but do not rely exclusively on it: you also need to read through the report after it is printed. The spell-checker will not, for example, pick up a 'there' that should be 'their', and it may not have heard of technical statistical terms – for instance, many spell-checkers turn 'outliers' on a scatterplot into 'outliners'.

- Layout – if you are going to put the work into a folder, leave big enough margins so that words do not disappear into the spine (this sounds obvious, but you do not want to irritate the person marking the report). Watch out for hanging headings (heading at the bottom of one page, text on the next). Use layout (bold lettering, centred text, etc.) to make the structure of your report clear.

- Do not adopt an excessively formal style – the report should not be 'chatty', but it does not need to adopt a clumsy passive voice all the time. The school chemistry experiment style ('A test-tube was taken . . .') is not necessarily the most readable.
- Consider which aspects of your work should be covered in the main body of the report, and which in appendices. Very often the details of the data can be relegated to the appendix, and this may apply also to the statistical calculations. If you find it hard to decide whether to put something into an appendix, ask yourself 'Could a reader decide not to read this bit and still make sense of the rest of the material?' If the answer is yes, then the section in question could well go into an appendix.
- Be punctilious about citing all your references – you do not wish to lay yourself open to a charge of plagiarism by quoting from other authors without acknowledgement. You should include a bibliography set out formally with details of publishers, dates and so on; your supervisor will be able to advise you on the precise conventions for referencing which you should adopt.
- Keep a clear picture of the reader in your mind while you are writing. Ask yourself 'Would I understand this if I didn't already know what it's about?'
- Finally, be concise – do not try to 'pad out' the report!

Examples

To start you thinking about the kinds of statistical investigation which you might incorporate into your own projects, here is a short list of examples based on work done by students whom I have taught. Remember that in most cases, the statistical work constituted only a small proportion of the total project, which also included literature reviews and qualitative considerations.

Example 1

Student A, who had a part-time job in a newsagent's shop, tested whether the proportions of people buying various daily newspapers in this shop were in accord with the national readership data obtainable from published sources. She had an initial idea that, because the shop was situated in a 'desirable' neighbourhood, the proportions buying quality newspapers should be higher than the national figure. The analysis involved using a χ^2-test for goodness of fit of the data she had collected with the theoretical figures, which did indeed confirm her initial 'hunch'. She was able to incorporate these findings into a discussion of the segmentation of the newspaper market.

Example 2

Student B, a part-time MBA student working for a large distributor of engineering products, investigated whether problems of late deliveries were attributable to particular distribution centres. By first stratifying the deliveries according to the value of the order, and then carrying out a series of hypothesis tests on the average time which elapsed between ordering and delivery for the various distribution centres, he was able to identify the one centre which had a significantly worse performance than the others on particular types of order. He then went on to explore means by which performance could be improved.

Interestingly, in this case it was the stratification of the data, rather than the hypothesis testing, that really gave insight into what was going on.

Example 3

Student C was interested in the way queues built up at the 'hole-in-the-wall' cash machines outside the Student Union at busy times. She therefore observed the lengths of the queues at various times of day over a period of several weeks, and was able both to carry out a time-series analysis (see Chapter 15) of the daily fluctuations in the queues, and to test whether the waiting times of individual customers varied significantly among time-slots (e.g. 11 a.m. and 1 p.m.). This analysis contributed to a wider discussion of the ways in which the service to customers could be improved.

Example 4

A group of full-time students working together obtained permission from a local motorway service area to carry out a survey of customers using the services. They were able to gather a substantial amount of data concerning the facilities used, amounts spent and demographic information relating to the customers. This was an exploratory investigation, designed primarily to give the management of the service area a better 'feel' for the market, so rather than carrying out many formal tests, the major challenge was to present the information, using diagrams, tables and an oral presentation, in such a way that the present management could make use of it in future planning.

Example 5

Student D, on placement with a large department store, was asked to investigate staff reactions to the recent introduction of new cash tills. Since he had the support of senior management, he was able to obtain a very good response rate to a survey in which staff were asked for their views on various aspects of the exercise, such as the training provided; most of the questions in this survey were answered using a five-point scale ranging from 'strongly agree' to 'strongly disagree'. Analysis included investigating issues such as whether younger staff responded more favourably to the new system than older staff. The findings were then incorporated into a project report which also examined the human resource implications of implementing major changes in working practices.

Example 6

Finally, student E, a part-time student who ran a small dairy herd in his spare time, wished to examine whether there was an association between the milk-yields of 'mother' and 'daughter' cows. Because he was obliged to keep very detailed records, both of the history of his herd and of milk yields, he had a great deal of data with which to address the question. The analysis proved quite complex, since factors such as the variation in yields with the age of the cow and the time of year had to be taken into consideration; however, he was eventually able to conclude, primarily via the use of regression, that there was some association, though not as strong as he might have predicted. The information would be used in making decisions about herd management.

These are just half-a-dozen examples, chosen to illustrate the range of possibilities open to you; if your institution keeps copies of former students' projects in the library, try looking at those to see whether they provide any ideas. And never forget that to produce a really good project, you should be asking 'What statistical methods can be used to help me answer this interesting business question?', not 'I understand regression – I'll look for some data that I could do a regression with'.

Further reading

This chapter has covered primarily issues related to quantitative methods in a research project. There are now a number of texts covering the whole business of choosing, carrying out and writing up a business-related project; these include advice on areas such as time management and scheduling the activities involved in the project; getting cooperation from individuals and organisations; and many other matters that we have not been able to touch on here. Two good ones to begin with are as follows:

Collis, J. and Hussey, R. (2009), *Business Research: A Practical Guide for Undergraduate and Postgraduate Students*, 3rd edn, Palgrave Macmillan.

Polonsky, M.J. and Waller, D.S. (2010), *Designing and Managing a Research Project: A Business Student's Guide*, 2nd edn, Sage.

APPENDICES

Appendix 1

A note on computer resources

Reference has been made throughout this book to the use of Excel spreadsheets in carrying out statistical calculations. However, I have not attempted to provide a general introduction to Excel, since it is likely either that you will already be familiar with the use of a spreadsheet, or that you will learn this in another part of your course, for example as part of an accounting module.

If you feel that you need to enhance your general Excel skills in order to be able to use it confidently in your statistical work, there are many good texts which you might find helpful. In particular, the 'For Dummies' series, published by Wiley, includes two useful volumes: *Excel 2007 for Dummies*, by Greg Harvey, and *Excel 2007 Data Analysis for Dummies*, by Stephen L Nelson.

It should be noted that all the examples in the book make use of Excel 2007; however, it may be necessary for you to customise Excel and include the Analysis Tools and Solver add-ins to follow the methods presented here.

I have not attempted to give examples using other statistical software, such as Minitab or SPSS. The methods discussed in the book can also be implemented using either of these, but the initial 'learning curve' required to become familiar with the software is much steeper than with Excel. If you are required to use either Minitab or SPSS for your course, then you should take the advice of your lecturer on acquiring the necessary skills.

Appendix 2

Random sampling numbers

78 41	11 62	72 18	66 69	58 71	31 90	51 36	78 09	41 00
70 50	58 19	68 26	75 69	04 00	25 29	16 72	35 73	55 85
32 78	14 47	01 55	10 91	83 21	13 32	59 53	03 38	79 32
71 60	20 53	86 78	50 57	42 30	73 48	68 09	16 35	21 87
35 30	15 57	99 96	33 25	56 43	65 67	51 45	37 99	54 89
09 08	05 41	66 54	01 49	97 34	38 85	85 23	34 62	60 58
02 59	34 51	98 71	31 54	28 85	23 84	49 07	33 71	17 88
20 13	44 15	22 95	98 97	60 02	85 07	17 57	20 51	01 67
36 26	70 11	63 81	27 31	79 71	08 11	87 74	85 53	86 78
00 30	62 19	81 68	86 10	65 61	62 22	17 22	96 83	56 37
38 41	14 59	53 03	52 86	21 88	55 87	85 59	14 90	74 87
18 89	40 84	71 04	09 82	54 44	94 23	83 89	04 59	38 29
34 38	85 56	80 74	22 31	26 39	65 63	12 38	45 75	30 35
55 90	21 71	17 88	20 08	57 64	17 93	22 34	00 55	09 78
81 43	53 96	96 88	36 86	04 33	31 40	18 71	06 00	51 45
59 69	13 03	38 31	77 08	71 20	23 28	92 43	92 63	21 74
60 24	47 44	73 93	64 37	64 97	19 82	27 59	24 20	00 04
17 04	93 46	05 70	20 95	42 25	33 95	78 80	07 57	86 58
09 55	42 30	27 05	27 93	78 10	69 11	29 56	29 79	28 66
46 69	28 64	81 02	41 89	12 03	31 20	25 16	79 93	28 22
28 94	00 91	16 15	35 12	68 93	23 71	11 55	64 56	76 95
59 10	06 29	83 84	03 68	97 65	59 21	58 54	61 59	30 54
41 04	70 71	05 56	76 66	57 86	29 30	11 31	56 76	24 13
09 81	81 80	73 10	10 23	26 29	61 15	50 00	76 37	60 16
91 55	76 68	06 82	05 33	06 75	92 35	82 21	78 15	19 43
82 69	36 73	58 69	10 92	31 14	21 08	13 78	56 53	97 77
03 59	65 34	32 06	63 43	38 04	65 30	32 82	57 05	33 95
03 96	30 87	81 54	69 39	95 69	95 69	89 33	78 90	30 07
39 91	27 38	20 90	41 10	10 80	59 68	93 10	85 25	59 25
89 93	92 10	59 40	26 14	27 47	39 51	46 70	86 85	76 02
99 16	73 21	39 05	03 36	87 58	18 52	61 61	02 92	07 24
93 13	20 70	42 59	77 69	35 59	71 80	61 95	82 96	48 84
47 32	87 68	97 86	28 51	61 21	33 02	79 65	59 49	89 93
09 75	58 00	72 49	36 58	19 45	30 61	87 74	43 01	93 91
63 24	15 65	02 05	32 92	45 61	35 43	67 64	94 45	95 66
33 58	69 42	25 71	74 31	88 80	04 50	22 60	72 01	27 88
23 25	22 78	24 88	68 48	83 60	53 59	73 73	82 43	82 66
07 17	77 20	79 37	50 08	29 79	55 13	51 90	36 77	68 69
16 07	31 84	57 22	29 54	35 14	22 22	22 60	72 15	40 90
67 90	79 28	62 83	44 96	87 70	40 64	27 22	60 19	52 54
79 52	74 68	69 74	31 75	80 59	29 28	21 69	15 97	35 88
69 44	31 09	16 38	92 82	12 25	10 57	81 32	76 71	31 61
09 47	57 04	54 00	78 75	91 99	26 20	36 19	53 29	11 55
74 78	09 25	95 80	25 72	88 85	76 02	29 89	70 78	93 84

Appendix 3

Cumulative binomial probabilities

The table gives the probability of *r or more* successes in *n* trials, with the probability *p* of success in one trial.

n	r	p = 0.05	0.1	0.15	0.2	0.25	0.3	0.35	0.4	0.45	0.5
1	10	1.0000	1.0000	1.0000	1.0000	1.0000	1.0000	1.0000	1.0000	1.0000	1.0000
	1	0.0500	0.1000	0.1500	0.2000	0.2500	0.3000	0.3500	0.4000	0.4500	0.5000
2	0	1.0000	1.0000	1.0000	1.0000	1.0000	1.0000	1.0000	1.0000	1.0000	1.0000
	1	0.0975	0.1900	0.2775	0.3600	0.4375	0.5100	0.5775	0.6400	0.6975	0.7500
	2	0.0025	0.0100	0.0225	0.0400	0.6525	0.0900	0.1225	0.1600	0.2025	0.2500
3	0	1.0000	1.0000	1.0000	1.0000	1.0000	1.0000	1.0000	1.0000	1.0000	1.0000
	1	0.1426	1.2710	0.3859	0.4880	0.5781	0.6570	0.7254	0.7840	0.8336	0.8750
	2	0.0072	0.0280	0.0608	0.1040	0.1562	0.2160	0.2818	0.3520	0.4252	0.5000
	3	0.0001	0.0010	0.0034	0.0080	0.0156	0.0270	0.0429	0.0640	0.0911	0.1250
4	0	1.0000	1.0000	1.0000	1.0000	1.0000	1.0000	1.0000	1.0000	1.0000	1.0000
	1	0.1855	0.3439	0.4780	0.5904	0.6836	0.7599	0.8215	0.8704	0.9085	0.9375
	2	0.0140	0.0523	0.1095	0.1808	0.2617	0.3483	0.4370	0.5248	0.6090	0.6875
	3	0.0005	0.0037	0.0120	0.0272	0.2148	0.0837	0.1265	0.1792	0.2415	0.3125
	4		0.0001	0.0005	0.0016	0.0039	0.0081	0.0150	0.0256	0.0410	0.0625
5	0	1.0000	1.0000	1.0000	1.0000	1.0000	1.0000	1.0000	1.0000	1.0000	1.0000
	1	0.2261	0.4094	0.5564	0.6723	0.7627	0.8320	0.8840	0.9222	0.9498	0.9686
	2	0.0225	0.0814	0.1649	0.2627	0.3672	0.4718	0.5716	0.6630	0.7439	0.8124
	3	0.0011	0.0085	0.0267	0.0579	0.1035	0.1631	0.2352	0.3174	0.4070	0.5000
	4		0.0004	0.0023	0.0067	0.0156	0.0308	0.0541	0.0870	0.1313	0.1874
	5			0.0001	0.0003	0.0010	0.0024	0.0053	0.0102	0.0185	0.0312
6	0	1.0000	1.0000	1.0000	1.0000	1.0000	1.0000	1.0000	1.0000	1.0000	1.0000
	1	0.2648	0.4686	0.6229	0.7379	0.8220	0.8822	0.9246	0.9533	0.9724	0.9845
	2	0.0327	0.1143	0.2236	0.3447	0.4660	0.5797	0.6809	0.7667	0.8365	0.8907
	3	0.0022	0.0159	0.0474	0.0989	0.1694	0.2556	0.3529	0.4557	0.5585	0.6563
	4	0.0001	0.0013	0.0059	0.0170	0.0376	0.0704	0.1174	0.1792	0.2553	0.3438
	5		0.0001	0.0004	0.0016	0.0046	0.0109	0.0223	0.0410	0.0692	0.1094
	6				0.0001	0.0002	0.0007	0.0018	0.0041	0.0083	0.0156
7	0	1.0000	1.0000	1.0000	1.0000	1.0000	1.0000	1.0000	1.0000	1.0000	1.0000
	1	0.3017	0.5218	0.6796	0.7904	0.8666	0.9177	0.0510	0.9713	0.9847	0.9922
	2	0.0444	0.1498	0.2836	0.4234	0.5551	0.6706	0.7662	0.8413	0.8975	0.9375
	3	0.0038	0.0258	0.0799	0.1481	0.2436	0.3529	0.4677	0.5800	0.6835	0.7734
	4	0.0002	0.0028	0.0122	0.0334	0.0706	0.1260	0.1998	0.2897	0.3917	0.5000
	5		0.0002	0.0013	0.0047	0.0129	0.0288	0.0556	0.0962	0.1529	0.2266
	6			0.0001	0.0004	0.0014	0.0038	0.0090	0.0188	0.0357	0.0625
	7					0.0001	0.0002	0.0006	0.0016	0.0037	0.0078

n	r	p = 0.05	0.1	0.15	0.2	0.25	0.3	0.35	0.4	0.45	0.5
8	0	1.0000	1.0000	1.0000	1.0000	1.0000	1.0000	1.0000	1.0000	1.0000	1.0000
	1	0.3366	0.5695	0.7275	0.8322	0.8999	0.9424	0.9681	0.0933	0.9915	0.9961
	2	0.0573	0.1869	0.3428	0.4967	0.6329	0.7447	0.8308	0.8937	0.9367	0.9649
	3	0.0058	0.0381	0.1052	0.2031	0.3214	0.4882	0.5721	0.6847	0.7798	0.8555
	4	0.0004	0.0050	0.0213	0.0563	0.1138	0.1941	0.2935	0.4060	0.5230	0.6367
	5		0.0044	0.0028	0.0104	0.0273	0.0580	0.1060	0.1738	0.2603	0.3633
	6			0.0002	0.0012	0.0042	0.0113	0.0252	0.0499	0.0884	0.1445
	7				0.0001	0.0004	0.0013	0.0035	0.0086	0.0181	0.0351
	8						0.0001	0.0002	0.0007	0.0017	0.0039
9	0	1.0000	1.0000	1.0000	1.0000	1.0000	1.0000	1.0000	1.0000	1.0000	1.0000
	1	0.3697	0.6125	0.7684	0.8659	0.9249	0.9595	0.9793	0.9898	0.9954	0.9982
	2	0.0712	0.2251	0.4005	0.5639	0.6996	0.8039	0.8789	0.9293	0.9615	0.9806
	3	0.0083	0.0529	0.1408	0.2619	0.3993	0.5371	0.6627	0.7681	0.8505	0.9103
	4	0.0006	0.0083	0.0339	0.0857	0.1657	0.2703	0.3911	0.5173	0.6386	0.7642
	5		0.0009	0.0056	0.0196	0.0489	0.0988	0.1717	0.2665	0.3786	0.5001
	6		0.0001	0.0006	0.0031	0.0100	0.0253	0.0536	0.0993	0.1658	0.2540
	7				0.0003	0.0013	0.0043	0.0112	0.0250	0.0498	0.0899
	8					0.0001	0.0004	0.0014	0.0038	0.0091	0.0196
	9							0.0001	0.0003	0.0008	0.0020
10	0	1.0000	1.0000	1.0000	1.0000	1.0000	1.0000	1.0000	1.0000	1.0000	1.0000
	1	0.4013	0.6513	0.8030	0.8926	0.9437	0.9717	0.9866	0.9940	0.9975	0.9991
	2	0.0862	0.2639	0.4556	0.6242	0.7560	0.8506	0.9141	0.9537	0.9768	0.9893
	3	0.0116	0.0702	0.1797	0.3222	0.4744	0.6171	0.7384	0.8328	0.9005	0.9454
	4	0.0011	0.0128	0.0499	0.1209	0.2241	0.3503	0.4862	0.6178	0.7340	0.8282
	5	0.0001	0.0016	0.0098	0.0328	0.0781	0.1502	0.2485	0.3670	0.4956	0.6231
	6		0.0001	0.0013	0.0064	0.0197	0.0473	0.0949	0.1663	0.2616	0.3770
	7			0.0001	0.0009	0.0035	0.0105	0.0260	0.0548	0.1020	0.1719
	8				0.0001	0.0004	0.0015	0.0048	0.0123	0.0274	0.0547
	9						0.0001	0.0005	0.0017	0.0045	0.0108
	10								0.0001	0.0003	0.0010

This table is taken in part from Table 1 of *Statistical Tables for Science, Engineering, Management and Business Studies* by J. Murdoch and J.A. Barnes, published by Macmillan, London and Basingstoke.

Appendix 4

Cumulative Poisson probabilities

The table gives the probability that *r or more* random events are contained in an interval when the average number of events per interval is *m*.

m =	0.1	0.2	0.3	0.4	0.5	0.6	0.7	0.8	0.9	1.0
r = 0	1.0000	1.0000	1.0000	1.0000	1.0000	1.0000	1.0000	1.0000	1.0000	1.0000
1	0.0952	0.1813	0.2592	0.3297	0.3935	0.4512	0.5034	0.5507	0.5934	0.6321
2	0.0047	0.0175	0.0369	0.0616	0.0902	0.1219	0.1558	0.1912	0.2275	0.2642
3	0.0002	0.0011	0.0036	0.0079	0.0144	0.0231	0.0341	0.0474	0.0629	0.0803
4		0.0001	0.0003	0.0008	0.0018	0.0034	0.0058	0.0091	0.0135	0.0190
5				0.0001	0.0002	0.0004	0.0008	0.0014	0.0023	0.0037
6							0.0001	0.0002	0.0003	0.0006
7										0.0001

m =	1.1	1.2	1.3	1.4	1.5	1.6	1.7	1.8	1.9	2.0
r = 0	1.0000	1.0000	1.0000	1.0000	1.0000	1.0000	1.0000	1.0000	1.0000	1.0000
1	0.6671	0.6988	0.7275	0.7534	0.7769	0.7981	0.8173	0.8347	0.8504	0.8647
2	0.3010	0.3374	0.3732	0.4082	0.4422	0.4751	0.5068	0.5372	0.5663	0.5940
3	0.0996	0.1205	0.1429	0.1665	0.1912	0.2166	0.2428	0.2694	0.2963	0.3233
4	0.0257	0.0338	0.0431	0.0537	0.0656	0.0788	0.0932	0.1087	0.1253	0.1429
5	0.0054	0.0077	0.0107	0.0143	0.0186	0.0237	0.0296	0.0364	0.0441	0.0527
6	0.0010	0.0015	0.0022	0.0032	0.0045	0.0060	0.0080	0.0104	0.0132	0.0166
7	0.0001	0.0003	0.0004	0.0006	0.0009	0.0013	0.0019	0.0026	0.0034	0.0045
8			0.0001	0.0001	0.0002	0.0003	0.0004	0.0006	0.0008	0.0011
9							0.0001	0.0001	0.0002	0.0002

m =	2.1	2.2	2.3	2.4	2.5	2.6	2.7	2.8	2.9	3.0
r = 0	1.0000	1.0000	1.0000	1.0000	1.0000	1.0000	1.0000	1.0000	1.0000	1.0000
1	0.8775	0.8892	0.8997	0.9093	0.9179	0.9257	0.9328	0.9392	0.9400	0.9502
2	0.6204	0.6454	0.6691	0.6916	0.7127	0.7326	0.7513	0.7689	0.7854	0.8009
3	0.3504	0.3773	0.4040	0.4303	0.4562	0.4816	0.5064	0.5305	0.5500	0.5768
4	0.1614	0.1806	0.2007	0.2213	0.2424	0.2640	0.2859	0.3081	0.3304	0.3528
5	0.0621	0.0725	0.0838	0.0959	0.1088	0.1226	0.1371	0.1523	0.1820	0.1847
6	0.0204	0.0249	0.0300	0.0357	0.0420	0.0490	0.0567	0.0651	0.0742	0.0839
7	0.0059	0.0075	0.0094	0.0116	0.0142	0.0172	0.0206	0.0244	0.0287	0.0335
8	0.0015	0.0020	0.0026	0.0033	0.0042	0.0053	0.0066	0.0081	0.0099	0.0119
9	0.0003	0.0005	0.0006	0.0009	0.0011	0.0015	0.0019	0.0024	0.0031	0.0038
10	0.0001	0.0001	0.0001	0.0002	0.0003	0.0004	0.0005	0.0007	0.0009	0.0011
11					0.0001	0.0001	0.0001	0.0002	0.0002	0.0003
12									0.0001	0.0001

continues overleaf

m =	3.1	3.2	3.3	3.4	3.5	3.6	3.7	3.8	3.9	4.0
r = 0	1.0000	1.0000	1.0000	1.0000	1.0000	1.0000	1.0000	1.0000	1.0000	1.0000
1	0.9550	0.9592	0.9631	0.9666	0.9698	0.9727	0.9753	0.9776	0.9798	0.9817
2	0.8153	0.8288	0.8414	0.8532	0.8641	0.8743	0.8838	0.8926	0.9008	0.9084
3	0.5998	0.6201	0.6406	0.6603	0.6792	0.6973	0.7146	0.7311	0.7469	0.7619
4	0.3752	0.3975	0.4197	0.4416	0.4634	0.4848	0.5058	0.5265	0.5468	0.5665
5	0.2018	0.2194	0.2374	0.2558	0.2746	0.2936	0.3128	0.3322	0.3516	0.3712
6	0.0943	0.1054	0.1171	0.1295	0.1424	0.1559	0.1699	0.1844	0.1994	0.2149
7	0.0388	0.0446	0.0510	0.0579	0.0653	0.0733	0.0818	0.0909	0.1005	0.1107
8	0.0142	0.0168	0.0198	0.0231	0.0267	0.0308	0.0352	0.0401	0.0454	0.0511
9	0.0047	0.0057	0.0069	0.0083	0.0099	0.0117	0.0137	0.0160	0.0185	0.0214
10	0.0014	0.0018	0.0022	0.0027	0.0033	0.0040	0.0048	0.0058	0.0069	0.0081
11	0.0004	0.0005	0.0006	0.0008	0.0010	0.0013	0.0016	0.0019	0.0023	0.0028
12	0.0001	0.0001	0.0002	0.0002	0.0003	0.0004	0.0005	0.0006	0.0007	0.0009
13				0.0001	0.0001	0.0001	0.0001	0.0002	0.0002	0.0003
14									0.0001	0.0001

m =	4.1	4.2	4.3	4.4	4.5	4.6	4.7	4.8	4.9	5.0
r = 0	1.0000	1.0000	1.0000	1.0000	1.0000	1.0000	1.0000	1.0000	1.0000	1.0000
1	0.9834	0.9850	0.9864	0.9877	0.9889	0.9899	0.9909	0.9918	0.9926	0.9933
2	0.9155	0.9220	0.9281	0.9337	0.9389	0.9437	0.9482	0.9523	0.9561	0.9596
3	0.7762	0.7898	0.8026	0.8149	0.8264	0.8374	0.8477	0.8575	0.8667	0.8753
4	0.5858	0.6046	0.6228	0.6406	0.6577	0.6743	0.6903	0.7058	0.7207	0.7350
5	0.3907	0.4102	0.4296	0.4488	0.4679	0.4868	0.5054	0.5237	0.5418	0.5595
6	0.2307	0.2469	0.2633	0.2801	0.2971	0.3142	0.3316	0.3490	0.3665	0.3840
7	0.1214	0.1325	0.1442	0.1564	0.1689	0.1820	0.1954	0.2092	0.2233	0.2378
8	0.0573	0.0639	0.0710	0.0786	0.0866	0.0951	0.1040	0.1133	0.1231	0.1334
9	0.0245	0.0279	0.0317	0.0358	0.0403	0.0451	0.0503	0.0558	0.0618	0.0681
10	0.0095	0.0111	0.0129	0.0149	0.0171	0.0195	0.0222	0.0251	0.0283	0.0318
11	0.0034	0.0041	0.0048	0.0057	0.0067	0.0078	0.0090	0.0104	0.0120	0.0137
12	0.0011	0.0014	0.0017	0.0020	0.0024	0.0029	0.0034	0.0040	0.0047	0.0055
13	0.0003	0.0004	0.0005	0.0007	0.0008	0.0010	0.0012	0.0014	0.0017	0.0020
14	0.0001	0.0001	0.0002	0.0002	0.0003	0.0003	0.0004	0.0005	0.0006	0.0007
15				0.0001	0.0001	0.0001	0.0001	0.0001	0.0002	0.0002
16									0.0001	0.0001

m =	5.2	5.4	5.6	5.8	6.0	6.2	6.4	6.6	6.8	7.0
r = 0	1.0000	1.0000	1.0000	1.0000	1.0000	1.0000	1.0000	1.0000	1.0000	1.0000
1	0.9945	0.9955	0.9963	0.9970	0.9975	0.9980	0.9983	0.9986	0.9989	0.9991
2	0.9658	0.9711	0.9756	0.9794	0.9826	0.9854	0.9877	0.9897	0.9913	0.9927
3	0.8912	0.9052	0.9176	0.9285	0.9380	0.9464	0.9537	0.9600	0.9656	0.9704
4	0.7619	0.7867	0.8094	0.8300	0.8488	0.8658	0.8811	0.8948	0.9072	0.9182
5	0.5939	0.6267	0.6579	0.6873	0.7149	0.7408	0.7649	0.7873	0.8080	0.8270
6	0.4191	0.4539	0.4881	0.5217	0.5543	0.5859	0.6163	0.6453	0.6730	0.6993
7	0.2676	0.2983	0.3297	0.3616	0.3937	0.4258	0.4577	0.4892	0.5201	0.5503
8	0.1551	0.1783	0.2030	0.2290	0.2560	0.2840	0.3127	0.3419	0.3715	0.4013
9	0.0819	0.0974	0.1143	0.1328	0.1528	0.1741	0.1967	0.2204	0.2452	0.2709
10	0.0397	0.0488	0.0591	0.0708	0.0839	0.0984	0.1142	0.1314	0.1498	0.1695
11	0.0177	0.0225	0.0282	0.0349	0.0426	0.0514	0.0614	0.0726	0.0849	0.0985
12	0.0073	0.0096	0.0125	0.0160	0.0201	0.0250	0.0307	0.0373	0.0448	0.0534
13	0.0028	0.0038	0.0051	0.0068	0.0088	0.0113	0.0143	0.0179	0.0221	0.0270
14	0.0010	0.0014	0.0020	0.0027	0.0036	0.0048	0.0063	0.0080	0.0102	0.0128
15	0.0003	0.0005	0.0007	0.0010	0.0014	0.0019	0.0026	0.0034	0.0044	0.0057
16	0.0001	0.0002	0.0002	0.0004	0.0005	0.0007	0.0010	0.0014	0.0018	0.0024
17		0.0001	0.0001	0.0001	0.0002	0.0003	0.0004	0.0005	0.0007	0.0010
18					0.0001	0.0001	0.0001	0.0002	0.0003	0.0004
19								0.0001	0.0001	0.0001

This table is taken from part of Table 2 of *Statistical Tables for Science, Engineering, Management and Business Studies* by J. Murdoch and J.A. Barnes published by Macmillan, London and Basingstoke.

Appendix 5

Areas under the standard normal curve

The table gives the area A under one tail:

z	0.00	0.01	0.02	0.03	0.04	0.05	0.06	0.07	0.08	0.09
0.0	0.500 0	0.496 0	0.492 0	0.488 0	0.484 0	0.480 1	0.476 1	0.472 1	0.468 1	0.464 1
0.1	0.460 2	0.456 2	0.452 2	0.448 3	0.444 3	0.440 4	0.436 4	0.432 5	0.428 6	0.424 7
0.2	0.420 7	0.416 8	0.412 9	0.409 0	0.405 2	0.401 3	0.397 4	0.393 6	0.389 7	0.385 9
0.3	0.382 1	0.378 3	0.374 5	0.370 7	0.366 9	0.363 2	0.359 4	0.355 7	0.352 0	0.348 3
0.4	0.344 6	0.340 9	0.337 2	0.333 6	0.330 0	0.326 4	0.322 8	0.319 2	0.315 6	0.312 1
0.5	0.308 5	0.305 0	0.301 5	0.298 1	0.294 6	0.291 2	0.287 7	0.284 3	0.281 0	0.277 6
0.6	0.274 3	0.270 9	0.267 6	0.264 3	0.261 1	0.257 8	0.254 6	0.251 4	0.248 3	0.245 1
0.7	0.242 0	0.238 9	0.235 8	0.232 7	0.229 6	0.226 6	0.223 6	0.220 6	0.217 7	0.214 8
0.8	0.211 9	0.209 0	0.206 1	0.203 3	0.200 5	0.197 7	0.194 9	0.192 2	0.189 4	0.186 7
0.9	0.184 1	0.181 4	0.178 8	0.176 2	0.173 6	0.171 1	0.168 5	0.166 0	0.163 5	0.161 1
1.0	0.158 7	0.156 2	0.153 9	0.151 5	0.149 2	0.146 9	0.144 6	0.142 3	0.140 1	0.137 9
1.1	0.135 7	0.133 5	0.131 4	0.129 2	0.127 1	0.125 1	0.123 0	0.121 0	0.119 0	0.117 0
1.2	0.115 1	0.113 1	0.111 2	0.109 3	0.107 5	0.105 6	0.103 8	0.102 0	0.100 3	0.098 5
1.3	0.096 8	0.095 1	0.093 4	0.091 8	0.090 1	0.088 5	0.086 9	0.085 3	0.083 8	0.082 3
1.4	0.080 8	0.079 3	0.077 8	0.076 4	0.074 9	0.073 5	0.072 1	0.070 8	0.069 4	0.068 1
1.5	0.066 8	0.065 5	0.064 3	0.063 0	0.061 8	0.060 6	0.059 4	0.058 2	0.057 1	0.055 9
1.6	0.054 8	0.053 7	0.052 6	0.051 6	0.050 5	0.049 5	0.048 5	0.047 5	0.046 5	0.045 5
1.7	0.044 6	0.043 6	0.042 7	0.041 8	0.040 9	0.040 1	0.039 2	0.038 4	0.037 5	0.036 7
1.8	0.035 9	0.035 1	0.034 4	0.033 6	0.032 9	0.032 2	0.031 4	0.030 7	0.030 1	0.029 4
1.9	0.028 7	0.028 1	0.027 4	0.026 8	0.026 2	0.025 6	0.025 0	0.024 4	0.023 9	0.023 3
2.0	0.022 75	0.022 22	0.021 69	0.021 18	0.020 68	0.020 18	0.019 70	0.019 23	0.018 76	0.018 31
2.1	0.017 86	0.017 43	0.017 00	0.016 59	0.016 18	0.015 78	0.015 39	0.015 00	0.014 63	0.014 26
2.2	0.013 90	0.013 55	0.013 21	0.012 87	0.012 55	0.012 22	0.011 91	0.011 60	0.011 30	0.011 01
2.3	0.010 72	0.010 44	0.010 17	0.009 90	0.009 64	0.009 39	0.009 14	0.008 89	0.008 66	0.008 42
2.4	0.008 20	0.007 98	0.007 76	0.007 55	0.007 34	0.007 14	0.006 95	0.006 76	0.006 57	0.006 39
2.5	0.006 21	0.006 04	0.005 87	0.005 70	0.005 54	0.005 39	0.005 23	0.005 08	0.004 94	0.004 80
2.6	0.004 66	0.004 53	0.004 40	0.004 27	0.004 15	0.004 02	0.003 91	0.003 79	0.003 68	0.003 57
2.7	0.003 47	0.003 36	0.003 26	0.003 17	0.003 07	0.002 98	0.002 89	0.002 80	0.002 72	0.002 64
2.8	0.002 56	0.002 48	0.002 40	0.002 33	0.002 26	0.002 19	0.002 12	0.002 05	0.001 99	0.001 93
2.9	0.001 87	0.001 81	0.001 75	0.001 69	0.001 64	0.001 59	0.001 54	0.001 49	0.001 44	0.001 39
3.0	0.001 35									
3.1	0.000 97									
3.2	0.000 69									
3.3	0.000 48									
3.4	0.000 34									
3.5	0.000 23									
3.6	0.000 16									
3.7	0.000 11									
3.8	0.000 07									
3.9	0.000 05									
4.0	0.000 03									

This table is taken in part from Table 3 of *Statistical Tables for Science, Engineering, Management and Business Studies* by J. Murdoch and J.A. Barnes, published by Macmillan, London and Basingstoke.

Appendix 6

Percentage points of the χ^2-distribution

The table gives the area α under one tail:

$\alpha =$		0.995	0.99	0.98	0.975	0.95	0.90
$\nu =$	1	0.0^4393	0.0^3157	0.0^3628	0.0^3982	0.003 93	0.0158
	2	0.0100	0.0201	0.0404	0.0506	0.103	0.211
	3	0.0717	0.115	0.185	0.216	0.352	0.584
	4	0.207	0.297	0.429	0.484	0.711	1.064
	5	0.412	0.554	0.752	0.831	1.145	1.610
	6	0.676	0.872	1.134	1.237	1.635	2.204
	7	0.989	1.239	1.564	1.690	2.167	2.833
	8	1.344	1.646	2.032	2.180	2.733	3.490
	9	1.735	2.088	2.532	2.700	3.325	4.168
	10	2.156	2.558	3.059	3.247	3.940	4.865
	11	2.603	3.053	3.609	3.816	4.575	5.578
	12	3.074	3.571	4.178	4.404	5.226	6.304
	13	3.565	4.107	4.765	5.009	5.892	7.042
	14	0.075	4.660	5.368	5.629	6.571	7.790
	15	4.601	5.229	5.985	6.262	7.261	8.547
	16	5.142	5.812	6.614	6.908	7.962	9.312
	17	5.697	6.408	7.255	7.564	8.672	10.085
	18	6.265	7.015	7.906	8.231	9.390	10.865
	19	6.844	7.633	8.567	8.907	10.117	11.651
	20	7.434	8.260	9.237	9.591	10.851	12.443
	21	8.034	8.897	9.915	10.283	11.591	13.240
	22	8.643	9.542	10.600	10.982	12.338	14.041
	23	9.260	10.196	11.293	11.688	13.091	14.848
	24	9.886	10.856	11.992	12.401	13.838	15.659
	25	10.520	11.524	12.697	13.120	14.611	16.473
	26	11.160	12.198	13.409	13.844	15.379	17.292
	27	11.808	12.879	14.125	14.573	16.151	18.114
	28	12.461	13.565	14.847	15.308	16.928	18.939
	29	13.121	14.256	15.574	16.047	17.707	19.768
	30	13.787	14.953	16.306	16.791	18.493	20.599
	40	20.706	22.164	23.838	24.433	26.509	29.051
	50	27.991	29.707	31.664	32.357	34.764	37.689
	60	35.535	37.485	39.699	40.482	43.188	46.459
	70	43.275	45.442	47.893	48.758	51.739	55.329
	80	51.171	53.539	56.213	57.153	60.391	64.278
	90	59.196	61.754	64.634	65.646	69.126	73.291
	100	67.327	70.065	73.142	74.222	77.929	82.358

$\alpha =$		0.80	0.75	0.70	0.50	0.30	0.25	0.20	0.10
$\nu =$	1	0.0642	0.102	0.148	0.455	1.074	1.323	1.642	2.706
	2	0.446	0.575	0.713	1.386	2.408	2.773	3.219	4.605
	3	1.005	1.213	1.424	2.366	3.665	4.108	4.642	6.251
	4	1.649	1.923	2.195	3.357	4.878	5.385	5.989	7.779
	5	2.343	2.675	3.000	4.351	6.064	6.626	7.289	9.236
	6	3.070	3.455	3.828	5.348	7.231	7.841	8.558	10.645
	7	3.822	4.455	4.671	6.346	8.383	9.037	9.903	12.017
	8	4.594	5.071	5.527	7.344	9.524	10.219	11.030	13.362
	9	5.380	5.899	6.393	8.343	10.656	11.389	12.242	14.684
	10	6.179	6.737	7.267	9.342	11.781	12.549	13.442	15.987
	11	6.989	7.584	8.148	10.341	12.899	13.701	14.631	17.275
	12	7.807	8.438	9.034	11.340	14.011	14.845	15.812	18.549
	13	8.634	9.299	9.926	12.340	15.119	15.984	16.985	19.812
	14	9.467	10.165	10.821	13.339	16.222	17.117	18.151	21.064
	15	10.307	11.036	11.721	14.339	17.322	18.245	19.311	22.307
	16	11.152	11.912	12.624	15.338	18.418	19.369	20.465	23.542
	17	12.002	12.792	13.531	16.338	19.511	20.489	21.615	24.769
	18	12.857	13.675	14.440	17.338	20.601	21.605	22.760	25.989
	19	13.716	14.562	15.352	18.338	21.689	22.718	23.900	27.204
	20	14.578	15.452	16.266	19.337	22.775	23.828	25.038	28.412
	21	15.445	16.344	17.182	20.337	23.858	24.935	26.171	29.615
	22	16.314	17.240	18.101	21.337	24.939	26.039	27.301	30.813
	23	17.187	18.137	19.021	22.337	26.018	27.141	28.429	32.007
	24	18.062	19.037	19.943	23.337	27.096	28.241	29.553	33.196
	25	18.940	19.939	20.867	24.337	28.172	29.339	30.675	34.382
	26	19.820	20.843	21.792	25.336	29.246	30.434	31.795	35.563
	27	20.703	21.749	22.719	26.336	30.319	31.528	32.912	36.741
	28	21.588	22.657	23.647	27.336	31.391	32.620	34.027	37.916
	29	22.475	23.567	24.577	28.336	32.461	33.711	35.139	39.087
	30	23.364	24.478	25.508	29.336	33.530	34.800	36.250	40.256
	40	32.345	33.660	34.872	39.335	44.165	45.616	47.269	51.805
	50	41.449	42.942	44.313	49.335	54.723	56.334	58.164	63.167
	60	50.641	52.294	53.809	59.335	65.227	66.981	68.972	74.397
	70	59.898	61.698	63.346	69.334	75.689	77.577	79.715	85.527
	80	69.207	71.145	72.915	79.334	86.120	88.130	90.405	96.578
	90	78.558	80.625	82.511	89.334	96.524	98.650	101.054	107.565
	100	87.945	90.133	92.129	99.334	106.906	109.141	111.667	118.498

α =	0.05	0.025	0.02	0.01	0.005	0.001
ν = 1	3.841	5.024	5.412	6.635	7.879	10.827
2	5.991	7.378	7.824	9.210	10.597	13.815
3	7.815	9.348	9.837	11.345	12.838	16.268
4	9.488	11.143	11.668	13.277	14.860	18.465
5	11.070	12.832	13.388	15.086	16.750	20.517
6	12.592	14.449	15.033	16.812	18.548	22.457
7	14.067	16.013	16.622	18.475	20.278	24.322
8	15.507	17.535	18.168	20.090	21.955	26.125
9	16.919	19.023	19.679	21.666	23.589	27.977
10	18.307	20.483	21.161	23.209	25.188	29.588
11	19.675	21.920	22.618	24.725	26.757	31.264
12	21.026	23.337	24.054	26.217	28.300	32.909
13	22.362	24.736	25.472	27.688	29.819	34.528
14	23.685	26.119	26.873	29.141	31.319	36.123
15	24.996	27.488	28.259	30.578	32.801	37.697
16	26.296	28.845	29.633	32.000	34.267	39.252
17	27.587	30.191	30.995	33.409	35.718	40.790
18	28.869	31.526	32.346	34.805	37.156	42.312
19	30.144	32.852	33.687	36.191	38.582	43.820
20	31.410	34.170	35.020	37.566	39.997	45.315
21	32.671	35.479	36.343	38.932	41.401	46.797
22	33.924	36.781	37.659	40.289	42.796	48.268
23	35.172	38.076	38.968	41.638	44.181	49.728
24	36.415	39.364	40.270	42.980	45.558	51.179
25	37.652	40.646	41.566	44.314	46.928	52.620
26	38.885	41.923	42.856	45.642	48.290	54.052
27	40.113	43.194	44.140	46.963	49.645	55.476
28	41.337	44.461	45.419	48.278	60.993	56.893
29	42.557	45.722	46.693	49.588	52.336	58.302
30	43.773	46.979	47.962	50.892	53.672	59.703
40	55.759	59.342	60.436	63.691	66.766	73.402
50	67.505	71.420	72.613	76.154	79.490	86.661
60	79.082	83.298	84.580	88.379	91.952	99.607
70	90.531	95.023	96.388	100.425	104.215	112.317
80	101.880	106.629	108.069	112.329	116.321	124.839
90	113.145	118.136	119.648	124.116	128.299	137.208
100	124.342	129.561	131.142	135.807	140.170	149.449

This table is taken from Table IV of Fisher and Yates: *Statistical Tables for Biological, Agricultural and Medical Research* published by Longman Group Ltd, reprinted by permission of Pearson Education Limited, and from Table 8 of *Biometrika Tables for Statisticians*, Vol. 1, Biometrika Trustees and Oxford University Press.

Appendix 7

The correlation coefficient

The table gives the values of the correlation coefficient for different levels of significance; v = number of pairs in sample $-$ 2.

	0.1	0.05	0.02	0.01	0.001
$v =$ 1	0.987 69	0.996 92	0.999 597	0.999 877	0.999 998 8
2	0.900 00	0.950 00	0.980 00	0.990 000	0.999 00
3	0.805 4	0.878 3	0.934 33	0.958 73	0.991 16
4	0.729 3	0.811 4	0.882 2	0.917 20	0.974 06
5	0.669 4	0.754 5	0.832 9	0.874 5	0.950 74
6	0.621 5	0.706 7	0.788 7	0.834 3	0.924 93
7	0.582 2	0.666 4	0.749 8	0.797 7	0.898 2
8	0.549 4	0.631 9	0.715 5	0.764 6	0.872 1
9	0.521 4	0.602 1	0.685 1	0.734 8	0.847 1
10	0.497 3	0.576 0	0.658 1	0.707 9	0.823 3
11	0.476 2	0.552 9	0.633 9	0.683 5	0.801 0
12	0.457 5	0.532 4	0.612 0	0.661 4	0.780 0
13	0.440 9	0.513 9	0.592 3	0.641 1	0.760 3
14	0.425 9	0.497 3	0.574 2	0.622 6	0.742 0
15	0.412 4	0.482 1	0.557 7	0.605 5	0.724 6
16	0.400 0	0.468 3	0.542 5	0.589 7	0.708 4
17	0.388 7	0.455 5	0.528 5	0.575 1	0.693 2
18	0.378 3	0.443 8	0.515 5	0.561 4	0.678 7
19	0.368 7	0.432 9	0.503 4	0.548 7	0.665 2
20	0.359 8	0.422 7	0.492 1	0.536 8	0.652 4
25	0.323 3	0.380 9	0.445 1	0.486 9	0.597 4
30	0.296 0	0.349 4	0.409 3	0.448 7	0.554 1
35	0.274 6	0.324 6	0.381 0	0.418 2	0.518 9
40	0.257 3	0.304 4	0.357 8	0.393 2	0.489 6
45	0.242 8	0.287 5	0.338 4	0.372 1	0.464 8
50	0.230 6	0.273 2	0.321 8	0.354 1	0.443 3
60	0.210 8	0.250 0	0.294 8	0.324 8	0.407 8
70	0.195 4	0.231 9	0.273 7	0.301 7	0.379 9
80	0.182 9	0.217 2	0.256 5	0.283 0	0.356 8
90	0.172 6	0.205 0	0.242 2	0.267 3	0.337 5
100	0.163 8	0.194 6	0.230 1	0.254 0	0.321 1

This table is taken from Table VII of Fisher and Yates: *Statistical Tables for Biological, Agricultural and Medical Research*, published by Longman Group Ltd, reprinted by permission of Pearson Education Limited.

Appendix 8

The *t*-distribution

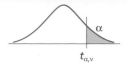

The tabulation is for one tail only, that is for positive values of *t*. For two-tailed tests, the column headings must be doubled.

α =		0.10	0.05	0.025	0.01	0.005	0.001	0.0005
ν =	1	3.078	6.314	12.706	31.821	63.657	318.31	636.62
	2	1.886	2.920	4.303	6.965	9.925	22.326	31.598
	3	1.638	2.353	3.182	4.541	5.841	10.213	12.924
	4	1.533	2.132	2.776	3.747	4.604	7.173	8.610
	5	1.476	2.015	2.571	3.365	4.032	5.893	6.869
	6	1.440	1.943	2.447	3.143	3.707	5.208	5.959
	7	1.415	1.895	2.365	2.998	3.499	4.785	5.408
	8	1.397	1.860	2.306	2.896	3.355	4.501	5.041
	9	1.383	1.833	2.262	2.821	3.250	4.297	4.781
	10	1.372	1.812	2.228	2.764	3.169	4.144	4.587
	11	1.363	1.796	2.201	2.718	3.106	4.025	4.437
	12	1.356	1.782	2.179	2.681	3.055	3.930	4.318
	13	1.350	1.771	2.160	2.650	3.012	3.852	4.221
	14	1.345	1.761	2.145	2.624	2.977	3.787	4.140
	15	1.341	1.753	2.131	2.602	2.947	3.733	4.073
	16	1.337	1.746	2.120	2.583	2.921	3.686	4.015
	17	1.333	1.740	2.110	2.567	2.898	3.646	3.965
	18	1.330	1.734	2.101	2.552	2.878	3.610	3.922
	19	1.328	1.729	2.093	2.539	2.861	3.579	3.883
	20	1.325	1.725	2.086	2.528	2.845	3.552	3.850
	21	1.323	1.721	2.080	2.518	2.831	3.527	3.819
	22	1.321	1.717	2.074	2.508	2.819	3.505	3.792
	23	1.319	1.714	2.069	2.500	2.807	3.485	3.767
	24	1.318	1.711	2.064	2.492	2.797	3.467	3.745
	25	1.316	1.708	2.060	2.485	2.787	3.450	3.725
	26	1.315	1.706	2.056	2.479	2.779	3.435	3.707
	27	1.314	1.703	2.052	2.473	2.771	3.421	3.690
	28	1.313	1.701	2.048	2.467	2.763	3.408	3.674
	29	1.311	1.699	2.045	2.462	2.756	3.396	3.659
	30	1.310	1.697	2.042	2.457	2.750	3.385	3.646
	40	1.303	1.684	2.021	2.423	2.704	3.307	3.551
	60	1.296	1.671	2.000	2.390	2.660	3.232	3.460
	120	1.289	1.658	1.980	2.358	2.617	3.160	3.373
	∞	1.282	1.645	1.960	2.326	2.576	3.090	3.291

This table is taken from Table III of Fisher and Yates: *Statistical Tables for Biological, Agricultural and Medical Research* published by Longman Group Ltd, reprinted by permission of Pearson Education Limited.

Appendix 9

Solutions to selected exercises

CHAPTER 1
Answers to test of basic mathematical skills

1. $(+)1$
2. -2.5 or $-2\frac{1}{2}$

$\left.\right\}$ If you got any of these wrong, read pp. 9–11.

3. $47/40$ or $1\dfrac{7}{40}$

4. $\dfrac{21}{40}$

5. 4

$\left.\right\}$ Problems with any of these? See pp. 11–12.

6. 0.125
7. 40
8. $0.416\,66\ldots$
9. $28/100$ or $7/25$

$\left.\right\}$ If you got any of these wrong, read pp. 13–16.

10. 67.5

See p. 14 if you got this wrong.

11. 1.28
12. 28.125%
13. £30

$\left.\right\}$ These three are covered on pp. 15–16.

14. x^6
15. x^8

$\left.\right\}$ See pp. 16–18 if either of these is wrong.

16. $5a + 4b$

See pp. 18–19 if you got this wrong.

17. $£\dfrac{24}{k}$

18. $£m/12$

$\left.\right\}$ See pp. 21–2 if either of these is wrong.

19. $f + m < 150$

This is covered on p. 22.

20. $x = 5$
21. $y = 32/7$

$\left.\right\}$ See pp. 19–27 if these caused problems.

22. $p = 4, q = -1.5$
23. At $t = -5/3$ or $-1\frac{2}{3}$

See pp. 22–4 if you couldn't do this.
See pp. 25–8 if you got this wrong.

24. (c)
25. Below and to the right

$\left.\right\}$ See pp. 28–9 if you got these wrong.

Exercise 1

1. −16	2. 0	3. 2	4. 32	5. 14	6. −3
7. −12	8. −6	9. (+)24	10. −9	11. (+)2	12. 25

Exercise 2

1. $\dfrac{7}{48}$ 2. $-\dfrac{1}{12}$ 3. $\dfrac{3}{22}$ 4. $\dfrac{1}{8}$ 5. $\dfrac{18}{7}$ or $2\dfrac{4}{7}$

6. $\dfrac{14}{20}$ or $\dfrac{7}{10}$ 7. 20 8. $\dfrac{15}{64}$ 9. $-\dfrac{9}{32}$ 10. $\dfrac{1}{6}$

Exercise 3

1. 0.444 2. 70 3. 14.4 4. 120 5. 17 000

6. $\dfrac{85}{100}$ or $\dfrac{17}{20}$ 7. 4.2 8. 0.1 9. 1 10. 0.02

Exercise 4

1. 3.2 2. 0.17 3. 42% to the nearest whole number 4. £15
5. £16 6. 952 7. 91% 8. 16% 9. 22.9 tonnes
10. Two years' interest will have been added, giving a total of £220.50.

Exercise 5

1. y^2 2. $x^{-\frac{1}{3}}$ 3. x^2 4. p^3q^3 5. n^{-3}

6. $\dfrac{b}{a}$ or $a^{-1}b$ 7. 1 8. $\dfrac{x}{3}$ or $\dfrac{1}{3}x$ 9. $x^{\frac{11}{2}}$ 10. $\pm 4x^2$

Exercise 6

1. $6x^2 - 18x$ 2. $a^2 + a - 2$ 3. $3xy + xz$
4. 32, 256 5. −33.75 6. $2x^3 - 2xy^2 - x^2 + y^2$
7. $5b - a$ (remember that the − sign in front of the second bracket multiplies everything inside the bracket).
8. The brackets are needed to show that the $B + F$ must be worked out first − giving the cost of one sandwich − and then multiplied by the number of sandwiches.
9. The 2 should have multiplied both terms in the first bracket, and the terms in the second bracket should both be multiplied by $-x$. The correct version is
$$2(x + y) - x(x + y) = 2x + 2y - x^2 - xy.$$
10. $x[2x - 3(y - 2)] = x[2x - 3y + 6] = 2x^2 - 3xy + 6x$

Exercise 7

1. $x = -5$ 2. $x = \dfrac{1}{2}$ 3. $x = 3$ or -3 4. $x = 1$

5. $f = \dfrac{v - u}{t}$ or $\dfrac{1}{t}(v - u)$ 6. $x = -2.5$ 7. $V = \dfrac{R - P + F}{n}$

8. $a = \pm 4\sqrt{c} - b$ 9. $y = \dfrac{27z^3}{x^2}$ 10. $x = 2$

Exercise 8

1. Cost $= (50 + 5m)$ pence 2. $1.5h + 1.25s < 12$
3. £1.60 4. $25 + (y - 12) \times 3$ pence or $(3y - 11)$ pence

Exercise 9

1. $x = 3, y = -3$ 2. $x = 1, y = 2$ 3. Equations are the same.
4. $x = 1.5, y = -2$ 5. $x = 3, y = 0$
6. The numbers are 6 and 12 (call the numbers x and y and solve the equations $x = 2y; x + y = 18$).
7. $a = 8, b = 3$
8. The equations are inconsistent, so there is no solution.
9. Peter is 17. Call the ages of the two boys A and P in an obvious notation. Then $P = A + 3$, and $P + A = 31$.
   Solving simultaneously gives $P = 17, A = 14$.
10. The first equation can be multiplied by y to give $x = 5y$. Solving $x = 5y$ and $2x + y = 33$ gives $11y = 33$ so $y = 3$, whence $x = 15$.

Exercise 10

1. (a), (c), (d)   2. (a) slope $= 2$; (c) slope $= 6$; (d) slope $= 5/2$

3.

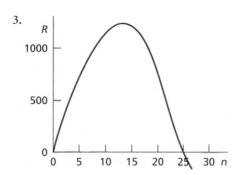

4.

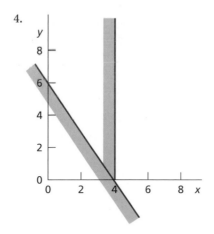

5. The graph is a straight line, passing through the y-axis at $y = 1$, with a positive slope of 2.
6. The graph crosses the x-axis where $y = 0$, giving $x = 3.5$.
7. If $y = x(x - 3)$, then when $x = 0, y = 0$ also. Thus the graph passes through the origin.
8. The graph crosses the n-axis when $p = 0$, giving $n = 4000$. In practical terms this means that if the price of the item were zero, so that it was being given away, then 4000 items would be demanded.
9. The region which satisfies the inequality lies below a line through $x = 10$ on the x-axis and $y = 4$ on the y-axis.
10.

n	0	1	2	3	4	5	6	7	8	9	10	11	12	13	14	15	16	17	18	19	20
C	0	−36	−64	−84	−96	−100	−96	−84	−64	−36	0	44	96	156	224	300	384	476	576	684	800

Exercise 11

1. Break-even at 1667 items approximately.
2. $x = 1$ and $x = 5$
3. 500 items

Exercise 12

1. 1394	2. 1096	3. −10
4. 11.45	5. 20.608	6. 239
7. 3.93	8. 869	9. 9.9
10. 11.3	11. £14.04	12. 3.15, 10.63, 12.99, 19.29, 28.35
13. 82.5	14. 29, 46, 55, 74, 91	15. £297
16. £19.98	17. 2.69	18. 0.64
19. 5.11	20. 6.2	21. 3.68
22. 0.18	23. −16	24. £431.52

CHAPTER 2

1. (a) Systematic – every tenth person arriving to collect payment.
   (b) Stratified by grade of employee, using payroll as sampling frame.
   (c) A difficult one – perhaps a quota subdivided by time of day and day of week.
   (d) Random – using randomly generated account numbers.
2. Continuous – (a) and (d) (unless (d) is measured as 'numbers of sacks'). Discrete – (b) and (c).
3. (a) Leading question.
   (b) Too vague.
   (c) Two questions in one.
   (d) Hypothetical – under what circumstances?
9. (a) This could be found from the point-of-sale scanning records, generated when the bar-code on each product is scanned as items pass through the checkout.
   (b) Train operators are obliged to publish these figures, and you will find them displayed on posters at major stations. You do, however, need to read the small print in order to find out exactly how 'on time' is defined.
   (c) You could only obtain this information by carrying out an experiment – that is, by testing a sample of lightbulbs. Because the test can only be based on a sample, there will be some uncertainty about the accuracy of the figures – a topic to which we will return in Chapter 8.

CHAPTER 3

1. Breakdown of customers

	Home	Overseas	Total
Regular	6270	1650	7 920
Occasional	2860	1100	3 960
Dormant	770	550	1 320
Total	9900	3300	13 200

(Last year's total: 11 000)
(Source: Company report.)

2. A compound bar chart with major bars representing 'home/overseas' and subdivisions for 'regular/occasional/dormant' is probably best, though there are other possibilities.
3. A bar chart with bars arranged horizontally and axis in the middle is perhaps best, so that positive and negative errors can be shown to left and right respectively.

4.

Distance travelled	Number of visitors
Under 5 miles	0
5 but under 15 miles	12
15 but under 25 miles	10
25 but under 35 miles	12
35 but under 45 miles	4
45 miles and more	2

This is only one possible version.

5. This should be a stepped graph.
11. One possibility would be as follows:

Company name	No. of shares at start	No. of shares at end	Change during year	Income/expenditure (£)
Equimix plc	500	0	−500	650
Farringdon Holdings	800	1000	+200	(160)
Greenbridge	400	200	−200	160
Heavicast Ltd	0	400	+400	(288)

Surplus for the year = £362.

There are many other possible layouts presenting various subsets of the data; it is difficult and probably not very useful to try to include all the information in a single table.

The changes in the portfolio – that is, information about the number of shares held without reference to their value – could best be presented by means of some kind of bar chart.

12.
No. of responses (% of row)

	Excellent	Fair	Poor	Total
Car owners	230 (66%)	72 (21%)	45 (13%)	347 (100%)
Non-car owners	29 (20%)	51 (36%)	63 (44%)	143 (100%)
Total	259 (53%)	123 (25%)	108 (22%)	490 (100%)

The percentages in this table bring out the strong difference in opinion between the two groups of customers. A multiple bar chart would emphasise this feature.

CHAPTER 4

1.

	Barsetshire	Cokeshire
Mean	£362 333	£338 167
Median	£342 000	£315 789
Mode	£320–360 000 class	£300–320 000 class
Standard deviation	£69 675	£67 342
Quartiles	£313 333 and £394 286 approximately	£300 000 and £349 333 approximately
Range	Indeterminate	Indeterminate

(To obtain the mean and standard deviation, the top classes have been closed at £700 000; other closing points will give slightly different answers.)

Both distributions have a longer right-hand tail, rendering the median perhaps more 'typical' than the means. Prices in Cokeshire are lower on average, and tend to be less variable (smaller standard deviation and interquartile range).

2. 2.73 in each case; adding a constant to a set of data does not alter its standard deviation.
3. 2.73 and 8.18 ($\approx 3 \times 2.73$); multiplying a set of data by a constant multiplies its standard deviation by the same constant.
10. £35.86 (the total will be eight times the mean, which is £468, so if you add the seven known values and subtract the total from £468, you will obtain the missing value).

CHAPTER 5

1. Base-weighted 107.6; current-weighted 107.9.
2. £16m, £17.31m, £21.27m.
3. From 245 to 265 is a rise of only 20/245 = about 8 per cent.
6. (a), (b) and (c). Note that answers may differ in the second decimal place due to rounding.

Year	A	B	Index A	Index B	Chain index A	Chain index B
2002	23.00	82.00	100.00	100.00		
2003	25.00	85.00	108.70	103.66	108.70	103.66
2004	28.00	91.00	121.74	110.98	112.00	107.06
2005	31.00	94.00	134.78	114.63	110.71	103.30
2006	35.00	99.00	152.17	120.73	112.90	105.32
2007	39.00	102.00	169.57	124.39	111.43	103.03
2008	44.00	108.00	191.30	131.71	112.82	105.88
2009	50.00	114.00	217.39	139.02	113.64	105.56

(d)

Year	A	B	RPI	Deflated A	Deflated B	Index A	Index B	Chain index A	Chain index B
2002	23.00	82.00	176.20	23.00	82.00	100.00	100.00		
2003	25.00	85.00	181.30	24.30	80.46	105.64	98.13	105.64	98.13
2004	28.00	91.00	186.70	26.43	79.20	114.89	96.59	108.76	98.44
2005	31.00	94.00	192.00	28.45	76.00	123.69	92.68	107.66	95.95
2006	35.00	99.00	196.10	31.45	72.40	136.73	88.30	110.54	95.27
2007	39.00	102.00	206.60	33.26	70.53	144.61	86.01	105.77	97.41
2008	44.00	108.00	214.80	36.09	68.82	156.93	83.93	108.51	97.58
2009	50.00	114.00	213.70	41.23	63.60	179.24	77.56	114.22	92.41

(e) The two index series based on 2002 enable us to compare the rates of growth of the two companies from that date. The resulting figures make it clear that Company B, while it has much larger turnover than A, has not grown nearly as rapidly.

The chain indices give an idea of the year-on-year growth rates. In the later years of the period, Company A has had yearly growth rates between about 11 per cent and 12 per cent, whereas Company B has hovered around 3 per cent to 5 per cent per annum.

When the deflated figures are used, so that the effect of inflation is removed, the picture is very different, with B's profits actually declining in real terms.

7. Pension for 2005 should be £9000 × 192/186.7 = £9255.49.

For 2006, pension = £9255.49 × 196.1/192 = £9453.13 (or £9000 × 196.1/186.7, which comes to the same thing – can you see why?).

8.

	Usage Q	Last year's price P0	This year's price P1	P0*Q	P1*Q
Screws	200	2.5	2.75	500	550
Washers	150	3.5	3.64	525	546
Clips	100	1.2	1.26	120	126
		Total		1145	1222

Index = $1222/1145 \times 100 = 106.72$.

9. $100 * 93/97 = 95.9$ Utopian pounds, to one decimal place.

10. £1212.83. You would be no better off in real terms because an investment which is index-linked simply keeps pace with increasing prices – the purchasing power of your money remains constant.

CHAPTER 6

1. $\frac{2}{3} \times \frac{3}{5}$ or $\frac{2}{5}$ (assuming independence)

2. (a) $\frac{1}{2}$; (b) $\frac{1}{5}$; (c) $\frac{1}{10}$.

3. (a) $\frac{4}{5} \times \frac{95}{100}$ or 0.76; (b) $\left(\frac{1}{5} \times \frac{95}{100}\right) + \left(\frac{4}{5} \times \frac{5}{100}\right)$ or 0.23.

4. (a) $\frac{4}{5} + \left(\frac{1}{5} \times \frac{3}{5}\right) + \left(\frac{1}{5} \times \frac{2}{5} \times \frac{1}{2}\right)$ or 0.96;

alternatively $1 - p(\text{no one finds error}) = 1 - \left(\frac{1}{5} \times \frac{2}{5} \times \frac{1}{2}\right)$.

(b) No – he weeds out the easy ones.

5. $\frac{4}{12} \times \frac{8}{11} \times \frac{7}{10} \times 3$ or 0.51.

6. Move – expected cost £220, as against £260 for staying.

7. No – expected cost of not paying is £2.50.

8. Sell now – expected result of keeping it is only £58.50.

11. Chance of rival marketing must be less than 5/12.

12. 2/250; standard charge would need to be > £2.50.

13. (a) The easiest way to deal with this problem is via a table. Assume that a random sample of 4 000 000 people has been taken (this number is chosen simply to make the arithmetic easier, but any total could be used). Then we would expect the situation to be as shown below.

	Has disease	Does not have disease	Total
Test +ve	19	79 999.6	80 018.6
Test −ve	1	3 919 980.4	3 919 981.4
Total	20	3 999 980	4 000 000

The chance that you have the disease if you have just tested positive is thus 19/80 018.6 or about 0.000 24. In other words, because of the comparative rarity of the disease, and the relative unreliability of the test, there is only a small chance that someone chosen at random who tests positive does in fact have the disease.

(b) Widespread screening for the disease with such an unreliable test and such a rare complaint will result in a great many people being unnecessarily worried, since the vast majority of those with a positive test do not in fact have the disease. Screening is probably only worthwhile if the reliability of the test can be substantially increased (you might like to think just how much it would need to be increased in order to give a better than 50 per cent chance that someone testing positive has the disease).

(c) The argument above will only apply if the test is given totally at random. If it is only given to those who have some reason to believe that they are likely to have the disease (such as exhibiting definite symptoms), then the position may be very different, since the proportion of people in the tested group with the disease may well be greater than that in the population at large.

CHAPTER 7

1. (a) 0.5940; (b) 0.1353 (Poisson, mean = 2).
2. 0.1298 (binomial, $n = 10$, $p = 0.15$).
3. (a) 0.0668; (b) 0.8413; (c) 0.910 45.
4. 0.8965; once (binomial, $n = 5$, $p = 0.25$; 'most likely' = having greatest probability).
5. 3 minutes approx.
6. 0.328 (binomial, $n = 5$, use $p(\text{no order}) = 0.1$).
7. 0.0014 (Poisson, mean = 4.8).
8. (a) 2.66 g; (b) 1005.45 g.
9. (a) 0.3770; (b) 0.3745.
10. (a) 0.4013; (b) 0.3935.
11. 0.1393 (using all values below 29.5).
12. (a) This is binomial, $p = 0.05$, $n = 10$.
     $p(\text{accept batch}) = 0.599$.
    (b) Here $p = 0.1$, $n = 10$, and $p(\text{accept batch}) = 0.349$.
    (c) $p = 0.15$, $n = 10$, $p(\text{accept}) = 0.197$.
     $p = 0.2$, $n = 10$, $p(\text{accept}) = 0.107$.
     The operating characteristic decreases rather slowly, indicating that this is not a very good inspection scheme – even very poor-quality batches have quite a high chance of being accepted. For a more discriminating scheme, a larger sample size would need to be used.

CHAPTER 8

1. 95% confidence interval is 47.1% to 56.9%.
2. (a) Between about 22.2% and 52.8%;
    (b) between about 17.8% and 57.2%.
3. Probability of a sample with this percentage or more who can distinguish is only 0.0418, so claim is open to doubt (though the group may not be a random sample of the general population).
4. Between about 5.4 and 5.6 minutes.
5. Approximately 16 640!
6. (a) £423 ± £36.80.
    (b) 141 people would be needed in total – an extra 76 people.
7. (a) STEP = 3, and the 95% interval is ±6%.
    (b) $n = 400$, STEP = 1.5; $n = 900$, STEP = 1%; $n = 1600$, STEP = 0.75%.
    (c) The variation of STEP with sample size is non-linear – in fact, STEP varies like $1/n$. In order to halve the size of STEP, we therefore need to quadruple the size of our sample.
    (d) Interviewing 2000 people rather than 1000 will be very much more expensive, but in absolute terms the improvement in accuracy will not be very dramatic. As we have seen, with $P = 10\%$ and $n = 900$, the 95 per cent interval will be ±2%, which is good enough for most purposes.

CHAPTER 9

1. Yes – the difference is significant (STEM = 75 pence).
2. No – the difference is not significant (STEP = 5.5%).
3. There is an association between sex and unionisation (χ^2 with Yates's correction is 4.69).

4. No ($\chi^2 = 0.55$, 2 degrees of freedom).
5. Yes ($\chi^2 = 2.56$, 2 degrees of freedom).
6. (a) 95 per cent confidence interval for the mean is 14 ± 1.14 journeys.
   (b) Change is not significant at the 5 per cent level – STEP = 5.48%.
   (c) There is a significant association between level of satisfaction and reason for use ($\chi^2 = 7.48$ with 2 degrees of freedom).

CHAPTER 10

1. Charts are shown below. They make it clear that although only a small proportion of toasters totally fail to function, when cost is taken into account this is the problem area which should be tackled first.

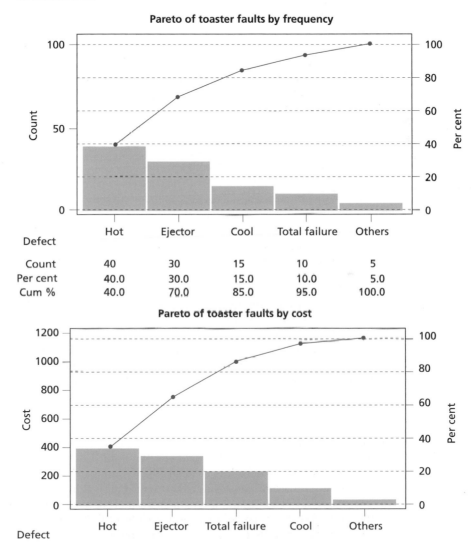

Pareto of toaster faults by frequency

Defect	Hot	Ejector	Cool	Total failure	Others
Count	40	30	15	10	5
Per cent	40.0	30.0	15.0	10.0	5.0
Cum %	40.0	70.0	85.0	95.0	100.0

Pareto of toaster faults by cost

2. (a) With $P = 60\%$ and $n = 50$, STEP $= \sqrt{60 \times 40/50} = 6.93\%$.
   The three standard error limits will thus be at $60\% \pm 3 \times 6.93\%$, or about 39% to 81%.
   (b) With $P = 80\%$ and $n = 50$, STEP $= \sqrt{80 \times 20/50} = 5.65\%$.
   Three standard error limits are therefore at $80\% \pm 3 \times 5.65\%$, or about 63.05% to 96.95%.
   (c) The limits in both cases are very wide, reflecting the relatively small size of the sample. There is little point in using limits based on a target which is very far from the current level of performance – all that will happen is that many points will fall outside the limits, resulting in much work in 'chasing' these cases and a possible drop in staff morale. It is probably

better at this stage to monitor the existing situation while taking steps to achieve gradual improvement, and then change the limits incrementally as improvements occur.

3. Process capability index $C_p = (24.5 - 21.5)/(6 \times 0.52) = 0.96$, so process marginally fails to meet the minimum requirement of a C_p of at least 1.

   Process is not properly centred on the target, so the situation is even worse than this value suggests. Proportion out-of-spec based on normal is $0.000\,97 + 0.004\,02 = 0.004\,99$ or about 0.5 per cent.

4. Mean of first 20 sample means = 27.007.
   Mean of first 20 sample ranges = 1.222.
   Sample size = 5.
   So limits for means chart are $27.007 \pm 0.58 \times 1.222 = 26.299$ to 27.716, using the constant from Table 10.2.
   For the range chart, the lower limit is zero.
   Upper limit = $2.11 \times 1.222 = 2.578$.
   None of the means in the next 20 samples is outside the limits, but the range in sample 5 exceeds the control limit – this point needs investigation.

5. (a) Between 11 and 12, because $p(12 \text{ or more}) = 0.007\,31$.
   (b) Between 0 and 1, because $p(1 \text{ or more}) = 0.994$, so $p(\text{zero}) = 0.006$.

6. (a) (i) 0.4013, (ii) 0.6513, (iii) 0.8926.
   (b) This scheme as it stands results in the rejection of a high proportion of batches with reasonable quality (5 per cent defectives) while allowing through over 10 per cent of batches with quality as poor as 20 per cent defective.
   (c) The probability of rejecting a batch with 5 per cent defective is 0.4013 as found in (a), so 40.13 per cent of 100 batches will be rejected – that is, approximately 40 batches.
       If these are, on average, only 5 per cent defective, then the number of OK items sent back will be $40 \times 5000 \times 95$ per cent = 190 000.
       So a great deal of acceptable material is rejected – a very wasteful procedure.

7. Limits will be at 19.42 mm and 20.58 mm.

8. The z-value corresponding to a call time of 3 minutes is $(3 - 2.6)/0.2 = 2$. Normal distribution tables then tell us that about 2.5 per cent of all calls will last longer than 3 minutes – so the target will not be met. This is a similar problem to that involved in the calculation of tolerance limits, but here the tolerance is one-sided – only those calls which are too long are a problem. The normal distribution is, however, unlikely to be a suitable model here – the lengths of calls cannot be less than 0 minutes, so the infinite 'tail' on the left of the normal distribution is not a good approximation, since it would involve negative call lengths. An unsymmetric distribution, with no values less than zero but with a long upper 'tail', is likely to be a better model.

9. Limits of ±2 standard errors would mean that approximately 5 per cent of samples would fall outside the limits, thus giving 'false alarms' 1 time in every 20 samples. This is clearly much too high for such a scheme to be a sensible control mechanism. However, limits of this kind are sometimes used as 'warning limits' in sampling schemes – no action is taken when a sample outside the 2 standard error limit is encountered, but in case this is the first warning of a drift in the process setting, another sample would be taken immediately. The chances of two consecutive samples giving means outside the 2 standard error limits are $1/20 \times 1/20$ or 1 in 400, so a second sample outside the limit would suggest that something is almost certainly amiss with the process.

10. The probability of at least one leaky cup in a sample of ten is 0.096 or nearly 10 per cent (find the probability of zero leaky cups and subtract from 1). So a whole hour's production is going to be scrapped roughly once in every ten hours, even when the underlying rate is steady at 1 per cent. This scheme is therefore wasteful and does not discriminate poor quality from acceptable quality well enough – in practice a much larger sample would be needed.

CHAPTER 11

1. $r_{rank} = 0.90$ – quite consistent.
2. (a) $r_{rank} = 0.95$; (b) the sign of r_{rank} changes.
3. (a) 0.98; (b) 0.90.
6. (a) $r = -0.43$ – a negative correlation, which is rather surprising.

CHAPTER 12

1. $y = 0.92x - 1.89$; 2.71 kg (use first six points only).
6. Time = $5.02 + 0.73 \times$ number of items.

   This equation would be quite reliable for predicting the time for three items, since the R-squared value of 0.79 (correlation coefficient 0.89) and the significant value of F suggest a fairly close linear relationship. For ten items, however, it would be less reliable, since this is an extrapolation well beyond the range of the given data.
7. In the equation derived in Exercise 6, the intercept represents the time required to pack zero items – in other words, it is a fixed time which represents the time taken by the staff to read the order and reach the correct area of the warehouse – this will be the same irrespective of the size of the order. This time is about five minutes. The slope of 0.73 then represents the 'typical' time in minutes required to pick an item.
8. The correlation coefficient between sales and week number is 0.94, which suggests that a linear relationship is quite a good fit.

   A suitable regression equation is: sales = $4.42 + 0.17 \times$ week number. This gives sales of 5.95, 6.12, 6.29 and 6.46 (in thousands) for the next four weeks.

   While the linear equation may be a good fit in the first few weeks that the bar in on the market, in the long run a linear model would predict continuing growth by an equal amount per week, whereas in fact growth is likely to level off at some point. So a curved relationship is likely to be more realistic in the long run.

CHAPTER 13

1. (a) ins = $29.05 + 34.507$inc $- 1.691$kids $- 0.082$age
   (b) Just over 67 per cent of variations in insurance levels are linearly associated with variations in the three variables inc, kids and age.
   (c) There are many points which could be drawn out of these results, but probably the most important is that income is by far the most significant determinant of amount of insurance held – in the presence of this variable, number of children and age are not significant.
2. (a) The p-value for location indicates that the coefficient of exp is not significantly different from zero at the 5 per cent level, so the true value in the population could well be zero or even negative.
3. (a) The p-value for location indicates that it does have a significant impact on sales, town-centre locations producing higher sales.
   (b) The actual size of the coefficients cannot be used to deduce their relative importance – it is their significance, as indicated by their p-values, which needs to be examined. Moreover, since the values of 'flow' will tend to be quite large numbers, the actual addition to sales produced by variations in 'flow' could be large even though the coefficient itself is small.
5. The output from an Excel regression of weight on height and exercise is as follows:

Regression Statistics

Multiple R	0.91
R Square	0.83
Adjusted R Square	0.77
Standard Error	5.19
Observations	8.00

ANOVA

	df	SS	MS	F	Sig F
Regression	2.00	678.57	339.28	12.57	0.01
Residual	5.00	134.93	26.99		
Total	7.00	813.50			

	Coefficients	Standard Error	t Stat	P-value	Lower 95%	Upper 95%
Intercept	−81.12	73.50	−1.10	0.32	−270.07	107.83
Height (cm)	0.93	0.40	2.34	0.07	−0.09	1.95
Hours of exercise per week	−3.11	1.31	−2.37	0.06	−6.48	0.26

The regression equation is thus weight = −81.12 + 0.93 × height − 3.11 × exercise.

The F-test indicates that the overall linear relationship between y and the two x-variables is significant, although the t-tests show that each of the coefficients of the individual x-variables is not significantly different from zero. The intercept (which is meaningless in this case – the weight of a person 0 cm tall! Doing no exercise!) also does not differ significantly from zero, so the true relationship might pass through the origin.

The adjusted R-squared statistics show that about 77 per cent of the variation in weight is explained by the linear combination of height and exercise.

In practice, a full report on these results would need to be more extensive and focus on the practical interpretation of the equation and other output.

6. The importance of the fact that all the students in the sample were male is that females tend, on average, to be shorter and lighter than males, and also to have a different metabolism. If a sample had contained data from both genders mixed together, therefore, any linear association such as that identified in Exercise 5 might have been obscured. If we wished to include people of both genders in the analysis, then one way to do so would be to introduce a dummy variable to represent gender, taking values such as 0 for male and 1 for female. The coefficient of this dummy variable would then indicate the flat amount by which the weight of a woman differs from that of a man, when both are of the same height and take the same amount of exercise.

7. The regression equation of number of employees on year number is

number of employees = 153.61 + 45.73 × year number.

Thus when the year number is 14, the predicted number of employees (rounded to the nearest whole number) is 794. This prediction is likely to be quite reliable, since year 14 is not far beyond the end of the data series, and the R-squared value of 0.87 and the value of the F-statistic indicate a fairly close and significant linear association between year and number of employees.

8. The regression including the squared term is

number of employees = 6.05 + 108.97 × year number − 4.86 × (year number)^2.

This gives a prediction of 579 employees to the nearest whole number. The difference in the two predictions is 215 employees – quite a large difference. The adjusted R-squared value for the quadratic regression is 0.95, as against 0.86 for the linear regression, suggesting that the former is a better fit. If you plot the actual data together with the two regression equations, you will see that the quadratic matches the decline in the number of employees in the last two years of the data series, whereas the linear equation continues to increase by a fixed number of employees per year. In practice you would also need to use your knowledge of the situation of the company in order to judge what type of equation might provide the best predictions.

9. The Multiple R, R-squared and Adjusted R-squared values are all 1, and all the p-values are effectively zero (though they may appear as very tiny numbers such as 1.38299E-95). This is of course because the points given lie exactly on a straight line with equation $y = 2.4x$ – the 2.4 appears as the coefficient of the x term in the regression output. Plotting the data would also show this.

10. Two dummy variables are required to represent the three-category variable morning/afternoon/evening. Calling these variables $x1$ and $x2$, and using 'morning' as the reference, we would then have $x1 = x2 = 0$ for 'morning', $x1 = 1$, $x2 = 0$ for 'afternoon', and $x1 = 0$, $x2 = 1$ for 'evening' (you could have the codings for 'afternoon' and 'evening' reversed).

With this coding, we find the following regression equation:

% successful = 12.94 + 0.39 × months of experience − 2.3 × $x1$ − 9.2 × $x2$.

The coefficients of the dummy variables indicate that the percentage of successful calls tends on the average to be 2.3 per cent lower in the afternoon and 9.2 per cent lower in the evening, as compared with the morning. However, the *p*-values indicate that only the coefficient of $x2$ is significantly different from zero, so only the evening success rate is significantly lower than that for the morning. The association with the 'months of experience' variable is also significant.

CHAPTER 14

1. Average weekly demand 45 boxes.
3. Order 30 boxes at a time.
4. Continue to order 30 (cost of this policy is £1.17 per week as against £1.62½ per week if orders are reduced to 20).
5. Reorder when two days' supply (= 15 are left, assuming a six-day week).
6. Make 30 000 at a time, taking ten days.
7.

Queuing time (minutes)	Percentage of customers	Random numbers
	0	601–06
	1	1107–17
	2	1818–35
	3	2536–60
	4	2161–81
	5	1482–95
	6	596–00

9. The distributions of random digits are as follows:

Length (minutes)	% of interviews	Random digits
8	8	01–08
9	14	09–22
10	23	23–45
11	30	46–75
12	18	76–93
13	7	94–00

Arrival	% of interviewees	Random digits
2 min early	12	01–12
1 min early	20	13–32
On time	40	33–72
1 min late	16	73–88
2 min late	12	89–00

Each simulation will be different, but as the average length of an interview is just over 10.5 minutes (you can check this by calculating the mean from the distribution of interview lengths), which is longer than the scheduled ten minutes, it is likely that over time the length of time that interviewees have to wait will increase. This is likely to be made worse by the fact that a higher proportion of people arrive early for their interview than late.

10. Distributions of random digits are as follows:

Time for repair	Percentage of repairs	Random digits
15 minutes	10	01–10
30 minutes	27	11–37
1 hour	35	38–72
2 hours	17	73–89
3 hours	11	90–00

Intervals between arrival of jobs (hours)	Percentage of occasions	Random digits
0.25	25	01–25
0.5	30	26–55
1	20	56–75
2	15	76–90
3	10	91–00

The simulation can be laid out in a similar way to that suggested for Exercise 9. Again, each simulation will be different, but as the average time between the arrivals of jobs is slightly less than the average time for repair, it is likely that the repair worker will eventually find it difficult to keep up with the arrival of jobs.

CHAPTER 15

1. The graph is as shown below:

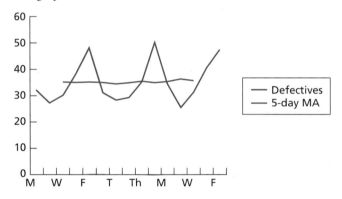

We use a five-day moving average because the pattern in the data repeats every week (= five days). This smooths the data effectively. The pattern shows higher levels of defectives on Monday and Friday than in the middle of the week. Perhaps on Monday the machines are warming up after being switched off at the weekend, and on Friday workers may be less careful as they are anticipating the weekend.

2. (a) The calculation is:

Month no.	Sales (packs)	Forecast	Error	$\alpha \times error$
1	117.00			
2	115.00	117.00	−2.00	−0.60
3	110.00	116.40	−6.40	−1.92
4	123.00	114.48	8.52	2.56
5	120.00	117.04	2.96	0.89
6	116.00	117.93	−1.93	−0.58
7	114.00	117.35	−3.35	−1.00
8	119.00	116.34	2.66	0.80
9	119.00	117.14	1.86	0.56
10	109.00	117.70	−8.70	−2.61
11	112.00	115.09	−3.09	−0.93
12	116.00	114.16	1.84	0.55
13	114.00	114.71	−0.71	−0.21
14	120.00	114.50	5.50	1.65
15	115.00	116.15	−1.15	−0.34
16	115.00	115.80	−0.80	−0.24
17	111.00	115.56	−4.56	−1.37
18	118.00	114.19	3.81	1.14
19		115.34		

Thus the forecast for month 19 is 115 packs to the nearest whole number.
(b) The next rows of the table are:

19	57.00	115.34	−58.34	−17.50
20	78.00	97.84	−19.84	−5.95
21	84.00	91.88	−7.88	−2.37
22	95.00	89.52	5.48	1.64

Thus the forecasts for months 19−21 are very inaccurate – only by month 22 does the accuracy of the forecast 'recover' from the shock of the sudden drop in sales. The lower the value of alpha, the longer the forecast will take to 'catch up' – try repeating this exercise with alpha = 0.1.

3. The graph with a log scale on the vertical axis is:

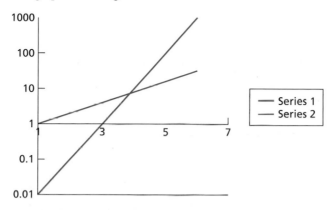

The lines are both straight – series 1 is steeper, since it represents a growth rate by a factor of 10 from one period to the next, while series 2 grows by a factor of 2.

4. The graph shows that the amplitude of the seasonal variations is increasing as the trend increases.

Multiplicative analysis (MA)

Period no.	Actual	3-period MA = trend	Actual as % of trend
1	22		
2	70	44	159.09
3	40	77	51.95
4	121	119	101.68
5	196	134	146.27
6	85	167	50.90
7	220	209	105.26
8	322	224	143.75
9	130		

Calculation of seasonal variation

Period				Average
1	–	101.68	105.26	103.47
2	159.09	146.27	143.75	149.70
3	51.95	50.9	–	51.43

Additive analysis

Period no.	Actual	3-period MA = trend	Actual minus trend	Expected (trend + seasonal)	Random (actual – expected)
1	22				
2	70	44	26	103	−33
3	40	77	−37	14.5	25.5
4	121	119	2	122.5	−1.5
5	196	134	62	193	3
6	85	167	−82	104.5	−19.5
7	220	209	11	212.5	7.5
8	322	224	98	283	39
9	130				

Calculation of seasonal variation

Period				Average	Corrected
1	−	2	11	6.50	3.5
2	26	62	98	62.00	59
3	−37	−82	−	−59.50	−62.5
				9.00	0.00

The seasonal variations from the multiplicative model total around 300 per cent because in a perfect model variations above and below 100 per cent should cancel out; thus for a three-period model the total will be 300 per cent.

5. (a) The plot should show pronounced peaks in March and September, with a smaller peak in June. The large peaks correspond to the twice-yearly issue of new registrations. Because buyers are waiting for the new registration plates, sales in February and August are particularly low.

(b) The data should be averaged over 12 periods (months) in this case.

(c) The centred moving averages are: 173.9417, 171.25, 164.8625, 157.375, 153.8333, 150.6208, 149.375, 149.6417, 151.2708, 154.4083, 158.3375, 162.3333, 165.2792, 167.05, 171.0125, 175.0125, 176.3042, 177.7792, 177.6375, 176.275, 174.4125, 171.5167, 169.2708, 167.45.

Seasonal variations on additive and multiplicative models are as follows:

	Add.	Mult.
January	−39.656 3	75.514 88
February	−103.958	36.135 98
March	189.208 3	215.475 2
April	−24.312 5	85.101 21
May	−22.054 2	86.452 24
June	17.058 33	110.288 5
July	−16.710 4	90.233 71
August	−105.25	37.793 22
September	178.812 5	206.346 9
October	−19.193 8	88.076 37
November	−36.218 8	77.276 26
December	−34.4	78.564 85

(d) The errors are slightly smaller with the multiplicative model, though there is little to choose between the two models.

(e) There appears to be some evidence from the plot that there is a cyclical pattern in operation – overall sales drop, then pick up, then start to decline again – so it would be difficult to obtain reliable forecasts without taking into account the economic factors which are affecting new car sales.

6. (a) The three forecasts are as follows (all rounded to two decimal places):

$$\alpha = 0.2, \text{ forecast } 24.32$$
$$\alpha = 0.3, \text{ forecast } 23.82$$
$$\alpha = 0.4, \text{ forecast } 23.53.$$

(b) The corresponding mean square errors are 8.26, 7.97 and 7.92, so on the minimum MSE criterion, $\alpha = 0.4$ is best. This is because there has been something of a drop in demand over the last three months, and the larger value of α catches up with this drop more quickly.

   (You can find a full worked solution to this problem on the student side of the Companion Website for Chapter 16.)

8. The graph shows that both costs and revenues give approximate straight lines when plotted on semi-log scales, so both are growing at constant rates. However, as the slope of the cost line is steeper, it will eventually intersect the revenue line.

   By extending the lines on the graph, we can see that this will occur around year 14 or 15. You can also show this by calculating the approximate per cent increase from year to year, which is about 6 per cent for costs and 4 per cent for revenues, and then continuing to increase each set of figures by the appropriate annual percentage until revenue becomes less than cost.

   It is unlikely that any firm would let this happen in practice – the narrowing gap between costs and revenues would be noticed, and steps taken to reverse the situation.

10. (a) There is likely to be some seaonality in annual leave data, since many people will take their main holiday in the period July/August, especially if they have children of school age. However, beyond this there may be quite a lot of variation in the times at which people take leave, so the seasonal pattern may not be very strong.

(b) Sales of electric heaters would probably show a strong seasonal pattern, with increased sales during the colder months. Unseasonal 'cold snaps' during spring and summer would appear as random disturbances to this pattern.

(c) An element of the sales of paper tissues might be expected to be seasonal, being associated with the winter period when people have colds and therefore use more tissues. However, a large part of the sales will be fairly constant over the year, so the seasonal effect will probably not be large compared with the overall level.

(d) Furniture sales are surprisingly seasonal – with peaks coinciding with the traditional periods of winter and summer reductions in prices.

(e) The numbers of logins to a direct sales website would exhibit peaks during special promotions, just after circulation of a new catalogue to customers etc.

(f) It is not likely that the numbers of people joining a motorists' breakdown service would be strongly seasonal – joining and renewal dates are likely to be spread across the year.

CHAPTER 16

1. £1402.55
2. No
3. (a) £1036.80; (b) £259.63
4. 6 months; £89.86
5. 'Excess'

6. £1154.87
7. £1309.86
8. Eskimo
9. Both machines make a loss.
10. £9129.97

CHAPTER 17

1. (a) 36 cabbages and 16 cauliflowers for 192 helpings. (b) Yes. (c) Only 177 helpings.
2. (a) Four Shadows and three Princesses costing £67. (b) 50p; between 32 and 42 guests.
   (c) $\dfrac{2}{3} \leqslant \dfrac{\text{Cost of Princess}}{\text{Cost of Shadow}} \leqslant 1$
3. There will be a whole set of solutions instead of one unique solution.
5. If P, L and B represent the number of kilos of Puce label, Olive label and teabags respectively manufactured per week, then the constraints are

$$0.2P + 0.4L + 0.2B \leqslant 1600$$
$$0.3P + 0.3L + 0.6B \leqslant 1200$$
$$0.2P + 0.6L + 0.2B \leqslant 1000.$$

   The cost of a kilo of each of the three products is as follows: for Puce label, £4.30, for Olive label, £4.90, and for teabags, £5.00. So profits per kilo are respectively 70p, £1.10 and £1.50. The objective function to be maximised is therefore (in pounds): $0.7P + 1.1L + 1.5B$.
   Solver gives the optimum solution as no Puce Label, 1200 kg of Olive label and 1400 kg of teabags, which leads to a profit of £3420. This uses up all the Ceylon and China tea, but only 760 kg of Indian tea.

6. The constraints are: $IC + DC + R \leqslant 80$
   $$IC \leqslant 15$$
   $$DC \geqslant 10$$
   $$IC/2 + R/5 + DC/10 \leqslant 40$$

   Objective is to maximise the profit which is $80IC + 100R + 60DC$, where IC, R and DC are the numbers of each type of bed.
   Solver shows that the optimal solution is to use all the beds for day-care, which gives a daily profit of £4800. In reality, of course, this might not be a viable solution since there may well be constraints other than those considered in this simplified model.

7. The graph shows that the maximum profit will be obtained from 50 aprons and 12.5 cushions – of course, in practice it is not realistic to make half a cushion. If 50 aprons and 12 cushions are made, the profit will be £211. The suggestion that only aprons should be made will not give the maximum profit because, although in theory 66.67 aprons could be made with the fabric, there is only enough binding for 50, so it is best to use the spare fabric to make cushions.

8. (a) The most profitable mix of coaches is five standard and five business class.
   (b) This gives a profit of £19 000 per journey.
   (c) The profit per coach in standard class would need to increase to £2000, which means that the profit per passenger would have to be £16.67 – an increase of £1.67.

9. (b) For minimum cost, 18 grade A and 12 grade B operative should be employed. At a cost of £234 per hour.
   (c) The constraint that a minimum of six grade B operatives should be employed is not tight at the solution point, so removing this constraint would have no impact on the solution.

CHAPTER 18

1. No increase in duration of job.
2. No increase required.
3. The critical activities remain the same but the time for the job is reduced to three hours.
4. (a) The shortest time (critical path) through the network is in fact 12 minutes.
   (b) If only two people are available, this will have no impact on the overall time.
5. The shortest time for the project is nine weeks. Labour costs will be £15 600.
6. (a) The shortest time for the project is 14 weeks.
   (b) There are in fact two critical paths here. Critical activities on one path are roof repairs, landscaping, furnishing and carpets. On the other, they are roof repairs, plumbing, fitting of catering area, furnishing and carpets.

(c) (i) If the gas fitting has to be carried out either before or after the plumbing, this will extend the time for the project by one week. (ii) If the decoration has to be delayed until the start of week 9 (that is, eight weeks after the start of the project), this will not extend the overall project time, since there is sufficient slack on this activity to allow for the delay.

7. (a) The students should allow 8.5 days.

  (b) Yes, in this case, an extra day will be required.

10. The precedence table is:

Activity	Preceding
A	None
B	A
C	A
D	B and C
E	C
F	D
G	E and F

The shortest time is 13 weeks.

Index

percentages 15–16
  estimating with STEP 208–12
  growth, forecasting 377
  sampling distribution of 204–7
perfect correlation 301
pictogram 67–8
pie chart 68–70
Poisson distribution 178–80
  features of 178
  Normal approximation tp 193–4
  tables for 179–80
population 42
positive correlation 294
positive integers 9
positive skewness 114
powers 17–18
precedence table 450
present value 412–15
price index 124–9
primary data 42, 43–50
principal in compound interest 409
print resources for secondary data 51
probability 141
  decision tables 157–9
  decision trees 159–62
  expected values 156–7
  exhaustive events 151
  mutually exclusive events 150
  or rule 149–50
  and rule 150–51
probability distributions 170–72
  binomial distribution 172–77
  normal distribution 181–91
    as approximation to binomial 192–3
    as approximation to Poisson 193–4
  Poisson distribution 177–80
process capability 268–74
process capability index 273
profit line in linear programming 434
profits, changes in linear programming 436
project planning see network analysis
proportion, hypothesis testing on more than
    one using chi-squared 239–49

quadrants 298
qualitative variables in multiple regression
    336–8
quality improvement 257–286
  importance of 259–60
  process capability 271–74
  sampling inspection 282–4

tools for 257–269
  cause-and-effect diagrams 263–5
  checksheets 261–2
  control charts 268–9, 274–281
  histograms 266–7
  Pareto charts 262–3
  scatterplots 267–8
  stratification 265–6
  tolerance limits 268, 271–74
  Total Quality Management (TQM) 260
  variability 270
quantitative data, tabulation of 73–7
quantitative investigations 470–78
quartiles 113–14
questionnaires 48–50
quota sample 46

R chart 279
random number table 367
random variations in time-series 385
  calculating 389
range 108–9
  controlling 279
  mean of 276
rank correlation 305–6
rankings 40
ratio scales 41
regression equation 316–7
regression line
  calculating 316–17
    with Excel 325–6
  confidence limits for 319–20
  extrapolation 319
  forecasting over time 323–4
  least squares 316
  predictions from 318–20
report writing 476–8
residual variation *see* random variation
Retail Price Index (RPI) 130–32
  uses of 132
roots 17–18
rounding 14

sample 44
  multi-stage 45
  quota 46
  simple random 44
  stratified 44
  systematic 46
sample mean, testing difference between two
    237–8